Management
Information Systems

Management Information Systems

Jaytilak Biswas

Faculty Member, Institute of Business Management of NCE Bengal, Jadavpur University, Kolkata

Los Angeles | London | New Delhi
Singapore | Washington DC | Melbourne

First published in 2020 by

SAGE Publications India Pvt Ltd
B1/I-1 Mohan Cooperative Industrial Area
Mathura Road, New Delhi 110 044, India
www.sagepub.in

SAGE Publications Inc
2455 Teller Road
Thousand Oaks, California 91320, USA

SAGE Publications Ltd
1 Oliver's Yard, 55 City Road
London EC1Y 1SP, United Kingdom

SAGE Publications Asia-Pacific Pte Ltd
18 Cross Street #10-10/11/12
China Square Central
Singapore 048423

Published by Vivek Mehra for SAGE Publications India Pvt Ltd. Typeset in 10/12.5 pt Minion Pro by AG Infographics, Delhi.

Library of Congress Cataloging-in-Publication Data

Names: Biswas, Jaytilak, author.
Title: Management information systems / Jaytilak Biswas, M.M.E. (Jadavpur), Ph.D. (I.I.Sc Bangalore), ACMA (India), Faculty member, Institute of Business Management, NCE Bengal, Jadavpur Member, Institute of Cost Accountants of India, Formerly, Member, Ordnance Factory Board, Ministry of Defence, Government of India, Formerly, Member, Indian Society for Training and Development.
Description: New Delhi, India; Thousand Oaks, California : SAGE Publications India, [2020] | Includes index.
Identifiers: LCCN 2020007896 (print) | LCCN 2020007897 (ebook) | ISBN 9789353883416 (pb) | ISBN 9789353883423 (epub) | ISBN 9789353883430 (ebook)
Subjects: LCSH: Management information systems. | Decision making. | Management.
Classification: LCC HD30.213 .B57 2020 (print) | LCC HD30.213 (ebook) | DDC 658.4/038011–dc23
LC record available at https://lccn.loc.gov/2020007896
LC ebook record available at https://lccn.loc.gov/2020007897

ISBN: 978-93-5388-341-6 (PB)

SAGE Team: Amit Kumar, Indrani Dutta, Vandana Gupta, Aishna Bhatt and Rajinder Kaur

To my parents, Late Dr Khagendra Nath Biswas and
Late Bakul Rani Biswas, with my deep regards.

Thank you for choosing a SAGE product!
If you have any comment, observation or feedback,
I would like to personally hear from you.

Please write to me at **contactceo@sagepub.in**

Vivek Mehra, Managing Director and CEO, SAGE India.

Bulk Sales

SAGE India offers special discounts
for bulk institutional purchases.

For queries/orders/inspection copy requests,
write to **textbooksales@sagepub.in**

Publishing

Would you like to publish a textbook with SAGE?
Please send your proposal to **publishtextbook@sagepub.in**

Subscribe to our mailing list

Write to **marketing@sagepub.in**

This book is also available as an e-book.

Contents

Detailed Contents

CHAPTER 13: Big Data Analytics and Cloud Computing   **411**

CHAPTER 14: Business Process Re-engineering   **483**

CHAPTER 15: Information Systems for Managerial Decisions: The Future   **497**

List of Figures

List of Tables

List of Abbreviations

1NF	First normal form
2NF	Second normal form
3NF	Third normal form
ABC	Activity-based costing
ACI	Application-centric infrastructure
ACK	Acknowledgement
AHP	Analytical hierarchy process
AIC	Akaike information criterion
AM	Amplitude modulation
AMI	Amazon machine image
AMT	Advanced manufacturing technology
ANN	Artificial neural network
API	Application programming interface
ARP	Address resolution protocol
AS	Autonomous system
ASCII	American Standard Code for Information Interchange
ASDL	Asymmetric digital subscriber line
ATM	Asynchronous transfer mode
AWS	Amazon web services
BaaS	Backend as a service
BCC	Blind carbon copy
BGP	Border gateway protocol
BI	Business intelligence
BIC	Bayesian information criterion
BOOTP	Bootstrap protocol
BPM	Business process mapping
BPR	Business process re-engineering
BPS	Bits per second
BSC	Balanced scorecard
BSP	Business system planning
CCITT	Consultative Committee for International Telephone and Telegraph

CGHS	Central Government Health Scheme
CICS	Customer information control system
CIF	Corporate information factory
CL	Connectionless
CLI	Command line interface
CMC	Computer maintenance corporation
CMS	Content management system
CMSM	Cross-media storage manager
CNN	Convolutional neural network
CO	Connection oriented
CRCs	Cyclic redundancy checks
CRM	Customer relationship management
CRUD	Creation, retrieval, updating and deleting
CSFs	Critical success factors
CSMA	Carrier sense multiple access
CSR	Corporate social responsibility
CSS	Cascade style sheets
CSU	Channel service unit
CTC	Cost to company
CVA	Credit valuation adjustments
CWIS	Corporate-wide information system
DBMS	Database management system
DDOS	Distributed denial of service
DFD	Data flow diagrams
DHCP	Dynamic Host Configuration Protocol
DIS	Data item set
DNS	Domain name system
DPR	Detailed project report
DS	Digital signal
DSL	Digital subscriber line
DSS	Decision support systems
DSU	Data service unit
DVA	Debt valuation adjustments
EC2	Elastic compute cloud
ECC	Elastic computing cloud
EDI	Electronic data interchange
EGP	Exterior gateway protocol
EIS	Executive information systems
EMR	Electronic medical records
EMV	Expected monetary value
EOT	End of transmission
EPOS	Electronic point of sale
ER	Entity relationship
ERD	Entity relationship diagram

ERP	Enterprise resource planning
ESS	Executive support system
EV	Expected value
EVPI	Expected value of perfect information
EXIF	Exchangeable image file
FCN	Fully connected network
FDM	Frequency division multiplexing
FM	Frequency modulation
FOIS	Freight operations information system
FRP	Fibre-reinforced plastic
FSM	Finite state machine
FTP	File transfer protocol
FVA	Funding valuation adjustments
GDSS	Group decision support system
GEO	Geostationary earth orbit
GMs	General managers
GPA	Grade point average
GPSS	General purpose simulation system
GUI	Graphical user interface
HDFS	Hadoop distributed file system
HP	Horsepower
HTML	Hypertext markup language
IaaS	Infrastructure as a service
ICANN	Internet Corporation for Assigned Names and Numbers
ICMP	Internet Control Message Protocol
ICU	Intensive care unit
IDS	Intrusion detection system
IFPS	Interactive financial planning system
IFRS	International Financial Reporting System
IGP	Interior gateway protocol
IGRP	Interior gateway routing protocol
IOFs	Indian ordnance factories
IOT	Internet of things
IPS	Intrusion prevention system
IPSec	IP security
IPV4	Internet Protocol Version 4
IRCTC	Indian Railways Catering and Tourism Corporation
IRR	Internal rate of return
IS	Information system
ISDN	Integrated services digital network
IS-IS	Intermediate system to intermediate system
ISPs	Internet service providers
ISs	Information systems
IT	Information technology

JDBC	Java database connectivity
JIT	Just-in-time
JS	JAVA scripts
JVM	Java virtual machines
KBUs	Key business units
KDD	Knowledge discovery in databases
KPIs	Key performance indicators
KS	Kolmogorov–Smirnov
LAN	Local area network
LED	Light emitting diode
LEO	Low earth orbit
LOB	Limit order book
LRU	Least recently used
LSTM	Long short-term memory
M&M	Mahindra and Mahindra
MAC	Media access control
MAN	Metropolitan area network
MAUT/MAVT	Multi-attribute utility/value theory
MBaaS	Mobile backend as a service
MBAN	Medical body area networks
MBO	Management by objectives
MBPS	Million bits per second
MCDA	Multiple-criteria decision analysis
MCQs	Multiple choice questions
MIS	Management information system
MTU	Maximum transmission unit
NAPT	Network address and port translation
NAT	Network address translation
NCE	National Council of Education
NFC	Near-field communication
NFS	Network file system
NIH	Network interface hardware
NIST	National Institute of Standards and Technology
NIU	Network interface unit
NLP	Natural language processing
ODBC	Open database connectivity
ODS	Operational data store
OEM	Original equipment manufacturer
OLAP	Online analytical processing
ONF	Open Networking Foundation
OR	Operation research
OS	Operating system
OSPF	Open shortest path first
OWL	Web ontology language

PaaS	Platform as a service
PAN	Permanent account number
PCM	Pulse code modulation
PGP	Pretty good privacy
POIS	Process, organization, information, resource and environment
POP	Post Office Protocol
POS	Point of sale
PRS	Passenger reservation system
PSL	Problem statement language
PVF	Present value factor
RADIUS	Remote Authentication Dial-in User Service
RARP	Reverse Address Resolution Protocol
RDSO	Research Development and Standardization Organization
RF	Radio frequency
RFC	Request for comment
RFID	Radio frequency identification device
RIP	Routing Information Protocol
RNN	Recurrent neural network
ROCE	Return on capital employed
ROI	Return on investment
ROM	Read-only memory
S3	Simple storage service
SaaS	Software as a service
SADT	Structured analysis and design technique
SAS	Statistical analysis system
SBI	State Bank of India
SBUs	Strategic business units
SCM	Supply chain management
SCP	Secure copy
SDH	Synchronous digital hierarchy
SDLC	System development life cycle
SDN	Software defined networking
SFTP	Secure File Transfer Protocol
SMART	Simple multi-attribute rating technique
SMDS	Switched multi-megabit data service
SMTP	Simple Mail Transfer Protocol
SOH	Start of header
SONET	Synchronous optical networking
SQL	Structured query language
SSH	Secured shell
SSL	Secure socket layer
SSN	Secondary NameNode
STP	Shielded twisted pair
SWOT	Strengths, weaknesses, opportunities and threats

TCP/IP	Transmission Control Protocol/Internet Protocol
TDM	Time division multiplexing
TFTV	Trivial File Transfer Protocol
TIFF	Tag image file format
TLD	Top-level-domain
TPM	Total productive maintenance
TQM	Total quality management
TTS	Text-to-speech
UDF	User-defined functions
UDP	User Datagram Protocol
UQ	Unit of quantity
UTP	Unshielded twisted pair
UTS	Unreserved ticketing system
UX	User experience
VM	Virtual machine
VPN	Virtual private network
VSATs	Very-small-aperture terminals
WAL	Write ahead log
WEP	Wired equivalent privacy
WIP	Work-in-process
XML	Extensible markup language
XOR	Exclusive or
YARN	Yet another resource negotiator

Foreword

Rapid development in information and communications technology has led to significant changes in the use of information systems in managerial decision-making over the years. The first- and second-generation computer systems of the 1960s and 1970s were massive in size and used to occupy big rooms. The computational speed was of the order of milliseconds, and data used to be stored in large magnetic tapes and disks. Today, multiple times faster computers with processing time of the order of nanoseconds and with data storage capacity of gigabytes (10^{12} bytes) or even more are available in laptops and palmtops and even smartphones!

In order to cope with the development in hardware, new software and communication systems have also evolved in the course of time. On the other hand, growing complexities in the business environment have further necessitated the advent of newer types of management information systems (MIS) using the new generation hardware, software and communication technology to facilitate effective and efficient managerial decision-making.

In the above context, this book titled *Management Information Systems* by Professor Jaytilak Biswas has got a special significance. It traces the evolution and transformation that have taken place over the years in this field of study, and the readers will greatly enhance their knowledge by going through the pages of the book. The coverage in it is wide and very comprehensive across the chronological developments in information systems. It will also help the readers to understand the concepts, organize their thoughts and get a first-hand idea about the phenomenal growth of information and communications technology and their application in business environments.

The language of the book is simple and student-friendly; the concepts have been discussed in a jargon-free manner, to enable students from various backgrounds to have an easy understanding of the basics of the subject. It will well serve the purpose of a textbook on MIS for the students pursuing both undergraduate and postgraduate degree courses in various B-schools including the Indian Institutes of Management. The examples cited in the book will be extremely helpful for the students. The case studies at the end of each chapter will make the readers understand the practical applications of modern developments in the decision-making process such as artificial intelligence, machine learning, artificial neural networks, deep learning, NoSQL databases, big data analytics using Hadoop and its ecosystems.

The material in the book spanning 15 chapters has been organized brilliantly. Chapters contain self-review questions at the end, which will enable the students to test their knowledge gained by reading the corresponding chapters. The chapter-end Bibliography will enable the readers to supplement their knowledge on MIS. The computer-based solutions of the problems and examples with screenshots, where relevant, have made the book very informative and engaging for the young readers.

My best wishes for the readers of this book; hope they find the journey into MIS thrilling and inspiring.

J. K. Das
Professor (Statistics), Department of Commerce and
Director, Internal Quality Assurance Cell (IQAC)
University of Calcutta

Preface

Of late, there has been a spurt in the activities relating to design and development of information systems for managerial decisions. Chief executives of Indian companies, who earlier used to consider their information technology departments as data-processing centres generating voluminous clerical reports, have started realizing the importance of information systems in achieving organizational success and growth. Information and knowledge management has evolved as a distinct management function. Further, there has been a phenomenal growth in information and communications technology all over the globe during the last two decades. Several institutes of information science and technology have been established in our country besides separate computer science courses being offered by Indian universities and institutes of higher learning.

For more than three decades, I worked with the information technology and management information system (MIS) departments of large engineering industries belonging to public sector enterprises and the government. Later, I have been teaching MIS and allied courses over the past 10 years for MBA programmes conducted by the Institute of Business Management of National Council of Education (NCE), Bengal, affiliated to Jadavpur University, Kolkata. Although I have covered the entire syllabus of MIS at the MBA level in the present textbook, it covers the topics included in the syllabus of MIS taught to the students pursuing various other programmes such as BE, BTech, BCA and MCA of Indian universities as well as professional courses run by the Institutes of Chartered/Cost and Management Accountants of India.

The present book cogently deals with a variety of topics such as decision support, expert systems, database management systems, systems analysis and design, data mining and warehousing, computer-based information systems, big data analytics, cloud computing, Internet of things and many allied topics. Latest developments on big data analytics adopting Hadoop, its ecosystems and NoSQL databases have been elaborately explained with real-life examples.

Management students, particularly at the MBA level, have different backgrounds: humanities, science, commerce, engineering, management, working executives as well as fresh graduates. The present book has been written comprehensively considering the diverse groups of management students as mentioned above. The illustrative examples and the case studies presented in the book are simple and relevant to Indian organizations. A list of carefully designed self-review questions has been provided at the end of nearly all chapters. This will enable the students to test their level of knowledge after reading the corresponding chapters.

During my long association with Indian industries as a practising manager, I observed a chasm between world-class information technology and the practices prevailing in Indian industries particularly in the manufacturing sector. I, therefore, felt the need to bridge this gap. The present book is an attempt in this direction. The book though primarily meant to be a textbook in MIS, nevertheless, targets the practising managers also.

The topics covered in this book have been selected basing on Indian and foreign books and papers published in various management journals. The book, thus, attempts to present all relevant and current topics at one place.

I am indebted to NCE, Bengal, for the encouragement and support extended to me while writing this book. My thanks are also due to the authorities of the Institute of Business Management of NCE, Bengal, for the facilities provided to me for writing the book.

I would like to thank the authorities of various industrial organizations in India for the necessary permission granted to me for collection and use of their organizational data.

I would also like to acknowledge the cooperation I received from my colleague faculty members and staff members of the Institute of Business Management of NCE, Bengal.

Credit also goes to my wife Rita, son Tamal, and daughter Smita, for their continued patience, support and interest in the progress of my work. I would like to thank Shri Maloy Das for typesetting and proofreading the entire book.

Finally, I would also like to thank my publisher for the publishing effort extended to me.

About the Author

 **Jaytilak Biswas** is a Faculty Member at the Institute of Business Management of NCE, Bengal, affiliated to Jadavpur University, Kolkata. Prior to this, he was a Member (Technical) of the Ordnance Factory Board, Department of Defence Production and Supplies under the Ministry of Defence, Government of India. He has worked about three-and-a-half decades at senior executive positions of various public sector enterprises and Government of India. He has been the General Manager of a number of ordnance factories such as Ordnance Factory Dumdum and Gun and Shell Factory, Cossipore, Kolkata.

Professor Biswas received his bachelor's and master's degrees in mechanical engineering from Jadavpur University, Kolkata, and PhD from the Industrial Management Department of the Indian Institute of Science, Bengaluru. He is also a member of the Institute of Cost and Management Accountants of India. He has been teaching courses in operations management and MISs to postgraduate students at the Institute of Business Management, Jadavpur, and has also conducted executive development programmes for senior managers from private and public sectors. He is a guest faculty to many leading institutions. He has published several papers in specialized national and international journals of repute. He has travelled extensively in India and abroad. His current areas of academic interest are MISs, operations management, supply chain management and project management.

CHAPTER

1

Concept and Role of Management Information System

1.1 Introduction

Growing complexities of modern organizations demand fast and complex managerial decision-making. Managers need appropriate information for effective and efficient decision-making.

Development of an effective management information system (MIS) is thus one of the primary tasks for efficient management today.

Researchers and designers of MIS have put forth many definitions of MIS. To mention a few, the following statements have been quoted:

A communication process in which information [input] is recorded, stored and retrieved [processed] for decisions [output] on planning, operating and controlling. Murdick and Ross (1977)

An organized method of providing past, present and projection information related to internal operations and external intelligence. Kennevan (1974)

Produced for all levels of management, the information required to make decisions in two areas:
(i) predicting what will happen by using historical data and simulation to give alternatives and
(ii) outlining or making change to a present procedure or decision to make predictions. Martino (1970)

Facilitates the management functions of planning, organizing, integrating, measuring and controlling. Breen et al. (1969)

An operational function whose parts corresponding to functional units are information subsystems of other operational functions. Blumenthal (1969)

The definition of MIS put forth by the MIS committee of the Financial Executives Institutes, UK, makes clear the relationship between management and information system (IS): 'MIS is a system designed to provide selected decision-oriented information needed by [the] management to plan, control and evaluate the activities of the corporation.'

In spite of certain variability in the above statements, there is a common and core component of MIS—appropriate quantum of information to be readily available to the management for taking effective and appropriate decisions towards the best interest of the organizations. The definitions also highlight certain essential features of MIS, such as its linkage to an organizational subsystem, its flexible and futuristic nature.

1.2 Schools of Management Analysis

Urwick has defined management as the responsibility for others' work. Bocchino has given a more appropriate explanation of the term management as the responsibility of optimum utilization of resources to attain the objectives of the organization. There is no doubt that the ultimate objective of management is to attain the organizational goals through effective and efficient utilization of available resources, such as men, material and machines, but the question arises: How do they achieve it? In other words, what are the management processes? Management processes are broad in scope and dimension. Hence, it is difficult to arrive at an all-comprehensive definition of management processes.

However, for the sake of convenience, the different management schools of thoughts may be organized as follows: behavioural, empirical, decision theory, quantitative and management process.

The behavioural school of management is one of the earliest theories of management. The proponents of this school can be divided between the human behaviour groups, such as Elton Mayo, Roethlisberger and Dickson and the social science groups, such as Maslow, Herzberg and Likert. The proponents of the first group believed that since management is a responsibility of getting work done through others, a manager must have knowledge of human relations and behavioural sciences.

The social science group went a step further and pointed out that an organization is a social system group where individuals with different ideas, attitudes and aspirations get together for a common purpose. Hence, the manager should study the group as a whole and not just individual behaviour.

The empirical school of management analysis belongs to many practising managers who believe that experience is the single factor that determines managerial success. They attempt to analyse management through practical case studies.

The next school of management analysis is the decision theory school proposed by Simon and others. According to this school, management is mainly decision-making processes. A manager at any level of the organization has to take fast and complex decisions. The more correct the decisions are, the more successful he or she is as a manager.

The quantitative school of management, also known as the mathematical school, describes management in terms of mathematical symbols, equations and models. Techniques such as operations research, linear programming and simulation were developed by this school for solution of the mathematical models. Development of high-speed computers facilitated the solution of the problems because of their capability of handling mathematical equations at a very high speed.

The last but most popular analysis of management is the so-called management process school propounded by Henri Fayol, Koontz, O'donnell and others.

The basic and universal functions of management as defined by the management process school are planning, organizing, staffing, directing and controlling.

The various schools of management analysis enumerated above are not mutually exclusive but they form parts of the total management system.

1.3 Management Process as Viewed for MIS

Management, for the purpose of MIS, consists of the activities carried out by managers. Planning, organizing, staffing, directing and controlling are five executive functions of management.

While each of the above functions needs relevant information, three particular areas, namely planning, organizing and control, need decision-making. MIS becomes a facilitating system for making decisions in planning, organizing and controlling in the best interest of the organizations.

According to Burch and Strater, planning, decision-making and controlling are the functions of management for the MIS design purpose. Bocchino has considered planning, analysing and controlling as the basic functions of management for the MIS design purpose.

1.4 Data and Information

Data and information are two separate entities. Data are nothing but isolated events or facts. Data, when processed and presented in a systematic mode to a manager for making specific decisions, become information. The process that converts data into information is known as data processing.

It should be noted that the difference between data and information lies in the mode of presentation, and that information must facilitate decision-making. Information which do not help a manager in his/her role of decision-making is not considered as information in MIS.

For example, annual sales figures (salesman-wise) when presented to the sales manager for decision on a reward scheme become information, whereas the same presented to a production manager are of no use and not considered as information in MIS.

1.5 Information and Decision-making

Information is vital for decision-making. It helps a manager in decision-making in two ways.

First, it reduces uncertainty in the decision-making process to a great extent, if not eliminated totally. Most of the managers' decisions, particularly at the top level, are future oriented. He or she is often ignorant of the future contingencies and takes decisions under uncertainty. The more the uncertainty, the more is the difficulty. Information helps a manager under such uncertain situations.

For example, a sales manager while forecasting future sales looks back to past sales figures to arrive at a reasonably accurate forecast.

Second, information provides a feedback to a manager to ensure that his/her decisions are in the right direction, and if not, he or she can amend the decisions at any time for corrective action without any adverse implications. Feedback is also vital for operational control level of the management where the decisions are very clear and decision rules can be automated or programmed.

Feedback information may be formal information such as periodic reports on actual production, sales and profit against targets or informal like behavioural feedback.

Every manager in an organization can be viewed as a point to which information flows and gives rise to decisions, which in turn produce further information in a closed loop. Miller and Starr developed this concept of information-decision into a model as shown in Figure 1.1.

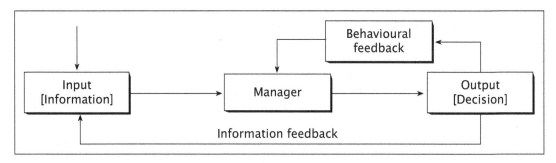

FIGURE 1.1   Miller–Starr Model of Information Decision

1.6 The System Approach

The term system has been extensively used in literature on business management, for example, business system, organization system and human system.

What is a system? More specifically, what makes a system?

Hopkins (1961) defined a system as a set of elements forming an activity or a processing procedure/scheme seeking a common goal or goals by operating on data and/or energy and/or matter in a time reference to yield information and/or energy and/or matter.

The following features characterize a system: (a) plurality of the parts (elements), (b) interdependency of the parts, (c) interaction of the parts with each other and with the environment, (d) common goal(s) and (e) synergy.

A business organization, for example, consists of a group of people, capital and machines as its elements which interact with each other for seeking a common goal, say, profit. The human body is another example of a system, consisting of many complex organs, which interact simultaneously to maintain homoeostasis.

The synergistic effect of a system is that which enables the parts or elements acting together simultaneously to achieve a combined effect which is greater than the sum of the individual effects of the parts if allowed to function in isolation. For example, sales, production and finance are three departments in a business organization, but they function in close liaison with each other for optimum profit. If, however, sales, production and finance try to optimize their activities in isolation, it may so happen that more than what can be sold might be produced and finance faces shortage of cash. The ultimate result is sub-optimized profit.

1.7 System Approach to MIS Design

MIS has got as its elements a group of people comprising functional managers, information technologists and programmers, a set of manuals and data-processing equipment, computers, communication networks, files and databases, which select, store, process and retrieve data and yield relevant information to managers at various levels in an organization when needed to facilitate management functions of planning, decision-making and controlling by reducing uncertainty in decision-making and providing feedback (common goal) to optimize the overall performance of the organization (synergy).

The position of MIS within an organization and its environment for three different types of organizations, namely a manufacturing unit, a service organization such as an institution of higher learning and a public-utility organization such as an electricity supply corporation, have been shown in Figures 1.2–1.4 respectively.

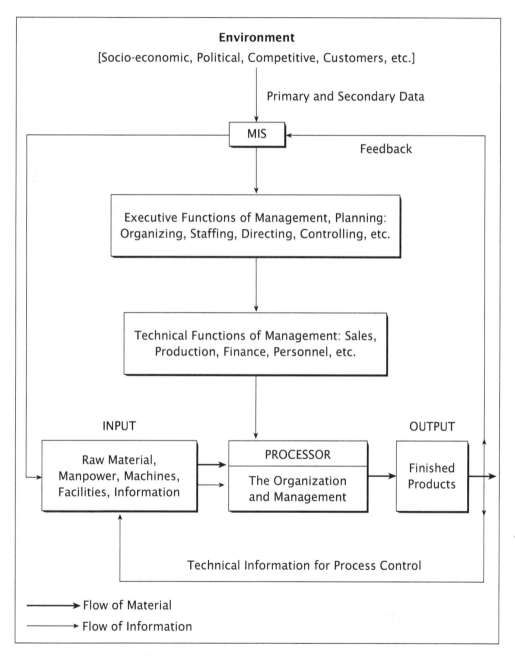

FIGURE 1.2 MIS in a Manufacturing Organization

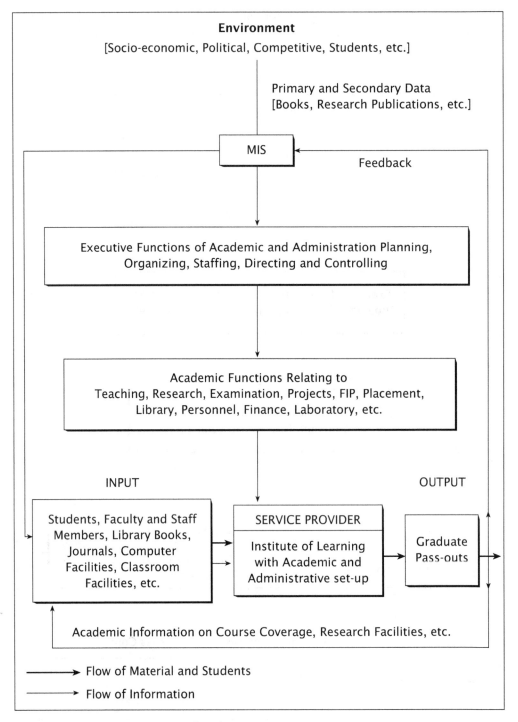

Environment
[Socio-economic, Political, Competitive, Students, etc.]

Primary and Secondary Data
[Books, Research Publications, etc.]

MIS

Feedback

Executive Functions of Academic and Administration Planning, Organizing, Staffing, Directing and Controlling

Academic Functions Relating to
Teaching, Research, Examination, Projects, FIP, Placement, Library, Personnel, Finance, Laboratory, etc.

INPUT

OUTPUT

Students, Faculty and Staff Members, Library Books, Journals, Computer Facilities, Classroom Facilities, etc.

SERVICE PROVIDER

Institute of Learning with Academic and Administrative set-up

Graduate Pass-outs

Academic Information on Course Coverage, Research Facilities, etc.

⟶ Flow of Material and Students
⟶ Flow of Information

FIGURE 1.3   MIS in an Institution of Higher Learning

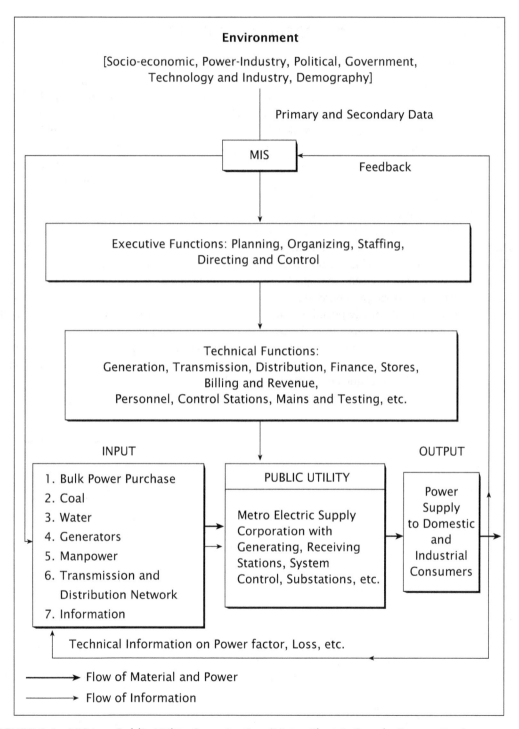

FIGURE 1.4 MIS in a Public-Utility Organization (Metro Electric Supply Corporation)

1.8 Organization and Management Control Systems

Anthony (1965) mentioned about three levels of management in an organization. These are the strategic planning level comprising the top management, the management control or the middle and operational control levels. Anthony's viewpoint was supported by Burch and Strater (1973) who named the three levels of management as the strategic, tactical and technical levels. Strategic planning is the management process of deciding on the long-term configuration which the organization will take in future in terms of inputs and outputs for survival and growth. For example, a strategic plan for a manufacturing industrial organization may include the volume of production and sales to be achieved after 10 years, customer profile, manpower inputs, financing pattern and so on; the management control level receives the strategic plan as an input from the top level and decides the tactical plan to achieve the strategy.

The tactical plans usually are the annual operating plans relating to the technical functional areas of sales, production, personnel, finance, R&D and so on and deployment of organizational resources effectively and efficiently to meet the operating plans. For example, an annual production plan and budget are tactical plans.

The operational control level is the bottom level in the management hierarchy and is concerned with the day-to-day operations to ensure that specific tasks are completed as per programme. Daily job shop scheduling, inventory ordering and purchase are all operational control activities. Although the executive functions of management, mainly planning and control, are being exercised in varying degrees by the three levels of management, planning is the essence of strategic planning level and control is less as compared with the operational control level which is heavily dependent on frequent feedback control, both formal and informal. Management control involves both planning and control. Operational control includes both technical control and administrative control.

It may be emphasized that the various levels of management are not mutually exclusive.

Bibliography

Anthony, R. N. *Planning and Control Systems: A Framework for Analysis*. Boston, MA: Division of Research, Harvard Business School, 1965.

Blumenthal, S. C. *Management Information Systems: A Framework for Planning and Development*. Englewood Cliffs, NJ: Prentice Hall, 1969.

Bocchino, W. A. *Management Information Systems: Tools and Techniques*. Englewood Cliffs, NJ: Prentice Hall, 1972.

Breen, R. E., H. Chestnut, R. R. Duersch, and R. S. Jones. *Management Information Systems*, 1. A Sub-Committee Report on Definitions. New York, NY: General Electric Co, 1969.

Burch, J. G., Jr., and F. R. Strater Jr. *Information Systems: Theory and Practice*. Santa Barbara, CL: Hamilton Publishing, 1973.

Hopkins, R.C. A systematic procedure for system development. *IRE Transactions on Engineering Management*, June 1961, p. 85.

Kennevan, W. J. 'MIS Universe.' In *Management of Information Handling Systems*, edited by Paul William Howerton, 63. Roselle Park, NJ: Hayden Book Company, 1974.

Koontz, H., and C. O'Donnell. *Principles of Management: An Analysis of Management Functions*. New York, NY: McGraw-Hill Book, 1972.

Martino, R. L. *Management Information Systems*. New York, NY: McGraw-Hill, 1970.

Miller, D. W., and M. K. Starr. *The Structure of Human Decisions*, 179. Englewood Cliffs, NJ: Prentice Hall, 1968.

Murdick, R. G., and J. E. Ross. *Information Systems for Modern Management*. New Delhi: Prentice Hall, 1977.

Simon, H. A. *The New Science of Management Decisions*. New York, NY: Harper and Row Publishers, 1960.

CHAPTER

Information Needs and Structure of MIS

2.1 The Information Needs

The information needs of a manager depend on his/her level in the organization. The type of information needed by a manager at the strategic planning level is different from the same required by managers at the tactical or operational control level of management in terms of important characteristics of the information. The characteristics of information needs are also known as the dimensions of information needs. The important dimensions are source, data volume, consolidation, frequency, accuracy, currency, scope, predictability, user dependence and real time or delayed. These dimensions of information needs for the decisions taken by various management levels are shown in Table 2.1.

A few examples of information needs in terms of the dimensions for typical organizational decisions have been shown in Table 2.2.

TABLE 2.1 Dimensions of Information Needs

Dimensions of Information Needs	Levels of Management		
	Strategic Planning	*Management Control*	*Operational Control*
Source	Mostly external	Mostly internal	Mostly internal
Scope	Wide [organizational]	Wide [functional]	Narrow [departmental]
Volume of data	High	High	Low
Consolidation	More	Less	Less
Frequency	Less	More	More
Accuracy	Low	High	High
Currency	Low	High	High
Predictability	Low	High	High
User dependence	Heavy	Low	Low
Real time/Delayed	Delayed	Delayed	Real time

TABLE 2.2 Dimensions of Information Needs for Various Organizational Decisions

Decisions	Source	Scope	Volume of Data	Consolidation	Frequency	Accuracy	Currency	Predictability	User Dependence	Real Time/ Delayed
Manufacturing										
1. Decision : Product diversification in next ten years	Mostly external	Wide	High	Modrate	Less	Low	Moderate	Moderate	Heavy	Delayed
2. Decision: Working Capital Requirement for a year	Mostly Internal	Wide	High	Less	Moderate	High	High	High	Less	Delayed
3. Decision : Daily scheduling of machines for various jobs	Internal	Narrow	Low	Less	More	High	High	High	Less	Real time
Public Utility [State Road Transport Corporation]										
1. Decision : New routes for passengers in next five years	External	Wide	High	High	Less	Low	Moderate	Moderate	High	Delayed
2. Decision : Public buses requirement for a particular year	Mostly Internal	Wide	High	Less	Moderate	Moderate	High	Moderate	Less	Delayed
3. Decision : Bus and crew scheduling for a particular day	Mostly Internal	Narrow	Moderate	Less	More	High	High	High	Less	Real time

2.2 Structure of MIS

Since any MIS is mainly to facilitate effective and efficient managerial decision-making related to the executive functions of management at various levels, the structure of MIS in any organization should be consistent with such decision-making as also with the various levels of management. The basic functions of management, namely planning, organizing, staffing, directing and controlling, require appropriate decisions and information. Since the proportion of these functions varies from level to level, the information needs and hence the MIS designs have to be necessarily different for those levels.

The IS for strategic planning needs to be designed mainly for supporting planning activities and hence has to cater to future-oriented decisions. The MIS for this level of management has to provide for exception reports and simulated or 'what-if' type of information apart from future projections. Such an MIS is also called executive information system (EIS), which also provides intelligent information—market intelligence, capital market intelligence and technology intelligence.

The MIS design for management control has to cater to the tactical needs and mainly includes prediction and optimization information. The management control level also needs information on actual performance as against the standards with variance analysis. The decision support system (DSS) for this level of management is semi-structured in nature and essentially comprises database, model base and a processor of the problems. DSSs have been elaborated in the subsequent chapters of this book.

The decisions at the operational control level are structured and programmable decisions. The IS pertaining to this level of management is mainly an automated decision-maker in nature as the decision rules are well defined. The management is so confident in the assumptions incorporated in this system that the optimum decisions are left to the IS itself. For example, the IS can monitor the stock level and initiate purchase order printing when the level reaches the reorder point. Similarly, the work order for preventive maintenance due for a particular plant or machinery, when the same becomes due, can be initiated by the maintenance IS. Office automation systems such as payroll and issue of meeting notices, and also automatic process control systems belong to the operational control level of management.

The structure of MIS as explained above has been shown in Figure 2.1.

2.3 MIS for Functional Management Areas

The structure of MIS as described in the previous paragraphs is applicable for the various functional areas of management which vary from organization to organization. For example, the typical management functions in organizations are operations including logistics, marketing, finance, personnel and support services. The MIS to cater to the information support for the various levels of management within the same structure will vary in terms of the actual types of information. The specific applications within these functional areas are broadly discussed below.

2.3.1 Operations, Production and Logistics

In general, the operations/production functions consist of the following:

- Operations/production planning and control
- Product/service design

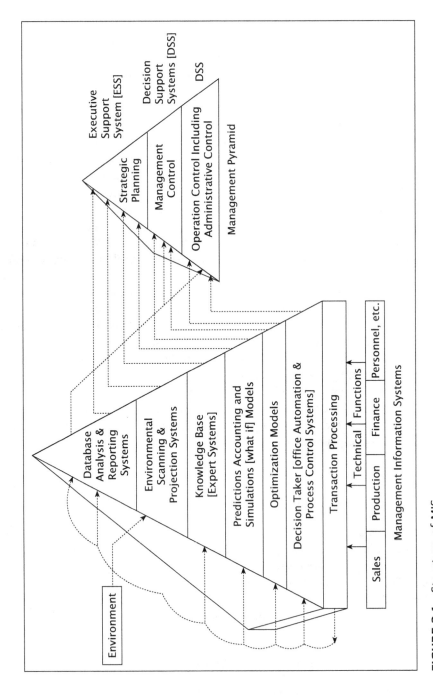

FIGURE 2.1 Structure of MIS

- Delivery/facilities planning
- Quality management of goods/services
- Logistics both inbound and outbound

2.3.2 Sales/Marketing/Revenue

In general, sales and marketing function includes the following:

- Sales
- Marketing
- Distribution
- Revenue collection for services
- Customers/consumers' feedback and after-sales services

2.3.3 Finance

In general, the finance function consists of the following:

- General ledger
- Final accounts
- Accounts payable and receivables
- Cash book
- Reconciliation
- Working capital
- Budgetary control
- Taxation
- Annual report
- Employee payroll
- Employee statutory benefits such as provident fund, bonus, gratuity, pension and group insurance
- Leave record
- Cost accounting and control

2.3.4 Personnel

In general, the personnel function consists of the following modules:

- Induction
- Training/skill development
- Placement/posting
- Career progression/promotion
- Wage/salary administration
- Transfers
- Attendance recording, leave sanction, leave rules
- Employee counselling, grievance handling

- Competency mapping
- Incentive scheme
- Performance appraisal
- Disciplinary proceedings
- Personnel data bank
- Administration of terminal benefits
- Safety and security aspects
- Negotiations with trade unions and so on

2.3.5 Support Services

The support services may include the following:

- Welfare activities—school, housing, recreation, healthcare and so on.
- Electricity, petrol, diesel, fuel, water, steam and air conditioning/refrigeration
- Environmental management plan including pollution control, forestation
- Material handling and transportation
- Telecommunication including telephone, fax and email

2.4 Important Factors for MIS Design

2.4.1 Nature of the Organization

The nature of the organization and its business activities play an important role in the design and complexity of its ISs.

A non-profit social organization will need many ISs to cater for diverse socio-economic applications rather than a very formal and precise IS suitable for a profit-making manufacturing unit producing consumer goods.

2.4.2 Critical Success Factors

The critical success factors (CSFs) for the industry type to which an organization belongs are also crucial in IS design. In most industries, there are usually three–six factors that determine success. These key-factor jobs must be done exceedingly well for a company to be successful. As a result, CSFs are areas of activities that receive constant and careful attention of management and the MIS must cater for information on these factors. The CSFs are mainly as follows:

1. Structure of the particular industry—the nature, competitive strategy, industry position, geographical location, size of the organization and its dispersion, forward, backward and vertical integration and so on
2. Environmental factors—such as government rules and control on industries
3. Political factors
4. Temporal factors such as local inflation and the effect of the economic cycle

2.4.3 Scale of Operation

The scale of operation and the volume of customers are important considerations for IS design. An Internet broadband service provider company, for example, has got a massive customer base as compared to its employee strength, and hence the IS design has to be necessarily different from the same for a city club having a limited number of members only.

2.4.4 Level of Information and Communications Technology

Another important factor that determines the nature of IS is the level of information and communications technology in the organization. For example, the IS for fully computerized and networked branches of a bank will be different from the banks which are not fully computerized. The other examples are supermarkets providing bar codes on the items, smart cards to customers for electronic purchase and payment, and smart cards provided by a health insurance company to the insured for admission and treatment at hospitals and nursing homes without cash payment.

2.4.5 Organizational Culture and Leadership Styles

The behavioural aspects of an organization also have a significant role in MIS design. The styles of management including the individual characteristics of the managers are also important in this regard. The important variables of organizational behaviour for the sake of IS design may be formal versus informal, rigid versus flexible, participative versus dictatorial and centralized versus decentralized. The number and nature of the legacy systems also affect the design of an integrated MIS. Another important behavioural aspect which the IS designer has to face is the people's resistance to change which is a basic and universal human attribute.

2.4.6 Number and Nature of User Interaction

The size of users and their nature of interaction with the IS also determine the nature of the same. For example, an airline seat reservation system has to be accessed by a large number of passengers all over the globe through the Internet and hence needs to be designed web-enabled, online and real time. On the other hand, a typical back office automation system like payroll processing having an entirely different number and nature of user interaction can be designed as a batch-processing system, since the idea is to improve processing efficiency and not customer service in terms of response time.

2.5 Some Guidelines for Successful Design of MIS

2.5.1 Business Process Re-engineering

The most important prerequisite to a successful design of MIS is business process re-engineering (BPR). The analysis and design of workflows and processes within an organization need to be carried out systematically, analysed and redesigned before the MIS is designed and implemented to have maximum benefit. A business process is a set of logically related tasks performed to achieve a defined business outcome. MIS development aims to integrate a large number of business functions. Enterprise resource planning (ERP), supply chain management (SCM), knowledge management system, groupware and collaborative system, human resource management system, customer relationship management (CRM) system and many such systems require a prior re-engineering of the business processes.

2.5.2 Top-Down Approach Rather Than Bottom-Up Approach

In the bottom-up approach, the subsystems are designed and developed in piecemeal or as and when required 'basis' without any overall initial planning. This approach is also known as inductive approach where the focus is on the parts rather than the whole. The subsystems are synthesized at a later stage to have an integrated system. In the process, incompatibility often arises and if the subsystems are not properly redesigned, the integrated system may run suboptimally. The top-down approach first decides on the total MIS and the overall objectives, and then requirements for the subsystems are framed before the design and implementation of the subsystems. The bottom-up approach is the approach frequently adopted by many organizations particularly in the Indian context where the design and development of the initial systems, such as payroll, personnel information and stock ledger, are completed in an unplanned way. Later on, at the time of development of an integrated system, the organizations face enormous difficulties.

2.5.3 Top Management Support and Involvement

In many cases, the failures of the MIS have been found to be due to lack of support of the top management. Apart from the financial sanctions, top management awareness and active support at every stage of MIS design and implementation are essentially needed for the success of the MIS designed and developed. The top management should hold periodic progress review meetings with the MIS team consisting of the users, the information technology (IT) specialists and the designers.

2.5.4 Users' Training

Users' training on the new MIS after implementation is vital for the success of the MIS. The users must be aware of the various aspects such as capabilities of the ISs, various reports, source data preparation, data feeding and benefits of the new MIS.

2.5.5 Employee Involvement

The active involvement of the employees is another key factor leading to the success of the MIS. Employees, particularly the managers of the organization, must realize that the ISs are for promoting productivity, efficiency, welfare and overall organizational development. On the contrary, if they treat the MIS as a threat to their authority, power and career prospect, the proposed IS is bound to be a failure. It is through employee training and awareness programmes that this type of misapprehension can be eliminated.

2.5.6 Phased Implementation

A successful MIS developer would undertake implementation in phases. Usually, a careful MIS developer would select the systems which are likely to yield significant benefits in a short time to the organization for the first phase of implementation. Often, the cost or investment consideration determines the systems to be implemented in the first phase. The above phased implementation strategy gives rise to adequate support within the organization for the integrated MIS.

2.6 Stages of Growth of MIS

Nolan (1979) mentioned about six stages of growth of electronic data processing and computerized applications. These stages are also applicable for the growth of MIS in organizations.

The first stage **initiation** starts with cost reduction applications in individual functional departments such as accounts, stores and purchase. The second stage **contagion** begins with the proliferation of applications in all functional areas such as production, sales, finance and personnel. The third stage **control** shifts emphasis from application proliferation to management control like budgetary control. In order to facilitate the same, the upgradation of documentation and restructuring of existing applications often become a necessity. In this stage, there is a transition from the management of the computer to the management of data resources in an organization. The fourth stage **integration** involves the use of database technology and increased user involvement in the control of data and information processing activities. The fifth stage **data administration** features organizational integration of information subsystems. A formal MIS department becomes functional at this stage. The sixth and the final stage **maturity** is the ideal stage but never really attainable in the dynamic environment in which organizations have to survive. However, at this stage, the emphasis shifts from the computer as a resource to information as a resource.

In the Indian context, the initiation stage in general is identified with the computerization of financial accounting and other clerical labour-saving applications like payroll. The contagion stage has witnessed development of ISs in other functional areas such as stores accounting and personnel IS, all in an unplanned way, and many a time, the growth is marked with IS relating to operational control.

In the control stage, the emphasis shifts towards the management control role of MIS such as variance analysis and reporting system for the middle and top levels of management.

The integration phase is marked by considerable investment in hardware and software and includes database creation in diverse functional areas. The use of communication technology in networking of remote locations through client-server technology is facilitated in this stage. The trading of National Stock Exchange and network banking operations are typical examples of integration.

Date administration envisaged corporate database creation and the Indian business organizations recognized information as a valuable organizational resource. The elaborate MIS planning and control for the passengers and goods traffic management by Indian Railways is a typical illustration of data administration. ERP implementation in various organizations is another example of data administration.

In the maturity stage, the ISs facilitated organizational growth and many Indian companies started forming subsidiary companies for information services such as Reliance, Siemens and Canara Bank. At this stage, top management along with the MIS team also determine MIS strategy and implementation priorities.

CASE STUDY: A SYSTEM APPROACH

Background

M/s ABC Company Limited (actual name is suppressed due to obvious reasons) manufactures electric motors, generators and heavy transformers for supply to various state electricity boards, metro-city electricity supply corporations and various manufacturing industries. The company also sells electric motors of lesser horsepower (HP) ratings to domestic users through its distribution channels.

The organization chart of the company has been as follows:

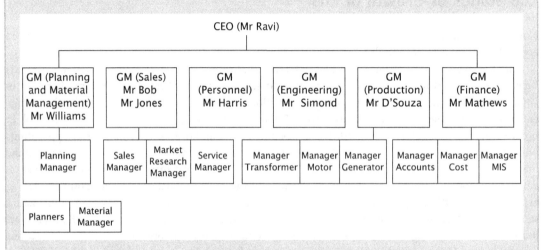

Planning and Reporting System of ABC Company Limited

The GM (Planning and Material Management) in consultation with the other GMs prepares five-yearly perspective roll-on plans which are then approved by the CEO following the company's policy, vision and mission. Besides, annual operating plans for all functions such as sales, production and finance are formulated in January each year, for the next financial year in the annual target fixation meeting chaired by the CEO, where all the GMs along with their supporting managers remain present.

In the same meeting, the GM (Finance) furnishes the previous financial year's figures of actual total sales revenue, production in quantity and cost item wise, profit before and after taxes and cost of capital.

He also provides his estimation of anticipated price escalation for the various finished products of the company.

Thereafter, the CEO sets the sales (revenue) target product-wise, considering the likely inflation of price of raw materials and bought-out components, increase in wages and salaries, support services such as electricity, other miscellaneous overhead cost and a growth rate in real terms consistent with the perspective plan.

The CEO also seeks the opinion of Mr Bob, GM (Sales), who used to invariably accept the sales target set by the CEO, without bothering for the sales forecast report forwarded to him by his managers. Mr Bob used to believe in achieving the sales target set by the CEO with aggressive push strategy for sales promotion.

Mr D'Souza, GM (Production), used to come prepared with his capacity plan for catering to the sales target. He used to overcome bottlenecks through outsourcing.

The GM (Planning and Material Management), GM (Engineering) and GM (Personnel) had only advisory roles in the annual target fixation meeting.

In the target fixation meeting for the financial years 2008–2009 and 2009–2010, Mr Bob, then GM (Sales), and Mr D'Souza, GM (Production), got high appreciation from the CEO for meeting the sales and production targets for the years 2007–2008 and 2008–2009. ABC Company Limited made profits for both the above years.

Mr Bob retired from service on attaining the retirement age on 31 May 2009. Thereafter, Mr Jones was directly recruited as the GM (Sales). The year 2009–2010 was however dismal for ABC company as the company for the first time incurred a loss of ₹100 million in the same year.

Actual sales in crores of INR for the above 3 years were 10, 12 and 8 as against the targets of 10, 11 and 12, respectively. Some figures from the balance sheet of the above mentioned three years for ABC Company Limited are reproduced and shown as a tabular statement as shown in the following table:

Figures Extracted from the Balance Sheets of ABC Co. Ltd (Figures: ₹ in Crores)

As on 31 March 2008				As on 31 March 2009				As on 31 March 2010			
Liability		*Asset*		*Liability*		*Asset*		*Liability*		*Asset*	
Capital	21	Land and building	5	Capital	22	Land and building	5	Capital	24	Land and building	5
Unpaid wages	40	P&M	10	Unpaid wages	25	P&M	9	Unpaid wages	30	P&M	8.1
		depreciation	−1			depreciation	−0.9			depreciation	−0.81
		net	9			net	8.1			net	7.29
Sundry creditors	2	WIP	1.5	Sundry creditors	2	WIP	1.5	Sundry creditors	2.5	WIP	0.50
Profit (+) Loss (−)	3.15	Finished goods	0	Profit (+) Loss (−)	4.09	Finished goods	0	Profit(+) Loss (−)	−0.10	Finished goods	0
		Sundry debtors	2.5			Sundry debtors	4			Sundry debtors	3
		Cash at bank	1.5			Cash at bank	0.05			Cash at bank	0.05

Mr Ravi was highly dissatisfied with the performance of Mr Jones, the new GM (Sales), for not achieving the sales target for the year 2009–2010. Mr Jones, however, pointed out that he could not achieve the target of ₹120 million as Mr D'Souza could not produce and supply the required number of transformers (a high value and high demand product of the company) in time, which led to lost sales. Mr D'Souza however put the blame on Mr Williams for not arranging the silicon sheets from M/s Rourkela Steel Plant and M/s GKW in time needed for the manufacture of transformers. Mr Williams, on the other hand, told Mr Ravi that the purchase requisition for silicon sheets was placed quite late by the production department in the month of June 2009. As a result, the purchase order for silicon sheets was placed on the above named two established sources in July 2009.

Mr Ravi, however, independently contacted the CEOs of M/s Rourkela Steel Plant and M/s GKW, but both of them told him that there had been no delay on their part in supplying the silicon sheets to M/s ABC Company Limited. However, they told Mr Ravi that some of their old bills were pending with the accounts department of M/s ABC Company Limited and requested Mr Ravi to look into the matter.

Mr Ravi was at a loss to understand as to why M/s ABC Company Limited, which had been making profits all along up to 2008–2009, suddenly ran into a loss in the year 2009–2010. He was thinking of engaging a consultant to find out where the system failed.

Note: The above case study is an exercise for the students to go through and find out what was lacking in the system which led to its failure. The students should also suggest remedial measures for ABC Company Limited.

Review Questions

1. Give three examples of MIS that you may like to install for a state bus transport corporation.

2. The information needs for a vice-president of the marketing department of a mobile telecom company are different from those for the after-sales service manager of the same company in terms of important dimensions. Illustrate with three examples.

3. Classify the following as office automation, executive support, decision support and transaction processing systems:
   i.   Word processing
   ii. Airline reservation system
   iii. Traffic simulation package
   iv. Mathematical programming software
   v.   Reporting system models
   vi. Remote sensing and control
   vii. Environmental scanning and projection

4. Trace the evolution of three well-known MIS applications and identify the stages outlined by Richard Nolan with them in the Indian context.

5. A courier company has got branches all over India. The top management of the company decided to monitor the various functions of the company on a monthly basis. What will be the source data and in what format and frequency the same should be collected by the branches and forwarded to the head office? How will the data be processed by the head office and furnished to the top management?

6. What are formal and informal sources of information?

7. How are data converted into relevant information?

8. What is BPR? How is it important in developing MIS?

9. What are the sources of information for environmental data for an organization?

10. Can the same data generate a variety of information? Explain.

Bibliography

Anthony, R. N., J. Dearden, and F. W. Vancil. *Management Control Systems: Text Cases and Readings*. Homewood, IL: Richard D. Irwin, 1965.

Drucker, Peter. 'The Effective Decisions.' *Harvard Business Review* 45, no. 1 (1965): 92–98.

McFarlan, W. F. 'Problems in Planning the Information System.' *Harvard Business Review* 49, no. 2 (1971): 75–89.

Nolan, R. L. 'Managing the Crisis in Data Processing.' *Harvard Business Review* 57, no. 2 (1979): 115–126.

O'Brien, J. J. *Management Information Systems, Concepts, Techniques, and Applications*. New York, NY: Van Nostrand Reinhold Co., 1970.

Patel, N. R. 'Locating Rural Social Service Centers in India.' *Management Science* 25, no. 1 (1979): 22–30.

Prince, T. R. *Information Systems for Management, Planning and Control*. Homewood, IL: Richard D. Irwin, 1966.

Rockart, J. F. 'Chief Executives Define Their Own Data Needs.' *Harvard Business Review* 57, no. 2 (1979): 81–93.

Zani, W. M. 'Blueprint for MIS.' *Harvard Business Review* 48, no. 6 (1970): 95–100.

Decision-making

3.1 Decision-making Process

All of us have to make decisions every day. It is an integral part of the management process involving all levels and functions of management. Some decisions are relatively simple such as whether to place a purchase order for a particular inventory item at a particular time depending upon the stock and the reorder level of the same. However, some decisions which managers have to take are quite complex in nature such as which employee should be selected for a particular job and how much quantity of consumer goods is to be produced the next year for sale. Simple decisions need a simple decision-making process which can be programmed by a suitable algorithm. However, difficult decisions arise due to the decision-making process involving complexity (in terms of many interrelated factors and multiple decision criteria), uncertainty, high risk, many options or choices available and unpredictable behavioural issues such as how other employees or groups will react to the decisions.

With the above difficulties, the best way to make a complex organizational decision is to design an effective decision-making process and decision rules. Such clear decision-making processes result in effective and efficient decisions in the best interest of the organizations.

3.2 Programmed and Non-programmed Decisions

Herbert A. Simon classified decisions into two categories, namely programmed and non-programmed decisions.

Programmed decisions are repetitive and routine in nature, and set procedures or decision rules can be defined for such decisions. These can be automated through algorithms describing the decision rule. These are also known as structured decisions and usually involve 'things' rather than people and are fit for delegation to the operational control level of management. Examples of programmed decisions are inventory control, job shop scheduling, discount to customers and accounting decisions.

Non-programmed decisions are novel, non-routine and unstructured in nature, which involve a high degree of uncertainty of the outcomes, and as such no clear decision rule can be defined. Non-programmed decisions cannot be automated and always involve people. Examples of non-programmed decisions are future sales/production planning, capacity augmentation, launching of new products, recruitment of personnel, mergers and acquisitions.

Programmed and non-programmed decisions are two extremes of the range of managerial and organizational decision-making.

Many decisions which involve characteristics of both the above extremes are semi-structured in nature. An example of semi-structured decision is a new incentive scheme for piece workers in a factory where the incentive payment for different levels of output and productivity can be precisely determined, but the actual effect of the scheme in motivating the employees and the extent of productivity increase remain uncertain. Pay Commission decisions for increase of pay and allowances of central government employees are also unstructured in nature because of many interrelated factors involved in the process.

3.3 ISs for Different Types of Decisions

The MIS for an organization provides information to support semi-structured and unstructured decision-making and also may take structured or programmed decisions. At the operational control level of management hierarchy, majority of the decisions are structured with known decision rules and objectives. Semi-structured and unstructured decisions are mostly taken at the management control and strategic planning levels. However, certain structured decisions, particularly which have organization-wide impact, are taken at a high level. For example, a very costly renovation decision in a manufacturing industrial unit which is likely to affect the operations of the entire unit and for which decision rules are available might be taken at the strategic level.

A broad overview of decision-making at the three levels of management and the related ISs have been shown in Figure 3.1.

The boundaries between structured and semi-structured or unstructured decisions are constantly changing with the development of decision tools and techniques.

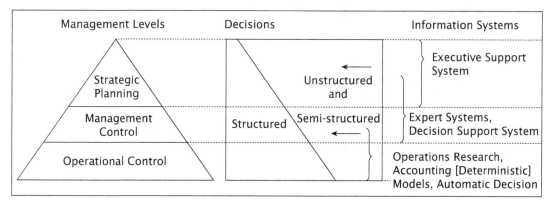

FIGURE 3.1 Decision-making and Information Systems

3.4 A Systematic Approach to Decision-making

Herbert A. Simon, in his decision theory, mentioned three phases of decision-making, namely intelligence, design and choice. The intelligence phase relates to environment scanning and finding conditions calling for decisions. The design phase is for setting goals, developing possible courses of action and analysis of the alternative courses of action. This involves processes to understand the problem, to generate solutions and the testing of solutions for feasibility.

Choice phase is for selecting one among the feasible alternatives available depending on set goals or objectives. A choice is made and then implemented. The implementation part is sometimes considered as a fourth phase of decision-making.

Let us illustrate the above phases of the decision-making process by a simple example. A licensed sporting rifle manufacturing unit in India through environmental scanning got the market intelligence that out of ₹5,000 million of sporting rifles purchased by the Shooters Association in India per annum on average, its share was only 10% (₹500 million) approximately. Through further survey and intelligence, the unit observed that about 70% sporting rifles of various bore sizes are imported from European manufacturers of small arms because the heavier metal components of rifles were replaced by fibre-reinforced plastics making the rifles lighter in weight and also cost-effective, and these features attracted Indian shooters. The top management of the Indian unit realized that there was a strong case in favour of developing fibre-reinforced plastic (FRP) components for the rifles for increasing customer base and thereby market share. This market condition called for a decision for action for development of plastic sporting rifles. This can be treated as Simon's first phase of decision-making, namely the 'intelligence' phase.

The second phase is the design phase when the corporate management set goals of replacing the metal components of their products with FRP components at a competitive price within a time schedule and an estimated investment cost. The alternative courses of action to achieve the above goals were also chalked out as follows:

1. To import the FRP technology through transfer of the technology route;
2. To indigenously develop the FRP technology through in-house R&D efforts;
3. To enter into a foreign collaboration agreement on a long-term basis with foreign manufacturers to import the FRP components and assemble the same in India;
4. To enter into a joint venture with a foreign manufacturer for co-production of rifles in India with profit sharing.

The feasibility of the four above alternatives has to be worked out with reference to the existing technology, input material availability in India, time and cost effectiveness and customer preferences. This phase can be called Simon's second phase, namely the 'design' phase.

In the next phase, one of the four alternative courses of action available as mentioned in the design phase needs to be selected based on the pre-set criteria for choice, judgement, intuition and 'bounded rationality'. The term bounded rationality has been explained elaborately in the subsequent paragraphs in this chapter. In this example, the manufacturing unit decided to go for the second alternative which was to indigenously develop the FRP technology through in-house R&D. This phase constitutes the third phase of the decision-making process, known as the 'choice' phase.

The implementation phase starts with the process of developing the FRP components with their own R&D efforts or by getting assistance from R&D institutes in India on FRP technology and the implementation phase ends when the regular production of FRP components commences.

It is pertinent to mention here that although there is a general flow from intelligence to design, choice and implementation of decision at every phase, there has to be a feedback and a review, and the whole decision-making process is an iterative process. In other words, it may so happen that the decision-maker may not find any suitable choice in the choice phase and may return to the design phase to explore more alternatives.

3.5 The Steps of Decision-making

The phases of decision-making as explained above can be organized into the following steps for an effective decision:

Step 1: Define what you want to achieve.

Step 2: Organize a team for involving the right people for environmental scanning for problem identification.

Step 3: Encourage team members to be participative and assertive during discussion for problem identification. The problems calling for decisions should be arrived at by a consensus opinion of experts and not by any compromise.

Step 4: Set objectives and goals.

Step 5: Generate ideas through brainstorming considering different perspectives.

Step 6: Organize the ideas into common themes and groups as various alternatives.

Step 7: Explore the alternatives considering feasibility, risks and implications of each of the alternatives.

Step 8: Choose the best alternative using various decision tools such as decision trees (described in subsequent paragraphs) and factor comparison analysis to determine the relative importance of various factors. The selection of the best alternative has to be necessarily with reference to the goals or objectives set.

Step 9: Review of the decision is essentially needed at every step mentioned above to ensure that the process is thorough and without any discrepancy at any stage.

Step 10: Communicate the decision to all affected by the same and also explain the same to those involved in the implementation of the decision. This may also need a change management to facilitate a smooth implementation.

3.6 Decision-making under Various Conditions

Decisions can be categorized into five broad categories depending upon the prior knowledge of the outcome of the various alternative decisions. The categories are as follows:

1. **Decisions under certainty:** When there is only one definite outcome for each alternative, there is a finite number of alternatives and exact knowledge about the outcomes, such decisions are deterministic in nature. Many managerial decisions mostly at the operational control level and management control level to some extent are taken under certainty.

2. **Decisions under risk:** When there are multiple possible outcomes for each alternative and a value and probability of occurrence of each outcome can be assessed, the decision under risk is taken

based on the value of each outcome and the probability of occurrence of that particular outcome with respect to the objective. The decisions under risk are therefore prone to certain risk since the outcome for a particular alternative is probabilistic in nature and the risk can only be assessed. Many decisions at the strategic and tactical levels are taken under risk. Sensitivity analysis is a method to insulate a decision-making process or model from risk. It is also referred to as 'what-if' or simulation analysis which in a way predicts the outcome of a decision given a certain range of variables. By creating a given set of variables the analyst can determine how changes in one variable impact the outcome. Vendors of perishable commodities such as fruits have to take decisions regarding the quantities of the commodities they have to purchase from wholesale markets based on their past experience. However, such decisions are associated with some risk.

3. **Decisions under uncertainty:** In case of decision-making under uncertainty, the probabilities of outcomes associated with the alternatives are not known to the decision-maker. In real business environment, the managers are often required to take decisions under varying degrees of uncertainty and in such situations the managers or decision-makers, particularly at the strategic level, exercise their experience and judgement based on available information to assess the uncertainties as probable risks. An example of decision under uncertainty is to select the venue (indoor or outdoor) for holding a party by a club house on a future date. The outcome of the decision is the level of enjoyment which obviously depends on the venue and the weather condition such as sunny, cloud, rainy, cold or hot. The weather condition on a future date is not known to the decision-maker at the time of selection of the venue.

   Managerial decision-making under uncertainties and risks is a sequential process where the decision-maker has to consider possible alternative actions in a logical sequence of the actions and the corresponding outcomes.

4. **Decision-making under conflicting environment:** Ranking and selection of an alternative among many feasible ones, based on a set of conflicting criteria, are important in case of multi-criteria decision-making problems as explained in the subsequent chapter.

5. **Decision-making in a fuzzy environment:** In a fuzzy environment, the goals and the constraints of the decision-making problem are fuzzy in nature, which means that those constitute classes of alternatives whose boundaries are not well defined. An example of a fuzzy goal is: 'return on investment (ROI) should be close to 20%'. Similarly, an example of a fuzzy constraint is: 'the price of an alternate item should not be much higher than the main item.' The bold words in the above examples create the fuzziness. Fuzzy situation often makes use of linguistic variables which consist of one or more words to represent some facts. For example, 'rich people' and 'hot climate' are linguistic variables.

Let us illustrate a few categories of the decisions as mentioned above with typical business decisions. A manufacturing unit requires component X as one of the components for its finished product Y. The component in machined and annealed condition can be bought from the market at a price of ₹110 per piece. The same component can be made in-house by purchasing raw material for the component at a cost of ₹60 per piece, the cost of machining and annealing being ₹40 and ₹20 per piece respectively. The production manager has to decide whether to buy or make the finished component. The objective is cost minimization.

This is a case of decision under certainty, since there are only two alternatives either to buy or to make and the outcome in terms of cost is known with certainty. If bought, the cost would be ₹110, and if made, the cost would be ₹(60 + 40 + 20) = ₹120. Hence, the choice is to buy the component since the cost will be less in case of buying.

An example of decision-making under risk is when a retail fruit seller has to decide how many crates of a particular fruit he has to purchase from wholesale market every day for selling the same in next two days.

The particular fruit is a perishable item and he earns a profit of ₹75 per crate in case the fruit seller can sell within two days, but incurs a loss of ₹50 per crate if he fails to do so. He has to decide how many crates he should purchase for two days' sales of fruits in order to earn maximum profit. The fruit seller is uncertain about the demand of the fruit in next two days. However, with his experience of past sales and judgement, he could convert the uncertainty into likely sales quantities with probabilities associated with such quantities and then can assess purchase quantity from the wholesale market to have maximum profit. However, there is a risk in his assessment.

He has estimated the sales for the next two days as follows:

Sales (Crates)	Probability (%)
0	5
1	30
2	45
3	20

Now the various alternatives available to him are purchasing 0, 1, 2 or 3 crates of fruits. Let us evaluate the outcome for each of these purchase quantities in terms of net expected profit/loss as follows:

Purchase [Crates]	Expected Profit [₹]			Expected Loss [₹]			Net Expected Profit/Loss [₹]
	Profit	Prob.	Expected Profit	Loss	Prob.	Expected Loss	
0	—	—	—	—	—	—	—
1	75	0.95	71.25	50	0.05	2.50	68.75
2	150	0.65	97.5	100	0.05		
				+			
				50	0.30	20	77.50
3	225	0.20	45	150	0.05		
				100	0.30		
				50	0.45	60	[15]

From the outcomes, it can be seen that if his choice is 2 crates, he earns an expected maximum profit. However, the risk involved is 5% loss in his decision.

3.6.1 Models of Decision-making

There are two models of decision-making, namely the prescriptive or normative model and descriptive model.

A prescriptive model is one which selects the optimum (best) alternative. Such models generally are mathematical models developed by operation researchers and economists. Linear programming, integer

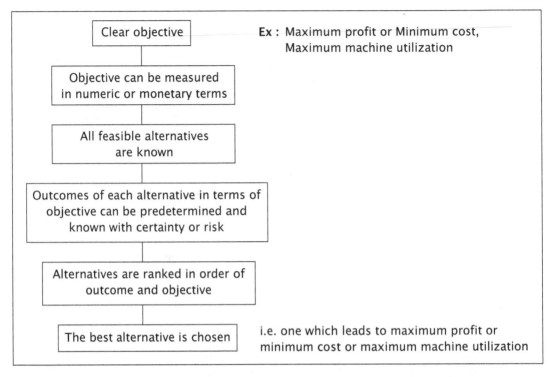

FIGURE 3.2   Rational Decision-making Process

programming, dynamic programming and models to automate decisions on process control, machine replacement and so on are examples of the prescriptive model. Basically, these models are optimizing techniques under conditions of certainty and also risk. The prescriptive model is also known as 'rational decision-making'. The model assumes perfect knowledge and information about all the factors relevant to the decision and adopts a rational and structured approach to arrive at the decision. Rational or prescriptive models of decision-making are more common with the operational control and management control decisions like optimum allocation of funds. Figure 3.2 shows the features of the rational decision-making process.

The descriptive model of decision-making also knows as the 'behavioural model', which was developed by behavioural scientists such as Herbert, A. Simon, J. Von Neuman, O. Morgenstein, A. Tversky and many others, seeks to describe the actual behaviour of the decision-maker while making a decision. This approach vindicates a concept proposed by Simon known as 'Satisficing' to describe the behaviour of decision-makers in a complex and partially unknown situation. Decision-makers in actual business environment are neither fully aware of all the alternatives available, nor is there always a single clear-cut objective. They often make only a limited search to discover a few satisfactory alternatives and finally make a decision that satisfies their aspiration level. The decision-making is heuristic in nature which generally yields a near optimal satisfactory decision as per their aspiration but not necessarily the optimum decision. In the descriptive model, there is not complete rationality as in the case of the prescriptive model, but there is bounded rationality due to imperfection in the information available to the decision-maker, his/her cognitive limitations to perceive alternatives and outcomes and also the time available for decision-making.

An important characteristic of this type of decision behaviour is the application of intuition, judgement and rules of thumb in making decisions rather than the use of explicit decision rules. Many of the decisions at the strategic and also tactical levels of management follow the bounded rationality approach. Let us illustrate this approach with the example of a housewife, while deciding on the investment for her savings in a particular period, the investment options available to her may be many such as small savings deposits with post offices, term deposits with banks, mutual funds, shares and debentures. She often considers a few satisfactory options and then decides to select one or more ways of investing her savings to get a satisfactory return on the same according to her aspiration level. Although her decision may not yield the maximum (optimum) return, due to her limitation of time and efforts to work out the return on all possible investment options and her inability to get the details of all investment schemes available, she has to adopt a bounded rationality while arriving at her choice or decision.

3.6.2 Decision Criteria

Managers or decision-makers while taking decisions under uncertainty without any knowledge of the probabilities of outcomes of various alternatives adopt various payoff criteria. The payoff criteria are mainly the following: (a) maximax, (b) maximin, (c) minimax regret (savage), (d) Hurwicz and (e) Laplace.

The payoff related to the alternative decisions varies depending upon the state of nature which remains unknown at the time of decision-making and the same is also beyond the control of the manager or decision-maker. The payoff can be profit, time, distance, cost or regret. Regret is the opportunity loss for any particular alternative under a particular state of nature.

Let us explain the above payoff criteria with the example of a particular investor who wants to invest for profit. There are three alternatives of investment available to the investor, namely gold, stocks and real estate. The state of nature is the economic condition such as boom, recovery or recession. The payoff table in this case is assumed as follows:

State of Nature (Economic Condition)

Alternatives	Boom	Recovery	Recession
Gold	3,000	1,100	300
Stocks	2,000	1,800	100
Real estate	1,100	1,000	1,000

Criterion 1: Maximax (optimistic) criterion. The alternative having the maximum among the maximum payoffs of all the alternatives is to be selected.

Alternatives	Maximum Payoffs	Maximax
Gold	**3,000**	3,000
Stocks	2,000	—
Real estate	1,100	—

Decision is to invest in gold if maximax is the criterion.

In case of cost, however, the optimistic criterion will be minimin which is minimum of the minimum costs (loss) for the alternatives.

Criterion 2: Maximin (pessimistic) criterion. The alternative having the maximum among the minimum payoffs of all the alternatives is to be selected.

Alternatives	Minimum Payoffs	Maximin
Gold	300	—
Stocks	100	—
Real estate	**1,000**	1,000

Decision is to invest in real estate if maximin is the criterion.

Criterion 3: Hurwicz, α = 0.8 (weighted average) criterion. The alternative having the highest weighted average payoff is to be selected. The weighted average for an alternative = α (maximum payoff) + $(1 - \alpha)$ (minimum payoff).

Since we have taken α as 0.8, the weighted averages for the alternatives are as follows:

> Gold: $0.8 \times 3,000 + (1 - 0.8) \times 300 =$ **2,460** (maximum weighted average)
> Stocks: $0.8 \times 2,000 + (1 - 0.8) \times 100 = 1,620$
> Real estate: $0.8 \times 1,100 + (1 - 0.8) \times 1,000 = 1,080$

Decision is to invest in gold if Hurwicz is the criterion with α = 0.8.

Criterion 4: Laplace (equally likely) criterion. The alternative having the highest average payoff is to be selected. In this case, the average payoff for each alternative is calculated as follows:

> Gold: $(3,000 + 1,100 + 300)/3 =$ **1,467** (maximum average payoff)
> Stocks: $(2,000 + 1,800 + 100)/3 = 1,300$
> Real estate: $(1,100 + 1,000 + 1,000)/3 = 1,033$

Decision is to invest in gold if Laplace is the criterion.

Criteria based on regret (opportunity loss). Regret (also known as opportunity loss) for any alternative for a particular state of nature is the difference between the highest payoff for that state of nature and the actual payoff of the particular alternative. Referring to our example, in case of stocks as the alternative, the actual payoff for the economic boom is 2,000. However, the highest payoff under the same condition of boom is 3,000 for the alternative gold. So, the regret or opportunity loss for the alternative stocks under boom is $(3,000 - 2,000)$ which is 1,000. Proceeding this way, we can calculate the regret values for all the alternatives under the various economic conditions and construct a regret table corresponding to our payoff table.

The regret table is as follows:

State of Nature (Economic Condition)

Alternatives	Boom	Recovery	Recession
Gold	0 (3,000 – 3,000)	700 (1,800 – 1,100)	700 (1,000 – 300)
Stocks	1000 (3,000 – 2,000)	0 (1,800 – 1,800)	900 (1,000 – 100)
Real estate	1,900 (3,000 – 1,100)	800 (1,800 – 1,000)	0 (1,000 – 1,000)

Criterion 5: Minimax regret (savage) criterion. The alternative with the minimum of the maximum regrets of the alternatives is to be selected. The maximum regret for each of the alternatives is as follows:

Alternatives	Maximum Regrets	Minimax Regret
Gold	**700**	700
Stocks	1,000	—
Real estate	1,900	—

So, the decision is to invest in gold following the minimax criterion.

3.6.2.1 Decision Criteria under Risk

In this case, the probabilities for the various states of nature are known. The criteria of decision-making under risk are: (a) expected value (EV) or EMV and (b) expected value of perfect information (EVPI).

Let us now find out the above criteria based on our previous example, assuming the probability values for boom, recovery and recession as 0.2, 0.5 and 0.3 respectively. The same payoff table along with the above probability values is as follows:

State of Nature (Economic Condition)

Alternatives	Boom	Recovery	Recession
Gold	3,000	1,100	300
Stocks	2,000	1,800	100
Real estate	1,100	1,000	1,000
Probability	0.2	0.5	0.3

1. **EMV** is calculated for each alternative as follows:
    i.   EMV (Gold) = $(3,000 \times 0.2) + (1,100 \times 0.5) + (300 \times 0.3) = 1,240$
    ii. EMV (Stocks) = $(2,000 \times 0.2) + (1,800 \times 0.5) + (100 \times 0.3) = 1330$ (maximum)
    iii. EMV (Real estate) = $(1,100 \times 0.2) + (1,000 \times 0.5) + (1,000 \times 0.3) = 1,020$

Hence, decision is to invest in stocks.

2. **EVPI** is the additional payoff for perfect information which is expressed as follows:
    i.   EVPI = EV (with perfect information) – EV (without perfect information) = EV (with perfect information) – maximum EMV; maximum EMV = 1330
    ii. Perfect information would reveal to the decision-maker the fact that gold, stocks and real estate would fetch highest payoffs under economic conditions of boom recovery and recession respectively. Hence, EV (with perfect information) will be:

    $(0.2 \times 3,000) + (0.5 \times 1,800) + (0.3 \times 1,000) = 1,600$; and EVPI = $1,600 - 1,330 = 270$.

3.7 Decision-making Tools

3.7.1 Decision Tree

A decision tree is a diagram which can organize a decision-making problem's alternatives, risks and uncertainty in the forms of activity forks and event forks associated with each activity.

This analysis consists of the following steps:

1. Identify all possible alternatives (activities) and the risks associated with each situation (event).
2. Calculate the consequences of each of the alternatives in EMV.
3. Determine the uncertainty (risk) associated with each alternative.
4. Combine 1, 2 and 3 into a tree diagram.
5. Determine the best alternative considering the EMV. A decision tree consists of three types of nodes. Decision nodes commonly represented by squares, chance nodes represented by circles and end nodes represented by triangles.

3.7.1.1 Examples of Decision Tree

Example 1: A company is considering whether to launch a new product or improve an existing product as per customer preferences. If it launches the new product, it has to hire a new plant exclusively for the new product which will cost ₹20 lakhs or work overtime with additional expenses on labour to the extent of ₹8 lakhs. If it decides to improve upon the existing product, it will incur an additional cost of ₹12 lakhs in modernizing its existing plants. A market survey has revealed the following data regarding the magnitude of sales of the new product and also the same for the improved product.

Magnitude of Sales	Probability		Resulting Profit in [₹ Lakhs]	
	New	Improved	New	Improved
High	0.50	0.40	40	30
Medium	0.30	0.35	18	12
Low	0.15	0.20	8	6
Nil	0.05	0.05	−10 [Loss]	−4

However, high sales cannot be fulfilled by working overtime or by improving upon existing products. Further, the cost of a new plant, additional cost for modernizing the existing plant and the additional expenses for working overtime have not been considered in the resulting profit calculations. The decision tree in this case is shown in Figure 3.3.

So, the EMV is maximum for a new product by working overtime (₹7.10), hence the decision is to develop a new product with overtime working.

Example 2: A student after higher secondary examination is to decide whether to study engineering or medicine for a graduation course of four years' duration. The probability that demand for engineering graduates will boom in the next four years is 0.40 (40%). Similarly, there is a probability of 0.50 (50%) boom in demand for medical graduates. If there is a boom in the demand for engineering graduates, the

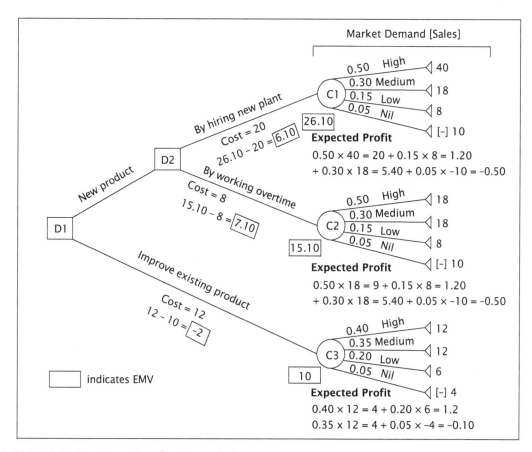

FIGURE 3.3   Decision Tree for Example 1

average annual cost to company (CTC) for a fresher is assessed to be ₹9 lakhs, otherwise the same is expected to be ₹5 lakhs. In case of fresh medical graduates, the corresponding figures are ₹8 lakhs and ₹7 lakhs respectively. Let us draw a simple decision tree in this case to find out which stream the student should select, without considering the cost of studies as a parameter for the decision. The decision tree is shown in Figure 3.4.

From the above decision tree, it can be seen that expected CTC is ₹7.50 lakhs for a fresh medical graduate after four years which is more than the same (6.60) for engineering streams. Hence, the choice is to select the medical stream.

Example 3: A multi-storey building owner is considering drilling a deep borewell to augment municipal water supply. In the past, only 60% of wells drilled in the area were successful at 300 feet depth. Moreover, on finding no water at 300 feet, some owners drilled further up to 350 feet but only 25% struck water. The cost of drilling is ₹40 per feet. The owner has estimated that the other alternative is to buy additional water from the municipal corporation at a cost of ₹1,800 per annum over the next 10 years. Let us draw an appropriate decision tree and determine the owner's strategy for minimum cost. The decision tree is as shown in Figure 3.5.

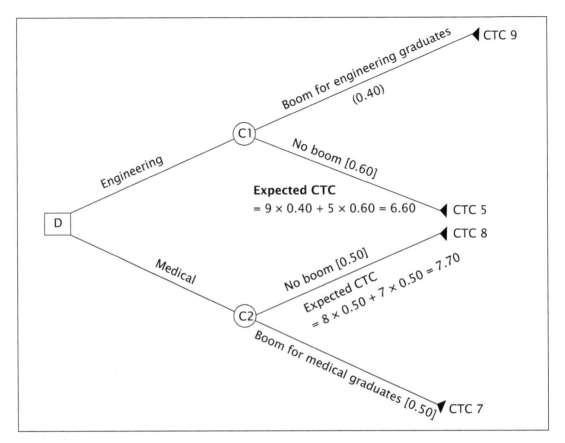

FIGURE 3.4 Decision Tree for Example 2

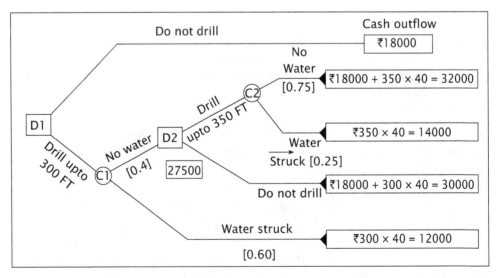

FIGURE 3.5 Decision Tree for Example 3

Decision point D2

1. Expected cash outflow for drilling up to 350 ft = (0.75 × 32,000) + (0.25 × 14,000) = 24,000 + 3,500 = 27,500
2. Cash outflow for not drilling up to 350 ft = 30,000

Decision point D1

1. Do not drill, cash outflow = 18,000
2. Drill up to 300 ft

   Expected cash flow = (27,500 × 0.40) + (12,000 × 0.60) = 11,000 + 7,200 = 182,000

Hence, decision is not to drill with minimum cash outflow of ₹18,000.

Example 4: A private inter-state bus transport company is considering operating on a new route. It has got two alternatives, Route 1 and Route 2, as the traffic is more compared to the available state bus service operating in either of these two routes. The company is also contemplating introducing four new buses either deluxe or ordinary, and the cost of a new deluxe bus would be ₹20 lakhs and that for an ordinary bus would be ₹15 lakhs. The company assessed passenger volume and likely resultant operating profit without considering depreciation of the buses over their total life span for both deluxe and ordinary bus service for the two routes separately. The assessed figures have been shown in the following table.

	Route 1					Route 2			
Volume of Passengers	Probability		Resultant Profit [₹ Lakhs]		Volume of Passengers	Probability		Resultant Profit [₹ Lakhs]	
	Ordinary	Deluxe	Ordinary	Deluxe		Ordinary	Deluxe	Ordinary	Deluxe
High	0.45	0.25	400	600	High	0.50	0.20	500	700
Medium	0.30	0.35	300	500	Medium	0.35	0.30	400	600
Low	0.25	0.40	200	300	Low	0.15	0.50	300	500

The company also feels that there is 60% chance of getting state government approval for operating in Route 1 and 70% chance for the same in case of Route 2.

Due to the minimum cooling-off period required between two consecutive trips for the buses running in Route 2, it is not possible to cope up with the high passenger volume in Route 2, and four buses running in Route 2 (being a long distance route) can handle only medium and low passenger traffic. The decision tree in this case has been shown in Figure 3.6.

Decision point D2

Deluxe bus:

Expected resultant profit
= (600 × 0.25) + (0.35 × 500) + (0.40 × 300)
= 150 + 175 + 120 = 445

Cost of deluxe buses = 80
EMV = 445 – 80 = 365

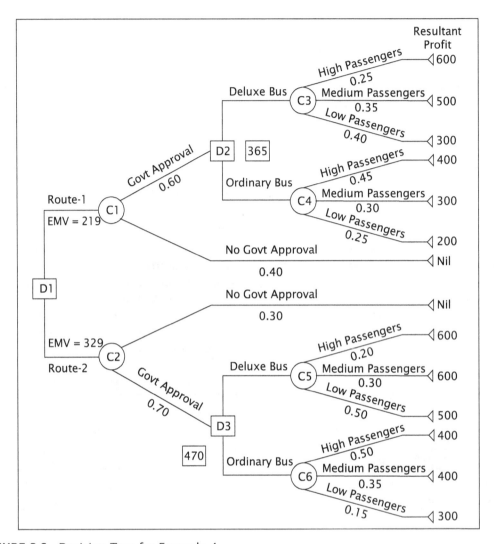

FIGURE 3.6   Decision Tree for Example 4

Ordinary bus:

Expected resultant profit
= (400 × 0.45) + (300 × 0.30) + (200 × 0.25)
= 180 + 90 + 50 = 320

Cost of ordinary buses = 60
EMV = 320 − 60 = 260

Net EMV at D2

= 365 for deluxe buses.

Decision point D3

Deluxe bus:

Expected resultant profit
= (600 × 0.20) + (600 × 0.30) + (500 × 0.50)
= 120 + 180 + 250 = 550

Cost of deluxe buses = 80

EMV = 550 – 80 = 470

Ordinary bus: Expected resultant profit

$= (400 \times 0.50) + (400 \times 0.35) + (300 \times 0.15)$

$= 200 + 140 + 45 = 385$

Cost of ordinary buses = 60

EMV = 385 – 60 = 325

Therefore, net EMV at D3 = 470 for deluxe buses.

EMV for Route 1 $= (0.60 \times 365) + (0.40 \times 0)$

$= 219 + 0 = 219$

EMV for Route 2 $= (0.70 \times 470) + (0.30 \times 0)$

$= 329 + 0 = 329$

Since EMV for Route 2 is higher than that for Route 1, the decision is to run deluxe buses in Route 2.

3.7.2 Decision Table

Decision tables are used to list out in tabular form all possible situations (set of conditions) which a business decision may encounter and to specify which action to take in each of those situations.

A decision table is a tabular form that represents a set of conditions and their corresponding actions. A decision table essentially consists of: (a) condition stubs, (b) action stubs, (c) rules consisting of the condition alternatives and combinations thereof and (d) the action entries.

Condition stubs describe the conditions or factors in different rows that will affect the decision or policy. They are listed in the upper part of a decision table.

Action stubs which form the lower part of the decision table describe in the form of statements, the possible action entries or decisions in different rows. Rules describe unique combination of conditions and the actions associated with each such combination.

	I. Condition Stub	*R1*	*R2*	*R3*	*R4*	*R5*	*R6*	*R7*	*R8*
					II. Rules [R1 ... to R8]				
	Condition C1	Y	Y	Y	Y	N	N	N	N
	Condition C2	Y	N	N	Y	N	Y	N	N
	Condition C3	Y	Y	N	N	Y	N	Y	N
	Action A1	X		X				X	
	Action A2		X		X	X			
III. Action Stub	Action A3			X		X			
	Action A4	X				X	X		

IV. Action Entries

Action entries contain the list of actions associated with each rule specified by putting a cross (x) in the appropriate columns of the action entries section of the decision table. The above sections can be represented in the form of four quadrants of a decision table as shown above. For example, Rule R2 is to take action A2 when conditions C1 and C3 exist but condition C2 does not exist.

A decision table can in a precise and compact way model complicated logic and decision rules. It can associate many independent conditions and their various combinations and the corresponding multiple actions in an elegant way like a checklist.

Apart from the basic four-quadrant structure, decision tables vary widely in the way the condition alternatives or rules and action entries are represented. Some decision tables adopt only true/false values (Y/N) to represent presence or absence of a condition, whereas other tables may use different data attribute values for the conditions, such as the gender of an employee (male or female) and age group (young, middle, senior). Some decision tables even use fuzzy logic or probabilistic representation for the conditions in a rule.

Action entries in a similar way can simply represent whether an action is to be performed (check the actions to perform as a checklist) or in more advanced decision tables the sequencing of actions to perform (numbering the actions as 1, 2, 3 and so on.)

3.7.2.1 *Methodology of Preparing a Decision Table*

The whole methodology of framing a decision table can be divided into following steps in a sequence:

Step 1: *Identify conditions and the values.* Identify all the conditions relevant to the situation and the possible values associated with the data attribute of each condition. For example, the possible values of the attribute states of a traffic signal can be 'red', 'green' or 'yellow' only. Similarly, the possible values of a condition that a machine is idle can be two, namely 'yes' or 'no'. 'Yes' if the machine is idle and 'no' if the machine is running.

Step 2: *Compute the maximum number of rules.* Multiply the number of values for each condition data attribute by each other. For example, if there are three conditions and each condition can have two values for attribute such as 'true' or 'false', the maximum number of rules will be $2 \times 2 \times 2 = 8$.

Step 3: *Identify possible actions.* Determine each independent action to be taken for the decision rule.

Step 4: *Enter all possible rules in the decision table.* Fill in the values of the condition data attributes in each rule column.

Step 5: *Define actions for each rule.* For each rule, mark the appropriate actions with an X in the decision table.

Step 6: *Verify the decision rules or policies.* Review completed decision table with end users.

Step 7: *Simplify the table.* By eliminating and/or consolidating rules which are unfeasible or repetitions, reduce the number of columns.

Step 8: For very complex business problems involving many rules make multiple decision tables and arrange the tables in a hierarchy of rules in the logical sequence of their application in the problem-solving scenario.

Example 5: A marketing company wishes to construct a decision table to decide the different discount rates to different categories of customers. The categories of customers are retailers and distributors, each having status of either registered with the company or not and the average volume of business per year: A (below ₹10 lakhs), B (between 10 and 20 lakhs) and C (over 20 lakhs). The company offers four discount rates, namely 5%, 8%, 10% and 12.5%. A discount of 5% is allowed to retailers who have average business below 10 lakhs, 8% discount is allowed to all retailers having volume of business between 10 and 20 lakhs, and 8% discount is allowed to all registered distributors having annual business volume less than 10 lakhs. All registered distributors having annual business between 10 and 20 lakhs are allowed 10% discount, 12.5% discount is allowed to all retailers and distributors having annual business volume over 20 lakhs. All distributors who want to make an annual business of ₹10 lakhs and above have to register themselves.

No discount is allowed to any unregistered retailer. However, a discount of 5% is allowed to all unregistered distributors having volume of business in a year less than ₹10 lakhs.

> **Step 1:** *Identify conditions and values.* The three data attributes tested by the conditions in this problem are category, with values retailers (R) and distributors (D); registration status with values Y (registered) and N (not registered) and average annual business volume with values A, B and C as stated in the problem.
>
> **Step 2:** *Compute maximum number of rules.* The maximum number of rules is $2 \times 2 \times 3 = 12$.
>
> However, all of them are not feasible.
>
> **Step 3:** *Identify possible actions.* The four actions are: offer discount rates of 5%, 8%, 10% and 12.5%.
>
> **Step 4:** *Enter all feasible rules.* The upper portion of the table would be as follows:
>
> It may be noted that all combinations of values are present.

					Rules							
Conditions	*1*	*2*	*3*	*4*	*5*	*6*	*7*	*8*	*9*	*10*	*11*	*12*
Category	R	D	R	D	R	D	R	D	R	D	R	D
Status of registration	Y	Y	N	N	Y	Y	N	N	Y	Y	N	N
Average annual business	A	A	A	A	B	B	B	B	C	C	C	C

Rules 3, 7, 8, 11 and 12 are not possible since unregistered retailers and also unregistered distributors having annual business of B and C are not allowed. Hence, the feasible rules are only seven as follows:

				Rules			
Conditions	*1*	*2*	*3*	*4*	*5*	*6*	*7*
Category	R	D	D	R	D	R	D
Status of registration	Y	Y	N	Y	Y	Y	Y
Average annual business [Lakhs]	A	A	A	B	B	C	C

Step 5: *Define actions for each rule.* The bottom of the table would look as follows:

	Rules						
Offer Discount	1	2	3	4	5	6	7
5%	X		X				
8%		X		X			
10%					X		
12.5%						X	X

Step 6: *Verify the policy.* Let us assume that the client agreed with the above discount policy.
Step 7: *Simplify the table.* There appears no infeasible rule. Note that rules 6 and 7 have similar action pattern (12.5% discount) and have two of the three condition values (status of registration and average annual business) as identical and all the two values of non-identical value (category) are covered, so they can be condensed into a single column 6. The revised table will be as shown in Table 3.1.

	Rules					
Conditions	1	2	3	4	5	6
Category	R	D	D	R	D	–
Status of registration	Y	Y	N	Y	Y	Y
Average annual business [Lakhs]	A	A	A	B	B	C

TABLE 3.1 Decision Table for Example 5						
	Rules					
Actions : Offer Discount	1	2	3	4	5	6
5%	X		X			
8%		X		X		
10%					X	
12.5%						X

Example 6: A Central Government Health Scheme (CGHS) beneficiary can avail the following medical facilities. He/she can consult the CGHS doctor and with his/her reference get the treatment performed in a CGHS recognized hospital or nursing home with full reimbursement of all costs including medicine cost. However, in case of emergency he/she can get directly admitted to the nearest hospital/nursing home without any reference. In that case, if the hospital/nursing home is not a CGHS recognized one, he/she can get reimbursement for nursing at the rates charged by the All India Institute of Medical Sciences for the same medical treatment.

However, if the hospital or nursing home happens to be a CGHS recognized one, he/she will get reimbursement at CGHS package rates only irrespective of the actual costs incurred. In either case of emergency admission and treatment, the cost of medicines consumed is reimbursable in full. However, in case of non-emergency, if anyone avails of any treatment without CGHS reference, he/she is not entitled to any reimbursement including cost of medicines. The decision table in this case can be formed as shown below.

	Rules							
Conditions	*1*	*2*	*3*	*4*	*5*	*6*	*7*	*8*
1. CGHS reference	Y	Y	Y	Y	N	N	N	N
2. CGHS recognised	Y	N	Y	N	Y	Y	N	N
3. Emergency case	Y	Y	N	N	Y	N	Y	N
Actions								
1. Full reimbursement	X		X					
2. Reimbursement at CGHS package rates					X			
3. Reimbursement at AIIMS rates							X	
4. No reimbursement						X		X
5. Reimbursement of actual cost of medicines	X		X		X		X	
		Infeasible case		Infeasible case				

The simplified decision table will be as shown in Table 3.2.

TABLE 3.2 Decision Table for Example 6

	Rules					
Condition	*1*	*2*	*3*	*4*	*5*	*6*
1. CGHS reference	Y	Y	N	N	N	N
2. CGHS recognized	Y	Y	Y	Y	N	N
3. Emergency case	Y	N	Y	N	Y	N
Actions						
1. Full reimbursement	X	X				
2. Reimbursement at CGHS package rates			X			
3. Reimbursement at AIIMS rates				X		
4. No reimbursement				X		X
5. Reimbursement of actual cost of medicines	X	X	X		X	

Example 7: A technical support company writes a decision table to sort out computer printer troubleshooting as shown in Table 3.3.

TABLE 3.3 Decision Table for Example 7

			Rules					
Conditions	1	2	3	4	5	6	7	8
1. Printer does not print	Y	Y	Y	Y	N	N	N	N
2. A red light is flashing	Y	Y	N	N	Y	Y	N	N
3. Printer is unrecognized	Y	N	Y	N	Y	N	Y	N
Actions:								
1. Check the power cable				X				
2. Check the printer-computer cable		X		X				
3. Ensure printer software is installed		X		X		X		X
4. Check/replace ink		X	X			X	X	
5. Check for paper jam			X		X			
								Infeasible Rule

The above decision table is a simple one, but even so, it demonstrates how decision tables can scale to several conditions, many possibilities and a checklist of actions associated with each decision rule.

Example 8: A preliminary decision table for the driver of a car in case of engine troubleshooting may be as shown in Table 3.4.

TABLE 3.4 Decision Table for Example 8

					Rules				
	Car Does Not Start	Y	Y	Y	Y	N	N	N	N
Conditions	Charge indicator is red	Y	Y	N	N	Y	Y	N	N
	Fuel indicator is red	Y	N	Y	N	Y	N	Y	N
Actions	Check/Fill fuel	X		X		X		X	
	Check battery/recharge	X	X						
	Check the dynamo belt/replace	X	X				X	X	
	Employ choke					X			
	Check/clean oil filter					X			
									Infeasible Rule

3.7.2.2 Hierarchy of Multiple Decision Tables in Case of Complex Problems

In many practical and complex decision-making situations, there may be many decision rules and the rules applicable may depend upon the actions taken and the outcome pursuant to an earlier decision rule. In other words, there may be levels of decision tables with an overall decision table at the first level and depending upon the outcome of the actions taken, there may be a greater number of decision rules at the second, third levels and so on. The following example of a medical diagnosis of a patient having fever will illustrate such hierarchy of decision tables.

Diagnosis of a patient having fever [Body temperature above 98.4° F]

Level-1 Decision Table

	Rules							
Condition of Patient	1	2	3	4	5	6	7	8
Body temperature above 100° F	Y	Y	Y	Y	N	N	N	N
Fever persists more than 72 hours	Y	N	Y	N	Y	N	Y	N
Having cough and cold	Y	Y	N	N	N	Y	Y	N
Actions [Prescribe]								
Paracetamol tablets	X	X	X	X				
General antibiotic	X	X	X	X	X	X	X	X
Cough syrup	X	X				X	X	
Pathological tests	X		X		X		X	
	↓		↓		↓		↓	
	Level 2		Level 2		Level 2		Level 2	

Level-2 Decision Table

	Rules							
Conditions	1	2	3	4	5	6	7	8
Urine Report OK	Y	Y	Y	Y	N	N	N	N
Sr Bilirubin OK	Y	N	Y	N	Y	N	Y	N
Malaria parasite present	Y	Y	N	N	N	Y	Y	N
Actions:								
Consult General Physician			X					
Consult Malaria Clinic	X	X				X	X	
Consult Urologist					X		X	X
Consult Liver specialist/Gastroentrologist		X		X				X

The above two decision tables are only illustrative examples for showing the hierarchy of decision tables at various levels and not an exhaustive case of actual diagnosis. Decision tables are often good methods of documentation of decision rules and actions relating to operational control and management control levels of decisions.

CASE STUDY: CREDIT RISK ASSESSMENT IS CARRIED OUT BY BANK OF AMERICA FOR MAKING CREDIT LENDING DECISIONS

Methodology Adopted by Bank of America

Bank of America uses credit risk scoring in making their credit-lending decisions. Credit scoring is not only applied to assess lending decisions, but also used for ongoing credit-risk management and collection strategies. A spectrum of scorecard development methodologies, such as logistic regression, decision trees, mathematical programming, survival analysis and modelling, is used by different lines of business. Among all these techniques, logistic regression is the most commonly used method for scorecard building at Bank of America. Logistic regression has been an optimal choice for developing credit-scoring models as it is designed to handle binary outcome and it provides probability values which cannot lie beyond the range of 0–1. Logistic regression uses maximum likelihood estimation process, which transforms the dependent variable into a log function and estimates the regression coefficients in a way that maximizes the log-likelihood.

For front-end approval/rejection decision-making, application scorecard (A-score) is used while for back-end customer-risk management, behaviour scorecard (B-score) is used. Both of these measure the likelihood of a customer becoming a defaulter over a certain period of time (known as performance window). The performance window for both A-score and B-score was chosen to be 12 months. Bank of America portfolio mostly consists of retail consumers, and the data set was extracted from external sources (bureau data) and internal data warehouses, which contained the following information:

- Customer information (e.g., customer ID, age, years in job)
- Product information (e.g., number of credit cards, credit limit of the cards)
- Internal behavioural information (e.g., number and amount of past dues and delinquency records)
- External information (e.g., credit bureau score)
- Macroeconomic indicators (GDP and unemployment rate by geographical areas)

As for the default, a definition of 'bad' behaviour is when a payment is 90 days or more overdue. The status of a customer is monitored over 12 months after the date of issuance of the card to predict any 'bad' behaviour.

The data set contained more than 200 predictor variables and a binary flag variable for default instances. The data set was partitioned into simple random samples of 70% observations for training set and 30% observation for validation set. Initial stage of model development process involved analysing distributions of predictor variables and checking for outliers and missing values. Data treatments were conducted to account for anomalies in data.

The model is built using statistical analysis system (SAS). SAS is a commercial statistical software. 'Proc logistic' was leveraged to estimate the model parameters. Information value (IV) statistic was used for selecting predictor variables for the binary logistic regression. Based on the average predictive performance of the independent individual variables, the variable selection cut-off point was set at IV of 0.1. Out of more than 200 predictor variables in the data set, 52 variables were selected for the final model. Once the short list of 52 variables was selected, further assessment was done to check for multicollinearity among the variables for the final model. Highly correlated variables with correlation coefficient more than 0.5 were dropped. Stepwise regression was carried out by an iterative process using forward selection of variables, which starts with no variable in the model, adding a single variable at each step using a chosen model comparison criterion. Predictor variables are added in their order of relative improvements to the model and the process is repeated until none of the remaining variables improves the model. Akaike information criterion (AIC) and Bayesian information criterion (BIC) were used for the final variable selection of the model based on stepwise forward logistic regression. The final model had 14 independent variables. Once the logistic regression model was built, the model performance on the testing sample for validation was done. Widely used statistics such as Kolmogorov–Smirnov (KS) chart and Gini coefficients were computed for the purpose of evaluating the improved odds to differentiate the good credit applicants from bad credit applicants.

Summary and Conclusions

Credit risk scorecard development is an iterative process and the resultant scorecard must satisfy a number of performance standards, including stability and interpretability. However, there is no unique quantitative framework that all organizations must follow, and the decision-making process varies for each organization, depending on a range of factors such as the available data and resources and the risk appetite of the organization. The industry standard for credit-lending risk is less than 2%, which implies that out of 100 cases of credit-lending decisions taken by a bank only in 2 cases there may be default. The banks and other financial institutions may design innovative and improved credit risk assessment methods to even reduce the chance of default to less than 2%.

⇒ Review Questions ⇐

1. What are programmed and non-programmed decisions? Illustrate with suitable examples.

2. What are the phases of decision-making as per Simon? Is the decision-making process iterative in nature? Explain.

3. What are the various ISs for the typical decisions taken by the different levels of management in an organization?

4. What is Simon's 'Satisficing principle'? Explain with suitable illustrations relating to organizational decisions.

5. A manager has a choice between: (a) a risky contract promising ₹8 lakhs with a probability of 0.7 and ₹5 lakhs with a probability of 0.3 and (b) a diversified portfolio consisting of two contracts with independent outcomes and each promising ₹4.5 lakhs with probability 0.55 and ₹2.5 lakhs with probability 0.45. Construct a decision tree using EMV criteria. Can you arrive at the decision?

6. ABC Co. is considering the manufacture of a new product. If manufacturing is started without research, it is estimated that there is a 60% probability of good sales, giving a net profit of ₹35,000 and a 40% probability of poor sales with a resultant net loss of ₹25,000. If research is undertaken (at a cost of ₹7,000), it is estimated that there is 90% chance it will indicate that sales will be high and a 10% probability that it will forecast low sales. It is possible, however, for research of this type when it gives a good indication, to be correct 70% of the time (when the net profit is calculated to be ₹45,000) and incorrect 30% of the time (when a net loss of ₹6,000 is incurred). If research forecasts poor sales, there is a 80% chance it is correct (with a net loss of ₹11,000) and 20% chance it is wrong (when profit is

₹9,000 net). Prepare a decision tree showing the various alternative lines of action open to the company and indicate the optimum strategy.

7. A doctor has to decide whether or not to perform a serious surgical operation on a patient suspected of malignant tumour in the upper abdomen. If the patient has tumour and the doctor operates, the chance of recovery is 65%; without an operation, the chance of recovery is only 15%. On the other hand, if the patient does not have tumour and operation is performed, there is 70% chance of survival of the patient whereas there is no chance of death without the surgical operation. Use the decision tree approach to determine whether to perform the operation or not. Assume only two possibilities—either recovery or death.

8. A car air-conditioner manufacturing unit is considering whether to release a new model in the market or to continue further testing to make it problem-free in operation. Releasing it immediately will ensure good sales, since no other competitor is there for this type of model. However, this would involve an estimated risk of 12% because of serious operational problems which may tarnish the image of the unit and result in decreasing the revenue from ₹150 lakhs to ₹75 lakhs. However, another four months testing would reduce the chance of problems to 6%, but there will be an estimated 8% risk of a competitor developing a similar model and in that case loss of revenue to the extent of 20% will result in. However, even after testing for four months if there is any problem, the revenue will become half. Use a decision tree to calculate the EMV of the options to decide what the unit should do.

9. Draw a decision table for the following discount policy of a distributor of mobile cell phones. If order is more than 5,000 units allow 3% discount. If delivery is within 35 km allow 2% discount, if not already given 3% quantity discount as above, otherwise only 1% discount to be allowed. A further discount of 2% will be allowed to a retailer, if the total purchase made during the last 12 months is 1 lakhs units or more.

10. An employee payroll system computes salary of the employees as follows:
The employees can be workers, supervisors or managers. If the employees work more than 160 hours in a month, they are given fixed salary plus extra amount per hour at the rate of ₹200, 100 and 50 for a manager, a supervisor and a worker respectively. In case any of them works more than 200 hours per month, he or she is given an additional allowance of ₹600 per month irrespective of the category of the employee.

Prepare a decision table to show the above decision rules and the associated extra payments for each category of the employees.

Bibliography

Bellman, R. E., and L. A. Zadeh. 'Decision-making in a Fuzzy Environment.' *Management Science* 17, no. 4 (1970): 141–164.

Quinlan, J. R. 'Simplifying Decision Trees.' *International Journal of Man-Machine Studies* 27, no. 3 (1987): 221–234.

Ross, R. G. 'Decision Tables, Part1~The Route to Consolidated Business Logic.' *Business Rules Journal* 6, no. 7 (2005). Available at: http://www.brcommunity.com/a2005/b240.html (accessed on 26 March 2020).

———. 'Decision Tables, Part2~The Route to Completeness.' *Business Rules Journal* 6, no. 8 (2005). Available at: http://www.brcommunity.com/a2005/b243.html (accessed on 26 March 2020).

Ross, R. G. 'Designing Decision Tables Part 1: Basics.' *Business Rules Journal* 15, no. 4 (2014, April). Available at: http://www.brcommunity.com/a2014/b754.html (accessed on 26 March 2020).

———. 'Designing Decision Tables Part 2: Fundamental Styles.' *Business Rules Journal* 15, no. 5 (2014). Available at: http://www.brcommunity.com/a2014/b759.html (accessed on 26 March 2020).

———. 'Designing Decision Tables Part 3: Representing Meaning (Semantics).' *Business Rules Journal* 15, no. 6 (2014). Available at: http://www.brcommunity.com/a2014/b764.html (accessed on 26 March 2020).

Simon, H. A. 'A Behavioral Model of Rational Choice.' *The Quarterly Journal of Economics* 69, no. 1 (1955): 99–118.

———. 'Bounded Rationality and Organizational Learning.' *Organization Science* 2, no. 1 (1991): 125–134.

Wagner, H. M. *Principles of Operations Research with Application to Managerial Decisions*, 2nd ed. Englewood Cliffs, NJ: Prentice Hall, 1975.

4
CHAPTER

Decision Support Systems

4.1 Introduction

IS designers, researchers and technology experts had been developing and investigating DSSs for nearly four decades. This development in DSS started with building model-driven DSS in the early 1970s, theory development in the late 1970s and the implementation of financial planning systems, spreadsheet DSS and group DSS in the early and mid-1980s. DSSs represent systems to support decision-making. In the context of business organizations, decision-making includes all types of decisions taken by managers at all levels in the hierarchy. In fact, DSSs are models which analyse business data into information to facilitate quality decisions. DSS applications are systems and subsystems that help managers to make decisions based on data from a wide range of sources.

4.2 Taxonomies

As with the definition, there is no universally accepted taxonomy of DSS. Different authors propose different classifications. Hatten Schwiler differentiates passive, active and cooperative DSS. A passive DSS is a system that aids the process of decision-making, but cannot bring out explicit decisions, suggestions or solutions. An active DSS can bring out such decisions, suggestions or solutions. A cooperative DSS allows the decision-maker (or its advisor) to modify, complete or refine the decision suggestions provided by the system, before sending them back to the system for validation. The system again improves, completes and refines the suggestions of the decision-makers and sends them back to them for validation. The whole process then starts again, until a consolidated solution is generated. Alter classified DSSs into six types. His classification was based on what the user does with them. The first and the simplest type of DSS is the one which retrieves isolated data items. A common example of this type of DSS is a shop floor IS, where the shop supervisor juggles this information to obtain productivity data by operation, machine or operator-wise. The second type of DSS is the one which both retrieves and analyses the data such as a portfolio analysis system in a bank. The third type of DSS is the one which uses multiple database and obtains pre-specified aggregation of data in the form of reports. The example of this type of DSS is the sales IS. The fourth type of DSS is the one which evaluates decisions using an accounting or simulation model.

The purpose is finding consequences of alternative decisions. Examples of this type of DSS are accounting models for source and application of funds, marketing decision systems such as levels of advertisement, pricing and many others. The fifth type of DSS proposes decisions by mathematical modelling and optimization techniques known as programming. An example of this type of DSS includes optimization of resource allocation and usage. Operation research (OR) techniques come under the purview of this category. The sixth and the latest type of DSS is one which makes decisions. This type of system is applicable in cases where the decisions are highly structured and programmable. The sixth type of DSS is usually online and real time in nature such as process control, airline reservations and many such applications.

Another taxonomy for DSS has been created by Daniel Power, according to the mode of assistance as the criterion, namely communication-driven DSS, data-driven DSS, document-driven DSS, knowledge-driven DSS and model-driven DSS. A communication-driven DSS supports more than one person working on a shared task such as Microsoft's 'NetMeeting' and 'Groove' for a peer to peer solution. A data-driven DSS or data-oriented DSS emphasizes access to and manipulation of a time series of organizational data and external data to yield decision-assisting information. A document-driven DSS manages, retrieves and manipulates unstructured information in a variety of electronic formats. A knowledge-driven DSS provides specialized problem-solving expertise stored as facts, rules, procedures in similar or in other forms. Certain expert systems are knowledge-driven DSSs.

A model-driven DSS emphasizes according to manipulation of a statistical, financial, optimization or simulation model.

Model-driven DSS uses data and parameters provided by users to assist decision-makers in analysing a situation; they are not necessarily data intensive. General Purpose Simulation System (GPSS), Arena 5.0 are examples of computer-driven simulation models.

Power mentioned about two different types of DSS, namely enterprise-wide DSS and desktop DSS. An enterprise-wide DSS is linked to large data warehouses and serves many managers at all levels in the organization. A desktop with single user DSS is a small system that runs on an individual manager's PC such as a spreadsheet model developed by a manager on his computer. In fact, there can be a third type known as group decision support system (GDSS) which facilitates decisions taken by a group of managers collectively.

A study and analysis of the DSSs for managerial decision-making reveals that not every DSS fits into one category or architecture exactly but the DSSs often are a mixture of more than one architecture. Holsapple and Whinston classified DSS into six frameworks. Those are text-oriented DSS, database-oriented DSS, spreadsheet-oriented DSS, solver-oriented DSS, rule-oriented DSS and compound DSS. A compound DSS is the most popular classification of a DSS. It is a hybrid system that includes more than one of the first five frameworks as mentioned above.

4.3 Components of a DSS

The main components or subsystems of a DSS are the following (Figure 4.1):

1. User interface subsystem
2. Database management subsystem
3. Model base management subsystem
4. The users (decision-makers) themselves

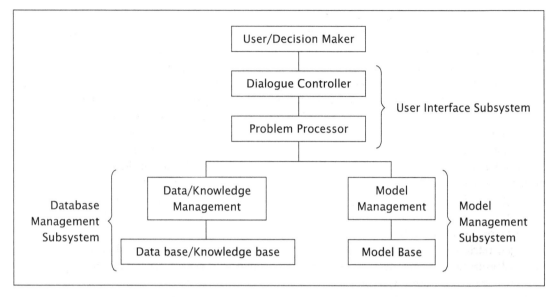

FIGURE 4.1 Components of a DSS

Generally, a DSS has three major components:

1. The data and knowledge management subsystem, which is a body of knowledge and data, selects the particular model that fits into the specific problem and also the data that must be fed into the model by manipulating the database.
2. The language system which is the total medium of communication between the decision-maker and the DSS for decision-making based on the data and models made available to him/her. The language system also provides help facilities to the user/decision-maker.
3. The problem processor is the interface between the language system (dialogue controller) and the knowledge and data subsystems. The problem processor contains algorithms for tools and techniques such as discrete simulation, statistical techniques for regression analysis, trend analysis and projection, linear programming, integer programming and dynamic programming.

4.4 Model Management System: Arena 5.0

As an illustration of a model management system, let us highlight the features of Arena 5.0. Arena 5.0 was developed by Rockwell Software, California, USA, for the purpose of computer simulation to mimic the behaviour of real systems on computer to enable decision-makers to have forward visibility of the systems on computer and to further enable decision-makers to test the outcome of what-if type of decisions relating to those systems. Unlike special purpose simulation language such as GPSS, SIMSCRIPT and SLAM, Arena 5.0 combines the ease of use found in high-level simulators with the flexibility of simulation languages and even all the way down to general purpose procedure languages such as the Microsoft Visual Basic programming system or 'C'. Arena 5.0 does this by providing alternative and interchangeable templates of graphical simulation modelling and analysis modules that one can combine to build a fairly wide variety of simulation models. For the ease of display, organizational modules are typically grouped into panels to compose a template. By switching panels, one can gain access to a whole different set of simulation modelling constructs and capabilities.

Arena 5.0 is flexible in modelling because of its hierarchical structure with a single-graphical-user interface consistent at any level of modelling. At the lower end of the hierarchy are user written codes in Visual Basic, C/C++ and at the higher end are user-created templates which are constructs on company specific processes. The intermediate levels of modelling may include elementary blocks of SIMAN simulation language, advanced process and transfer panels, basic process panels and application solution templates such as assembly and testing lines. Arena 5.0 enables a manager/decision-maker to do the following:

1. Model processes to define, document and communicate
2. Simulate the future performance of the business, to understand complex relationships among various parameters and to identify areas of improvement
3. Visualize the operations and flow processes with dynamic animation graphics
4. Plan for facilities for delivery of goods and services
5. Analyse how the business system will perform in its current configuration and under a set of feasible 'to-be' alternatives so that one can confidently choose the best way or 'satisficing' way to run the business

Modelling and simulation enable the decision-makers to take decisions leading to business process improvement. The purpose of simulation models is to compare the current business processes with the unlimited realm of 'would be' processes in the best interest of the business. All these experiments are performed without disrupting the day-to-day operations.

Since the 1980s, business process improvement and simulation have become leading methodologies to allow corporations to deliver high-quality products and services through business process modelling (BPM). Businesses are seeking not only to automate existing operations, but to re-engineer business processes to achieve customer satisfaction through delivery of products and services on time at competitive price. Simulation models have got wide scope and application for decision-making relating to BPR in diverse industries such as manufacturing, petrochemical, food processing, transport, power transmission and distribution and also service sector.

4.4.1 Salient Features of Arena

The main features of Arena are as follows:

1. **Basic process panel:** The basic process panel consists of flow-chart modules and data modules. Flow-chart modules comprise create, process (resource), decide, assign, separate, record and dispose. The data modules consist of entity, queue, resource, schedule, set and variable. Figure 4.2 shows the pictorial representation of these modules of the basic process panel in Arena 5.0.
2. **Statistical distributions:** Arena 5.0 contains a set of built-in functions for generating random numbers involving the commonly used probability distributions, such as beta, continuous,

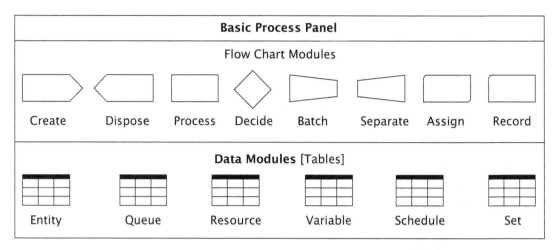

FIGURE 4.2   Basic Process Panel (Arena 5.0)

discrete, Erland, exponential, gamma, Johnson, log-normal, normal, Poisson, triangular, uniform and Weibull.

3. **Picture libraries:** The picture libraries in Arena 5.0 consist of pictures of basic process, buildings, equipment, faces, factory, machines, medical objects, office and office equipment, people, symbols, vehicles and workers.

Illustrative Example To illustrate the decision support capability of the Arena 5.0 system, let us consider the following facilities planning example for delivering public service by the regional transport authority of a state for delivering road permits to owners of light vehicles. The owners are divided into three types based on their car registration numbers. The owners arrive and enter one of the three queues before the three counters. The three independent arrival streams follow exponential inter-arrival time distribution with a mean of 10 minutes for each stream. Each counter is manned by a single clerk who processes the application forms and accepts payment for the road permit. The service time is uniform (8, 10) minutes for all the three counters. After completing the formalities in the counters, all owners are sent to a second clerk who checks the payment receipts and issues the permits for all types of owners. The service time for this activity is uniform (2.66, 3.33) minutes for all types of owners. Let us develop a model of this system and run the simulation for 10 days of 6 hours of working each day and obtain the results. Also, let us consider a BPR by making a single counter with three clerks to cater to the checking of application forms and receive payment, where all types of owners can arrive with the same statistics of inter-arrival time and let us find the results for a similar time period. Finally, in order to decide on the service strategy of having either three separate reporting counters with one clerk for each counter or having a single counter with three clerks, let us compare the results to decide the better strategy for service quality in terms of average waiting time.

The create simulation model is as shown in Figure 4.3 where the three types of owners (1, 2 and 3) arrive in three different streams and line up before the application processing and payment (cash) receipt counters 1, 2 and 3 respectively. The create 1, 2 and 3 are the basic process modules for creating entities (owners of the three types) with inter-arrival time exponentially distributed with a mean of 10 minutes.

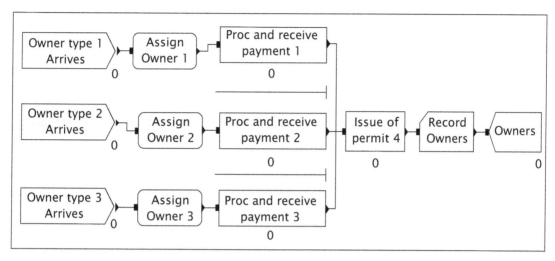

FIGURE 4.3 Simulation Model with Three Processing Counters in Parallel

The entities created by the create modules 1, 2, 3 are assigned attributes of arrival time ('TNOW' the parametric representation of the same by Arena 5.0) by the modules assigned 1, 2 and 3 respectively. The entities seize the resources (counter 1, 2 and 3 respectively) depending upon their types (owner 1, 2 and 3) for the processing of applications and obtaining cash receipts for payments made by them and the process involves delay (processing time). Finally, the entities release (leave) the resource (respective counter) for the next entity (owner for that counter). The waiting time for an entity consists of the processing time (time taken by the clerk at the counter) plus waiting time if any in the queue before the counter. The processing time of an application including the payment receipt time has been assumed to have a uniform distribution within 8 and 10 minutes. The entities (all types of owners) next arrive at counter 4 for issue of their permits and the process of issue of permits has also been assumed to have a uniform distribution within 2.66 and 3.33 minutes. The waiting time for each entity in this counter similarly consists of the waiting time, if any, in the queue plus the time for issue of permit by the clerk. Finally, from the counter 4, the entities are disposed of depicted by the disposal module which records the statistical results of the simulation run. Before the disposal module, there is a record module also to record certain attribute statistics of the entities, for example, time interval between arrival time and disposal time.

The model has been run for 10 days consisting of 6 hours working by the clerks per day and the number of replications was 1. The picture on completion of the run is as shown in Figure 4.4. It can be seen that 1,056 numbers of entities were created (328 + 377 + 351) and finally 1,040 numbers were disposed of and 16 numbers (2 + 9 + 3 + 2) are in queue and under processing in counters 1, 2, 3 and 4 respectively.

Next, the arrangement is changed by making only one processing of application and payment receipt counter having three clerks who can process any of the applications and the owners of all types have to line up before the counter. The inter-arrival time for the three types of owners and the processing time have been assumed to be same as in the previous model. The capacity of the counter has been made three in each six-hours-day working. The second model has been shown in Figure 4.5 and the picture on completion of the simulation run in Figure 4.6. The second model is also run for 10 days of 6 hours

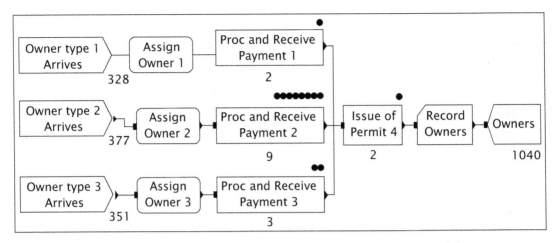

FIGURE 4.4 Status after Completion of the Simulation Run for the First Model

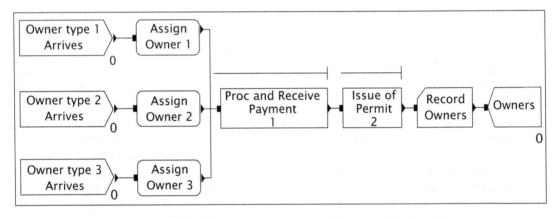

FIGURE 4.5 Simulation Model with One Processing and Payment Receipt Counter

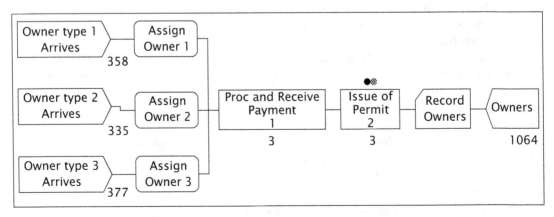

FIGURE 4.6 Status after Completion of the Simulation Run for the Second Model

working each day. The statistical results relating to queues and resource utilization for Model 1 and Model 2 have been shown in Figures 4.7–4.10 respectively. It can be seen from the same figures that Model 2 has shown better performance results as compared to the same for Model 1 in terms of both waiting time and resource utilization.

Queues		
		Replications: 1
Replications: 1 Start Time: 0.00 Stop Time: 3,600.00 Time Units: **Minutes**		
Queue Detail Summary		
Time	**Other**	
Waiting Time	Number Waiting	
Issue of permit Queue 2.00	Issue of permit Queue 0.58	
Proc and receive payment 1. Queue 18.00	Proc and receive payment 1. Queue 1.64	
Proc and receive payment 2. Queue 46.87	Proc and receive payment 2. Queue 4.91	
Proc and receive payment 3. Queue 28.42	Proc and receive payment 3. Queue 2.76	
Total 95.29	**Total** 9.89	

FIGURE 4.7   Queues Statistical Results for Model 1

Resources					
					Replications: 1
Replications: 1 Start Time: 0.00 Stop Time: 3,600.00 Time Units: **Minutes**					
Resource Detail Summary					
Usage			**Other**		
	Number Busy	Number Scheduled	Utilization	Number Times Used	Schedule Utilization
Counter 4	0.86	1.00	0.86	Counter 4 1041.00	0.86
Counter 1	0.81	1.00	0.81	Counter 1 327.00	0.81
Counter 2	0.92	1.00	0.92	Counter 2 369.00	0.92
Counter 3	0.87	1.00	0.87	Counter 3 349.00	0.87

FIGURE 4.8   Resource Utilization Statistical Results for Model 1

Queues				
				Replications: 1
Replications: 1	Start Time:	0.00 Stop Time:	3,600.00	Time Units: **Minutes**
Queue Detail Summary				
Time			**Other**	
	Waiting Time			Number Waiting
Issue of permit Queue	2.29		Issue of permit Queue	0.68
Proc and receive payment Queue	12.31		Proc and receive payment Queue	3.66
Total	14.60		**Total**	4.34

FIGURE 4.9 Queues Statistical Results for Model 2

Resources					
					Replications: 1
Replications: 1	Start Time:	0.00 Stop Time:	3,600.00	Time Units: **Minutes**	
Resource Detail Summary					
Usage				**Other**	
	Number Busy	Number Scheduled	Utilization	Number Times Used	Schedule Utilization
Counter 1	2.66	3.00	0.89	Counter 1 1070.00	0.89
Counter 2	0.88	1.00	0.88	Counter 2 1065.00	0.88

FIGURE 4.10 Resource Utilization Statistical Results for Model 2

4.5 DSS Generators

DSS generators are computer software that facilitate developing DSSs by the decision-makers to enable them to take effective and efficient decisions. Spreadsheets such as Microsoft Excel are one of the DSS generators. Extensive use of spreadsheet software is made by managers or decision-makers for financial planning systems such as interactive financial planning system (IFPS) developed by Wagner. The earlier spreadsheet software was further developed into the programmable spreadsheets for ease of generating DSSs. Let us consider a simple example of a five-year plan for manufacturing and sales of an industry unit using spreadsheet as a DSS as shown in Tables 4.1 and 4.2 and the graphical output of the model in Figure 4.11 respectively. The plan is for the period from the financial year 2010–2011 to 2014–2015 considering the base year as 2010–2011.

TABLE 4.1 Spreadsheet Sample Model for Manufacturing Planning

Profit = Sales – Total cost (TC)

Sales = Units × Price

TC = Fixed cost (FC) + Variable cost (VC) units (nos.) = 10,000, previous × growth

Fixed cost (₹) = 600,000, previous × escalation-1 (ESC-1) Variable cost = Units × Unit variable cost (UVC)

Unit variable cost (₹) (UVC) = 240, previous × escalation-2 (ESC-2) Price = Total unit cost (TUC) + Margin

TUC = (FC + VC)/Units

Margin (%) = 25; Growth (%) = 10; ESC-1 [%] = 4; ESC-2 [%] = 3

TABLE 4.2 Results of Spreadsheet Sample Model

	Years				
Variables	*2010–11*	*2011–12*	*2012–13*	*2013–14*	*2014–15*
Growth		0.10	0.10	0.10	0.10
Units [Nos]	10,000	11,000	12,100	13,310	14,641
ESC-1		0.04	0.04	0.04	0.04
FC [₹]	600,000	624,000	648,960	674,918	701,915
ESC-2		0.03	0.03	0.03	0.03
UVC [₹]	240	247	255	262	270
VC [₹]	2,400,000	2,717,000	3,085,500	3,487,220	3,953,070
Margin	0.25	0.25	0.25	0.25	0.25
TUC [= (FC + VQ/Units (₹)]	300	304	309	313	318
Price [TUC + 0.25 × TUC]	375	380	386	391	398
Sales [₹]	3,750,000	4,180,000	4,670,600	5,204,210	5,827,118
Total Cost [₹]	3,000,000	3,341,000	3,734,460	4,162,138	4,654,985
Profit [₹]	750,000	839,000	936,140	1,042,072	1,172,133

The important characteristics of the spreadsheet DSS models are:

1. Capabilities to support mathematical and statistical functions and operations which enable it as a good DSS model generator particularly involving financial decision-making
2. Multiple what-if type of scenario analysis
3. Programming features as in Microsoft Excel

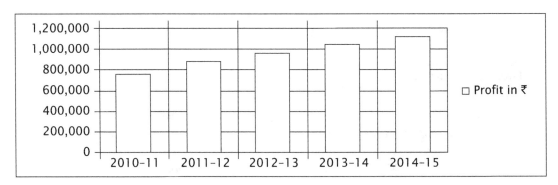

FIGURE 4.11   Graphical Representation of the Spreadsheet Sample Model on Profit Plan

4. Goal-seeking capabilities
5. Sensitivity analysis leading to optimum solution of a problem
6. Built-in capability to support corporate database and scanning the same
7. Powerful report generation and graphical user interface (GUI)

4.5.1 Analytica Software as a DSS Generator

Lumina Decision Systems, Inc., California, USA, has developed a software Analytica (4.2) beyond the spreadsheet, which uses Influence diagram concept to model the essential qualitative nature of the decision problem to arrive at either the optimum or near-optimum solution of the problem. Using a visual point and click approach, one can draw nodes and arrows to depict the relationship among the model components which can be variables, modules, decision variables, objectives, chance variables and so on. Another important feature of Analytica is the use of intelligent arrays which allows one to add or remove dimensions such as time periods, locations, various conditions and the associated parameters. The added features of Analytica over the spreadsheets are:

1. Analytica separates the dimensions from relationship so that one need not repeat formulae when new dimensions are added, or existing dimensions are deleted.
2. It is faster in speed of computation.
3. Each node or object in an Analytica model has a window that displays the inputs and outputs of the node, definitions, descriptions and units of measure whose features make Analytica easier and more user-friendly. Further, Analytica also has a built-in capability of integrated risk and sensitivity analysis for analysing models with uncertain inputs. It has also got powerful facilities for time-dependent dynamic situations, powerful GUI and more than 200 financial, statistical and scientific functions inbuilt with the software.

4.5.1.1 Influence Diagram

An Influence diagram is a graphical representation of a model, showing the relationships and interactions among the different variables (factors) in a model. A typical influence diagram consists of a number of nodes connected by arrows. The nodes may include modules to represent a hierarchy of Influence diagrams to depict a complex model, where the lower-level modules are represented as modular nodes in the higher-level diagrams. The typical nodes used in Analytica are shown in Figure 4.12.

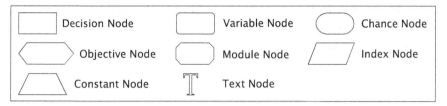

FIGURE 4.12 Nodes in Analytica Figure

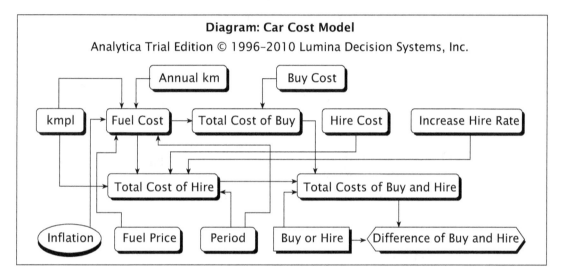

FIGURE 4.13 Influence Diagram for Car Cost Model

Illustrative Example 1: Let me illustrate the Influence diagram with a simple car-cost model as shown in Figure 4.13. Annual fuel cost in rupees for a car over a period of years depends on the annual kilometres run by the car (assumed 12,000 km), kilometres per litre of fuel (petrol or diesel) defined as 15 for a new car and 11 for a hired second-hand car and fuel price per litre is ₹45 for current year and the expected rate of inflation of fuel price per year assumed normally distributed with mean 3.5% and standard deviation 1.5% and the period (in this model assumed from 5 to 10 years in steps of 1 year). This has been depicted by the way of connecting the nodes for annual kilometres, km/l, inflation (a chance variable), fuel price and period with arrows terminating at fuel cost node. The total cost of buying (if the decision is to buy a new car) is dependent on fuel cost for a new car (at15 km/l) and the buying cost of a new car (assumed ₹3 lakhs, that is, three hundred thousand). This is represented in the Influence diagram by connecting the nodes for buying cost and fuel cost to the total cost of buying with arrows. Similarly, the total cost of hiring a car (if the decision is to hire a second-hand car) is dependent on the hire cost (assumed in this case ₹10,000 per month), contractual rate of increase in hire rate every year (assumed 5% on the previous year rate) over the period under consideration by the decision-maker (to decide whether to buy or to hire) and the fuel cost for hiring a second-hand car (at11 km/l). This has been represented by connecting the nodes accordingly with the node for total cost of hire. Next, the decision whether to buy or hire is dependent on the total cost of buying vis-à-vis hire. This is represented by the variable node of the total costs of buying and hire indexed by buy or hire which is a decision variable as represented by the 'buy or hire' node which is a decision node. Therefore, the variable nodes representing total cost of buy, total cost of hire and the decision variable buy or hire (which is a list of 'buy' and 'hire') are connected with arrows with the total cost of buy and hire node. Finally, the objective has been represented as the difference between total cost of buy and total cost of hire over the period of time which decides the choice of the decision-maker.

The definitions of some of the variable nodes, decision node, chance node and the objective node as explained above have been shown in Figures 4.14–4.17 respectively, which show the windows of the

FIGURE 4.14 Variable and Chance Nodes

Object: Fuel Cost

Analytica Trial Edition c 1996–2010 Lumina Decision Systems, Inc.

◯ **Variable**   Fuel_cost   **Unit :** ₹

          Title : Fuel cost

   Description :

              expr

   Definition : Annual_kms*Fuel_price*period*[1 + I/100]^Period/kmpl

      Inputs : ◯ Annual_kms   Annual kms

              ◯ Fuel_price   Fuel Price

              ◯ I   Inflation

              ◯ Kmpl   kmpl

              ◯ Period   Period

   Outputs : ◯ Total_cost_of_buy   Total cost of buy

              ◯ Total_cost_of_hire   Total cost of hire

FIGURE 4.15   Variable Node Fuel Cost

nodes separately as obtained by double clicking on the node icons. Any of the nodes can be deleted or new nodes can be added or connected without repeating the definition and modifying the formulae of the affected nodes which are automatically modified by Analytica. The results associated with any module of the car-cost model can be obtained by clicking only once on the module and then clicking on the result button on the tool menu bar. The result as obtained with the values of the model for the module of total costs of buying and hire has been shown in Figure 4.18 for the period varying from 5 years to 10 years. The result shows that for a period up to 7.5 years, it is economical to hire a car but beyond that it is economical to buy a car. The same result has been shown in Figure 4.19 in the graphical form. Analytica has also got options for showing the results in various statistical forms such as probability bands and cumulative probability distribution of probable values. The decision-maker who decides whether to buy a new car or hire a second-hand car can vary the range of variables such as his usage in terms of annual kilometres, fuel price for petrol or diesel car and also the hiring period and rate, and buying cost of various models of cars and find out the best decision for the objective of minimum total cost.

Illustrative Example 2: Let us consider a two-branch decision tree for deciding a location for arranging a party. The decision tree has been shown on the upper portion of Figure 4.20. The equivalent Analytica model (influence diagram) has been shown in the lower portion of the same figure. The decision-maker's problem is to select a clubhouse location for a party which will provide the optimum value to the decision-maker. The value depends on the weather, temperature and the location. Three locations have been considered, namely outdoor, porch and indoor. The weather condition is a chance variable and can

---

Object : Total cost of buy

Analytica Trial Edition c 1996–2010 Lumina Decision Systems, Inc.

Variable   Total_cost_of_buy   Units : ₹

    Title : Total cost of buy

Description : Total Cost of buying a car

    expr

Definition : Buy_cost + Fuel_cost [Kmpl = "Buy"]

    Inputs :   Buy_cost   BUY COST

              Fuel_cost   Fuel Cost

              Kmpl   kmpl

  Outputs :   Total_costs_of_buy_a   Total costs of buy and hire

Variable   Total_cost_of_hire   Units : ₹

    Title : Total cost of hire

Description : Total Cost of hiring a second hand car

    expr

Definition : Fuel_cost [Kmpl = 'Hire'] + Hire_cost*12*[1 + Increase_hire_rate/100]^
Period

    Inputs :   Fuel_cost   Fuel Cost

              Hire_cost   Hire cost

              Increase_hire_rate   Increase hire rate

              Kmpl   kmpl

              Period   Period

  Outputs :   Total_costs_of_buy_a   Total costs of buy and hire

---

FIGURE 4.16 Variable Nodes

be either sunny or rainy and is defined as a probabilistic table indexed by weather table (list of two labels, i.e., sunny or rainy) as shown in Figure 4.21.

The input to the weather is the probability of sunshine (p), which is the probability that the sun will be shining on the day of the party. This is the range of probabilities from 0 to 1, and the decision-maker has to select one value or all, using the pop-up menu. In this example, p has been assigned the value 0.4. The temperature is also a probability table indexed by temperature (which can be cold, warm or hot) as shown in the domain of list of labels in Figure 4.21. The discrete probabilities associated with these labels are cold: 0.2, warm: 0.5 and hot: 0.3 respectively. The value to the decision-maker is the objective node

Object: Buy or hire

Analytica Trial Edition c 1996–2010 Lumina Decision Systems, Inc.

▢ **Decision**   Buy_or_hire   **Units :**

Title : Buy or hire

Description : Buy or hire

Definition : | Buy
| Hire

Outputs : ⬭ Diff_of_buy_and_hire   Diff. of buy and hire
⬭ Total_cost_of_buy_a   Total costs of buy and hire

⬭ **Variable**   Total_cost_of_buy_a   **Units :** ₹

Title : Total costs of buy and hire

Description : Total costs of buy and hire

| 1, 2 |

Definition : Edit Table   indexed by Buy or hire

Inputs : ▢ Buy_or_hire   Buy or hire
⬭ Total_cost_of_buy   Total cost of buy
⬭ Total_cost_of_hire   Total cost of hire

Outputs : ⬭ Diff_of_buy_and_hire   Diff. of buy and hire

⬭ **Objective**   Diff_of_buy_and_hire   **Units :** ₹

Title : Diff. of buy and hire

Description : Difference of buy and hire

expr

Definition : Total_costs_of_buy_a [Buy_or_hire= 'Buy']-Total_costs_of_buy_a [Buy_or_hire = 'Hire']

Inputs : ▢ Buy_or_hire   Buy or hire
⬭ Total_cost_of_buy_a   Total costs of buy and hire

FIGURE 4.17 Decision Variable and Objective Nodes

that computes the value to the decision-maker for each possible outcome of location—weather—temperature, by assigning a rupee value to each combination. Decision-maker selects the prospect (party location) which has the highest EV. The EV (mean value) for a given location is the average of the values of the outcomes for that location, weighted by their probabilities.

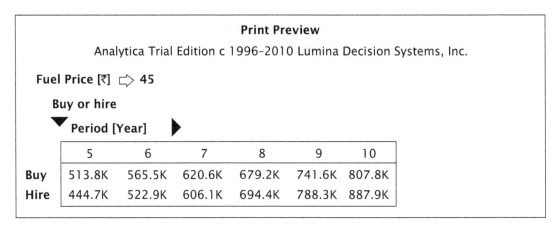

FIGURE 4.18   Total Costs of Buy and Hire

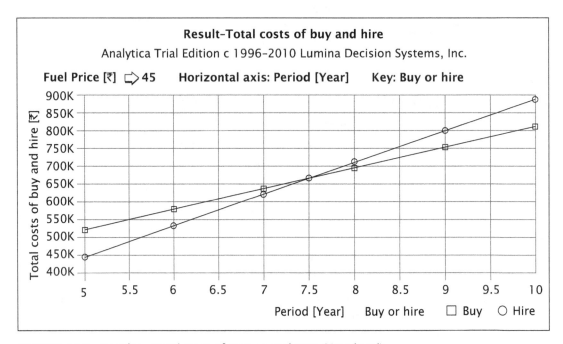

FIGURE 4.19   Results—Total Cost of Buying and Hire (Graphical)

The value to the decision-maker is defined as a multidimensional deterministic table indexed by temperature, weather and party location. The deterministic values are as shown in Figure 4.22. The results of the model (mean value to the decision-maker) are as shown in Figure 4.23. Also shown in Figure 4.23 are the cumulative probabilities for possible values to decision-maker associated with each of the three locations. It may be noted that Analytica simulates all probability distributions and calculates the expected (mean) value of a distribution by computing the average of the samples. For a discrete

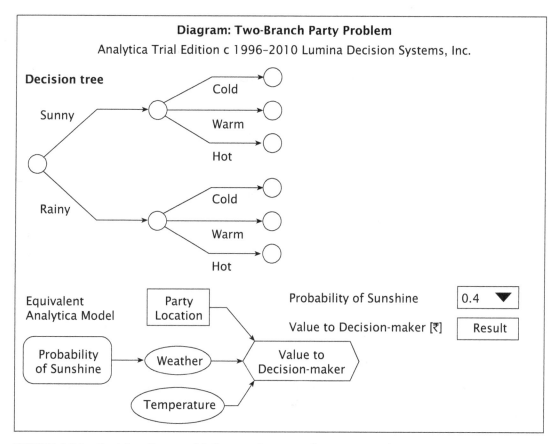

Diagram: Two-Branch Party Problem

Analytica Trial Edition c 1996–2010 Lumina Decision Systems, Inc.

Decision tree

Sunny — Cold, Warm, Hot

Rainy — Cold, Warm, Hot

Equivalent Analytica Model

Party Location

Probability of Sunshine → Weather → Value to Decision-maker

Temperature

Probability of Sunshine 0.4

Value to Decision-maker [₹] Result

FIGURE 4.20 Decision Tree and Influence Diagram for Two-Branch Party Location Problem

distribution (like the party location model), the computed mean converges, with increasing sample size towards the value obtained by multiplying the probabilities with the discrete outcome values. According to the result shown in Figure 4.23, the location 'indoors' for the party returns the highest EV to the decision-maker of ₹2,300 and hence the same has to be chosen.

The idea behind showing the above illustrative examples of applications of Analytica is only to demonstrate how to generate DSS models using Analytica. However, those readers who are interested in knowing the details including advanced features of Analytica may refer to Analytica Tutorial Release 4.2.

4.6 Multiple-criteria Decision Analysis (MCDA)

Decision-making in a real-life situation is typically a complex and confusing analysis, characterized by trade-offs between multiple criteria such as cost, quality, sociopolitical and economic factors such as growth, employment and pollution. Cost–benefit analysis is often used for such projects as building a new railway station or a new technology-based oil refinery. Sensitivity and risk analysis are also often

---

Object –Weather

Analytica Trial Edition c 1996-2010 Lumina Decision Systems, Inc.

◯ **Chance**   Weather   **Units :**

       Title : Weather

    Description : Weather has two possible values : sunny or rainy. It is defined as a discrete distribution, using the Probability of Sunshine

          ⊞ 1, 2

    Definition : Prob Table   indexed by Weather

    Domain :   **List of Labels**

          sunny
          rainy

     Inputs :   ◯ P   Probability of Sunshine

    Outputs : ◇ Value_to_me   Value to Decision maker

◯ **Chance**   Temperature   **Units :**

       Title : Temperature

    Description : Temperature is modeled as being cold, warm, or hot. It is defined as a discrete probability distribution

          ⊞ 1, 2

    Definition : Prob Table   indexed by Temperature

    Domain :   **List of Labels**

          Cold
          Warm
          Hot

    Outputs : ◇ Value_to_me   Value to Decision maker

FIGURE 4.21   Chance Variables: Weather and Temperature

carried out among the competing factors. However, unlike a single criterion optimization decision problem, MCDA calls for consideration of the competing multiple objectives. Further, some of the criteria cannot be easily condensed into a monetary value, which complicates the integration problem inherent in making comparisons and trade-offs. Even if it is possible to convert multiple criteria into a common unit, this approach is based on subjective assessment and may not always include all stakeholders' preferences which may be lost in the process.

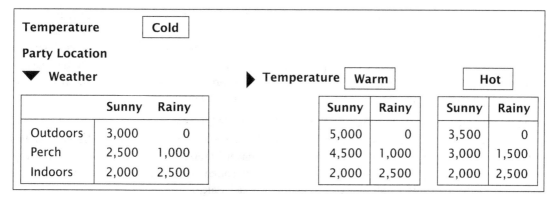

FIGURE 4.22 Value to Decision-maker in Rupees Regarding Party Location

Party Location

	Expected values [₹]
Outdoors	1,687.50
Porch	2,180.00
Indoors	2,300.00

Party Location

Possible values to Author [₹]

	0	1,000	1,500	2,000	2,500	3,000	3,500	4,500	5,000
Outdoors	0.6	0.6	0.6	0.6	0.6	0.67	0.785	0.785	1
Porch	0	0.415	0.6	0.6	0.67	0.785	0.785	1	1
Indoors	0	0	0	0.4	1	1	1	1	1

FIGURE 4.23 Results of the Model for Example 2

Considerable research in the areas of MCDA has developed practical methods for applying scientific decision approaches to multiple-criteria problems.

4.6.1 MCDA Methods

There are many MCDA methods evolved over the years. They are based on different theoretical foundation and behavioural science such as optimization, goal aspiration or outranking or a combination of them. However, the four popular approaches to MCDA are the following:

1. **Elementary methods:** These methods intended to convert complex problems to a singular basis for selection of a preferred alternative. For example, an elementary method may rank alternatives in terms

of number of performance or criteria threshold met or exceeded and the one achieving the maximum number may be chosen. Some of the elementary methods are pros and cons analysis such as strengths, weaknesses, opportunities and threats (SWOT) analysis, decision-tree analysis and influence diagrams. However, the elementary methods, though simple and can be executed even without the help of computer software, are best suited for single decision-maker problems involving a few alternatives and criteria and as such not suited to real-life situations involving MCDA.

2. **Multi-attribute utility/value theory (MAUT/MAVT):** MAUT/MAVT is a technique for formally drawing multiple perspectives and evaluations into the decision-making process. The goal of this approach is to find simple expression for the decision-makers' preferences. Through the use of utility/value functions, this approach transforms diverse criteria (often conflicting in nature) such as price, safety, reliability and comfort into one common dimensional scale of utility/value.

The main considerations used in MAUT/MVAT are: (a) how great is the score and (b) the relative importance (weightage) of the criteria being measured compared to all the other criteria. MAUT/MVAT follows a systematic approach of identifying the key attributes of a problem and then the top-level attributes are split into finer attributes in a top-down fashion. The steps in the MAUT/MVAT analysis are as follows:

> **Step 1:** Identify the key attributes (criteria).
> **Step 2:** Define weightage for the attributes based on decision maker's preferences.
> **Step 3:** Define the attribute levels and the scoring scale.
> **Step 4:** For each alternative, we have to define the level (rating) for the qualitative attributes based on subjective assessment and considering all the other alternatives. For the non-qualitative attributes, the actual quantitative values are to be assigned for each alternative.
> **Step 5:** Convert the levels for qualitative attributes into scores as per the scale (Step 3). For non-qualitative attributes only actual quantitative values need remain.
> **Step 6:** For non-qualitative attributes, the best and worst levels are assessed and defined.
> **Step 7:** Normalization of the scores for all attributes is done.
> **Step 8:** For all alternatives, the weighted average normalized scores (utility) are calculated and the alternative achieving the highest such score is considered.
>
> The goal of MAUT/MVAT approach is to maximize the utility/value, which is a compensatory optimization approach. Nevertheless, MAUT/MVAT leads to a complete ranking of all the alternatives based on the decision-maker's preferences. The goal is not only to reach a forced 'consensus' through averaging different decision-makers/stakeholders weightages, but also to clarify the position and to test the feasibility of the objectives.

MAUT/MVAT relies on the assumption that the decisions-maker is rational, that is, he/she prefers more to less, his/her preferences do not change, he/she has perfect knowledge and the preferences are transitive.

Implementation of considerations for MAUT/MVAT led to the development of the simple multi-attribute rating technique (SMART), which comprises simple utility relationships. SMART allows for use of shorter range of utility scales, if the data do not discriminate widely. For example, in case of SMART alternatives, which are not significantly different with respect to a particular criterion can be assigned equal scores.

Illustrative Example—MAUT: A buyer of a car has to decide which car out of three choices, namely Alto, Swift Dzire and Santro Xing to select based on the criteria of price, fuel efficiency, performance, comfort, safety and reliability. This is a good case of MAUT application for the decision-maker. Let us proceed step by step as explained earlier.

Step 1: Identify the key attributes (criteria) which are price, fuel efficiency, performance, comfort, safety and reliability.

Step 2: Define weightages for the criteria based on the decision-maker's (buyer) preference. Let us assume the following weightage:

Attributes	Weightage
Price	100
Fuel efficiency	20
Performance	30
Comfort	30
Safety	20
Reliability	20

Step 3: Decide the attribute levels and the scoring scale. Let us assume the same as follows:

Attribute	Attribute Level and Scores				
	Worst	Poor	Average	Good	Best
Price	0	25	50	75	100
Fuel efficiency	0	25	50	75	100
Performance	0	25	50	75	100
Comfort	0	25	50	75	100
Safety	0	25	50	75	100
Reliability	0	25	50	75	100

Step 4: For each alternative, the decision-maker has to assign a level for the qualitative attributes based on his subjective assessment and for the non-qualitative attributes, the actual values are to be assigned for each of the alternatives assumed as follows: (Figures are illustrative.)

Attribute	Attribute Levels		
	Alto	Santro Xing	Swift Dzire
Price (₹)	200,000	300,000	400,000
Fuel efficiency	20	15	18
Performance	Poor	Average	Average
Comfort	Good	Poor	Best
Safety	Good	Average	Best
Reliability	Best	Average	Good

Step 5: Convert the levels for the qualitative attributes into corresponding scores as per the scale decided in Step 3. For non-qualitative attributes, the actual values will remain.

Attribute	Attribute Scores		
	Alto	Santro Xing	Swift Dzire
Price (₹)	200,000	300,000	400,000
Fuel efficiency	20	15	18
Performance	25	50	50
Comfort	75	25	100
Safety	75	50	100
Reliability	100	50	75

Step 6: For non-qualitative attributes, the best and worst levels are assessed by the decision-maker. Let us assume, the best price is 100,000 and worst price is 600,000. Similarly, best fuel efficiency is 30 and worst fuel efficiency is 5.

Step 7: Normalization of the scores using the formula:

$$\text{Normalized score} = 100 \times (\text{Actual score} - \text{Worst})/(\text{Best} - \text{Worst})$$

The normalized scores for the attributes are accordingly computed and are as follows:

Attribute	Normalized Scores		
	Alto	Santro Xing	Swift Dzire
Price (₹)	80	60	40
Fuel efficiency	60	40	52
Performance	25	50	50
Comfort	75	25	100
Safety	75	50	100
Reliability	100	50	75

Step 8: For each alternative, apply the weightage as shown in Step 2 for the attributes to the normalized scores to arrive at the weighted average scores for utility for the same alternative and finally the choice is the one which gets the highest utility score.

$$\text{For Alto} = (80 \times 100) + (60 \times 20) + (25 \times 30) + (75 \times 30) + (75 \times 20)$$
$$+ (100 \times 20)/(100 + 20 + 30 + 30 + 20 + 20) = 71.36$$

$$\text{Santro Xing} = (60 \times 100) + (40 \times 20) + (50 \times 30) + (25 \times 30) + (50 \times 20)$$
$$+ (50 \times 20)/(100 + 20 + 30 + 30 + 20 + 20) = 67.27$$

$$\text{Swift Dzire} = (40 \times 100) + (52 \times 20) + (50 \times 30) + (100 \times 30) + (100 \times 20)$$
$$+ (75 \times 20)/(100 + 20 + 30 + 30 + 20 + 20) = 59.27$$

Alto, having the lightest multi-attribute utility of 71.36 is to be considered by the buyer.

3. **Analytical hierarchy process (AHP):** The AHP is a MCDA process developed by Saaty in 1980. Like MAUT, AHP also completely aggregates various aspects of the multiple-criteria decision problem into a single objective function. AHP also selects the alternative that results in the greatest value of the objective function. However, AHP adopts a quantitative comparison method based on a pairwise comparison of the decision criteria or attributes rather than utility and weightage assigned to all the criteria or attributes by the decision-maker. Behavioural scientists believe that a human being can better compare two criteria at a time on their relative importance to him/her rather than comparing a number of criteria at a time and assigning weightage in order of relative importance. In other words, the AHP method relies on the supposition that human beings are more capable of making relative judgements than absolute judgements. In case of AHP, evaluators express the intensity of a preference for one criterion versus another (pairwise comparison) using a nine-point scale as follows:

1: If the two criteria are equally important.
3: If one criterion is weekly/moderately more important than the other.
5: If one criterion is strongly more important than the other.
7: If one criterion is very strongly more important than the other.
9: If one criterion is absolutely/extremely more important than the other.

In AHP, all individual criteria or attributes are compared against all others and results are compiled in a matrix form. It may be stated that if a criterion i is compared with a criterion j and a value of importance of i with respect to j is a_{ij}, then the reciprocal score is awarded to the opposite relationship, that is, say if $a_{ij} = 5$ then, $a_{ji} = 1/5$. Obviously, $a_{ii} = 1$. The normalized weight is calculated for each criterion by dividing each element in a column of the matrix by the sum of all the elements in the same column. For a perfectly consistent decision-maker, each column should be identical. However, in case of small inconsistencies in the decision-making process, the same is corrected by averaging across each row and the average figure will then represent the relative weight on the criterion as shown against that row. The normalized weights (after averaging) for all the criteria (all rows) should add to 1 but may vary slightly because of half rounding or truncation of figures during computation. Let me illustrate the AHP by bringing the same example (as in case of MAUT) of deciding by a buyer which car to purchase out of three choices, namely Alto, Santro and Swift, considering the preferences based on criteria of price, fuel efficiency, performance, comfort, safety and reliability.

Step 1: To determine the preferences for the criteria mentioned above by pairwise comparison on the nine-point-scale and after getting all preferences the following matrix is formed.

i	Price	Fuel Efficiency	Performance	Comfort	Safety	Reliability
Price	1	5	3	3	5	5
Fuel efficiency	$1/5$	1	$1/3$	$1/3$	1	1
Performance	$1/3$	3	1	1	3	3
Comfort	$1/3$	3	1	1	3	3
Safety	$1/5$	1	$1/3$	$1/3$	1	1
Reliability	$1/5$	1	$1/3$	$1/3$	1	1

Step 2: Normalize the figures (elements) in each column of the matrix as obtained in Step 1 by the sum of all the elements in that column. For example, (price-safety) entry would end up as (5/[5 + 1 + 3 + 3 + 1 + 1]) = 0.35. The matrix finally obtained will be as shown below.

	Price	Fuel Efficiency	Performance	Comfort	Safety	Reliability	Average
Price	0.44	0.35	0.5	0.5	0.35	0.35	0.42
Fuel efficiency	0.09	0.07	0.06	0.06	0.07	0.07	0.07
Performance	0.15	0.12	0.17	0.17	0.21	0.21	0.18
Comfort	0.15	0.12	0.17	0.17	0.21	0.21	0.18
Safety	0.09	0.07	0.06	0.06	0.07	0.07	0.07
Reliability	0.09	0.07	0.06	0.06	0.07	0.07	0.07
							$\Sigma = 0.99$

All the columns should be identical, but we find small inconsistencies and hence we correct by averaging the figures in a row and the same have been shown in the average column and the average figures added up to 0.99 (should be 1 if no truncation, half rounding).

Step 3: Next, we evaluate all the three cars on each criterion separately. For instance, if we consider price, the importance of Alto will be more than either Santro or Swift because of lowest price and we might get a matrix as follows:

Criterion: Price

	Alto	Santro	Swift
Alto	1	3	5
Santro	$1/_3$	1	3
Swift	$1/_5$	$1/_3$	1

By normalizing and averaging we get the following matrix:

Criterion: Price

	Alto	Santro	Swift	Avg.
Alto	0.652	0.690	0.550	0.630
Santro	0.217	0.230	0.330	0.250
Swift	0.130	0.100	0.110	0.110
				$\Sigma = 0.99$

In a similar way, we can obtain for Alto, Santro and Swift, the relative weights for preferences with respect to fuel efficiency, performance, comfort, safety and reliability. We get the matrices for relative scores for all the criteria as shown below.

Criterion: Fuel Efficiency

	Alto	Santro	Swift	Avg.
Alto	0.60	0.60	0.60	0.60
Santro	0.20	0.20	0.20	0.20
Swift	0.20	0.20	0.20	0.20
				$\Sigma = 1$

Criterion: Performance

	Alto	Santro	Swift	Avg.
Alto	0.14	0.14	0.14	0.14
Santro	0.43	0.43	0.43	0.43
Swift	0.43	0.43	0.43	0.43
				$\Sigma = 1$

Criterion: Comfort

	Alto	Santro	Swift	Avg.
Alto	0.25	0.40	0.24	0.29
Santro	0.05	0.08	0.10	0.07
Swift	0.75	0.56	0.70	0.67
				$\Sigma = 1.03$

Criterion: Safety

	Alto	Santro	Swift	Avg.
Alto	0.24	0.33	0.22	0.26
Santro	0.08	0.11	0.13	0.11
Swift	0.72	0.55	0.65	0.64
				$\Sigma = 1.01$

Criterion: Reliability

	Alto	Santro	Swift	Avg.
Alto	0.65	0.55	0.22	0.64
Santro	0.13	0.11	0.11	0.11
Swift	0.22	0.55	0.33	0.26
				$\Sigma = 1.01$

Then, the relative scores for the criteria for all the three types of cars can be combined into one matrix as follows:

	Alto	Santro	Swift
Price	0.63	0.25	0.11
Fuel efficiency	0.6	0.2	0.2
Performance	0.14	0.43	0.43
Comfort	0.29	0.07	0.67
Safety	0.26	0.11	0.64
Reliability	0.64	0.11	0.26

Step 4: Now, with the weights of the criteria as determined in Step 2 and the relative score for the criteria for all the three cars as determined in Step 3, we get a score for each car as follows:

Alto: $(0.63 \times 0.42) + (0.60 \times 0.07) + (0.14 \times 0.18) + (0.29 \times 0.18) + (0.26 \times 0.07) + (0.64 \times 0.07) = 0.447$

Santro: $(0.25 \times 0.42) + (0.20 \times 0.07) + (0.43 \times 0.18) + (0.07 \times 0.18) + (0.11 \times 0.07) + (0.11 \times 0.07) = 0.224$

Swift: $(0.11 \times 0.42) + (0.20 \times 0.07) + (0.43 \times 0.18) + (0.67 \times 0.18) + (0.64 \times 0.07) + (0.26 \times 0.07) = 0.321$

Therefore, Alto getting the highest value can be considered as the choice by the decision-maker (buyer).

4. Outranking: The concept was first defined by B. Roy in 1970. Unlike MAUT and AHP, outranking is based on the principle that one alternative or choice may have a degree of dominance over the other rather than a single-best choice or alternative. The alternatives are compared in pairs, on each criterion, an alternative a1 is said to outrank the other alternative a2, if a1 performs better than a2 in some criteria and at least equally well in all the other criteria. In this case, a1 is said to be the dominant alternative and a2 the dominated one. Under no circumstance or no combination of weightage will a2 (the dominated alternative) would be preferred by the decision-maker. In outranking method, preferences between the paired alternatives (say, X and Y) are expressed for each criterion as one of the following four types:

1. XPY strict preference of X over Y
2. XQY weak preference of X over Y
3. XIY indifference between X and Y
4. XJY inability to compare the actions

In the outranking method, preference and indifference thresholds are introduced for each criterion to avoid exaggerating the importance of small differences in performance. The indifference threshold is the difference level below which the decision-maker considers no preference as the distinction is too small. Likewise, the preference threshold is the difference level above which the decision-maker prefers one alternative to another. In other words, the preference threshold is the smallest value, that is, a deciding factor when comparing two alternatives, while the largest value of no preference represents the indifference threshold.

In case of outranking, the preference function can take different forms for different criteria and decision-makers, but certain forms may be suggested generally to assess the performance of the criteria, depending upon the nature of the criteria. For quantitative criteria such as cost and price, the preference function may be a linear function; for semi-quantitative criteria such as prestige value (high, medium or low), the function may be a stepped one; and for non-quantitative criteria such as colour and appearance, the function may be a set of choices/preferences, for example, colour red and yellow are preferred and violet and blue are not in the list of choice.

Outranking is a partial compensatory method and does not rely upon optimization. The emphasis is on understanding trade-off and a structured comparison of strengths and weaknesses of the alternatives. Also, outranking method is flexible in allowing the decision-makers to change their preferences by adjusting inter-criteria weightage, introducing new criteria and alternatives during the analysis phase.

4.7 Group Decision Support Systems

A GDSS is a class of electronic meeting system which is a collaboration technology designed to support meetings and group work leading to group decisions. A GDSS contains most of the elements of DSS plus software to provide effective support in group decision-making.

4.7.1 Components of a GDSS

The important components of a GDSS are:

- Database
- Model base
- Communication capability
- GDSS processor
- Groupware, which is a special software which facilitates people located all over the globe to work on the same project, same document and files efficiently and at the same time

Examples of groupware supporting group decision are the IBM Lotus Notes, Promino 8.0 and the commercial software products, such as Smartspeed Connect, FacilitatePro and think tank, which work over the Internet in both synchronous and asynchronous settings.

- Dialogue manager
- External databases including other corporate databases
- Users and hosts

4.7.2 Characteristics of a GDSS

The characteristics of a GDSS are as follows:

- Special design
- Ease of use

- Flexibility
- Decision-making support
- Delphi approach—a consensus decision-making approach where decision-makers (experts in various fields) are geographically dispersed
- Brainstorming
- Electronic mail system
- Group consensus
- Nominal group technique
- Anonymous input
- Reduction of negative group behaviour
- Parallel communication
- Automated record keeping
- Cost, control, complexity factors
- Flash plug-in of the browser

GDSSs can be categorized into various types depending upon the location and decision frequency into decision room, local area GDSS network, wide area GDSS network or teleconferences and so on. Decision room and local area GDSS network are meant for low decision frequency and close location of group members, whereas, wide area GDSS network and teleconferences are for groups of decision-makers located around the world and working on common problems also known as virtual work groups.

4.7.3 Online Electronic Meeting Systems

Online electronic meeting systems usually have got the following tools for:

1. Automatic meeting minutes and reports generation
2. Meeting set-up
3. Building an agenda either from scratch or from a template
4. Online meeting tools:
   i. Brainstorming with electronic flip charts
   ii. Voting and analysis
   iii. Discussion
   iv. Notebook
   v. Presentation
   vi. Action tracking

4.7.4 Group Decisions

Many business decisions are collectively taken by a group of managers/individual decision-makers, and therefore a need arises for a consensus decision for a group consistent with individual choices or preferences. In actual practice, inconsistencies often arise in group decisions which have been pointed out by various authors from time to time. For example, Pareto optimality condition attempts to eliminate such inconsistencies by restricting the list of alternative group decisions to a few important ones which can be considered for final choice based upon one or more criteria.

Likewise voting, although is considered as a method for group decision-making with the majority principle to decide the best, often suffers inconsistencies due to possible bias in the process of selection.

Finally, the famous Arrow's 'impossibility theorem', also known as 'Arrow's paradox', rules out any consistent or fair group decision in view of the incompatibility of the conditions of unanimity, non-dictatorship and independence of irrelevant alternatives.

In spite of the complexities involved in group decision-making for arriving at consistent and rational decisions, GDSSs, as described earlier, attempt to eliminate some of the limitations by way of software and adopting tools such as 'Delphi', brainstorming, analysis and nominal group techniques. For details of these features, interested readers may refer to popular GDSS software like Smartspeed Connect.

CASE STUDY: APPLICATION OF ANALYTIC HIERARCHY PROCESS (AHP) IN SUPPLIER SELECTION

Background

In the present competitive environment, selection of right suppliers for input items and outsourced components is vital for the success of any manufacturing organization.

Supplier selection is a complex process involving multi-criteria decision-making. A trade-off between the qualitative and quantitative criteria is essential for the selection of the optimum supplier.

The present case study relates to a manufacturing factory located in Malaysia and producing a variety of specialized factory automation equipment such as conveyors, elevators, automatic sorting and ware-housing systems. Of late, the factory has been exporting finished equipment to Singapore, Indonesia, Thailand, Vietnam and Philippines. Although the factory produced a lot of components in-house, the study focused on a particular sensor component which was outsourced. There were three potential suppliers 'A', 'B' and 'C' (actual names not mentioned due to obvious reasons) and the application of AHP was for the selection of the best out of the three suppliers.

AHP Model

The criteria considered for the supplier selection in this study were price, service, quality and logistic. The AHP model with its three levels has been shown as follows:

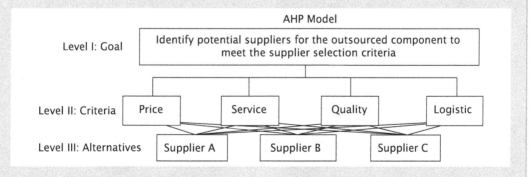

At the top level is the goal of the model followed by the four criteria at level II and the three suppliers at level III are the alternatives. They are to be evaluated in order to select the best supplier.

Methodology and Data Collection

All the primary data relating to pairwise comparison of the suppliers were collected based on interview of the employees concerned with the process of selection of the suppliers. These data were analysed using Microsoft Excel in order to interpret the data in a simple and comprehensible way. Two managers looking after purchase and engineering were interviewed to get their pairwise judgements for assessing the weights of the four criteria.

Result and Discussion

A four-point rating scale (1, 2, 3 and 4) was designed and the priority weights of the criteria as well as the weights of the suppliers for each criterion were determined. The pairwise comparison matrix for the criteria formed with the pairwise judgement has been shown as follows:

Criterion	Price	Service	Quality	Logistic
Price	1	1/3	1/4	1/2
Service	3	1	3	4
Quality	4	1/3	1	3
Logistic	2	1/4	1/3	1

After normalization of each column with sum to 1.0 or 100% and averaging the values of the elements in each row, the priority vector denoting the approximate weights for the criteria of price, service, quality and logistic was obtained as follows:

$$\begin{pmatrix} \text{Price} \\ \text{Service} \\ \text{Quality} \\ \text{Logistic} \end{pmatrix} = \begin{pmatrix} 0.097 \\ 0.487 \\ 0.286 \\ 0.130 \end{pmatrix}$$

Evaluating the alternative suppliers with respect to the criteria was the next step. The pairwise comparison matrix for the three suppliers with respect to price formed with the primary data was as follows:

Criterion: Price

Supplier	A	B	C
A	1	1/3	1
B	3	1	4
C	1	1/4	1

Following the normalization and averaging of the row elements, the priority vector, showing the weights for the three suppliers for the criterion of price, was obtained and shown as follows:

$$
\begin{array}{cc}
\text{Supplier} & \text{Price} \\
\begin{pmatrix} A \\ B \\ C \end{pmatrix} = & \begin{pmatrix} 0.192 \\ 0.633 \\ 0.175 \end{pmatrix}
\end{array}
$$

Proceeding the same way as for price, pairwise comparison matrices and the priority vectors for service, quality and logistic were obtained. The pairwise comparison matrices are shown as follows:

Criterion: Service

Supplier	A	B	C
A	1	2	1/2
B	1/2	1	1/3
C	2	3	1

Criterion: Quality

Supplier	A	B	C
A	1	3	2
B	1/3	1	1/3
C	1/2	3	1

Criterion: Logistic

Supplier	A	B	C
A	1	1	1/4
B	1	1	1/4
C	4	4	1

The priority weights of the three suppliers for the four criteria obtained following the normalization and averaging of the values of the row elements have been shown as follows:

Criterion Supplier	Price	Service	Quality	Logistic
A	0.192	0.297	0.525	0.167
B	0.633	0.164	0.141	0.167
C	0.175	0.539	0.334	0.667
Sum	1.000	1.000	1.000	1.000

Based on the priority weights of the criteria as shown earlier and the priority weights of each supplier with respect to the criteria as shown in the table above, the overall rankings of the suppliers were calculated as follows:

Supplier A = $(0.192 \times 0.097) + (0.297 \times 0.487) + (0.525 \times 0.286) + (0.167 \times 0.13) = 0.33512$
Supplier B = $(0.633 \times 0.097) + (0.164 \times 0.487) + (0.141 \times 0.286) + (0.167 \times 0.13) = 0.20330$
Supplier C = $(0.175 \times 0.097) + (0.539 \times 0.487) + (0.334 \times 0.286) + (0.667 \times 0.13) = 0.46170$

Supplier C with the highest score of 0.46170 was selected.

Conclusion

The case study shows the application of AHP for identifying the potential suppliers for input materials and outsourced components required by manufacturing organizations based on set criteria of performance on the part of the suppliers.

Source: Ramlan and Qiang (2014).

•Review Questions•

1. What are DSSs? Illustrate with suitable examples.

2. What are the main components of a DSS? Explain their roles.

3. What constitutes the knowledge system in a DSS environment?

4. What are DSS generators? Is Arena 5.0 a DSS generator? Explain.

5. In what ways Analytica is different from Spreadsheet software such as Microsoft Excel? What are the advantages of Analytica as a DSS generator?

6. What is an influence diagram? Explain with a suitable example.

7. What are the distinguishing features of MAUT and AHP?

8. What is outranking method? How is it different from AHP? Explain.

9. What is the implication of Arrow's paradox for group decisions?

10. What are GDSSs? How do they facilitate group decision-making?

Bibliography

Alter, S. 'How Effective Managers Use Information Systems.' *Harvard Business Review* 64, no. 6 (1976): 97–104.

Arrow, K. J. 'A Difficulty in the Concept of Social Welfare.' *The Journal of Political Economy* 58, no. 4 (1950): 328–346.

Bose, U., A. M. Dave, and D. L. Olson. 'Multi-Attribute Utility Methods in Group Decision Making: Past Applications and Potential for Inclusion in GDSS.' *Omega, International Journal of Management Sciences* 25, no. 6 (1977): 691–706.

Holsapple, C. W., and A. B. Whinston. *Decision Support Systems: A Knowledge Based Approach*. Saint Paul, MN: West Publishing, 1996.

Janakiraman, V. S., and K. Sarukesi. *Decision Support Systems*. New Delhi: PHI, 2008.

Keeny, L., and H. Raiffla. *Decisions with Multiple Objectives: Preference and Value trade-offs*, Cambridge: Cambridge University Press, 1976.

Linkov, I., A. Varghese, S. Jamail, T. P. Seager, G. Kiker, and T. Bridges. 'Multi-Criteria Decision Analysis: A Framework for Structuring Remedial Decisions at Contaminated Sites.' Proceedings of the Comparative Risk Assessment and Environmental Decision Making Conference, Nato Science Series: IV: Earth and Environmental Sciences, 38, pp. 15–54, 2004.

Power, D. J. *Decision Support Systems: Concepts and Resources for Managers*. Westport, CT: Greenhood Publishing Group, 2002.

Ramlan, Rohaizam, and Lee Wen Qiang. 'An Analytic Hierarchy Process Approach for Supplier Selection: A Case Study.' 3rd International Conference on Global Optimization and Its Application, September 2014, Yogyakarta, Indonesia.

Saaty, T. L. 'Decision Making with the Analytic Hierarchy Process.' *International Journal of Services Sciences* 1, no. 1 (2008): 83–98.

Velasquerz, M., and P. T. Hesrter. 'An Analysis of Multi-Criteria Decision Making Methods.' *International Journal of Operations Research* 10, no. 2 (2013): 56–66.

Executive Information Systems

5.1 Introduction

Executive information systems (EISs) are of paramount importance for the senior executives such as functional heads and CEOs of organizations. The evolution of EISs was necessary in view of the very nature of information requirements for the decisions taken by the senior managers of any organization. The traditional MISs fail to provide such information. This development was further facilitated because of a gradual shift from a batch of an interactive environment and also an increase in information focus and integration. Each of these transitions results in technological and organizational changes. The information and decision-making needs of senior executives can be provided by easy access to both internal and external information relevant in meeting the strategic goal of an organization. It is commonly considered as a specialized form of a DSS.

5.2 Definition of EIS

An EIS is a set of tools supporting the information and decision-making needs of senior managers through timely, summarized and relevant information available within the organization and also external information in an analytical framework.

The purpose of an EIS is to provide senior executives or managers, at the strategic and tactical levels in an organization, access to the relevant data/information either directly online or through periodic reports. The idea is that the managers can identify trends, measure performance and raise queries to facilitate managerial learning and thus decide for the future course of action.

5.3 Characteristics of an EIS

The important characteristics of an EIS can be listed as follows:

1. Tailored to senior executives' information needs.
2. Reports are of executive summary or exception type.

3. 'Drill-down' process associated with each summary information/data item.
4. Online and interactive type.
5. User-friendly with GUI.
6. Performance indicators and factors are highlighted (a recent concept is the performance dashboards explained in the succeeding paragraphs in this chapter).
7. Provides access to both organizational database and external business intelligence (BI).
8. New concepts of BI, performance dashboards and so on.
9. Provision for information of both hard and soft nature.

5.4 History of Evolution of EIS

The term 'executive information systems' was introduced in 1982 by Rockart and Treacy to describe the kind of systems which a few senior corporate officers were using on a regular basis to retrieve information needed by them for decision-making. In 1988, Rockart and Delong defined the term executive support system (ESS) to refer to systems similar to EIS but with a broader set of capabilities than EISs. These, apart from providing information, also might include communication support, such as emails and teleconferencing, data analysis facilities such as spreadsheets, influence diagrams, query languages, DSSs to evaluate decisions of simulated or 'what–if' types, artificial intelligence (AI) and expert systems and organizing tools such as electronic calendars and electronic flip charts. Rockart (1979) mentioned about four major approaches of defining top executive information needs, namely by-product approach, null approach, key indicator approach and the total study method. In the 'by-product' method, a little attention is paid to any formal study of information needs of the top executives. More attention is focused on data processing such as payroll, accounts receivable and payable and billing customers, and the information by-products of these data-processing systems are made available to the interested executives and at the most, some aggregation of data such as total sales over a period of time is passed to the top executives. In the 'null approach', the proponents such as Mintzberg (1976) point to the uselessness of any formal MIS for top executives. According to them, top executive activities are dynamic and ever changing, so one cannot predetermine exactly what information will be needed at any point of time. A great deal of top executive information needs is met by informal sources such as words, hearsay and gossip. Hard data such as written reports are of little use for this purpose. The 'key indicator' system is based on three concepts. The first concept is that for every organization, irrespective of the type, there are a set of key indicators of the health of the organization and data are collected on the basis of each of these indicators. The second concept is the principle of exception reporting. It means that managers should be provided with only those indicators where performance is significantly different from expected results. Senior executives, therefore, need to focus their attention on areas where the actual performance is different from the planned targets. The third concept underlying the key indicator system is the expanding use of visual displays such as computer consoles, digital displays and other video displays.

In the fourth approach in the study of information needs of top executives, known as the total study process, a large sample of managers are interviewed about their information needs and the results are compared with the existing IS. The gap is bridged by designing subsystems to provide information currently not available. IBM's business system planning (BSP) is the most widely used total study process. It is aimed at a top-down analysis of the information needs of an organization. There are two phases in it. In the first phase, executives starting from top are interviewed to determine their environment, objectives, key decisions and information needs. This helps the analyst to form an overall understanding of the business and the existing IS. The second phase consists of designing new information subsystems and implementing them to provide necessary information currently unavailable.

Each of the above-mentioned approaches to the study of the senior executive's information needs has its advantages and limitations. The by-product method is aimed at paperwork processing inexpensively, rather than fulfilling real management information needs. The null approach with its emphasis on soft, diverse and ever-changing information needs of a top executive has saved many organizations from building useless ISs and expenses. It, however, places too much stress on the executives' strategic and inter-personnel roles and overlooks the management control role of the executives. The key indicator system provides a significant amount of useful information. It, however, tends to be all inclusive rather than on target to a particular executive's specific information needs. The total system process is expensive in terms of manpower and all-inclusive in terms of scope.

One of the important current approaches to the study of executives' information needs is the CSFs method developed by a research team of the Sloan School of Management Information Systems at Massachusetts Institute of Technology (MIT). The CSF approach is actively researched and applied at the MIT centre too. The CSF approach is based on the identification of CSFs, that help in attaining organizational goals. In most industries, there are usually three to six factors that determine success. These key jobs must be done exceedingly well for an organization to be successful. As a result, CSFs are areas of activity that receive constant and careful attention of management. The four prime factors that determine critical success for any industry are: (a) structure of the particular industry, that is, the nature of the industry, competitive strategy, industry position and geographical locations, (b) environmental factors such as socio-economic environment, (c) political factors and (d) temporal factors such as inflation, sensex fluctuations and oil price.

Four frameworks for EIS development, namely (a) evaluation, survey, prototype, review, implement and transfer (ESPRIT); (b) structural; (c) path and (d) structurational have been described in the following sections.

5.5 ESPRIT Framework

The first framework ESPRIT is a sequential framework in the form of a six-phase development project. It is essentially an evolutionary prototyping method and starts with a feasibility study and follows on to other stages of development until installation of the final system and training of users. The second phase is the survey of business needs followed by the third phase of prototyping the current requirement. The fourth phase is the review of the benefits. The fifth phase is the implementation phase, and the sixth and the final phase is the transfer of the skills in-house. This last phase involves the design and implementation of training courses for the users of the system.

5.6 Structural EISs Framework

The structural framework stems from practical experience in developing EIS, a large number of literature on EIS and discussions with EIS vendors, consultants and EIS staff members. There are three components which comprise the structural framework. The first component is a structural perspective of the development of EIS and describes the key elements such as internal and external environment and data, executive sponsor, operating sponsor, executive users, functional areas, organizational database, the information science and technology group, vendors, consultants and builders and their interactions with each other and the EIS. The second component of the framework is relating to issues relevant to the development process such as development time, methodology and the spread of the system among the other members of the organization. The third component is the user–system dialogue. The user–system dialogue is concerned with issues such as user knowledge to operate the EIS, response time, the user-system interface and mode of presentation of the information.

5.7 Path Framework for EIS

The path framework draws attention to the importance of timing and coordinating EIS development so that it is appropriately matched with the organization's level of decision-making maturity and technical capabilities. It also describes how EIS evolves from MIS foundation to cater to the senior executives' integrated, focused and easily accessible information needs for decision-making. The evolution of an EIS from traditional MIS requires changes in stages mainly in two areas. First, there has to be a shift from a batch to an interactive environment, and second an increased focus and integration of information organization-wide. Each of these transitions results in technological and organizational changes. Table 5.1 summarizes the evolution stages of the path framework of EIS.

The 'focus and integration' dimension is concerned with the system's ability to provide and integrate information about specific performance measures relevant to various functional areas in the organization. The 'mode of operation' differentiates between batch systems (designed for periodic reporting) and online systems (allowing interactive retrieval of information). The two-dimensions result in four types of systems, as shown in the Table 5.1. Typically, the starting point is the operation of a traditional MIS

TABLE 5.1   A Path Framework for EIS

		Batch	Online
Focus and Integration	High	**3. Batch EIS** • Key performance indicators • Critical success factors • Integrated information • Periodic paper reports	**4. On-line EIS** • Selective, ad-hoc monitoring • Key indicators and back up detail
	Low	**1. MIS** • By-product • Bottom-up approach • Isolated, scattered high volume reports	**2. Query** • Selective, ad-hoc access for query and analysis used by staff

Source: Kaniclides and Kimble (1994).

and the 'online EIS' stage representing the most advanced stage in this framework. There can be various paths of evolution of ISs from the MIS to an online EIS in an organization.

5.8 Structurational Framework

The structurational framework of EIS development is based on a systematic study and investigation of the interaction between human actors and the social structure during the development of the EISs.

The structurational framework was brought out by Orlikowski and Robey in 1991. Orlikowski and Robey's framework has been described in Table 5.2. The utility of this framework is in the fact that it provides a means of integrating the elements in a coherent manner and linking them explicitly to human action.

Each of the four frameworks mentioned in Table 5.1 has a considerably different perspective of EIS development. This is mainly due to differences in purpose, nature, emphasis and focus of each framework. Nevertheless, they together describe the various aspects of successful EIS development.

Kaniclides and Kimble (1994) put forward a new framework of EIS development, namely, the 'PAS' framework, where 'PAS' stands for the People, Activities and Systems of the framework. The 'PAS' framework can be described using Set theory. Each of the three main components can be considered to be sets containing elements present in an organization during system development. The set of people {P} in an organization comprises subsets or elements such as people who are neither involved in the development of EIS nor using the resulting EIS, the people who are involved in the development process but are not users of the system, the people who are actively involved in the development process and are also users of the EIS and the people who are not involved in the development process

TABLE 5.2 Orlikowski and Robey's Framework

	System Developers Are	System Developers Work	System Developers Draw
Realm of social structure	Informed by systems development methodologies and knowledge about their organizations to build information systems.	Within the constraints of time, budget, hardware, software and authority to build information systems.	On the values and conventions of their organization occupation and training to build information systems.
Modalities	Interpretive schemes	Resources	Norms
Realm of human action	System developers create meaning by programming assumptions and knowledge into information systems.	System developers create IS through the organizational power capabilities they wield in their organizational roles.	System developers create sanctions by designing and programming legitimate options and conventions into information systems.

but are users of the system. Similarly, the activities {A} set comprises subsets of organizational activities not directly related to EIS but can influence the development or use of EIS, activities directly connected with EIS developmental efforts, and the subset of activities representing post-implementation efforts.

The set of systems {S} comprises other organizational systems operational in the organization, the subset of the systems in the organization representing the EISs applications operational in the organization and the subset of systems including enhancements, or expansion to the initial implementation. Besides an integral part of the framework of EIS development is the environment in which the organization operates and the time dimension for each activity. The detailed interactions of the above components and elements employing the set theory in EIS development can be studied from the paper of Kaniclides and Kimble (1994).

5.9 EIS and BI

In recent years, the term EIS has become less popular, while BI techniques (with the sub-areas of reporting, analytics and digital dashboards and so on) have become more popular for the sake of information and decision-making particularly at senior management echelons.

The BI refers to computer-based techniques used in locating, digging out and analysing business data, such as sales revenue by products and/or departments. The BI technologies provide historical, current and predictive views of business operations. Common functions of BI technologies are reporting, online analytical processing (OLAP), analytics, data mining, business performance management and control through digital dashboards, benchmarking and predictive analytics.

The BI can be applied to the following business purposes in order to derive business value:

1. Measurement of progress against business goals through a hierarchy of performance metrics and benchmarking. The idea is to manage the business processes accordingly.
2. Analytics through program that builds quantitative processes for a business to arrive at optimal decisions and to perform business knowledge discovery. This frequently involves data mining, statistical analysis (such as risk and sensitivity analysis), predictive modelling and BPM. The concept of data mining has been discussed in subsequent chapters of this book.
3. Enterprise reporting through a program that builds infrastructure for strategic reporting to serve the strategic management of a business such as customer service, sales promotion, market analysis of new products, trend analysis, inventory control, sales decisions and similar ones. Enterprise reporting frequently involves data visualization, EIS and OLAP described in a subsequent paragraph of this chapter.
4. Collaboration platform through a program that gets different areas (both internal and external to the business organization) to work together through data sharing and electronic data interchange (EDI).
5. Knowledge management through a program to make the company data driven through strategies and practices to identify, create, represent, distribute and to enable adoption of insights and experiences which are true business knowledge. Knowledge management leads to learning management and regulatory compliance.

5.10 BI and Data Warehousing

Often, BI applications use data gathered from a data warehouse or a data mart. However, neither all data warehouses are used for BI, nor do all BI applications require a data warehouse. Data warehouses have been characterized with the following features:

1. **Subject-oriented:** Data are organized according to major subjects or processes of an organization such as products, customers, materials, machines, vendors and employees. The subjects are common for various application-oriented operational systems.
2. **Integrated:** The data from various subject areas should be rationalized with one another. The integration is achieved through the data model and physical tables or databases in the warehouse.
3. **Non-volatile:** Data in a data warehouse, unlike data of online operational databases, are not updated. Once a data record is properly stored in the warehouse, it is not subjected to change. For example, a particular customer record will be retained with the period of tenure even if the customer ceases to be a customer subsequently. The data records in a data warehouse are snapshots and time stamped, and updates are not allowed.
4. **Time variant:** A data record is accurate only as of some moment in time. In some cases, the moment in time is a single moment. In other cases, it is a span of time. However, in any case, the values of data found in a data warehouse are accurate with reference to the particular time moment or time span.
5. **Facilitator of managerial decisions:** Data warehouses are created for the purpose of managerial decisions. The operational systems provide for operational information for facilitating day-to-day operations of a company, whereas data warehouses are basically ISs to facilitate managerial decisions for deriving value to the business.

    Apart from the above characteristics which defined the data warehouse, the additional features are:
    i.   Detailed or granular data;
    ii. Historical data;
    iii. Faster Navigation through related data and information;
    iv. Heterogeneous data set transformed into a common format.

A data warehouse is a physically distinct place from online operational applications.

5.11 Architecture of a Data Warehouse

The typical architecture of a data warehouse is as shown in Figure 5.1. The architecture is a top-down one where the departmental data marts (explained in subsequent sections) have been shown as subordinate to the main data warehouse and created from the same.

    The important components are:

1. **Operational data sources**, which consist of the following:
    i.   External systems such as the Internet, commercially available database or database associated with the suppliers or customers of the organizations and the database of the statutory or regulatory authorities such as the government.

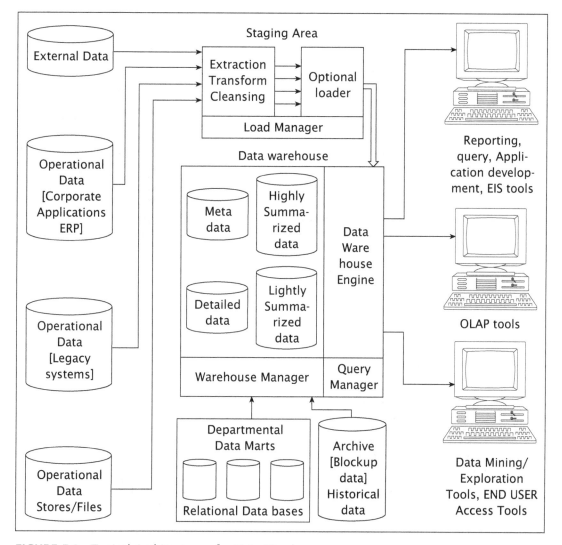

FIGURE 5.1 Typical Architecture of a Data Warehouse

    ii. Corporate applications including ERP, legacy systems such as payroll, stores ledger and similar ones.

2. Operational data stores/files which are **stores of current and integrated operational data.** The operational data store is often structured and supplies data in the same form as to be stored in the warehouse but may often act as a staging area for the data to be loaded into the data warehouse.

3. **Load manager,** also known as the front-end component of the data warehouse architecture, performs all operations such as extraction of data from the operational systems, transformation of data into internal format and structuring of the data warehouse, cleansing to improve quality of data and loading of the data into the warehouse. The four processes from extraction through

loading are often called collectively 'data staging'. Let us elaborate on the four processes as follows:

i. *Extract:* It is necessary to extract only the data relevant and useful for decision-making processes from the operational databases before including in the warehouse. The extract process specifies:

    a. Which data files and tables are to be accessed in the source databases?

    b. Which fields of the data records are to be extracted from a above? For example, in case of a goods receipt note record, the delivery truck or lorry number field may not be relevant for decision purpose whereas the supplier field is very relevant and needs to be extracted.

    c. What are the extracts to be incorporated in the resulting database?

    d. What are the target and database format of the output?

    e. The schedule of the extraction process.

ii. *Transform:* Transform process deals with rectifying any inconsistency among the data from different sources. The idea is to transform the data into a common form for storing in the data warehouse. The inconsistencies are mainly due to the following:

    a. Attribute naming inconsistency, for example, customer name may be cust_name, custname and so on.

    b. Mixed text containing upper and lowercases.

    c. Numerical data in different formats in different databases.

Examples of data transform process

Source	Employee Name	Date of Birth	Salary	Target	(Warehouse) DOB	(Warehouse) Salary
Payroll system	BANERJEE ♭ SOUREN	30.11.1949	60000.00	SOUREN ♭ BANERJEE	11301949	60000.00
Personnel Information System	SOUREN ♭ BANERJEE	NOV 30, 1949	60000.00	SOUREN ♭ BANERJEE	11301949	60000.00
ERP HR Module	Souren ♭ Banerjee	NOV 30, 1949	60000.00	SOUREN ♭ BANERJEE	11301949	60000.00

    d. Date formats are different, for example, ddmmyy, mmddyy or 30NOV1949 and so on.

    e. Different units of measure, for example, ₹/$, number/dozen and so on.

    f. Coded data in different formats, for example, male/female, M/F.

    All the above inconsistencies need to be eliminated by transform and convert to a common format, for example: (a) all characters can be converted into ASCII, (b) texts may be converted into uppercase, (c) common format for numeric and date fields, (d) one unit of measure for similar physical quantities and (e) coded data must be in an uniform format.

iii. *Cleansing:* The quality of information is one of the key considerations which determine the value of information to a manager. The process of data cleansing is to eliminate errors in the data as far as possible to make it error free before entry into the data warehouse. The possible errors which need elimination are missing data, abnormal value of data, invalid data, inconsistent data and conflicting data arising out of more than one source. Examples of such errors are numbers in the name field, alphanumeric characters in the value field, two different date of births for the same employee, missing serial numbers in vouchers, date of birth and age as on a particular date do not tally; for example, if date of birth is on 30 November 1949 and age as on 1 January 2017 is 70 years.

iv. *Loading:* Loading implies physical movement of the data from the computers storing the source database to the data warehouse database, assuming the two are different. Loading takes place after extraction, transformation and data cleansing. The most common channel for data transfer and loading is a high-speed communication link. Loading puts raw/detailed data in the form of fact tables and also generates a report of the data loaded into the warehouse.

4. A **warehouse manager** performs all the operations associated with the management of the data in the warehouse. The operations performed by the warehouse manager within the data warehouse include analysis of data to ensure consistency, time stamping, creation of indexes and views such as bitmap indexes and join indexes which considerably reduce data scanning, partitioning of data to create multidimensional views of the same, de-normalization and aggregations, creation of data marts, archiving and backing up of historical and other data. The storage of data in various forms is explained in subsequent sections in detail.

5. **Detailed/granular data,** lightly and highly summarized data, in the form of various schemas and data models achieve backup data in a warehouse (explained subsequently).

6. A **query manager** is also called back-end component as he/she performs the task of managing user queries for data/information. He/she is the interface between warehouse and end-user access tools and directs the queries to the appropriate tables (fact tables and dimensional tables explained in next section of this chapter) and also schedules the execution of queries.

7. **Metadata** is an essential feature of the warehouse. Metadata is data/information about the data in the warehouse. It contains information about the components of the corporate information factory (CIF) as named by Bill Inmon known as the father of data warehouse. Metadata has two major functions to describe the data found in the architectural component of a data warehouse and to exchange metadata with other components. Besides, metadata in the data warehouse plays several roles such as describing the location of various data in the warehouse for usage, coordinating between different operations starting with extract, transform, load (ETL) to information access for facilitating various queries and other end-user access modes.

8. There can be different **types of metadata** such as technical metadata which describe the structure and content of different types of data, operating metadata which are generated as metrics (measures) of day-to-day operations of the data warehouse such as number of records accessed or transferred from one component to another, total number of records in a table or a database and business metadata which consist of business definitions, formulae, rules and conditions, glossaries and dictionaries of business which people understand.

9. **End-user access tools** can be categorized into five main groups: data reporting and query tools, application development tools, EIS tools, OLAP tools for analysis such as aggregation (total sales, percentage of sales of a particular product to total sales), comparison (budget versus actual), ranking (top 10, quartile, percentile analysis), access to detailed data (drill) and aggregate data (roll-up), complex criteria specification, visualization and data mining developed from research into statistical analysis and AI which is the process of extracting previously unknown information patterns and linkages from large database to facilitate proactive information delivery leading to knowledge for the decision-makers such as senior managers/executives. Data mining helps building predictive models for future values of target variables. The process has been successfully used for credit analysis, fraud detection, target marketing, banking and insurance, healthcare and

many other areas of applications. For example, Electronic Point of Sale (EPOS) data analysis of the shopping baskets in a shopping mall is often applied by mall managers to find relationships among the product mix of choice of the buyers in order to refine purchasing, display and promotional decisions by the shopping mall.

5.12 Some Important Physical Aspects of a Data Warehouse

5.12.1 Data Model

The design of a data warehouse begins with a data model. At the highest level, a data model represents an entity relationship diagram (ERD). Each entity represents a subject such as customer, product, vendor, machine and employee. Each entity is further defined at a lower level of data modelling called the data item set (DIS). The DIS specifies a lower level of detail than the entity does, such as keys and attributes as well as structure of the keys and attributes. The DIS is further broken down into a lower level of physical design creating the physical characteristics of the data such as alpha and numeric. Figure 5.2 shows a nursing home data model as an illustration.

5.12.2 Physical Tables

The data warehouse is made up of interrelated tables or physical databases. Within the data warehouse, there are different physical areas. Each subject area may comprise one fact table and a number of dimension tables related to each other by means of a shared key or foreign key relationship. Collectively the different tables along with their relationships form a data warehouse. The dimension tables arise

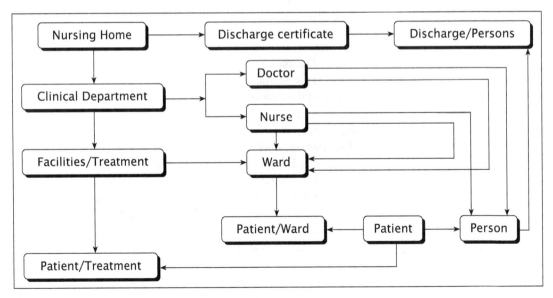

FIGURE 5.2   A Nursing Home Data Model

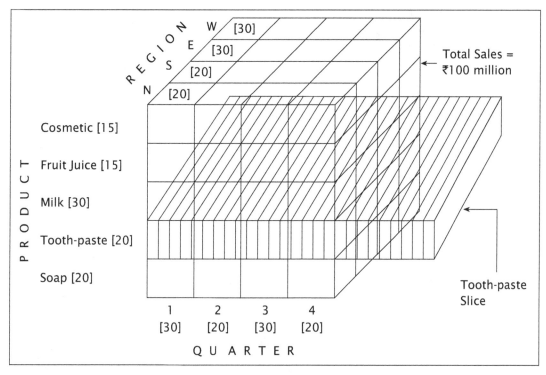

FIGURE 5.3 Multidimensional Data

because of the multidimensional data in a warehouse. The dimensions may be product, region, time and so on. For example, a sales revenue of ₹100 million of a consumer goods company in a year may comprise products sold such as soap, toothpaste, milk, fruit juice and cosmetics. The total sales may again consist of sales of all products region-wise such as North India, South India, East India and West India. Similarly, the total sales of ₹100 million may be split up into quarterly, monthly, weekly and daily sales for 4 quarters, 12 months, 52 weeks and 365 days. The multidimensional sales data as mentioned above can be represented as shown in Figure 5.3.

The multidimensional data leads to 'slicing and dicing' for data analysis and query response. For example, the total sales of ₹100 million as shown in Figure 5.3 comprises slices such as the toothpaste slice. The slices constitute the cube (dice) of total sales of ₹100 million.

5.12.3 Corporate Data Model Architecture

The corporate data model is the intellectual road map for the development of the data warehouse. The architecture of the data model in a data warehouse comprises: (a) Third normal form (3NF), (b) star, fact constellation and snowflake schema and (c) data vault.

The above architecture is based on the data tables collectively along with their relationships.

1. **3NF:** The 3NF is a normal form used in database normalization and the concept has been described elaborately in a subsequent chapter on database management systems (DBMSs) of this book.

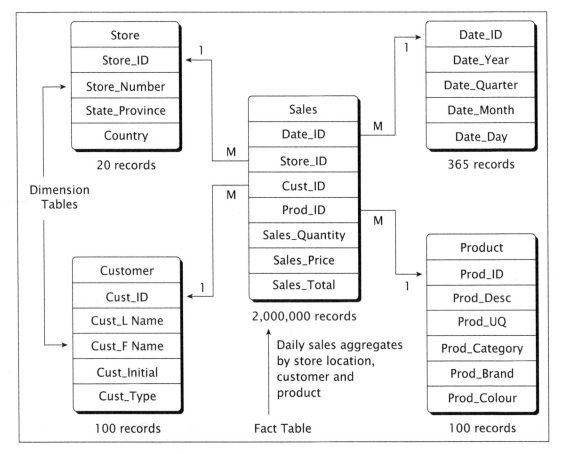

FIGURE 5.4 Star Schema for Sales

2. **Star schema:** The star schema has been described in Figure 5.4. It comprises a fact table which contains all the records of aggregate transactions of a subject (in the example daily sales) and the dimension tables which in the example shown in Figure 5.4 are store location, time (period of sales), product and customer tables containing different number of records.

3. **Snowflake schema:** The snowflake schema is similar to star schema. However, the difference is that in snowflake schema, dimensions are normalized into multiple related tables, whereas in star schema dimensions are denormalized with each dimension represented by a single table. The example shown in Figure 5.4 is normalized and shown as a snowflake schema as shown in Figure 5.5.

4. **Fact constellation schema:** For each star schema, it is possible to construct fact constellation schema (e.g., by splitting the original star schema into more star schemas, each of them describes facts on another level of dimension hierarchy). The fact constellation architecture contains multiple fact tables that share many dimension tables. This schema is used mainly for the aggregate fact tables or where we want to split a fact table for better comprehension. The split of fact tables is done when we want to focus on aggregation over few facts and dimensions. The main

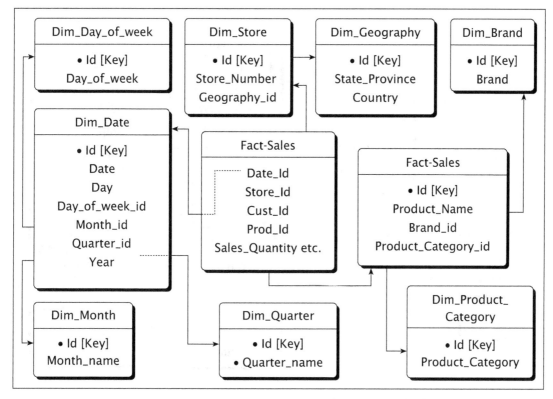

FIGURE 5.5 Snowflake Schema for Sales

shortcoming of the fact constellation schema is a more complicated design because many variants for particular kinds of aggregation must be considered and selected. Moreover, dimension tables are still large. Figure 5.6 is an example of fact constellation schema.

5. **Data vault:** Data vault concept of data modelling in warehouse was first developed in the late 1990s and released in 2000 onwards. The proponent was Dan E. Linstedt, USA. The data vault is a detail-oriented, historical tracking and uniquely linked set of 3NF tables that support one or many functional areas of business. It is a hybrid approach with the best features of 3NF and star schema as explained in earlier sections. It is the latest concept of data model and is the architect to meet the needs of enterprise data warehouse. A data vault can act as operational data store (ODS) and at the same time can handle large sets of granular data in the range of terabyte in a smaller, more normalized physical space in comparison to both 3NF and star schema. Inside the data vault are familiar structures that match traditional definitions of star schema and 3NF that include dimensions, many-to-many linkages and standard table structures. The distinctive features are the relationship representations, field structuring and granular time-stamped data storage. The data vault consists of the following minimum and essential components:

i. Hub entities or hubs are a single table carrying a minimum unique list of primary business keys, for example, employee number, customer number, supplier number, item number, machine number and so on. These keys are those utilized by businesses for day-to-day

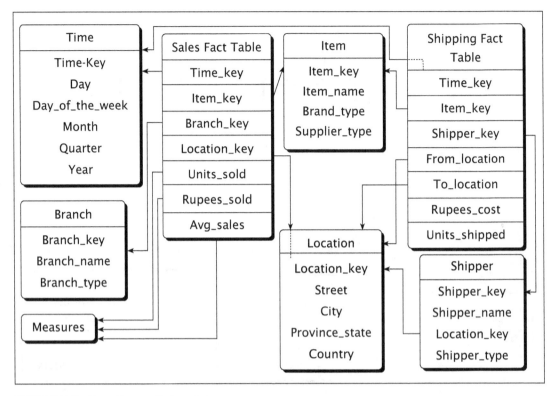

FIGURE 5.6 Fact Constellation Schema

operations. Other attributes in the hub are surrogate keys, that is, optional components such as sequence number, load date-time stamp recording from the first instance of time of the arrival of the key and record source for traceability of the source system of the key.

ii. The second component of the data vault is the link entities which are a physical representation of a many-to-many 3NF relationship. The link represents the relationship or transaction between two and more business components (two and more keys). The link also contains the entities of surrogate key, hub 1 key to hub N key, load date-time stamp and the record source for traceability.

iii. The third component is satellite entities or satellites which are hub-key context information to describe the hub key. The satellite information is subject to change over time, and the structure of the satellite is capable of storing new or altered data at the granular level. For example, a particular milling machine may be retrofitted with an add-on component (feature) to make it not a milling machine but a special purpose gear-cutting machine. The attributes of the satellite are—the satellite's primary key, that is, the hub or link primary key migrated from hub or link into the satellite, load date-time stamp which records the time of the context information that first came to exist in the warehouse, satellite's optional primary key and sequence surrogate number utilized for satellites that have multiple values and record source for data traceability.

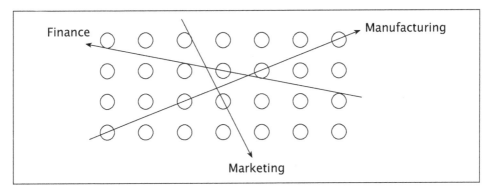

FIGURE 5.7 Granular Data Allows the Source Data Viewed in Different Ways

Building a data vault involves modelling the hubs, links, satellites and point-in-time tables which is a satellite derivative.

Other aspects of a data warehouse are as follows:

1. **Granular data:** The data found in a data warehouse are very granular in nature. This implies that the data in a warehouse is placed in a very detailed form. The data may then be shaped by an application so that it can be viewed in a distinct manner. The granular data at the core of data warehouse provide many benefits. A primary benefit is that the same data can be viewed in different ways but there is a single source of reconciliation. Figure 5.7 shows how the same granular data can be examined in different ways by three departments in an organization.

   Usually, each grain of information in the data warehouse represents some finite unit of business activity for the company such as an order, a sale, manufacture of an item, a payment and a telephone call. All the above grains of information may be uniquely specified by the date, the item, the amount, length of call, the customer, the person making the payment or the call and the person receiving the payment or the call as the case may be.

   Each grain of information can be combined with other grains to provide a different perspective of data. For example, a sale can be combined with the corresponding order (another grain) to find whether the order was executed in time.

   In addition to allowing data to be viewed differently by different parties, another benefit is that granular data may lie in the data warehouse for unknown future requirement. So, we can say data warehouse keeps the senior executives in a proactive position rather than a reactive one for new needs of information.

2. **Historical data:** A data warehouse contains a robust amount of historical data. Many companies keep year-wise history of data in the data warehouse for the past 5–10 years.

   A data warehouse can benefit many organizations such as metro city municipal corporations, universities, offices of the registrar of assurances and courts by replacing huge record rooms associated with the problem of space and preservation of the old records. The retrieval of old data/information also becomes faster and easier. Although historical data have many applications, perhaps the most potent is the ability to step backward in time and extrapolate the future trend or perform a 'what-if' analysis.

Discrete Data records		Continuous Data records	
☐	15 January	☐	14–29 January
☐	27 February	☐	15–22 February
☐	11 April	☐	1 March–1 July
☐	12 December	☐	30 November–21 December

FIGURE 5.8 Time Stamping of Either Continuous or Discrete Records

3. **Time stamping and data relationships:** The units of data stored in a data warehouse are time stamped so that each unit of data record in the data warehouse has some element of time associated with the same. Time stamping of records in a data warehouse is either continuous or discrete as shown in Figure 5.8. In case of a discrete record, there is one instant in time for which the record is accurate, and this is true in case of fast changing variables such as gold price and share value. In case of continuous records, there is a span of time for which the record is accurate such as variables that change slowly and for which there is an advantage in knowing information over time. The records in data warehouse have a distinctive structure including (a) a time stamp, (b) a key, (c) a primary data and (d) a secondary data. For example, in case of an order record, there will be a time stamp corresponding to the order date, order number, product or products ordered, quantity, amount and delivery date and so on which are primary data and the secondary data are package type, mode of delivery and so on. The different types of data found in a data warehouse relate to each other by means of foreign keys pointing to actual keys. For example, an end product EP1 requires a component COMP1. There would be an end product record for end product EP1, as well as a separate component record for the component COMP1. The component record COMP1 in its body would have a foreign key reference to end product EP1.

It may be noted that the data relationships found in the data warehouse are delimited by time. This implies that when a relationship is indicated in the data warehouse, the relationship is only valid for the moment in time indicated by the time stamps found on the participating records. This interpretation of data relationship in case of a data warehouse is quite different from that of referential integrity found in case of online database environment.

4. **Data volume in a data warehouse:** Today the usual volume of data in a data warehouse is of the order of terabyte (10^{12} bytes) or petabyte (10^{15} bytes)! As volume of data increases in a data warehouse, the ratio of inactive to active data increases at a very high rate and in case of a terabyte warehouse, it may be as high as 90%. This makes cost of the warehouse very high and at the same time, data access very slow. It is therefore the practice to periodically remove inactive (dormant) data from main storage and place the same to alternate storage. This results in significant reduction in cost of active data storage and increases the speed of access to the active data in the data warehouse. However, in order to make the active data and inactive (dormant) data in separate storage to work well, a cross-media storage manager (CMSM) technology is utilized. The CMSM acts as a link between main storage and alternate storage and manages the traffic between the two so that the end users are presented with a seamless view of the data residing in the data warehouse.

5. **Data marts:** Data marts are simple forms of data warehousing, and in the case of top-down architecture, they are supposed to be created out of and subordinate to the data warehouse. However, data marts can also be created independently for various functions and then, they may collectively represent a corporate data warehouse as a bottom-up approach. In other words, data marts are scaled-down versions of data warehouse and created with specific objectives or functions of the company. The functions specific to data marts are related to functions such as marketing, manufacturing, personnel and logistics.

The advantages of creation of data marts are low cost and less time requirement. Data marts are also often created with specific focus. For example, data marts may be created for purchase department of a company with supplier's information only to develop better sources of supplies. This kind of approach is useful so far as relevant information base to cater to managerial decisions is concerned. Instead of creating a full-scale data warehouse, data marts sometimes provide tremendous service to meet immediate and specific information need.

The data warehouse gave birth to different forms of environment that accomplished very different types of information processing. At the centre of all the different architectural structures such as operational data stores, alternative forms of storage, data marts, data mining and so forth is the data warehouse. The data warehouse provided the granular data that was reshaped into many different forms in order to feed many different forms of decision support process. The architectural framework that emerged is called the 'corporate information factory' as shown with a simple illustration in Figure 5.9.

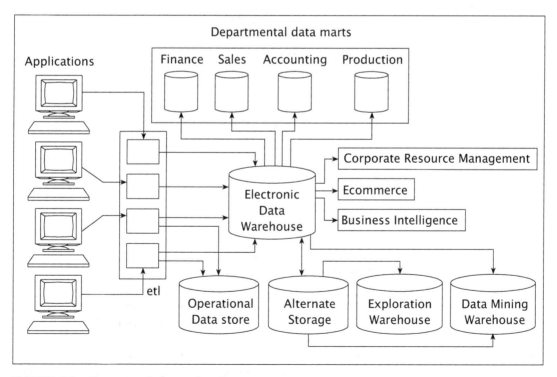

FIGURE 5.9 Corporate Information Factory

5.13 Some Popular Data Warehouse Software

Some of the popular software products and tools relating to data warehouse ETL and data mining are listed below:

1. Warehouse products:
   i. 'CA—Ingress'—Computer Associates
   ii. 'AllBase/SQL'—HP
   iii. SQL Server—Microsoft
   iv. 'Informix XPS'—Informix
   v. Oracle 8, 'Oracle Parallel Server'—Oracle
   vi. SQL Server 11.0—Sybase
2. Data-mining products:
   i. 'Mine Set'—on silicon graphics platform
   ii. 'Intelligent Miner'—IBM
   iii. 'Knowledge Seeker'—Angloss
   iv. 'Neuroagent'—Data Mind
   v. 'IDIS3'—Information Discovery
   vi. 'SAS/Neuronets'—SAS Institute
3. ETL tools:
   i. 'Passport'—Carleton Corporation
   ii. 'Data Junction' ETL Tool—Data Junction Corporation
   iii. 'Data Mapper' for transform—Applied Database Technology
   iv. 'Prism warehouse Manager'—Prism Solutions
4. OLAP and EIS:
   i. 'Pablo'—Andyne computing
   ii. 'Plato'—Microsoft
   iii. 'Express'—Oracle
   iv. 'Metacube'—Informix
   v. 'SAS/EIS', 'OLAP + +'—SAS Institute
5. Reporting tools:
   i. 'Discoverer 2000'—Oracle
   ii. 'Infomaker'—Power software
   iii. 'Vision'—Sterling Software

5.14 Business Dashboards

A dashboard is a user interface that somewhat like an car's dashboard organizes and presents information in a way (usually in the form of charts, graphs and dials, etc.) that is easy to read and interpret. However, a business dashboard usually in the form of computer dashboard is an interactive one through which the users, usually the senior business executives, can visualize the data or information relating to the key performance indicators (KPIs) of the business they are interested in and also in a fashion of their choice so as to pay their attention where needed.

A dashboard more or less resembles GUI. However, some product developers consciously employ this metaphor (and sometimes the term) so that the user instantly recognizes the similarity.

Dashboards usually integrate information from multiple components into a unified display. For example, a dashboard may obtain information from the local operational database of a computer, from one or more applications running concurrently and also from remote location on web servers and present them on the same display board (dashboard). A project monitoring and control centre dashboard can monitor the progress of projects located in various distant locations. Hewlett Packard (HP) developed the first dashboard for customizing windows desktops.

The HP dashboard was subsequently acquired by Borland, and then a company called Star Fish was established. Microsoft's digital dashboard tool incorporates web-based elements such as news and stock quotes together with corporate elements (such as email and applications) into outlook. Dashboards may be customized in a multitude of ways and named accordingly, for example, enterprise dashboard, CEO dashboard and executive dashboard.

5.14.1 Examples of Dashboards

Example 1: Let us illustrate a simple dashboard for monitoring and control of inventory level for a manufacturing unit by the senior materials manager. The dashboard is for showing raw material and work-in-process (WIP) inventory both in value and in days of average consumption for raw materials and days of production for WIP. The dashboard shows only quarterly figures for each quarter completed which are compiled with the figures for the three consecutive months of the quarter. The dashboard consists of bar charts, pie charts and dials as shown in Figure 5.10.

Example 2: A sales analysis dashboard to facilitate sales promotion drive has been shown in Figure 5.11.

There are many dashboard software available in the market and the available software invariably has got the open database connectivity (ODBC) feature to get the source data from various types of files such as Microsoft Excel, dBase, Oracle, MySQL, DB2 and Access. The dashboard software also has got excellent interactive features, by dint of which the users can select the type of visual display such as chart, pie or dial and score speedometer. The users of dashboard have also got the options to select data range, define regions on the displays as 'bad', 'warning' or 'good' to attract attention when the performance measure is not satisfactory.

In case of Excel files, the data rows/columns can be suitably defined to indicate values associated with the KPIs and also the date hierarchy (day/month/quarter/year and so on) corresponding to the performance indicators.

The dashboard software through ODBC accesses the Excel data files and converts the data in the form of display as defined by the user relating to fiscal quarter, fiscal month and so on.

5.14.2 Some Important Features in a Dashboard Design

Some very important aspects that make a good dashboard application and which decide the choice of the dashboard software are:

1. Customizable reports, charts and graphs
2. Options to adjust the measures of performance

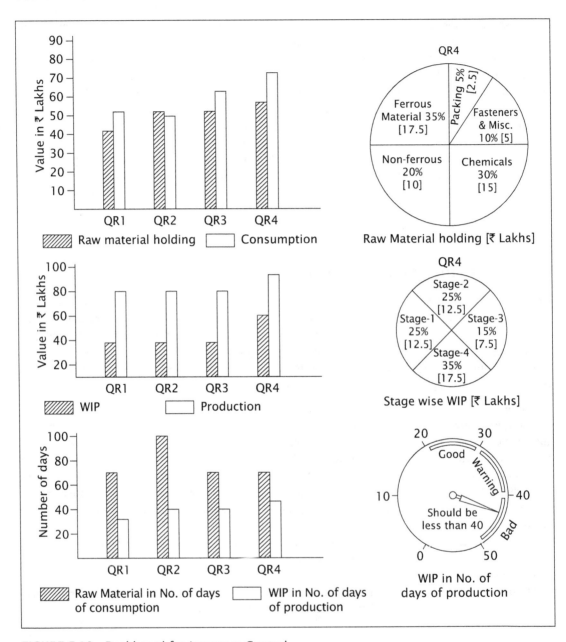

FIGURE 5.10 Dashboard for Inventory Control

3. Sharing of the dashboards with other team members of the company
4. Option to present an automatic report generation date and time
5. Collection and analysis of data according to a preselected set of rules as opposed to merely recording

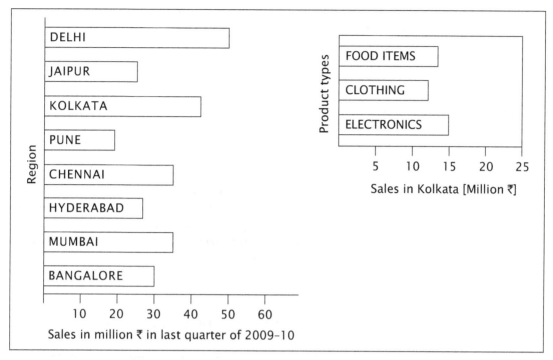

FIGURE 5.11 A Dashboard for Sales Analysis

6. ODBC to various types of files and web-enabling features
7. User-friendly with no need for coding; easy to use and easy to learn

5.14.3 Practices to Design Good Dashboards

The points that should be kept in mind while designing a dashboard are as follows:

1. The dashboard should be designed to have a diagnostic approach to business problems.
2. Before designing the dashboard, the designer should choose wisely and decide the most important data points for the management team. In other words, the designer needs to know the KPIs and the CSFs for the organization for which the dashboard is designed
3. The dashboard should be simple and must not be cluttered with too many unnecessary graphs, charts and so on which may distract attention so that important things may be overlooked.
4. The dashboard screen design should be such that no horizontal scrolling is necessary. It is best if the dashboard is a single-page design without any scrolling at all.
5. In order to get concise results, the period of time over which reports are generated should be kept to a certain minimum. If need arises to compare data over a longer period of time, it is better to generate two dashboard graphs for comparison.
6. The design should be such that there is adequate interactivity such as selection of a certain region, drilling down which add to perceived usability.

5.15 Artificial Intelligence

There can be more than one definition of AI such as:

1. AI is the study of how to make machines (rather computers) do certain things which human beings can also do using their intelligence.
2. AI is a branch of computer science, which deals with the automation of intelligent behaviour.
3. AI is the study of computational processes and techniques for performing tasks that apparently require intelligence performed by humans.

All the above definitions have a commonality, which is that AI is similar to human intelligence which when ascribed to computers or machines makes them perform tasks as humans can also perform using their intelligence. Hence, AI is machine or computer intelligence which functions like human intelligence. A comparison and contrast of machine intelligence versus human intelligence in the perspective of AI have been shown in Table 5.3.

TABLE 5.3 Comparison and Contrast of Human and Machine Intelligence

	Human Intelligence		*Machine Intelligence*
1.	Human intelligence is derived out of knowledge stored in human brain.	1.	Machine intelligence is derived out of knowledge stored in the machine.
2.	Knowledge is acquired through the process of learning (formal or informal education).	2.	Knowledge is acquired out of learning (instructions).
3.	Knowledge is gained out of experience (expertise).	3.	Knowledge is gathered through perception (machine vision).
4.	New knowledge is created out of existing knowledge and expertise (derived knowledge).	4.	New knowledge is created out of existing knowledge (derived knowledge).
5.	Human intelligence is derived out of knowledge possessed by human beings by dint of memory, comprehension, logic, mental arithmetic, perception and recognition and so on.	5.	Machine intelligence is derived by processing of knowledge through searching of knowledge base, language understanding, symbolic representation through logic and frames, rules, program, pattern matching, reasoning, resolution and so on.
6.	Human beings also derive intelligence by way of consultation with domain knowledge experts.	6.	Intelligence is also derived out of computer programs that are able to exhibit expert-like performance in a specific domain of application.

Human Intelligence		Machine Intelligence	
7.	Intelligence (actions) arises because of stimulus (perception), understanding of languages and foresight.	7.	Intelligence (actions) arises because of natural language processing, machine (computer) vision and environmental scanning and projections.
8.	Knowledge is stored in human memory (brain).	8.	Knowledge is stored in machine (computer) by way of knowledge representation methods.
9.	Complex problems are solved by intuition to arrive at optimal or near optimal solution.	9.	Complex problems are solved by heuristic problem-solving methods.
Contrast		**Contrast**	
10.	Human intelligence and behaviour are subject to emotions and sentiments.	10.	Machine intelligence and behaviour are not subject to emotions and sentiments.
11.	Human intelligence deteriorates with ageing.	11.	Machine intelligence does not deteriorate with ageing.

5.15.1 Areas of AI

5.15.1.1 Natural Language Processing (NLP)

This involves the understanding of natural human languages such as English, speech understanding, machine translation and language generation. Making computers understand English allows non-programmers to use them with little training. Natural language understanding in specific application areas such as access to a database is easy.

Natural language generation is easier than natural language understanding and can be accomplished through inexpensive output devices.

Machine translation is usable translation of text and is important for organizations having global operations.

5.15.1.2 Perception

It facilitates recognizing shapes, features and so on by machines automatically and to initiate automatic action. Perception involves machine vision, speech understanding, tactile sensation and so on. Machine vision can be developed by interfacing a camera to a computer which gets an image into the computer memory. The problem is with matching the image with patterns already stored in the computer system and understanding what the image represents.

Speech understanding systems are available now, and some systems need to be trained for individual users and require parse between words. However, understanding continuous speech with large vocabulary may be difficult to perceive by machines. Tactile sensation is common with computer touch screens, robot tasks and so on. Perception leads to actions (tasks) by intelligent robots.

5.15.1.3 Machine Learning

It is a method of programming a computer which learns from experience with reference to some specific type of tasks, and the performance for the tasks of the same type also improves with the experience. In other words, it is the ability of a machine to improve its own performance through the use of algorithms that employs techniques to mimic the ways by which humans seem to learn, such as repetition and experience.

Learning techniques are broadly classified as learning from examples, advice of experts and analogy. Learning from examples and analogy gives rise to knowledge induction in the form of induction algorithm. Input to the induction algorithm is classified examples, and output from the same algorithm is a decision tree with features labelling interior nodes and the classifications labelling the leaves of the tree. Depending upon the combination of various features as observed in the learnt examples, there can be multiple classifications as illustrated in the Figure 5.12.

In the example shown in Figure 5.12, the classifications, features and the domains are as follows:

Classifications: (Scooter, bicycle, auto-rickshaw, cycle rickshaw, trailer, car, bus)
Features: (Number of wheels, engine, weight)
Domains:
Number of wheels = (2, 3, 4)
Engine = (Yes, No)
Weight = (Low, Heavy)

New objects can be classified using the decision tree.

The algorithms for rule of knowledge induction have inputs of instances, a set of training examples, known as training set and the associated features known as the feature vector $(f_1, f_2, ..., f_n)$.

The algorithms employ various selection strategies for features such as (a) random selection to make a decision tree consistent with the training set and with no guarantee of optimality, (b) information theoretic selection to select features which maximally divides the training set and (c) minimum cost selection which considers evaluation of features. For example, the feature of blood group may be costly to determine in a group of mammals.

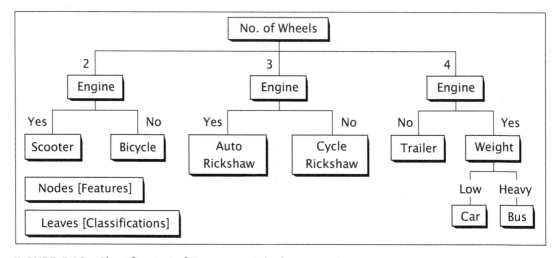

FIGURE 5.12 Classification of Transport Vehicles According to Features

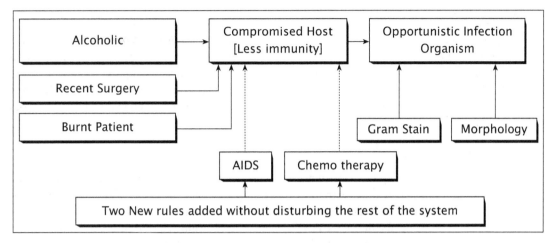

FIGURE 5.13 A Conceptual Island

Learning from the advice of experts is based on the assumption that it is easier for experts to demonstrate his/her expertise in respect of the learning than to record all of his/her knowledge. Interactions with experts often reveal new knowledge and rules. For example, for a young male patient of 19 years of age, the symptoms of persistent knee and ankle joint pains, swelling of joints and muscular inflammation necessitate the correct diagnosis consistent with the symptoms which is osteoarthritis. However, experts opined that osteoarthritis could never be expected in a male patient at this young age. This results in a new rule added to the existing knowledge to rule out osteoarthritis in young male patients.

Conceptual Islands

Conceptual islands are tools for collecting knowledge from experts about a domain. These concepts reduce the number of rules required for the knowledge and also facilitate introducing new rules to become effective along with the rest of the system knowledge.

A classic example of a conceptual island is the expert system 'MYCIN', that diagnosed blood diseases with a compromised host as shown in Figure 5.13.

However, there are many tasks for which it is impossible or rather difficult to design and implement machine learning software with expert advice. A few of such cases are as follows:

1. There are problems where human experts are unable to demonstrate their expertise, for example, handwriting experts. In such cases, machines are provided with examples of inputs and correct outputs to those inputs for future knowledge extraction.
2. There are totally new problems for which no human expertise exists, for example, launching spacecraft towards Mars with human beings for the first time.
3. There are problems where significant events are rapidly changing such as foreign currency exchange rates, behaviour of stock market and so on. In these cases, a continuous learning program on a real-time system constantly modifies and fine-tunes the learnt prediction rules.
4. Customized applications for each user separately, for example, a program to eliminate unwanted email messages.

Learning Tasks

Learning tasks can be classified according to many different dimensions, and one such dimension is distinction between empirical and analytical learning. Empirical learning is learning which relies on some form of external experience, while analytical learning needs no external inputs. The various types of empirical learning tasks are supervised learning, unsupervised learning, reinforcement or Q-learning and so on, while speed-up learning is a form of analytical learning. Let us explain in brief the above types of empirical and analytical learning.

Supervised Learning

The task of supervised learning is to construct a classifier, given a set of classified training examples such as photographs of sports personalities with the games they play. A pair consisting of an object along with the associated class is called a labelled example and the set of such labelled examples is known as the training set. The training set facilitates the development of the learning algorithm. Apart from learning classifiers, supervised training also includes learning functions to predict numerical values. The task is called regression. For example, given the three-dimensional view of a building, a civil engineer might like to predict the construction cost, years elapsed since its construction and so on. A major challenge to supervised learning is the problem of generalization. The generalization accuracy depends upon the (a) size and complexity of the classifiers and also (b) upon the volume of training data (examples). The accuracy improves with the increased size of classifiers up to a certain maximum and then decreases with further increase. However, the accuracy increases with the increase of training data volume.

Unsupervised Learning

Unsupervised learning is to describe a wide range of different learning tasks which analyse a given set of objects that do not belong to defined class labels. The unsupervised learning tasks are generally of the following types:

1. **Object completion:** Object completion task involves predicting missing parts of an object or a situation and then constructing the full object or completely describe the situation, given a partial description of the object or situation.

    For example, if it is told 'Ram went to the fruit shop and paid money to the shopkeeper for some fruits and then left', we may as well as find out the missing situation 'Ram picked up some fruits from the shop and put the same into his bag' before he left. Another example which can be cited for object completion is if one sees the front side of a car visible around the corner of a building, he or she can predict what the rest of the car looks like and then complete the picture of the car.

2. **Understanding and visualization:** The idea of understanding and visualization is basically to study the relationships existing among a large collection of objects in order to arrange them into a hierarchy of classes known as clusters based on the relationships. The relationship among the objects in a hierarchical cluster is based on one or more attributes such as length, height, width, colour, density and chemical composition. For example, income taxpayers can be arranged into hierarchical clusters as shown in Figure 5.14.

3. **Density estimation and anomaly detection:** This type of unsupervised learning task is based on probability distribution of the attribute values of a random sample of objects. The objects which

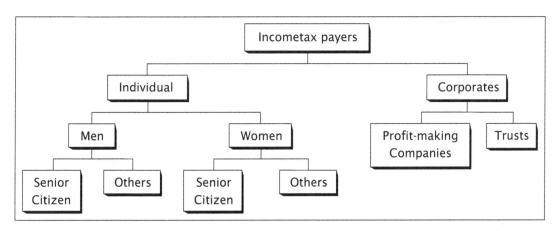

FIGURE 5.14 Hierarchical Clusters

do not belong to the underlying probability distribution are considered as anomalous. Statistical quality control procedure adopted in manufacturing falls under the purview of unsupervised learning to identify anomalous products produced by a defective machine or process.

4. **Data compression:** This involves identifying and returning the essential aspects of data. Data compression is a method of storing frequently occurring substrings or subimages of objects into a dictionary. Then each occurrence of such substrings and subimages can be replaced by a much precise reference to the corresponding dictionary entry for those substrings or subimages. Data compression in case of unsupervised learning is associated with modelling and coding. Coding is much easier for machines as compared with humans since it requires computation based on history. For example, if an algorithm is used to compute the probability of occurrence of a string S, P(S) in a natural language, the same algorithm can be duplicated while decompressing. Further, there are efficient algorithms for mapping strings to codes given any distribution P(S) of such arithmetic coding.

Example 1: A numeric figure as 51.55555 can be expressed as 51.(5)5 meaning after decimal there are five numbers of '5'. The decompressor will use the same algorithm exactly to decompress 51.(5)5 into 51.55555. However, humans may decompress it as 51.56. Modelling is, however, easy for humans as compared to machines since humans with their real-world knowledge and good ability of applying the same are in a better position to distinguish between high-probability strings and low-probability strings.

Example 2: Let us consider two strings, the 'sky is blue' and the 'sky blue is'. Human beings are able to identify the former as the high-probability string and latter as the low-probability string. This is precisely the hard problem that a text compressor must solve so that it can assign shorter codes to more probable strings. However, the fact remains, that no two humans are going to agree exactly on P(S) for all S. Moreover, P(S) to a person changes overtime as he or she learns and forgets.

5. **Information retrieval:** Another type of unsupervised learning task is to retrieve objects (documents, images, fingerprints) from a large collection of objects. Clustering methods can be applied to this type of unsupervised learning tasks.

Reinforcement Learning

Also known as Q-learning is a type of learning facilitating sequential decision-making. In the case of supervised and unsupervised learning tasks, the decisions made by the machine or computer system after learning are non-sequential in nature, that is, if the machine or computer system commits a mistake on one decision, the same will have no effect on the subsequent decisions. For example, if the barcode reader misreads a barcode for the price of a particular item in a shopping mall, the billed amount for that item will be reflected wrongly, but that will have no effect on the next item. Contrary to the above, if a pilot of an aircraft makes a mistake at one decision point during the flight, this will affect the situation that the pilot has to take care in the next decision point. In other words, in case of sequential decision-making the decision-makers' decisions at any point have to consider the consequences of his/her previous decisions also. Sequential decision-making tasks arise in case of many control systems such as control of spacecrafts, oil refineries and nuclear plants.

Reinforcement learning is the task of learning a control policy by interacting with an unknown environment. It can be either model based or without the same. In case of model-based reinforcement learning, the learner performs an action (a) in the state of the control system (S) and observes the next state (S') and the rewards (r) associated with the change from S to S' and records his/her observation in the form of a quadruple tuple (S, a, r, S'). For example, for a driver controlling the movement of a car, the state of the car can be a vector expressed as (velocity, position, acceleration) and the driver also notes the result (reward [r]) as to whether the car is moving on the proper position on the road or displaced from the proper track and then controls the car by the next action. After performing a large number of actions and noting the change of states with each action, the learner (the driver in the above example) can learn the probability of transition from one state (S) to another state (S') by an action (a), P(S', S, a) and the result (reward [r]) associated with S, a and S' as a function R (S', a, S). Once the transition probability and the reward function are known, a dynamic programming algorithm can be formulated to find the optimum control policy. This is known as model-based reinforcement learning. However, reinforcement learning algorithms can be developed as Q-learning where the control policy is learnt by directly interacting with the environment without learning the transition probability and reward functions.

Analytic Learning

As already stated earlier, analytic learning does not require any external input. Instead, the emphasis is on speed and the reliable inferences and decisions performed by the machine or computer. This type of learning is therefore known as speed-up learning. For example, a mason can mix cement, sand and stone-chips in various proportions, check the strength, then find the proportion which maximizes the concrete strength, and note down the same in his handbook. After that, when another mason wants to make concrete, the same handbook can be referred to find the proper proportion of mixing of the ingredients of concrete. A form of speed-up learning is the explanation-based learning. For example, the mason might have discovered that it is important to add cement, sand and stone-chips slowly while mixing it with water. The generalized explanation of this is that when adding fine particle ingredients to a liquid, adding them slowly facilitates homogeneous mixing.

Deep Learning

One of the big challenges with traditional machine learning is that it is not suitable for high dimensionality of data where managers or decision-makers have to deal with very large number of inputs and outputs. Moreover, machine-learning models are not able to solve complex and crucial AI problems involving natural language processing, voice and image recognition. The above-mentioned limitation of machine learning arises due to lack of a process called feature extraction during the learning phase of complex problems such as object or handwriting recognition. A machine-learning model cannot of its own detect all the right features for a complex problem. Deep-learning models are, however, capable to focus on the right features by themselves, requiring little guidance from the programmers.

Deep-learning models learn through actual examples during training phase and do not perform any specific task programmed by a programmer. These models can also solve the data dimensionality problem as mentioned earlier. Deep learning emerged as a subset of machine learning. Though the concept of deep learning was developed much earlier in 1985, it could not be exploited fully because of the limitation of the computing power of the computers which existed during that time. However, the next significant evolutionary step for deep learning took place in 1999 when computational speed increased 1,000 times. Deep learning as a subset of machine learning gained wide popularity from 2006 onwards. Deep-learning models were developed and applied for commercial use from 2010 onwards.

Neural Networks and Deep Learning   Deep learning makes use of neural networks to simulate human thinking and decision-making. The motivation behind neural networks is the biological neuron as shown below:

The biological neuron consists of the cell nucleus, the dendrite which receives input a tail-like thing known as axon, and at the end of axon a synapse, which transmits the output of the neuron to the dendrite of the next neuron as input. The neurons are connected with one another, and each one receives signals as inputs from other neurons or body parts and then gets activated or not based upon the inputs, such as a binary gate.

The human brain consists of innumerable neurons through which it functions. Similarly, the artificial neural network (ANN) is based on the principle of the human brain and its smallest component is an artificial neuron also known as perceptron. Figure 5.15 shows an artificial neuron. It has got a central unit which receives inputs which, for example, may be pixels for image processing. The inputs x_1, x_2, ..., x_n multiplied with corresponding weights w_1, w_2, ..., w_n are added up in the central unit and to the sum is added a bias multiplied by its weight. The bias value (offset) is always +1 for all neurons, and bias weights only vary to change the offset. The weights can be positive, negative or very near to zero depending upon the influence of the inputs. Initially, random values are assigned as input weights.

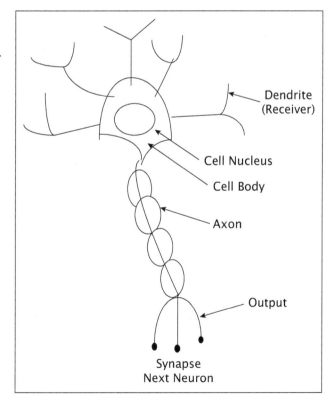

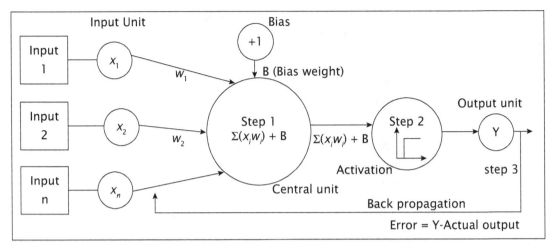

FIGURE 5.15 Artificial Neuron

The output of Step 1 as obtained above is fed as input to an activation function in Step 2. The purpose of the activation function is to convert the input into an output Y depending upon the type of activation function. Some types of activation functions convert the input into binary output (0 or 1), which decides whether the neuron should fire (1) or not (0). However, there are other types of activation functions also which do not generate binary output and in that case depending upon some threshold value, the neuron will either fire or not fire. The output Y of the neuron is compared with the actual or expected value also known as the labelled information, and the difference is the error which is fed to the neuron for updating the weights of inputs and the bias such that the output Y conforms to the actual or expected value either exactly or as closely as possible. The process of feeding the error as feedback to the neuron or neural network is called back propagation. The process of updating the weights through back propagation is an iterative one, and the iteration continues till the error becomes either zero or close to zero. The whole purpose of training a neural network is to update the weights of the inputs and the bias to achieve the minimum error in the output of the network. The rate at which the ANN is trained to adjust the weights for its inputs and bias in order to attain convergence of its output with expected or labelled values is known as the learning rate of the ANN.

1. **Activation functions:** An activation function takes the 'weighted sum of inputs plus bias' as the input to the function and returns an output which decides whether the neuron will fire or not depending upon the threshold. The main purpose of an activation function is to induct non-linearity in the output. There are different types of activation functions and the output is different for the different types. The common activation functions are as follows:

    i. *Sigmoid function*: In case of sigmoid function, the output is always between 0 and 1 as shown in the figure below. It is used for situations where the output is required to be expressed as a probability. The function is expressed as:

    $$Y(X) = 1/(1 + e^{-x})$$

    where X is the input and Y is the output of the function.

ii. *Step function:* Step function is also a threshold-based activation function but unlike sigmoid function, the output for step function is only 0 or 1 and not any value between 0 and 1 as shown in the figure below. The function is expressed as:

$$Y(X) = 1, \text{ if } X > 0 \text{ else}$$
$$= 0, \text{ if } X < 0$$

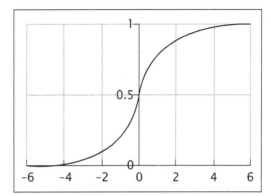

iii. *ReLU function:* ReLU, also known as the Rectified Linear Unit, is the most widely used activation function. The function returns an output value equal to zero if the input value is zero or less than zero, and an output value equal to the input value if the input value is greater than zero as shown in the figure below. Mathematically, ReLU function is expressed as:

$$Y(X) = \max(X, 0)$$

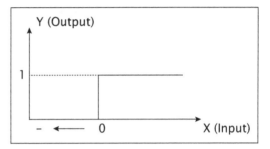

iv. *Hyperbolic tangent function:* This function is similar to the sigmoid function except that it returns an output which is bounded between –1 and +1 for all values of input as shown in the figure below. The function can be expressed as:

$$Y(X) = (1 - e^{-2x}/(1 + e^{-2x}))$$

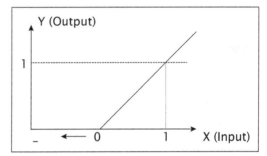

The choice of the particular activation function depends upon the type of neural network model and the application for which the model is used.

Deep learning is performed with deep networks, which are neural networks with multiple hidden layers in between the input and the output layers. All the nodes of hidden layers are activation nodes, and the outputs of any particular hidden layer will become inputs for the next layer with corresponding weight. However, the

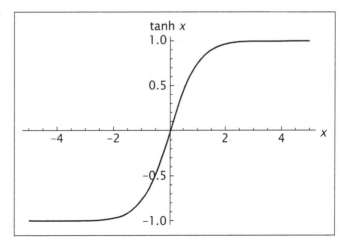

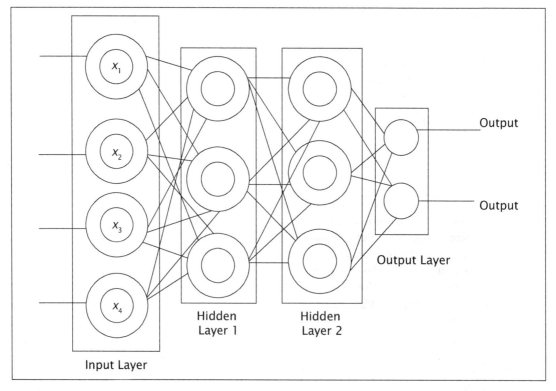

FIGURE 5.16 Deep Neural Network with Two Hidden Layers

output of any node of any layer may also be the input to a node of the previous layer, and in that case the neural network is termed as a recurrent neural network (RNN) which has been explained in a subsequent paragraph. The hidden layers may be fully connected in which case the nodes of the same layer may also be connected with each other or partially connected. Figure 5.16 shows a deep neural network with two hidden layers.

Example: Let us illustrate deep learning with a simple example. Suppose students after passing their higher secondary examination appear in an entrance examination for admission to state medical colleges. The subjects of the examination are three, namely physics, chemistry and biology. The students who pass out the entrance examination are called for interview for the final selection. The criteria of passing the entrance examination are either a pass in all the three subjects or a pass in physics or chemistry with distinction (80% or more marks) in biology. A deep neural network for this example which can be trained for adjusting the weights for output ('0' for fail and '1' for pass) conforming to the above criteria can be as follows (Figure 5.17):

Let us initially assign the weights as follows:

$$w_{11} = 1, w_{12} = 1, w_{13} = 1, BW_{11} = 1, BW_{12} = 1, w_{21} = 1, w_{22} = 1 \text{ and } BW_{21} = 1$$

However, in this case for a student who has passed in physics and biology only but has not got distinction in biology, the output of the deep neural network is 1 (selected for interview), which is not

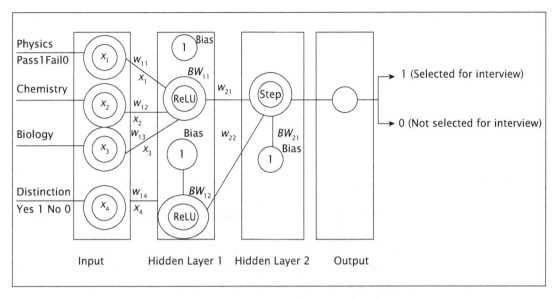

FIGURE 5.17 Deep Neural Network for the Example

the correct output since the student with passing marks in physics and biology cannot be selected for interview unless he or she secures distinction in biology. Hence, the back-propagation process will update the weights through iterative trials. It can be seen that for the following weights, the network will be fully accurate conforming to correct output for all valid input.

$$w_{11} = 2, w_{12} = 2, w_{13} = 2, BW_{11} = -5, BW_{12} = 1, w_{21} = 1, w_{22} = 1 \text{ and } BW_{21} = 1.$$

Types of Neural Networks   There are various types of neural networks with different features and the selection of the proper type mainly depends upon the particular application. Some of the popular types of networks and their distinctive features are as follows:

1. **Feed forward neural network:** It is a very simple form of ANN where the data or input travels in one direction from the input nodes to the output nodes. Feed forward neural networks may have or may not have hidden layers. Such networks have front propagation only and no back propagation. Generally, they work on classifying activation function. Feed forward neural networks find use in computer image and voice recognition where due to the very nature of the computer images and voice, classifying the target classes is very difficult and complicated. This type of neural network finds wide application in X-ray images fusion, which is the process of superimposing one image over the other based on the edges. MRI and CT images can be overlaid into a fused image.
2. **Recurrent neural network:** RNN works on the principle of saving output of a layer and feeding the same back to the input to help in predicting the outcome of the layer. This implies that each neuron will remember the information it had in a previous time step $(t - 1)$ which can be compared with the current information at time (t). In order to achieve the same feature, each neuron or node acts like a memory cell in case of making a computation.

Example of RNN:

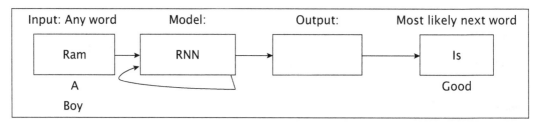

Recurrent neural network is perhaps the most widely used ANN, and it is used in text processing, text-to-speech conversion (TTS), stock price prediction and many other applications.

3. **Long short-term memory (LSTM):** This artificial recurrent neural network is used in deep learning. Unlike feed forward neural network, LSTM possesses feedback connections. It can process sequential data such as speech, video or time series data. A usual LSTM has got an 'input' gate, an 'output' gate and a 'forget' gate. The gates enable an LSTM to remember values over arbitrary time intervals and also to control the flow of information from its input to output. LSTM networks are well suited for making predictions based on time series data.

4. **Convolutional neural network (CNN):** CNN is perhaps the most important deep learning neural network for computer vision, which facilitates image classification with a high degree of accuracy. For example, a computer can recognize an image of an animal and classify it as a dog, a cat or a horse. However, CNN can be applied in other areas of deep learning also such as trend analysis using time series data.

The computer is able to perform image classification by looking for low-level features such as edges and curves and then building up more abstract concepts through a series of convolutional layers. The basis of functioning of a CNN is the biological visual cortex which has got small regions of cells which are sensitive to specific regions of visual field.

The first convolutional layer is basically a filter which slides or convolves around the input such as an image. As it convolves, it multiplies the values of the filter with the original pixel values of the image for each location on the image, and the values of the multiplications for all the locations on the image are summed up to have a single value. The purpose is to detect low-level features on the image such as curves or edges.

The output of the first convolution layer is fed as input to the second convolutional layer. The input to the second layer is the activation maps that result from the first layer. The output of the second and subsequent convolutional layers are the activations that represent higher levels of features such as semi-circles or squares which are only combinations of several curves or straight edges. As we go through deeper convolutional layers, we get activation maps representing more and more complex higher-level features.

The last convolutional layer is connected to a fully connected network (FCN) at the end of the network. FCN basically takes the output of the convolutional or ReLU or pool layer preceding it and generates outputs which are the probability values for the input image to match with the different classes such as dog, cat or horse. This is, in short, the function of a CNN. A classic CNN architecture is as follows:

Input → Convolution → ReLU → Convolution → ReLU → Pool → FCN

Important Applications of Deep Learning   The deep learning method is adopted in a variety of applications such as:

* Cancer detection by early identification of cancerous tumors in the human body
* Robot navigation for manufacturing operations
* Oil exploration
* Surveillance and security
* Self-driving cars
* Music composition
* Colourization of images
* Machine translation of languages such as Spanish, French or German

5.15.1.4. Knowledge Representation

Since AI is created through computer's knowledge of the world, it is necessary to represent the computer's knowledge by some kind of data structures in the memory of the computer. Apart from traditional computer databases which deal with large amount of structured data, AI programs need to deal with complex entities having complex relationships on a conceptual level. In the case of AI, several kinds of knowledge need to be represented—factual knowledge which are known facts such as 'sun rises in the east', universal rules or principles such as 'every cow is a mammal', hypothetical data which the computer has to consider in order to reason about the effects of actions which are contemplated.

There are also several ways of knowledge representation as described in the following paragraphs. There are also several issues in knowledge representation such as knowledge storage, knowledge retrieval applicable to a problem, reasoning (logic) to derive implied knowledge.

Rule-based Knowledge

Knowledge-based systems often represent knowledge by if–then type rules. The expert systems, which will be discussed in a subsequent section, are built on if–then rules. For example, a medicine specialist with years of clinical experience can create knowledge based on rules as follows:

> **Rule 1:** If (Body temperature above 100°F AND no cough) THEN prescribe 'Calpol' and antibiotic tablets.
> **Rule 2:** IF (Body temperature below 100°F AND fever persists for more than 2 days) THEN advise blood test and prescribe antibiotics.
> **Rule 3:** IF (Fever accompanies with tremor) THEN advise tests for malaria parasites.
> **Rule 4:** IF (Mild fever persists AND pale-yellow eyes) THEN advise treatment for 'jaundice'.

Ontology Tools

Ontology describes the relationships among entities on a conceptual level. It also describes hierarchy of classes and subclasses for an object entity together with the relationships, contrasts, constraints and other information about objects.

Example: Ontology for the Judiciary of India.

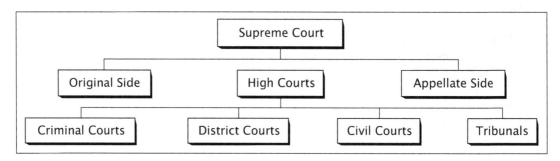

Ontology tools such as the Protégé (frames and editors), knowledge acquisition systems, Gene ontology tools and 'DARPA' facilitate knowledge acquisition, representation and also generation of new knowledge out of existing knowledge.

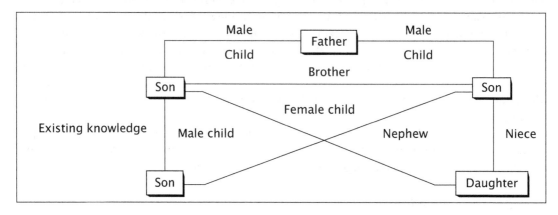

Leads to a new knowledge as follows:

Ontology provides vital information to search agents, intelligent agents and databases. Agents use ontology and perform powerful reasoning to represent knowledge. Ontology is modelled using web ontology language (OWL) and gives rise to web encyclopaedia of knowledge.

Logic

Knowledge representation methods based on mathematical logic retrieve intelligence by the use of first order predicate logic. A predicate resembles a function that returns either true or false for a proposition. While propositional logic deals with simple declarative propositions, first-order logic incorporates, predicates and quantifies additionally. For example, 'Kalidas is a poet' and 'Tagore is a poet' are two unrelated propositions. However, in predicate logic, these two propositions can be expressed with a syntactic entity 'Poet' as Poet (x) which asserts that the object represented by x is a poet. If x is Kalidas, then Poet (x) represents the first proposition, whereas if x is Tagore, Poet (x) represents the second proposition. An assignment of semantic meaning as explained above is called an interpretation. First order logic allows reasoning about properties that are shared by many objects. For example, if Poet (x) asserts that x is a poet and if Linguist (x) asserts that x is also a linguist, then the formula

$$\text{Poet (x)} \rightarrow \text{Linguist (x)}$$

asserts that if x is a poet, then x is also a linguist. The symbol $\rightarrow$ is used to denote a condition. The hypothesis lies to the left of the arrow and the conclusion to the right. Now, if we assume that for every x, if x is a poet, then x is also a linguist, the first order sentence will be expressed as follows using the universal quantifier $\forall$

$$\forall x \text{ (Poet (x)} \rightarrow \text{Linguist (x))}$$

The universal quantifier $\forall$ expresses the idea that the above claim holds for all choices of x.

If the universal claim that 'if a poet then a linguist' is false, then there has to be some poet who is not a linguist. This counter claim against universality can be expressed in first order logic with existential as quantifier $\exists$

$$\exists x \text{ (Poet (x)} \wedge \neg \text{ Linguist (x))},$$

where $\neg$ is negation operator and means that $\neg$ linguist (x) is true if and only if Linguist (x) is false or in other words if x is not a linguist. $\wedge$ is the conjunction operator which asserts that x is a poet and also not a linguist.

In the above example, predicates Poet (x) and Lingu (x) take only one parameter each. First order can also express predicates with multiple parameters. For example, 'there is some employee x, who can be relied upon for every work y', can be expressed as:

$$\exists x \text{ (Employee (x)} \wedge \forall w \text{ (work(y) can Rely (x, y)))}$$

The range of the quantifiers is the set of objects that can be used to satisfy them and known as the domain of discourse or universe for the quantifiers.

Through logic and reasoning, information is derived that is implied by existing knowledge but not stored directly.

Knowledge representation through predicate calculus has definite strength of logical power and a mathematical foundation. However, it has got inherent weaknesses of low speed and rigidity.

Knowledge representation and retrieval in predicate calculus is through storing of facts in a propositional database, and facts can be retrieved in response to patterns as illustrated below:

Fact:

```
            RAM
        (PRAISES)
            SITA
```

Retrieval of facts:	Does Ram praise Sita?	(PRAISES RAM SITA)
	Whom does Ram praise?	(PRAISES RAM?X)
	Who praises Sita?	(PRAISES?X SITA)
	All pairs of appraiser and appraisee	(PRAISES?X?Y)

Knowledge is stored as logical axioms which can be used for deductions. For example, the rule that 'all dogs bark' can be represented as:

```
(ALL X (IF(DOG X) (BARK X)))
              OR
     (IF(DOG?X) (BARK?X))
```

Deduction, induction and abduction: These are various methods of application of principles to infer or explain facts logically.
Deduction applies a general principle to infer a fact.

Example: Deduction
Given: Every dog barks. Sweety is a dog.
Inference: Sweety barks
Induction: It assumes a general principle that subsumes many facts.

Example: Induction
Given: Rose, jasmine and lotus are flowers. Rose, jasmine and lotus are fragrant. Bakul is a flower. Bakul is fragrant.
Assume: Every flower is fragrant.
Abduction guesses a new hypothesis that explains some facts.

Example: Abduction
Given: Every dog barks. Sweety barks.
Guess: Sweety is a dog.
   Deduction is sound, whereas induction and abduction are not, but essential for intelligence. However, logic is a preferred method of representation and reasoning in cases where the data are discrete and there is absolute truth. Such applications include (a) mathematical theorem proving, (b) proofs of correctness of computer programs and (c) proofs of correctness of logic designs.

5.15.1.5 Semantic Networks and Frames for Knowledge Representation

An alternative to logic for knowledge representation formalism is semantic networks and frames. The term frame was first introduced by Malvin Minsky of Massachusetts Institute of Technology, USA.
   Frame-based knowledge representation captures a set of related facts about an object, image or a situation in the form of a frame. Frames are important because they allow deep understanding of new situations about which only minimal information is directly available. They represent our understanding of regularities in the universe that allows intelligent action based on minimal clues. A frame can represent an individual object or a class of similar objects. Instead of properties, a frame has slots. A slot is like a property but can contain more kinds of information (sometimes called facets of the slot). According to Minsky, 'We can think of a frame as a network of nodes and relations. The top levels of a

frame are fixed and represent things that are always true in the supposed situation. The low levels have many slots that must be filled with specific instances or data.'

Example of knowledge frame

Slot Name	Data
Mammal	True
Legs	4
Gender	
Food habit	

The above frame captures information about all mammals having four legs in the world. However, the same frame as shown below will capture information regarding all mammals having four legs, male and who eat flesh such as dog.

Slot Name	Data
Mammal	True
Legs	4
Gender	Male
Food habit	Carnivorous

Frames can thus capture both the concepts of generalization and specialization which facilitate representation of knowledge. A semantic network is a collection of related frames which link together into a frame system. The different frames of a semantic network have got the same terminals, which feature makes it possible to coordinate information gathered from different points of view of objects. The semantic networks are linked in turn by an appropriate information retrieval network. A semantic network is a directed or uni-directed graph consisting of vertices, which represent concepts and edges that connect pair of vertices as shown in Figure 5.18.

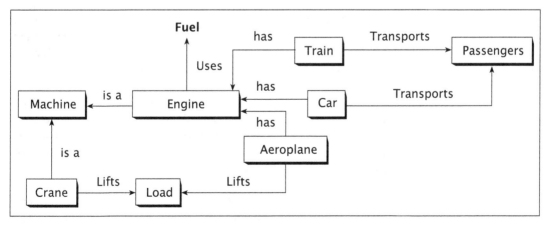

FIGURE 5.18 Example of a Semantic Network

There can be various types of semantic networks. A few examples are as follows:

Word Net

It is an example of semantic network which is a lexical database of English vocabulary. It groups English words into sets of synonyms called synsets and provides the various relations between the synsets. If A and B represent two synsets, then the relationships between A and B can be: synonym (A and B denote the same thing), antonym (A denotes the reverse of B), meronym (A is a part of B, expressed as B has A as a part of itself), holonym (B is a part of A expressed as A has B as a part of itself) and so on.

Winston in 1971 proposed a 'similarity network' wherein pointers from each description of an object/ concept point to other descriptions of similar objects/concepts, with each pointer labelled by a difference marker. Complaints about mismatch are matched with the difference pointers leaving the frame and thus may propose a better candidate frame. From example, a furniture network with chair, couch, table, stool, desk and so on and their similarities and differences can be represented as follows:

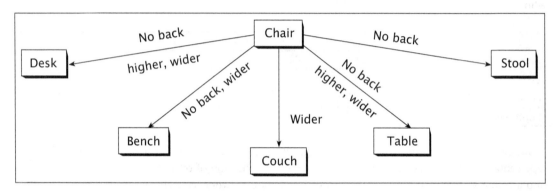

It can be observed from the above examples that semantic networks capture a far deeper knowledge representation through multiple relationships, implication, set and subset association, generalization, specialization, instantiation and so on.

Search

Search programs find a solution for a problem by trying different sequences of actions (operators) until a solution is found. For example, a program can be written to play chess using search if one knows the rules of chess, it is not necessary to know how to play good chess. However, there is an inherent disadvantage of search if the search space is very large as is the case with many problems (such as game playing). For example, chess has been estimated to have 10,120 possible games and a search, in such case, requires huge memory space and computer time also. However, with the application of 'combinatorial explosion' facilitating combinations of possible moves, the problem can be simplified. Search is necessary as there are practical problems which cannot be modelled precisely for exact computation. Moreover, any intelligent system must encounter surprises. Such problems need to be solved dynamically, starting with observed data. Search arises in almost all areas of AI such as:

1. **Theorem proving:** Searches for a sequence of proof steps that will prove a desired conclusion.
2. **Natural language processing:** A writer or composer searches the vocabulary to find words and structure to assign meaning to ambiguous sentences.

3. **Planning:** A planner searches for action plans to achieve goals in the best possible way.
4. **Learning:** A learning program searches for a compact description of a set of training instances.
5. **Perception:** Searches for consistent interpretation of input signals or feedback.
6. **Expert systems:** Adopt rules applicable to the current problem.

Broad categories of search include state space search, problem reduction search including game tree search, simulated annealing and Waltz filtering. The various strategies for search include depth-first, breadth-first, hill climbing, heuristic search, uniform cost search, bidirectional search, iterative deepening and so on. Let us briefly explain the concept of state space search and heuristic search strategy with suitable illustrations since these are of considerable significance in problem solving using AI.

State Space Search   A state space represents a problem in terms of states and operators that change states. It consists of:

1. A representation of all possible states of a system. Each state is an abstract representation of the system configuration. For example, in a board game, the board represents the current state of the game.
2. Initial state: The description of the starting configuration of the system.
3. An action/operator that takes the system from one state to another state. For example, in a board game, the operators have the legal moves from any given state. The actions/operators are also known as the production rules or programs that change a state representation to represent a new state. A state can have a number of successor states.
4. A plan is a sequence of actions or production rules.
5. A set of final states: some of these may be desirable (goals), others undesirable. Goal states are often specified by a goal test and a program implicitly detects the goal states.
6. Path cost is the sum of the costs of all steps leading from initial state to the terminal states.

Example of state space search: Using two empty water jugs of 4 litres and 5 litres capacity. It is required to fill 3 litres of water from a tap into either of the jugs.

Here, the state can be represented as a set of ordered pair of integers as:

$$(X, Y) \text{ where } X = 0, 1, 2, 3 \text{ or } 4 \text{ (Quantity in 4-litre jug)}$$
$$Y = 0, 1, 2, 3, 4 \text{ or } 5 \text{ (Quantity in 5-litre jug)}$$

Start state is (0, 0).
Goal states are (3, n) or (n, 3).
The operations or production rules are as follows:

Production Rules [PR]	Initial State	Final State	Operation
1.	[X, Y] if X< 4	→ (4 — (4, Y)]	Fill 4-litre jug
2.	[X, Y] if Y < 5	→ (X, 5)	Fill 5-litre jug
3.	[4, Y]	→ (0, Y)	Empty 4-litre jug

Production Rules [PR]	Initial State	Final State	Operation
4.	[X, 5]	→ (X, 0)	Empty 5-litre jug
5.	[X, Y]	→ (X – (5 – Y), 5)	if X + Y >= 5 and X > 0, Pour water from 4-litre jug into 5-litre jug until 5-litre jug is full
6.	[X, Y] if X + Y >= 4 and Y > 0	→ (4, Y – (4 – X))	Pour water from 5-litre jug into 4-litre jug until it is full
7.	(X, Y) if X + Y <= 4 $\xrightarrow{\text{and } Y > 0}$ (X + Y, 0)		Pour all water from 5 Litre jug into 4 Litre jug
8.	(X, Y) if X + Y <= 5 and X > 0	→ (0, Y + X)	Pour all water from 4-litre jug into 5-litre jug

The production rules applied in sequence and the state space for the state changes and paths leading to goal states have been shown in Figure 5.19.

The paths from start state (both jugs empty) to one of the goal states (any jug having 3 litres of water) as shown in Figure 5.19 are having the actions denoted by production rules as:

1. PR1—PR5—PR1—PR5 (4 actions) and
2. PR2—PR6—PR3—PR8—PR2—PR6—PR3—PR7—PR2—PR7 (10 actions)

Since Path 1 has got a smaller number of actions, it is preferable to Path 2.

Heuristic Search   There are practical state space search problems where the state space becomes enormously large and involves considerable search time as also computer storage space to reach the goal state. In such situations, the magnitude of the search can be significantly reduced by resorting to heuristic

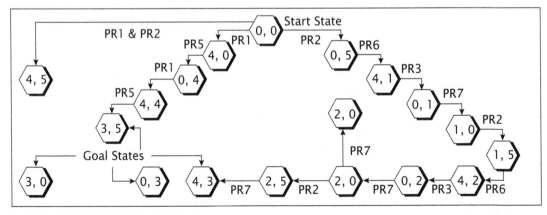

FIGURE 5.19   State Space and Paths for Production Rules and Change of States Leading to Goal States for the Two Water Jugs Problem

search. Heuristics use domain specific knowledge to estimate the quality of intermediate states or potential of partial solutions. The domain-specific knowledge may be established knowledge such as science or intuition acquired through experience. In order to explain how heuristics facilitate state space search, let us cite the example of the famous game of eight numbered tiles as follows:

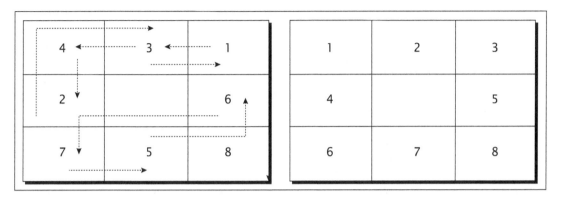

Consider the arrangement of the eight tiles on the left-hand side to a pattern on the right by moving one square at a time into the empty slot.

Let us introduce a term called 'distance' in terms of units of one tile moving either horizontally or vertically one slot. For example, in the case of the pattern on the left, if the tile number 3 is shifted down into the empty slot below, the distance moved is 1 unit. Similarly, if either tile 2 is moved to the right or tile 6 moved to the left into the empty slot, the distance moved is 1 unit only. Now the heuristics in this case is that in order to arrange the tiles into the pattern on the right, the total distance (in units) moved by all the tiles from their initial position (left-hand side arrangement) by whatever state space search path will obviously always be equal to or greater than the individual distance in units measured for each tile from their initial position and the same totalled for all the eight tiles. Let me list below such distances for each tile (the distance are shown through dotted arrows in the pattern shown above).

Tile Number			Distance (units)
1	...	...	2
2	...	...	2
3	...	...	1
4	...	...	1
5	...	...	2
6	...	...	3
7	...	...	1
8	...	...	0
Total			12 Units

The above total of 12 units is the lower bound of the number of shifts of the tiles by state space search for arranging the tiles from the state on the left to the pattern on the right. Hence, the heuristic in this state space search problem suggests that at each state, the action for the next state (till the goal state is reached) is to move one of the tiles one slot at a time and the tiles to be considered for this move are those involving minimum distances from the present position to the goal state position.

Simple language processing: Earlier generation AI program, ELIZA, developed by Joseph Weizenbaum simulated a psychotherapist and achieved very good performance simply by matching the patient's input to patterns.

> **Pattern:** (I AM FEELING *)
> **Response:** (WHY ARE YOU FEELING *)
> The * above matches anything; and the same is repeated in the response.
> **Patient:** I am feeling nervous.
> **Doctor:** Why are you feeling nervous?
> However, ELIZA and a general natural language grammar represents two extremes of language processing. ELIZA is too restricted and requires huge number of patterns as otherwise there can be lack of real understanding as illustrated below:
> **Patient:** I feel like jumping in the river.
> **Doctor:** Tell me more about the river.

The response of the doctor lacks real understanding.

General natural language grammar on the other extreme contains hundreds of interpretations of ordinary sentences and is full of ambiguity.

5.16 Expert Systems

Expert systems are knowledge-based systems which provide specific knowledge about narrow problem domain through the use of knowledge stored in the knowledge base and an inference (reasoning) procedure to solve problems that would otherwise require human competence or expertise.

Features of expert systems are as follows:

1. They are usually computer systems which try to mimic human expertise.
2. Produce decisions that do not require judgement.
3. They assist decision-makers but do not substitute them.

Expert systems are a sub-area of AI. While AI is a group of technologies that attempt to emulate certain aspects of human behaviour such as reasoning and communicating with the primary objective of evolving strategies of general problem-solving using intelligence, expert systems concentrate on problem solving in specific problem domains. Examples of expert systems are oil exploration, medical diagnosis, crime investigation and so on.

5.16.1 Components of Expert Systems

A typical expert system consists of a knowledge base, inference engine, knowledge acquisition module and an explanatory interface as shown in Figure 5.20. The knowledge base is a representation of both book knowledge about a problem domain and the accumulated wisdom of an expert acquired through years of study and experience. The expert knowledge is stored in the knowledge base as rules of thumb used by the human experts in the domain. The knowledge base is built up through a knowledge acquisition module used by experts to enter rules or facts with the help of a knowledge engine. The inference engine controls

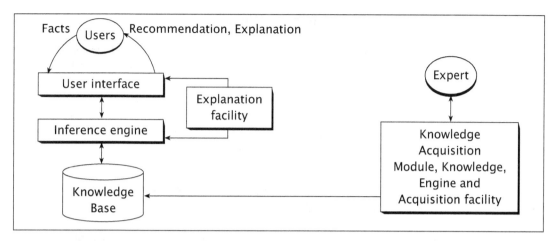

FIGURE 5.20 Components of an Expert System

the order in which the production rules (described elaborately in subsequent paragraphs of this chapter) are applied to solve the problem and resolve conflicts if more than one rule apply. Inference engine functions on a 'reasoning' process. The explanatory interface is the user interface wherein users input the facts of the case and query with the expert system and obtain recommendations/query explanation.

Explanatory interface subsystem of an expert system also shows the trail of reasoning it used to reach a decision, that is, (a) explains the facts used, (b) the rules applied and (c) the order in which the rules were applied.

5.16.2 Knowledge Representation in an Expert System

As already stated, earlier knowledge representation in expert systems is in a variety of ways including (a) rules and (b) case-based reasoning. Let us explain these in detail:

Rules: Rules are heuristics obtained from experts and consist of an IF part and a THEN part. IF <condition> THEN <action>.

Example: Heuristic rule

IF good customer and
credit requested < ₹10,000
and loan term < 2 years
then grant credit

Case-based reasoning: In case of case-based reasoning, the expert system draws inferences by comparing a current problem or case with hundreds of similar past cases. It is best suited when the situation involves too many nuances and all the delicate differences need to be generalized into rules.

Example: The chance of survival of a critically ill patient admitted in the intensive care unit of a hospital can be predicted by entering the vital statistics of the patient including the medical history and so on into the expert system which draws records of thousands of previous intensive care patients with similar illness to predict the chance of survival of the patient.

5.16.3 How Does an Expert System Work?

User presents a set of facts describing a situation to the expert system. Inference engine compares facts of the case with the knowledge base. System then either gives a recommendation or asks for more information.

The inference strategy for rule-based system can be either to prove that a conclusion (goal) is true or to verify the conjecture that a particular premise is true. The former strategy of inference is called forward chaining, whereas the latter strategy is known as backward chaining. Forward chaining is data driven where inference moves from facts to a goal. In case of backward chaining, inference moves from a possible goal state to premise that will satisfy it.

Example: A general physician with considerable experience has expressed his expertise for treatment of a patient with fever particularly in the form of simplified rules as follows:

Rule 1: IF (Body temperature 98.4°F or above AND body ache) THEN prescribe antibiotics.
Rule 2: IF (Fever more than 3 days AND body ache) THEN prescribe Cifran tablets.
Rule 3: IF (Viral infection AND prescribe antibiotic) THEN prescribe Cifran tablets.
Rule 4: IF (Viral infection) THEN body ache.
Rule 5: IF (Prescribe Cifran tablets) THEN prescribe dose 500 mg.

FACT: Assume a patient Mr X has a temperature of 101°F and viral infection; Query is what should be the prescription for Mr X?

The rules can be written down then as follows:

R1: IF (A & C) THEN E
R2: IF (D & C) THEN F
R3: IF (B & E) THEN F
R4: IF (B) THEN C
R5: IF (F) THEN G

With these simplified rules, and input facts being A and B, if our objective is to prove G is true or not, we can proceed either by forward chaining or backward chaining as shown below.

1. **Forward chaining:**

		Rules Applicable					
Iteration	Facts/Updated Facts	R1	R2	R3	R4	R5	New Fact
1.	A, B	N	N	N	Y	N	C
2.	A, B, C	Y	N	N	—	N	E
3.	A, B, C, E	—	N	Y	—	N	F
4.	A, B, C, E, F	—	N	—	—	Y	G

So, we have reached our claim that G is true by firing R5 at iteration 4.

Notes: 1. Firing a rule at any iteration leads to a new fact.
2. After a rule is fired at any iteration, subsequently the question of firing the same rule will not lead to any new fact.

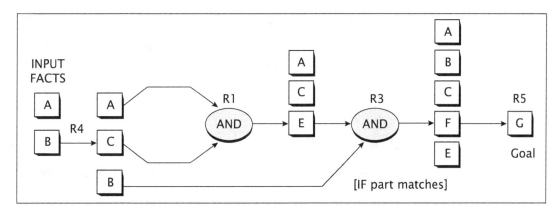

FIGURE 5.21 Inference Diagram Showing Forward-chaining Process

The above iterative forward-chaining process can be described by an inference diagram as shown in Figure 5.21.

2. **Backward chaining:** As stated earlier, backward-chaining process attempts to solve the problem by moving backward from the goal and trying to locate only the rules whose consequences are the goal and sub-goals and to verify whether the antecedents can be established from the facts available.

For the example stated above, let us start from goal G and scan the rules which have G as their consequence. We find only R5 has G as consequence. However, we cannot fire R5 at this stage since we do not know whether F is true. Hence, our sub-goal is now to prove whether F is true by applying backward-chaining process. Again, scanning through the rules, it can be seen that R2 and R3 have F as their consequence. Next, we look at rule R2 and find that it can be fired only if both D and C are true. However, there is no rule to prove whether D is true. Hence, R2 cannot be fired. Next we look at R3. Since B is true, we have to establish that E is true to prove that F is true. Now E is the consequence of R1, if only both A and C are true. A is true; hence our sub-goal is to establish C is true. C is the consequence of R4 and R4 can be fired since B is true. Hence, all the sub-goals stand established and obviously the goal that G is true gets established. The backtracking process has been described in the Figure 5.22.

The backward-chaining process is sometimes cumbersome but neverthe-less has been found to be faster, and computer-based expert systems adopt backward-chaining process for inference.

In the process of backward chain-ing, often problems are faced when more than one rule are applicable for the same consequence. In such situa-tions, the strategies for deciding the order of firing of the rules include: (a) natural order, (b) fact order (recently updated), (c) priority order for the rules.

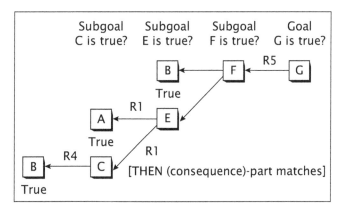

FIGURE 5.22 Backward-chaining Process

5.16.4 Application Domain for Expert Systems

Expert systems have applications involving technical disciplines with large bodies of complex information such as diagnosis, analysis, interpretation, consultation and design. They further facilitate situations requiring decisions and also articulate decision rules that a decision-maker uses. Typical applications of expert systems include the 'MYCIN' project.

5.16.5 Rule-based Expert Systems

Rule-based expert systems were highly developed and published in case of typical medical applications. A very notable among them is the 'MYCIN' project at Standford university, California. 'MYCIN' diagnosed infectious blood diseases using a backward chained (exhaustive) control strategy.

There are other applications also such as XCON, a project of Digital Equipment Corporation to configure equipment related to VAX minicomputers, PROSPECTOR for mineral prospecting through observations obtained in exploratory drilling and DENDRAL developed at Stanford University for chemical applications for possible structure of molecules.

5.16.6 Expert System Shells

Expert system shells are inference engines (described earlier in this chapter) consisting of computer programs that derive answers from a knowledge base. Similar to DBMS software for creation and management of database and also retrieval of data from the database, expert system shell provides all tools including the inference engine, for the creation and management of a knowledge base for an expert system. EMYCIN (which stands for empty MYCIN) was the first widely used expert system shell. EMYCIN as a shell was the outcome of efforts made to build expert systems similar to MYCIN using the structure, interface and control mechanism of MYCIN redefined with the new system. This facilitates much faster development of expert systems.

EMYCIN was also found having the following features:

1. Good for learning expert systems
2. Limited in applicability to 'finite classification' problems such as medical diagnosis and identification
3. Good explanatory capabilities
4. Inbuilt certainty factors

Today, several derivative versions of EMYCIN exist.

Other popular expert system shells include OPS5, VP-expert which runs on PCs, EXSYS and so on.

5.16.7 Advantages of Expert Systems

The main advantage of expert systems is that on the demise of an expert, his/her knowledge and expertise will not be lost, if the same has been captured by an expert system. Further, the knowledge of experts can be made available to one and all at reasonable and affordable cost by the expert systems. Through the expert systems, others who are less experienced may be trained with the distilled expertise of many human experts. Finally, expert systems facilitate documenting the expertise for future generations.

5.17 PROLOG and LISP

The programming languages PROLOG and LISP are associated with AI, expert systems and computational linguistics. PROLOG (programming logic) has its roots in first-order logic and unlike many other procedural programming languages, PROLOG is declarative. A declarative programming is a programming paradigm that expresses the logic of a computation without describing its control flow by way of explicitly provided algorithm. While PROLOG initially was adopted for natural language processing, the language has, in course of time, stretched far into other areas such as theorem proving, expert systems, games, ontology and other sophisticated control systems.

In PROLOG, programming logic is expressed in terms of relations and a computation is initiated by running a query over these relations. Relations are represented by clauses. The label of the clauses is known as predicate, and the objects of the clause are called arguments.

5.17.1. Data Types

PROLOG's single data type is the term. Terms are either atoms, numbers, variables or compound terms.

An atom is a general-purpose term with no inherent meaning such as X, Y and green. A number can be a float or an integer. Variables are denoted by a string consisting of letters, numbers and underscore characters and beginning with an uppercase letter or underscore. A compound term is composed of an atom called a 'functor' and a number of 'arguments' which are again terms. Examples of compound terms are:

Car_model ('Maruti', 800) and manager_subordinates (Johun, [Jones, Smith, Marie]).

5.17.1. Rules and Facts in PROLOG

An unconditional clause is a fact, while a conditional clause is a rule.

A rule is of the form

Head: Body

and is read as 'Head is true if Body is true'. Clauses with empty bodies are called facts, for example, cat (Micky).

The adjacency information for neighbouring Indian states in Figure 5.23 is represented in PROLOG through the following unit clauses or facts.

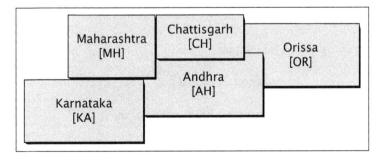

FIGURE 5.23 Five Adjacent Indian States

Note: For simplicity, we have assumed regular shapes and boundaries.

```
adjacent (MH, CH)   adjacent (CH, MH)
adjacent (MH, KA)   adjacent (KA, MH)
adjacent (MH, AH)   adjacent (AH, MH)
adjacent (CH, OR)   adjacent (OR, CH)
adjacent (CH, AH)   adjacent (AH, CH)
adjacent (OR, AH)   adjacent (AH, OR)
adjacent (KA, AH)   adjacent (AH, KA)
```

If the above clauses are loaded into PROLOG, we can observe the following behaviour of some goals:

```
?          —    adjacent (MH, KA)
yes
?          —    adjacent (OR, KA)
no
?          —    adjacent (AH, X)
X = 1;
X = 2;
X = 3;
X = 4;
No
```

Example 1: Program for change for a hundred-rupee note.

```
/* Program for generating change adding up to a ₹100 note*/
Change {{H, S, T, F, R}}: —/* not taking two-rupee note */
member {H, {0, 1, 2}}/* Fifty Rupee notes */
member {S, {0, 1, 2, 3, 4, 5}}/* Twenty- Rupee notes */
member {T, {0, 1, 2, 3, 4, 5, 6, 7, 8, 9, 10}}/* Ten-rupee
notes */
member {F, {0, 1, 2, 3, 4, 5, 6, 7, 8, 9, 10,/* Five-rupee
notes */
11, 12, 13, 14, 15, 16, 17, 18, 19, 20}}
A is 50 * H + 20 * S + 10 * T + 5 * F,
A = < 100
R is 100 - A
```

Several kinds of goals are possible, for example:

```
?—change {{H, S, T, F, R}}
```

will list all possible ways of giving change for a 100-rupee note, and

```
?- change {{0, 2, 3, 4, 6}}
              no
```

Since two 20-rupee notes, three 10-rupee notes, four 5-rupee notes and 6 rupees do not make 100-rupees and

```
?–change {{1, 2, 1, 0, 0}}
            T
Also? –change {{0, 2, 3, 4, P}}
            P = 10
```

The most important feature of this example is to show how a member can be used to generate choices for values of some variable in order to satisfy some constraints! PROLOG's backtracking mechanism then automatically pursues each of the alternatives.

Example 2: Towers of Hanoi puzzle.

The object of this famous puzzle is to move N disks from the left peg to the right peg using the centre peg as an auxiliary holding peg as shown in Figure 5.24 for a set-up for N = 3 disks.

At no time can a larger disk be placed upon a smaller disk. The puzzle can be solved using a recursive PROLOG program. The recursive program solves the problem by breaking the problem into a collection of smaller problems and further breaking these smaller problems into even smaller problems till a solution is reached. The steps for this recursive approach are:

Step 1: Label the pegs X, Y, Z, ... These labels may move at different steps to follow.
Step 2: Number the discs from 1 (smallest topmost) to N (largest, bottom most)
Step 3: Move (N – 1) discs from X to Y. This leaves N alone on peg X.
Step 4: Move disc N from X to Z.
Step 5: Move (N – 1) discs from Y to Z so that they sit on disc N.

The above (step 3 to step 5) is a recursive algorithm (recursion is the process of repeating items in a self-similar way) since to carry out steps 3 and 5, the same algorithm is to be applied for N – 1 discs again. After a finite number of recursions, the number of discs remaining on peg X will be 1 and which is a trivial process to move a single disc from X to Z.

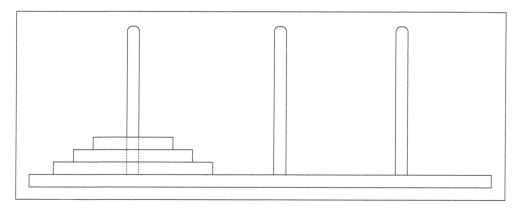

FIGURE 5.24 Towers of Hanoi Puzzle

The recursive PROLOG program consists of two classes as shown below:

```
move (1, X, Y, _): —
Write ('move top disk from'),
Write (X),
Write ('to'),
Write (Y)
nl.
move (N, X, Y, Z): —
N > 1,
M is N - 1
move (M, X, Z, Y)
move (1, X, Y, _),
move (M, Z, Y, X)
```

The variable filled in by '_' (underscore) is 'do not care' variable, which PROLOG allows to freely match with any structure, but no variable binding results from this gratuitous matching.

The first clause in the above program describes the move of a single disk. The second clause declares how a solution could be obtained recursively. For example, for N = 3, X = left, Y = right and Z = centre, the clause is

```
move (3, left, right, centre) if
move (2, left, centre, right) and
move (1, left, right, centre) and
move (2, centre, right, left).
```

The output of the program is:

```
?—move (3, left, right, centre)
Move top disc from left to right
Move top disc from left to centre
Move top disc from right to centre
Move top disc from left to right
Move top disc from centre to left
Move top disc from centre to right
Move top disc from left to right true.
```

5.17.3 LISP

LISP was invented by John McCarthy in 1958 at the Massachusetts Institute of Technology, USA. From the very inception, it was associated with the AI research workers. Since its first implementation, LISP had various versions such as Stanford LISP, standard LISP and common LISP available for wide-ranging platforms. LISP was originally developed as a practical mathematical notation and symbol for computer programs. Soon it became a favoured programming language for AI. LISP stands for 'list processing'. Major data structures and LISP source code are made up of linked lists and other lists. A function is written as a list with the function or operator's name first, and the arguments following, such as function f with two arguments will be invoked using (f arg1 arg2). Common LISP reads an expression entered by the user and the LISP prompt evaluates the expression and then prints the result.

Example:

```
USER(1):  (*2(Cos 0)(*2 3)
12.0
```

It may be noted that LISP represents a function f(x) as (f x) such as Cos(0) as (Cos 0); LISP expressions are case-insensitive. LISP evaluates function calls in applicative order, that is, all the argument forms (except conditionals) are first evaluated before invoking the function containing the arguments. LISP has got built-in usual numeric functions such as '+', '−', '*', '/', 'abs', 'max' and 'min'.

Example:

```
USER(2):  (max 7 11 13)
13
USER (3):  (/28 2)
14
```

Introductory comments are preceded by ';; '. LISP allows user-defined functions (UDF) also.

```
; triple the value of a number
defun triple (x)
'Compute three times X.'; inline comments can
                (*3 X); be written here
                USER(4): (triple 4)
                12
```

5.17.3.1 Recursions and Conditionals in LISP

LISP includes relational operators and expressions such as (= xy) x is equal to y; (/ = xy) x not equal to y; (< x y) x less than y; (> x y) x is greater than y (< = x y) x is less than or equal to y and (> = x y) x is greater than or equal to y. 'If' form checks the condition of the relational expression and returns values either 'T' if true or NIL if false. LISP allows recursions also. In other words, the definition of a function may involve invocation of itself. Recursion facilitates looping behaviour in programming.

Example: Let us write down a recursive definition of XY (X raised to the power Y), assuming both X and Y are non-negative and non-zero integers.

```
              (defun power (X Y)
   'Compute the value of X raised to the power Y'
              (if ( = Y 1)
                 X
    (*X (power(X (-Y 1)))))))
```

The 'if' form is not a strict function (as strict functions evaluate their arguments in applicative order). Instead, the 'if' form evaluates the condition (= Y 1) before further evaluating the other two arguments. If the condition evaluates to true (Y is equal to 1), then only the second argument is evaluated, and its value is returned as the value of the 'if' form; otherwise, the third argument is evaluated and its value is returned.

In order to facilitate the recursion, we can make use of the debugging facility 'trace' as follows:

```
USER (5): (trace power)
    (Power)
USER (6): (power (2 6))
    0: (POWER (2 6))
       1: (POWER (2 5))
          2: (POWER (2 4))
             3: (POWER (2 3))
                4: (POWER (2 2))
                   5: (POWER (2 1))
                   5: returned 2
                4: returned 4
             3: returned 8
          2: returned 16
       1: returned 32
    0: returned 64
```

Multiple recursions are also possible.

Example: Sum of N Fibonacci numbers. By definition, the first two Fibonacci numbers are 1, 1 and each subsequent number is the sum of the preceding two, for example, 1, 2, 3, 5, 8, 13, ... The Nth number is Fib(N) = Fib(N–1) + Fib(N–2) for N > 1. The above definition can be directly translated to the following LISP code:

```
(defun fibonacci(N)
'Compute the Nth Fibonacci number.'
(if ( = N1) or (zerop N))
1; for N equal to 0 or 1 the
; value is 1
(+ (fibonacci (-N1)) (fibonacci(-N2))))
```

The function (zerop N) tests if N is Zero. Like 'or' LISP allows other logical operators such as 'and'; 'not' also.

The above function definition for Fibonacci number involves two recursions:

First recursive evaluation for (fibonacci [–N1]) and second recursive evaluation (fibonacci [–N 2]) and finally return their sums.

5.17.3.2 Lists

LISP supports symbolic computing in addition to numeric computing. The fundamental LISP data structure for supporting symbolic manipulation is lists. Lists are containers that support sequential traversal. List is also a recursive data structure. In order to better appreciate a recursive abstract data type and develop recursive operations on the same, the data types need to be presented in terms of its constructors, selectors and recognizers. Let me explain these three terms as follows:

Constructors are forms that create new instances of a data type (possibly out of some simpler components):

Example 1. Nil: Evaluating nil creates an empty list
2. Cons (AB): Creates a list containing A followed by the elements in B

Instead of typing 'Cons' if we already know the elements in a list, we could as well enter the list as list literals by way of 'quote' or ""

USER (7): quote(A B C D E F)
    (A B C D E F)
USER (8): '(A B C D E F)
    (A B C D E F)

The second ingredient of an abstract data type is its 'selectors'. A 'selector' form returns one of the components out of a composite object made up of several components.

Examples:
USER (9): (first '(7 8 9))
7
USER (10): (rest '(7 8 9))
(8 9)
USER (11): (rest (rest '(7 8 9)))
(9)
USER (12): (rest (rest (rest '(8 9))))
NIL

The last ingredient mentioned earlier is 'recognizers', which tests how an object is constructed. Corresponding to each 'constructor' of a data type is a 'recognizer'. For example, it is 'null' for 'nil'.

Constructors, selectors and recognizers of lists enable one to develop recursive functions that traverse a list. This requires use of a function for determining list length recursively; we can define such a function as follows:

```
            (defun recursive-list-length (L)
    "A recursive implementation of list-length". (if (null L)
                          0
          (1 + (recursive-list-length (rest L)))))
```

The recognizer null is to differentiate how list L was constructed. In case L is nil, 0 will be returned as its length. Else L was a list created by the constructor cons and in that case 1 plus the length of rest (L) is returned recursively. For example:

```
USER (13): (trace recursive-list-length)
(RECURSIVE-LIST-LENGTH)
USER (14): (recursive-list-length '(1 2 3 4)
    0: (RECURSIVE-LIST-LENGTH (1 2 3 4)
      1: (RECURSIVE-LIST-LENGTH (2 3 4)
        2: (RECURSIVE-LIST-LENGTH (3 4)
          3: (RECURSIVE-LIST-LENGTH (4))
            4: (RECURSIVE-LIST-LENGTH NIL)
            4: returned 0
          3: returned 1
        2: returned 2
      1: returned 3
    0: returned 4
4
```

5.17.3.3 Symbols

LISP allows lists with symbols, alpha numeric and special characters
Such as '—'. LISP is also case insensitive.

Example:

```
USER (15) :'(What is your name?); A list of symbols
(WHAT IS YOUR NAME?)
USER (16) :'(1 + 3 * A * B); A list of symbols and numbers
(1 + 3 * A * B)
USER (17) :'(Jaytilak (Biswas M)); A list containing 'Jaytilak and
'(Biswas M)
(Jaytilak (Biswas M))
```

Note that the list as above only has a length 2.

Example:

```
USER (18) : (nth 0 '(c a t))
C
USER (19) :(nth 2 '(c a t))
T
```

nth is a function is LISP as (nth N L) which returns the Nth member of the list L assuming members are numbered as zero onwards.

Like first L, LISP has a built-in function (last L) that returns the last cons structure in a given list L.

Example:

```
USER (20): (last '(Ram Shyam Jadu))
(Jadu)
```

Append: LISP defines a function append that appends one list to another.

```
USER (23) : (append '(R A M) '(C H A N D R A))
(R A M C H A N D R A)
```

Using lists as sets: Lists are ordered sequences, whereas sets are not. Further, sets do not have multiple occurrences of the same element, whereas lists do have multiple occurrences. For example, (x y z) and (y x z) are two different lists although the elements of both the lists are same. Similarly, (x x y z) and (x y z) are two different lists. LISP defines functions such as (intersection L1 L2), (union L1 L2) and (difference L1 L2) for Boolean operations on sets.

Example of intersection:

```
USER (24) : (trace list-intersection) (LIST-INTERSECTION)
USER (25) : (list-intersection '(A C E G) '(A B C D))
0 : (LIST-INTERSECTION (A C E G) (A B C D))
    1 : (LIST-INTERSECTION (C E G) (A B C D))
                       2 : (LIST-INTERSECTION (E G) (A B C D))
                       3 : (LIST-INTERSECTION (G) (A B C D))
                       4 : (LIST-INTERSECTION NIL (A B C D))
                       4 : returned NIL
    3 : returned NIL
    2 : returned NIL
    1 : returned (C)
0 : returned (A C)
(A C)
```

The above examples are only to illustrate certain features of LISP. It may be mentioned that with the features of linear recursions, member, append and Boolean operations such as intersection, union and difference, LISP enables pattern matching and retrieval of knowledge, thus making it a powerful language along with PROLOG for artificial intelligence as well as expert systems.

CASE STUDY: DEEP LEARNING—CRYPTO CURRENCY EXCHANGE PRICE PREDICTION USING LIMIT ORDER BOOK

Background

High-frequency trading or algorithmic trading is popular in stock exchanges. In current stock markets over the globe, a sizeable portion of the daily trading volume is carried on by specialized companies adopting those techniques. In the elaborated stock market, it is not possible for individuals to get fast access to data to gain any advantage out of the stock trading without heavy computing machines and technology as because margins and arbitrages are closed in the fraction of a second.

The case pertains to the development of a deep machine learning model using an RNN for predicting future price of digital assets such as cryptocurrency like bitcoin based on input data obtained from the limit order book. It may be mentioned that the limit order book captures all pending order data for 'bids' and 'asks' with the reserved price limit. A snapshot of the limit order book represents the demand and supply position of any asset at a certain point in time in the exchange market.

Cryptocurrency is a type of digital currency that uses cryptography for security and anti-counterfeiting measures. It usually uses 'blockchain' technology. Although a digital asset was chosen in the present model development, the principles and methods are applicable to any asset or stock which is tradable in an exchange. The RNN-based model was developed based on real-time data such as limit order book snapshots, price history and data from an exchange to predict future price of the cryptocurrency.

Identification of the right feature set from the data, selection of the correct model architecture, and configuration of the hyper parameters and choice of the cost function were the challenges faced by the development team.

Data Acquisition

Data were obtained by sampling the Bittrex exchange every minute using the API provided and storing the data. About 3,000 samples representing 3 weeks of trading data were collected. The data were not 100% consecutive because of networking disturbances and related disruptions. Since every order in the limit order book has two parameters (quantity and price), the data could not be used as it was. A small modification was applied to the data to extract training sets. Bins of 10 US$ were defined and the quantities relating to each bin were added together. Hundred bins were created for 500 bid orders representing the last price and up to last price minus US$1000.

Models of Neural Networks Adopted and the Results

Five different models were applied in order to improve the accuracy of prediction of future price of the bitcoin.

1. The initial model was a fully connected network (FCN) architecture as shown below:

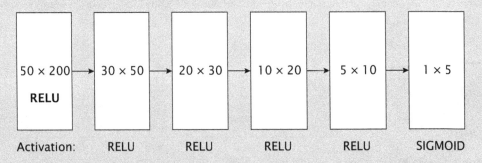

The key objective of this model was to find correlation and validate the data from the order book as valid predictor. Twenty-one thousand training samples with training/dev sets as 80%/20% split were fed to the model and the model compared bitcoin prices 1, 2, 3, 5 and 10 minutes into the future with the current price. The fully connected network architecture achieved approximately 95% accuracy on the training set and 64% accuracy on the dev set at around 31,000 epochs.

2. RNN architecture with same inputs and outputs of the fully connected network:

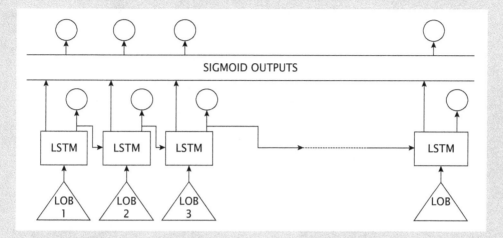

Limit order book (LOB) provides input to an LSTM network followed by a sigmoid output prediction of an increase or decrease like the fully connected network. By adding L2 regularization (L2 regularization is a technique to reduce over fitting of the model to improve its performance with highly variable input data) 10% increase in dev accuracy was achieved while the training accuracy was reduced close to dev accuracy.

3. RNN with fully connected network acting as encoder to provide RNN input:

In this model limit order book, data were encoded using a FCN and the activations from the last but one layer of the FCN were fed into the RNN. Performance was similar to the previous RNN architecture where the order book was directly fed as input.

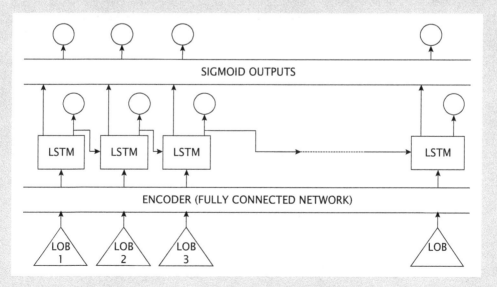

4. RNN with single limit order book spliced into multiple time steps:

   Input was split into equal number of parts and fed to time steps in the LSTM network. Two hundred feature inputs split into 10 parts of 20 each were fed to the LSTM network with 20-time steps. An accuracy of 95% plus was achieved on the training set and 66% accuracy was achieved on the dev set, which was 3% more compared to accuracy of the fully connected network.

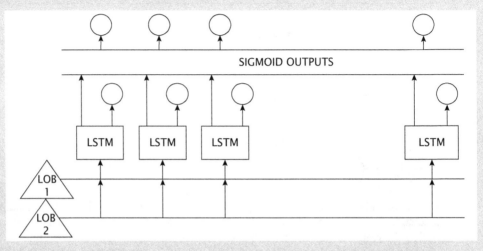

5. In the categorical model, the output labels were grouped under three categories as follows:
   i. Category with output more than a threshold percentage;
   ii. Category with output less than the threshold percentage;
   iii. Category with output equal to threshold percentage.

The signal in the categorical model was created with four dimensions—the first one being the threshold (0.1%, 0.2%, 0.3%, 0.4% and 0.5%), and second dimension being the future prediction look ahead (1, 2, 3, 5 and 10 minutes). Other two dimensions were the RNN time step or window size and the batch. Best result was achieved with a two-minute look-ahead prediction and 0.2% threshold change.

Categorical model architecture had three convolutional layers of one dimension each connected to two layers of LSTM RNN with 256 hidden nodes each and one softmax layer with three categories for the output. The architecture for the categorical model is as follows:

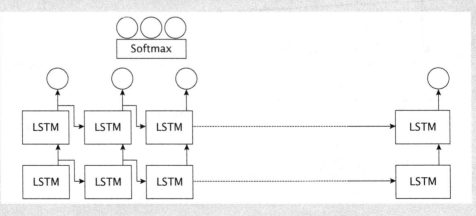

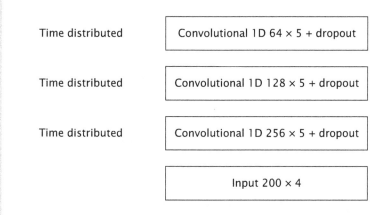

Sample label distribution and result obtained: 25,000 sample labels distribution was as follows:

	Increase	No Change	Decrease
Training set	3,126	16,310	3,060
Dev set	278	1,928	290

With the sample distribution as shown earlier, the following results were obtained for the categorical model:

	Increase	No Change	Decrease
Ground truth (Dev set)	278	1,928	290
Predicted increase	87	247	17
Predicted no change	181	1,505	196
Predicted decrease	10	176	77

Using the categorical model and the network described above, 70% accuracy for the training set and 67% accuracy for the dev set were obtained.

Conclusion

The case study shows a clear correlation between LOB and future price. Further, it was found that RNN performs better than a fully connected network for the price prediction problem of this kind. However, using a categorical model with threshold, modifying the loss function and adding convolutional layers the best result was obtained.

Source: Padmanabhan, Gilboa and Biswas (2018).

Review Questions

1. What is an EIS? Mention the broad types of EIS.

2. What is BI? Explain.

3. What capabilities a machine or computer must have in order to pass the Turing test?

4. Mention few tasks which you feel computers or machines are not able to do now and also in the near future.

5. Design few questions which you would like to ask a man and a machine for the sake of the Turing test.

6. What is machine learning? What is supervised learning? Is reinforcement learning a type of supervised learning? Explain your answer.

7. What are the different methods of knowledge representation for AI?

8. Distinguish between forward chaining and backward chaining with a suitable example. Why do computer-based expert systems use backward chaining for inference?

9. What is 'heuristic'? How does heuristics facilitate state space search?

10. What are expert system shells? Mention any expert system shell you are familiar with.

11. Mention two possible applications of expert systems.

12. What is declarative programming? How is it different from procedural programming? Is PROLOG a declarative programming?

Bibliography

Gordon, S. Novak Jr. 'Lecture Notes on Artificial Intelligence' (CS343). Austin, TX: University of Texas at Austin, 2007.

Inmon, W. H. Claudia Imhoff, and Ryan Sousa. *Corporate Information Factory*, 2nd ed. New York, NY: Wiley, 2002.

Kaniclides, T., and C. Kimble. 'Executive Information Systems: A Framework for Their Development and Use.' *YCS247*, Department of Computer Science, University of York, UK, 1994.

Koutsoukis, N. S., and G. Mitra. *Decision Modelling and Information Systems: The Information Value Chain*. Boston, MA: Springer Science, Business Media, 2003.

Linstedt, D. E. 'Data Vault Series 1 to 5.' *The Data Administration Newsletter* (September 2012).

McCarthy, J. 'Recursive Functions of Symbolic Expressions and Their Computation by Machine, Part I.' *Communication of the ACM* 3, no. 4 (1960): 184–195.

Minsky, Marvin. 'A Framework for Representing Knowledge.' *MIT-AI Laboratory Memo* 306, 1974. Available at: https://courses.media.mit.edu/2004spring/mas966/Minsky%201974%20Framework%20for%20knowledge. pdf (accessed on 24 January 2020).

Mintzberg, H. 'Planning on the Left Side and Managing on the Right.' *Harvard Business Review* 54, no. 4 (1976): 49–58.

Orlikowski, W. J., and D. Robey. 'Information Technology and Structuring of Organizations.' *Information Systems Research* 2, no. 2 (1991): 143–169.

Padmanabhan, A. S., Ben Gilboa, and Tamal Biswas. 'Crypto Exchange Price Prediction Using Limit Order Book Project.' Report No. CS230, University of California, Los Angeles, CA, 2018. Available at: https://cs230. stanford.edu/projects_spring_2018/reports/8289864.pdf (accessed on 24 February 2020).

Rockart, J. F. 'Chief Executives Define Their Own Data Needs.' *Harvard Business Review* 57, no. 2 (1979): 81–93.

Rockart, J. F., and M. Treacy. 'The CEO Goes On-Line.' *Harvard Business Review* 60, no. 1 (1982).

Weizenbaum, J. 'Eliza: A Computer Program for the Study of Natural Language Communication Between Man and Machine.' *Communication of the ACM* 9, no. 1 (1966): 36–45.

Winston, P. H. 'Learning Structural Descriptions from Examples.' *AI Technical Reports of Computer Science and AI Lab*. Cambridge, MA: MIT, 1970.

6 CHAPTER

Information System for Planning

6.1 Introduction

Planning is the managerial process of deciding in advance what has to be done, how it has to be done, who has to do it, when it has to be done and what resources are to be provided for doing it. It bridges the gap from where the organization is to where it has to go in a defined time span. It may be noted that planning is an activity of managers which is very much integrated with decision-making and control. It provides the guidelines necessary for decision-making and resulting action throughout the organization.

6.2 Need for Planning

Planning is essentially needed for an organization to decide its course of action or strategy to cope up with the changes in the environment of the organization for its very survival and growth. An organization has to function within an industry where its competitors also act and the industry as a whole is to operate within the broader socio-economic and political environment. The competitive forces within the industry determine the position of the organization in the industry, and with those external environmental forces, the organization has to plan the strategy considering its inherent strengths and weaknesses. Planning together with industry analysis, competitor analysis and strategic positioning is therefore an essential practice of management particularly at the strategic level. Michael E. Porter (2008) in his famous 'five forces model' had mentioned about five competitive forces which jointly determine the intensity of industry competition and thereby the profitability of the industry. The Porter model has been shown in Figure 6.1.

Further analysis of industry environmental factors reveals that statutory regulations and technological changes also play vital roles for organizations to plan their strategy.

Broader social expectations and corporate social responsibility are also important factors external to an organization that affect the planning of a strategy.

Porter's five forces and the other factors external to an organization as mentioned above force an organization to plan its course of action for the future or the strategy. However, there are factors internal to the organization such as its inherent strengths and weaknesses, personal values of the top management

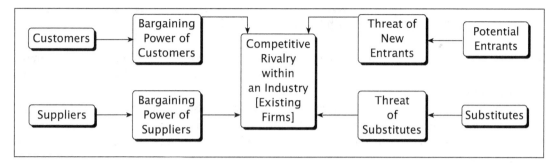

FIGURE 6.1 Porter Five Forces Model

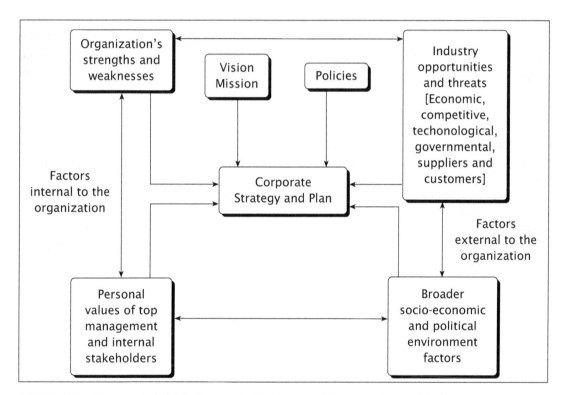

FIGURE 6.2 Context in Which Corporate Strategy and Plan Are Formulated

including prominent shareholders, the value system and ethics prevalent in the organization, which collectively determine the internal limits (to the organization) for the formulation of plans which the organization can successfully adopt. All these factors, external and internal, to the organization necessitate the formulation of a corporate strategy and plan for an organization as shown in Figure 6.2.

It may be observed from Figure 6.2 that the corporate strategy and plan also called the strategic plan (described in detail subsequently in this chapter) is guided by the other planning parameters such as vision and mission and also influenced by the policies of the organization. The terms vision, mission and policies have been described in the subsequent paragraph.

6.3 Planning Terms and Their Interrelationship

Strategic intent is a term coined by Prahlad (1965) and is the ambition of an organization. For example, a B-school might have a strategic intent that one day in future it will be reckoned as one of the top five B-schools in India.

Vision can be said to be the future aspiration that leads to an inspiration to be the best in one's field of activity. It may be mentioned that the strength of the vision statement for an organization is not in the wording of the statement, but the statement must truly reflect the aspirations of the stakeholders of the organization (employees, customers, suppliers, shareholders and so on).

Examples of vision statements
Honda: 'To be a company that our shareholders, customers and society want.'
Infosys: 'We will be a globally respected corporation.'
Mission of an organization is the description of the purpose of the organization as a whole and relates it to the society. A mission statement ensures that all employees are working towards a common purpose, enables employees to identify themselves better with the organization and serves to state explicitly or implicitly the organization's beliefs, values and aspirations. The vision of an organization is only a broad indication of the organization's intentions. The aspiration level embodied in the vision is often too lofty. A vision becomes tangible when it is expressed in the form of a mission statement.

Examples of mission statements
Infosys: 'To achieve our objectives in an environment of fairness, honesty and courtesy towards our clients, employees, vendors and society at large.'
Coca-Cola: 'To refresh the world, to inspire moments of optimism and happiness, to create value and make a difference.'
Goals
Goals describe future expected outcomes or states. They provide programmatic direction and focus on ends rather than means.

Example of organizational goals
A company in the IT sector—'To provide high-quality information services that satisfy user needs.'

Objectives are clear, realistic, specific, measurable and time-bound statements of action, which when completed will move the organization towards goal achievement. Objectives will tell how to meet a goal. They can be either outcome objectives which address ends to be achieved or process objectives which specify means to achieve outcome objectives.

Examples of objectives:
For a company in IT:

1. **Outcome objectives:** 'By end of financial year 2020–2021, 50% of all employees will be aware of three library services.'
   'By 31 March 2021, achieve an objective of 75% customer satisfaction rating on the basis of requests entertained.'
2. **Process objectives:** 'To provide online database search training to all users of the service.'

It may be noted that whereas goals are general and broad in nature, objectives are specific, quantifiable and time-bound in nature.

Plans are statements of specific activities to achieve the objectives of an organization. Plans are the means and objectives are ends. For example, the capacity augmentation plan of a manufacturing industrial unit may be to increase the current level of output to 100% in the next 10 years.

The values and ethics are the belief that define a company's culture and help managers to set priorities and guide the day-to-day operations.

For example, the top management may give highest importance to transparency and integrity on the part of employees. Likewise, fairness and impartial treatment of all customers may be practised in an organization.

Policies are statements that attempt to inform and guide employees so that the totality of actions by individuals are consistent with the sense of direction of the company. Policies are of two types: (a) they provide limits for discretionary action by specified individuals and (b) they specify a procedure or action under specific circumstances. Thus, policies are representations of both the methods of implementing plans and methods of controlling such implementation.

Examples of Policies:

Function	Policy	Examples
1. Production	Make or buy	Make if price difference exceeds cost of capital.
	Price discount	Do not hold raw materials more than 60 days of consumption
2. Sales and marketing	Price discount	10% discount on lots of 1,000 pieces or more.
	Credit sales	Credit sales not more than 20% of total sales.
3. Finance	Working capital	Maintain [2:1] acid test ratio.
	Capital procurement	Through retained profit only.
4. Personnel	Promotion	Based on last three years' appraisal report on performance.
	Training	All executives have to attend one week training every year with an external institute in India in his or her areas of interest.
5. General	Competitive actions	No collusion in any way with the competitors to increase prices of products.

Corporate plans may be of various types depending upon the different dimensions of the plans as illustrated below.

Dimensions	Illustrations of Plans		
Time	Long term	Medium term	Short term
Level	Corporate	Managerial	Operation
Function	General management	Marketing	Production
Purpose	Strategy	Tactical	Task-oriented
Scope	Company wide	Functional	Departmental

The types of corporate plans will be described further in detail in subsequent paragraphs of this chapter as the information requirements are different for the different types of planning.

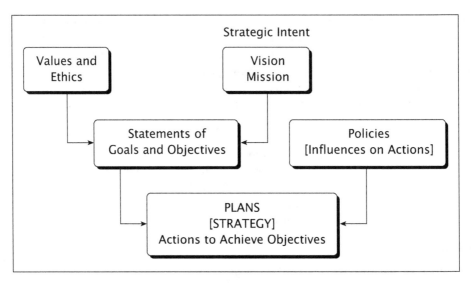

FIGURE 6.3 Relationship among Planning Parameters

The relationship among the planning parameters defined and explained in the previous paragraphs is shown in Figure 6.3.

6.4 Types of Plans

All levels of management plan but obviously the type of planning done at each level varies in scope and time frame as already explained earlier. The planning commences with the strategic planning at the top level of the management hierarchy, and all other plans are for a shorter time frame and consistent with the strategic plan. The strategic plan is long term in nature and consists of the (a) strategy and (b) steps, the time and costs associated with the steps. Strategy in the context of strategic planning is the desired configuration of a company at a future specified date. The configuration may be expressed in terms of the following:

1. **Scope of business:** Scope of the business of the company in future in terms of products or services, customer profile, markets, suppliers, price and quality and other characteristics of the products and services.
2. **Competitive edge:** Special market segment, niche market, product distinction, financial strength, unique technical and managerial skills and so on.
3. **Future inputs:** Specification of future inputs in terms of financing, manpower, plant and machines, facilities and so on.
4. **Future targets:** Specifications of targets both financial and non-financial such as quantitative statements of size of the company, turnover, profitability, ROI, market share, assets and trade-off between risk and reward.
5. **Allocation of resources:** Allocation of long-term capital, investment and divestment, deployment of manpower, emphasis on functional areas such as marketing, production and operations, management development and market segments.

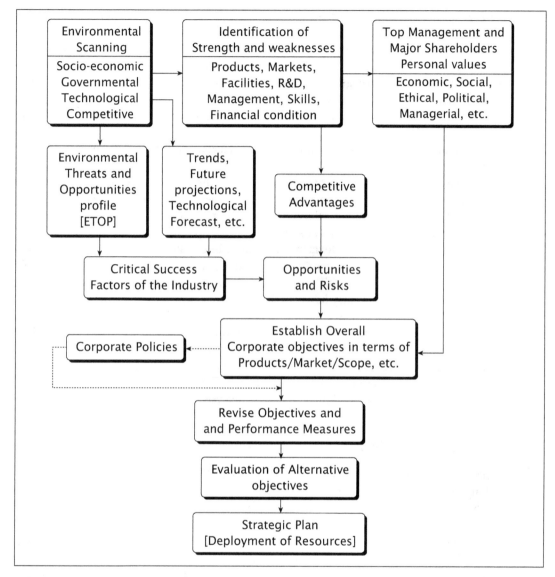

FIGURE 6.4 The Strategic Planning Process

6.4.1 Strategic Planning Process

The strategic planning process consists of the following steps as shown schematically in Figure 6.4.

Step 1: Environmental scanning. The scanning of the socio-economic, governmental, technological, market and competitive environment, both existing and future, conditions will enable the strategic planners to identify the environmental threats and opportunities for the organization on the one hand and to make projection for the future in terms of technological forecast, economic growth and so on, on the other hand.

Step 2: A systematic study and analysis of the environmental threats and opportunities together with future projections will also lead to the determination of the CSFs for the particular type of industry to which the organization belongs. For example, in the food processing industry, the nutritional value of the products is one of the factors leading to success.

Step 3: Identification of strengths and weaknesses. A systematic review of products, markets, facilities, value addition processes, R&D, management skills and financial conditions will enable the strategic planners to identify the strengths and weaknesses within the organization and in turn the competitive advantages.

Step 4: Opportunities and risks. Steps 1 to 3 described above will reveal the opportunities and risks for the organization.

Step 5: Establish overall corporate objectives. Based on the opportunities and risks as revealed in Step 4 and considering the personal values of top management and major shareholders relating to economic, social responsibility, ethical, political, religious and so on, the overall corporate objectives are set in terms of product or service, market, scope and so on.

Step 6: Revise objectives and performance measures. In this step, the strategic planners revise the overall corporate objectives according to corporate policies and also formulate, if possible, alternative objectives together with performance measures associated with each alternative objective. Quantitative targets may be established for parameters such as annual growth rate for sales, profit, ROI and market share.

Step 7: The alternative objectives, if any, as determined in Step 6 are evaluated based on predetermined evaluation criteria and compared with each other.

Step 8: Strategic plan. Finally, in this step the best alternative objective is selected as the strategic plan which covers the pattern of deployment of resources such as men, machines and facilities in the long term. The process is also known as SWOT analysis.

6.4.2 Development Plan

The strategic plan described earlier is specific but not detailed because although the strategic plan establishes long-term configuration or goals to be achieved by an organization, the same must be backed by detailed short-term plans known as development plans in line with the current environmental and competitive conditions. The long-term goals of the strategic plan set the constraints for the intermediate and short-term goals in the form of development plan and the operations plan, usually the annual operating plan. The development plans focus mainly on the capacity augmentation, acquisitions and diversifications, modernization, R&D, market, product and so on. The time horizon of the development plan depends upon the time horizon of the strategic plan and various other factors both internal and external to the organization.

6.4.3 Operating Plan

Operating plan, also known as the annual operating plan, is mostly financial in nature such as the annual performance budget which sets the objectives and standards of performance in financial terms. The basic idea is to decentralize the profit responsibility to profit centres and cost control to cost centres. The determinants for such decentralization of profit and cost are sales turnover, cost of sales and further split

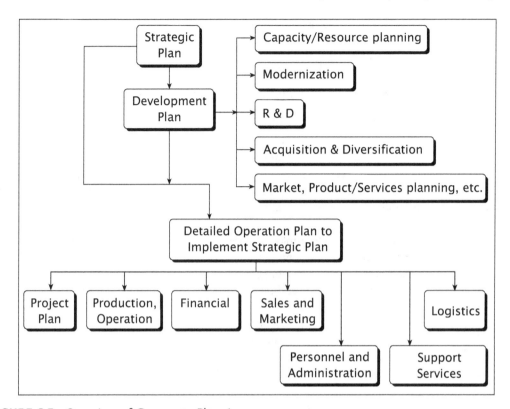

FIGURE 6.5 Overview of Corporate Planning

into elements such as investments in fixed assets, inventory, cash, accounts receivables, direct material, direct labour and overheads. The advantage of the annual operating plan lies in the identification of determinants of profit for separate organizational entities and also in providing measurable performance yardsticks for those entities. However, the plan being short-term operational in nature, its contributions to the long-term objectives is not generally assessed. The overview of corporate plans described above has been shown in Figure 6.5.

6.5 Information for Planning

The first, second and third steps in the planning process of developing environmental threats and opportunities profile, future projections and identifying internal strengths and weaknesses, depend heavily upon the availability and utilization of vital information.

The planning information needs of an organization can be classified into the following broad categories:

1. Environmental information;
2. Competitive and industry-related information;
3. Internal information.

Each of the above categories needs detailed elaboration.

6.5.1 Environmental Information

Environmental information needs can be classified and described as follows:

1. **Demographic and socio-economic trends:** The products, services or outputs of most firms and organizations are affected by the population strength and its dispersion. Social trends and consumer buying behaviour are important inputs for planning.

    Similarly, the economic trends such as GNP level and consumer disposable income, price, wage level and cost of living index are vital for planning at the corporate level in almost all organizations. Other economic indicators such as employment, productivity and capital investment provide valuable planning information.

2. **Technological:** Because of rapid technological innovation resulting in technological obsolescence of existing products and processes, it becomes necessary for many organizations to forecast the technological changes in their industry in general and the individual organization in particular. Companies such as Lockheed Martin and Intel forecast key technological advances in all fields for a period of 20 years.

3. **Political and governmental factors:** Information relating to political stability of the state as well as the federal government is very relevant for forecasting long-term plans. Different political parties forming a government may have different priorities relating to agriculture, industry and so on which have vital repercussion on the strategic plans of organizations. Further, statutory government regulations, controls and the fiscal policies are to be taken into account by strategic planners as such factors have significant impact on the planning decisions particularly the long-term ones.

4. **Factors of production and services:** Information pertaining to the factors of production are source, cost, availability, accessibility, quality and productivity of major factors (inputs) of production and services such as raw materials and components, labour, capital, power, water and other utilities.

6.5.2 Competitive and Industry-related Information

A competitive analysis of an industry and its competitors requires a great deal of data, some of which are difficult to obtain. There are three specific types of information concerning factors which affect the operations of a company within an industry. The three types are:

1. **Industry demand:** Because the sales/level of operations for any single unit within an industry largely depends upon the level of demand for the given industry, firms or units in the industry must have information on industry demand to facilitate strategic planning.

2. **Firm demand:** The demand for products and services of the individual unit or firm, which is a function of the total industry demand and the resources, capabilities and actions of the individual firm as compared to those of the other competing firms in the industry.

3. **Data of competitors:** Data of competitors are very vital for long-term forecasting of individual demand which in turn facilitates strategic plan to achieve the forecast. This information generally can be divided into three types:

i. Past performance of competitors on profitability, market share, ROI, growth in market share and so on which often provides a yardstick for setting performance objective for individual unit or firm.
ii. Present activities relating to competition, such as price strategy, advertising campaigns and changes in distribution channels.
iii. Plans concerning new products, acquisitions, modernization, R&D efforts and other plans that affect the individual firm's future.

6.5.3 Internal Information

Internal information influences the planning decisions of almost all the levels in the organization.

The information pertaining to business environment and premises surrounding competitive industry mainly facilitate planning decision-making by relatively few managers in a firm, mainly top managers and marketing managers. However, internal information such as a budget or production plan once framed become essential planning data for a number of connected plans such as material plan, capacity utilization plan and manpower deployment plan.

The internal information for planning are of the following types:

1. Marketing and sales information on performance, revenue, market shares, channels of distribution, retail outlets and franchise stores, customer feedback and so on. Sales forecast is another vital planning information in an organization and all other plans for allocation of company resources are derived from the sales forecast.
2. Financial information on profit, cost, cash flow, investment, ROI and so on. The budget is the financial plan of an organization and involves the entire organization and links all activities of the organization in monetary terms.
3. Production and operational information on assets, rated and available capacities, product mix, capacity utilization, lead time, quality standards, support facilities and so on.
4. Personnel information on skills availability, industrial relations, training and development facilities and so on.
5. Source, availability and limitations of supply factors like manpower, capital, plant and machines and others.
6. Research and development activities on new products, intellectual property rights, knowledge base and so on.
7. Basic policies are relatively fixed for long-run purposes and cannot readily be changed to permit flexibility in developing alternate courses of action in the short run.

6.6 Sources of Data for Industry Analysis

A systematic and organized approach is necessary for conducting industry survey for collecting data—both primary data from field and secondary data from published sources.

1. **Primary data from field:** In collecting primary data from field, it is important to develop a framework for possible source identification. The major sources of primary data for industry analysis are the firms or competitor units in the industry, suppliers, distributors, customers,

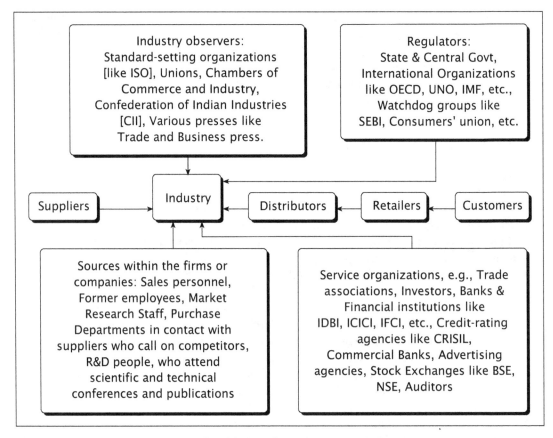

FIGURE 6.6 Important Sources of Field Data for Industry Analysis

service organizations such as bank and trade associations, industry observers such as financial community and the regulators including government. Out of all the above sources, industry competitors may not be always eager to furnish data about their units because of apprehension on their part that if they furnish data, it may harm them. The service organizations such as bankers, auditors, experts and trade associations also often maintain confidentiality of data relating to their clients. The most perceptive sources of primary industry data are the suppliers, customers, retailers and wholesalers, who take keen interest in the entire range of industry participants over a long time period. Figure 6.6 shows the important sources of field data for industry-related information to facilitate corporate planning.

The initial contact for collection of field data can be with any of the sources shown in Figure 6.6. In order to get the background for collection of industry data, it is appropriate to make contact with some person who is knowledgeable about the industry but at the same time who has not any competitive or direct economic stake in the industry.

2. **Secondary data for industry analysis from published sources:** The published sources of data are mainly as follows:

   a. **Journals and bulletins:** Trade journals in customer, distributor or supplier industries are often useful sources of industry-related data.

b. **Study reports for industries**: Industry study reports often provide important data for industry analysis.

c. **Annual reports of various companie**s: A quick review of the annual reports of a number of companies over a 10- or 15-year period facilitates understanding of the industry. Industry analysts as well as strategic planners should look for the reasons given for good as well as bad financial results, which, in turn, will expose the CSFs for the type of industry under analysis.

d. **Business press publications**: Business standards, business periodicals and index, RBI bulletins, *Dalal Street Journal* and so on.

e. **Company directories**: Statistical data can be obtained from Company directories like the Million Dollar directory, CRISIL ratings, Dun and Brad Street business information report and similar global publications.

f. **Government publications**: Such publications furnish statistics on manufacturers, retail traders, mineral industries, etc.

g. **Publications of trade associations**: Many industries have trade associations, which serve as clearing houses for industry data and sometimes publish detailed industry statistics.

The broad categories of data for the purpose of planning information are:

a. **Industry participants:** A list of major industry participants specially the leading companies.

b. **Product lines:** Company and year wise.

c. **Major customers**: Customer preferences.

d. **Complementary and substitute products**: Specifications of those products.

e. **Industry growth:** Rate, pattern (seasonal, cyclical and so on) and determinants of growth.

f. **Production and distribution:** Technology, life cycle, cost structure, value addition, economics of scale, logistics, labour and other factors of production/operation.

g. **Market:** Segmentation, marketing practices and so on.

h. **Suppliers:** Types, sources of innovations, supply channels, (indigenous/import), ancillary units and so on.

i. **Competitors:** Their strategy, goals, strengths and weaknesses and so on.

j. **Socio-economic, political and legal environment**: At macro-level.

6.7 Classification of Planning Models

The typical planning models are mathematical models consisting of mathematical expressions including financial statements. The models are either deterministic or probabilistic in nature. However, the scope and applicability of deterministic models are limited for corporate planning in view of uncertainties involved in external and competitive environments. Probabilistic models are better in this regard. The planning models being adopted by organizations can be broadly divided as optimization models (deterministic in nature), simulation models which can be either deterministic or probabilistic in nature to simulate various conditions and provide 'what-if' type of information to the corporate planners. In addition, there can be heuristic models. Models are mostly computer-based and use the processing power of the computer to enhance a manager's analytical ability. The various types of computer-based planning models and their typical business applications have been shown in Figure 6.7.

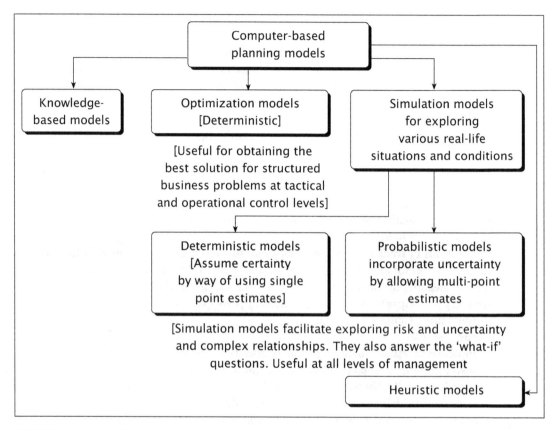

FIGURE 6.7 Classification of Planning Models

6.8 A Simple Planning Model

A simplified example of a deterministic simulation model involving profit planning based on output of a particular product manufactured by a manufacturing unit is as follows:

Output = Input variable
Sales = Price × Output
Price = ₹450 (price is fixed, the item being covered under rate contract)
Cost of sales = Direct cost + Overhead cost
Direct cost = Direct material cost + Direct labour cost
Direct material cost = Output × 200
Direct labour cost = Output × 50
Overhead cost = Variable overhead + Fixed overhead
Variable overhead = Output × 50
Fixed overhead = 40,000
Profit before tax = Sales – Cost of sales

Taxes = 0.50 × Profit before tax
Net profit = Profit before taxes – Taxes
Assuming, output = 1,000 units

The profit plan for a particular year, say 2019–2020, is as follows:

Output = 1,000
Sales = 450 × 1,000 = 4,50,000
Less: Cost of sales = 1,000 × 200 + 1,000 × 50 + 50 × 1,000 + 40,000 = 3,40,000
Profit before tax = 1,10,000
Less: Taxes = 55,000
Net profit = 55, 000

The above planning model is a very simple example illustrating the form of a planning model. However, more complicated and yet comprehensive business planning models can be developed in a similar fashion for planning sales, production, capacity utilization, level of advertising, level of outsourcing, pricing at micro- (unit level) and at macro-level, estimation of gross national income (GNP), disposable consumer income, planning of manufacturing and service sector industries and so on.

However, the planning models irrespective of the complexities involved must include the following:

1. A set of input data to the model;
2. The processing formulae, logic, equations and flow charts and so on to operate on the input data;
3. A format for presenting the results obtained after processing by the model.

6.9 Risk and Sensitivity Analysis of Planning Models

With most planning models, it is possible to assess risk by way of sensitivity analysis. The process of sensitivity analysis is to study the effect of any variable at a time on the result or outcome of the model. The objective of the analysis is to identify the 'critical' or 'sensitive' variables, which are variables having more than proportionate effect on the result. For example, a simulation model involving financial investment might include variables such as unit cost, unit price, volume of sales and amount to be invested. Sensitivity analysis in such a case might show that the resulting profit arising out of the investment is little affected by unit cost or price, but significantly affected by the volume of sales.

6.10 Balanced Scorecard

Balanced scorecard (BSC) is a new tool to strategic management developed by Robert Kaplan and David Norton, which comprises a performance measurement system, strategic management system and a communication system. The performance measurement system not only retains the traditional financial measures such as ROIs and profit but also includes the drivers of future economic performance and value creation through investment in customers, suppliers, employees, technology and process innovation. The financial measures are mainly indicators of past performance and hence called lag indicators, but

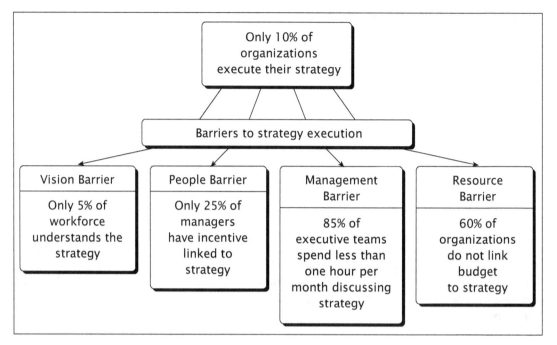

FIGURE 6.8 Barriers to Implementing Strategy

Source: Adapted from material developed by Robert S. Kaplan and David P. Norton.

the future drivers of economic performance and value creation are known as lead indicators such as customer satisfaction, employee skills and reduced process cycle time.

The performance measures as mentioned above, both the lag and lead indicators in a BSC, are derived from the organizations' mission statements and overall business. BSC translates the organization's strategy into specific, quantifiable objectives and monitors the organization's performance in terms of those objectives. The BSC also aligns budget to strategy and helps in developing an enterprise performance management system.

The BSC is additionally a communication tool in an organization as it communicates the vision and strategy translated in terms of performance measures to all levels of employees insofar as they are individually or jointly concerned.

The communication role of the BSC facilitates strategy execution by removing the barriers of vision, people, management and resource as shown in Figure 6.8.

6.11 Four Perspectives of a BSC

While the scorecard retains the traditional financial measures, it takes a total view of an organization by complementing the financial perspective with three other distinct perspectives: the customer perspective, internal business process perspective and learning and growth perspective. The BSC developed objectives, metrics (measures), targets, initiatives to collect data and analyse the same related to each of

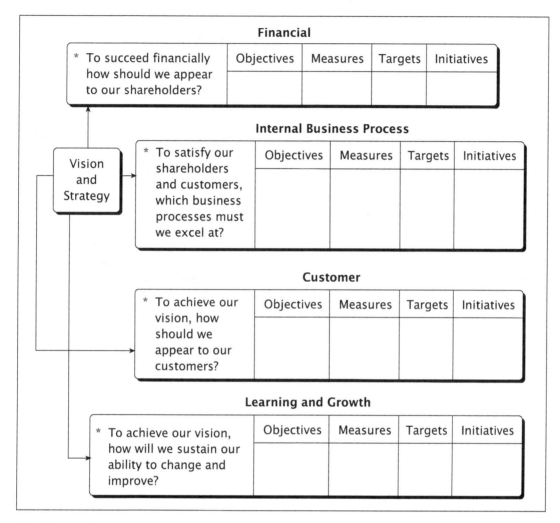

FIGURE 6.9 The Balanced Scorecard

Source: Kaplan and Norton (1996).

these perspectives. Figure 6.9 shows the framework of the BSC with vision and strategy at the centre of the scorecard and with the four perspectives as mentioned above around it.

Let us explain the four perspectives along with the performance measures for each of them.

6.11.1 Customer Perspective

Organizations have, in recent times, realized the paramount importance of customer focus and customer delight in any business. If customers are not satisfied, they will eventually find alternate suppliers who will meet their needs. Poor performance from this perspective will lead to future decline in growth even though the current financial scenario may appear satisfactory.

In developing objectives and measures for this perspective, two important factors must be considered—the target customers (focus) and the value proposition for the products or services provided to them. The value propositions may include:

1. Operational excellence leading to cost leadership as in case of Walmart.
2. Product leadership through constant product innovation as is the case with Nike, a product leader in the field of athletic footwear.
3. Customer intimacy by way of developing long-term relationship through deep understanding of customer needs and providing solutions. For example, Dr Fixit of Pidilite Industries Limited providing long-term waterproofing and allied solutions epitomizes the customer-intimate organization.

6.11.2 Internal Business Process Perspective

In the internal process perspective of the scorecard, the key processes, at which the organization must excel in order to continue adding value to customers, are identified. This requires that business organizations identify entirely new internal processes through re-engineering rather than concentrating on incremental improvement of existing processes and activities.

6.11.3 Learning and Growth Perspective

The learning and growth perspective includes employee skills, satisfaction, availability of information, corporate cultural attitude, employee training, learning and development. In a knowledge worker organization, employee—the repository of knowledge is the main resource. The measures in the learning and growth perspective of the BSC are really the enabler for the other three perspectives. Like the other perspectives of the scorecard, there will be a mix of core outcome (lag) measures and performance (lead) measures to represent the learning and growth perspective.

6.11.4 Financial Perspective

Traditional financial measures are important components of the BSC. In the case of profit organizations, the classic financial lag indicators include: revenue, profitability and budget variances. In the case of non-profit and public sector organizations, financial measures ensure that the organizations are achieving results in an efficient manner that minimizes cost.

6.12 Application of BSC in Private Sector in India

BSC has been very successfully applied in the private sector in India. Tata Motors was the first company in India to win the BSC Hall of Fame award. In the corporate private sector in India, the adoption rate of BSC is about 45%.

BSC example in private sector
The application of BSC in case of Air Deccan is as shown below:

Vision: 'To be the preferred airline of air travellers in India.'

Mission: 'To demystify air travel in India by providing reliable, low-cost air travel to the common man by constantly driving down the air fares as an ongoing mission.'

Air Deccan started its operations in civil aviation as a low-cost airline and had been able to compete with full-service airlines such as Indian Airlines by adopting cost-saving measures as follows:

1. **Food cost:** Food is not provided onboard since domestic flights are of short duration.
2. **Extra seats:** Since no food is provided, no space is required for food and the space could be utilized for providing extra seats. It was possible to provide 40 seats more than the number of seats provided by the other full-service airlines.
3. **Sale of tickets is done online** through the Internet and with the booking, the passengers get the boarding pass at the airport. This change in the ticket sales saved the cost of engaging travel agents and also the stationery and printing charges of tickets.
4. **Turnaround time management:** Turnaround time is reduced to 20 minutes only, nearly 50% reduction as compared to the same for other airlines. This was possible since the time for loading and unloading of meals is saved along with the cleaning time, thereby resulting in increased flying time.
5. **Repair and maintenance cost:** Air Deccan had only one type of aircraft in its fleet, and hence it held a smaller number of maintenance spares as compared with the same for other airlines. Further, the repair and maintenance function is outsourced partially to economize cost on repair and maintenance.
6. **Pricing strategy:** Apart from low fares, Air Deccan offered various incentives to passengers like a 'frequent flier' scheme. From the above data obtained from an article published by Dr Mukesh Chauhan, a strategy map for Air Deccan can be developed which will facilitate drawing the BSC for Air Deccan as shown in Figure 6.10.

6.13 Application of BSC in Public Sector Not-for-Profit Enterprises

The scope and applicability of BSC in public sector non-profit enterprises and government are enormous. The public sector enterprises, unlike the private sector where profit is the prime objective, have to cater to the needs of all stakeholders such as customers, community, physical environment and the people at large.

The performance measurement system for non-profit organizations has to essentially address the following areas:

1. **Financial accountability:** The performance measurement system includes standard of financial accounting, documentation and reporting relating to proper utilization of funds for the purpose for which the same are provided by the funding agencies.
2. **Products and services delivered:** This category represents the classical measurement efforts for counting the number of products and services delivered and the number of people served.
3. **Adherence to the quality standards of service delivery:** Quality of service delivery is of paramount importance in case of public sector enterprises and the government.
4. **Customer-need-based measures:** These measures are taken to ensure those in-service delivery.

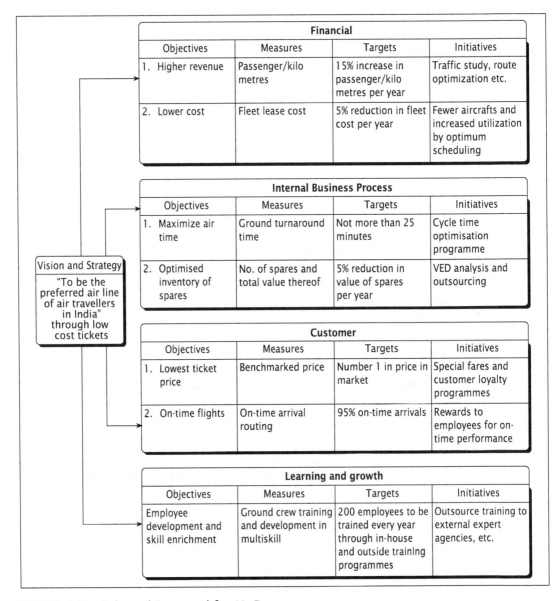

Financial			
Objectives	Measures	Targets	Initiatives
1. Higher revenue	Passenger/kilo metres	15% increase in passenger/kilo metres per year	Traffic study, route optimization etc.
2. Lower cost	Fleet lease cost	5% reduction in fleet cost per year	Fewer aircrafts and increased utilization by optimum scheduling

Internal Business Process			
Objectives	Measures	Targets	Initiatives
1. Maximize air time	Ground turnaround time	Not more than 25 minutes	Cycle time optimisation programme
2. Optimised inventory of spares	No. of spares and total value thereof	5% reduction in value of spares per year	VED analysis and outsourcing

Vision and Strategy

"To be the preferred air line of air travellers in India" through low cost tickets

Customer			
Objectives	Measures	Targets	Initiatives
1. Lowest ticket price	Benchmarked price	Number 1 in price in market	Special fares and customer loyalty programmes
2. On-time flights	On-time arrival routing	95% on-time arrivals	Rewards to employees for on-time performance

Learning and growth			
Objectives	Measures	Targets	Initiatives
Employee development and skill enrichment	Ground crew training and development in multiskill	200 employees to be trained every year through in-house and outside training programmes	Outsource training to external expert agencies, etc.

FIGURE 6.10 Balanced Scorecard for Air Deccan

5. **KPIs:** KPIs can serve as a repository for all areas of measurement such as cost of service provided and response time for customer complaints.
6. **Client satisfaction:** Among the indicators of satisfaction that are measurable important ones are: overall satisfaction, accessibility and so on.
7. **Corporate social responsibility (CSR):** CSR is becoming more and more important for public sector and government sector since the aspects of environmental, social and cultural impacts and related issues are also related to good governance of the organizations.

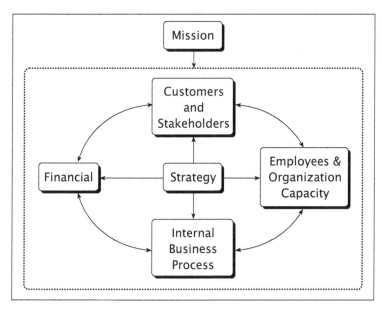

FIGURE 6.11   Public Sector Balanced Scorecard

Figure 6.11 displays the BSC model applicable to public sector non-profit enterprises. The salient differences between the private and public sector use of the scorecard are as follows:

1. Mission is at the top of BSC in case of the public sector unlike the private sector where improving value to the shareholders is of prime importance and the management is accountable to their financial stakeholders. In case of public sector enterprises, apart from efficient allocation and utilization of funds, the enterprises function to serve higher social purposes such as 'public safety', 'green environment' and 'eradication of poverty'.
2. Strategy remains at the core of the BSC. In case of public sector and non-profit enterprises, it is very difficult to define a clear and concise strategy as in case of private enterprises with profit motive.
3. Customer perspective is elevated, and customer here includes not only financial stakeholders but also all those whom the organization aims to serve. The important issue involved is who are the customers for public sector and non-profit enterprises and how the enterprises create value for the customers. Establishing the real customers in many ways depends on the perspective of the designers of BSC. For example, in case of a metro city municipal corporation, the unauthorized hawkers who sit on the pedestrian footpath and are periodically evicted are also treated as customers or stakeholders, as the municipal corporation has to deal with them to keep the footpath free from any encroachment.

6.14 BSC for a State Government

The strategy map relating to the top level of a state government administration has been shown in Figure 6.12. The four perspectives are customer, financial, internal administration processes and the state government's capacity for learning and improvement. The BSC has been shown in Figure 6.13.

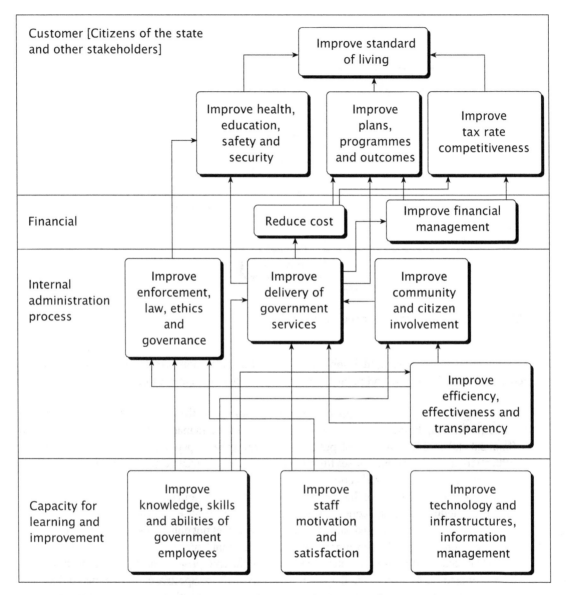

FIGURE 6.12 Strategy Map for State Government Administration

6.15 Information and Organizing Function

According to Murdick and Ross, 'organizing is required of managers because it is the method by which effective group action is obtained. A structure of roles must be designed and maintained in order for people to work together in carrying out plans and accomplishing objectives'.

MISSION

Improve Standard of Living and 'Gross State Happiness' through [i] Health, education, Safety, Security, Employment measures, [ii] Sustainable Development, [iii] Good Governance and [iv] Preservation and promotion of cultural values.

Citizens & other stakeholders

Objectives	Measures	Targets	Initiatives
1. Improve health of people	Healthcare	100 health centers and 10 super speciality hospitals to be opened by 31.12.2019	Medical Education, modernised health care measures etc.
2. Improved education	1. Adult literacy programmes 2. Higher educational facilities	Literacy level to be increased to 70% in next three years. seats for higher education to be doubled in next four years	Recruitment of teachers, upgradation of teaching & research facilities

Strategy

Efficient governance with full involvement of public

Financial

Objectives	Measures	Targets	Initiatives
Reduce Expenditure	Government expenditure under various heads	5% reduction in non-plan expenditure in next two years	Austerity measures
Financial management	Self-sufficient in financing the state plan and Programmes	GDP growth rate not less than 8%, tax revenue to increase by 5% every year	Rapid industrialization, Tax collection drive, etc.

Internal Administration Process

Objectives	Measures	Targets	Initiatives
Law and order, safety enforcement	Crime, accident rates	No. of crimes and accidents to reduce by 30% in current year	Modernisation of police department etc.
Speedy delivery of govt services, Maximise benefit/cost to public	Time, cost and No. of outlets for delivery of services	Delivery of essential service time not more than three days	Improved service delivery mechanism
Improve Productivity through technology innovation	Publication of pilot technology strategy document	By October 2022	Facilitate strategic technology plan for the state

Learning & Improvement

Objectives	Measures	Targets	Initiatives
Close skill gaps	No. of Employees trained in a year	100 employees of all categories to undergo two weeks training in a year	Outsourcing of training activities to reputed institutions
Achieve positive employee climate	Employee Productivity, satisfaction index	Satisfaction intex to be 6 out of 10 in a 4-point scale	Reward Incentive schemes for good performance
Improved technology Infrastructure & information management	Development of common data base for technology and infrastructure development plan for the state	By 31.3.2021	Strategically focused guides to facilitate progress towards growth initiatives

Note : Employee satisfaction

Index : 0 for no satisfaction, 3.5 for somewhat satisfied, 6 for satisfaction and 10 for highly satisfied

FIGURE 6.13 An Illustration of Balanced Scorecard for State Government Administration

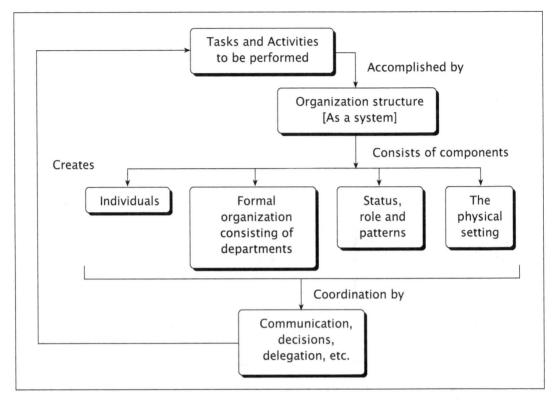

FIGURE 6.14 Integration of the Organizational System through the Management Process of Organizing

Organizing is a key function of management, and the process of organizing involves the following:

1. Grouping of activities and tasks necessary to achieve the plans.
2. The assignment of the tasks to various departments by allocation of responsibilities and commensurate delegation of authority.
3. To make provision for effective coordination of the tasks, activities and responsibilities of the work groups and departments.

The management process of organizing, as described above, addresses itself to the structural system for achieving responsibility allocation, coordination and delegation of authority as shown in Figure 6.14.

6.16 Classical Vis-à-Vis Systems Approach to Organizing

The classical, also known as the pyramidal organization, structure is hierarchical and at one time was most widely accepted by business organizations and is the foundation upon which all adaptations and modifications are constructed. The keywords of the hierarchical organization structure are: **structure** and **formal**. The basic ideas of the classical organization structure are: specialization of work (departmentalization), span of control (supervision of a limited number of subordinates), chain of command (authority delegation) and the unity of command (no subordinate has more than one superior).

Although the classical organization structure is easily understood and was widely applied in business organizations, due to its inherent limitation, such as too structured to adopt to change, it inhibits innovation, too mechanistic and job-centric and not human-centric, the classical approach has become outdated with the current needs of business and hence the systems approach to organizing has developed. The systems approach to organizing is based on the following concepts:

1. Integration of subsystems to make up the whole organization;
2. Decentralization leading to improved morale and motivation of managers;
3. Centralized control with decentralized operations through information flows;
4. Process orientation rather than structure;
5. The system approach to organizing lays emphasis on the system as opposed to organizational functions such as sales, finance and personnel.

The systems approach to organizing is very much dependent on the integration of the subsystems through information flows. Each organizational entity, such as the subsystem, the responsibility centre or the manager can be viewed as an IS having input (information), processor (for example, the manager) and the output which is the decision or else input information for the other entities. Each organizational entity becomes a decision point. It may be emphasized here that organizations consisting of the entities must be designed around information flow and the information must facilitate the planning and control of performance. However, frequently organizational structures and performance reporting do not match with each other. In such cases ISs cannot facilitate proper planning and performance reporting.

Organizations have to change with the changes in the environment and other internal changes in structure, management and so on. It is therefore essentially needed that with the above changes the ISs also change. In case the ISs are not changed matching with a change in organizational responsibilities and the needs of managers, the result will be 'information lag' as mentioned by Murdick and Ross.

CASE STUDY: AN INTEGRATED CAPACITY EXPANSION PLAN FOR MANUFACTURE OF A PRODUCT AND ITS FUTURE REQUIREMENT OF SPARES

Background

The case study can be divided into two parts. The first part relates to the development of an empirical model for realistic assessment of future requirement of spares for an end product in service based on the initiation of the end product into service and past consumption pattern of spares depending upon the age profile of the population of the end product in use.

The second part considers the integrated capacity expansion plan of a manufacturing organization involved in producing the end product which is a complex engineering product and the spares needed to meet the replacement demand for worn-out components. Precisely, the study shows how to earmark the net requirement of capacity at any machine centre during any future period in the planning horizon both for meeting the demand for the end product and also for its spares.

An interesting aspect of the study is that the demand for spares increases as more and more quantity of the end product is inducted into service and so with the ageing of the population of the end product in service. However, the demand for the end product is dependent on the user requirement for the same for immediate need and also for replacement of the old end products which may be beyond economic repair.

Often the requirement of capacity for manufacture of spares is significantly less than those for regular manufacture. Nevertheless, the need for planning for this part of plant capacity cannot be discarded in view of the corporate commitment to supply spares for operating the products in use particularly for products manufactured for exclusive use by the armed forces. In general, once a customer buys a product of a particular brand, the same customer will be totally dependent on the specific original equipment manufacturer (OEM) for the supply of spares for the product in future. The OEM may also be bound by contractual obligation for meeting the spares requirement during the entire life cycle of the product even if the same product model is phased out due to obsolescence. The above-mentioned situation offers both an opportunity and a challenge for the manufacturer as the profit margin for sale of spares is normally higher in a captive market for the sale of spares for the original equipment.

The specific product considered in this study relates to the supply of a particular defence use product and its related spares manufactured by the Indian Ordnance Factories (IOFs). The product has been in use of the Indian army and other paramilitary forces in India for a considerable period. The IOFs are captive production units under the Ministry of Defence, Government of India, and the units manufacture a variety of products used by the armed forces as well as the paramilitary forces. As a matter of policy, the Government of India does not allow the manufacture of these products by private manufacturers. Thus IOFs are the sole manufacturer of their products and the related spares.

Methodology Adopted for Formulation of the Model for Capacity Expansion Plan

A lag regression model was formulated with past requirement of capacity at machine centres, calculated based on historic data on spares consumption as the dependent variable and the corresponding quantities of the product initiated into service earlier as the independent lag variables. A lag regression model can be expressed as:

$$Y_t = \beta_0.X_t + \beta_1.X_{t-1} + \ldots + \beta_s.X_{t-s} \tag{1}$$

In equation 1, Y_t is the value of the dependent variable Y at time t and is expressed as a function of the current (at time t) and s is the previous values of an independent variable X. In the above equation, X_t, X_{t-1} and so on are called lag variables, s is the lag period and β_0, β_1 are called the coefficients of lag regression.

In our present study, the dependent variable is the total capacity requirement for spares for any time period and the lag variables are the number of end-products inducted into service during the particular time period and the previous lag period.

Almon's methodology for transformation of lag variables and principal component analysis had been adopted in the development of the lag regression model to find out the coefficients of the lag regression equation. Almon's method is an approach to overcome the difficulty associated with the reduction in degrees of freedom with increase in length of lag period, and principal component analysis was done to overcome the problem of multi-collinearity associated with lag regression models.

Readers may refer to the book titled *Econometric Methods* (2nd ed., 1972) by J. Johnston, and the book titled *Classical and Modern Regression with Applications* (2nd ed., 1990) by H. Myers Reymond,.

The lag regression model was used for estimation of future capacities of different machine centres based on anticipated entry of quantities of the product into service.

An integer linear programming model was also formulated for modelling the aggregate capacity expansion problem for meeting the future requirement of capacity. The model also takes into consideration the erosion of existing capacity and capacity replacements. General cost functions for capacity expansion were considered besides maintenance and operating costs. The model seeks to minimize the total present worth of all costs associated with future capacity expansion plans.

Statistical tests were conducted to prove the validity of the capacity estimation model for spare parts manufacture. The model was also externally validated using independent observations. The model is applicable in situation where the manufacturer of a product is also the exclusive supplier of the spares for the product. The product for the study was an assembly of 120 different components, out of which 40 were plastic components, fasteners and other simple components and those were procured from the market in 'ready to use' condition. The remaining 80 components were manufactured in-house by the manufacturing unit (ordnance factory in this case). In all, 15 different types of machining processes were involved in the in-hose manufacture of these components by four machining centres. As manufacture of this product was established many years ago and there had been many capacity expansions, an exact estimate of the capacity of the different machine centres for manufacture of these components during the past is not readily available. However, the supply of these components towards spares requirement had generally not been adequate in the past. The actual annual requirements of spares converted to aggregate requirement of manufacturing capacity required at the four-machining centres during 15 years from 1975–1976 to 1989–1990 are shown in the following table:

Actual Requirement of Capacities for Spares Manufacture (Machine Hours Per Year)

Year	Machine Center 1	Machine Center 2	Machine Center 3	Machine Center 4
1975–1976	4,760.84	2,648.94	2,554.58	4,249.61
1976–1977	7,309.11	6,588.67	4,765.24	2,744.23
1977–1978	9,181.50	11,732.06	5,149.56	3,401.87
1978–1979	16,868.28	10,992.18	11,081.38	5,923.80
1979–1980	11,075.26	9,702.87	6,283.64	21,154.12
1980–1981	22,487.61	15,769.39	13,263.88	10,404.85
1981–1982	21,183.29	10,707.14	10,800.92	9,505.81
1982–1983	25,113.82	17,792.20	18,920.99	10,881.01
1983–1984	32,603.62	25,669.34	25,129.64	16,622.98
1984–1985	41,261.62	31,703.71	33,762.21	17,627.67
1985–1986	26,845.25	15,262.85	15,649.96	11,339.55
1986–1987	28,829.26	20,552.03	15,729.91	13,141.00
1987–1988	30,939.94	20,963.34	16,428.76	15,874.59
1988–1989	23,220.06	19,082.44	14,397.26	13,417.02
1989–1990	29,167.92	22,674.13	18,678.37	11,001.12

The annual production figures of the end product from 1963 to 1993–1994 are as follows:

Year (March–April)	Production during the Year (Numbers)	Year (March–April)	Production during the Year (Numbers)	Year (March–April)	Production during the Year (Numbers)	Year (March–April)	Production during the Year (Numbers)
1963–1964	13,882	1971–1972	51,612	1979–1980	20,000	1987–1988	20,300
1964–1965	37,500	1972–1973	68,336	1980–1981	20,005	1988–1989	20,000
1965–1966	48,800	1973–1974	52,225	1981–1982	20,000	1989–1990	18,570
1966–1967	41,500	1974–1975	52,415	1982–1983	20,005	1990–1991	20,300
1967–1968	36,000	1975–1976	53,004	1983–1984	17,000	1991–1992	25,760
1968–1969	38,260	1976–1977	45,005	1984–1985	12,000	1992–1993	30,425
1969–1970	44,541	1977–1978	35,010	1985–1986	12,002	1993–1994	26,000
1970–1971	29,545	1978–1979	22,920	1986–1987	18,300	1994–1995	Not available

Validation of the Model

The lag regression model was validated internally using the significance tests for the t-statistic associated with the regression coefficients, the overall F-statistic of the regression model and the R-square statistic. Additionally, the model was also externally validated. This was done by splitting the data collected for the selected model into two portions. The first portion (data corresponding to 1975–1976 and 1986–1987) was used to develop a lag regression model and internally validate it. The second portion (data corresponding to 1987–1988 and 1989–1990) which was independent from the first was then used to compare with predicted results from the model.

Results of the Study

Results of the regression analysis for a particular machine centre have been shown in the following table as an illustrative sample. Similar results were also obtained for the other three machine centres.

Results of Lag Regression Analysis for Machine Centre 1
The above table shows the variation of the F-statistic, mean squared error S of regression, mean of observed values of the dependent variable (capacity required at the machine centres during the years), observations omitted from the analysis based on R-student statistic and the ratio C_v, the coefficient of variation corresponding to lag periods varying from 10 to 25 years. For each lag period, the combination that gave the best value of the F statistic was chosen. The final choice of the lag regression model was based on the highest F value. The details of the chosen lag regression model for estimation of capacity for machine centre 1 are given in the following table.

Length of Lag (Year)	Order of Polynomial	Regression Variance (S)	Coefficient of Regression (F)	Mean of Observed Dependent Variables	Coefficient of Variation (CV)	Years Corresponding to Data Not Included in the Analysis
10	4	9,612.00	32.51	22,056	0.4358	—
12	2	8,259.80	58.12	22,056	0.3745	—

Length of Lag (Year)	Order of Polynomial	Regression Variance (S)	Coefficient of Regression (F)	Mean of Observed Dependent Variables	Coefficient of Variation (CV)	Years Corresponding to Data Not Included in the Analysis
15	3	3,829.00	158.07	20,685	0.1851	1984–1985
16	4	3,765.00	122.95	19,768	0.1905	1983–1984, 1984–1985
17	2	3,514.00	239.55	20,685	0.1699	1983–1984, 1984–1985
18	3	3,113.50	612.30	19,768	0.1575	1983–1984, 1984–1985
19	2	3,104.00	725.33	20,685	0.1501	1984–1985
20	2	2,971.00	793.00	20,685	0.1436	1984–1985
21	4	3,236.00	333.65	20,685	0.1564	1984–1985
22	4	3,304.50	319.77	20,685	0.1598	1984–1985
23	4	3,240.00	222.25	20,685	0.1566	1984–1985
24	4	3,247.00	331.39	20,685	0.1570	1984–1985
25	4	3,281.00	324.46	20,685	0.1586	1984–1985

Details of the Lag Regression Model for Estimation of Capacity at Machine Centre 1 for Manufacture of Spares

Parameters and their combination for the best value: F-Statistic: 793; coefficient of variance: 0.1436; lag period: 20 years; S: 2971.00

Total number of observations: 15; number of observations deleted: 1; number of observations used: 14.

Result of residual analysis:

Year	Actual Capacity Required as Observed (Hours/Year)	Capacity Required as Computed from Equation (i) (Hours/Year)	Residues (Absolute)	Residues (R-student)
1975–1976	4,760.84	3,292.97	−1,467.87	−0.48055
1976–1977	7,309.11	6,625.98	−683.13	−0.22238
1977–1978	9,181.50	8,289.18	−892.32	−0.29170
1978–1979	16,868.28	21,241.72	4,373.45	1.57043
1979–1980	11,075.26	6,879.84	−4,195.42	−1.50438
1980–1981	22,487.61	26,562.32	4,074.72	1.46690
1981–1982	21,183.29	20,434.38	−748.91	−0.25162
1982–1983	25,113.82	24,388.28	−725.54	−0.24731
1983–1984	32,603.62	36,559.44	3,955.82	1.48068
1985–1986	41,261.62	25,234.43	−1,610.82	−0.56114
1986–1987	26,845.25	29,266.68	437.42	0.15052

Year	Actual Capacity Required as Observed (Hours/Year)	Capacity Required as Computed from Equation (i) (Hours/Year)	Residues (Absolute)	Residues (R-student)
1987–1988	28,829.26	33,040.16	2,100.22	0.73982
1988–1989	30,939.94	17,428.59	–5,791.47	–2.44345
1989–1990	23,220.06	29,895.81	727.88	0.25094

The requirement of capacity as shown in the above table was computed from Equation 1 based on the actual number of products inducted in service for the lag period of 20 years and the coefficients of lag regression as shown in the following table for machine centre 1. The lag regression coefficients were obtained following the Almon's methodology and the principal component analysis as mentioned earlier.

Lag Year	1	2	3	4	5
Coefficient of Lag Regression	0	0.000283	0.001105	0.002464	0.004361
Lag Year	11	12	13	14	15
Coefficient of Lag Regression	0.027038	0.03270	0.038900	0.045637	0.052913
Lag Year	6	7	8	9	10
Coefficient of Lag Regression	0.006795	0.009768	0.013279	0.017327	0.021913
Lag Year	16	17	18	19	20
Coefficient of Lag Regression	0.060727	0.069078	0.077968	0.087395	0.097360

The F-statistic, which is a measure of the association of the dependent variable with the independent variable, increases with increase in the length of lag period up to a maximum value. Significant improvement in performance of the above model was noticed when lag length reaches 15 years. Thereafter, the result continued to improve but beyond a definite lag length the strength of the association started declining and the F-value too declined. In case of machine centre 1, a lag period of 20 years resulted in the highest F-value.

From the results of external validation, it was observed that in majority of the cases the observed values were within the 95% confidence interval of prediction and in all cases within 95% confidence interval for individual observation thereby proving the validity of the lag regression model.

Conclusion

The above analysis proves the suitability of the lag regression model for estimation of capacity for manufacture of spares.

Review Questions

1. Define the terms: (a) vision, (b) mission, (c) strategic intent, (d) strategy, (e) goals, (f) objectives and (g) policy.

2. What is corporate strategy? How is it formulated?

3. What are the five forces mentioned by Michael E. Porter? How do they facilitate industry analysis?

4. What are the different types of corporate plans? Illustrate.

5. What is environmental scanning? How does it facilitate strategic planning in an organization?

6. What are the main sources of planning information?

7. What is a planning model? Describe briefly any planning model which you know.

8. What is a BSC? What are its major perspectives? Illustrate with a suitable example.

9. How do BSCs for public sector not-for-profit enterprises differ from the same for profit making private enterprises?

10. What is system approach to planning and organizing?

Bibliography

Hamel, G., and C. K. Prahalad. 'Strategic Intent.' *Harvard Business Review* 67, no. 3 (1989): 63–76.

Kaplan, R. 'Strategic Performance Measurement and Management in Non-profit Organizations.' *Non-profit Management and Leadership* 11, no. 3 (2001): 353–370.

Kaplan, R., and D. P. Norton. 'The Balanced Scorecard–Measures That Drive Performance.' *Harvard Business Review* 70, no. 1 (1992): 71.

Murdick, R. G., J. E. Ross, and J. R. Clagett. *Information Systems for Modern Management*, 3rd ed., New Delhi: Prentice Hall India, 1985.

Porter, M. E. 'The Five Competitive Forces That Shape Strategy.' *Harvard Business Review* 88, no. 1 (2008): 78–93.

7

CHAPTER

Information System for Control

7.1 Control as a Management Function

Control is a primary function of management and also the management process which ensures that (a) operations or performance proceeds according to plans and (b) the plans themselves result in attaining the objectives or goals of the organization.

Basically, the control process consists of three steps, namely (a) setting the standards of performance or plans, (b) measuring actual performance against the standards or plans and (c) correcting deviations, if any, from standards or plans.

Any organization, whether it is a manufacturing unit, a public utility such as a metropolitan electricity supply corporation or a non-profit social organization such as a school or a club has to produce goods, services or other facilities to fulfil its objectives—profit, quality service at reasonable cost and so on. In order to facilitate the same, planning must be undertaken as a first step, and once the plans have been formulated, control needs to be exercised to ensure conformity to the plans and relevancy of the plans in the future. The first step in control in an organization is setting the standards of performance, which involves defining for employees at all levels what is expected of them in terms of job performance or individual targets. The standards which are criteria against which results are measured and compared can be either quantitative or qualitative. For example, the quantitative target for the works manager of a factory can be 5% increase in labour productivity in a particular year as compared to the previous year. The qualitative standard may be maintaining satisfactory industrial relations. Besides employee performance standards as mentioned above, many organizations have identified key result areas relating to overall performance. Indeed, by evaluating organizational performance in these key areas, the top management monitors progress towards the basic objectives. General Electric Company of the USA mentioned about eight such key areas as follows:

1. Productivity
2. Profitability
3. Market position
4. Personnel development
5. Innovation and product leadership
6. Employee attitude
7. Public responsibility
8. Balance between short- and long-term goals

For each of the above key areas, performance targets are established for the activities. The targets have dimensions of profit, cost, time, quantity and quality. Furthermore, the targets can be tangible or

TABLE 7.1 Criteria of Performance within Key Result Area

		Dimensions			
Key Result Area	*Criteria of Performance*	*Cost*	*Time*	*Quantity*	*Quality*
Productivity	Output in standard man-hours per employee per annum		√	√	
Profitability	Return on investment	√	√	√	
Market position	Market share			√	
Personnel development	Ratio of number of employees fit for promotion to total number of employees in a particular trade			√	
Employee attitude	Positive attitude towards change and innovation				√

intangible. Tangible targets or standards are physical measures such as colour, hardness, quantitative measures (man-hours, machine hours, kilos of materials and so on), monetary values in terms of cost of operations, revenue such as sales, profits and programmes involving physical performance with respect to time. Intangible targets are performance standards not measurable in quantitative terms such as employee morale and motivation, peace and happiness. Table 7.1 illustrates a few criteria of performance along with the dimensions within the key areas as mentioned above.

7.1.1 Measurement of Actual Performance

Once the standard of performance has been established, it is necessary to measure actual performance against the standard. This needs to be done in an accurate, speedy and unbiased manner using the same relevant units as specified in the standards such as time taken, expenditure in rupees and output in standard man-hours. Measurement of performance may be through personal observations or reporting which may be either oral or written. Personal observation is one of the most prevalent methods of performance measurement, in which case the managers visit the shops, fields, offices and departments to gather first-hand information about the state of affairs and performance. However, this form of measurement is more suitable at the operational control level of management. Oral reporting about performance is in the form of interview, group discussion and meeting such as periodic production review meeting, finance liaison meeting, budget meeting and various unit level management committee meetings.

Both personal observation and oral reporting do not result in any permanent record of performance, except that in case of meetings, minutes are kept for record purpose. Increasingly, performance reporting is in written form due to use of computer-based IS for performance reporting. Written reports of performance measures provide permanent records and may take various forms such as narrative reports, statistical reports, graphical reports such as charts, summary and exception reports.

The last but not the least important step in the control process is correcting deviations if the actual performance deviates adversely from the standards. Methods and techniques for correcting deviations take the form of review of the original standards, modification of the same if needed, organizing, staffing and directing. All these actions are required to be taken by the control unit of any organization either to alter performance to adhere to the standards or to modify the standards as mentioned above.

7.2 Control of Physical Systems and Organizational Control

In case of physical systems including mechanical systems, control is in-built and is an integral part of the system design. Control in such cases is based on direct measurement of physical parameters such as temperature, speed and weight through sensors. Examples are the control systems for thermostats, engine governors, overload circuit breakers and so on.

In case of management and operation control systems of organizations, the need to monitor activities is not necessarily so apparent and the control systems are appropriately designed throughout the organization. Another important difference between the organizational control and mechanical control system is that the former is based on the use of appropriate information flow throughout the organization, whereas the latter is based on direct measurement of physical parameters. Managers in an organization mostly exercise control on the basis of information about the activities which take place in the organization, and hence designing formal ISs is of paramount importance for all levels of management and in particular for the operational and management control levels.

7.3 Types of Control Systems in an Organization

Control in an organization can be usually categorized into two groups, namely operating and management control. Operating control systems are simple, deterministic in nature and can be automated with the help of computers. Such systems hardly require management intervention and are based on routine information flows.

Management control systems, on the contrary, are complicated and attempt to control numerous factors including behavioural aspects and hence are mostly based on human control through managerial decision with the help of various information, formal and informal in nature.

However, before we analyse the details of ISs for the above types of organizational control, let me explain some salient features of control in subsequent paragraphs.

7.4 Closed- and Open-Loop Systems

The system of feedback described in the Miller and Starr model explained in an earlier chapter of this book is a closed-loop feedback system, where control is an integral part of the system and feedback based on output measurement is fed to the controller (manager) to make appropriate decisions to modify the inputs to the organizational system. Closed-loop systems are more appropriate for mechanical systems as well as operational control systems in organizations such as stock-control system. The stock-replenishment orders are dependent on the actual measurement of stock level and compare the same with the reordering level.

Open-loop systems, on the other hand, are those where no feedback loop exists, and control is external and not an integral part of the systems. Open-loop control systems are more suitable in organizations where the environmental factors are rather unpredictable and more adaptation is required. In such cases management intervention is necessary and open-loop control systems are adopted. For example, unpredicted factors such as emergence of a new competitor and liberalization of the import policy of the government need appropriate actions on the part of strategic planners through open-loop control.

Positive and negative feedback: Positive feedback causes a system to move in the same direction as the measured deviation. Negative feedback, on the contrary, dampens or reduces deviations from the standard. The corrective action in case of negative feedback is in the opposite direction of the observed deviation. Positive feedback is generally incorporated with open-loop control systems where managerial intervention is required to deal with changing environmental circumstances. Negative feedback, on the other hand, is mostly incorporated with operational and tactical levels of management to ensure that operations and activities conform to plans.

Examples: A company might diversify into four types of new businesses and plan equal amount of investment in each of the new businesses. However, after one year of investment, it was found that one of the new businesses was more profitable than the others, necessitating positive feedback for managerial intervention for enhanced investment on the profitable business as compared to the others.

Budgetary control involves negative feedback as, if the actual expenditure on any budget head exceeds the budgeted amount, then control is exercised to curtail expenditure.

Information equivalents: Any control system needs information regarding the tangible inputs to the system and the outputs from the system. Such information which represent the physical inputs and outputs are called the information equivalents.

These information equivalents, which may take various forms such as printouts, vouchers, fax messages and emails, provide the basic inputs to the ISs which facilitate control.

For example, information equivalents to physical inputs and outputs may be represented in case of a healthcare system as shown in Figure 7.1.

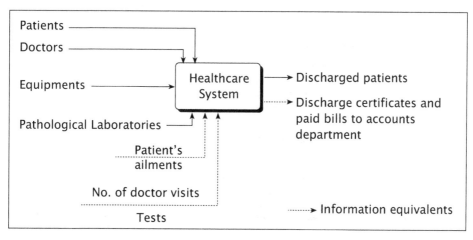

FIGURE 7.1 Information Equivalents for a Healthcare System

Single-loop and multi-loop feedback: A single-loop feedback is a simple feedback where the performance standards or plans are more or less fixed and the actual variations are relatively small in magnitude so that corrective actions can be taken without any difficulty to bring the actual output or performance in-line with the plan. Typical examples of single-loop feedback include inventory control, cost control, budgetary control and many other operational and tactical control systems.

The single-loop feedback control systems are very much suitable for computerization and automated decision-making.

The multi-loop feedback is primarily designed to ensure that the plans, performance standards and the operational and management control systems themselves are changed to suit the changes in environmental conditions for the very survival and growth of the organization. A double-loop feedback control for daily provisioning in a restaurant is shown in Figure 7.2. The multi-loop feedback is also necessary in organizations to synchronize the multiple activities, each of which may be controlled by a single loop feedback system. This is achieved through nesting of multiple control loops as shown in Figure 7.3.

The double and higher-order feedback systems are more common with the strategic management level which has to deal with environmental uncertainties relating to socio-economic and political change, the change in competitors' action, consumer behaviour and tastes, technological innovation and new legislation.

There are mainly three types of system control, namely feed forward, concurrent and feedback control.

Feed forward control, also known as preliminary or preventive control, aims at controlling the inputs to the system by anticipating the environmental disturbances and problems in advance to

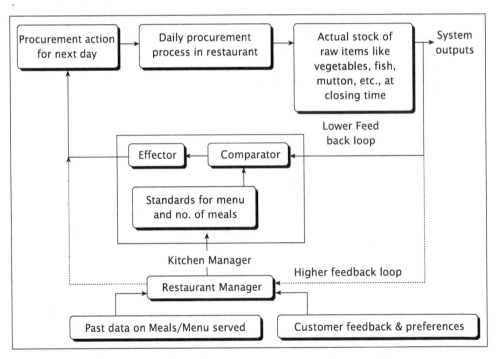

FIGURE 7.2 A Double Loop Feedback System for Restaurant Procurement

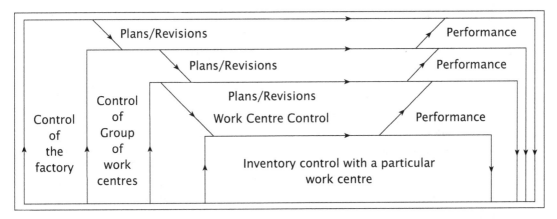

FIGURE 7.3 Nesting of Control Loops

prevent any deviation in the system output from the standard. Feedback control, on the contrary, monitors the output in terms of quantity and quality to detect any deviation from the standard and correct the same to adhere to the standard. Feedback control is therefore also called post-action or output control.

Concurrent control monitors the ongoing activities or processes and thereby ensures that the processes or activities being undertaken are consistent with the standards. Concurrent control concentrates on the ongoing processes to ensure that the same are under control. Statistical quality control and statistical process control are typical examples of concurrent control. The three types of control as described above are diagrammatically represented in Figure 7.4.

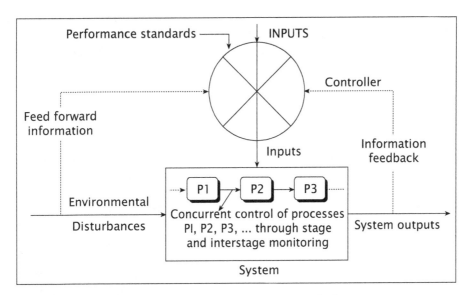

FIGURE 7.4 Feed Forward, Feedback and Concurrent Control of a System

Examples of the three types of controls:

1. **Feed forward control:** (a) Inspection of input materials at receipt stage to avoid rejections during processing, (b) training and selection of skilled manpower, (c) control of capital investment through financial risk management and (d) socio-economic and political disturbances are anticipated in advance to take corrective actions.
2. **Feedback control:** (a) Final inspection of an automobile in the assembly shop provides feedback to the production managers about the quality of the automobile components produced, (b) student result and feedback provide feedback control to improve teaching and (c) customer survey provides feedback to sales managers to control the after sales service and so on.
3. **Concurrent control:** (a) Total quality management adopting statistical process control and so on, (b) employees try to control themselves in order to adapt to the culture of the organization they belong to.

It may be noted that feed forward control requires a thorough knowledge about the behaviour of input variables to the system and their relationships both individually and jointly with the results (output). Only then it is possible to monitor and change the inputs in order to attain the desired output. However, in case of organizational control with environmental changes, it is not always possible to derive a precise relationship between the input variables and the output. Moreover, such a relationship changes with time and is dynamic in nature.

In any organization, it is unlikely to have only feed forward control. Control is exercised through both feed forward and feedback. Feed forward control is risky, whereas feedback control has got the inherent delay associated with the control action to correct any unfavourable deviation of the output from the standard set. In practical situations, organizational control is exercised through a combination of feed forward, concurrent control and feedback. Harold Koontz and Robert W. Bradspies (1972) illustrated the feed forward approach to cash budgeting as shown in Figure 7.5. In Figure 7.6, a typical feedback control system relating to operation and maintenance of a city passenger transport system has been shown. In order to cite an example of both feed forward and feedback control simultaneously, the training and development system for industrial employees in a manufacturing type of industry has been shown in Figure 7.7.

7.5 Information for Control

In the earlier sections of this chapter, we have seen control as a function of management consisting of three steps: (a) setting the standards of performance or the plans, (b) measuring the actual performance against the plans and (c) correcting deviations, if any, from the standards or plans. It is then obvious that relevant information are essentially required to set standards of performance or plans. Similarly, for controlling the actual performance, the same needs to be communicated to the controllers (managers at various levels in an organization) in the form of formal reports or informal feedback. The control information to be fed to managers vary depending upon the levels of the organization to which they belong to and the functional areas such as operations, personnel, finance, logistics and R&D. However, before we describe the IS for organizational control, mainly to facilitate operational control and

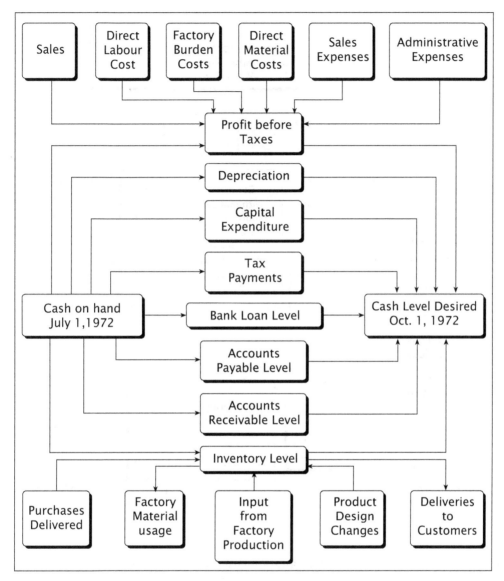

FIGURE 7.5 The Feed Forward Approach to Cash Budgeting

Source: Koontz and Robert (1972).

management control, certain important factors must be considered while designing a control system to make it successful. The factors are listed as follows:

1. Setting standards of performance or plans should be related to overall long-term objectives and growth of the organization.
2. Participation of all connected with the performance at any level in the organization needs to be ensured while setting the standards or plans.

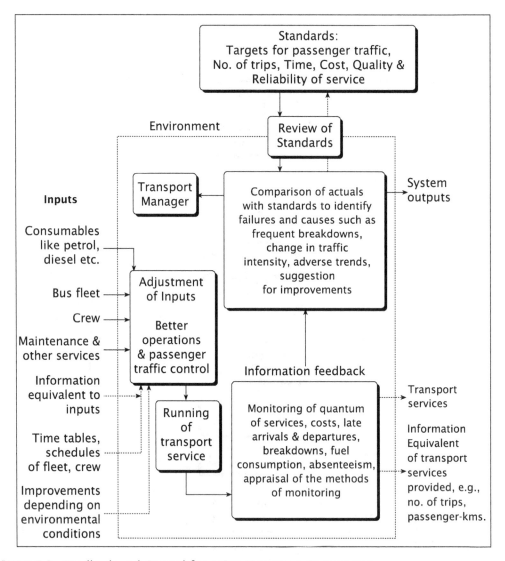

FIGURE 7.6 Feedback and Control for a City Transport Corporation

3. Each level of plans has to provide the standards of performance for the next lower level of operations.
4. The control system should be designed relating to the organizational structure.
5. The control system should facilitate decentralized decision-making to improve organizational efficiency.
6. The control system should consider both the quantitative performance levels and the behavioural factors described in the subsequent paragraphs.
7. The information to facilitate control should be timely, relevant and with proper aggregation to reduce information burden on managers.

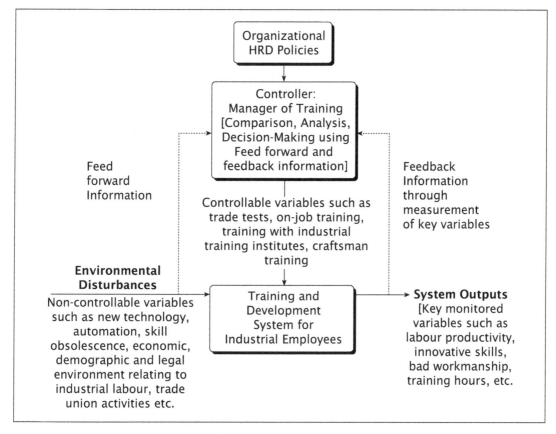

FIGURE 7.7 Feed Forward and Feedback in Training and Development System for Industrial Employees

8. Informal feedback through meetings, personal contacts and so on should be suitably incorporated in the control system to foster human contacts.
9. The control system should be designed to control performance at each level of the organization with adequate flexibility for freedom of operations at those levels, to encourage initiative and drive.

7.5.1 Operational Control

Operational control in an organization takes place at the operational level of the organization and is exercised to monitor and control the day-to-day operations. Monitoring and control at this level can be broadly divided into operational management, which is basically offline in nature, and online monitoring and control. Whereas the former is mostly model-based operational planning including optimization of the activities and processes, the latter is well structured and repetitive in nature with deterministic rules and pre-set standards for control of operations.

The online monitoring and control of operations in an organization can either be real time which is automatic closed-loop control of plants, machines or processes or may be programmed into a supervisory

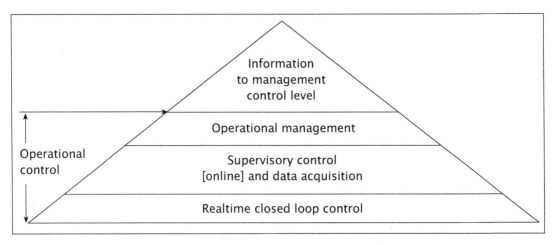

FIGURE 7.8 Information System Hierarchy for Operational Control in an Organization

control and data acquisition system with human operator intervention in alarm or emergency situation only through human–machine interface. Operational management is the function of technical and managerial personnel who are not directly involved with online monitoring and control of the IS hierarchy for operation control in an organization as shown in Figure 7.8.

A systematic and detailed study and analysis of the characteristics of the above-mentioned discrete functional levels for operational control reveal the traits as shown in Table 7.2.

TABLE 7.2 Discrete Functional Levels of Operational Control and Associated Traits

Discrete Functional Levels of Operational Control	Traits	
1. Real-time control (closed loop system)	1.	Data required are real time.
	2.	Closed loop control achieved through programmable logic controllers [PLCs]
	3.	Operations/process parameter are measured through sensors and fed to PLCs
	4.	Data validation through signal processing and noise elimination.
	5.	Data for control are mostly technical and internal to process/operations.
	6.	Control is stable and usually no human intervention.
	7.	Data for control are exact, reliable and consistent.
	8.	Suitable for continuous processes, for example, chemical processing, water treatment and so on.

Discrete Functional Levels of Operational Control	Traits
2. Supervisory control and data acquisition	1. Data for control are current and online.
	2. Data fed through transaction processing. This includes also recording of transactions, file maintenance, periodic generation of transaction summary and totals.
	3. Data validation through limits, abnormality checks and so on.
	4. Data may be monetary or non-monetary.
	5. There is need for human operator intervention in case of emergency or alarm situation through human-machine interface (HMI).
	6. Data acquisition and archiving is mostly through internal sources.
	7. Predetermined decision rules, procedures and standards.
	8. Scope is precise.
	9. Control is repetitive, stable and prescribed.
	10. Control can be linked to multiple processes, activities and work centres spread over a wide geographical area.
	11. Control is basically reactive in nature.
	12. Provides feedback to workers relating to their performance against targets, generates various control reports such as 'exception reports', 'scorecards' and so on regularly and also handles numerous enquiries from operational management.
3. Operational management system	1. Control is offline and proactive.
	2. Short-term current perspective is pre-dominant.
	3. It is often mathematical-model-based.
	4. Facilitated through decision support systems. Information needs are fulfilled through data archiving, analysis and reporting.
	5. Data validation is also manual and requires audit trails.
	6. Cost data are engineered.
	7. Operational planning and optimization are the essence of operational management.

7.5.2 Examples of Operational Control Systems

Typical examples of operational control systems as mentioned in preceding paragraph for business organizations based on functional divisions and further subdivisions of tasks are shown in Table 7.3.

TABLE 7.3 Operational Control Systems for Business Organizations

	Operational Control Systems		
Functions	Real Time [Closed Loop]	Online [SCADA]	Offline [OMS]
Production of goods and services.	Job/process control in nuclear reactor, chemical plant, refinery and so on.	Machine loading, predictive management, stock control, power transmission and distribution, traffic monitoring and control in a marshalling yard, quality management system.	Scheduling, supply-chain management, planning of transport and distribution of power and so on.
Sales and marketing.		Invoicing, packaging, customer order processing and so on.	CRM, planning after sales service, optimization of advertising budget and so on.
Human resource management		Electronic attendance recording system, payroll, security, safety	Optimum deployment of personnel, productivity analysis and reporting, safety and security planning and so on.
Financial management including accounting		Time booking, payroll accounting, computerized journal, ledger keeping, cost data tabulations and so on.	Cost variance reporting, credit control.

(**NB:** The list of functions as shown above is illustrative only and not exhaustive)

7.6 Management Control Systems

Management control systems are organizational systems which evaluate the performance of the organizational resources through pertinent information and thereby controls the behaviour of the organizational resources such as human, physical and financial to ensure that organizational strategies are achieved. Unlike operational control systems that deal with a limited number of factors, management control systems are more complex and deal with multiple control factors such as productivity, human resource development, employee morale and attitude, market share, ROI, innovation, corporate social responsibility, and short- and long-term goal congruence.

The multiple control factors include performance levels in quantitative terms as well as behavioural factors such as leadership, employee involvement and motivation, team spirit, cooperation among employees, employee aspirations and satisfaction. These behavioural factors need to be controlled by the managers at the management control level to ensure that employees work towards achieving the organizational objectives.

Management control has a broader function than merely monitoring performance to adhere to the original plan or target. In many cases, the management control system facilitates review of plans set for the operational control level though higher-level feedback. Management control systems must consider both long-term and short-term objectives to be an effective control system. For example, human resource development, total productive maintenance, modernization, research and development are long term in nature, whereas profitability is a short-term factor. However, if a manager concentrates on profitability only the long-term factors as mentioned above might be ignored.

Robert N. Anthony (2007) defined management control as the process by which managers influence other members of the organization to implement the organization's strategies.

According to Horngreen et al. (2005), management control system is an integrated technique for collecting and using information to motivate employee behaviour and to evaluate their performance.

7.6.1 Management Control Systems Are Interdisciplinary

According to Maciariello et al. (1994), management control is concerned with coordination, resource allocation, motivation and performance measurement. It is obvious that the practice of management control and design of management control systems are therefore based on disciplines such as management accounting for performance measurement, managerial economics and operations research for resource allocation, organizational behaviour studies for motivation, effective communication and coordination. This interdisciplinary approach to management control system design has been shown in Figure 7.9.

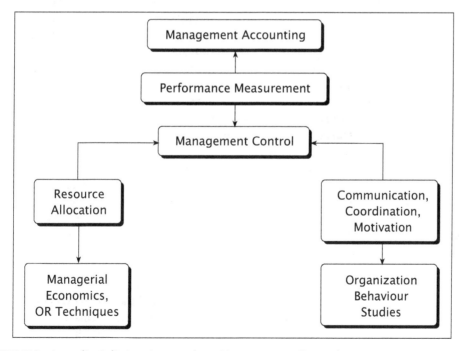

FIGURE 7.9 Interdisciplinary Approach to Management Control

7.6.2 Functional Categorization of a Management Control System

Like any other system, a management control system has certain characteristics such as realistic standards or plans, performance measurement system, comparison of actual performance with the standards, variance analysis if any and a reporting system meant for the concerned authorities for appropriate and timely corrective actions, which may necessitate alteration of predetermined standards.

These functional criteria are achieved through organizing, planning and budgeting, accounting, variance analysis and revision/adjustments. Organizing involves the work breakdown and allocation of responsibilities based thereupon through functional lines. Besides, two other important factors of organizing which have significant influence on the effectiveness of the management control system are the structure and culture of the organization. The organization structure determines the various positions of managers at decision-making levels and their relationships. The structure depends on the type of work, the process or technology adopted, competitive edge and similar uncontrollable external factors. The organization's culture which also affects the effective functioning of a management control system is the set of beliefs, values, norms and ethics shared by the people in the organization such as the belief for many organizations that quality is the most important factor for customer satisfaction.

7.6.3 Performance Measurement Systems

Performance measurement is an essential function of management control. It facilitates dual role. The first role is output control or results control in which specific outcomes are measured and compared with the expectations, and variations are corrected through administrative controls or actions that involve formal rules, procedures and handbooks. The measurement of results will also lead to rewards for satisfactory performance. The second role of performance management involves behaviour controls, which direct the behaviour of use of physical, financial and human resources in order to achieve the strategic objective of an enterprise.

Various performance measurement systems evolved time to time starting with the traditional standard costing system of measurement. However, there were chronological improvements in the performance measurement systems to cater to the new and world class technology and management methods such as just-in-time, lean and six sigma. It was also felt that apart from measurement of financial parameters, non-financial parameters such as customer delight, market share, internal business processes and innovation were also important to meet the financial and other strategic objectives of an enterprise. It was further observed that the performance measurement system and the measurement parameters thereof need to take care of profit, not-for-profit, service and manufacturing types of organizations. It was also observed that performance measurement systems for large organizations may not suit the small organizations such as a proprietary or partnership firm.

Lynch and Cross (1991) first developed a new approach to performance management—the 'BSC'. The emphasis of this BSC was on integrating financial and non-financial measurements.

Thereafter, by the early 1990s, Kaplan and Norton (1992) introduced the popular version of BSC. In their approach, Kaplan and Norton linked performance measurements to strategy management in a 'top-down' model of measurement and control. During this time, need was also felt for a 'bottom-up' methodology by experts such as Lynch, Cross and others, wherein the objective was to measure performance relating to operational level to reflect the strategy.

Both the 'top-down' or 'bottom-up' approaches to development of performance measurement systems have several drawbacks as mentioned below:

1. They do not create value in their metrics system. For while customer perspective is important in BSC, direct measure of the company's performance in the eye of the customer was not incorporated.
2. Causal interrelations among the classical perspectives of learning and growth, internal processes, customers and finance do not or may not necessarily exist under all circumstances.
3. Environmental, social and other external groups such as competitors are not considered.
4. The models often prove to be misfit for small and service type organizations.
5. The models do not show linkages with other key performance measurement concepts, such as CSFs and KPIs.
6. The models did not explicitly tie in performance rewards to the overall measurement model.

A chronology of performance measurement models with a brief description of the models has been shown in Table 7.4. It may be noted that in the chronology of the development as shown in the table, there is a change in focus from performance management and control to strategic management. This strategic development of the BSC of Kaplan and Norton in 1992 was made possible by introducing the lead and lag indicators which provided the two directional cause-and-effect chains. The lead indicators are the 'performance drivers' which lead to be on track to achieve the strategic goals, whereas the lag indicators are 'outcome measures'. Lead indicators without lag indicators may focus on short-term performance of the enterprise but will not be able to confirm that long-term objectives will be achieved. For example, 'on-time delivery' is a lead indicator for the outcome of customer satisfaction which can be measured by the lag indicator of reducing number of 'customer complaints'. The ultimate purpose of selecting performance metrics is to enable management to track performance towards goals.

TABLE 7.4 A Chronology of Performance Measurement Models

Authors and Models	*Description*
Epstein and Manzoni (1997) Bourguignon et al. (2004) Pezet (2009) The *tableau de bord*	The concept of the *tableau de bord* has been in use, in some way or other, since the late 19th century. However, it was not until the 1950s that it was formalized as a tool in the service of corporate management. The various Tableau de Bord are not limited to financial indicators but are developed in the context of the mission and objectives of each unit. This involves translating the vision and mission of the unit into a set of objectives from which key success factors are identified and then transformed into a series of quantitative key performance indicators.
Keegan et al. (1989) The performance measurement matrix	The performance measurement matrix categorizes measurement as being 'cost' or 'non-cost' and 'internal' or 'external'. Key to the model is the use of the key metric approach and the 'determine and decompose' method. This involves decomposing departments into functional equivalents and assessing how the departments support the business.

Authors and Models	Description
Lynch and Cross (1991) The strategic measurement and reporting technique (SMART) pyramid	This also supported the need to include internally and externally focused measures of performance and added the notion of cascading measures down the organization so that measures at department and work centre level reflect the corporate vision as well as internal and external business objectives.
Fitzgeral et al. (1991) The results and determinants framework	This model classified measures into two basic types: those relating to results (competitiveness, financial performance) and those that focus on the determinants of those results (quality, flexibility, resource utilization and innovation). A particular strength of the results-determinants framework is that it reflects the concept of causality.
Kaplan and Norton (1992) The balanced scorecard	The balanced scorecard reflects many of the attributes of other measurement frameworks but links measurement to the organization's vision. It grew out of the realization that no single performance indicator can capture the full complexity of an organization's performance. The balanced scorecard translates the vision of a business into objectives and performance measures in four perspectives: financial, customer, internal business process, learning and growth.
Brown (1996) The input–process–output–outcome framework	This macro process model links the five stages of a business process and the measures of their performances.

7.6.4 The Performance Wheel

The different performance measurement models mentioned in Table 7.4 can be reduced to one overarching model known as 'the performance wheel' developed by Watts and McNair (2012). The performance wheel incorporates and addresses the identified weakness of previous models such as 'top-down' or 'bottom-up' orientation, linking of performance metrics with CSFs, KPIs and value creation. Moreover, the performance wheel can be adapted to large organizations of various types such as service, not-for-profit, profit and manufacturing. The performance wheel laid out straight and as shown in Figure 7.10 adds value to the CSFs and creates a linkage to the external stakeholders performance wheel. The performance wheel is subdivided into three sub-groups: (a) those controlled by top management, (b) those under the purview of the middle management and (c) those which only operational managers, supervisors and other operational control level of employees can alter. These three divisions coincide with strategic objectives, CSFs and KPIs.

7.6.5 The Performance Wheel in Case of Not-for-profit Organizations

The applicability of the performance wheel in case of a service organization has been shown in Figure 7.11 for the vehicle licence authority of a state government, known as the Regional Transport Authority. It differs clearly, in that the work it performs takes place in the public domain and is service based. Its primary

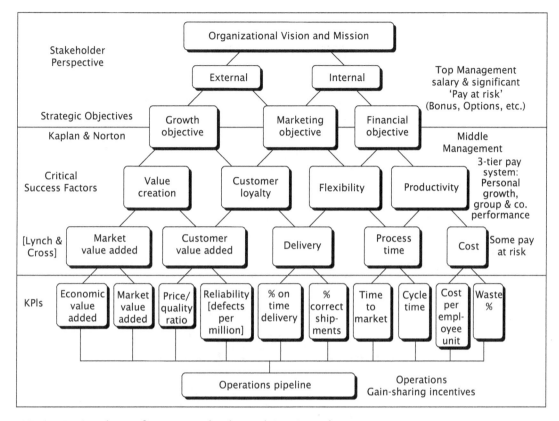

FIGURE 7.10 The Performance Wheel—Laid Out Straight

objective is to attain a high level of service delivery and also to control hazards due to vehicle emission, breakdowns and accidents on roads. Whereas a manufacturing company might focus on productivity and efficiency for profit maximization, the primary goal of the vehicle inspectorate is effective and efficient service to reduce accidents.

7.6.6 The Small Business Performance Pyramid

The small manufacturing and service organizations present different challenges—to simplify the model and to keep the integral nature of the model intact. The performance wheel can be modified for small business organizations to form the small business performance pyramid as shown in Figure 7.12. It can be seen from Figure 7.12 that the middle of the flattened version of the performance wheel (Figure 7.10) has been removed reflecting the fact that middle management is non-existent in small business. The key factors to the survival and growth of a small business are sustainability, productivity and liquidity.

These three dimensions are then expanded to a set of operational measures that allow the small business owner to plan for and control the operational pipeline that connects the small business to the customer. It may be observed that the KPIs for small business also capture information relating to

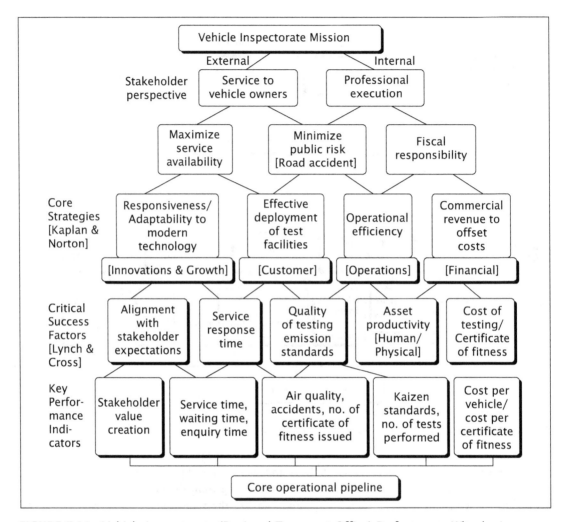

FIGURE 7.11 Vehicle Inspectorate (Regional Transport Office) Performance Wheel—An Integrated View

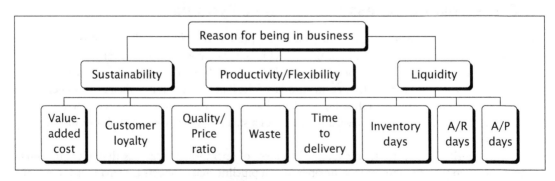

FIGURE 7.12 The Small Business Performance Pyramid

customer satisfaction and thereby customer loyalty because the customer is never far away from the operational control level. Therefore, in small business, value is always created for the customer from the bottom up.

7.7 Behavioural Aspects of Management Control

One of the aims of an effective management control system is to motivate the managers to be effective and efficient in attaining the organizational goals. The behavioural aspects of management control are important factors to motivate the managers. For example, while setting the standards of performance or plans of an organization, the managers who will be required to meet the plans need to be involved in the process. They will, in that case, be encouraged to see that the standards of performance or plans set by them are fulfilled. Further, performance standards should be set by managers with input from employees whose performance is measured.

A fiscal budget process can be either 'top-down', in which case senior managers set the budget for the lower levels, or 'bottom-up' wherein the lower level managers set the budget amounts. The top-down approach hardly works because of lack of commitment on the part of lower level managers. The bottom-up approach of budgeting, although encourages budgeters to meet the budget in their respective areas of responsibility, may not match the corporate objectives unless carefully controlled. Therefore, actually an effective budget process blends the two approaches as mentioned above.

Management control originates from the individuals, and therefore the successful operation of a management control system requires the study of the social and psychological characteristics of the people involved and their attitude and aspiration.

Every individual employee in an organization has individual goals as well as his/her contribution towards organizational goals. Behavioural aspect of management control demands that the actual performance results of the employees and rewards for the same should be such as to orient individual expectations/goals towards the organizational goals. According to Horngreen et al. (2005) management control system is an integrated technique for collecting and using information to motivate employee behaviour and to evaluate performance. A formal IS partially represents the management control process. For example, a formal production achievement report would contain nothing about the bargaining, negotiations, conflicts, direct and indirect workers involved with the production in the shop floor. A manager's control behaviour is influenced, by numerous factors and interactions as shown in Figure 7.13.

7.7.1 Avoiding Behavioural Problems in Management Control

Managers exercise control for effective and efficient utilization of organizational resources and need information for the same. The nature of information or reports varies depending on the individual characteristics and styles of control of the managers. There cannot be any uniform standardized system of reporting and control. Control systems which are designed and operated without considering the behavioural factors can produce various adverse effects such as reduction of overall organizational efficiency, lack of goal congruence between short-term and long-term goals and formation of unreliable and informal information and control systems within the organization.

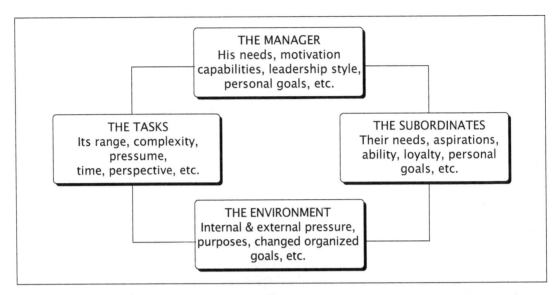

FIGURE 7.13   Influences on the Manager's Control Behaviour

Source: Lucey (2017).

Some of the measures which can be adopted to avoid such behavioural problems are as follows:

1. Managers should encourage participation of all concerned employees in the process of design of the control system.
2. Control reports should be designed to suit the individual needs and capabilities of the manager who will use the reports.
3. Reduce the information load on managers by way of proper design of reports, exception reporting and executive summary.
4. Improve the level of contacts and interaction among employees through committee meetings and the like.

7.8 Management Control for Sustainability

The performance measurement systems for management control such as the Kaplan and Norton's BSC basically link operational and non-financial corporate activities with the firms' long-term strategy through causal chains. In other words, the BSC takes into account the non-financial strategic perspectives such as customer, internal business process, learning and growth which have got significant effect on the financial prosperity of the business. Since, as of today, organizations have to deal with environmental and social aspects of the business also, it is appropriate to incorporate those aspects into the management control system of the firms or business enterprises. This can be facilitated suitably by integrating the three pillars of sustainability, namely economic, social and environment performance of firms into a single and overarching performance management system. Conceptually, value-based sustainability management seeks to address the issue of contribution of firms towards sustainability. Figge et al. (2002) mentioned about 'sustainability BSC' as a tool for value-based sustainability management. They have mentioned about three different approaches of integrating the environment and social aspects into the BSC of a firm. The first approach is to integrate the social and environmental aspects into the four standard perspectives. This means that environmental and social aspects are integrated into the four perspectives through respective strategic core elements or performance drivers for which lagging and leading indicators as well as target and measures are formulated. For instance, in the customer perspective, a firm may include in the lagging indicator of 'market share' a dimension for environment-friendly products. Similarly, the leading indicator 'product features' could have an environment dimension of 'recycling of the waste'.

The second approach is the introduction of an additional non-market perspective into the BSC to take care of the social and environmental aspects. The rationale behind this approach is that environmental and social aspects as social constructs can become strategically relevant for firms through mechanisms other than the market exchange process, such as sociocultural, legal and regulatory spheres. The necessity for an additional non-market perspective arises when environmental or social aspects significantly affect a firm's performance or success in all four perspectives of the conventional BSC and at the same time such aspects cannot be included within the same four standard perspectives due to their strategic relevance.

The third approach to integrating sustainability into the BSC is the deduction of an environmental and/or social scorecard derived as an extension to the two variants of BSC described in the earlier paragraphs.

The possibility of such a derived scorecard is of particular interest to environmental and/or social management departments which are mainly concerned with cross-sectional and coordinative management tasks. The choice of the particular approach for integrating the strategically relevant environmental and social aspects with the core BSC during the process of formulating sustainability BSC has to be taken during the process itself. Figure 7.14 illustrates the strategy map of a typical chemical plant for a sustainability BSC. It may be seen that while some of the strategic environment and social aspects such as import content in the end products have been incorporated into the conventional internal process and customer perspectives, aspects such as adult and skilled workers have been shown in the non-market perspective.

7.9 Techniques for Management Control

Management control system uses many techniques for effective and efficient utilization of organizational resources such as:

1. Activity-based costing (ABC)
2. BSC
3. Budgeting
4. Capital budgeting
5. Just-in-time (JIT)
6. Kaizen
7. Kanban
8. Target costing
9. Programme-management techniques
10. Total quality management (TQM)
11. Total productive maintenance (TPM) and many other techniques.

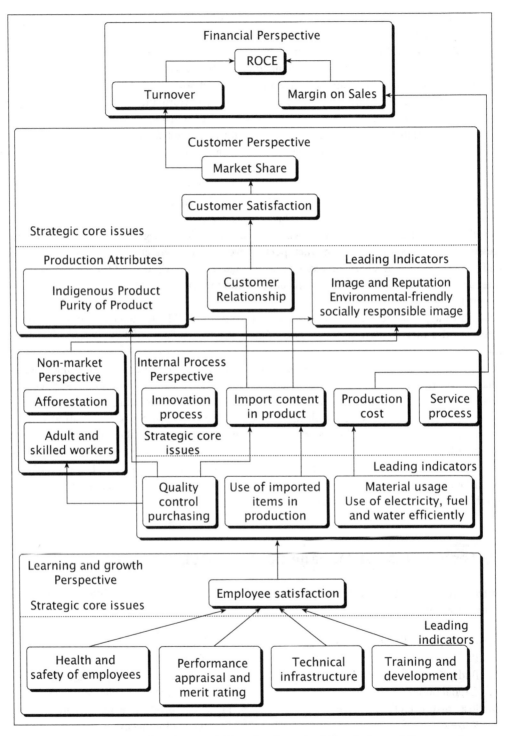

FIGURE 7.14 Strategy Map of a Chemical Plant for Sustainability Balanced Scorecard

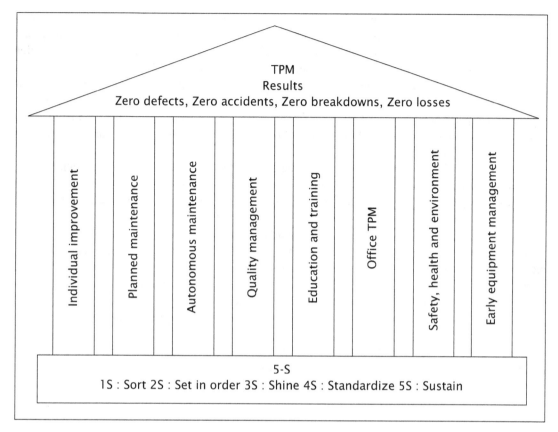

FIGURE 7.15 The Traditional TPM Model

Advanced manufacturing technology (AMT) and JIT systems have TPM in which zero defects, zero accidents, zero breakdowns and zero losses are the acceptable levels of quality, safety, reliability and resource utilization. These levels of organizational performance can be achieved through the eight pillars of TPM as shown in Figure 7.15.

The eight pillars are built on the foundation of the Japanese concept of 5S. The goal of 5S is to create a clean and organized work environment necessary for implementing TPM through the eight pillars.

The first pillar of TPM is the individual improvement (*kobetsu kaizen* in Japanese) to create an engine for continuous improvement by employees either individually or in small groups for overall equipment efficiency and productivity through elimination of all types of losses such as failure losses and defect losses. Continuous improvement also leads to identification of and solution of chronic problems existing in the workplace.

The second pillar of TPM refers to planned maintenance, which includes scheduled maintenance activities such as time-based and condition-based maintenance, control of replacement of parts, failure analysis and preventive measures and lubrication control. The purpose of this pillar is significant reduction of unplanned downtime and control of spare parts leading to improvement of overall efficiency of the maintenance department.

The third pillar of TPM is autonomous maintenance (*jishu hozen* in Japanese), which is meant for assigning the responsibility for routine maintenance of equipment such as cleaning, lubricating and inspection by the respective operators themselves. This pillar requires prior training of operators for gaining proficiency in the operation of the equipment. Autonomous maintenance involves seven steps: initial clean up, countermeasures against contamination or ingress of dirts, creation of standards of autonomous maintenance, general inspection, autonomous inspection, standardization and all-out goals management.

The fourth pillar of TPM is quality management. The main idea behind this pillar is to apply root cause analysis for quality defects and their elimination. The ultimate objective is to achieve zero defects in products.

The fifth pillar of TPM is early equipment management. The purpose of this pillar is to facilitate faster equipment development and to reduce the prototyping time. Because of early equipment management, operators gain practical knowledge and understanding of the operations of the equipment prior to installation thereby leading to easy maintenance of the equipment.

The sixth pillar of TPM, namely the education and training pillar, deals with introducing technical education for operators, maintenance personnel and managers so that operators can maintain equipment regularly and identify troubleshooting. Maintenance personnel can perform preventive maintenance and managers get acquainted with TPM principles as well as with employee training and development.

The seventh pillar of TPM is office TPM to create efficient offices to provide supporting service to production departments. Office TPM facilitates elimination of wastes in administrative operations such as order processing, procurement and scheduling.

The eighth pillar of TPM is the safety, health and environment pillar which serves the purpose of creating a healthy, safe and environment friendly working environment to achieve an accident-free workplace with healthy and motivated employees.

CASE STUDY: THE CITY OF CHARLOTTE— A BSC SUCCESS STORY

History and Background

The city of Charlotte, North Carolina, USA, implemented BSC in 1996 and is considered by many people as the best example of successful implementation of BSC in a public sector and not-for-profit organization. The BSC has paid substantial returns to the city of Charlotte's efforts towards performance management efforts.

Prior to the implementation of BSC by the then city manager, Mr Pam Syfert, top management echelon was practising Management by Objectives (MBO). However, the city mayor and Council of Charlotte were very much interested and also looking for a new measurement and reporting system on their strategy which they thought would facilitate improved decision-making.

Initially Mr Pam Syfert and three other key implementers had to make the following changes to the typical Kaplan and Norton model of the BSC for the private sector enterprises to suit the needs of the city of Charlotte, a public sector organization:

1. The first change was to place the customer perspective on the top of the other perspectives. This change was necessary as the key implementers felt that being a public sector organization

catering to the services for the citizens, who are also taxpayers, it is of utmost importance for the city of Charlotte to meet the needs of citizens who are the customers for them.

2. The perspectives were renamed to be consistent with the terminologies internally used by them. The word 'internal processes' was replaced with the word 'running the business'. The word 'customer' was changed as 'serve the customer'. Similarly, 'financial perspective' was renamed as 'manage resources'. The term of 'employee learning and growth' perspective was changed to a new terminology 'develop employees'.

3. The implementers of the BSC for the city of Charlotte retained the terms objective, measure, target and initiative in consistence with the model of scorecard framed by Kaplan and Norton. However, they expanded measures into four types, namely activity measures, input measures, output measures and outcome measures.

Employee training and development was accorded very high priority all along the implementation phase. For the same purpose, handbooks, newsletters, glossaries of terms and scorecard training sessions were frequently utilized.

A top level 'corporate scorecard' was constructed for the city first followed by development of scorecards for five focus areas of community safety, communities within the city, transportation, economic development and restructuring government. Each of the focus areas has a cross-functional team which meets regularly to identify strategic initiatives and measures for achieving overall vision of the focus areas. The scorecard was cascaded to all key business units (KBUs) throughout the city. Each KBU with its cascaded scorecards identifies the resources required to achieve the BSC objectives. A sample of Charlotte's corporate-level scorecard measures has been shown as follows:

Perspective	Objective	Sample Measure	Target
Serve the customer	Strengthen neighbourhoods	Number of stable neighbourhoods as measured by the Quality of Life index	102 stable neighbourhoods
Run the business	Develop collaborative solutions	Percentage of strategic transportation and land use projects utilizing integrated land use and transportation planning	100%
Manage resources	Expand tax base and revenue	Percentage change in tax valuation in targeted neighbourhoods	10% increase in tax valuation
Develop employees	Recruit and retain skilled and diverse workforce	Percentage increase in city average turnover rate	5% increase in turnover

Resultant Benefits Achieved by the City of Charlotte

Many benefits accrued to the city of Charlotte consequent upon implementation of the BSC as mentioned above. Some of the major benefits are as follows:

1. Before the BSC, the city had to monitor more than 900 performance measures which dropped down to a more manageable 375 measures spread across 14 KBUs after the launching of the BSC.

2. Awareness and understanding of strategy increased significantly among the employees. Almost 70% of the employees reported that they understood the goals of their respective business units.

3. Linkage between budget and strategy was established.
4. Improvement in the process of management decision-making was made.
5. The BSC enabled the city of Charlotte to report outcomes to the communities and citizens of Charlotte, the taxpayers.

Source: Niven (2003).

Review Questions

1. What are the basic steps of a control process?

2. What is the difference between control of a physical system and an organization?

3. What is feedback with reference to a control system? How is it different from feed forward?

4. Why is information important for management control?

5. What are single and double-loop feedback?

6. What is an open-loop feedback system? How is it different from closed-loop feedback system? Illustrate both with suitable examples.

7. What is positive feedback? What is negative feedback?

8. What are the basic differences between operational and managerial control?

9. What is real-time control of a system? Illustrate.

10. What is the meaning of control in management control?

11. Why are behavioural aspects important in management control? How can behavioural problems be avoided in management control?

12. What are the roles of a 'performance measurement system' in management control?

13. What are 'top-down' and 'bottom-up' approaches to development of performance measurement systems?

14. What are the important perspectives of a BSC? What do you understand by 'leading' and 'lagging' indicators of a BSC?

15. What is the drawback of a BSC?

16. What is a 'performance wheel'? Illustrate how it overcomes the drawbacks of other performance measurement models.

17. What is a 'performance pyramid'? What is its applicability?

18. What is a 'sustainability BSC'? What are the different approaches of formulating the same?

19. What is TPM? What are its objectives?

20. What are the pillars of TPM? Explain how TPM facilitates management control.

Bibliography

Anthony, R. N., and V. Govindarajan. *Management Control Systems*, 12th ed. Boston, MA: McGraw-Hill Irwin, 2007.

Figge, F., T. Hahn, S. Schaltegger, and M. Wagner. 'Development of a Sustainability Balanced Scorecard: Translating Strategy into Value-based Sustainability Management.' *Journal of the Asia Pacific Centre for Environmental Accountability* 8, no. 1 (2002): 269–284.

Fitzerald, L., R. Johnson, and S. Brignall. *Performance Measurement in Service Business*. London: CIMA, 1991.

Horngreen, C. T., A. Bhimani, S. M. Datar, and G. Foster. *Management and Cost Accounting*, 3rd ed. Harlow: Pearson, 2005.

Johnson, I. M. 'Information System Architecture for Operational Management and Control.' *Journal of Computing and Information Technology* 1, no. 4 (1993): 265–272.

Kaplan, R. S., and D. P. Norton. 'The Balanced Scorecard: Measures That Drive Performance.' *Harvard Business Review* 70, no. 1 (1992): 71–79.

Koontz, H., and R. W. Bradspies. 'Managing through Feed Forward Control.' *Business Horizons* 15, no. 3 (1972): 25–36.

Lucey, T. *Management Information Systems*, 8th ed., 13. New Delhi: BPB Publication, 2017.

Lynch, R., and Cross K. F. *Measure up! Yardstick for Continuous Improvement*, 1st ed. USA: Blackwell, 1991.

Niven, Paul R. *Balanced Scorecard Step-by-step for Government and Non-profit Agencies*, 271–285. Hoboken, NJ: John Wiley & Sons, 2003.

System Analysis

8.1 Characteristics of a System

A system is characterized by plurality of parts, which along with their properties define the structure of a system. Systems in the context of business or ISs have specific inputs, processing and outputs of material, energy and/or information. The parts of a system interact with each other and are interdependent in order to attain the common goal and synergy of the system. A system is also characterized by its boundary which isolates the parts of the system from the surrounding environment.

8.2 Classification of Systems

8.2.1 Physical or Abstract Systems

Physical systems are tangible, whereas abstract systems are conceptual in nature and not physical entities. Computer systems, automobiles, human beings, organizations and so on are examples of physical systems. Abstract systems can be mathematical models representing a real-life system, ethics and value systems and so on.

8.2.2 Open or Closed Systems

Open systems interact with their environment to achieve their goals. Obviously, open systems need to be dynamic in nature to cope with the changing environment. Mostly, all practical systems are open systems and have interfaces with the environment to receive input from the environment and to deliver output to the environment. A business enterprise is an open system. Closed systems are those systems which do not interact with their environment. A closed system does not exist in reality and is only a concept.

8.2.3 Static or Dynamic Systems

The parts of a static system usually do not change their properties with respect to time. A classroom, for example, consists of static parts such as tables, chairs and blackboards. ISs are dynamic in nature since data, information, reports and applications can change according to the users' needs.

8.2.4 Formal or Informal ISs

Formal ISs deal with the flow of information within an organization in the form of written reports, instructions, procedure manuals, electronic mails, text messages and formal minutes of meetings. The channels of information flow are predefined and usually routine in nature.

Informal ISs are employee based and non-routine in nature. Hearsay, gossips, rumours and personal contacts constitute informal channels of informal flow within an organization.

8.2.5 Analogue or Digital Systems

Analogue systems are physical systems which receive inputs from their environment in the form of physical parameters or signals such as pressure, temperature, length, humidity and density. Digital systems are also physical systems which receive inputs through numbers or characters (bits). A digital computer used for business data processing is an example of a digital system.

8.2.6 Real-time or Delayed Systems

Both real-time and delayed systems function on feedback control principle. However, they differ in the response time of the system to adjust itself to any environmental change before any adverse impact due to such change occurs. Real-time systems are those systems which can react to any environmental disturbance or change and adjust the system functioning before any adverse impact takes place on the system due to such environmental change. For example, an airline reservation system is a real-time system since any particular request for seat booking instantly disables the entire reservation system from taking any further booking request momentarily in order to avoid double booking of seats. Real-time systems are early warning systems and are usually operation control systems. Delayed systems, on the other hand, take corrective actions only after environmental changes affect the systems.

8.3 System Analysis

System analysis is a method of problem solving that disintegrates a system into its constituent parts for the purpose of studying how well those parts function individually and interact with each other to accomplish the common goal and synergy of the system. The analysis involves critical examination of the existing system and improvements thereof by addition, modification and/or deletion of system parts, if considered, necessary to meet the requirements of the system from the users' point of view.

8.3.1 ISs Analysis

ISs analysis mainly focuses on business objectives, business problems and requirements of information for managers at all levels in order to implement a solution to the problems. A systematic study and analysis of the information requirements of managers and the resources they handle is essentially needed to find solutions to many business problems. The various methods of identifying information needs of managers have been mentioned in subsequent paragraphs of this chapter.

8.4 Model-based Approach to Problem Analysis

The approach to problem solving lays emphasis on the drawing of system models in pictorial form to document and validate both the existing and the proposed systems. The proposed system model forms the blueprint of developing an improved system. There are many model-driven approaches to problem analysis. A few important ones out of those have been described in the following paragraphs.

8.4.1 Structured Analysis

The structured analysis method is based on function-based decomposition while modelling a problem. It focuses on the flow of data through the various functions or processes in the problem domain which converts input data into processed output data. The output of a process may again form input to other processes in the domain. The model so developed through structured analysis is called data flow diagram (DFD) and its associated data dictionary. DFD is effectively used for the study and analysis of a system. It treats a system as a function or process (called a bubble) which transforms input into desired output.

This transformation will not be performed in a single step, but data will undergo transformations through a series of processes (or bubbles) within the system. A DFD shows the flow of data through different transformation processes in a system. The processes are represented by circles with appropriate names within them, and data flows are shown by named arrows entering (inputs) or leaving (outputs) the bubbles. A rectangle in a DFD represents a source (originator) or a sink (consumer) of data. Figure 8.1 shows a DFD for an indoor patient billing system that produces bills for medical services availed of by indoor patients in a nursing home.

In this DFD, there are four basic input data flows: the daily occupancy list originating from the patients, daily test/clinical procedures list emanating from laboratories, daily medicine bills generated from pharmacy and doctors' bills raised by the attending doctors. The basic output is net bill payable, the sink for which is the patient party. In this system, patient record is retrieved using patient ID which links it with the patient occupancy register. The daily rates for beds in wards as well as in intensive care units (ICU) are obtained from the patient record. It may be stated that the daily occupancy rate for a bed in a ward or in an ICU is not the same for all patients and may vary depending upon male, female, child, company sponsored, senior citizens and patients availing of cashless facilities offered by health insurance companies. These rates together with the days in bed and days in ICU (obtained from patient occupancy register) are used to compute total nursing home accommodation charges. After the bed/ICU charges are determined, the charges for in-house laboratory tests and clinical procedures are added to the same

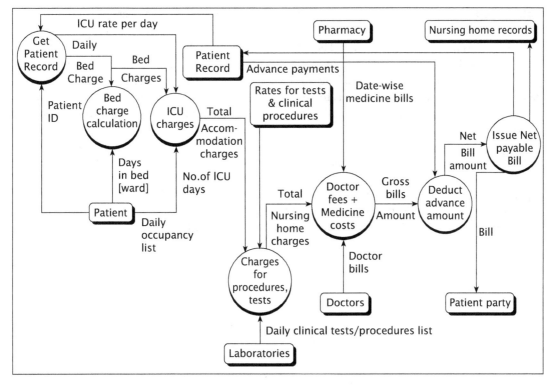

FIGURE 8.1 Data Flow Diagram for Indoor Patient Billing System

to arrive at the total nursing home charges. Next, the visiting doctors' fees for attending to the patient and also the costs of medicines supplied to the patient by the pharmacy are calculated based on bills raised by doctors for visits on different dates and the bills sent by the pharmacy for the patient linked through the patient name and ID number respectively. The charges for these two services are added to the total nursing home charges to arrive at the gross bill amount. Next, any advance amount paid by the patient at the time of admission in the nursing home is deducted from the gross bill amount to arrive at the net amount payable by the patient for indoor treatment in the nursing home and the bill is presented to the patient party for payment. The net amount billed to the patient is also recorded in the records of both the patient and the nursing home.

The DFD shown in Figure 8.1 is an abstract representation of the indoor patient billing system of a nursing home irrespective of whether the system is a manual or a computer-based one. The DFD can also be refined to indicate further details, minor data paths, error checks and report generation. For example, detection of discrepancies if any in the patient occupancy register such as more than one patient shown occupying the same bed and occupancy by a patient even after discharge have not been shown in the DFD. Similarly, checks can be introduced in the system to avoid over billing.

It may be pointed out that a DFD shows only the flow of input data into a process and the corresponding output of the process. It does not however show the procedure or how the input data are converted into the output within the process. A DFD is also different from a flow chart. Flow chart shows the flow of control whereas DFD shows the flow of data only.

Data dictionary: In a DFD, data flows are shown by named arrows. The names are so chosen that they convey some idea about the data and uniquely identify the data flow. However, the precise structure of the data flow is not shown in the DFD. The structure of each data flow in a DFD is shown in the data dictionary which is a collection of descriptions of all data flows in the DFD. Data dictionary thus helps programmers, system analysts and others who need to refer to those data descriptions. The data dictionary also specifies the components in the structure of data flows and the structures of files shown in the DFD. The data dictionary pertaining to data flows relating to indoor patient billing has been shown as follows:

```
Daily occupancy list = Patient_ID + Patient_name + (Ward_Bed_
number|ICU_bed_number)
Daily_bed_charge = Patient_ID + ₹_amount
ICU_rate_perday = Patient_ID + ₹_amount
Daily_tests_clinical_procedures = Patient_ID + {(test_code + test_name) |
                                  [procedure_code + procedure name)}*
Doctor_bills = Patient_ID + Patient_name + (Doctor_name + Date + No_of_
               visits + Total_ Fees)*
Daily_medicine_bills = Patient_ID + Patient_name + (Medicine_name +
price + quantity)*
Patient_ID = digit + digit + digit
Patient_name = (MR/MS) + Lastname + Firstname + Middlename
test_code = digit + digit + digit
test_name = characters(50)
procedure_code = digit + digit
procedure_name = characters(50)
Date = mm/dd/yyyy
Price = unit + Rupees_amount
Doctor_name = Lastname + First name + Middle name
Medicine_name = characters(50)
```

In the above data dictionary, the symbol '+' has been used to denote concatenation; vertical bar 'I' has been used to denote one OR the other and '*' has been used to denote multiple occurrences.

Context diagram: Structured analysis is based on a top-down approach with levels of DFDs. The reason for this is that systems often are too large and complicated for a single DFD to describe the data flows in detail with clarity. Therefore, a level-by-level decomposition and abstraction mechanism is adopted for such large systems. The analysis starts with a top-level DFD, known as the context diagram, wherein the whole system is considered as a single process with all major inputs to the system from its environment and major outputs from the system to the environment are considered as the data flows.

Figure 8.2 shows a context diagram for a nursing home of which the DFD for the indoor patient billing system has been shown in Figure 8.1.

In the context diagram, doctors, nursing and other staff, nursing home managers have been considered a part of the total nursing home and not shown separately. Starting with the context diagram, the refinement process starts with the description of the different parts of the system and the data flows among them in a logical sequence. This leads to a levelled set of DFDs till the final level of refinement.

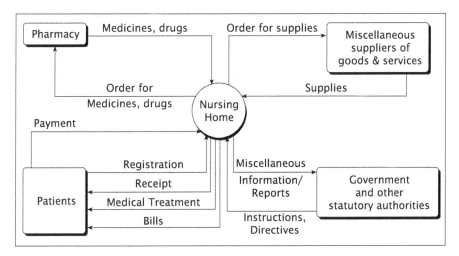

FIGURE 8.2 Context Diagram for a Nursing Home

The system analyst, however, has to ensure that consistency is maintained and net input and output are preserved during this level by level refinement of the DFDs.

Structured analysis is an important tool to analyse a system and represent information about it. The various processes and the data flow facilitate a good understanding of the existing system, which indirectly helps the system analyst to design a new and improved system.

8.4.2 Object-oriented Analysis

The study and analysis of a system in case of object-oriented analysis is based on partitioning of the system with respect to objects, which are physical entities or concepts. Physical objects are computers, chair, table and so on, while concepts are formula, mathematical models, processes, projects and so on. Object-oriented analysis and modelling techniques view a system as a set of interacting objects through their actions (services they provide) in order to identify the system requirements and develop system specifications in terms of an object model of the system. Some objects also interact with the system users who get the desired services through them. The main difference between object-oriented analysis and the structured analysis is that in case of the former, the analysis is organized around identifying objects, which integrate both encapsulated data and functions. The encapsulated data are the values of attributes which define some properties of the object. The values of the attributes of the object at any time determine its state at that point of time. The functions of the object are the behaviour of the object and which are externally visible activities of the object. Objects interact with each other and the users for their behaviour or action, and after completion of such activities change their states. For example, a regular stock item is an object with two important attributes as name (static attribute) and quantity (dynamic attribute) in stock. If some quantity of the item is issued by the storekeeper (an activity by the object storekeeper) the value of the attribute of quantity decreases, thereby changing the state of the same item object.

The main tasks involved in object-oriented analysis are the following:

1. Identifying the objects both physical and conceptual;
2. Arranging the objects in an orderly fashion depending on their relationships into an object model diagram;
3. Defining the attributes of the objects;
4. Defining the object behaviour or actions;
5. Describing the interactions among the objects.

8.4.2.1 Concepts and Notations Used in Object-oriented Modelling

Class

A class represents a collection of objects having some common properties and behaviour. Object is a particular instance of a class only. A class can also represent a collection of objects which constitute the parts of the class. Let me cite some examples of class.

Mammal is a class consisting of human, dog, cat, elephant and so on with some common properties of possessing hair, mammary glands and others. Each of them represents an instance of mammal. However, the class 'mammal' is different from the class 'birds' since birds do not possess all the common characteristics of mammals.

Another example of a class is a library, which consists of books, journals, librarians and so on, which are separate objects but are parts of the aggregate class 'library' also known as the 'container' class. The usual notations for representing the above classes in object-oriented analysis are shown in Figure 8.3.

In an object diagram, which represents the object model graphically, an object class is represented by a rectangle divided into three parts. The uppermost part contains the name of the class such as 'mammals' shown in the example in Figure 8.3, the middle part lists the attributes that objects belonging to the particular class possess such as height, weight and number of legs, and the lower part lists the services or actions provided by objects of the class such as 'move' and 'hear'.

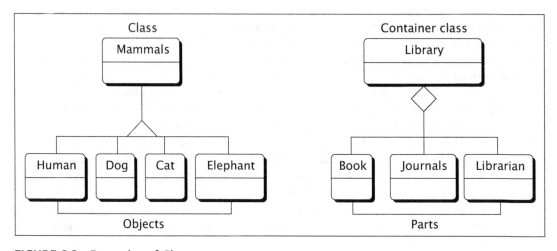

FIGURE 8.3 Examples of Class

Inheritance

Objects and classes are related through inheritance in the real environment. Inheritance is the mechanism that permits specialized classes to be created out of a general class, by adding some special attributes or services to the general class. The structure through which inheritance is derived is known as 'generalization—specialization', which represents a hierarchy of relationship between the general class (known as super class) and the specialized classes (known as subclasses) which inherit the attributes and services of the former class. It may be noted that many specialized classes can be created from a general class. For example, 'doctor' is a general class of all who provide medical treatment to patients. The specialized classes arising out of this class are the classes known as 'cardiologist', 'radiologist', 'urologist' and many others. All these specialized classes of doctors inherit the attributes and services of the class 'doctor' like all of them are medial graduates and all offer medical treatment. However, each subclass such as 'cardiologist' has got specialized knowledge and skill of a particular organ of human beings, such as heart.

Aggregation

The aggregation structure models the whole-part relationship between the container class and the parts comprising the same. This has already been shown in Figure 8.3.

Associations denote the relationships among the objects (instances) pertaining to the various classes in the object model. For example, the class 'employer' of a particular company has multiple associations with all the instances of the class 'employee' since one employer has got many employees. An association is shown in an object diagram by a straight line joining the two classes. An association between two classes can be of three types: (a) one-to-one (one instance of one class is related to only one instance of the other class), (b) one-to-many (one instance of one class is related to many instances of the other class) usually represented by a solid dot (.) on the line adjacent to the class representing zero or more instances and (c) optional association (one instance of a class with another class may be optional, i.e., zero or one). Optional association is usually represented by a hollow circle (o) on the line next to the class whose association is optional.

Encapsulation (Data Hiding)

Data encapsulation, also known as data hiding, is a basic property of an object which encapsulates or hides data, information and their implementation details from the users. It only provides a set of services to the users from outside through an interface. The internal operations of the object do not form any part of the interface. Encapsulation has two major advantages. First, the internal data, information and operations thereof cannot be manipulated from outside. Hence, the integrity of the data and information is preserved. Second, as long as the interface between the object and the users is preserved, implementation of an object can be changed without affecting the users of the object, who continue to get the defined services from the object through the interface. For example, the object employee register of a company provides through its interface user operations such as add employee (), change employee data () and find employee (). There are, however, internal operations within the object 'employee register', such as insert () and sort () which are used to support the user services through the interface but do not form any part of the interface and thus not accessible to the users. Moreover, the object may alter the arrangement of the employee data for implementation from a stack to linked list structure while preserving the user interface at the same time enabling the user to get the earlier defined operations in the object and get the desired services out of it.

Message Passing

Objects interact with each other by passing message. An object can send or receive message or information. Through message passing, objects and users can get the desired services from other objects. Message passing involves a message which is a function. The function has to be applied on the object with an information associated with it.

8.4.2.2 Object-oriented Analysis Techniques

Object-oriented analysis uses the following techniques in conjunction with each other. The techniques are:

1. Object modelling;
2. Dynamic modelling;
3. Functional modelling (already described earlier in structured analysis).

The object modelling technique first of all identifies objects in the system and groups them into different classes. The second step is to establish relationships among the classes in the form of structures, which represent either generalization–specialization or whole–part hierarchy as already explained earlier. The third step defines the object attributes. For example, for the object, 'student', the attributes can be roll number, name, sex, courses opted and so on. The fourth step is to define operations or services that can be performed on the objects. A pre-defined service is performed by an object when it receives a message for the same either from any other object or from the user. Objects change their states by providing the desired services, and thus the services are responsible for state change and the dynamism in the object-oriented modelling. Also, a system provides the functional services to the users through the object services. Fifth step in object modelling is to identify the associations among the objects pertaining to various classes in the object model. The associations can be one of the types 1: 1, 1: M (many) or M: M and the same are derived from the point of view of the problem domain and the objects in the system.

Finally, after following the five steps, an object model diagram of the system is constructed.

For example, let us consider the case of a paint shop which sells varnishes, paints and primers of various types.

All the products of a typical paint shop have a definite shelf life and accordingly, the manufacturing date as well as the expiry date of a product are embossed by the manufacturer on the product container. The paint shop owner manages all sales through counter salesmen. Each salesman every day sells the products to customers and collects the total amount for the products sold to each customer through cash memos. The cash memo is dated and shows the serial number, salesman identification number, name of customer, the products along with the quantities sold and the total amount of the cash memo. The object model represents the system to be designed for a paint shop to compute the total sales for a particular period of time for all products of the shop through the sales effected by each salesman of the shop during the same period. The system also additionally highlights the products due for placement of supply orders because of nil stock and also because the time expired products require their removal from the active stock bins. The object model diagram for the system has been shown in Figure 8.4.

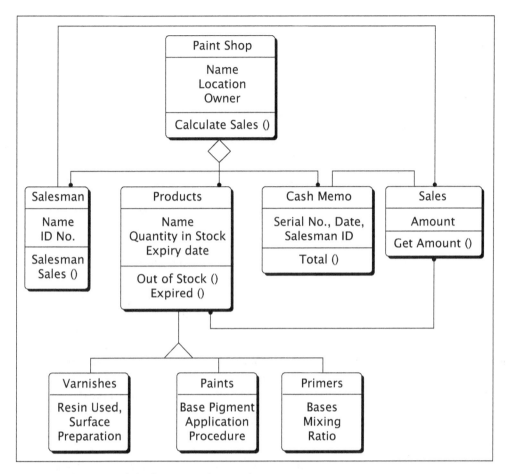

FIGURE 8.4 Object Model of a Paint Shop

The system in this case has got eight classes of objects, each with a name, attributes and services. For example, the paint shop is a an aggregation of the classes 'product', 'salesman' and 'cash memo', which implies that the paint shop is composed of products, salesmen and cash memos. The products are varnishes, paints and primers. Product is a super class having attributes name, quantity in stock, expiry date and so on and services such as out of stock () (requiring placement of orders for products having nil stock) and expired () (to list products expired and requiring removal from the shop). The classes varnishes, paints and primers are specialized subclasses of the class 'product' and inherit all the attributes and services of the class 'product'. Additionally, varnish class have attributes such as resins used and surface preparation. Similarly, paint class has additional attributes of base pigments, application procedure and so on and primer class has additional attributes such as base and mixing ratio. The various associations in the model have also been shown in Figure 8.4. The association between products and sales is many to many since one sale may comprise many products and vice versa. Similarly, the paint shop is associated with product, salesman and cash memo. Salesman and cash memo are individually associated with sales.

8.4.2.3 Dynamic Modelling

Dynamic modelling studies the behaviour of a system with respect to time and events which can be either internal in nature triggered by other objects within the system or external events caused by the outside environment. The steps involved in dynamic modelling are as follows:

1. Identification of the possible states of each object in terms of object attributes;
2. Analysis of the applicable actions and consequent events which lead to change of states;
3. Construction of the dynamic model diagrams comprising the state transition diagrams and interaction diagrams;
4. Validation of the above-mentioned diagrams.

A graphical representation of the state transition diagram is known as state machine diagram which models the entire transition of a single object, specifying the sequence of states that it undergoes during its entire life period in response to events. The states are represented by rounded rectangles with the name of the state written inside and the transitions by solid directed arrows. A transition consists of five parts, namely source state, event trigger, guard condition, action and destination state. The five parts are illustrated with the example of a ballistic missile operation involving the various steps as shown in Figure 8.5.

The initial and final states are denoted by a filled circle and a hollow circle with a dot inside, respectively, and both states may also be labelled with a name. The action (fire) is executed with the event trigger which is the launch time and the guard condition written within parenthesis {} indicates the condition for the transition of the object (missile from stationary to flying state) which in this case is the OK signal by the commander of the missile operation.

In dynamic modelling, the state machine diagrams need to be drawn for all the objects included in the problem domain of the system.

Interaction Diagram

The interactive behaviour among the different objects in an object-oriented model is represented through interaction diagrams, which capture the snapshot of a dynamic system at any particular point of time. There are basically two types of interaction diagrams, namely the sequence diagram and the collaboration diagram. The sequence diagram represents the message flow among the objects in sequence of time, whereas the collaboration diagram represents the arrangement of objects in the system, which takes part in the above-mentioned message flow. Figures 8.6 and 8.7 are examples of the sequence diagram and the collaboration diagram for an online air ticket purchase system. The sequence diagram as shown in Figure 8.6 has got passenger as the user of the system and four objects, namely home page,

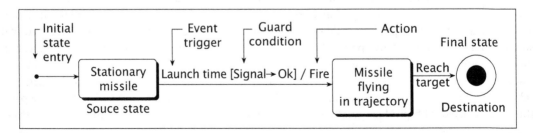

FIGURE 8.5 State Machine Diagram for a Missile

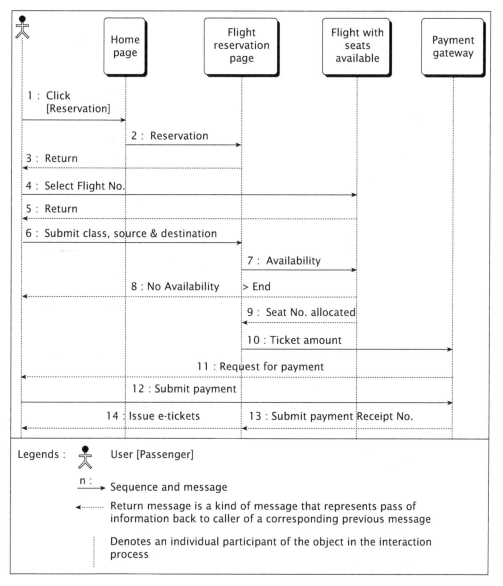

FIGURE 8.6 Sequence Diagram for Online Air Ticket Purchase System

flight reservation page, flight numbers with seat numbers available and payment gateway. The time sequence of the message flows has been indicated by arranging them vertically from top to bottom. The various legends used in the sequence diagram have been shown in Figure 8.6 itself.

Collaboration diagram has been shown in Figure 8.7 for the same online air ticket purchase system. Collaboration diagram can be compared with sequence diagram. Every sequence diagram has got an equivalent collaboration diagram and vice versa. Both show interaction among objects. However, collaboration diagrams show interaction without the time dimension, but do include object links. Sequence diagrams are helpful because they capture visually the sequence of events over time.

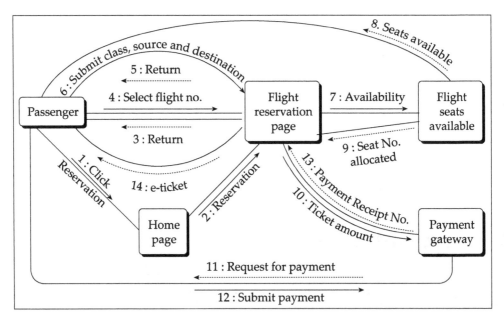

FIGURE 8.7 Collaboration Diagram for Online Air Ticket Purchase System

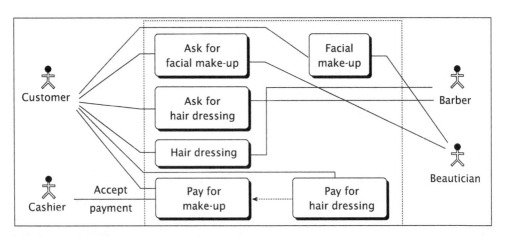

FIGURE 8.8 Use Case Diagram for a Beauty Parlour

Collaboration diagrams, on the other hand, capture more directly the interactions among actors and objects. Besides the object model, state machine model and the interaction model consisting of the sequence and collaboration diagrams, system use case model is also quite useful in object-oriented analysis of a system, particularly while systematically studying the user's interaction with the system. The use-case diagram can be used to describe the usage requirements for a system from user (external to the system) point of view.

Figure 8.8 illustrates a use case diagram for a beauty parlour assumed to be a system where customers get hair dressing and/or facial makeup service. The users of the parlour system are the customers, the beautician, the barber and the cashier.

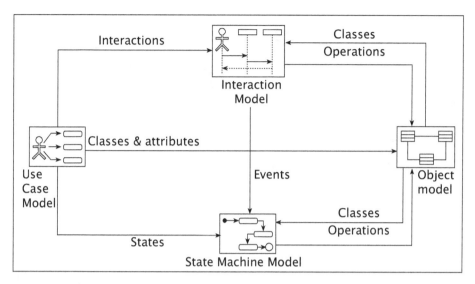

FIGURE 8.9 Interdependency among Interaction, State Machine and Object Models Derived from Use Case Model

System use case model leads to the development of the object model, interaction model and the state machine model iteratively and they are all interdependent as shown in Figure 8.9.

Many languages and related tools and techniques have been developed by analysts and researchers for system analysis. Some of them worth mentioning are structured analysis and design technique (SADT) for information processing systems, the problem statement language (PSL) designed to specify requirements of ISs and language for real-time control systems. Readers who may be interested in the above-mentioned techniques may refer to the references listed at the end of this chapter.

8.4.3 Entity Relationship (ER) Modelling

ER modelling can be effectively adopted for designing databases relating to ISs. The ER model develops the conceptual schema (the model) for the data items and their relationships from the users' perspective. ER model is a canonical conceptual data model which represents the true data interrelationships and can be used to design various database models such as relational, network and hierarchical. ER model consists of entities, entity types and their attributes and relationship between entity types. Entities are either physical things in the real world such as chair, table and person or concepts, such as profession and course of study. Entities are similar to objects in object-oriented modelling explained in earlier paragraphs of this chapter.

Entity types are similar to classes in object-oriented modelling and represent the general structures of entities of a particular type such as professors, lawyers and managers. Attributes are the features that describe a particular entity type. For example, entity type doctor has attributes such as name, specialization, department and hospital name. An attribute may be a composite attribute consisting of sub-attributes. For example, attribute name has got sub-attributes as last name, first name and middle name. Entities have associations among themselves and such associations are expressed as relationships in the ER model. For example, entity type doctor has got relationship with the entity type patient.

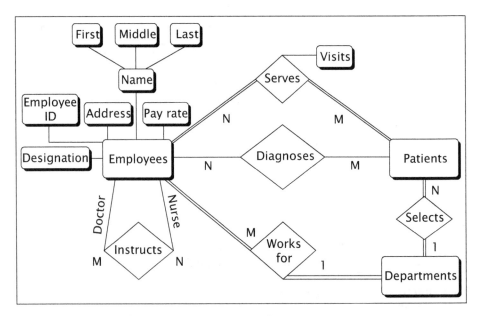

FIGURE 8.10 ER Diagram for a Nursing Home Database

Relationship types may also have attributes. Figure 8.10 describes ER model for a nursing-home database with the associated diagrammatic notations.

Entity types are represented by rectangles as shown in Figure 8.10. In this example, there are three entity types, namely employees, patients and departments. The relationship between entities are represented by single straight line for partial relationship and double lines for total relationship. The relationship in this example is a binary relationship (with degree 2) since the relationships indicate association between entities of any two types. There can be ternary association with degree 3 also. Relationship types are indicated by diamonds and these are diagnoses, serves, works for and instructs in this example. Partial relationship indicated by single line exists when some entities of one type may not be related to any entity of the other type, whereas total relationship exists when each entity of a type is related to at least one entity or instance of the other type in the relationship. For example, Diagnoses is a relationship between employee and patient representing that some employees of the nursing home (doctors) diagnose patients. In this case, the relationship is partial for employees since all employees do not diagnose, and the same for patients is total since all patients are diagnosed by employees (doctors).

Cardinality ratio denotes the number of relationships, which one entity instance of a particular entity type can participate with another entity type. The three types of cardinality ratios are one-to-one (1:1), one-to-many (1:M) and many-to-many (M:M). For example, the relationship diagnoses between employee and patients is M:M since one employee (doctor) can diagnose many patients and vice versa. The relationship ratio between employee and departments is M:1, since one department consists of many employees, whereas one employee is attached with only one department. Attributes as well as composite attributes are denoted by oval shapes attached with the entity with the attribute names written inside. A relationship can have attributes also. For example, the relationship 'serves' has got attribute 'visits' which indicates the number of visits the employee (doctor or nurse) have made for the patient. It may be noticed that relationship can exist between entities of the same type. For example, in the case with 'Instructs', the two entities of the same type 'Employee' are 'Doctor' and 'Nurse'.

The ER modelling focuses on data and relationships between data items in the IS, and therefore the model is suitable for database applications.

8.5 Fact Finding and Information Gathering

A systematic study and analysis of an existing system and the organization including various modelling approaches as described in the previous paragraphs need fact finding and relevant information gathering by the system analysts. The various kinds of information needed for the purpose can be broadly divided into the following categories:

1. Information about the organization such as its vision, mission, policies, goal, objectives and organization structure.
2. Information relating to the users of the system such as their functions, authorities and responsibilities, resources handled by them and information needs.
3. Financial reports, system documentation and procedure manuals, forms, memos, business, plans, policy statements, other miscellaneous organizational chart, information about the operations and processes of the organization such as workflow, methods and procedures, work schedules and flow process charts.

8.5.1 Sources of Information

There are mainly internal and external sources of information about the organization to be studied. Internal sources are the employees, mainly staff, managers, professionals, internal auditors, users of system and so on and the written documents from within the organization. The external sources are stakeholders such as customers, vendors, competitors, government, concerned public including shareholders of the company, government publications, annual reports of the company, various newspapers such as the *Business Standard*, *The Economic Times*, trade and professional journals.

8.5.2 Tools and Methods of Information Gathering and Fact Finding

The various tools and methods applied by the system analysts for information gathering and fact finding are mainly:

1. **Review of various reports, forms and procedures:** Review of reports, forms and procedures involves a critical study of their importance to the users in the context of objective of the organization and its subsystems. The study also leads to addition, deletion, modification,

simplification, standardization and redesigning of the existing forms and reports, if any, required to facilitate understanding of the problems and better decision-making by the users.

2. **On-site observations:** On-site observations involve the observation and study of the system while it is actually running. They also include the function of identifying the key persons involved in running the system in order of their relative importance. If the on-site observation happens to be for a subsystem, its nature and role in comparison with other subsystems and the organizational system as a whole are also observed on site. Observations also lead to important findings such as the chronological developments of the system from inception to its present stage and most important whether the system, as it is working, fulfils its desired role towards attainment of the objectives of the organizational system as a whole. On-site observations can be made either directly or indirectly. In case of direct on-site observations, the observer or the system analyst actually observes himself/herself the subject or the system at work. In case of indirect observation, the system analyst uses audio and video recording devices to record all information about the system while it is working and later on analyses the recorded matter about the system. Direct observation by the system analyst often becomes obtrusive in nature where the persons involved with the working of the system become aware of the situation that they are being observed. Indirect observation can be made unobtrusive by placing the recording devices in secret positions.

3. **Interviews:** Interview is a face-to-face interpersonal interaction in which the interviewer asks pre-designed questions to another person who may be an employee, user of the system or manager, called the interviewee, to gather information or find facts relating to a problem in the system.

   Interview as a technique of information gathering has got many advantages such as exploring complex areas, validation of the gathered information and people being interviewed enjoy and become assertive irrespective of the problem area. However, for successful conduct of an interview, the interviewer needs to be prepared well in advance. The questions to be asked should be properly designed and sequenced properly in a questionnaire. A well-designed questionnaire facilitates reliable responses from the interviewee and recording of the same precisely and accurately. There should be a friendly atmosphere during the interview so that the respondents feel themselves at ease. Prior appointment made by the interviewer with the interviewee with proper place and time of interview is an essential requirement to ensure privacy and minimal interruption during the interview to make it successful. The interviewer should strictly adhere to the appointed time period. The interviewer should ask questions clearly and try to avoid arguments during the interview. The entire proceedings of the interview should be properly recorded for subsequent analysis. Above all, the interviewer should give patient hearing to the interviewee and must not interrupt or influence the responses of the interviewee.

4. **Questionnaires:** Questionnaires contain questions to which individuals (employee, user or manager and so on) respond and in the process, information and facts about the existing system and problems are gathered. The design of the questions and their proper sequence in questionnaire are vital for information and/or facts gathering. A questionnaire may be used as a guide for personal interview or can be distributed to a large number of individuals to collect their responses simultaneously to save the analyst's time and cost of information gathering. There are other advantages of questionnaires, such as uniformity of questions posed to individuals, respondents

get more time to think and submit more accurate information and candid responses against the questions. The questions can be either open-ended or close-ended. In case of open-ended questions (such as 'what are your views on the present system of training and development'?) the respondents submit their subjective responses freely and spontaneously in their own words. An open-ended question requires no specific or structured response on the part of the respondents. In case of close-ended questions, however, the responses have to be presented from among prescribed set of alternatives of the following types:

i. Fill in the blanks
ii. 'Yes' or 'No' type questions
iii. Multiple choice questions (MCQs)
iv. Select the most appropriate type questions
v. Ranking-scale questions such as comparing a list of goods or services in order of their importance to the respondent or ranker. For example, please rank cost, quality, maintainability and durability in order of importance to you as 1–4; 1 being most important and 4 the least important.
vi. Rating-scale questions, for example, how do you rate the quality of food in the scales of 'very poor', 'poor', 'OK', 'good', 'very good'? Close-ended questions being structured in nature facilitate ease of analysis of the collected data and information through responses against such questions.

8.6 Tools Used for Data and Information Analysis

Commonly used tools are DFDs already described in earlier paragraphs, system flow charts, connectivity diagrams, grid charts, decision tables and so on.

System flow charts display an IS such as a snapshot of the various resources and related business processes. It shows clearly the origin of data/information, users/managers who handle the information and how information is summarized for the sake of decision-making and controlling events. The various symbols used in a flow chart are shown in Figure 8.11.

Figure 8.12 shows a flow chart pertaining to an inventory control system to find out the stock items due for reordering. There are a total N number of items.

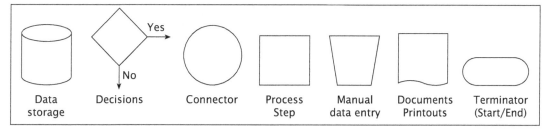

FIGURE 8.11   Various Symbols of Flow Chart

Connectivity diagrams show how the various system modules (components or subsystems) are logically connected with each other. Connectivity diagram for a local area network (LAN) showing how the users or clients are connected to the communication server through a hub and router has been shown in Figure 8.13.

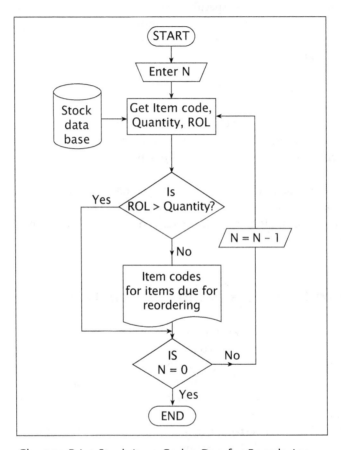

FIGURE 8.12 Flow Chart to Print Stock Item Codes Due for Reordering

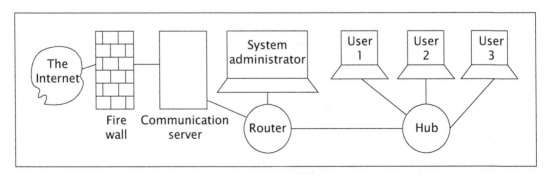

FIGURE 8.13 Connectivity Diagram for a Local Area Network

A **grid chart** is a tabular statement which shows the relationship between input data items in forms and the corresponding output reports generated out of one or more of those data items. Grid charts are used to study the duplication of information present in various reports in order to eliminate unnecessary reports, standardize or simplify existing reports. Table 8.1 shows example of a grid chart for a perpetual inventory system.

TABLE 8.1 A Grid Chart

	Report [Output]		
[Input] Forms	Material Receipt Summary	Consumption Summary	Priced Stores Ledger
Receipt Vouchers	√		√
Demand Notes		√	√
Return Notes		√	√

CASE STUDY: CUSTOMER ORDER PROCESSING SYSTEM FOR A MANUFACTURING ORGANIZATION PRODUCING DEFENCE STORES

Background of the Case

The case pertains to a manufacturing organization, which produces defence stores for use of defence forces. The organization has got a corporate head office located in a metro city that controls a number of manufacturing units located in various geographic locations. The units are of two categories: the finishing units which make the complete end-products for issuing to the customers (defence forces in this case) and the feeder units, which manufacture components and sub-assemblies required for the end-products and supply the same to the finishing factories. Both the feeder units and the finishing units also purchase some trade items needed for the manufacturing activities through local as well as foreign suppliers.

The earlier customer order processing system is such that the head office receives the orders directly from the customers and based on the same, it forwards the manufacturing orders for end-products specifying delivery schedule to one or more appropriate finishing units with proper allocation of quantity based on the capacity of each unit.

The finishing units after receiving the manufacturing orders from head office send manufacturing orders for components and sub-assemblies to one or more appropriate feeder units with proper allocation of quantity based on the capacity of each feeder unit and the bill of components and sub-assemblies. The feeder units thereafter manufacture components and sub-assemblies and issue those to the respective finishing units who then further process the same into end-products for issue to the customers.

The above-mentioned system of customer order processing was found to be unsatisfactory as in many occasions in the past, the finishing units could not supply the end-products to the customers and meet the delivery schedules stipulated by the customers. The finishing units, however, ascribed the delay in supplies to customers to late receipt of components and sub-assemblies from the feeder units.

Methodology Adopted for Analysis of the System

A structured analysis with function-based decomposition was adopted. DFD were developed for the present system. The context diagram and the level 1 DFD in a simplified form have been shown as follows:

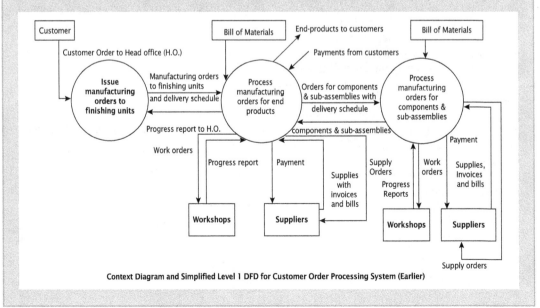

Context Diagram and Simplified Level 1 DFD for Customer Order Processing System (Earlier)

It was observed that the customer order processing system was defective as because the feeder units who had to start their manufacturing activities first received the manufacturing orders from the respective finishing units last in the sequence of information flow. Hence, the system was modified.

Modified Customer Order Processing System

The level 1 DFD for the modified system is as follows:

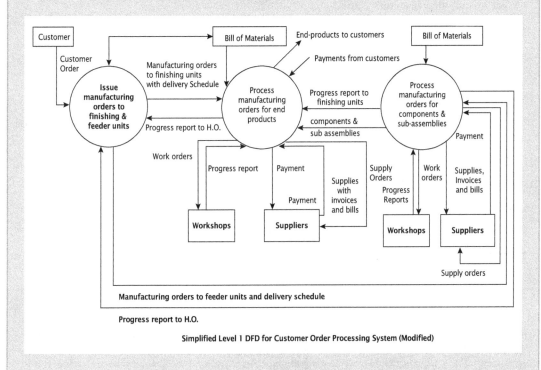

Simplified Level 1 DFD for Customer Order Processing System (Modified)

In the modified system, the head office on receipt of the customer orders converts the same into manufacturing orders for the finishing units and at the same time generates and sends manufacturing orders for components and sub-assemblies to the feeder units based on the end products and the bill of materials of the finished end-products. In order to facilitate the same, the head office has got access to the bill of material files of the finishing units also.

Result and Conclusion

The modified customer order processing system considerably reduced the delay in meeting the customer delivery schedules from 30% to nearly 4% in terms of number orders met with delay. This delay of 4% was also due to delayed receipt of trade supplies from local and foreign suppliers.

The case study shows how application of system analysis techniques can help diagnose organizational problems for designing better organizational systems and procedures.

•Review Questions•

1. Define a system. What are the characteristics of a system?

2. What are the important classifications of a system?

3. What is the necessity of system analysis for developing MIS?

4. What is structured analysis? How does it facilitate system analysis?

5. What is a data-flow diagram? Illustrate.

6. What is a context diagram? Is it a data flow diagram?

7. What is the principle of object-oriented analysis of a system?

8. What are the important concepts underlying object-oriented modelling?

9. What do you understand by the term 'encapsulation and data hiding'?

10. What is dynamic modelling? What are the important diagrams which represent the dynamic model of a system?

11. Describe ER modelling with a suitable example.

12. What are the important methods of fact finding adopted by a system analyst?

13. What is a connectivity diagram? Illustrate.

14. What is a grid chart? What is its role in system analysis?

Bibliography

Gabbert, P. 'Systems Analysis: The Challenge of Integrating Two Competing Technologies.' *Journal of Computing Sciences in Colleges* 16, no. 2 (2000): 193–200.

Hawryszkiewycz, I. T. *Introduction to Systems Analysis and Design*, 2nd ed. New Delhi: Prentice Hall India, 1991.

Jacobson, I. *Object-oriented Software Engineering: A Use Case Driven Approach*. Boston, MA: Addison-Wesley, 1992.

Jalota, P. *An Integrated Approach to Software Engineering*, 2nd ed. New Delhi: Narosa Publishing House, 1997.

Kenneth, C. L., and P. L. Jane. *Management Information Systems: Managing the Digital Firm*, 9th ed. New Delhi: Prentice Hall India, 2006.

Lynch, R., and K. F. Cross. *Measure UP! Yardsticks for Continuous Improvement*. Oxford: Blackwell Business, 1991.

Maciariello, J. A., and C. J. Kirby. *Management Control Systems*, 2nd ed. Pearson, 1994

Marca, D., and C. McGowan. *Structured Analysis and Design Technique*. New York, NY: McGraw-Hill, 1987.

Murdick, R. G., J. E. Ross, and J. R. Clagett. *Information Systems for Modern Management*, 2nd ed. New Delhi: Prentice Hall India, 1977.

Ohlhorst, F. *Big Data Analytics: Turning Big Data into Big Money*. Hoboken, NJ: John Wiley & Sons, 2012.

Pressman, R. *Software Engineering: A Practitioner's Approach*, 7th ed. New York, NY: McGraw-Hill, 2009.

Rumbaugh, J. *Object-oriented Modelling and Design*. New Delhi: Pearson Education, 2004.

Preda, P., and T. Watts. 'Contemporary Management Accounting Techniques in Australia: Manufacturing Versus Service Organizations.' *Journal of Applied Management Accounting Research* 2, no. 2 (2004): 17–27.

Watts, T., and C. J. McNair. 'New Performance Measurement and Management Control Systems.' *Journal of Applied Accounting Research* 13, no. 3 (2012): 226–241.

9 CHAPTER

System Design and Development

Based on user requirements and the detailed analysis of the existing system as already described in Chapter 8, the new and improved system is designed. The conceptual system design arrived as a result of system analysis is converted into physical system design. Generally, system design is divided into two stages, namely the preliminary or gross design as the first stage followed by the second stage called the detailed system design.

9.1 Gross System Design

In the gross design, the features of the new system and the feasibility for meeting the objectives of the IS and user requirements get specified. The output of gross design is a set of documents showing how the system will broadly work. The same documents describing the ISs will enable the technical personnel to begin the detailed system design.

The important activities during gross system design are discussed further.

9.1.1 Setting the System Objective in Detail

System objective should be specific and relate to each functional subsystem of an organization in terms of information needs to improve managerial effectiveness. Precisely, system objective should be expressed in terms of what managers can do after the ISs meet their information needs. A statement of system objective should include what the system is supposed to do to improve managerial effectiveness and by which means the same improvement can be evaluated. Table 9.1 illustrates some important objectives for a few organizational subsystems:

9.1.2 Identifying Information Needs for Users (Managers) and the Sources of Such Information

Burch and Strater (1973) suggested three different approaches to study the information needs of managers. The first approach is the decision-level analysis. The main rationale for this approach is that

| TABLE 9.1 | Organizational Subsystems and Objectives |

Subsystems	Few Objectives
Purchase	To provide information on price negotiations with vendors so that price variance can be controlled within set limits
Training and development	To provide information on effectiveness of industrial training programmes in increasing productivity of industrial workers
Cost control	To identify cost variances within one month to institute stringent cost control
Maintenance	To provide information on breakdowns in a particular time period to assess efficiency of preventive maintenance

all managers, irrespective of their positions in the hierarchy, need an IS that provides information about the use of resources handled by them and not a system that provides information only by organizational functions. Once the resources of the organization (both tangible and intangible) are identified and categorized, the IS analyst breaks each one of the resources into decision points or levels so as to identify information required for each decision level. Once this is done, the next step is to ascertain the sources of data which generate the required information. For example, one resource is inventory which consists of raw materials, work in progress and finished stores. This resource can be broken down into major decision points concerned with it as shown in Figure 9.1. A distinct advantage of this approach is that it enables the system analyst to know the interaction of the decisions made by one manager on the others. For example, production planning decisions affect stock-level decisions and reorder decisions.

The second approach proposed by Burch and Strater to identify the managers' information needs is the information flow analysis. The analyst is concerned with what information a manager needs from

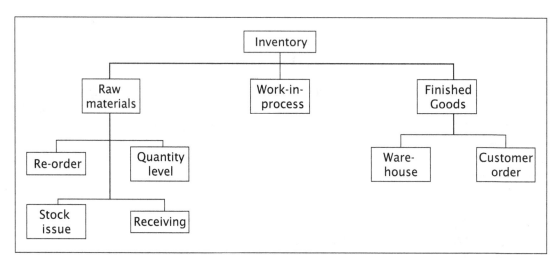

FIGURE 9.1 Decision Points Based on Inventory Resource Breakdown

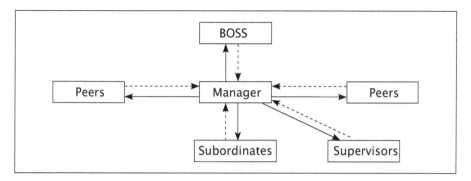

FIGURE 9.2 Information Flow in an Organization

others such as his supervisors, peers and subordinates and what information is required from him by others such as his own boss. This approach is illustrated in Figure 9.2.

The third approach is input/output analysis. When the analyst is investigating the existing system to gain an understanding of what is being done, facts can be collected in terms of inputs and outputs to the system. In this approach, each input and each output are only described. Nothing is said about how the input was converted to the corresponding output, or about decision-making, information requirements and information flows. For example, in a computer-based personnel IS, the inputs can be the biodata of employees and the outputs are various reports such as seniority list of employees, retirement analysis, promotion prospect reports.

9.1.2.1 Information Sources

Information needs can hardly be met unless matching information sources are determined. Information sources can be either external or internal to the organization. External information is obtained from a number of sources such as newspapers, trade journals, government statistics, Reserve Bank of India bulletins on trade and commerce, annual reports of companies and similar publications. Internal sources of information are the records, files, statistical and accounting documents, various reports on sales, production, personnel and so on.

Sources of information may also be categorized as follows:

1. **Internal sources**: These include internal files, records, various reports, procedure manuals, circulars, office notes, letters, memoranda, existing system documentation and so on, which can be either hard copies or soft copies in digital form on computer storage devices.
2. **External sources**: External sources include external data and information relating to socio-economic, political, technological, demographic, competitive environment and government rules and regulations.
3. **Informal sources**: Informal information obtained through interviewing of managers and other employees, committee meetings, group discussions and the like are also important sources of information to satisfy the information needs of users of an IS. However, unlike written reports and records, information gathering through informal sources as mentioned above involves communication problems, which can be eliminated to a large extent by proper planning and gaining confidence of the concerned persons.

TABLE 9.2 Information Needs/Information Sources Matrix

Subsystems	Information Needs	Information Sources
Inventory	Items with stock equal to or less than reorder level	Bin card showing stock quantity and reorder level quantity
Production	Prime cost variance more than 10%	Material, labour abstracts
Accounts receivables	Credit sales, overdue for payment	Sundry debtor's ledger
Project control	Progress against plan for critical path events	Project time sheet

4. **Various mathematical and statistical models:** These models generate information adopting simulation, estimation, forecasting, work sampling and various other techniques. These techniques are adopted to facilitate input/output analysis and multidimensional flows.

5. **Input/output analysis,** which has already been mentioned in earlier paragraphs of this chapter is done on a two-dimensional matrix in which inputs (information sources) are listed as rows and the corresponding outputs (information needs) as column headings and the relationships are shown by tick marks ($\checkmark$) at the point of intersection. The analysis helps eliminating duplicate sources. Table 9.2 shows a matrix to illustrate the matching of information needs with the information sources for a few subsystems.

6. **Multidimensional flow** is another technique of organizing information source to match the information needs in the existing design of a subsystem.

7. **The flow of information** from origin to destination in a chronological sequence through the organizational subsystems is shown as a flow chart. Apart from identification of information sources, the frequency, volume, time, cost and physical distance of information flow can also be shown in such a flow chart additionally.

9.1.3 Setting the System Constraints

Constraints are the restrictions imposed upon the system design and are the conditions under which the system objectives are to be achieved. By their very nature, constraints can be classified as internal or external to the system. External constraints are related to customers, legal and government regulatory frameworks, suppliers, shareholders, technology and so on. Customer-related constraints demand that customer needs, insofar as the interface of the system being designed with the customer system is concerned, be fulfilled. For example, while designing system outputs such as format of invoice, bills, cost breakup and receipt for payments, the needs of the customers, particularly the compatibility with input to their various subsystems, must be considered.

The legal and regulatory framework imposed by the government (central, state or local authorities) covers the security and privacy of data, bookkeeping and financial reporting as per prescribed standards such as companies and other relevant acts.

Suppliers, like customers are also important for designing subsystems which interface with their subsystems. For example, notice inviting quotations may be sent in electronic form through e-procurement system. SCM demands total compatibility of the systems of the suppliers and customers with the subsystems of the manufacturers and service providers. Shareholders demand that performance of the organization during a specified period be reported in a prescribed format such as International Financial Reporting System (IFRS). Finally, technological innovations such as ERP, data warehouse, data vaults, the Internet and World Wide Web, social networks and other information and communications technology impose restrictions on gross system design.

Internal constraints on gross system design arise out of organization and its policy, employees including managers, available resources, legacy systems, cost–benefits, top management involvement in the system design, user involvement and technology compatibility. Illustration of internal constraints imposed on the system design has been shown in Table 9.3.

TABLE 9.3 Internal Constraints on System Design

Internal Constraints Arising Out of	Nature of Constraints
Cost-benefit	Cost associated with the new system is a major limitation. The cost to achieve the objective of the system should be commensurate with the benefit derived out of the system. Cost consideration demands optimum utilization of resources allocated for the new system.
Top management involvement	Top management support is essentially needed to make any new system design and development a success. This constraint can be to a great extent overcome by involving top management in the conceptual system design.
User involvement	Like top-management involvement, user involvement is also equally important for ultimate acceptance of the new system.
Technology compatibility	In designing the system to achieve objectives, the designer has to scale down several requirements to make the system fit for existing technology.
Organization and its policy	Organizational structure including the heads of the cost, profit and responsibility centres influences the flow of information and system outputs. Company policies relating to operations, marketing, finance, personnel, information technology and R&D have a vital role to impose restrictions on system design. For example, an in-house R&D policy would have an effect on the system design to build research aptitude among technical personnel. Audit and accounts policy also imposes restrictions on system design.
Employees including managers	Employee knowledge and experience are important considerations in system design. A sophisticated computer-based system may prove futile if computer literacy level is poor among employees. Personal characteristics including the psychological type among managers also play a vital role in system design.
Resource availability	Computer hardware, software and manpower are important considerations for design of computer-based information systems.
Legacy systems	Any new system design needs to consider the conversion of existing data base and utilization of technology available with the legacy systems.

9.1.4 Developing Alternative Gross Designs of the System and Selecting One

Development of a gross IS design is a creative process which involves many alternatives in respect of pattern and channels of information flow across the managers of the organization. Moreover, the gross design must also include a linkage of the IS with all functional subsystems of the organization such as personnel, finance and accounts, operations and marketing. Depending upon the nature of such linkage, there can be more than one variation of gross or conceptual IS design. Let us illustrate alternative gross designs with a simple example. A heavy vehicle manufacturing company has four plants located in various distant geographical locations in India. Three of the plants manufacture different components and sub-assemblies and supply the same to the fourth plant which assembles the complete end product (heavy vehicle) for the customers. The headquarter of the company is located very near to the assembly plant. According to the existing system of production planning and control, marketing division of the head quarter receives customer orders for heavy vehicles and, in turn, furnishes the production target for the end product to the assembly plant of the company. The assembly plant based on the production target for the complete heavy vehicle calculates the requirements of components and sub-assemblies and provides manufacturing targets for the three component and sub-assembly manufacturing units in turn.

The above-mentioned system of regulating production and inventory of the manufacturing plants gives rise to frequent delay in delivery to customers because the manufacturing units for components and sub-assemblies who have to initiate the manufacture of the required components and sub-assemblies for a customer order get the information about their manufacturing targets from the assembly plant quite late. Therefore, a better conceptual or gross design of the IS may be one wherein the headquarter marketing division, who receives customer orders should set targets not only for the assembly plant but also work out the targets for component and sub-assembly manufacturing units and provides the same to the corresponding units simultaneously in order to avoid any delay in initiating manufacture of components and sub-assemblies by the respective plants. It is obvious that every alternative gross design has its own merits and demerits. The selection of the one among the alternative designs will be on the basis of a number of criteria, such as the fulfilment of the system objectives, cost effectiveness of the designs and quality of information and the time lag for information to be made available to managers to facilitate decision-making relating to organizational functions.

9.1.5 Documenting the Gross System Design

The system concept developed during the gross design needs to be documented properly for the next phase of detailed system design. The documentation essentially includes the following:

1. **System flow chart**: A system flow chart shows the flow of information through the system reaching the various decision points. Further, the various functional subsystems and their integration through the flow of information are clearly depicted in the chart. The gross design flow chart is similar to the system flow chart described in Figure 8.12. However, additionally, system objective, system constraints—both internal and external, information needs, information sources, various decision rules connected with the decision points, various inputs and outputs connected with the information flow process are suitably incorporated and designated into the chart.

2. **System inputs**: System inputs and their formats for capturing data obtained from sources outside the firm such as customer order, invoices and bills raised by the vendors are also included in the gross design document. The input formats should be designed and documented considering compatibility, conversion and collation of the input data by the subsystems. In case of inputs received from other subsystems within the company also, the formats need to be designed for integrating the subsystems through common data items having compatibility. Further, since inputs must be checked for validity, the editing procedures for accepting valid inputs by the system should be specified in the gross design documentation. The format of input data should also consider the subsystem which will accept the data and process the same to facilitate decisions. As example, the input transaction formats for updating store records for decisions regarding reordering of items have been shown in Table 9.4. The essential data elements are the code for the type of input such as, say, '01' for material receipt vouchers through purchase, '02' for material issue vouchers for consumption, item code (say five numeric digits), unit of quantity (say km, kg, kl and so on) comprising two alpha characters and the quantity of material either received in store in case of receipt vouchers or issued out of the available balance in the store warehouse. Quantity is a numeric field of width 11 digits inclusive of 2 digits after decimal.

TABLE 9.4 Input Format for Inventory Re-ordering Subsystem

Code '01' or '02'	Item code 5 numeric digits	Unit of quantity (2 alpha characters)	Quantity NNNNNNNN–NN (N: A numeric digit)

The processing logic is such that if the transaction item code and unit of quantity match with the same in the stock file record, the available balance will be increased by the transaction quantity if the transaction code is '01', otherwise if the code is '02', the available balance will be decreased to the extent of transaction quantity. However, before accepting the transaction for updating the stock record as above, the validity of the data fields of code, item code, unit of quantity and quantity will be checked by the subsystem.

If, however, the same type of input transactions is considered for updating priced stores ledger for inventory valuation subsystem, the formats will undergo a change as reflected in Table 9.5.

TABLE 9.5 Input Format for Inventory Valuation Subsystem

Code '01' or '02'	Item code 5 numeric digits	Unit of quantity 2 alpha characters	Quantity NNNNNNNN–NN (N: A numeric digit)	Value of receipt or issue (₹ NNNN–NN)

3. **System outputs**: System output formats for three illustrative subsystems, namely inventory control, machine capacity utilization and customer complaints handling which are required to be designed to satisfy the information needs of managers to facilitate decisions relating to the above subsystems, have been shown in Table 9.6.

TABLE 9.6 Output Formats Related to Three Subsystems: Inventory Control, Capacity Utilization and Customer Complaint Handling

Daily Stock Review Report										*Date: 09.19.2015*
Item Code	*Nomen-clature*	*Unit of Quantity*	*EOQ*	*ROL*	*Balance*	*Out-standing Orders*	*PDS[a]*	*Received Awaiting Inspection*	*Action*	
101	Washer	Doz.	200	100	95	200	09.12.15	—	Expedite supplier	
102	Bearing	Nos.	50	20	18	50	08.27.15	30	Inspect 30 nos. received	

Note: [a]PDS: Probable date of supply (as per supply order).

Machine Capacity Utilization Report										*Date: 09.18.2015*
Machine No.	*Descrip-tion*	*Shop*	*Unit*	*Available Time*	*Preventive Mainte-nance Time*	*Loading Time*	*Actual Loading Time*		*Utiliza-tion Per-centage*	*Action*
101	Horizontal milling centre	Machine shop A	Hrs.	16	02	14	Job. No.	Time	71.40	Analyse idle time
							Jo1	4		
							Jo2	6		
						Total		10		
102	Vertical turning centre	Machine shop A	Hrs.	16	04	12	J10	3	100	Nil
							J11	4		
							J12	5		
						Total		12		

Customer Complaints Report							Week Ending: 09.19.2015
Customer	Nature of Complaint	Complaint Received on	Complaint Attended to and Resolved on	Type of Fault	Remedial Action	Days Taken to Resolve	Reasons for Delay in Resolving Complaint If Beyond 48 Hours
M/S Zenith Co.	Machine not getting 'On'	09.14.2015	09.15.2015	Starter switch burnt	Starter switch replaced	1	NA
M/S Machino Techno Industries	Lubricant leakage from machine T001	09.15.2015	09.18.2015	Lubricant seal broken	New seal inserted	3	Seal was not available in local market and had to be brought from outstation

Apart from the output format design to suit the information needs of managers, the other important factors for output data and information are as follows:

i. Destination of the output reports in terms of its recipients
ii. Distribution of output—number of copies to be sent to various recipients and mode of distribution such as online and through courier
iii. Frequency and timing of output distribution
iv. Form of output data, such as hard copy, data terminal and soft copy
v. Detailed or summarized
vi. Routine, on demand or exception reporting.

4. **Activity sheet and the system narrative:** The other frequently used means of documenting the gross system design are the activity sheet and the system narrative. Activity sheet is a description of inputs, outputs and various files associated with a subsystem in terms of transaction volume for the inputs, outputs and the records of the files. Table 9.7 illustrates an activity sheet for the production-control subsystem, consisting of customer order, scheduling and production progress reporting.

The system narrative is basically a written narrative about the system details such as the functional subsystems, the decision points or managers, the resources handled by them, the flow of materials and other resources including information within the subsystems. The routine operations performed by the various individuals within the functional areas are also mentioned in the system narrative.

5. **Gross design report:** The gross design report is a report prepared by the design team leader for forwarding the documentation of the conceptual or gross design and is meant for the top management to accept the same for the detailed system design to follow and also to approve the necessary expenditure of funds and organizational changes needed for the conceptual system designed. In a sense, the gross design report is similar to the detailed project report (DPR) for a project for seeking approval of the competent authority for the same. Gross design report should

TABLE 9.7 Activity Sheet for Production Control Subsystem

		Activity: Production Control	
Customer order subsystem:	**Key**	**Name**	**Volume**
As received		**Inputs**	
Inputs	10:	Customer orders	10 per day
Scheduling subsystem:	11:	Despatch to customers	10 per day
Daily	12:	Defectives returned by customers	1 per day on an average
Inputs		**Outputs**	
Production progress reporting:	20:	Pending order status	500 per day
Monthly	21:	Overdue orders for expediting	50 per day
Inputs	22:	Production schedules	5 per day (For 5 shops)
	22:	Work-in-process status (work centre-wise)	200 per day
	23:	Production plan	5 per month (shop wise)
		Files	
	30:	Customer order file	1,000 records
	31:	Work-in-process file	1,000 records
	32:	Manufacturing estimate file	2,000 records
	33:	Capacity master file	1,000 records
	34:	Finished products dispatch file	1,500 records

Note: The volume indicated is only illustrative.

be concise and summarized mentioning the problems necessitating the system, objectives, reasons why the particular conceptual design was chosen from among the alternatives, the time schedule, manpower and other resources required to design, develop and implement the system and the performance metrics for the system. Along with the above summary, the complete conceptual design documentation described in earlier paragraphs such as the system flow chart, input and output formats, activity sheet and system narrative should be enclosed.

9.2 Detailed System Design

Detailed design of the system commences after the conceptual framework has been chalked out. The conceptual or gross design shows the broad concept of the system along with its overall performance specifications. The detailed design, however, yields the construction and operating specifications.

The idea of detailed design is to provide a detailed description of operating subsystems which fulfil the objective of the gross design requirements. The detailed description is represented through different types of flow charts and activity sheets showing the inputs, outputs and decision rules. Design of database and master files, specification of computer hardware and software, personnel requirement and the final performance parameters including cost of installation, implementation and operations are also furnished.

9.2.1 Detailed Design Steps

9.2.1.1 Review of the Conceptual Design

Review of the conceptual design is done in order to redefine the subsystems if necessary.

9.2.1.2 Identification of Dominant and Trade-off Criteria of the System

Dominant criteria for a system define an activity as to be of utmost importance to dominate all other activities. For example, a dominant criterion might be that the system operates without any delayed supply to the customers. This criterion might override the other criteria such as cost of production and machine utilization. Zero-delay criterion as above usually holds in case of supply made to the defence forces by the manufacturing units such as ordnance factories and defence public sector undertakings. Any delay in such a case might jeopardize defence preparedness. There can be other examples of dominant criteria such as zero-defect product, zero machine breakdown, no-stock out and no wastage. Trade-off criteria are those where one criterion may be improved while deteriorating the other. In other words, they are criteria associated with two activities which are negatively correlated. For example, the criterion of low inventory cost might be traded-off against the low stock-out cost. The identification of dominant and trade-off criteria is a necessity before the subsequent detailed system design steps. The detailed design involves identification of decision-makers (managers), who have to achieve the dominant criteria and also make trade-offs. The detailed MIS should be so designed as to provide the necessary information to the above-mentioned decision-makers.

9.2.1.3 Detailed Break-up of Subsystems

The next step is to break down the major blocks of subsystems of the gross design into functional components, tasks, subtasks and finally the operational elements which activate functional components. For example, Figure 9.3 is a system flow chart which is a simplified representation of gross system concept for a hospital. The flow chart is however not exhaustive but is only a simple illustration. The billing and cash collection subsystem needs to be broken down into a hierarchy of functional component, task, subtask and operational element as shown in Figure 9.4. The various activity operations along with the information inputs and outputs relating to the billing activity have been shown in Figure 9.5. It is important to mention that the IS must be based upon the operating system. Once the operating system has been outlined by the general system concept as shown in Figure 9.4, the basic relationships among major activities become generally established such as the relationship between the billing and cash collection activity with the patient registration activity. However, during the process of breakdown of major activities, considerable flexibility is achieved in establishing the detailed activities including the

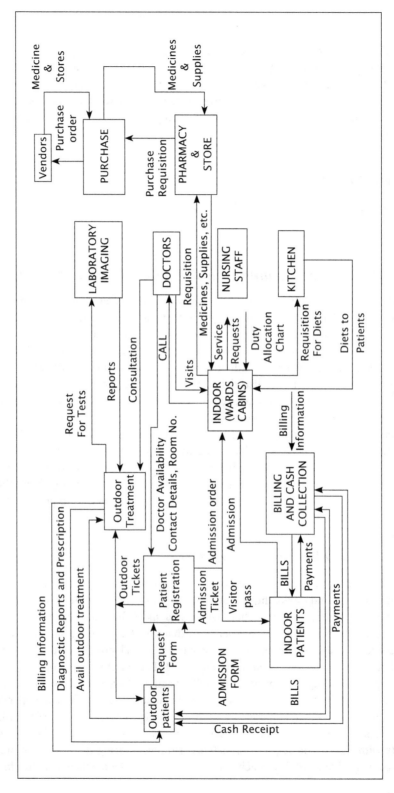

FIGURE 9.3 Simplified Representation of Gross System Concept for a Hospital

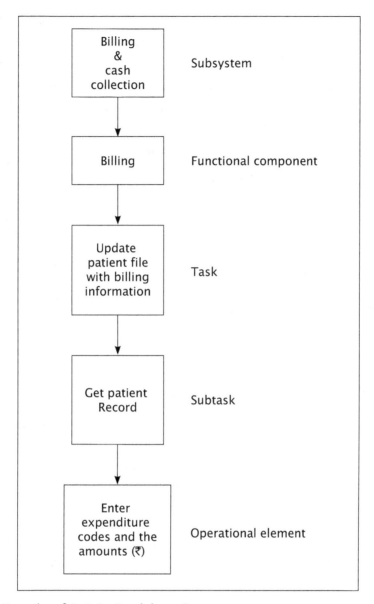

FIGURE 9.4 Hierarchy of Activity Breakdown Structure

operational elements and their inter-relationships. The detailed activities once identified and defined may be related among themselves in a flow chart as shown in Figure 9.6 for two detailed activities relating to the billing activity.

The degree of breakdown of the major activities as mentioned above depends upon the nature of the system including the size and complexity. It should be sufficiently detailed to reveal the operating elements, information and the decisions and also to facilitate examination of various options of

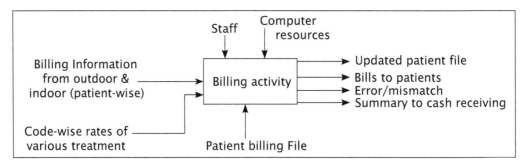

FIGURE 9.5 Activity Operations and Information Inputs and Outputs

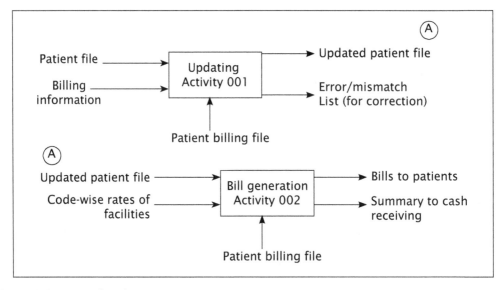

FIGURE 9.6 Interrelated Activities

regrouping the activities. Table 9.8 is a typical form of an operation activity sheet for the billing activity of a hospital. Similar operation activity sheets facilitate the development of description of each activity during detailed system design.

9.2.1.4 Regrouping of the Activities

This step is to regroup the activities starting with the operational elements and synthesizing them into subtask, task and finally develop activity network at the functional component level. Once activity networks are developed to include each major activity of conceptual design, the subsystems can be redefined with the help of various information such as performance specifications obtained from the conceptual design, dominant and trade-off criteria for the operating and ISs combined, available resources, required activities and their inter-relationships, major decision points, control positions, specific input information and output required for all subsystems.

TABLE 9.8   Operation Activity Sheet

Activity: Billing Activity	*Activity Number: 002*	
Purpose and Description		
With the updated patient billing file and the rates for various codes of facilities, individual bills for each category of patients are generated and also a summary statement of total billed amount is printed for the cash office.		
Inputs	Media	
1. Updated patient billing file	off-line magnetic storage	
2. Code-wise rates of facilities	off-line magnetic storage	
Outputs	Media	
1. Patient bills	Hard copy (printouts)	
2. Summary of bills	Hard copy (printouts)	
Sequence of Element of Activity	**Performer**	Decision rule
Only one activity	Billing section in-charge	

9.2.1.5 Representing Detailed Operating Subsystems through Flow Charts

Operating subsystems and information flows are represented through flow charts. Usually, three types of flow charts are used to sketch the detailed design of the operating subsystems, namely task-oriented, forms-oriented and program flow charts. Task-oriented flow charts are block diagrams showing the various tasks or activities and their relationships. For example, Figure 9.7 is a task-oriented flow chart for the billing and cash collection module of the hospital IS. Forms-oriented flow charts show the forms used in communicating or reporting relevant information within a system. Additionally, these flow charts also show the number of copies, the colour of the copies meant for different recipients such as managers and the sequence of movement of the forms in chronological order. Figure 9.8 is an example of a form-oriented flow chart for indirect material purchase subsystem from purchase requisition up to ordering stage.

Program flow charts are block diagrams prepared by computer programmers to pass instructions to the computer. These flow charts basically describe the computer algorithms. Figure 9.9 shows a program flow chart for computing the factorial of a number. The flow charts are sketches describing the detailed system design by the information flows and relationships with the inputs and outputs in gross form.

9.2.1.6 Specification of the Inputs, Outputs and Database

The specifications for the construction of the detailed MIS design also include the format for inputs, outputs and design of database and associated master files.

Each operating subsystem receives information as input and also produces output information which in turn will act as input to other subsystems. In order to achieve compatibility with the different

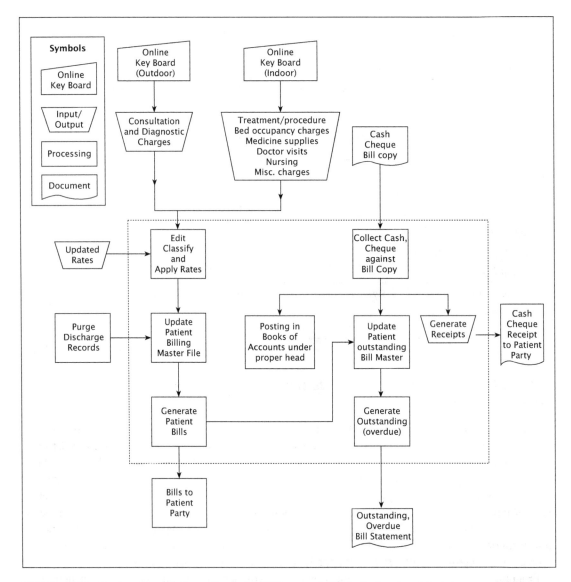

FIGURE 9.7 Task-oriented Flow Chart for Billing and Cash Collection Module

subsystems, it is essentially needed to specify the inputs and outputs and forms for inputs and outputs designed properly during detailed design process. The best practice is to design the inputs and outputs in consultation with the users who will actually use those forms.

The database is the repository of the total business system data stored for future retrieval for managerial decision-making including automated decisions. It is therefore of paramount importance that the total management needs for information to facilitate decisions be studied in depth and an integrated approach adopted to design the database to avoid any redundancy.

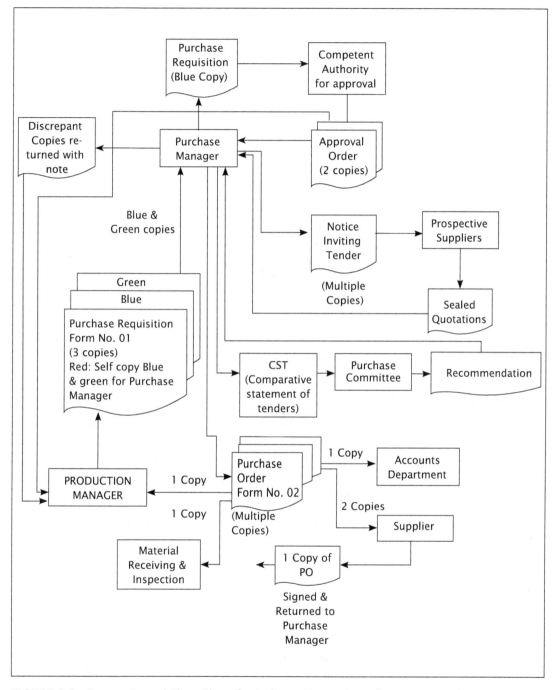

FIGURE 9.8 Form-oriented Flow Chart for Indirect Material Purchase up to Ordering Stage

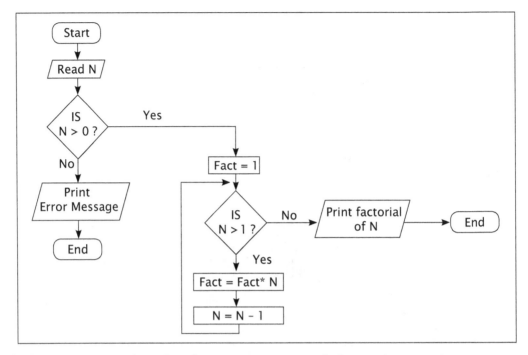

FIGURE 9.9 Program Flow Chart for Computing Factorial of a Number

9.2.1.7 Inform and Involve People at All Levels of the Organization

The awareness of the employees, particularly the top management, about the new system and involvement of all levels of managers, particularly the users during the detailed system design stage itself, are also pre-requirements for acceptance of the new MIS at all levels in the organization. Top management support is essentially needed to get funds necessary for design, development and implementation of the new system. Last, but by no means least important, is that the final users of the system/subsystems be explained about the system in detail. Acceptance at the level of final users is essential for the success of the new MIS. It is therefore necessary to include as many members in the study and detailed design of the system as possible to involve them and get their support and acceptance. Furthermore, it is equally important to reassure the employees through various awareness programmes that the new system, when implemented, will benefit all of them both financially and otherwise.

9.2.1.8 System Testing

System testing at the detailed design stage is of paramount importance as it is very easy and cheaper to fix any problem or defect relating to the functions of the MIS at the design stage itself rather than at implementation stage or even the operational stage. Testing during design of MIS mainly concentrates on the following aspects of the MIS:

1. Business processes are tested to ensure that those meet their intended functional requirements which the user needs.

2. Risks that may jeopardize the system functioning are identified.
3. The interfaces of the subsystems (modules) and the cross-module impacts are systematically studied and analysed.
4. Compatibility of legacy systems with the new MIS designed is studied to determine the conversion efforts needed during the subsequent implementation stage.
5. Quantitative ranges for valid inputs and outputs and their relationships are determined.
6. Time and reliability responses for the operations involving the system are studied.
7. Security aspects including security restrictions are studied during system testing.

Various types of system testing are (a) integration testing to find out the bugs in complete functions and processes within the subsystems and among them. This testing basically ensures correct linking of the subsystems, (b) system testing to validate that the system performs functionally as specified in the design, (c) input–output testing to ensure that the valid ranges of inputs and outputs are accepted by the system and the transfer functions are the same as specified in the design and (d) user testing to provide the opportunity to the users of the system to validate functionality of the system prior to implementation.

System testing plans should cover the level of details including the conditions to be tested for each subsystem and the overall system being designed. Inputs, outputs and databases will have separate test plans. Test plans also include appropriate test conditions for valid as well as invalid situations.

There are three methods of system testing. These are as follows:

1. **Modelling** is basically to determine the quantitative ranges for inputs and outputs and establishing relationships between them. It also considers the time response and reliability of the system operations. Decision modelling may take the form of either decision tables or set of mathematical equations. Decision tables have been elaborately described in a previous chapter of this book.
2. **Simulation testing** is suitable for large and complex systems for which actual testing, debugging and modifications of the system, subsystems and functional components during conversion to the new system and changeover may become too expensive and may also be detrimental to the morale of the implementation team. In case of such systems, simulation may be adopted to test the functional subsystems and the components of the large system. In such cases, simulation further facilitates performance evaluation of the system against the performance specification of parameters such as speed and throughput.

    Simulation testing of a management is carried out in the following steps:
    i. By the Monte Carlo technique, random values of exogenous variables within the ranges of their values as specified in the IS designed are generated. For example, random values may be generated for manufacturing lead time, procurement lead time, demand and supply of raw materials, cost of raw materials, inflation rate and so on for an inventory control system. Non-quantitative input variables such as employee morale are usually selected randomly from among the various alternative attributes of such variables.
    ii. The second step is to simulate the effect of the random values of the exogenous variables as obtained in Step i.
    iii. The third step is to examine the outputs of various subsystems obtained following the Steps i and ii described above. The outputs should be checked for consistency and adherence to the specified limits as stipulated in the conceptual design.
    iv. Steps i through iii are to be repeated many times to test the system by simulation.

3. **Test planning** pre-defines the strategy to be followed for testing the new MIS, resources to be deployed for testing, the testing environment, test data, test cases, schedule of activities relating to testing and the shortcomings of testing. It also covers the features and the deliverables of the new MIS that need to be tested. Basically, test planning formulates the quality assurance plan for the new MIS.

9.2.1.9 Documenting the Detailed Design

Finally, like any other design, it is necessary that at the end of the detailed design, the same be recorded in the form of suitable documentation for later implementation. The documentation usually consists of the following:

1. A summary flow chart similar to one shown in Figure 9.9;
2. Detailed flow charts showing interrelated activities;
3. Operations/activity sheets showing inputs, outputs and their relation;
4. Specifications of inputs, outputs and the database;
5. Requirement of computer hardware and software resources in broad terms;
6. Personnel requirements for the new system specifying the type of skills;
7. Final performance specifications;
8. Estimated cost of installation, implementation and operation of the system;
9. Program for maintenance, modification and termination of the system;
10. An executive summary of the detailed system design, particularly meant for the top management in order to enable them to get an essence of the system including the general configuration, estimated cost and benefit of the system for the company as a whole.

9.3 System Development Life Cycle

ISs are created to solve problems related to managerial decision-making. System life cycle is an organizational process of problem investigation, analysis, design, development and maintenance of the system including review of the same with the changing scenario. IS development involves various activities performed in various phases which constitute the system development life cycle (SDLC). The various phases of SDLC are as follows:

1. Initial need recognition
2. Feasibility study
3. System analysis
4. Conceptual system design
5. Detailed system design
6. Implementation
7. Post-implementation, maintenance and review of the system.

The different phases of SDLC are shown in Figure 9.10.

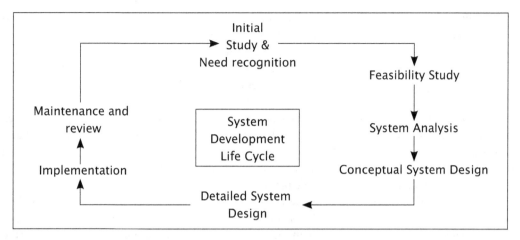

FIGURE 9.10   Phases of System Development Life Cycle

9.4 Phases of SDLC

Let us now describe the different phases and related activities of the SDLC.

9.4.1 Initial Study and Need Recognition

This is the first phase of SDLC and mainly covers the following activities:

1. Problem identification and project initiation
2. Background analysis
3. Recognition of needs for a new system
4. Justification for a new system
5. Preparation of a system proposal for obtaining management approval for 'go-ahead' or otherwise.

The initial study must address the scope of the proposed system and the perceived problems, opportunities, constraints and the requests of the stakeholders that triggered the idea of the proposed system. The management may accept the proposal or reject the same or even suggest suitable modifications of the proposal.

9.4.2 Feasibility Study

In case the system proposal is accepted by the management, the next phase of SDLC is the study of the feasibility of the system. There are basically five types of feasibility related to ISs which are usually addressed in this phase, namely technical feasibility, economic feasibility, schedule feasibility, motivation feasibility and operational feasibility. Technical feasibility assessment is focused on gaining an understanding of the present technical resources of the organization such as hardware, software, legacy systems and skill of technical personnel to meet the expected needs of the proposed system. Technical feasibility study ensures whether the proposed system can be made feasible with the available technical resources of the company. For example, a computer-based inventory control system can be technically feasible, only if the operational staff are computer literate.

Economic feasibility assessment is to find out the positive economic benefits that the proposed system is likely to bring to the organization. The assessment includes identification of both expected benefits with as much quantification as possible as well as the costs involved. Economic feasibility study is basically a cost–benefit analysis of the proposed system. For example, a proposed computer-based project control system is expected to bring benefits like savings in project time and cost while incurring a little cost in design and development of the proposed system.

Schedule feasibility is estimating the time needed to develop the system. If the time schedule for development is too long, the proposed system may not be of any use because of technological, organizational and environmental changes in the meantime. Schedule feasibility is further to check the reasonableness of the time frame of design and development of the proposed system against the backdrop of available technical expertise.

Motivational feasibility study is the investigation of the impact of human factors on the proposed IS development. The complexity of the design of the proposed system, the technical challenges and the available development tools have got important bearing on the motivation of the system developers which in turn affects the development process. In short, motivation feasibility is to study and analyse the motivation of the system developers.

Operational feasibility is a measure of how well the proposed system solves the problems and satisfies the requirements identified during the analysis phase of the system. The important aspects covered under operational feasibility study are the throughput, response time, quality of information, accuracy, operational and managerial control and so on arising out of the proposed system.

In short, operational feasibility study finds answers to the questions whether the current organizational practices and procedures will support the proposed system and will the proposed system, when developed, become workable?

During the feasibility study phase, the cost and the likely benefits out of the proposed system are estimated as accurately as possible to find out the ROI of the proposed system. It is worth mentioning that there may be both tangible and intangible costs and benefits. The intangible costs and benefits cannot be quantified but nevertheless, they need to be identified and assessed as far as practicable. At the end of the feasibility study as mentioned above, a feasibility report is prepared and submitted to the management for acceptance, rejection or acceptance with modifications. The SDLC can proceed to the next phase, only if the feasibility report is accepted by the management.

9.4.3 System Analysis

This phase of SDLC has already been explained elaborately in Chapter 8 of this book.

9.4.4 Conceptual and Detailed System Design

This phase has also been explained elaborately in earlier paragraphs of this chapter.

9.4.5 Implementation

Implementation is the stage where the system designed and accepted by the users is actually put into practice. Implementation is a very important stage in the entire SDLC and it ensures the success of the new MIS. If not implemented properly, even a well-designed system can fail. Further, it is worth mentioning that implementation stage involves considerable time and cost as compared to the other stages of the total SDLC.

The major steps involved during implementation are briefly explained as follows:

1. **Acquiring and installation of the necessary hardware, software and supporting services:** The required hardware and the relevant software have to be installed and made fully operational. Prior to acquisition of hardware and software, vendors for the same need to be selected. Along with hardware and software, support services such as electricity, air conditioning and also computer-related materials such as furniture, stationery items and data storage like compact discs need to be provisioned.

2. **Conversion of existing data files, creation of new files and databases:** The data from the old legacy systems need to be converted for being compatible with the formats of the new system. The database needs to be set up with proper backup, security and recovery procedures. During this step, all the programs developed for the system are loaded on the computers of the users of the new system.

3. **Training of the users:** A comprehensive awareness-cum-orientation programme needs to be organized for the management and support personnel to make them aware of the various features of the new system, its nature and objectives and benefits to the organization derived out of it. The awareness programme may be a seminar or a workshop of short duration of about a week or so. The training of the users of the system should be a comprehensive one, covering all important aspects of the system particularly the operational details such as:
   i. What the new system is supposed to do?
   ii. What are the salient differences in the operation of the new system with the previous one, if any?
   iii. How to execute the system?
   iv. How to feed the input data to the system?
   v. What are the scrutiny and internal checks to be exercised with the system?
   vi. The processing details of the system to convert data into meaningful information must be understood.
   vii. What are the various reports and their formats? How to make use of the reports?
   viii. What are the measures of performance of the system and the operating personnel?
   x. What new skills are to be developed by the users as well as their subordinates?
   x. What changes have to be made in the existing system and procedures? Elaborate and formal training programmes should be conducted for the operating personnel of the system who perform daily operations such as computer operators and file maintenance personnel.

4. **Changeover:** Changeover is basically the shifting of working from the existing to the new system. The changeover is usually completed in one of the following ways:
   i. **Direct changeover:** This is the complete cut-off of the existing system and installation of the new system. Direct changeover is risky and there is a time gap during changeover during which no system (existing or new) is in operation. This is suitable for very small MIS.

    ii. **Parallel run and cut off:** In parallel run, both the existing and the new systems are run simultaneously for a predefined period of time depending upon the size, complexity and importance of the system being implemented. This method of changeover though expensive, is less risky as the new system becomes foolproof. It is suitable for essential systems such as payroll and billing.

    iii. **Changeover in segments:** This method of changeover is basically phased replacement of the existing system with the new one. In this case, the subsystems of the existing system are replaced by the same from the new system in a phased manner and in logical sequence. This method is less risky than the direct changeover method.

5. **Documentation:** Documentation is of paramount importance in SDLC. It ensures the continuity of the system with the employees leaving the organization. Moreover, documentation is essentially needed in case of troubleshooting, modification and upgrading the system to cope up with organizational changes. There are usually two types of documentation, namely user or operator documentation and system documentation. User documentation is primarily meant for the users of the new system and contains operational details such as how to operate the system, how to feed data or information to the system, how to generate various management information reports, various types of error messages to be faced by the users and the remedial actions thereof. User documentation takes the form of user manual. System documentation facilitates understanding of the system. It is also vital for developing an altogether new MIS, if need arises due to organizational changes.

    System documentation contains the details of system design, software development, programs, coding, description of master files, database, data processing and retrieving of data and information and so on.

6. **Maintenance and review of the new system:** The maintenance function commences after the system has been implemented fully. Maintenance of the system is needed to reduce or eliminate errors during its working life arising out of design and environmental changes. It is an ongoing monitoring process with an objective of improving the effectiveness and efficiency of the system within the cost constraints. The review of the system is done for understanding the full capabilities of the system and its performance and for identifying the required changes, which may be needed pursuant to the following changes:

    i. Policy change

    ii. Change of management resulting in a change in reports

    iii. Changes in forms

    iv. Operating system and procedural changes

    v. Changes in hardware and software

    vi. Changes due to internal controls, checks and security needs.

Maintenance and review of the system may also become necessary due to environmental changes related to changes in government rules, regulations and legislation, general economic conditions, industry and market competition and emerging technologies. In short, there is a continual flow of organizational and environmental changes that require constant updating of the MIS in an organization.

CASE STUDY 9: MEDALLION THEATRE—TICKET SALES SYSTEM

Background

Dr Thomas Waggoner, a professor of ISs with an American university, came to Will Call window at the Medallion Theatre to pick up two tickets he had reserved for himself and his wife for celebrating their marriage anniversary. However, to his utter surprise, he found that his tickets for the reserved seats were sold to another patron due to an oversight. Fortunately, the box office manager could arrange for Dr Waggoner and his wife two box seats which had not been claimed by any other patron.

In the course of conversation with the box office manager, Dr Waggoner came to know that similar types of mistakes due to oversight was frequent and he offered to help the Medallion theatre management to analyse, redesign and develop their ticket sales system to avoid this type of problem in future and to improve customer satisfaction.

Objective

The objective of this case study is to provide an insight for MIS students to apply their knowledge of data modelling, process modelling and user interface design. Moreover, they can also apply their knowledge and skills to design class diagrams/entity relationship diagram as well as create a physical database based on IS requirement specifications for this case and similar other cases. This case study presents a small but realistic example of system analysis, design and development.

Specific requirements of the ticket sales system:

The Medallion theatre ticket sales office has to monitor the patrons, productions, performances, seats and tickets. So far as a computerized system is concerned, for each of the above entities the following information needs to be kept.

> **Patron:** Unique patron number, last name, first name, street address, city, state, pin code, telephone number and email address.
> **Productions:** Production name and production type (such as play or concert).
> **Performance:** Date of the performance and the time of performance (such as matinee, evening or night performance). A production can have multiple performances on different dates and also a production can have multiple performances (such as matinee, evening and night) on the same date.
> **Seats:** Unique seat number, seat category (such as orchestra, mezzanine, balcony and box) and the ticket price.
> **Tickets:** Ticket number, seat number and ticket price.

When patrons either call or get down to reserve or purchase tickets, their names, addresses and contact information are recorded, if those are not already there in the computer files. Patrons then select the production, performance date and time and their seats from the available seats as displayed or shown to them. A ticket identifies a particular seat for a specific performance.

Appropriate and user-friendly data entry/edit screens need to be designed and created to enter and edit data for patrons, performances as well as ticket sales for various seat types. The ticket sale system should generate and display information on seats sold or seats vacant for a particular performance.

The system should also generate the seats reserved/purchased by patrons (patron number or name wise) for any specific performance.

Solution

The proposed solution has been made based on object-oriented analysis and design. The use-case diagram, class diagram and the user-interface design in the form of create/edit screens have been shown as the following diagrams:

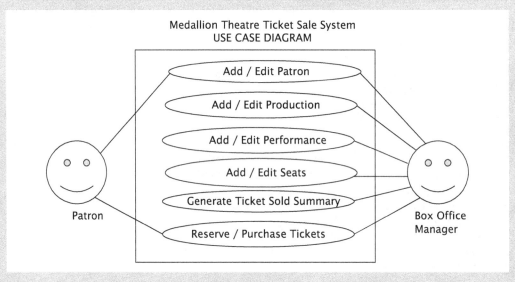

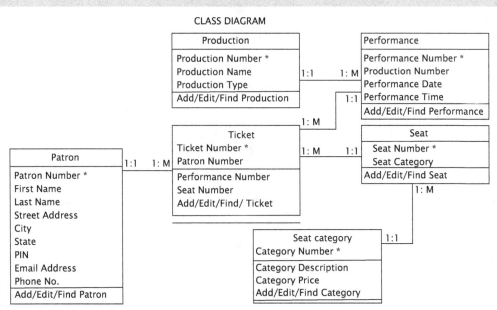

USER INTERFACE DIAGRAMS
Patron Information CREATE/ EDIT Screen

Patron Information

Patron No.　　　3005

First Name　　　RITA　　　　Last Name　　BISWAS

Street　　　　　301 Middleton

City　　　　　Kolkata　　　State　　West Bengal　　PIN　　700068

Phone No.　　　(033)24730014

Email Address　rita1955@gmail.com　　　| ADD | FIND | MAIN MENU |

Production and Performances CREATE / EDIT SCREEN

Production

Production No.　　　101

Production Name　　Chandalika

Production Type　　Dance Drama

Performances

Performance	Date	Time
1050	20/10/2018	7:30PM
1051	21/10/2018	3:00PM
1052	22/10/2018	3:00PM
1053	22/10/2018	7:30PM

Record #	4	ADD	EDITS	SEARCH

ADD	FIND	MAIN MENU

SEATS AND SEAT CATEGORIES

SEATS

Category Code	BAL ▽
Description	Balcony
Category Price	₹100

SEATS

Seat
G28
G29
G30
H1
H2

Record No. _____

ADD	FIND	MAIN MENU

TICKET SALES SCREEN

TICKET SALES

Patron   SOM NITIN ▽

Tickets

Ticket#	Production :	Performance		Seat	Price
30	A TALE OF TWO CITIES ▽	09/20/2018	7:30PM ▽	A11	₹300
31	A TALE OF TWO CITIES ▽	09/20/2018	7:30PM ▽	A12	₹300

Find Patron	Main Menu

REPORT OF SEATS SOLD BY PERFORMANCE

SEATS SOLD BY PERFORMANCE				
Production : A Tale of 2 Cities				
Performance Date	Performance Time	Seat Number	Ticket #	Patron Name
09/20/2018	7:30 PM			
		A11	30	Som Nitin
		A12	31	Som Nitin
09/21/2018	2:30 PM	Seat Number	Ticket #	Patron Name
		H5	21	Kar Sachin
		H6	22	Kar Sachin
		H7	23	Kar Sachin
		H8	24	Kar Sachin

REPORT OF SEATS SOLD TO PATRONS

Seats Sold to Patrons			
Patron Name : Kar Sachin			
Phone : (033) 24726106	Email: Kars@gmail.com		
Production Name	Date	Time	Seat #
A Tale of Two Cities	09/21/2018	2:30 PM	H5
	09/21/2018	2:30 PM	H6
	09/21/2018	2:30 PM	H7
	09/21/2018	2:30 PM	H8
Patron Name : Som Nitin			
Phone : (033) 24719286	Email: somn@gmail.com		
Production Name	Date	Time	Seat #
A Tale of Two Cities	09/20/2018	7:30 PM	A11
	09/20/2018	7:30 PM	A12

Conclusion

This case study is an application of concepts and techniques of system analysis and design, database and system development.

Source: Fox (2017).

• Review Questions •

1. What are the popular approaches to study the information needs of managers?

2. What is conceptual design of a system? What are the key tasks associated with it?

3. What are the criteria for comparing alternative conceptual designs?

4. Match the items in column A with those in column B.

Column A	Column B
System	Purchase control
Subsystem	Enter supply order details
Functional component	Update supplier file
Task	Find supplier record
Subtask	Vendor rating package
Operational element	Supplier file processing

5. What are the different types of charts used to sketch the detailed system design? Explain the charts.

6. What is SDLC? What are the important phases of SDLC?

7. What is system feasibility study? What are the different types of feasibility study? Briefly explain.

8. What are the important task covered under the implementation phase of SDLC?

9. Briefly explain the two major types of system documentation.

10. What are the major reasons for system maintenance?

Bibliography

Burch, J. G., Jr., and F. R. Strater Jr. *Information Systems: Theory and Practice*. Santa Barbara, CA: Hamilton Publishing, 1973.

Fox, T. L. 'Teaching Note: Systems Analysis, Design and Development Case Study: Medallion Theatre—Ticket Sales System.' *Journal of the International Academy for Case Studies* 23, no. 2 (2017), 11–17.

Murdick, R. G., and J. E. Ross. *Information Systems for Modern Management*. Englewood Cliffs, NJ: Prentice Hall, 1971.

Senn, J. A. *Analysis and Design of Information Systems*, 2nd ed. New York, NY: McGraw-Hill, 1989.

10
CHAPTER

Database and Database Management Systems

10.1 Introduction and Database Definition

The concept of MIS is to convert business data into appropriate management information to facilitate decision-making. Business decisions are supported by information or processed data and the data are stored and retrieved from a database. The information as obtained from the database is provided to various database users or decision-makers.

According to James Martin, 'A database is a collection of data that is shared and used for multiple purposes.' A company database is a repository or store of all types of company data which are captured, validated and stored into proper physical locations in the database for subsequent retrieval as information to various categories of users. A database caters to the information needs of the managers belonging to the various functions such as sales, manufacturing, purchase, finance and personnel as well as to various levels in the hierarchy of the organization such as strategic planning, management control and operational control.

10.2 Data Aggregates

The data stored in a database are in the form of files such as customer file, product file and employee file. The files comprise data records which are also known as individual instances or entities in a file. For example, an employee file consists of many employee records. Each record in turn consists of individual fields or elements known as the attributes of a record such as for an employee record, the data fields may be employee identification number, name, date of joining, grade and salary. Figure 10.1 shows the concept of data aggregates in a database. It may be mentioned here that the classic database was based on the above concept. However, with the recent development in big data analysis, the concept of data aggregates has undergone modification, where data records are not only entities with fields of data attributes consisting of text, numeric data and dates but the records may be in the form of documents, images (photographs) in addition to conventional data records as described above. Such types of databases have been described later.

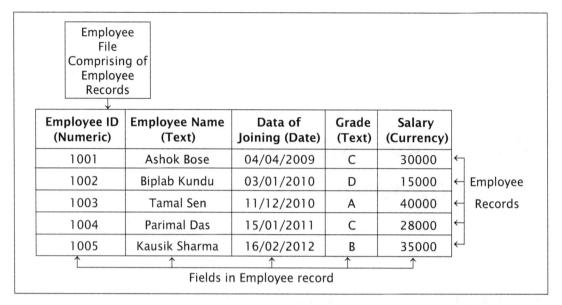

FIGURE 10.1   Data Aggregates in a Database

10.3 Data Organization in a Database

The physical arrangement of data records in a database determines the location of the data records in the database as well as the structure of the arrangement. The organization of data in the database can take various forms known as database models such as:

Hierarchical model: In case of hierarchical model as shown in Figure 10.2, the data records in a file are arranged into echelons or levels, the records in a higher level are the parent records for the corresponding child records which are placed in the next lower level or echelon. Each parent record can have multiple child records in one-to-many relationship. However, a child record cannot have more than one parent record. The records bearing parent–child relationship are connected through links (fields which indicate the relationship). Hierarchical storage structure of data records is also known as the tree structure.

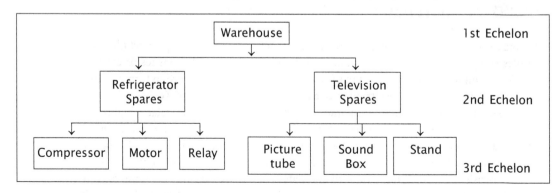

FIGURE 10.2   Hierarchical Arrangement of Data Records

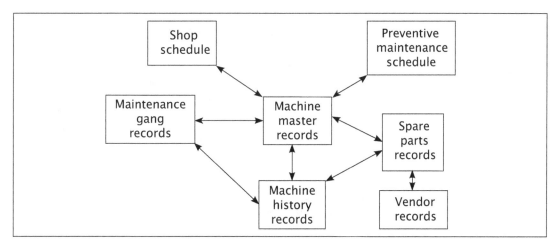

FIGURE 10.3 Network Arrangement of Data Records

Referring to Figure 10.2, if we wish to obtain a record pertaining to the third echelon, say, a 'relay' of a particular make and model, we have to first go to the particular warehouse which stores 'refrigerator spares' and search records for the same until we reach the records of 'relay' and then finally search the particular 'relay'.

Network model: In a network model, complex associations are organized among data records belonging to related groups. Figure 10.3 shows a network database relating to a maintenance system.

An employee ordering the spare part of a machine will search for the machine to be ordered, then will search for the machine records for the particular machine in the machine master to find the link (pointer), which will locate the frequency of replacement of the spare in the machine history records. It may be mentioned here that the physical representation of the above structure including the linkages is very complex and beyond the scope of the conceptual point of view presented here.

Relational model: In case of a relational database, the data are stored in the form of tables (known as relations) consisting of rows and columns. The individual rows known as the tuples are the data records or entities, and the columns constitute the fields or the attributes of the data records as already shown in Figure 10.1. The relational approach to database model is perhaps the most popular one among various classic database models because of the ease of the procedural tasks related to creation, retrieval, updating and deleting (CRUD) of data records. The features of relational database and its programming have been elaborated in subsequent paragraphs of this chapter.

Physical and logical data records in a database: The physical data records in a database are the physical arrangement of the data records in their respective locations. However, logical data records represent the relationship among the records irrespective of their physical locations or arrangements in a database. Further, for a particular physical organization of data records, there can be more than one logical relationship among the records. The above views of a database records have been illustrated in Table 10.1 where the same physical arrangement of employee records in a table as shown in Figure 10.1 has been reproduced. The physical arrangement of the five employee records is as shown in Table 10.1 (a). However, relationships among the records can be more than one as shown in Table 10.1 (b), (c) and (d) depending on the name in alphabetical order, grade and salary in ascending order of value.

TABLE 10.1 Physical and Logical Arrangement of Data Records

Employee ID (Numeric)	Employee Name (Text)	Data of Joining (Date)	Grade (Text)	Salary (Currency)
1001	Ashok Bose	04/04/2009	C	30000
1002	Biplab Kundu	03/01/2010	D	15000
1003	Tamal Sen	11/12/2010	A	40000
1004	Parimal Das	15/01/2011	C	28000
1005	Kausik Sharma	16/02/2012	B	35000

(a) Physical Arrangement: 1001 → 1002 → 1003 → 1004 → 1005

(b) Logical relationship (1)

    In alphabetic order of Name: 1001 → 1002 → 1005 → 1004 → 1003

(c) Logical relationship (2)

    In alphabetic order of Grade: 1003 → 1005 → 1001 → 1004 → 1002

(d) Logical relationship (3)

    In ascending order of Salary: 1002 → 1004 → 1001 → 1005 → 1003

10.4 Data Independence (Schemas and Subschemas)

A database integrates the data files pertaining to the various applications of interest to the users of data of an organization. The purpose is mainly to eliminate redundant data files being maintained by the different applications as also to avoid duplication of efforts in maintaining separate data files for the separate applications. Moreover, such stand-alone and isolated data files may also cause further complications, if such files are used or shared by a number of application programs in an organization. The above statements are clarified with a simple example as shown in Figures 10.4 and 10.5 respectively.

In Figure 10.4, job allocation and employee pay are two separate tables and are used by job allocation manager and accounts manager. In this arrangement, the two tables have got both employee name which is a duplication and therefore needs more data storage space and also duplication of efforts while updating employee names in both the tables. However, the two tables can be integrated as shown in Figure 10.5 where unlike employee name being stored twice, a separate table with employee ID and name has been created and linked with the job allocation table as also the employee pay table. Any subsequent updating of employee name (addition of new employee name, deletion of name or amendment of name) can be performed only on the employee name table. It may be, however, noted that two tables, namely job allocation and employee pay, use data from the employee name table. Therefore, changes of the employee name table structure are likely to call for changes in both the application programs related to job allocation and employee pay. Likewise, any change in one of the two above-mentioned application programs is likely to necessitate changes in employee name table directly and in the other application program indirectly.

Job Allocation Table

Job #	Job Description	Employee #	Employee Name
J01	Pin grinding	E001	Arun Gupta
—	—	—	—
—	—	—	—
—	—	—	—

Separate tables

Employee Pay Table

Employee #	Employee Name (₹)	Basic Pay (₹)	Allowance
E001	Arun Gupta	8000	4000
—	—	—	—
—	—	—	—
—	—	—	—

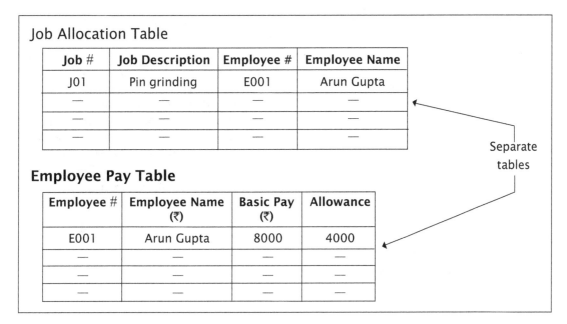

FIGURE 10.4 Job Allocation and Employee Pay Tables

Job Allocation Table

Job #	Job Description	Employee #
J01	Pin Grinding	E001
—	—	—
—	—	—
—	—	—

Employee Pay Table

Employee #	Basic Pay (₹)	Allowance (₹)
E001	8000	4000
—	—	—
—	—	—
—	—	—

Employee Name Table

Employee #	Employee Name
E001	Arun Gupta
—	—
—	—
—	—

FIGURE 10.5 Job Allocation, Employee Pay and Employee Name Tables

The above difficulty led to the concept of physical data independence as an essential requirement of an integrated database. Precisely, it means that physical data structure in a database can be changed independent of the application programs. For example, an employee table consisting of employee#, name, date of joining, salary as attributes can be changed with respect to the attributes date of joining and salary in whatever way, without affecting an application program using or viewing the employee# and name only.

This can be achieved by a three-tier architecture of an integrated database. The three tiers are known as internal schema, conceptual schema and external schema (or subschema) in database parlance.

Internal Schema shows the physical storage structure of data in the database. It describes the complete data storage in the database and the paths to access the data. Conceptual schema also known as the logical organization of the database hides the details of physical storage structures and concentrates on describing entities, data attributes and their types, relationships and their operations and constraints.

External Schema also known as the subschema is a subset of the database in which a particular application or user group is interested. Thus, the database software also known as the DBMS (to be described later) provides different views or subschema to different users of the database depending upon individual needs without exposing the entire conceptual or internal schema of the database to the users. The application programmer's view is referred to as the subschema or the local view as compared to the global view or conceptual schema. This feature facilitates the concept of data independence as shown in Figure 10.6.

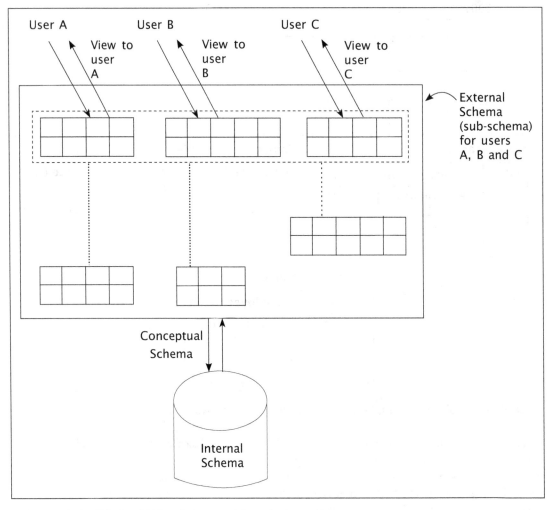

FIGURE 10.6 Schema, Sub-schema and Data Independence

10.4.1 Metadata

Metadata is only data about the data, which actually exist in the database storage. The three schemas, namely internal schema, conceptual schema and the external schema are only metadata describing the actual data.

Any user request for specific data (external schema) needs information in metadata in order to accomplish mapping among the conceptual schema and then into the internal schema. The mapping among the levels is accomplished through metadata which precisely describes the location and the type of data in the database.

10.4.2 Database Schema and Database Instances

In any database model, it is important to differentiate between the overall description of the database and the database itself. The former is called the database schema, while the latter is known as database instance.

Database schema show the overall description of the data in the database including locations through a set of definitions or mappings which is specified during database design and which does not frequently change.

Database instance, on the other hand, is the content or actual data at any particular instant, and the same may change frequently during database operations to be described later in this chapter. It only depicts the database state at any point of time. For example, when a database defined through the schema remains in empty state and data are subsequently loaded into it, the initial state is obtained.

10.5 Features of a Relational Database

A relational database consists of tables which are the building blocks of the database. As earlier stated also, each table consists of rows and columns similar to a spreadsheet. Each row in a table contains data related to the same kind of thing. However, each table contains data related to a particular thing. For example, you may have one table for data related to your customers where each row contains data related to one single customer only. Similarly, we may have different tables in the database for data related to employees, inventory, customer orders and so on. Each repeating row in an employee table contains same formatted data about one single employee. Each column in a table contains a particular piece of data related to that row. For example, in the employee table, we may have columns representing employee name (text), date of birth (date), grade (numeric) and salary (currency). However, the columns, once defined, become fixed insofar as the types of data are concerned. For example, we cannot store text data in the grade column or the date of birth column. The structure of each table, which depicts the type of data it contains as explained above, is defined initially and also subsequently during day-to-day operation of the database. Data can be modified, retrieved or deleted from the tables, but strictly conforming to the initially defined structures of the tables at any point of time. This concept of data manipulation is known as 'CRUD' which has been explained in Figure 10.7. A table is also known as a relation in which each row is an entity known as 'tuple' and each column is an 'attribute'.

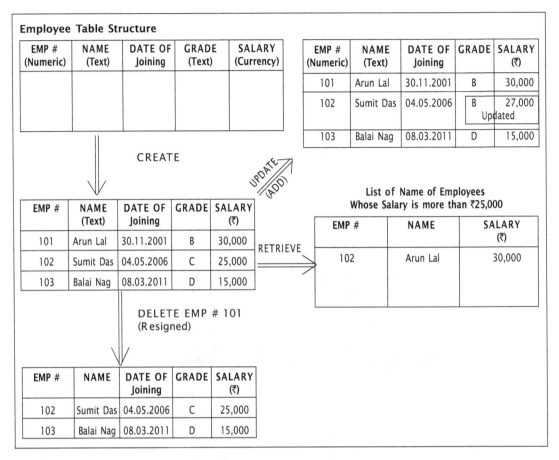

EMP # (Numeric)	NAME (Text)	DATE OF Joining	GRADE (Text)	SALARY (Currency)

EMP # (Numeric)	NAME (Text)	DATE OF Joining	GRADE	SALARY (₹)
101	Arun Lal	30.11.2001	B	30,000
102	Sumit Das	04.05.2006	B	27,000 Updated
103	Balai Nag	08.03.2011	D	15,000

CREATE

UPDATE (ADD)

EMP #	NAME (Text)	DATE OF Joining	GRADE	SALARY (₹)
101	Arun Lal	30.11.2001	B	30,000
102	Sumit Das	04.05.2006	C	25,000
103	Balai Nag	08.03.2011	D	15,000

RETRIEVE

List of Name of Employees Whose Salary is more than ₹25,000

EMP #	NAME	SALARY (₹)
102	Arun Lal	30,000

DELETE EMP # 101 (Resigned)

EMP #	NAME	DATE OF Joining	GRADE	SALARY (₹)
102	Sumit Das	04.05.2006	C	25,000
103	Balai Nag	08.03.2011	D	15,000

FIGURE 10.7 CRUD Concept of a Relation

10.5.1 Attributes

Attributes (columns in a relation) are the characteristics which together specify an entity. The attributes can be classified into five different types, namely simple or composite, keys and non-keys, single or multiple value, stored or derived and required or optional attributes. Let the above types of attributes be explained with simple examples:

Simple attributes cannot be split into smaller parts, whereas composite attributes can be divided into sub-parts. Age and date of joining of an employee are simple attributes, whereas name of an employee is an example of composite attribute since it consists of last name and first name.

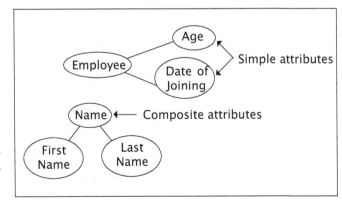

Keys are employee ID, product ID and department ID, which uniquely define an entity in a relation, whereas age, salary, address and so on are non-key entities since two employees (entities) can have same value for these attributes.

Single-value attributes are those which can have only one single value for any one entity, whereas in case of multi-valued attributes there can be more than one value for any particular entity. For example, last name of an employee is a single-valued entity since an employee can have one last name only. However, cell phone number is a multi-value attribute since one employee can have more than one cell phone.

Derived attributes are those whose values can be derived based on other attributes known as stored attributes. For example, date of birth of an employee is a stored attribute, while age of an employee is a derived attribute which can be arrived at from his/her date of birth.

Required attributes are essentially needed to have values such as employee ID and name, whereas optional attributes may or may not be having any value such as spouse of an employee, which a particular employee may or may not have.

In a table, there can be unique and non-unique columns. Unique columns are those where the data corresponding to all rows in that column are unique and no two values are same at any point of time. For example, name, date of joining, grade and salary can be non-unique columns since there can be instances that name or date of joining or grade or salary for two employees may be same. However, employee number (employee #), which is generated for each employee record, is unique for each employee.

A column in a table which is a generated unique one is called the primary key of the table. The primary key uniquely identifies any row of a table in a database. Incidentally, it may so happen that a column other than the generated primary key may be unique. For example, if we add a column in the employee table shown earlier to include the permanent account number (PAN) allotted by the income tax department, the column obviously will be an unique one as no two employees can have the same PAN. However, any DBMS always generates the primary key known as the generated primary key or the surrogate primary key irrespective of whether the table already has got one unique column. The primary key, in addition to uniquely identifying any row (entity), also helps in establishing a relationship among tables as explained in the following paragraph.

10.5.2 Tuple

A 'tuple' is a particular row in a table. For example, in an Employee table there will be as many tuples (rows) as the number of employees. Each tuple is uniquely identified in the above-mentioned Employee table by the employee identification number. Each tuple in a table is one distinct entity.

10.5.3 Establishing Relationships among Tables—Foreign Keys

The tables in a database contain data which are naturally connected, and therefore in a database, tables need to be connected through their relationships. For example, in case of a college database, we may define a student table, a faculty member table and a department table, each one of which has got a primary key for its entities. However, there exist relationships among the tables because students are taught by the faculty members and students belong to the departments. Although the data contained by the three tables are different, there exist relationships among them.

The relationships among the tables are established through foreign keys which are primary keys in one table, but non-unique in the other table and which establish relationships between the two tables.

For example, Figures 10.8a and 10.8b describe tables for students and departments of a college. The primary keys for the two tables are the student ID and the department ID respectively. Now, any student belongs to a particular department only, but a department has got many students. This is a case of one-to-many relationship. In order to establish a relationship between the student table with the department,

Student Table

Student ID	Student Name	Tel. No.	E-mail	Present Class
101	Joyeeta Basak	9830612881	basakj@.....	B.Sc First year
102	Arnab Saha	9435712096	arnab@.....	B.A. Second year
103	Partha Banerjee	9737145111	banerjeep@.....	B.Sc Third year
—	—	—	—	—
—	—	—	—	—
—	—	—	—	—

↑
Primary Key

FIGURE 10.8a Student Table

Department Table

Department ID	Department Name	Name of HOD	Tel. No.	E-mail of HOD
11	Physics	Dr. Santanu Roy	9431012095	santanu@.....
12	Chemistry	Dr. Ila Mitra	8411225150	mitra.ila@.....
13	English	Dr. Robin Das	9830132424	rabindas@.....
—	—	—	—	—
—	—	—	—	—
—	—	—	—	—

↑
Primary Key (Unique)   Link 1

Student Table with a Foreign Key   Non-unique

Primary key (Unique)   Foreign Key

Student ID	Student Name	Tel. No.	E-mail	Present Class	Department
101	Joyeeta Basak	9830612881	basakj@.....	B.Sc First year	11
102	Arnab Saha	9435712096	arnab@.....	B.A. Second year	13
103	Partha Banerjee	9737145111	banerjeep@.....	B.Sc Third year	11
—	—	—	—	—	—
—	—	—	—	—	—
—	—	—	—	—	—

Link 2

FIGURE 10.8b Foreign Key Connecting Student Table with Department Table

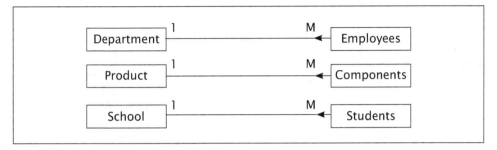

FIGURE 10.9 One-to-many (1:M) Relationships

we need to add a column in the student table to accommodate the department ID from the department table against the student ID row-wise, and this extra column thus establishes the connection between the two tables as shown in Figures 10.8a and 10.8b.

It may be noted that the department ID shown in the student table, which connects student entity with the concerned department of the student, is however, non-unique although the same is a unique prime key in the department table. This is because the same department ID can occur more than once (such as in the example department, ID '11' has appeared twice) in the student table though the same is unique in the department table. This is because more than one student belong to a particular department but not the other way, that is, one student cannot belong to more than one department. A key which is unique in one table and is the prime key in that table may not be unique in another table, but still, it is a key in the table though non-unique. Such a key, which is non-unique in a table is known as the 'foreign key'. In Figure 10.8, the department ID, though a unique and 'prime key' in department table, is the non-unique 'foreign key' in the student table. The foreign key establishes contacts between two tables as shown as Link 1 and Link 2 in Figure 10.8b.

Another feature of the relationship shown in Figure 10.8b is the 'one-to-many' relationship. That is to say, one department has many students, but one student cannot have more than one department. The 'one-to-many' relationship exists in many business situations as shown in Figure 10.9.

10.5.4 Representing Many-to-Many (M: M) Relationships in Relational Database

Unlike one-to-many relationship, we cannot express many-to-many relationship directly by a foreign key. The relationships in such cases are established between the two tables indirectly by creating a third table for linking through two one-to-many relationships. The method has been explained with an example shown in Figure 10.10. The figure shows a student table and a faculty member table of a college. The relationship between them is a many-to-many one. Because a student can be taught by many faculty members, at the same time, a faculty member can teach many students. The relationship is established through a linking table, namely faculty member-student table.

It may be noted that the faculty member table and the student table remain isolated and the link is established with a faculty member-student table through two one-to-many relationships as shown in Figure 10.10 and the student ID and faculty member ID relationships (many-to-many) are found in the same linking table. We can go from student ID in student table to the faculty member-student ID and map the student ID in an all faculty-member ID in the same linking table. We can also start with faculty-member ID and then map the faculty-member ID in the all student ID in the linking table.

Faculty Member Table

Faculty Member ID	Faculty Member Name	Tel. No.	Email (ID)	Designation
11	Dr. Santanu Mitra	9431012095	santanum@gmail.com	Professor
12	Dr. Bijon Sarkar	8431122515	sarkarb@...	Associate professor
13	Mr. Subrata Kar	9830132424	skar@...	Assistant professor

Faculty Member—
—Student Table

Faculty Member ID	Student ID
11	103
11	101
12	102
13	103

Linking table

Student Table

Student ID	Student Name	Tel No.	Email ID	Present Class
101	Jayeeta Basak	9830612881	basakj@...	B.Sc 1st year
102		9435712096	arnab@...	B.A. 2nd year
103		9737145111	banerjeep@...	B.Sc 3rd year

FIGURE 10.10 Many-to-many Relationships with Linking Table

10.5.5 Composite Keys

Sometimes, it may so happen that there is no unique column in a table which can identify each row in the table uniquely. In such a situation, though one value does not uniquely identify a row, two values together uniquely identify a row. In that case, we can combine the two column values to make a unique key which is known as a composite key. Let me illustrate a composite key with an example shown in Table 10.2, which shows a database relation containing records of the office bearers of a club for different years.

The attributes are the post held, year, last name, first name and membership number of each office bearer of the club during the different years. It may be seen from the above table that no single column has got values to identify each row uniquely. Same value can be found in more than one row of each column. Therefore, we are not in a position to find a primary key except generating a surrogate key uniquely. However, without the same, we can find a combination of the values in columns post held and year as a unique combination which can uniquely identify each row. In this case, post held, and year combined constitute a composite key. For example, president for the year 2014 is a unique value. Composite keys are useful in joining tables together to create multiple relationships.

TABLE 10.2 Composite Key Example

Club-Office Bearers

Post held	Year	Last Name	First Name	Membership No.
President	2014	Mehra	Anil	116
Secretary	2014	Baruah	Santosh	201
Treasurer	2014	Saxena	Sanjeev	220
President	2015	Mehra	Anil	116
Secretary	2015	Sarkar	Jayanta	230
Treasurer	2015	Bajaj	Deepak	305

10.5.6 Transactions and the ACID Test

Data in a database get updated or changed with transactions. A transaction is therefore very important for the operations on databases. If the DBMS does not take care of certain essential features of any transaction, which changes the data in a database, there will be error in the data of the database. For example, a database pertaining to the inventory management system might contain two tables, namely the stock table and the inventory consumption table. There may be other tables also. Now if there is a withdrawal of a certain quantity, say, X units of a particular item of material, the DBMS will first subtract the quantity X from the stock value of the item in the stock table and then will add the same X to the material consumption figure contained in the record of the item in the inventory consumption table. However, it may so happen that the above transaction (material withdrawal) may update the stock in the stock table but fails to update the inventory consumption table because of any temporary glitch in the system such as power failure. The result will be an erroneous data in the inventory consumption table. Therefore, the DBMS must ensure that in such cases, the data updated in the stock table must be changed back to the original value. This brings the concept of atomic nature of the transaction, which means that all the changes made to a database by a transaction must be done together. Otherwise, the transaction must not do any of the changes. The other features relating to transactions for database data updating are the consistency, isolated and durable and all these features give rise to the acronym 'ACID'. Consistency implies that any transaction must change the database from one valid state to another valid state based on the rules of the database. Even if a transaction is successfully atomic, it cannot still result in a violation of the integrity rules of the database, such as the referential integrity which means that if B references A, then A must exist. Isolation refers to the data and the transaction being essentially locked during the occurrence of the transaction. Durability refers to the transaction being considered robust and the change made by it remains guaranteed even in case of any hardware disruption such as power failure. Majority of DBMS take care of ACID features as explained above.

10.5.7 Relationship Rules and Referential Integrity

Referential integrity basically is a constraint that does not allow any entry in a row of a table if the foreign key for that entry does not exist in the table which has got the prime key. Let us illustrate the

End product

End Product ID	Description	Unit of measure	Price (₹)
101	Stop cock	Number	570
102	Plastic tap	Number	50
103	Valve	Number	600

Components

Component ID	Nomenclature	Unit of measure	Price (₹)	End product ID
301	Inner pass	Number	100	101
302	Spindle	Number	150	101
303	Spring washer set	Number	40	103
304	Shower Nozzle	Number	200	110

× Not allowed due to Referential Integrity

FIGURE 10.11   Referential Integrity and the Relationship Rules

relationship rules and the referential integrity with an example. Figure 10.11 shows two tables, one being an end-product table and the other the component table. The components are assembled to make up the end products.

It may be noted that due to referential integrity, the DBMS does not allow one to create a record with component ID 304 in the component table since the foreign key 110 does not appear in the end-product-ID table. Similarly, if one entity (end-product ID 101) needs to be deleted from the end-product table, first the records in the component table pertaining to that particular end-product ID (in this case component ID 301 and 302) need to be deleted first and then the record with end-product ID 101 can be deleted.

10.6 Database Modelling: Normalization

Normalization is a process of database modelling where one applies a set of formal criteria and rules known as normalization in database parlance. Normalization facilitates optimization of database design considering data storage, ease of data manipulation, minimum redundancy in data and more reliability to work with the database. The normal forms were developed by Edgar Codd, called the father of relational database.

The important normal forms are the first normal form (1NF), second normal form (2NF) and 3NF. However, there are also normal forms higher than 3NF.

10.6.1 First Normal Form (1NF)

The First Normal Form (1NF) stipulates that each column and each table in a database should contain one value and there should not be repeating groups in a table. For example, let us consider an employee table as shown in Figure 10.12 having employee ID (primary key), first name, last name, email ID and mobile number as the columns of the table. Now, it may so happen that any employee can have more than one mobile telephone and we want to store the same in the employee table. One way of doing the same is to store the multiple mobile numbers in the mobile number column separated by delimiters (,) but that violates 1NF as there cannot be more than one value in any field or column. The other way is to create multiple columns for storing more than one mobile number which again violates 1NF as repeating groups are not permitted in 1NF. Hence, in order to comply with 1NF, a separate table has to be created with mobile numbers and employee ID columns. Employee ID in this linking table is a foreign key and the relationship between the employee table and the employee ID—mobile number table is a one-to-many relationship as shown in Figure 10.12.

Employee ID	First Name	Last Name	E-mail ID	Mobile No.
101	Ashoke	Bose	bashok@........	9431112096
102	Sachin	De	dsachin@........	9832288428
103	Partha	Banerjee	bpartha@........	9433101281

Employee ID	First Name	Last Name	E-mail ID	Mobile Numbers
101	Ashoke	Bose	bashok@..	9431112096, 9831115092
102	Sachin	De	dsachin@..	9832288428, 9731177010
103	Partha	Banerjee	bpartha@..	9433101281, 9432012096

Violates INF since more than one value of mobile numbers in a column.

Employee ID	First Name	Last Name	E-mail ID	Mobile No.1	Mobile No.2
101	Ashoke	Bose	boshok@...	9431112096	9831115092
102	Sachin	De	dsachin@...	9832288428	9731177010
103	Partha	Banerjee	bpartha@...	9433101281	9432012096

Repeating group of columns

Violates 1NF since there are repeating groups in mobile numbers data.

Primary Key

Foreign Key

Employee ID	First Name	Last Name	E-mail ID
101	Ashoke	Bose	boshok@...
102	Sachin	De	dsachin@...
103	Partha	Banerjee	bpartha@...

Employee ID	Mobile No.
101	9431112096
101	9831115092
102	9832288428
102	9731177010
103	9433101281
103	9432012096

One to many relationship
Compliance with INF

Separate Linking Table

FIGURE 10.12 First Normal Form

The solution to the 1NF is through the creation of a new table and the relationship between the two tables though in the above example is one-to-many, it might even require in some cases many-to-many relationship with a linking table.

10.6.2 Second Normal Form (2NF)

2NF of a relational database is applicable when and only when the following two conditions are satisfied by all the tables of the database.

Condition Number 1: The database has to be in the 1NF. That is, there is no repeating values in any column position for any particular row.

Condition Number 2: Any non-key field should be dependent on the entire primary key.

Now referring to condition number 2, the non-key field means the actual value in a particular non-key column position for a particular row. The Second Normal Form (2NF) may become an issue only when there is a composite primary key and not otherwise. Let me illustrate the above stipulations relating to the 2NF with an example shown in Figure 10.13. The example is about a tour operator operating package tours in various places of tourism in India. The package tour table shown in the upper part of Figure 10.13 is in 1NF since there is no duplicate data or repeating groups in any row.

However, it violates condition number 2 of 2NF since in this case a non-key, namely package tour name does not depend entirely on the composite prime key consisting of two attributes namely tour ID and the start date but it depends on the tour ID only which is a portion of the composite key. Hence, it violates 2NF. However, it can be made to comply with 2NF by removing the package-tour name from the

Package Tour Table

Tour ID	Start date	Package Tour Name	Capacity	Availability	Accommodation
AN 01	10.20.2016	Andaman	40	11	Hotel
KAS 02	07.29.2016	Kashmir	40	18	Hotel
AN 01	12.14.2016	Andaman	50	20	Resort
GOA 03	11.30.2016	Goa	30	15	Guest house
KAS 02	10.31.2016	Kashmir	30	25	Guest house

Composite Primary key   Not in Second Normal Form

Package Tour Table

Tour ID	Start date	Capacity	Availability	Accommodation
AN 01	10.20.2016	40	11	Hotel
KAS 02	07.29.2016	40	18	Hotel
AN 01	12.14.2016	50	20	Resort
GOA 03	11.30.2016	30	15	Guest house
KAS 02	10.31.2016	30	25	Guest house

Tour ID	Package Tour Name
AN 01	Andaman
KAS 02	Kashmir
GOA 03	Goa

Second Normal Form

FIGURE 10.13 Example of Second Normal Form

original package-tour table and creating a separate linking table with tour ID and the corresponding package-tour name as the attributes.

This table then creates one-to-many relationship with the package-tour table which now does not contain any non-key field not dependent entirely on the composite prime key.

10.6.3 Third Normal Form (3NF)

The Third Normal Form (3NF) of a relational database is applicable when and only when the following two conditions are fulfilled by all the tables of the database.

Condition 1: The database has to be in the 2NF. This condition obviously implies that the database is also in 1NF.

Condition 2: Every non-prime attribute of any relation (table) is non-transitively dependent on every prime key (including composite key) of the relation (table).

By transitive dependency, we mean if X is functionally dependent on Y and Y is functionally dependent on Z, then Z is transitively dependent on X via Y. Condition 2 implies that every non-prime attribute of the relation depends on the prime key (including composite key) only and not on any other non-prime key. This means that in case of 3NF, there cannot be any dependence among the non-prime attributes in any row. Figures 10.14 and 10.15 show two cases of 3NF. Figure 10.14 starts with the same package-tour table in the 2NF shown in Figure 10.13.

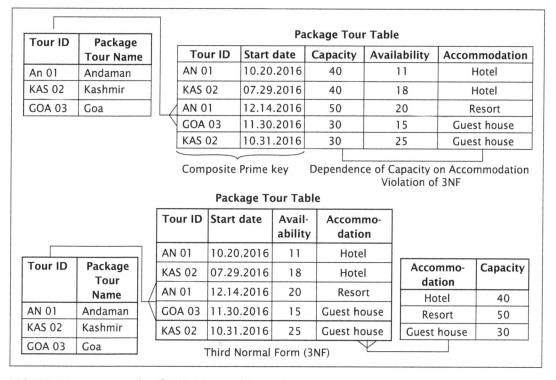

FIGURE 10.14 Example of Third Normal Form (3NF)

Product Table

Product ID	Product Description	UQ	Quantity	Price (₹)	Value (₹)
100	Desktop	No.	50	25,000	1,250,000
101	Laptop	No.	200	35,000	7,000,000
102	Scanner	No.	40	3,000	120,000
103	Laser Printer	No.	50	7,000	350,000

Not in Third Normal Form.
Since Value is depended upon Quantity and Price

Product ID	Product Description	UQ	Quantity	Price (₹)	
100	Desktop	No.	50	25,000	Value =
101	Laptop	No.	200	35,000	Quantity ×
102	Scanner	No.	40	3,000	Price
103	Laser Printer	No.	50	7,000	

Value is not an attribute but can be computed as Quantity × Price

FIGURE 10.15 Third Normal Form

The package-tour table in the 2NF contains two non-key attributes, namely capacity and accommodation. However, capacity depends on the accommodation as can be seen from the table. For example, capacity for hotel accommodation is 40, for resort it is 50 and for guest house it is 30. Hence, the table in 2NF violates the 3NF. However, the package-tour table can be made to comply with the 3NF by removing the capacity attribute and instead making a linking table with accommodation and capacity as the attributes as shown in Figure 10.14. Now, there is no dependence among the non-key attributes, which are only availability and accommodation. Figure 10.15 shows another relation (table) consisting of product ID, product description, unit of quantity (UQ), quantity, price and value as the attributes for products in a warehouse. It may be noted that in this case, the non-key attribute 'value' is dependent on the other two non-key attributes that are quantity and price and can be derived from those two. Hence, the table is not in 3NF. However, in such cases when a non-key attribute is derived from other non-key attributes, we can remove the same attribute from the table ('value' in this case) and compute its value by the appropriate formula for derivation.

Therefore, we can summarize that the process of normalization from 1NF → 2NF → 3NF vastly improves the quality of data and also facilitates avoidance of redundant data being stored while maintaining the referential integrity.

10.7 Creating Queries through Structured Query Language (SQL)

SQL, the abbreviated form of Structured Query Language, is not a procedural general purpose programming language, but it is a small declarative query language focused primarily for working with relational databases and handling queries relating to the data stored in such databases.

SQL is used to select and retrieve or read data from the data tables. It can also create data into the tables, update data tables and delete data from a relational database. All the above operations pertaining to a relational database are known as CRUD as already mentioned in an earlier paragraph of this chapter.

10.7.1 Creating SQL Queries and the Major SQL Keywords

SELECT: This keyword is used to select and retrieve information from a particular table in the database. The formats of SELECT query are as follows:

```
SELECT <attribute>
FROM <table>;
SELECT Last name
FROM Employee;
```

The above query will return all the last name of all employees (rows) from the Employee table:

```
SELECT last name, first name, Basicpay
FROM Employee;
```

This will return last name, first name and basic pay of all employees from the Employee table:

```
SELECT*
FROM Employee;
```

The asterisk (*) after SELECT returns every column from the Employee table.

WHERE: This keyword when applied with the SELECT query will return values of SELECT columns for those rows when the particular rows fulfil some specified conditions of data in that row. The format of the keyword WHERE is as follows:

```
SELECT Lastname, Firstname
FROM    Employee
WHERE   Salary > 30000
```

The above query will return the last name and first name of all the employees from the Employee table whose salary exceed 30,000:

```
SELECT*
FROM Employee
WHERE firstname = 'Amar'
```

WHERE clause also allows multiple conditions using AND, OR such as:

```
SELECT*
FROM Employee
WHERE firstname = 'Amar' AND Salary > 30000
```

ORDER BY: This will return query results in sorted order (ascending or descending order).

Example: SELECT firstname, lastname, Age, Salary

```
FROM Employee
WHERE Salary > 30,000
ORDER BY Age, lastname;
```

If the Employee table is as shown in Table 10.3, the above SQL query will return the following result:

First Name	Last Name	Age	Salary
Ashoke	Basu	32	34000
Chitta	Bhadra	32	49000
Ashim	Deb	56	45000
Maya	Mukherjee	56	50000

The default order is ascending only as in the above example. However, if descending order is desired, then the keyword DESC to be inserted at the end of the ORDER BY line as follows:

```
ORDER BY Age, Last Name DESC;
```

TABLE 10.3 Employee Table Example

Employee ID	First Name	Last Name	Age	Salary (₹)
10	Maya	Mukherjee	56	50,000
11	Ashim	Deb	56	45,000
12	Chitta	Bhadra	32	49,000
13	Ashoke	Basu	32	34,000
14	Soumitra	Dutta	28	25,000

Aggregate functions: COUNT, MAX, MIN, AVG, SUM and GROUP BY are the keywords used in SQL to get the result of various calculations on a set of data stored in tables. For example, COUNT is an aggregate function which returns a single value which is the aggregation of the number of rows in a table and is used in conjunction with SELECT and/or WHERE.

Example: SELECT COUNT (*)
    FROM Employee;

This will return the value 5 since there are 5 employees (rows) in Employee table shown in Table 10.3. Similarly, the query:

```
SELECT COUNT (*)
FROM Employee;
WHERE Salary > 34000;
```

will return the single value 3 since there are three employees (rows) having salary greater than 34,000.

```
SELECT MAX (Salary)
FROM Employee;
```

will return the maximum salary from the Employee table, which is 50,000:

Similarly, `SELECT MIN (Salary)`
`FROM Employee;`

will return the minimum salary which is 25,000 and

```
SELECT AVG (salary)
FROM Employee;
```

will return the average value of salary of all the rows which in this case is (50,000 + 45,000 + 49,000 + 34,000 + 25,000)/5 = 40,600

```
SELECT SUM (Salary)
FROM Employee;
```

will result in the sum of salaries of all employees (rows) which is (50,000 + 45,000 + 49,000 + 34,000 + 25,000) = 203,000.

Joining tables: In a relational database, if there are multiple tables, SQL enables us to join columns from two or more different tables. Let us explain with an example shown in Figure 10.16 where there are two tables, namely the employee table and a department table having one-to-many relationship.

Now, suppose, we want to join the two tables such that the columns Department Name and Cost Centre Code from the Department table are appended with the Employee Table, the SQL keyword for this is JOIN and the syntax of the SQL statement is as follows:

```
SELECT Firstname, Lastname, Age, Salary, Department ID,
Department Name, Cost centre code
FROM Employee JOIN Department ON Employee.
Department ID = Department.Department Id
```

Employee Table

Employee ID	First Name	Last Name	Age	Salary	Department ID
10	Maya	Mukherjee	56	50000	1
11	Ashim	Deb	56	45000	4
12	Chitta	Bhadra	32	49000	5
13	Ashoke	Basu	32	34000	6
14	Soumitra	Dutta	28	25000	6
15	Subhash	Sen	26	24000	(Null)

Department Table

Department ID	Department Name	Cost Centre Code
1	Sales	CC01
2	Finance	CC02
3	HR	CC03
4	Purchase	CC04
5	Production	CC05
6	Maintenance	CC06

Many

FIGURE 10.16 Two Tables Having One-to-many Relationship

will result in a new table as follows:

Employee ID	First Name	Last Name	Age	Salary (₹)	Department ID	Department Name	Cost Centre Code
10	Maya	Mukherjee	56	50,000	1	Sales	CC01
11	Ashim	Deb	56	45,000	4	Purchase	CC04
12	Chitta	Bhadra	32	49,000	5	Production	CC05
13	Ashoke	Basu	32	34,000	6	Maintenance	CC06
14	Soumitra	Dutta	28	25,000	6	Maintenance	CC06

It may be noted that in the above combination of the two tables, only the rows from the two tables having matching Department ID have been joined. For example, in the Employee table, the row having Employee ID of 15 has been ignored since it does not have a Depart ID value which is (Null). Similarly, from the Department table, the rows pertaining to Department ID, 2 (Finance) and three (HR) have been ignored since there is no employee in the employee table having Department ID either 2 or 3.

This type of JOIN of two tables is called INNER JOIN which is the default option of JOIN. However, in case of joining of two tables with all the rows of one of the tables, retained after joining, we use the keyword OUTER JOIN. Again, if we want that the table name on the left side of the OUTER JOIN retains all its rows, we use the keyword LEFT OUTER JOIN. Similarly, if we use the keyword RIGHT OUTER JOIN, the joining will retain all the rows of the table name appearing on the right side of the keyword JOIN.

Example:

```
SELECT First Name, Last Name, Age, Salary, Department ID,
Department Name, cost centre code
FROM Employee LEFT OUTER JOIN Department ON EMPLOYEE.
Department ID = Department.Department ID
```

will form the following table:

Employee ID	First Name	Last Name	Age	Salary	Employee. Department ID	Department Name	Cost Centre Code
10	Maya	Mukherjee	56	50,000	1	Sales	CC01
11	Ashim	Deb	56	45,000	4	Purchase	CC04
12	Chitta	Bhadra	32	49,000	5	Production	CC05
13	Ashoke	Basu	32	34,000	6	Maintenance	CC06
14	Soumitra	Dutta	28	25,000	6	Maintenance	CC06
15	Subhash	Sen	26	24,000	(Null)	(Null)	(Null)

However,

```
SELECT Firstname, Lastname, Age, Salary, DepartmentID,
DepartmentName, Costcentre code
FROM Employee RIGHT OUTER JOIN Department ON Employee.
Department ID = Department.Department ID
```

will form the following table:

Employee ID	First Name	Last Name	Age	Salary	Employee. Department ID	Department Name	Cost Centre Code
10	Maya	Mukherjee	56	50,000	1	Sales	CC01
(null)	(null)	(null)	(null)	(null)	(null)	Finance	CC02
(null)	(null)	(null)	(null)	(null)	(null)	HR	CC03
11	Ashim	Deb	56	45,000	4	Purchase	CC04
12	Chitta	Bhadra	32	49,000	5	Production	CC05
13	Ashoke	Basu	32	34,000	6	Maintenance	CC06
14	Soumitra	Dutta	28	25,000	6	Maintenance	CC06

INSERT INTO: This keyword creates ('C' of CRUD) new records in a table in a relational database.

Example:

```
INSERT INTO Employee
(Firstname, Lastname, Age, Salary)
VALUES ('Ram', 'Singh', 40, 40000)
```

This will create a new row into Employee table as follows:

Employee ID	First name	Last name	Age	Salary
15	Ram	Singh	40	40000

(Auto generated)

```
UPDATE
SET
WHERE
```

updates (changes) a column value for a particular row of a table.

Example:

```
UPDATE Employee
SET Age = 45
WHERE Employee ID = 15
```

Employee ID	First name	Last name	Age	Salary
15	Ram	Singh	45	40000

The Age of Employee ID 15 has changed from 40 to 45

```
DELETE FROM
WHERE:
```

Deletes an entire row depending upon WHERE Condition.

Example:

```
DELETE FROM Employee
WHERE EMPLOYEE ID = 15
```

will delete the entire row pertaining to Employee ID = 15 from the table.

Data definition language (DDL): The SQL keywords and the statements explained in the earlier paragraphs such as SELECT, INSERT, UPDATE and DELETE are only examples of data manipulation of an already existing relational database and therefore they form only a part of SQL—data manipulation language known as DML in abbreviated form. DML is not all of SQL as it does not allow us to create a new table or to alter the structure of an existing table. Further, DML does not control the access permissions for the users of a database. Therefore, there are two more languages other than DML known in SQL as data definition language (DDL) and data control language (DCL). DDL has got three keywords which are CREATE, ALTER and DROP and these keywords allow us to create a new table or change the structure of a data table or delete a complete table.

Examples:

```
CREATE Employee
(Employee ID INTEGER PRIMARY KEY,
First name VARCHAR (30) NOT NULL,
Last Name VARCHAR (30) NOT NULL,
Age INTEGER
Salary INTEGER
);
```

This will create the structure of a table named Employee with Employee ID as an integer and the primary key, First Name and Last Name as the columns of variable characters not exceeding 30 and not null (blank), Age as an integer field or column and Salary as another integer column for the salary of an employee. It may be noted that CREATE only creates the structure of the table named Employee but the table remains blank until data are filled in by the INSERT statement described earlier as DML.

```
ALTER TABLE Employee
ADD Department VARCHAR (20);
```

This will add a new column Department which is a data type of variable length character not exceeding 20 characters.

```
DROP TABLE Employee
```
 will delete the entire Employee table.

Data control keywords: The two keywords for data control in SQL are GRANT and REVOKE for granting permission and revoking permission to users of the database. However, such keywords are part of the access control of the operating system which is a part of the DBMS.

The above mentioned three types of the SQL statements have been schematically shown in Figure 10.17.

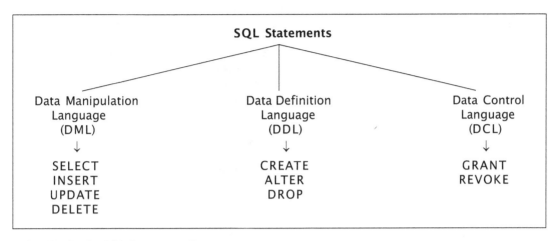

FIGURE 10.17 SQL Statement Types

10.8 Database and DBMS

Database is the repository of data of an organization in storage devices. For example, a company may have one integrated database storing all the corporate data or it may like to have separate databases—one for its customer data, one for all employee data, one for product data and so on. Accordingly, the databases may be named as Customer, Employee and Product. Depending upon the type of data and the arrangement of the data elements or items in a database, we can have various types of databases such as hierarchical, network, relational database as already described in the earlier paragraphs of this chapter. Besides, there are other types of databases such as HBase, MongoBase and Couchbase, all of which belong to a more recent type of database containing structured, semi-structured and unstructured data and known as NoSQL database which has been discussed in a subsequent paragraph.

DBMS, on the other hand, is a software which manages the organizational databases. Data definition, data manipulation and data control are all taken care of by the DBMS. One DBMS can manage one or more types of databases. This concept of database and DBMS has been shown in Figure 10.18.

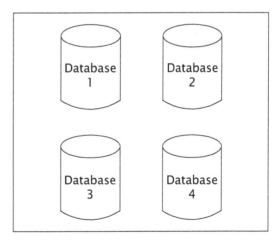

FIGURE 10.18 DBMS Software for Databases

A DBMS performs the following tasks relating to a database:

1. Organizes the data in a database according to the data definition language.
2. Integrates data in a database to rule out duplication.

Hierarchical DBMS	Network DBMS	Relational DBMS Examples: — ORACLE — SQL Server — DB 2 — MYSQL — Postgre. SQL — SQLITE — MS ACCESS (with GUI)	NOSQL DBMS — Cassendra — Couch base — Mongobase — Hbase

FIGURE 10.19 Types of DBMS

3. Filters data according to the need of the application programmers or users.
4. Controls data storage and retrieval for the application programmers or users.
5. Protects valuable data against unauthorized access, physical damage due to system failure, interruptions and simultaneous updating.

There are various types of DBMS available today, and the popular ones have been shown in Figure 10.19. The selection of a DBMS depends upon multiple factors. The more important ones are as follows:

1. **Nature of data—structured, unstructured or semi-structured data:** Structured data are those where attributes of the data entities are fixed such as employee data. Unstructured data are those where the attributes of the data change and there may be variety of data types such as text, integer, image and float in the same field. In other words, in case of unstructured data, there is no predefined schema as is the case with structured data. Semi-structured data fall within these two extremes, that is, they have a mix of fixed and flexible schema.
2. Ease of updating database
3. Volume of the database
4. Data accuracy
5. Data integrity and privacy
6. Data redundancy
7. Data are essentially needed and any business organization cannot afford to lose any data.

By far the relational DBMS is the most common and widely used DBMS because of the principles of RDBMS facilitate understanding of the other database systems.

10.9 NoSQL Database Systems

Recently, NoSQL database systems have been developed mostly by big web players, such as Amazon and Google, to cater to the needs of databases for web-scale data which are characterized by volume, variety, velocity—the Vs of big data that have been explained in Chapter 13 of this book. NoSQL databases unlike the SQL relational databases deal with voluminous data (magnitude of the order of terabytes or petabytes) of variety, having not only structured data but also semi-structured data consisting of characters, strings, number, date, time and images. Furthermore, they cater to data generated at very high velocity which is known as 'streaming data'. 'NoSQL' stands for 'not only SQL' and they are different from the relational databases which have structured data in the form of tables of rows and columns with fixed schema. NoSQL databases are mostly schemaless and have flexibility in storing a variety of data of semi-structured type such as the log files of users associated with various web applications. Further, most of the NoSQL products belong to the open source community. Although NoSQL databases can store relational data, they have been designed really for non-relational data with no structure or semi-structure.

Another important characteristic of NoSQL databases is their high scalability which implies that they can be distributed or partitioned on various physical storages automatically to scale very high volume of data such as terabytes (10^{12} bytes) or even petabytes (10^{15} bytes). Because of the non-relational and high scalability of the NoSQL database, they lose the transactional consistency of the data stored. In other words, unlike RDBMS, the NoSQL data because of being scaled can be in an inconsistent state. Table 10.4 shows a comparison of a SQL and a NoSQL database.

TABLE 10.4 A Comparison of SQL and NOSQL Database

SQL Database	*NOSQL Database*
1. Relational database	1. Non-relational database
2. Structured data	2. Usually semi-structured or unstructured data
3. Data stored as tables of rows and columns consisting of text, integer, float, currency and date.	3. Data stored as documents (word document or PDF), wide columns, graphs structured with interconnected nodes and the data consist of text, integer, float, currency, date, sensor data and image also
4. Fixed schema	4. Flexible schema
5. Transactional consistency	5. Inconsistency due to high scalability
6. No scalability because of volume of data not high	6. High scalability due to high volume of data
7. Volume of data is not very high. Usually consists of tables having few thousands or few millions of rows	7. High volume of data of the order of terabytes or petabytes
8. Not usually open source databases	8. Open source databases
9. Availability is high when data volume is not high	9. High availability with high volume of data
10. SQL database systems are compatible systems	10. NOSQL databases are of different types

10.10 Categories of NoSQL Databases

There are about 150 categories of NoSQL databases available as of now. However, those can be broadly grouped under five major heads: document store, key-value store (volatile or persistent), wide column store, graph store and object databases. The five heads and the subheads within them with popular examples have been shown in Figure 10.20.

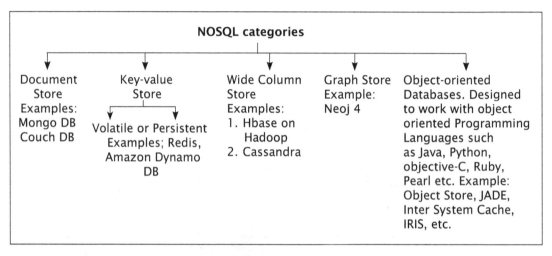

FIGURE 10.20 Categories of NoSQL Databases

10.10.1 Distinctive Features of NoSQL Databases Categories

10.10.1.1 Document Store

In this type of NoSQL database, the database integrates documents which are structured typically as JSON objects. The documents have unique ID and are schemaless. Documents again have fields having field name and value (data as text, number, dates and so on). However, pictures (images) can be attached to any field of a document as binary files. Data retrieval specifying search criteria is also possible. Similarly, query and retrieving of images from documents of the database are possible.

Figure 10.21 shows a schematic diagram of a document database for a college.

The college database as shown in Figure 10.21 is document oriented and has got number of documents. Each document is identified by a document ID which is generated as a hash by the DBMS and has got a revision number which shows the number of revisions the particular document has undergone since its creation as a document.

Each document having structured format such as JSON or XML has got fields, each of which has a name and a value as shown in Figure 10.21. Attachments of pictures (images) can be there with any field and the attachments generally are in the form of binary files. Each document has its unique structure.

MongoDB and CouchDB are two very popular document-store DBMS. It is possible to query a document by its fields.

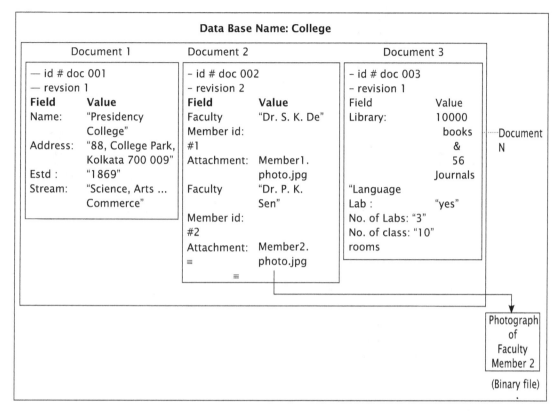

FIGURE 10.21   Document Database of a College

10.10.1.2 Key-value Store

Key/value NoSQL database has got keys and corresponding values. They are basically hash tables. Key/value databases accept queries based on the key only. NoSQL databases of this type have just keys and values and totally schemaless. A key/value database consists of a number of key-value pairs where key is the name and value is the content of an item of data. Table 10.5 shows an example of key-value store. Key-value store can be volatile in memory or persistent on storage.

TABLE 10.5	Key/Value Database Consisting of Key/Value. 'Redis' and 'Amazon Dynamo' Are Examples of Key/Value Database

Key	Value
Name	John Smith
Age	23
Colour	White
City	Phoenix
Sex	Male

10.10.1.3 Wide Column Store

A wide column store is another type of NoSQL database which has tables of rows and columns similar to a relational database, but the names and formats of the columns are flexible unlike relational database

TABLE 10.6 Wide Column Employee Table Showing Column Families

Row#	Column Family 1			Column Family 2		
101	Name	Age	Address	Deptt.	Salary ₹	
	Shyamal Bose	43	143J. Street	Sales	40000	
102	L name	F Name	Tel. No.	DOB	DOJ	Salary
	Biswas	Ashoke	9433112181	30.11.59	01.02.16	30000
103	Name	Age	email	DOJ	Deptt.	
	S. Basu	44	sbasu@gmail.com	03.03.10	Finance	

and can vary from row to row in the same table. Column spaces may be empty also, and hence the wide column store is a sparse column set database. Wide column database is also called 'schema light' as the columns are having flexible schema as explained earlier. Wide column databases are named after Google 'Bigtable' implementation. Only wide column databases have column families having various cells which vary from row to row. Table 10.6 is a schematic representation of a wide column database with column families relating to Employee table.

Cassandra and HBase with Hadoop are examples of wide column database. HBase tables are created through HBase shell running on Hadoop shell.

10.10.1.4 Graph Store

A graph database is a database which consists of graph-oriented data structures. It consists of data as nodes having name and properties and connected among themselves through relationships with or without properties.

A simple graph model is as follows:

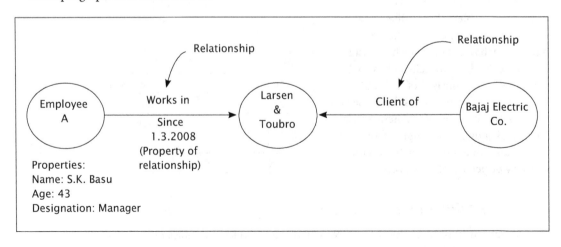

The above is a directed graph as all the relations have specific direction. There can also be graphs where the edges (relations) are not having specific direction as shown as follows:

The advantage of the graph database over the relational database is the fast retrieval with complex query and searches involving more than one level of data hierarchy. Moreover, the fast response for query is facilitated in case of graph database by way of recursive search as shown in Figures 10.22a and 10.22b.

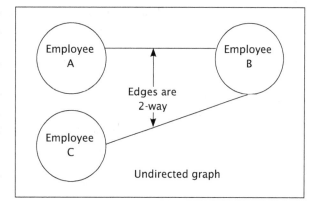

It may be noted that in Figure 10.22a, a query about list of citizens of Kolkata who reside in area having pin 700068 and who are subscribers of Airtel is replied in a single recursive search which first finds the link from 'Citizens of Kolkata' node to the 'Residents of Pin 700068' node, which further finds its links to the 'subscribers of Airtel' node and finally through back (recursive) links to the 'Citizens of Kolkata' node.

Similarly, Figure 10.22b handles a query, which are the award-winning movies, in which actors other than the lead actor of the film 'Sholay' acted? The query is replied through links in the graph database shown in the same figure.

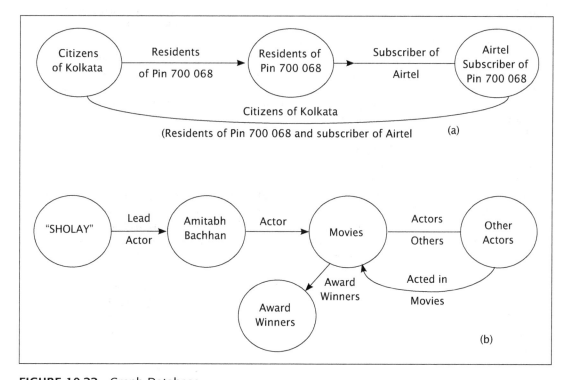

FIGURE 10.22 Graph Database

A graph database stores data, where connected data (nodes) are directly linked together without any index or join table with foreign keys as in the case of relational database. A typical graph database is Neo4j.

The other advantages of graph databases over the relational databases lie in their scalability, schemaless, efficient storage of semi-structured information and fast deep traversal instead of slow SQL queries which require many table joins. Moreover, graph database such as Neo4j supports ACID transactions with roll backs.

It is very easy to represent connected data and relationships through graph database. The traversal rate for Neo4j is about 4 million nodes per second.

CASE STUDY: MONGO DATABASE

Background

Craigslist Inc. is a popular American classified advertisement website with sections devoted to jobs, housing for sale, items wanted, community and other services. It also serves as a discussion forum in English, French, German, Dutch, Spanish, Italian and Portuguese. Craigslist was established in 1955 and incorporated in 1999 with its headquarters located in San Francisco, USA. The Craig network presently serves 570 cities in 70 countries including India and posts about 1.5 million classified advertisements every day.

Initially, Craigslist stored its data records and information in a MySQL cluster but with the massive increase of classified advertisements, Craigslist found it extremely difficult to manage billions of records due to lack of flexibility and data management costs associated with MySQL.

Solution: In order to archive billions of records in many different formats and to query and report on those archives at runtime, Craigslist in year 2011, transferred more than two billion documents to MongoDB data store for its scalability and flexible schema. The original Craigslist archive application copied the existing live database data to the archive system. However, using a relational database system not only restricted flexibility but also caused considerable delay because changes in the database schema needed to be incorporated to the system archive. While making amendments to billions of rows in their MySQL cluster, Craigslist could not move data to the archive and consequently archive-ready data used to pile up in the production database. As a result, performance of the live database deteriorated.

In order to prevent further barriers to the growth of the company and to serve the customers who used to post classified advertisements, Craigslist decided to go for MongoDB. The reason is that MongoDB, because of its sharding capability, provides built-in scalability. Sharding is the process of storing data records across more than one machine in order to cater to the demand of data growth. This is also called horizontal scalability. Each post of advertisement and its metadata can be stored as a single document. Further, as the schema changes on the live database, MongoDB can accommodate these changes without costly schema migrations.

Craigslist used auto-sharding across commodity hardware and deployed the same initially to hold over 5 billion documents of size 2 KB each and the corresponding 10 terra bytes (TB) of data. The cluster topology comprises 3-machine replica sets with each set serving a shard of Craigslist archive database cluster. The configuration is three replica sets in each collocation centre to handle initial build up.

Benefits Accrued to Craigslist for Switching over to MongoDB

Craigslist can put data into MongoDB faster than getting the same data out of MySQL during the migration. Moreover, MongoDB concepts and features are similar in many respects to relational databases and so the transition to MongoDB was a seamless one.

• Review Questions •

1. What is a database? What are the typical forms of database models?

2. What is a DBMS? Is MySQL a database?

3. What is a relational database? Explain with example 'primary keys', 'foreign keys' and 'composite keys'.

4. What are 'schemas' and 'sub-schemas'?

5. What are 'ACID' transactions?

6. What are the different kinds of relationships in a relational database? What do you understand by 'referential integrity'?

7. What is normalization? What are the first, second and third normal forms?

8. What are 'data definition language', 'data manipulation language' and 'data control language'?

9. What is SQL? Which of the following is not a valid SQL query?

    a. SELECT * FROM Employee WHERE Salary > 50,000
    b. SELECT * FROM Employee WHERE salary > 40,000
    c. SELECT * FROM Employee WHERE department = 'Finance'

10. What are NoSQL databases? What are its important features? What are the advantages of NoSQL databases?

11. Explain the different types of NoSQL databases.

Bibliography

Date, C. J. *An Introduction to Database Systems*, 8th ed. Beijing: Pearson Education Asia, 2004.
Harrison, G. *Next Generation Databases—NoSQL and Big Data*, 1st ed. New York, NY: Apress, 2015.
Martin, J. *Principles of Database Management Systems*. New Delhi: Prentice Hall of India, 1985.
Perkins, Luc., E. Redmont, and J. R. Wilson. *Seven Databases in Seven Weeks: A Guide to Modern Databases and the NoSQL Movement*, 2nd ed. Raleigh, NC: The Pragmatic Programmers, LLC, 2018.
Vaish, G. *Getting Started with NoSQL*, 1st ed. Birmingham: Packt Publishing, 2013.

11
CHAPTER

Computer-based Management Information Systems

11.1 Introduction

MIS developers have made extensive use of application software to develop various models of MIS in typical Indian organizations. The models can be broadly classified into broad groups, based on the type of software adopted by the developers, as follows:

1. Models based on spreadsheet such as Microsoft Excel various versions;
2. Models based on optimization techniques such as Operations Research (OR) models developed on computer;
3. Models based on computerized database;
4. Models based on web design and the Internet.

In the following paragraphs, a few models of MIS of the above-mentioned types have been discussed.

11.2 Spreadsheet Models

11.2.1 Model 1 (Finished Inventory Analysis System)

Many of the benefits of inventory of finished products analysis software arise from the analysis of finished products in hand, manufacturing cycle time and profit margin of the products. For example, this particular model pertains to M/s ABC, which manufactures and sells a variety of sprockets for various types of customers such as manufacturers of bicycles, power-driven two wheelers and other power transmission equipment. ABC Company used to maintain the inventory holding of finished sprockets of various nomenclatures on a computer spreadsheet, and the status as on 31 March 2015 is as shown in Table 11.1. However, Mr X, the managing director of the company, felt that information furnished in this form does not facilitate proper decision-making for production planning, since each type of sprocket

TABLE 11.1 Inventory Holding as on 31.03.2015 of ABC Manufacturing Co.

ABC Sprocket Manufacturing Co. Pvt Ltd

Item Code	Nomenclature	Unit Cost (₹)	Unit Price (₹)	Stock in Hand	Units Sold in 2014–2015	Mnfg Cycle Time (Mins)
SP1001	6mm bore 21mm OD 9 teeth	69	94	50	450	8
SP1002	6mm bore 23mm OD 10 teeth	81	101	53	490	9
SP1003	6mm bore 32mm OD 14 teeth	110	139	48	144	13
SP1004	6mm bore 40mm OD 18 teeth	135	174	20	170	17
SP1005	6mm bore 50mm OD 23 teeth	160	226	54	500	19
SP2001	10mm bore 60mm OD 18 teeth	165	215	71	466	20
SP2002	10mm bore 78mm OD 24 teeth	250	310	36	276	28
SP2003	12mm bore 84mm OD 26 teeth	260	349	67	280	30
SP2004	12mm bore 87mm OD 27 teeth	280	371	44	220	32
SP2005	12mm bore 90mm OD 28 teeth	301	379	25	156	35
SP2006	12mm bore 96mm OD 30 teeth	320	425	20	100	37
SP3001	16mm bore 72mm OD 16 teeth	257	342	46	138	31
SP3002	16mm bore 73mm OD 18 teeth	287	383	28	86	35
SP3003	16mm bore 74mm OD 20 teeth	310	413	10	80	36
SP3004	16mm bore 76mm OD 22 teeth	370	490	20	240	43
SP3005	18mm bore 78mm OD 24 teeth	409	536	11	88	49
SP3006	18mm bore 80mm OD 26 teeth	580	779	8	8	67
SP4001	18mm bore 82mm OD 28 teeth	155	200	37	148	18
SP4002	18mm bore 83mm OD 30 teeth	200	263	61	183	23
SP4003	18mm bore 84mm OD 32 teeth	300	344	27	80	35
SP4004	20mm bore 88mm OD 34 teeth	370	486	22	88	43
SP4005	20mm bore 89mm OD 36 teeth	475	641	17	68	55
SP4006	20mm bore 90mm OD 38 teeth	530	720	15	60	60
SP4007	20mm bore 91mm OD 40 teeth	730	985	80	180	80
SP5001	20mm bore 93mm OD 42 teeth	402	550	20	68	46
SP5002	22mm bore 94mm OD 44 teeth	422	562	23	92	48
SP5003	22mm bore 95mm OD 46 teeth	464	619	24	80	53
SP5004	22mm bore 96mm OD 48 teeth	473	631	25	75	55
SP6001	22mm bore 97mm OD 50 teeth	350	463	20	46	40
SP6002	22mm bore 98mm OD 52 teeth	400	528	19	88	45
SP6003	22mm bore 99mm OD 54 teeth	450	598	18	72	51

consumes manufacturing time which was a resource constraint, and further each type of sprocket fetches different profit margins. Mr X, therefore, felt the necessity to redesign the spreadsheet by introducing additional columns which would make the spreadsheet an important MIS and accordingly instructed the MIS department of the company. A new spreadsheet was developed with additional columns as shown in Table 11.2. The formulae for the additional columns of the finished inventory analysis spreadsheet have been shown in Table 11.3.

Finally, for the purpose of decision-making, a spreadsheet was developed by sorting the spreadsheet of Table 11.2 in descending order of gross profit per unit of manufacturing cycle time as the major column and within that stock-in-hand in days of sales as the minor column. The final spreadsheet developed in the above way has been shown in Table 11.4.

11.2.2 Model 2 (Financial Feasibility Analysis)

This model pertains to a cost–benefit analysis using the net present value method through spreadsheet. The model was adopted by M/s PQR Forklift Truck Manufacturing Company located in a metro city, manufacturing different capacity forklift trucks for material-handling purpose. The management of the company decided to install a shop floor job-tracking software package since the present manual system of job tracking was considered to be inefficient, time consuming and costly. Many of the tangible benefits of job tracking software arise from the automation of manufacturing and other allied business processes. Further, the tracking software has got in-built statistical quality control features. However, there are tangible costs associated with such automation apart from the one-time cost of the software package, the necessary hardware required for the same and recurring maintenance cost of the hardware as well as the software. Management of the company assessed the tangible benefits recurring annually as shown in Table 11.5. The one-time costs and the recurring costs assessed have been shown in Tables 11.6 and 11.7 respectively.

The cost–benefit analysis performed on the spreadsheet has been shown in Table 11.8. The recurring costs and benefits have been discounted to their present value. The recurring costs and benefits at various future years have been multiplied by the corresponding present value factor (PVF) given as:

$$(\text{PVF})_N = 1/(1 + i) \wedge N$$

where i is the discount rate and N is the year.

The net present value of all benefits or costs is obtained by summation of all benefits or costs of all years including the current year, and accordingly the formulae have been applied in the worksheet appropriate cells. The overall net present value is the difference between the net present value of all benefits and the net present value of all costs. In order to make the model flexible with regard to various discount rates, the same has been used as a variable in the formulae of present value of recurring costs and benefits. The discount rate can be changed, and all the formulae referencing this value will automatically recalculate the values for analysis. In Table 11.8, with a discount rate of 0.14 the overall net present value calculates to ₹684.37 lakhs and the break-even point (point at which net present value of benefits equals the net present value of costs) appears somewhere in the third year. Internal rate of return (IRR) is the discounting rate at which net present value of all benefits becomes exactly equal to the net present value of all costs over the entire life cycle of the software package. In this model, it works out to 48.60% approximately. Management can apply different discount rates to find the overall net present value of the software package with varying discount rates.

TABLE 11.2 Additional Columns for Analysis of Stock in Hand as on 31.03.2015 of ABC Manufacturing Co.

ABC Sprocket Manufacturing Co. Pvt Ltd

Item Code	Nomenclature	Annual Sales 2014–2015 (₹)	Cost of Unit Sold 2014–2015 (₹)	Annual Gross Profit 2014–2015 (₹)	Cost of Stock in Hand (₹)	Gross Margin 2014–2015	Margin on Cost 2014–2015	Stock in Hand (Days of Sales)	Gross Profit/Mins of Mfg Cycle Time
SP1001	6mm bore 21mm OD 9 teeth	42,300	31,050	11,250	3,450	0.27	0.36	33.33	3.13
SP1002	6mm bore 23mm OD 10 teeth	49,490	39,690	9,800	4,293	0.20	0.25	32.45	2.22
SP1003	6mm bore 32mm OD 14 teeth	20,016	15,840	4,176	5,280	0.21	0.26	100.00	2.23
SP1004	6mm bore 40mm OD 18 teeth	29,580	22,950	6,630	2,700	0.22	0.29	35.29	2.29
SP1005	6mm bore 50mm OD 23 teeth	113,000	80,000	33,000	8,640	0.29	0.41	32.40	3.47
SP2001	10mm bore 60mm OD 18 teeth	100,190	76,890	23,300	11,715	0.23	0.30	45.71	2.50
SP2002	10mm bore 78mm OD 24 teeth	85,560	69,000	16,560	9,000	0.19	0.24	39.13	2.14
SP2003	12mm bore 84mm OD 26 teeth	97,720	72,800	24,920	17,420	0.26	0.34	71.79	2.97
SP2004	12mm bore 87mm OD 27 teeth	81,620	61,600	20,020	12,320	0.25	0.33	60.00	2.84
SP2005	12mm bore 90mm OD 28 teeth	59,124	46,956	12,168	7,525	0.21	0.26	48.08	2.23
SP2006	12mm bore 96mm OD 30 teeth	42,500	32,000	10,500	6,400	0.25	0.33	60.00	2.84
SP3001	16mm bore 72mm OD 16 teeth	47,196	35,466	11,730	11,822	0.25	0.33	100.00	2.74
SP3002	16mm bore 73mm OD 18 teeth	32,938	24,682	8,256	8,036	0.25	0.33	97.67	2.74
SP3003	16mm bore 74mm OD 20 teeth	33,040	24,800	8,240	3,100	0.25	0.33	37.50	2.86
SP3004	16mm bore 76mm OD 22 teeth	117,600	88,800	28,800	7,400	0.24	0.32	25.00	2.79
SP3005	18mm bore 78mm OD 24 teeth	47,168	35,992	11,176	4,499	0.24	0.31	37.50	2.59
SP3006	18mm bore 80mm OD 26 teeth	6,232	4,640	1,592	4,640	0.26	0.34	300.00	2.97
SP4001	18mm bore 82mm OD 28 teeth	29,600	22,940	6,660	5,735	0.23	0.29	75.00	2.50
SP4002	18mm bore 83mm OD 30 teeth	48,129	36,600	11,529	12,200	0.24	0.32	100.00	2.74

Item Code	Nomenclature	Annual Sales 2014–2015 (₹)	Cost of Unit Sold 2014–2015 (₹)	Annual Gross Profit 2014–2015 (₹)	Cost of Stock in Hand (₹)	Gross Margin 2014–2015	Margin on Cost 2014–2015	Stock in Hand (Days of Sales)	Gross Profit/ Mins of Mfg Cycle Time
SP4003	18mm bore 84mm OD 32 teeth	27,520	24,000	3,520	8,100	0.13	0.15	101.25	1.26
SP4004	20mm bore 88mm OD 34 teeth	42,768	32,560	10,208	8,140	0.24	0.31	75.00	2.70
SP4005	20mm bore 89mm OD 36 teeth	43,588	32,300	11,288	8,075	0.26	0.35	75.00	3.02
SP4006	20mm bore 90mm OD 38 teeth	43,200	31,800	11,400	7,950	0.26	0.36	75.00	3.17
SP4007	20mm bore 91mm OD 40 teeth	177,300	131,400	45,900	58,400	0.26	0.35	133.33	3.19
SP5001	20mm bore 93mm OD 42 teeth	37,400	27,336	10,064	8,040	0.27	0.37	88.24	3.22
SP5002	22mm bore 94mm OD 44 teeth	51,704	38,824	12,880	9,706	0.25	0.33	75.00	2.92
SP5003	22mm bore 95mm OD 46 teeth	49,520	37,120	12,400	11,136	0.25	0.33	90.00	2.92
SP5004	22mm bore 96mm OD 48 teeth	47,325	35,475	11,850	11,825	0.25	0.33	100.00	2.87
SP6001	22mm bore 97mm OD 50 teeth	21,298	16,100	5,198	7,000	0.24	0.32	130.43	2.83
SP6002	22mm bore 98mm OD 52 teeth	46,464	35,200	11,264	7,600	0.24	0.32	64.77	2.84
SP6003	22mm bore 99mm OD 54 teeth	43,056	32,400	10,656	8,100	0.25	0.33	75.00	2.90

TABLE 11.3 Finished Inventory Analysis Worksheet Formulae

Column Heading		*Formula used to Calculate*
Annual gross profit	=	(Annual sales) – (Cost of goods sold)
Annual sales	=	Unit sales price × units sold in the year
Cost of stock-in-hand	=	Unit cost × Stock-in-hand
Gross margin	=	$\dfrac{\text{Annual gross profit}}{\text{Annual sales in units}}$
Margin on cost	=	$\dfrac{\text{Unit price} - \text{Unit cost}}{\text{Unit cost}}$
Stock-in-hand in terms of number of days of sales	=	$\dfrac{300 \times \text{Stock-in-hand}}{\text{Annual sales in units}}$
Gross profit earned per unit of machining cycle time	=	$\dfrac{\text{(Annual gross profit)}}{\text{(Units sold in year x Machining cycle time)}}$

Note: 300 working days in the year have been considered.

TABLE 11.4 Items Arranged in Descending Order of Gross Profit per Unit of Manufacturing Cycle Time of ABC Manufacturing Co.

ABC Sprocket Manufacturing Co. Pvt Ltd

Item Code	*Nomenclature*	*Annual Sales (₹)*	*Annual Gross Profit (₹)*	*Stock in Hand (Days of Sales)*	*Gross Profit/ Minute of Mfg Cycle Time*
SP1005	6mm bore 50mm OD 23 teeth	113,000	33,000	32.40	3.47
SP5001	20mm bore 93mm OD 42 teeth	37,400	10,064	88.24	3.22
SP4007	20mm bore 91mm OD 40 teeth	177,300	45,900	133.33	3.19
SP4006	20mm bore 90mm OD 38 teeth	43,200	11,400	75.00	3.17
SP1001	6mm bore 21mm OD 9 teeth	42,300	11,250	33.33	3.13
SP4005	20mm bore 89mm OD 36 teeth	43,588	11,288	75.00	3.02
SP3006	18mm bore 80mm OD 26 teeth	6,232	1,592	300.00	2.97
SP2003	12mm bore 84mm OD 26 teeth	97,720	24,920	71.79	2.97
SP5003	22mm bore 95mm OD 46 teeth	49,520	12,400	90.00	2.92
SP5002	22mm bore 94mm OD 44 teeth	51,704	12,880	75.00	2.92
SP6003	22mm bore 99mm OD 54 teeth	43,056	10,656	75.00	2.90

Item Code	Nomenclature	Annual Sales (₹)	Annual Gross Profit (₹)	Stock in Hand (Days of Sales)	Gross Profit/ Minute of Mfg Cycle Time
SP5004	22mm bore 96mm OD 48 teeth	47,325	11,850	100.00	2.87
SP3003	16mm bore 74mm OD 20 teeth	33,040	8,240	37.50	2.86
SP6002	22mm bore 98mm OD 52 teeth	46,464	11,264	64.77	2.84
SP2004	12mm bore 87mm OD 27 teeth	81,620	20,020	60.00	2.84
SP2006	12mm bore 96mm OD 30 teeth	42,500	10,500	60.00	2.84
SP6001	22mm bore 97mm OD 50 teeth	21,298	5,198	130.43	2.83
SP3004	16mm bore 76mm OD 22 teeth	117,600	28,800	25.00	2.79
SP3002	16mm bore 73mm OD 18 teeth	32,938	8,256	97.67	2.74
SP3001	16mm bore 72mm OD 16 teeth	47,196	11,730	100.00	2.74
SP4002	18mm bore 83mm OD 30 teeth	48,129	11,529	100.00	2.74
SP4004	20mm bore 88mm OD 34 teeth	42,768	10,208	75.00	2.70
SP3005	18mm bore 78mm OD 24 teeth	47,168	11,176	37.50	2.59
SP2001	10mm bore 60mm OD 18 teeth	100,190	23,300	45.71	2.50
SP4001	18mm bore 82mm OD 28 teeth	29,600	6,660	75.00	2.50
SP1004	6mm bore 40mm OD 18 teeth	29,580	6,630	35.29	2.29
SP1003	6mm bore 32mm OD 14 teeth	20,016	4,176	100.00	2.23
SP2005	12mm bore 90mm OD 28 teeth	59,124	12,168	48.08	2.23
SP1002	6mm bore 23mm OD 10 teeth	49,490	9,800	32.45	2.22
SP2002	10mm bore 78mm OD 24 teeth	85,560	16,560	39.13	2.14
SP4003	18mm bore 84mm OD 32 teeth	27,520	3,520	101.25	1.26

TABLE 11.5 Annual Recurring Benefits of Proposed Shop Floor Job Tracking Software

Recurring Benefits Arising Out of	Approximate Value (₹ Lakhs)
Increase in productivity	300
Reduction in work-in-process	25
Reduction of scrap and waste	40
Reduced rework	38
Reduction in idle time	30
Better planning and scheduling	100
Reduction in supervisory staff	30
Total	**563**

TABLE 11.6 One-time Costs for Proposed Shop Floor Job Tracking Software

One-Time Costs	Approximate Value (₹ Lakhs)
Cost of software	300
Initial training cost of operating personnel and users	50
Software related hardware purchase	100
Data conversion, database and so on	40
Site preparation including air-conditioning	100
Miscellaneous supplies	40
Total	**630**

TABLE 11.7 Annual Recurring Costs for the Proposed Shop Floor Job Tracking Software

Recurring Costs	Approximate Value (₹ Lakhs)
Software maintenance	50
Hardware maintenance	25
Miscellaneous supplies	50
Salary of IT personnel	60
Cost of electricity, air-conditioning and so on	40
Total	**225**

Further, in order to add flexibility to the model to include additional items of benefits and costs, not foreseen in the initial stage, there can be two separate worksheets, one for item-wise costs (one-time and recurring) and the other for benefits with blank rows in each worksheet to allow additional entries in the model. The year-wise totals of the worksheets can be then linked with the appropriate cells of the summary worksheet shown in Table 11.8.

11.3 Models Based on Optimization Techniques

11.3.1 Model 3 (Distribution of Electricity in a Metro City at Optimum Cost)

An important operational control decision for a metro city electricity supply corporation which has to be taken very fast and at the same time efficiently is how the transmission and distribution system for electricity will operate. Precisely, it means where from the distribution system will receive power

TABLE 11.8 Cost-Benefit Analysis of a Proposed Job Shop Order Tracking Software

PQR Forklift Truck Manufacturing Co. Pvt. Ltd

Year (Present Year Is Shown as 0)	0	1	2	3	4	5	6	Totals
Costs:								
One-time costs	−630							
Recurring costs		−225.00	−225.00	−225.00	−225.00	−225.00	−225.00	
Discounting factor for present value		0.877193	0.76946753	0.67497152	0.59208028	0.51936866	0.45558655	
Present value of recurring costs		−197.37	−173.13	−151.87	−133.22	−116.86	−102.51	
Net present value of all costs	−630	−827.37	−1000.50	−1152.37	−1285.59	−1402.44	−1504.95	−1,504.95
Benefits:								
Recurring benefits	0	563.00	563.00	563.00	563.00	563.00	563.00	
Discounting factor for present value	1	0.877193	0.76946753	0.67497152	0.59208028	0.51936866	0.45558655	
Present value of recurring benefits net	0	493.86	433.21	380.01	333.34	292.40	256.50	
Present value of all benefits	0	493.86	927.07	1307.08	1640.42	1932.82	2189.32	2189.32
Overall net present value								684.37
Break-even point for discount rate = 0.14				3rd Year				
Internal rate of return (IRR) = 48.60% (approx.)								

(electricity) and distribute the same to which destinations. The sources of power are the generating stations generating electric power and the receiving stations purchasing power from other agencies. The cost per unit of power varies depending upon the source. Moreover, the sources of power are located at different distances apart from the load centres, thereby causing varying transmission losses. Hence, the pattern of distribution of power from the sources to different destinations technically called the load centres or substations has got an important bearing on the overall economy of the electricity supply corporation. The problem can be formulated as an optimization model based on operations research technique as follows:

Mathematical formulation: Let there be *i*th number of sources of power, which include the generating stations as well as the receiving stations and *j*th number of destinations technically known as substations which receive power and distribute the same among the consumers in a particular zone of the metro city, where

$$i \text{ can be } 1, 2, ..., n \text{ and}$$
$$j \text{ can be } 1, 2, m$$

B_i: The rated capacity of power supply from the *i*th source
D_j: The demand for power for the *j*th substation
C_i: The cost per unit of power per second for the *i*th source
X_{ij}: The quantum of power supplied by the *i*th source to the *j*th destination
D_{ij}: The distance between *i*th source and the *j*th destination
α: The transmission loss per unit of power transmitted per unit distance

The distribution model is a linear programming model as follows:

$$\text{Minimize cost} \sum_{i=1}^{n} \sum_{j=1}^{m} C_i \cdot X_{ij}$$

Subject to,

$$\sum_{j=1}^{m} X_{ij} < Bi, \text{ for all } i,$$

$$\sum_{i=1}^{n} X_{ij} \cdot (1 - \alpha d_{ij}) = D_j, \text{ for all } j$$

$$X_{ij} > 0, \text{ for all } i \text{ and } j$$

The problem can be converted into a transportation problem with the cost per unit of power transmitted from *i*th source to *j*th destination including the cost of transmission losses. In other words, the cost of transmitting one unit of power from *i*th source to *j*th destination can be written as:

$$C_{ij} = \frac{C_i}{(1 - \alpha \cdot d_{ij})}$$

The above model was applied in case of a metro city electric supply corporation. The approximate geographical locations of the generating stations, receiving stations and the substations within the city have been shown in Figure 11.1. Two out of the three generating stations were located at the same place and have been shown as one (generating Station 1). The distances between the generating/receiving stations and the substations for distribution of electricity have been shown in Table 11.9.

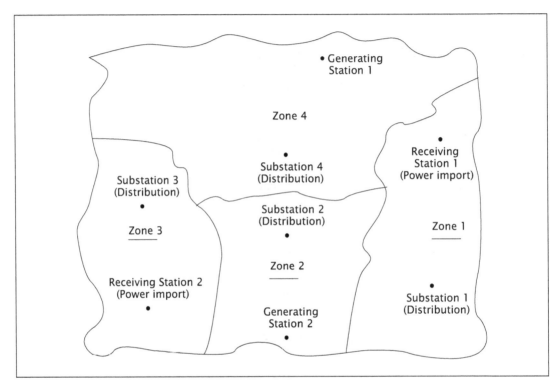

FIGURE 11.1 City Distribution Zones and Locations of Generating, Receiving and Substations of the Electricity Supply Corporation (Not to Scale)

TABLE 11.9 Distance Matrix in Kilometres (d_{ij})

From i to j	GS1 (i = 1)	GS2 (i = 2)	RS1 (i = 3)	RS2 (i = 4)
SS1 (j = 1)	14	5	4	16
SS2 (j = 2)	11	6	10	10
SS3 (j = 3)	12	10	18	6
SS4 (j = 4)	5	13	9	10

Note: SS: Substation; GS: Generating Station; RS: Receiving Station.

The cost per unit of power per second and the rated capacities of the generating/receiving stations are shown in Table 11.10 and 11.11, respectively. The transportation problem as formulated with the help of distance matrix and cost per unit of electric power at source has been shown in Table 11.12. The transmission loss α has been assumed as 0.001 per MW of electricity transmitted per kilometre distance. The optimum solution of the problem has been shown in Table 11.13, and the optimum cost is ₹297.69 per second which is less than the cost at which the system was actually operated by the metro city electric supply corporation on the particular day with the particular load demand pattern shown by ₹2.10 per second. A saving of ₹2.10 in distribution cost per second implies a total saving of approximately ₹662 crores per annum!

Since the load demand as also the availability of power is highly fluctuating in nature, the whole exercise can be computerized, and the computerized results can be used to operate the power supply system at optimum cost. However, such a system has to be online and real time in nature.

TABLE 11.10 Cost per Unit of Power per Second (C_i)

$i = 1$	$i = 2$	$i = 3$	$i = 4$
56	56	63	63

Note: Paisa/megawatt/second

TABLE 11.11 Rated Capacities (B_i) in Megawatt

$i = 1$	$i = 2$	$i = 3$	$i = 4$
145	125	175	110

TABLE 11.12 Power Transportation Problem

Sources Destinations	$i = 1$	$i = 2$	$i = 3$	$i = 4$	Demand (D_j)
$j = 1$	56.80	56.28	63.25	64.02	120
$j = 2$	56.62	56.34	63.64	63.64	110
$j = 3$	56.68	56.57	64.15	63.38	120
$j = 4$	56.28	56.74	63.57	63.64	150
Capacities (B_i)	145	125	175	110	

Note: Value in cells in paisa.

TABLE 11.13 Optimum Solution for Electric Power Distribution

Sources Destinations	$i = 1$	$i = 2$	$i = 3$	$i = 4$	Demand (D_j)
$j = 1$	0	5	115	0	120
$j = 2$	0	110	0	0	110
$j = 3$	0	10	0	110	120
$j = 4$	145	0	5	0	150
Capacities (Bi)	145	125	175	110	

Note: Optimum Cost = 29,769; paisa = ₹297.69 per second.

11.4 Models Based on Computerized Database

11.4.1 Model 4 (Gold Swimming Club Database)

The model pertains to Gold Swimming Club located in a metro city in India and catering to the swimming practice of various age groups of men and women including fresh learners. The service of the club is very beneficial for the parents of children who reside in the metro city because of convenient central location of the club in the metro city. The club is a newly established one and currently has got about a hundred members enrolled for learning/practice sessions of 1 hour duration each during 8–11 AM in the morning and between 5 and 8 PM in the evening for 6 days in a week, Monday being a closed day for the club. Because of its international standards, including proper temperature control and purification of the pool water, the club has been registering five fresh enrolments per week on an average. Presently, the record-keeping system for members data is a manual one. However, with increasing member strength, the paperwork as also data volume increases significantly. It is found that at times information storage and retrieval for effective and efficient decision-making relating to allotment of time slots to trainers and for fresh enrolment, resource levelling for the busy and lean slots in various week days and other important areas of the club activities take so much time that appropriate decisions are not forthcoming. Therefore, the management of the club decided to develop a computer DBMS for tracking the data of the members (swimmers), available time slots for new enrolments, trainers duty roster and other monitoring parameters of the swimming club.

The club management entrusted the job of designing and developing a suitable computer database linked with GUI to a computer professional, who has proposed the following tables with proper linkages among the tables.

The above relational database tables are created and subsequently updated with addition of records as and when new enrolments are made, deletion when a member discontinues membership or when a trainer leaves his/her job. A basic form design for creation and addition of records in the data tables as described above has been shown in Figures 11.2 and 11.3 respectively.

Information/reports: The management of Gold Swimming club requires two routine reports on a weekly basis, which can be generated using the report generation module of the database software. The reports are

---

Gold Swimming Club
Application Form for Membership (Colour: Pink)

Name of member: _____   _____
                                              (Last name)   (First name)

Sex: Male/female (tick one)

Date of birth   DD   MM   YYYY

Street address:

City: Pin Code:

Phone no: Email address (if any):

                                                            Signature of Applicant

(To be filled up by staff after getting from computer)

Membership no.:

Slot no. allotted:

Trainer no.:

Monthly fees:

Date of enrolment:

FIGURE 11.2   Application Form for Membership

Gold Swimming Club
Trainer Employment Form (Colour: Blue)

Trainer no.   (To be filled up by staff after getting from computer)

Name of trainer: Mr/Ms   _____   _____
                                                         Last name   First name

Street address:

City: Pin code:

Telephone no:

                              (To be filled up by staff)

Working shift: Morning/evening   Monthly pay (₹):
                              (Tick one)

Email address (if any):

FIGURE 11.3   Application Form for Employment of Trainer

---

the trainer schedule and the updated membership list. Since the trainer schedule report requires data both from member table (Table 11.14) and the trainer table (Table 11.15), it is necessary to build a select query with the two tables linked through the trainer number (TNO) field and thereafter the report can be generated. Figure 11.4 shows a sample trainer schedule report as on as particular date.

TABLE 11.14 Member Table Structure

Field Name	Data Type	Field Description	Field Size	Remarks
MNo.	Auto generated number	Is a unique identification for each member	Integer 3 digits (001 to 999)	Serves as a primary Key
M last name	Text	Last name of a member	25	Required field
M first name	Text	First name of a member	25	Required field
M sex	Text	Sex of member M (Male); F (female)	1	Required field
M DOB	Date	Date of birth of member	8 (MMDDYYYY)	Required field
M street	Text	Street address of member	25	Required field
M city	Text	City name of member	10	Required field
M pin	Text	Pin code of member address	6	Required field
M phone	Text	Telephone number of member	10	Required field
M email	Text	Email address of member	20	Required field
M fees	Currency	Monthly membership fee for the member	₹xxx.xx	Required field
Last payment month	Month/year	Month and year up to which fees paid	mm yyyy	Required field
Slot	Number	Time slot allotted to the member	Integer one digit[a]	Required field
TNo.	Number	Trainer, no. of the trainer assigned with the member	Integer 3 digits	Required field
Enrol date	Date	Indicates the date of membership enrolment	8 MMDDYYYY	Required field
Comments	Memo	Contains any additional Relevant information		Required field

Note: [a] Slot: 1 for 8–9 AM; 2 for 9–10 AM.; 3 for 10–11 AM; 4 for 5–6 PM; 5 for 6–7 PM; 6 for 7–8 PM.

TABLE 11.15 Trainer Table Structure

Field Name	Data Type	Field Description	Field Size	Remarks
TNo.	Numeric	Unique identification number of the trainer	Integer 3 digits	Required for linking
T last name	Text	Last name of a trainer	25	Required field

T first name	Text	First name of a trainer	25	Required field
T sex	Text	Sex of trainer M (male); F (female)	1	Required field
T DOB	Date	Date of birth of trainer	8 (MMDDYYYY)	Required field
T street	Text	Street address of trainer	25	Required field
T city	Text	City name of trainer	10	Required field
T pin	Text	Pin code of trainer address	6	Required field
T phone	Text	Phone number of trainer	10	Required field
T email	Text	Email address of trainer	20	Required field
T shift	Text	Shift of trainer M (morning); E (evening)	1	Required field
T pay	Currency	Monthly rate of remuneration	₹ xxxx.xx	Required field
T employ date	Date	Date of appointment	8 (MMDDYYYY)	Required field
Comments	Memo	Contains any additional information about the trainer		

Note: A trainer is appointed for a particular shift only.

		Gold Swimming Club Trainer Schedule				Date: Report Date
Trainer No.	**Trainer**	**Name**	**Shift**	**Slot**	**Members to Be Attended**	
015	Biswas	Anil	M	1	Chanda	Mira
					Deb	Paresh
					Samanta	Chandan
			M	2	Adhikary	Pinky
				2	Basu	Gopal
			M	3	Saha	Bimal
					Paul	Joyeeta
					Roy	Samar
011	Chatterjee	Satya	M	1	Mitra	Debabrata
	...			2	Roy	Sudip
	...			3	Poddar	Barun
002	Majumdar	Ranjan	E	4	Sengupta	Arya
	...					
	...					

FIGURE 11.4 Trainer Schedule Report

Note: M: Morning, E: Evening, 1 : 8–9 AM.; 2 : 9–10 AM.; 3 : 10–11 AM.; 4 : 5–6 PM.

The trainer schedule report is generated in the ascending order of the last names of the trainers and within that slot, number-wise in ascending order. The sorting in the same order is performed on the file built up using the select query as mentioned in the earlier paragraph. Further, the trainer schedule report has been prepared for the morning shift first followed by the evening shift by splitting the trainer file built up using the select query.

The sample membership list as on a particular run date has been shown in Figure 11.5 below:

			Gold Swimming Club					Date: Run Date
			Membership List					
Membership No.	Name of Member	Street Address	City	Pin	Telephone No	E-mail	Last Fees Paid for (MM/YYYY)
010	Basu Gopal	531, Gariahat Road	Kolkata	700068	9431166700	—	12/2015
008	Chanda Sumit	F 53 New Alipore Road	Kokata	700053	9830312961	—	03/2016
	...						
	...						

FIGURE 11.5 Membership List Report

The membership list has been generated in the ascending order of the last name of the club members by performing the required sorting operation on the member table. The computerized database as described in the preceding paragraphs can also provide answers to various queries of club management such as:

1. How many members are trained by each trainer on an average?
2. What is the total fees collected as membership fees during a particular month?
3. What is the outstanding dues payable by the members of the club as on a particular date?
4. What is the monthly remuneration paid to the trainers for any particular month?
5. Which slot is having maximum number of members and which slot is having minimum number of members in any week?

All the above types of queries can be answered using SQL formulations. Further, the answers to queries can be displayed on screen in graphical form by interfacing with GUI.

11.4.2 Model 5 (Database Model)

This model pertains to creation of employee database to facilitate employee training of Precision Tools and Equipment Company Limited. It is a manufacturing company in the eastern part of India, producing a diverse range of precision tools and equipment for supplying to capital goods industries. Because the very nature of the manufacturing process demands continuous upgrade of technology and necessary training of employees at all levels in the company, the top management of the company is contemplating to develop a full-fledged employee training scheme to be operated by the training division of the company. Presently, the training activities are decentralized and training of employees is being organized departmentally by the heads, and employees are deputed to outside training institutes for attending courses of various durations. Sometimes the departmental heads also arrange for in-house training programmes with the assistance of own experts as well as by hiring outside experts also. The selection of employees working in a particular department for any specific training is done on the basis of the recommendation of their immediate superiors. The course and with the training institute imparting the same course are selected by the departmental heads in consultation with the training division of the company. However, the above system of selection of employees for training has an inherent drawback that no consideration is paid to the past training programmes attended by the concerned employees as well as the company policy for training of employees. The present company policy regarding training of all categories of employees is as follows:

- All technical and supervisory persons should attend specialized courses on manufacturing technology and allied areas conducted by reputed technical institutes including supervisory training institutes for a duration of not less than 3 weeks every year.
- All skilled and semi-skilled workers should attend skill-development programmes arranged either in-house conducted by the training division of the company or by deputing the workers to various artisan/industrial training institutes for at least 4 weeks in a year.

Although the company has got a laid down training policy as above, often superiors do not like to spare essential subordinate staff with the apprehension that if employees are sent for training, departmental work may be hampered. As a result, it has been found by the top management of the company that some employees are repeatedly being sent for training to different training institutes, whereas employees who are required to undergo training to develop themselves to contribute much better towards the interest of the company are not spared to undergo training. The above situation also has resulted in under-utilization of training funds allocated annually in the past.

The top management of the company, therefore, engaged a consultant to develop a database covering the employee data, available training courses offered by the various institutes in India every year and other relevant details. Training division has to update the database for preparing a comprehensive annual training plan for all categories of employees keeping into consideration the real training needs of the employees, company's training policy and funds allocated for training for the particular year. The plan should be prepared in advance to be ready in the month of March every year for the next financial year. The process of preparation of the annual training plan as proposed in short is as follows:

During the month of March preceding the plan year, the available training programmes from various institutes for the next financial year and the recommendations of superiors for training of their subordinate employees are received by the training division of the company. The available training programme report makes the training division aware of the various training programmes available with the cost per participant as well as the overall fund allocated for each such programme during the plan year. The total training budget for the plan year is also made known to the training division after the company budget has been approved. The departmental heads then meet along with the head of training division and study the recommendations for each employee for training, the company training policy, the available training programmes and the fund availability for training. After studying the process as described above, the consultant has decided that two database tables are primarily required to be created, which are the available training programmes and the employee data tables. The consultant accordingly designed two tables, which have been shown as Tables 11.16 and 11.17 respectively.

TABLE 11.16 Training Programme Table Structure

Field Name	Data Type	Field Description	Field Size	Comments
Progno	Integer	Serves as primary key	3 digits	Required field
Programme name	Text	Specifies the name of the programme	50	Required field
Inhouse	Yes/No (Y/N)	Indicates whether the programme is in-house or conducted by outside institute	Y or N	Required field
Instcode	Integer	Indicates the code number of the institute for in-house code no. is '01'	2 digits	Required field
Instname	Text	Indicates the name of the institute	40	Required for outside programmes only
Start date	Date	Indicates the course commencement date	8 MM DD YYYY	Required field
Durwks	Numeric	Course duration in weeks	Integer 2 digits	Required field
Fee	Currency	Course fee per participant	₹ XXXXXX	Required field
Maxno	Numeric	Maximum number of participants allowed	Integer 1 digit	Required field
Guide	Memo	Provides the eligibility criteria for participants		

Note: A fee is charged notionally for in-house programmes by the training division to defray the expenses such as remuneration to experts hired for the programme.

TABLE 11.17 Employee Table Structure

Field Name	Data Type	Field Description	Field Size	Comments
Empno	Integer	Employee identification number which serves as a primary key	4 digits	Required field and primary key to establish relation with other tables
Lname	Text	Last name of the employee	25	Required field
Fname	Text	First name of the employee	25	Required field
Address	Text	Street address of the employee	25	Required field
City	Text	City of the employee address	10	Required field

Pin	Text	Pin code of address of the employee	6	Required field
Telno.	Text	Telephone number of the employee	10	Required field
Deptcode	Text	Department code of the employee	2	Required field
Desgn.	Text	Current designation of the employee	20	Required field
Category	Text	Employee category 01: Manager 02: Engineer 03: Supervisor 04: Clerical; 05: Skilled; 06: Unskilled	2	Required field
Policy	Numeric	Training policy for the year in terms of the minimum number of weeks of training for the employee category	2	
DOB	Date	Date of birth of employee	8 MM DD YYYY	Required field
Grosspay	Currency	Present gross pay of the employee in a month	₹ XXXXXX	Required field
Jointdt	Date	Joining date of the employee in theservice of the company	8 MM DDYYYY	Required field
Recommend	Memo	Recommendation of the superiors regarding training needs		Required field

In the Employee table (Table 11.17), there is a recommendation memo field which contains the recommendation submitted by the superiors of the employees through a recommendation form suitably designed as an input to the employee data table. The Employee table has several fields which are more or less static in nature such as employee identification, name, contact address, department code, current designation, gross pay, data of birth, date of joining, employee category and training policy.

The third table which contains the annual training plan of the company precisely is developed based on the Employee table, available training programme table and the past training records of the employees. The structure of the annual training plan so developed has been shown in Table 11.18.

A study of the Table 11.18 reveals that two basic relationships are necessary. First, a relationship between the training programme table and the annual training plan table needs to be established. This is done through the programme identification number. Second, a relationship between the annual training plan and the employee table is necessary. As both the annual plan and the employee tables have

TABLE 11.18 Annual Training Plan

Field Name	Data Type	Field Description	Field Size	Comments
EMPno	Integer	Employee identification number	4 Digits	Primary key to establish relation with employee table
Progno	Integer	Programme identification number for the programme for which the employee has been selected	3 Digits	Required field for relation with available training program table
YRSTART	Date	The commencement date of the plan year	8 MMDDYYYY	Required field
REMARKS	Memo	Provides the criteria of selection		Optional but preferred for transparent selection process

got the employee number as a field, the same can be used to establish the second relationship. The consultant also decided to enforce referential integrity for each of the above two relationships.

Input specifications: The creation and subsequent updation of the Training programme table and the Employee table require programme and employee forms. The programme form enables training division to update information about available training programmes and also to add or delete records. The employee form creates and subsequently updates data in two tables, namely the Employee table and the past Training Records table, which stores information about the past training programmes attended by the employees. This table shown in Figure 11.17 uses a combination key consisting of programme identification number and employee identification number. Figures 11.6 and 11.7 show the sketches of the programme and employee forms respectively.

Precision Tools and Equipments Co. Pvt. Ltd
Training Division   Programme Form

Programme No. (auto-generated)   Financial Year: 2016–2017

Programme Name: In-house: Yes/no (tick one)

Institute Code: Start Date:

Institute Name: Duration (weeks):

Eligibility   Fee per participant (₹):

Criteria: Total no. of participants allowed:

[ADD]   [DELETE]   [FIND]   [PRINT]

FIGURE 11.6 Programme Form

Precision Tools and Equipments Co. Pvt. Ltd
Training Division   Employee Form

Employee ID no. (auto-generated)

Last name: _____

First name: _____

DOB: _____
Joining date: _____
Monthly gross pay (₹):

Street : _____
City : _____
Pin : _____
Tel no. : _____

Dept. code : _____
Designation : _____
Category : _____
Training
policy (weeks) : _____

Comments:

	Previous Training Attended			
Program Number	Program Name	Institute	Duration	Year

ADD	DELETE	FIND	PRINT

FIGURE 11.7 Employee Form

Figures 11.8 and 11.9 show the tentative sketches for the main and form switchboards. The query and report switchboards should use a similar format as the main and form switchboards. In order to perform the Exit function, a macro needs to be created and assigned to the Exit to M/s Precision Tools and Equipment Company database button. Several other queries and associated macros are also designed and incorporated in this database model.

Table 11.19 shows the annual training plan printed with the help of report generator invoked by selecting the Reports button on the main switchboard and using the Annual Training Plan table.

M/s Precision Tools and Equipment Company Training Scheme

☐ Forms

☐ Queries

☐ Reports

☐ Exit to precision company database

FIGURE 11.8 Main Switchboard

M/s Precision Tools and Equipment Company Training Scheme

☐ Employee

☐ Training programme

☐ Return to main menu

FIGURE 11.9 Form Switchboard

TABLE 11.19	Annual Training Plan of Precision Tools and Equipment Company						
Precision Tools and Equipment Company *Training Division Annual Training Plan Year: 2016–2017*							
Dept Code	*Employee Code*	*Employee Name*	*Program Name*	*Duration Weeks*	*Fee (₹)*	*Institute*	*Start Date*
01	1245	Bhattacharyya Rabin	Motivation and leadership	2	80,000	IIM, Bangalore	06/14/16
	1280	Ghosh Sukumar	Tool and cutter design	1	20,000	CMTI Hyderabad	08/01/16
20	1341	Adhikary Gautam	TPM and 5S	2	40,000	NPC Chandigarh	11/11/16

The database model as described above can handle various management queries such as:

1. What is the average programme fee per participant?
2. How many participants have been earmarked for training in outside institutes from a particular department?

In order to handle such queries, we can build SQL formulations, and the answers to the queries can be displayed with any GUI.

11.5 Models Based on Web Design

Valuable management information can be provided through pages suitably designed using various web skills, tools and techniques, which facilitate web design and thereafter hosting the designed web pages consisting of a homepage and the detailed pages. Let me illustrate a web-based MIS through the following case pertaining to a metro city beautification-cum-fitness centre named 'Inspire'.

'Inspire' is located in the heart of a metro city providing beautification and fitness service for adult male and female customers who wish to avail of either beautification or fitness service according to their convenient day and time. Ms Lovely Singh, a beautician by profession owns and operates 'Inspire' with employees consisting of experienced beauticians, dieticians, masseurs, physiotherapists and fitness-cum-slimming experts. 'Inspire' has been in operation for several years and the list of its customers was increasing rapidly. Since its inception almost 10 years ago, the centre had grown from six beautification beds to its present 18 beds and a full-fledged fitness centre. Besides, 'Inspire' sells a variety of cosmetic products of reputed brands to its customers. The centre is open six days in a week (Monday to Saturday except public holidays) from 10 AM to 8 PM. Although walk-ins are appreciated, 'Inspire' Beauty Parlour and Fitness Centre appointments can also be booked in advance over telephone.

TABLE 11.20 Current Price List of 'Inspire' Beauty Parlour and Fitness Centre

Beauty parlour	₹
1 Session	1,000.00
4 Sessions	3,500.00
8 Sessions	7,000.00
10 Sessions	10,000.00
One month unlimited	8,000.00
Yearly enrolment (new)	90,000.00
Old customers (yearly)	80,000.00
Fitness centre	
6-month membership	40,000.00
Annual membership	70,000.00
Products	
Ponds body lotion 100 ml	65.28
Ponds oil control 350 gm	153.60
Boroplus advance moisturizing lotion 100 ml	57.60
Moisturising cold cream 100 ml	129.60
Lakme black kajal	165.00
L'oreal Paris excellence	254.00

The beauty parlour provides herbal beauty treatment, hair style, haircut, facial treatment, waxing, makeup, permanent makeup tattoo, manicure, pedicure, skincare, nail polishing and a host of other services. The fitness centre is a top-class facility equipped with state-of-the art, sports equipment, jacuzzi, steam rooms and saunas, jogging path, free weights, treadmills, exercise bicycles and so on. When a client joins the fitness centre, a fitness evaluation is done for him/her and he/she is provided with a fitness programme chalked out by a fitness expert. The current price list of 'Inspire' is shown in Table 11.20.

Ms Lovely Singh appreciates the power of the web and she desires to provide customers, both existing and potential, with information about the parlour, fitness centre and beautification products through the web and she likes to design a web page for the same and upload it through some hosting company.

11.5.1 Design Specifications

The web page should be informative and at the same time presentable in visual appearance. The main information which Ms Lovely Singh wants to furnish in the web page are the working hours, weekly holiday, the various services and price for the same. Further, she feels that the web page be so designed that the visitors can navigate the same fast and with ease. Figures 11.10 and 11.11–11.15 show the tentative design sketches of the home page and internal web pages of 'Inspire', respectively.

The web pages as designed above have been developed using 'Webfix', and examples are shown subsequently (Figures 11.16–11.19).

Web design has evolved and has now become a technology with blend of different technologies. In the initial stage of development, all that was really needed to design a web page was a little bit of hypertext markup language (HTML) and creation of link to place images on the page. However, the scenario now is much more extensive and different, where so many new technologies and processes exist and web designers specialize in specific technologies of web design. A generalist, however, is a web designer having adequate skill in core technologies of web design, namely HTML, Cascade Style Sheets (CSS) and JavaScripts (JS). Using the above three core skills, the generalists create websites from scratch through planning, designing, prototyping, testing and developing.

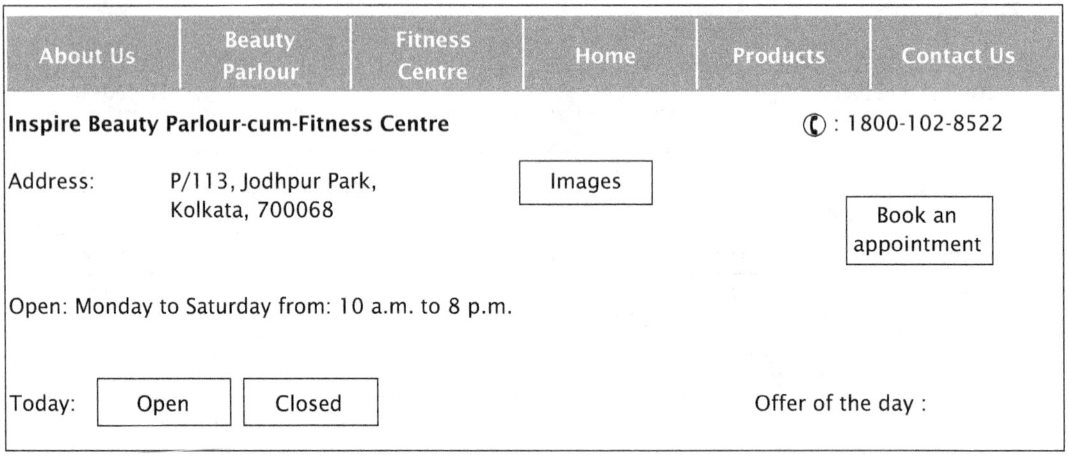

About Us	Beauty Parlour	Fitness Centre	Home	Products	Contact Us

Inspire Beauty Parlour-cum-Fitness Centre　　　　　　　　　　　(: 1800-102-8522

Address:　　　P/113, Jodhpur Park,　　　[Images]
　　　　　　　Kolkata, 700068
　　　　　　　　　　　　　　　　　　　　　　　[Book an appointment]

Open: Monday to Saturday from: 10 a.m. to 8 p.m.

Today: [Open] [Closed]　　　　　　　　　　Offer of the day :

FIGURE 11.10　Home Page Design of 'Inspire'

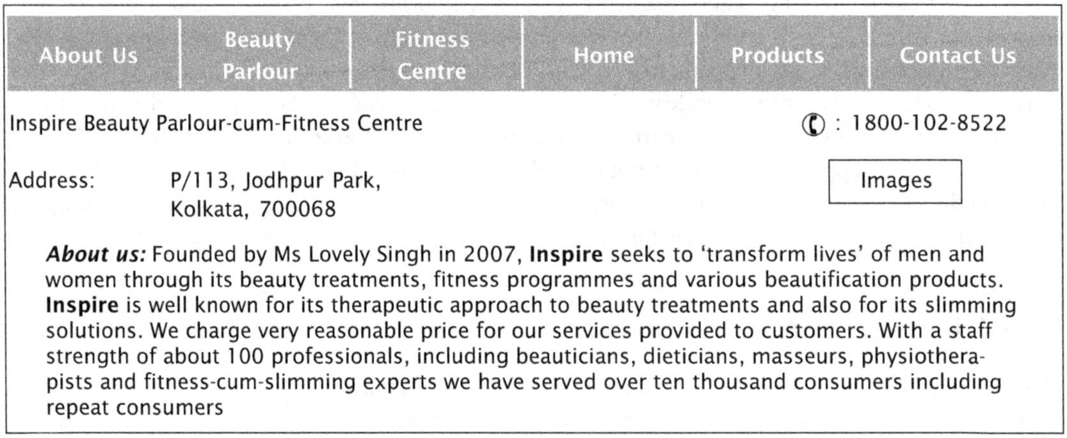

About Us	Beauty Parlour	Fitness Centre	Home	Products	Contact Us

Inspire Beauty Parlour-cum-Fitness Centre　　　　　　　　　(: 1800-102-8522

Address:　　　P/113, Jodhpur Park,　　　　　　　　[Images]
　　　　　　　Kolkata, 700068

About us: Founded by Ms Lovely Singh in 2007, **Inspire** seeks to 'transform lives' of men and women through its beauty treatments, fitness programmes and various beautification products. **Inspire** is well known for its therapeutic approach to beauty treatments and also for its slimming solutions. We charge very reasonable price for our services provided to customers. With a staff strength of about 100 professionals, including beauticians, dieticians, masseurs, physiotherapists and fitness-cum-slimming experts we have served over ten thousand consumers including repeat consumers

FIGURE 11.11　Internal Web Page Design of 'Inspire'

About Us	Beauty Parlour	Fitness Centre	Home	Products	Contact Us

I Inspire Beauty Parlour-cum-Fitness Centre

Address: P/113, Jodhpur Park, Kolkata 700068

Images

© : 1800-102-8522

Beauty parlour: In the beauty parlour there are 16 beds. We offer cosmetological, dermatological, nutritional and physiotherapy consultations free of cost to our customers willing to join any of our programmes. We offer personalized solutions for each and every customer. Some of our services include:

* Hair style and hair treatments	* Herbal beauty treatment
* Facial treatment	* Skincare
* Waxing and make-up; permanent make-up tattoo	* Pedicure
* Manicure	* Nail polishing

Our price List for Beauty parlour :

1 Session	₹ 1,000
4 Sessions	₹ 3,500
8 Sessions	₹ 7,000
10 Sessions	₹ 10,000
1-month unlimited	₹ 8,000
Yearly enrolment (new)	₹ 90,000
Yearly enrolment (old)	₹ 80,000

FIGURE 11.12 Internal Web Page Design of 'Inspire'

The other specialized technologies are visual design, user experience (UX), motion graphic designs, content management system (CMS), blogs building and so on. Visual designs of sites and interfaces involve colour, layout, typography and graphics.

UX designs focus on user experience, and a true UX designer has to study human behaviour and tendencies in order to facilitate the design of web. Interactive web designers focus on creating interfaces for seamless interactions between users and websites. They work in close coordination with UX designers but are more focused on behavioural technologies using JS which allow them to modify static HTML interfaces into interactive experiences. Motion graphic designers are the traditional animators, who work on animation required in web design. They mostly use 'Flash' for animation and games on the web. However, they also make use of JS and HTML 5 technologies such as 'Canvas'.

Another area of specialized web design is the CMS such as Drupal, Joomla and WordPress which are used to build sites very fast and at the same time with powerful functionality.

Blogs have evolved as powerful tools which can compete with many fully featured sites in terms of capabilities. Many platforms feature free blogs which can be activated for building blogs very fast to get

About Us	Beauty Parlour	Fitness Centre	Home	Products	Contact Us

I Inspire Beauty Parlour-cum-Fitness Centre

Address: P/113, Jodhpur Park, Kolkata, 700068

Images

(C) : 1800-102-8522

Fitness centre:

Facilities include:

* State-of-the art sports equipments.

* Jacuzzi

* Steam rooms and saunas

* Jogging path

* Free weights

* Treadmills

* Exercise bicycles

Services include:

• Weight loss—body shaping

• DNA-based dietary modification

• Muscle toning and firming

• Removal of body aches, pains, improved postures and fitness.

Membership fees:	
For 6 months:	₹ 40,000
For 12 months:	₹ 70,000

FIGURE 11.13 Internal Web Page Design of 'Inspire'

About Us	Beauty Parlour	Fitness Centre	Home	Products	Contact Us

I Inspire Beauty Parlour-cum-Fitness Centre

Address: P/113, Jodhpur Park, Kolkata, 700068

(C) : 1800-102-8522

Images of the Products

Our products: We market the reputed brands of products for beautification and fitness.

Price of products	:	
Ponds body lotion 100 ml	:	₹ 65.28
Ponds oil control 350 gms	:	₹ 153.60
Boroplus advance moisturising lotion 100 ml	:	₹ 57.60
Moisturising cold cream 100 ml	:	₹ 129.60
Lakme black kajal	:	₹ 165.00
L'oreal Paris excellence	:	₹ 254.00

FIGURE 11.14 Internal Web Page Design of 'Inspire'

About Us	Beauty Parlour	Fitness Centre	Home	Products	Contact Us

Inspire Beauty Parlour-cum-Fitness Centre   ☏ : 1800-102-8522

Address: P/113, Jodhpur Park, Kolkata, 700068

Contact us:

Inspire Beauty Parlour-cum-Fitness Centre

P/113, Jodhpur Park,

Kolkata, 700068

Phone	:	(033) 24730015
Fax	:	(033) 24730016
Email	:	lovely.inspire@gmail.com
Website	:	www.inspire.in

FIGURE 11.15   Internal Web Page Design of 'Inspire'

FIGURE 11.16   Example of a Web Page

FIGURE 11.17 Example of a Web Page

online quickly. It may be incidentally mentioned that front-end web developers focus more on the functionality of sites through client-end scripting. With the help of JS and powerful JS libraries, they facilitate processing of scripts directly on the browser rather than on the server side. However, for dynamic web pages we can use PHP code or ASP.NET which are server-side popular programming or scripting languages and embedded into the HTML page.

With the help of the above, we can write simple code for web pages to make the same dynamic. The output of PHP or ASP.NET is fed to the client-side browser as HTML only. However, PHP or Microsoft ASP.NET processes data obtained from the database which is either MySQL or SQL server. Both MySQL and SQL server are two leading databases that support front-end applications related to various domains. Figure 11.20 shows how .PHP processes data from MySQL database at back end and feeds the output of processed data as HTML to the browser at the client side (front end) to make the web pages interactive as well as dynamic (Figure 11.21).

Home *About Us* Beauty Treatment *Fitness Center* *Our Products* *Contact Us*

Open Everyday...
Timings: from 10 am to 10 pm*

INSPIRE BEAUTY PARLOUR & FITNESS CENTER

Beauty Treatment...

We offer a holistic approach, we care for your body, mind, and spirit. We offer cosmetological, dermatological, nutritional and medical consultations free with every programme in order to understand the underlying causes and correct them with lasting results. So when you walk in for a skin/hair concern, our doctor/beauty head and nutritionist/dietician also confer with you besides the appointed professional. We offer personalized, solution oriented skin and hair therapies with necessary interventions and treatments being administered from time to time by experts. Each service is analyzed by a specialist– Beauty Consultant/ Doctor/ Dermatologist to determine whether a single sitting would suffice or an entire course would be required

OUR SERVICES

- **SKIN CARE TREATMENT**
  - Anti Aging Treatment
  - Pigmentation and Tan Removal
  - Acne Treatment
- **HAIR CARE TREATMENT**
  - Hair Fall Treatment
  - Hair Damage Repair
  - Ozone Treament For Hair Growth
- **REGULAR BEAUTY SERVICES**
  - Facial
  - Manicure - Pedicure
  - Hair Spa
  - Hair Coloring
  - Hair Straightening
  - Gorgeous Bridal Makeup
  - Party Makeup
  - Stylish Groom
  - Threading
  - Waxing

FIGURE 11.18 Example of a Web Page

Home *About Us* *Beauty Treatment* Fitness Center *Our Products* *Contact Us*

Open Everyday...
Timings: from 10 am to 10 pm*

INSPIRE BEAUTY PARLOUR & FITNESS CENTER

Use of Gym facilities -
- **Cardio vascular section**
- **Yoga**
- **Weight training**
- **Kick Boxing**
- **Functional Training**
- **Pilates**

Our present day busy lifestyle has made good health a concept that is universally desired. At INSPIRE, we endeavor to turn this desire into an achievable state of healthy living, by offering a harmonious blend of the latest scientific technologies along with nutritional and lifestyle counseling in leading a happy, healthy and stress free life."A condition of good physical, mental and social health, is achieved and maintained by proper diet, exercise and lifestyle management"

Gym packages -
- **1 month : Rs 1500**
- **3 months : Rs 4000**
- **6 month : Rs 7500**
- **1 year : Rs 14000**

FIGURE 11.19 Example of a Web Page

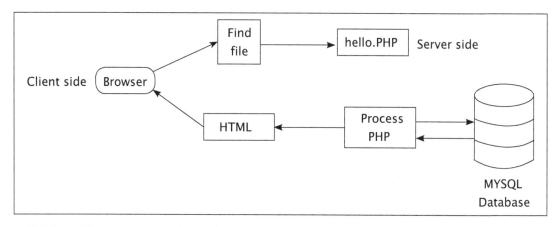

FIGURE 11.20 Processing of Data from MYSQL by .PHP and Feeding the Output as HTML

FIGURE 11.21 Example of a Web Page

11.5.2 Web Hosting

After designing and developing web pages, we have to choose a web host to upload our web pages. The selection or choice should be guided by the following broad considerations:

1. Price should not be the sole driving factor.
2. The amount of storage (hosting space) required by the site.
3. Data transfer rate.
4. What type of site has been built? Is it a simple blog, e-commerce or does it need server-side scripting?
5. Future changes envisaged for the site so that we can properly select the host who can scale with the site as it changes over the years.

CASE STUDY: BREAK-EVEN ANALYSIS OF EXCESS STOCK OF SLOW-MOVING ITEMS BY A FURNITURE MANUFACTURING UNIT

Background

The case pertains to a furniture manufacturing unit, located in the state of West Bengal, India. The unit was facing a problem of holding excess stock of some items of raw materials. The items were regularly procured based on consumption pattern commensurate with customer demand for the end products. Earlier the customer demand was very high for the particular end products and hence the items were fast-moving. However, due to change of customer preferences for new design of furniture, the demand for the earlier end-products decreased considerably and as a result, the items procured earlier in large quantities became slow-moving resulting in excess stock holding.

The management of the unit were in a fix to decide whether to sell the entire stock of the items to reduce inventory-holding cost associated with those items or to hold the items as there was a risk also that if the items are disposed off and in future, the customer demand might increase, the same items would have to be purchased at a higher price due to escalation. The manufacturing unit engaged a management consultant to develop a computer-based model to perform break-even analysis of excess stock of such items as mentioned above.

Mathematical Formulation of the Model

The economic ordering quantity of the items based on the present actual consumption pattern of the same items was determined with the holding cost of each of the items per unit per annum, ordering cost per order, and the procurement lead time of the items as the parameters. This was followed by the development of the model to determine the break-even quantity of excess stock for each of the items. The model was developed as follows:

Notations used:

M = Monthly usage of the item in units
i = Rate of interest on capital per annum, %

P = Price of the item, ₹/Unit
C = Inventory carrying cost per month per ₹ stock
E = Excess stock of the item
X = Rate of increase of price of the item per month, %
D = Discount offered while selling excess stock of the item
Q = Economic ordering quantity
B = Ordering cost in ₹ for the item
R = Cost of processing a sale of excess stock in ₹ per unit

Now, If the excess stock E is sold,

Cash return = D.P.E. (1)

If the excess stock E is sold, then holding cost saved can be expressed as:

$$\text{Holding cost saved} = \text{P.C.} \sum_{j=0}^{E/M}(E-jM) \tag{2}$$

Present worth of gross holding cost saved as shown in 2 above can be expressed as:

$$\text{P.C.} \sum_{j=0}^{E/M}(E-jM)/(1+i/12)^j \tag{3}$$

Selling cost and repurchase penalty if excess inventory would have been sold may be given as:

$$R + \sum_{j=1}^{E/Q}\{B+P\cdot Q\cdot(1+X)^{jQ/M}\}/(1+i/12)^{jQ/M} \tag{4}$$

Combining equations 1, 2, 3 and 4, net gain, G for holding of excess inventory:

$$G = R + \sum_{j=1}^{E/Q}\{B+P\cdot Q\cdot(1+X)^{jQ/M}\}/(1+i/12)^{jQ/M} - \text{D.P.E} - \text{P.C.}\sum_{j=0}^{E/M}(E-jM)/(1+i/12)^j \tag{5}$$

However, for break-even value of $E = E^*$, $G = 0$ and from equation (5):

$$G = 0 = R + \sum_{j=1}^{E^*/Q}\{B+P\cdot Q\cdot(1+X)^{jQ/M}\}/(1+i/12)^{jQ/M} - \text{D.P.E}^* - \text{P.C}\sum_{j=0}^{E^*/M}(E^*-j\cdot M)/(1+i/12)^j \tag{6}$$

From Equation 6, the recommended excess quantity, E can be found out.

Results Obtained

The net gain for holding different quantities of excess inventory was calculated from the parameters shown in the table below for a particular item and plotted in a graph as shown in the following page. It is found from the same graph that break-even quantity $E^* = 55$ kg, which is greater than the EOQ (38 kg). Further, it can be seen that up to the break-even point (E^*) it is profitable to hold excess stock and beyond that holding excess stock is not profitable. The maximum gain can be achieved if excess inventory is kept at 43 kg as can be seen from the graph.

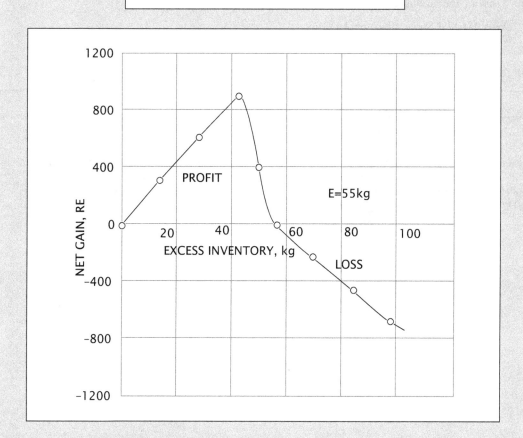

R	₹3.00 per kg
B	₹4.50 per order
i	15%
C	9.6%
D	70%
X	6%

A computer algorithm was developed to solve the equation for net gain and determine the excess stock for maximum gain for all the slow-moving items.

Conclusion

Similar computer-based mathematical models can be developed to facilitate managerial decisions related to holding of excess stock of slow-moving items.

• Review Questions •

1. What are the broad groups of models of computer-based MIS?

2. Mention some common spreadsheet models for facilitating management decisions.

3. Can you think of some limitations of the optimization models in their application in real-life situations?

4. 'MIS models based on computer database need an efficient DBMS'. Explain with suitable illustrations.

5. Web-based models of MIS have become very popular because of distinct advantages. What are the advantages?

6. What are the various technologies involved in web design?

7. What is CMS? Name some popular CMS.

8. What are the functions of PHP and ASP.NET in Web design?

9. What are the criteria of choosing a web host?

Bibliography

Biswas, J. 'A Study and Development of Models of Management Information Systems in Typical Indian Organizations'. PhD thesis, Department of Industrial Management, IISc, Bangalore, India, January 1982.

Miller, L. *MIS Cases: Decision Making with Application Software*, 3rd ed. London: Pearson Education, 2009.

Robbins, J. N. *Learning Web Design: A Beginner's Guide to HTML, CSS, JAVASCRIPT and Web Graphics*, 4th ed. Sebastopool, MA: O'Reilly Media, 2007.

12

CHAPTER

Computer Networking and Communication Technology

12.1 Introduction

During the last two decades, computer networks have grown extensively. Computer networks and the Internet have become an important infrastructure for communication and control in every sphere of our activities such as business, education, healthcare, defence and corporate management involving IT. Some of the latest developments such as mobile computing, e-commerce, e-governance, social networks and IOT have been made possible mainly because of this explosive growth in computer networking.

Today, the Internet has made it possible to connect millions of people all over the globe. It connects and transmits information across large multinational corporations, schools, colleges and universities, state and central government offices. In addition, it connects private houses and individuals through dial-up telephone systems, cable modulator–demodulator (modems), satellites, digital subscriber lines (DSL) and wireless technologies.

The Internet has grown from its early research project to a global communication channel, encompassing about 3,566 million Internet users as in June 2016. The rate of growth of Internet users all over the world since 2000 AD is fantastic as shown in Table 12.1.

12.2 Data Transmission Basics

12.2.1 Transmission Media

1. **Copper wires:** Copper wires are used by conventional computer networks. The data in the form of electric signals are transmitted through insulated copper wires. In order to minimize interference due to emitting of electromagnetic waves, there are three basic types of wiring.

   Unshielded twisted pair wiring consists of a pair of wires insulated with insulating material such as plastic and then the pair is twisted together in order to avoid interference with other wires. **Coaxial cable** consists of an inner wire surrounded by insulation and then a metal shield and

TABLE 12.1 Growth of World Internet Users since 2000

World Region	Population 2016 (EST)	Population as % of World	Internet users (30.6.2016)	Penetration as % of Population	Growth 2000– 2016 (%)	Users as % of World
Africa	1,185,529,578	16.20	333,521,659	28.10	7288	9.40
Asia	4,052,652,880	55.20	1,766,289,264	43.60	1445.3	49.50
Europe	832,073,224	11.30	614,974,023	73.90	485.2	17.20
Latin America/ Caribbean	626,054,392	8.50	374,461,854	59.80	1972.4	10.50
Middle East	246,700,900	3.40	129,498,735	52.50	3842.4	3.60
North America	359,492,293	4.90	320,067,193	89.00	196.1	9.0
Oceania/ Australia	37,590,704	0.50	27,508,287	73.20	261.0	0.80
World Total	7,340,093,980	100.00	3,566,321,015	48.60	887.9	100

Source: Internet World Stats: www.internetworld stats.com/stats.htm

finally a layer of outer insulation. The metal shield forms a cylinder around the inner wire such as a cylindrical capacitor and provides a barrier to electromagnetic radiation and higher protection from interference than a twisted pair. A **shielded twisted pair**, however, has a metal shield around the twisted pair to reduce interference.

2. **Optical fibres:** Optical fibres are made of flexible glass fibres and use light to transmit data in computer networks. Data are transmitted in the form of pulses of light emitted by light emitting diode (LED) or LASER at one end of a fibre which travel down the optical glass fibre. Optical fibres have many advantages such as large distance of transmission of pulses (signals) than copper wires, no electrical interference, a single optical fibre can carry more data than a pair of copper wires needed to form a complete circuit. However, optical fibres require special manufacturing equipment and processes and further in case of breakage of a fibre in a network, it is difficult to repair the same.

12.2.2 Electromagnetic Radiation

Electromagnetic radiation at radio frequency (RF) can be used to transmit computer data without any direct physical connection among the computers in a network such as copper wires or optical fibres. Each computer in the network is attached to an antenna, which can act as a transmitter or receiver of RF.

12.2.3 Microwave

Microwave is electromagnetic radiation beyond the frequency range used for radio and television. It can be used to transmit information as both voice and data over long distance. However, microwaves travel in a single direction unlike low frequency RF transmission and moreover, they cannot penetrate metal structures. As a result, microwave transmission is possible when a clear path exists between the transmitter and the receiver.

12.2.4 Infrared

Computer networks can also use infrared technology for data communication. Such communication does not require any antenna. However, infrared communication is limited to a small distance such as computer in a network within a small room.

12.2.5 Laser

Laser beams can be used to transmit data in a straight line over a long distance. However, because of the fact that it travels in straight line and cannot penetrate trees and weather conditions such as snowfall and fog, laser transmission for computer network has limited application.

12.2.5 Satellites

RF technology can be used along with communication satellites to allow transmission over a long distance over the earth surface with curvature. Satellites are placed in orbit around the earth. A satellite consists of transponders which can receive RF transmission signal sent by a ground station antenna, amplify the signal and transmit the amplified signal back to another ground station (receiving station) in a slightly different direction. Figure 12.1 illustrates how a communication satellite in orbit around the earth can provide a network connection over a mountain range.

A single satellite contains multiple transponders. Each transponder operates under a different RF channel, thus making possible simultaneously multiple users communication. Moreover by sharing, a single satellite can serve many users connected through a computer network.

Depending upon the height at which they orbit, communication satellites can be categorized as (a) geosynchronous or geostationary earth orbit (GEO) satellites and (b) low earth orbit (LEO) satellites.

A geosynchronous or geostationary satellite is placed in an orbit that is exactly synchronized with the rotation of the earth. The satellite, when viewed from the ground, appears to remain exactly at the same point in the sky at all times. For example, a geostationary satellite in a circular orbit over the Pacific

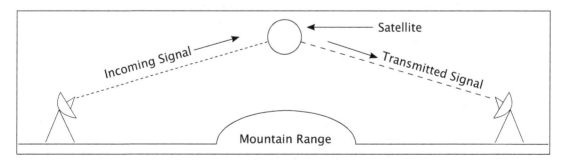

FIGURE 12.1 A Satellite Used to Provide Communication across a Mountain Range

Ocean can transmit signals between Japan and North America at all times because the satellite remains above the same spot over the ocean. Applying the laws of physics, we can find out that the distance from earth for the geosynchronous orbit is 35,785 km or 22,236 miles. In order to avoid interference, a minimum distance of separation must be maintained between any two satellites in the geostationary orbit which also depends upon the signal strength of the transmitter. Usually, the angular separation is about 4–8 degrees. Thus, there can only be from 45 (360/8) to 90 (360/4) satellites in the geostationary orbit above the equator.

12.2.6 LEO Satellites

LEO satellites operate in orbit only at a much lesser height from earth than the geostationary earth orbit. They usually are 200–400 miles above the earth surface. Because the speed of rotation of LEO satellites is faster than the rotation of earth, they do not appear stationary to an observer on the earth and appear to be moving across the sky. The obvious disadvantage is that the satellite can only be used to transmit signals during the time it orbits between two ground stations. In order to enable LEO satellites for continuous communication, a set of LEO satellites are launched. In that case, although each individual satellite appears to be moving across the sky, at any point of time, the set of orbiting satellites guarantees that at least one satellite is available to transmit between two ground stations. Further, in addition to transponders to communicate with ground stations, an array of LEO satellites contain radio equipment used to communicate with each other in the array. This feature facilitates continuous transmission of signals received from one ground station to any intended ground station through the array of satellites.

12.2.7 Local Asynchronous Communication (RS–232)

Computers use binary digits (bits) to represent data. Therefore, transmission of data is through bits which can be encoded and decoded by the transmitting and receiving end computers. Local asynchronous communication (RS–232) uses electric current to transfer data in digital form (bits) over a short distance such as sending characters from a keyboard to a computer. The term asynchronous implies that the sender and the receiver of data do not need to coordinate or synchronize before every transmission. For example, in case of a keyboard, data are generated and sent to computer when a user touches a key and no data flows from keyboard to computer when the keyboard is idle. This is asynchronous communication only.

The Electronics Industries Association (EIA) standard RS–232C specifies details of physical connection such as the connected distance less than 50 feet as well as electrical properties, that is, –15 volts to +15 volts to transmit data bits. RS–232 has become a popular standard for serial communication (bit by bit) over short distance of less than 50 feet usually between a computer and an American Standard Code for Information Interchange (ASCII) terminal or a computer and a modem. RS–232 sends each character with seven data bits, serially preceded by a start bit and followed by a stop bit representing an idle period. Each bit is sent in exactly the same period of time.

Figure 12.2 shows how the voltage on a wire fluctuates between –15 volts (representing '1' bit) and +15 volts (representing '0' bit) to send the start bit (0 bit), stop bit (1 bit) and in between the seven bits representing character 'A'. The above sequence is repeated for transmitting the character 'B' from keyboard to a computer using RS- 232C. It may be mentioned that the seven bits representing 'A' and 'B' are '1000001' and '1000010' respectively.

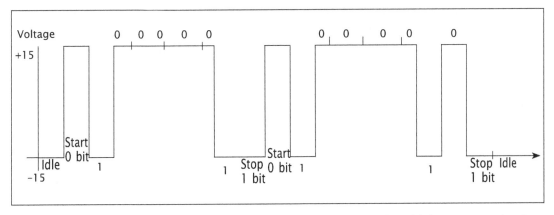

FIGURE 12.2 Electric Voltage on a Wire as the Two Characters 'A' and 'B' Are Transmitted Using RS-232C

Baud rate is the number of bits (0 or 1) transmitted as signal per second and for RS-232 it is 33,600 bits per second, that is, 33.6 kbps. In case the sending and receiving computers and associated hardware are not configured to use the same baud rate, errors known as 'framing errors' will occur as the receiver's timer will not wait same length of time as that of the sender for each bit. Therefore, the baud rate for each computer and hardware can be set physically by setting switches on the hardware when it is installed in a computer.

12.2.8 Half- and Full-duplex Asynchronous Communication

Full-duplex communication takes place when data are transmitted simultaneously in two directions. Half-duplex transmission also known as simplex transmission allows data transmission in both directions but permits transmission in one direction only at any given time. In other words, simultaneous transmission of data in two directions is not possible in case of half-duplex or simplex communication.

Full-duplex connection often uses three wires, two for transmitting data in each of two directions simultaneously and a common ground wire for the return path shared by each. Figure 12.3 illustrates a three wire full-duplex transmission.

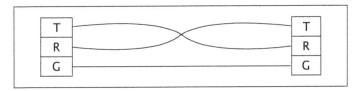

FIGURE 12.3 Three-Wire Full Duplex Transmission Sharing a Single Ground Wire

12.2.9 Bandwidth and Maximum Data Transmission Rate

Each transmission system has a limited bandwidth, which is the maximum rate of change of signal by the transmission device or hardware. For example, in case of RS–232, the maximum rate of change of voltage (say, from –15V to +15V) determines its bandwidth. Bandwidth is measured in cycles per second or hertz (HZ). Obviously, bandwidth of a transmission system has a relation with the maximum data rate which is the maximum speed of sending bits. Nyquist theorem provides the relationship between maximum data rate in bits per second (D) and the bandwidth (B) as follows:

$$D = 2B \, \text{Log}_2^k$$

where ^{k} is possible values of voltage. Applying
Nyquist theorem as above to RS–232, where

$$^k = 2;$$

and we get

$$D = 2B$$

Nyquist theorem provides the maximum theoretical data rate that is not possible to be achieved in practice because of ground interference, known as noise. Another researcher Shannon propounded a theorem known as 'Shannon's theorem', which gives a limit on the maximum data rate in presence of noise. Shannon's theorem is as follows:

$$C = B \log_2 (1 + S/N)$$

where C is the effective limit on the channel capacity in bits per second, B is the hardware bandwidth, S is the average signal power and N is the average noise power. S/N which is called signal-to-noise ratio is usually expressed as $10 \log_{10} S/N$ and measured in decibels (dB). For example, a ratio of S/N equal to 100 is $10 \times \log_{10} 100 = 10 \times 2 = 20$ dB and similarly, ratio of 1,000 is 30 dB.

In a voice telephone system, (S/N) is approximately 30 db and bandwidth approximately 3,000 HZ. Then, according to Shannon's theorem, the maximum transmission rate in bits per second in a real voice telephone system under noise due to background interference is = 3,000 $\log_2$ (1 + 1,000) or 30,000 bps approximately.

12.3 Long-distance Communication

A signal in the form of electric current cannot be transmitted over a long distance through copper wire because of transmission loss which makes the current weaker during propagation. As a result, the signal in the form of electric current cannot be detected by the receiver placed at a long distance. Such loss is due to the resistance to electric current by the copper partially converting electric energy to heat. Communication scientists, however, studied and discovered that in case of long-distance transmission, a continuous, oscillating signal usually in the form of a sine wave, propagates farther than any other signal. This continuously oscillating sine-wave signal is known as the carrier which is, however, subjected to modifications (technically called modulations) by the transmitter. The receiver receives the incoming carrier, detects modulation, reconstructs the original data (signal) and then discards the carrier. A question arises as to how the transmitter modulates the carrier. It is either amplitude modulation (AM)/ frequency modulation (FM) or a pulse shift modulation (PSM) depending upon the technique adopted by the network technology. Amplitude modulation varies the strength of the carrier wave in proportion

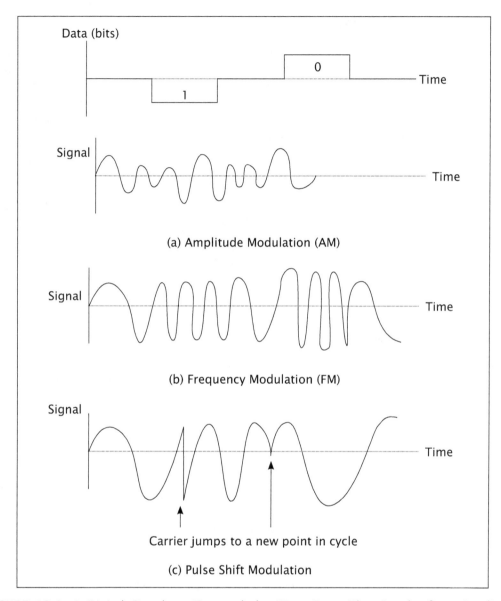

FIGURE 12.4 A Digital Signal on Top and the Wave Form That Results from Amplitude Modulation, Frequency Modulation and a Pulse Shift Modulation

to the information being sent; frequency modulation varies the frequency of the underlying carrier in proportion to the information being sent. PSM, which is often adopted by computer networks, changes the timing of the carrier wave abruptly to encode data. Each such change is known as a 'phase shift'. PSM has got an advantage due to its ability to encode more than one-bit value per change. After a 'phase shift', the carrier jumps to a new point in its oscillating cycle. Figures 12.4a, 12.4b and 12.4c show examples of AM, FM and PSM respectively.

12.3.1 Modem Hardware

A hardware device that accepts a sequence of data (bits) and modulates a carrier wave to represent the data bits is called a modulator. Likewise, a hardware device that accepts a modulated carrier wave to recreate the sequence of data bits, which was used to modulate the carrier is called a demodulator. However, in case of most network systems, the transmission is full duplex, and hence the modulators and demodulators have been combined into a single hardware device known as 'modem'. One such device is kept at each end of a long-distance connection as shown in Figure 12.5.

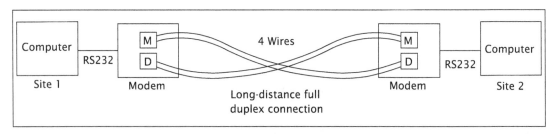

FIGURE 12.5 Modem for Long-distance Full-duplex Connection

12.3.1.1 Types of Modem

In addition to dedicated wires, modems can be used with optical (glass fibres), radio frequency and conventional telephone connections. In case of conventional telephone system, dial-up modems are used to connect computers at long distance apart as shown in Figure 12.6.

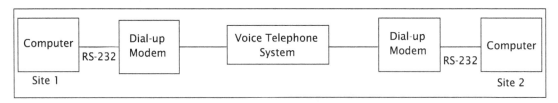

FIGURE 12.6 Dial-up Modems Used with Voice Telephone System to Communicate between Two Computers

Dial-up modems appear to be a telephone to the voice telephone system. As the telephone system is designed to carry sound, a dial-up modem contains circuit to send and receive audio over the telephone line in addition to sending and receiving a carrier.

12.3.2 Carrier Frequencies and Multiplexing

Multiplexing is the principle of sending two or more signals using different carrier frequencies through a single medium simultaneously without interference. Computer networks use the above principle to permit multiple communication using a single shared physical connection. This is technically known a frequency division multiplexing (FDM) as shown in Figure 12.7.

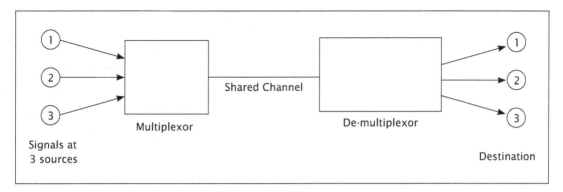

FIGURE 12.7 Illustration of Frequency Division Multiplexing

12.3.2.1 Multiplexing Technologies

The multiplexing technologies are as follows:

Broadband and baseband technologies: In order to achieve higher throughput, the underlying hardware for multiplexing often uses a larger part of electromagnetic spectrum or in other words a larger bandwidth which is called a broadband technology. On the contrary, the technology that sends only one signal at a time over a medium using a small electromagnetic spectrum is known a baseband technology.

Wavelength division multiplexing: Wavelength division multiplexing is applicable in case of optical FDM. It operates multiple lights of different wavelengths through a single optical fibre. At the receiving end, an optical prism is used to separate the light waves with different wavelengthes and therefore different frequencies.

Spread spectrum: Spread spectrum uses a transmitter to send the same signal on a set of carrier frequencies to improve reliability of transmission. The receiver checks for all carrier frequencies in the spectrum and selects the desired one.

Time division multiplexing (TDM): It is basically a time-sharing multiplexing in which sources share a single medium according to turn.

TDM can be either synchronous in which case sources take turns in a round-robin fashion with time slices allotted to each source or statistical multiplexing in which case, if a given source does not have data, the same will be ignored.

12.4 Packet Networks

Packets are small blocks of data, which a network system sends individually. Packet networks, also known as the packet switching networks, send data in packets, and the technology is known as packet technology. The use of packets facilitates two things.

First, it ensures proper coordination of sender and receiver to see that data in packets arrive correctly to the receiver from the sender. Second, communication circuits and the associated modems being expensive, multiple computers often share underlying connections and hardware. The network permits

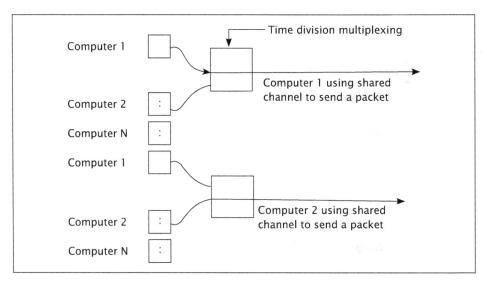

FIGURE 12.8 Illustration of Time Division Multiplexing with Packets

one computer to send a packet at a time and then waits for other computers to send packets according to their turn before being allowed to send a second packet. This sending of packets in a sharing mode by each computer is taken care of by the network system using packet switching technology. This is illustrated in Figure 12.8.

Dividing data into small packets facilitates TDM as all data sources (computer 1, 2, ..., N) get equal share of time for transmitting one packet each at a time.

Packets are associated with frame which defines a packet used with any specific type of network. A frame consists of a block of data preceded by an unprintable ASCII character known as start of header (SOH) and followed by another unprintable ASCII character to mark the end of transmission (EOT) of the frame. An example of frame is shown as follows:

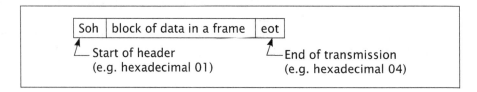

The main advantage of sending data in a frame with a character at the beginning and end of a frame arises when there is large delay in transmission of data due to crashing of computer system. Rebooting using two characters to delimit a frame takes care of such eventualities. However, there is an obvious disadvantage of extra overhead associated with extra bits between blocks of data (one EOT and one SOH between two successive blocks).

In order to permit a frame to carry arbitrary data, the same must be modified before transmission and restored after reception. Techniques used for modification are referred to as data or byte stuffing because the modification involves inserting extra bits or bytes.

12.4.1 Transmission Errors, Parity Bits and Checks

Data transmission through electronic circuits or copper wires is susceptible to error due to interference caused by lighting, power surges and other form of electromagnetic interference. Such interference changes the electrical signal representing data causing the receiver to misinterpret one or more bits of data. This gives rise to transmission errors. Networks are therefore designed to enable hardware and software mechanisms with checks to detect such errors and rectify those. RS–232 circuits in addition to declaring an error, in case a fixed voltage does not remain during expected duration of each bit or if the stop bit does not occur at an appropriate time, use a second mechanism to ensure that each character arrives intact. This mechanism is technically known as a 'parity check', which requires the sender to compute an additional bit, known as a 'parity bit' and attach it to each character before transmitting. The receiver receives all bits of a character and then removes the parity bit and does the same computation as done by the sender and checks that the computation results in the same value as per the parity bit. If there is any loss of bit during transmission, the computation done by the receiver will not tally with the parity bit and the receiver will send an error message to the sender. Parity checks may be even or odd as shown below:

Transmission Character	Parity Check for 1' Bits	Parity Bit
0100101	Even	1
0101101	Even	0
0100101	odd	0
0101101	odd	1

Parity bit has been selected so as to make the total number of '1' bits even or odd depending upon the even or odd parity check.

However, it may be noted that in case of any transmission error involving loss of even number of bits, parity check will fail to detect the same.

12.4.2 Checksum as Error-Detecting Mechanism

Often computer networks make use of checksum as a mechanism for detection of errors. The sender computes checksum as the sum of a sequence of binary integers which represent the data transmitted. This is illustrated in the Figure 12.9.

Checksum mechanism has advantages such as smaller transmission overhead as checksum technique uses either a 16-bit or a 32-bit checksum, and hence a single checksum is computed for an entire packet. Moreover, the computation of checksum is much easy being simple addition of binary integers. However, checksum cannot detect all common errors as shown in the example in Figure 12.10.

Data Item in Binary	Checksum Value
00010	2
00001	1
00100	4
00010	2
Total	9

FIGURE 12.9 Illustration of a Checksum Value

Data Item in Binary	Checksum Value		Data Item in Binary	Checksum Value
00010	2	Transmission	00011	3
00001	1	Error converts	00000	0
00100	4	Data item in	00000	0
00010	2	binary as	00110	6
Total	9			9

FIGURE 12.10 Example of a Checksum Failing to Detect Transmission Errors

12.4.3 Error Detection with Cyclic Redundancy Checks (CRC)

CRC techniques can detect more errors in a computer network system than checksum. CRC employs two simple hardware components, namely an exclusive or (XOR) unit and a shift register. Figure 12.11 shows an XOR unit and the output table corresponding to four combinations of two inputs to the XOR unit. The output will be true (1) when two inputs differ, otherwise false (0).

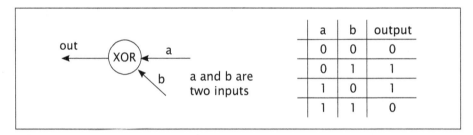

FIGURE 12.11 Exclusive OR Unit with Output Value Corresponding to Different Input Values

The other device used to compute a CRC is a shift register. A shift register has an output that gives the value of the leftmost bit. The shift register further reads an input on its right side only when a shift operation occurs. For example, Figures 12.12a and 12.12b show that although input is '0', the rightmost bit in the shift register remains '1' until the instant the shift takes place.

The CRC method is based on division of a polynomial of degree m (where m + 1 represents the bits of the message sent from receiver to sender) by another polynomial whose degree n determines the length of the CRC shift register. The second polynomial of degree n is called the generator (G) which is

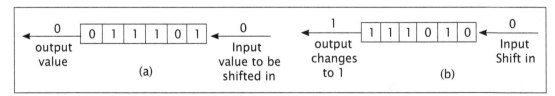

FIGURE 12.12 A Shift Register (a) before and (b) after a Shift Operation

known to both the receiver and the sender of the message of length (m + 1). The following example shows how the CRC works to detect error. Let the message represented by the polynomial M is:

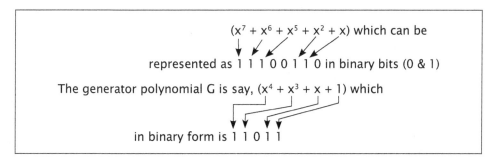

Therefore, the CRC shift register will be of length of (5–1), that is, 4 which is the degree of the G polynomial.

The division of M by G is taken care of by the hardware components performing X or (represented as +) and the CRC shift register in following steps separately shown for sender and receiver.

Sender:

Step 1: Initialize the shift register with all 0's and append equal number of 0's to M

CRC Shift Register   M with appendix

| 0 | 0 | 0 | 0 | | 1 | 1 | 1 | 0 | 0 | 1 | 1 | 0 | 0 | 0 | 0 | 0 |

Step 2: If the order bit (leftmost) of shift register is '0'; shift the leftmost bit of CRC and the left most available bit of M together; otherwise if the leftmost bit of CRC is '1'; shift CRC by one leftmost bit and M by the left most available bit and perform XOR on CRC by n low order bits of generator G of degree n. Since in this case the leftmost bit in CRC is 0, we shift both shift registers with the leftmost bit of message M giving rise to:

CRC   (M – 1)

| 0 | 0 | 0 | 1 | | | 1 | 1 | 0 | 0 | 1 | 1 | 0 | 0 | 0 | 0 | 0 |

Again, since leftmost bit of CRC is 0, we perform same shift operations giving rise to

CRC   (M – 2)

| 0 | 0 | 1 | 1 | | | | 1 | 0 | 0 | 1 | 1 | 0 | 0 | 0 | 0 | 0 |

Again, since leftmost bit of CRC is 0, we perform same shift giving rise to

CRC   (M – 3)

| 0 | 1 | 1 | 1 | | | | | 0 | 0 | 1 | 1 | 0 | 0 | 0 | 0 | 0 |

Again, since leftmost bit of CRC is 0; we perform same shift giving rise to

Now, leftmost bit of CRC is '1', we perform shift first and then X or with four (degree of generator) low order bits of G which is 1011, resulting in as follows:

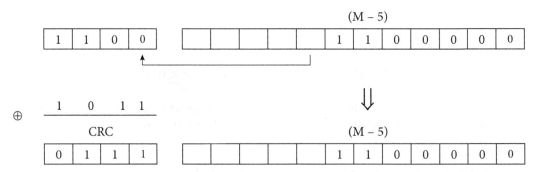

Now, leftmost bit of CRC is '0', so we perform only shift operations giving rise to

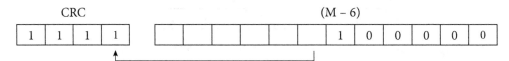

Since, leftmost bit of CRC is '1' we perform shift operation first and then XOR as before with 1011 giving rise to

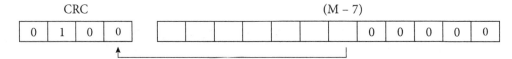

Now leftmost bit of CRC is '0', so we perform only shift operations giving rise to

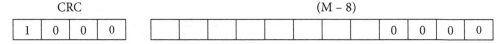

Now, leftmost bit of CRC is '1'; hence we perform shift first and then XOR as before with 1011 giving rise to

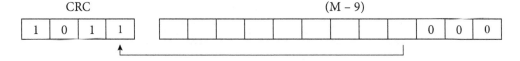

Now, leftmost bit of CRC is '1' hence we proceed with shifts first and then XOR with '1011' giving rise to

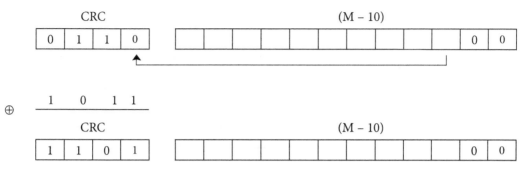

Now, leftmost bit of CRC is '1' hence we proceed with shift first and then XOR with '1011' giving rise to

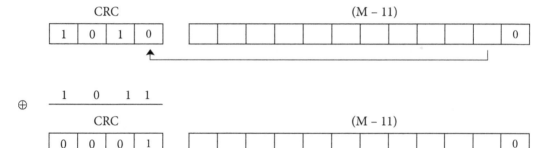

Now, leftmost bit of CRC is '0' hence we proceed with same shift giving rise to

We are left with the message as blank.

Since now no bit is left in appended message, CRC content '0000' is the remainder which the sender will append with the message and transmit to receiver as follows:

1	1	1	0	0	1	1	0	0	0	0	0

Now, in order to ensure error-free transmission, the receiver will either perform the same steps as done by sender on the main message by eliminating the last four low order bits appended and arrive at the same remainder of '0000' or perform the steps with the received message as it is and arrive as '0000' remainder. If the result of either operation as mentioned above is different, receiver will report transmission error to sender. Let us perform the second alternative in steps as performed by receiver.

CRC   (Message of received with CRC checksum)

| 0 | 0 | 0 | 0 | | 1 | 1 | 1 | 0 | 0 | 1 | 1 | 0 | 0 | 0 | 0 | 0 |

⇓

| 0 | 0 | 0 | 1 | | | 1 | 1 | 0 | 0 | 1 | 1 | 0 | 0 | 0 | 0 | 0 |

⇓

| 0 | 0 | 1 | 1 | | | | 1 | 0 | 0 | 1 | 1 | 0 | 0 | 0 | 0 | 0 |

⇓

| 0 | 1 | 1 | 1 | | | | | 0 | 0 | 1 | 1 | 0 | 0 | 0 | 0 | 0 |

⇓

| 1 | 1 | 1 | 0 | | | | | | 0 | 1 | 1 | 0 | 0 | 0 | 0 | 0 |

⇓

| 1 | 1 | 0 | 0 | | | | | | | 1 | 1 | 0 | 0 | 0 | 0 | 0 |

⊕   1   0   1   1 (overlined)

| 0 | 1 | 1 | 1 | | | | | | | 1 | 1 | 0 | 0 | 0 | 0 | 0 |

⇓

| 1 | 1 | 1 | 1 | | | | | | | | 1 | 0 | 0 | 0 | 0 | 0 |

⇓

| 1 | 1 | 1 | 1 | |

⊕   1   0   1   1 (overlined)

| 0 | 1 | 0 | 0 | | | | | | | | | 0 | 0 | 0 | 0 | 0 |

⇓

1	0	0	0

								0	0	0	0

⇓

0	0	0	0

⊕

1	0	1	1
1	0	1	1

									0	0	0

⇓

0	1	1	0

										0	0

⇓

⊕

1	0	1	1

1	1	0	1

										0	0

⇓

1	0	1	0

											0

⊕

1	0	1	1
0	0	0	1

⇓

											0

⇓

0	0	0	0

Blank

CRC remainder

0	0	0	0

The remainder is '0000', which shows that there is no transmission error.

12.5 LAN Technology and Network Topology

Direct point-to-point connection requires a dedicated connection for each pair of computers in the network which is obviously disadvantageous since there will be many number of dedicated connections for the computers belonging to two locations. Therefore, the technology adopted for LAN is designed for sharing of the communication line instead of separate modems and cables for each pair.

12.5.1 LAN Topologies

Networks are classified into different categories known as topologies such as star, ring and bus. They are described as follows:

Each computer (C1, C2, C3,…, C8) is attached to a central hub. For example, asynchronous transfer mode (ATM) is an electronic switch developed by telephone companies. ATM is connected to multiple computers each one being connected to the switch through a pair of optical fibres, each fibre transmits data in one direction only at a speed of 155 mbps or faster.

Computers (C1, C2, C3, C4) are connected to one another in a ring.

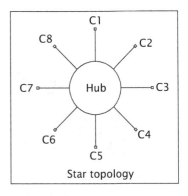

Star topology

12.5.2 Token Passing

Computers attached in a ring topology network use a token, which is a short message to coordinate error-free transmission of data. The bit pattern of the token is different from the data frame bits. The token rotates around the ring and allows one computer at a time to transmit exactly one frame and then passes the data frame to all other computers and then reaches back to the sender computer to return the same frame. The sender computer compares the frame transmitted with the frame received from the token and if both are found same, error-free transmission is ensured. During the cycle of

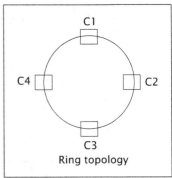

Ring topology

rotation of the token with a frame of data, when the token reaches the destination computer (recipient of the frame), the same makes a copy of the frame and allows the token to pass to the next computer. The token allows the computers to send one frame at a time each in rotation and if no computer has data to transmit, the token cycles round the ring (known as 'token ring') at a very high speed. Figure 12.13 shows a 'token ring' with flow of bits of a frame in it.

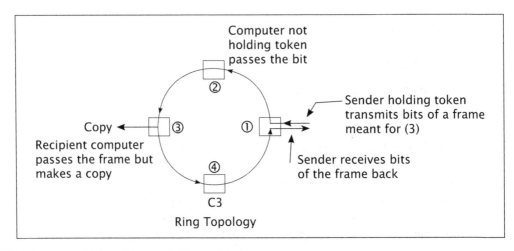

FIGURE 12.13 Token Ring with Flow of a Frame

12.5.3 Self-healing Token Ring

In case of a normal token ring, any failure of a single computer attached to the ring will make the complete token ring inoperative since each computer attached to the ring must pass the frame to the next one in the cycle. Hence, self-healing token rings have been designed to take care of failure of any computer by bypassing the same one and completing the cycle with the other computers through another inner ring (cable). Necessarily, therefore, self-healing token rings have two concentric rings connecting the computers. The outer ring is used for normal transmission of data and the inner ring is unused for data transmission except in case of any failure, and the inner ring facilitates completing the path by looping back by the computer adjacent to the failed computer as shown in Figure 12.14.

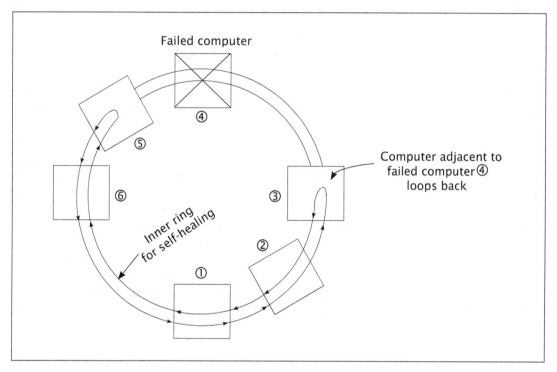

FIGURE 12.14 Self-healing Token Ring

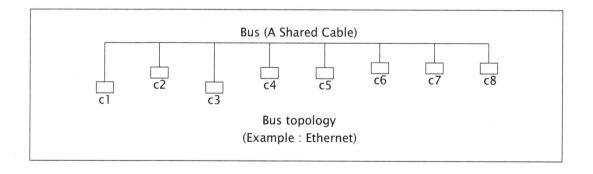

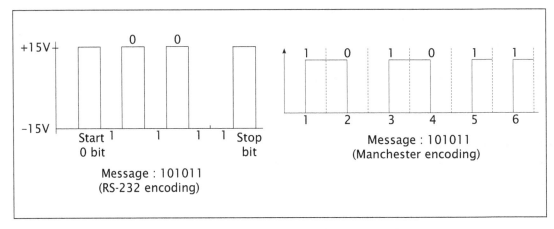

FIGURE 12.15 Comparison between RS-232 and Manchester Encoding

In bus topology, a single long cable known as bus is being used and to which computers are attached. Any computer attached to a bus can send a signal when all other attached computers receive the signal. However, the transmission is coordinated in such a way that one computer is allowed to send a signal at any time. Popular ethernet is a bus network first developed at Xerox Corporation's Palo Alto Research Centre in the early 1970s. It consists of a single coaxial cable (bus) to which multiple computers are connected. Ethernet has a limitation of 500 metres length and a minimum separation distance of 3 metres between each pair of computers connected to ethernet. The original ethernet of the 1970s had a speed of 10 mbps, however the speed was enhanced subsequently to 100 mbps or even 1 gbps (gigabyte per second) in case of gigabit ethernet. Ethernets use Manchester encoding in which case bits (0 or 1) are represented by changes in voltage rather than fixed voltage as in case of RS–232. A change from positive to zero voltage represents a '0' bit, and a change from zero to positive voltage represents a '1' bit. This is because researchers observed that a hardware device detects a change in voltage more promptly than a fixed voltage value. A comparison of the encoding according to RS–232 with the Manchester encoding used by Ethernet for the same message '101011' transmitted is shown in Figure 12.15.

Ethernet allows any one computer to transmit a frame at a time and all other computers wait till the transmission is over. The frame bits pass one by one across the cable to all computers connected and the destination computer receives a copy of each bit. The bus technology is adopted by a multi-access shared network in order to detect by any computer at any time whether the cable is engaged with any electrical signal (technically called carrier) before transmitting any signal. The network is known as carrier sense multiple access (CSMA) network. In order to ensure that no two computers transmit simultaneously causing collision, the sending station monitors signals on the cable and if it finds that the signal on the cable is different from the one it is sending, it will realize that a collision has occurred and immediately it will stop transmission. Technically, the process of detecting any collision during transmission through a 'cable carrier sensing' is known as CSMA with collision detection (CSMA/CD) mechanism. Although the ethernet is very popular bus technology LAN, other technologies such as 'LocalTalk' invented by Apple Computer Corporation (through 230.4 kbps) use bus topology for connecting Macintosh computers. It is a low-cost network.

12.5.4 Collision Avoidance through Carrier Sensing in Case of Wireless LANs

Wireless LAN adopts a modified form of CSMA/CD, known as CSMA with collision avoidance (CSMA/CA). The sender sends first a control message to the receiver before transmitting the frame. The receiver responds by sending another control message indicating that it is free to receive a frame. After the sender receives the same control message as response from the receiver, it starts transmitting a frame. Since control messages are generally much shorter than a frame, the collision of control messages, if it occurs, can be handled at first instance only by back off by the sending stations, and the chance of a second collision is almost ruled out and eventually one of the two control messages arrives as it is to the receiving computer and the same then transmits a response. Institute of Electrical and Electronics Engineers (IEEE) standard 802.11b known as 'Wi-Fi' operates at 11 mbps and 2.4 GHz frequency range. A standard known as a 'Bluetooth' which specifies a short distance wireless LAN technology employs CSMA/CA method.

12.6 Hardware Addressing and Frame Type Identification

The hardware of a computer attached to a network consists of two main components. The first component is the Network Interface Hardware (NIH) which basically transmits and receives frames on the LAN. The second component is the processor and the memory unit which handles incoming data, processes the data and generates outgoing data. This component constantly interacts with the NIH. Figure 12.16 shows schematically the organization of the LAN hardware and the CPU and memory.

Hardware addressing is very important for direct communication among the network computers. The frame transmitted by any computer in a shared network (LAN) essentially contains the address of sender, the source address and the intended recipient, the destination address. Therefore, each computer on the LAN is assigned a unique numeric address, called its physical address. Different LAN technologies employ different formats or types of physical addresses of the hardware, which are of three main categories, namely:

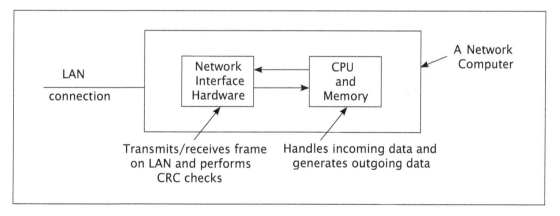

FIGURE 12.16 Hardware Organization of a Network Computer

Preamble	Destination Address	Source Address	Frame Type	Data in Frame	CRC
8	6	6	2	46—1500	4

|← ———————— Header ———————— →|← — Pay load — →|

FIGURE 12.17 Frame Format Used with Ethernet

Note: The number in each field gives the field size in 8-bit octets; for example, preamble is of 8 × 8, that is, 64 bits.

1. Static physical address which is assigned by the hardware manufacturer and is fixed for a particular hardware.
2. Configurable physical address which is set by the customer (user) when the hardware is first installed in a LAN.
3. Dynamic physical address which is automatically assigned to a computer when the computer in the network first boots. Dynamic addressing is facilitated by some randomizing algorithm to ensure that assigned address is not already being used by any other computer in the network.
   i. **Addressing mechanism for broadcasting and multi-casting:** Broadcasting makes a copy of the transmitted data available to all computers on the network so that the particular computer for which the message is applicable would respond. Multi-casting is a restricted form of broadcasting introduced to take the advantage of broadcasting without wasting CPU resources of all other computers on a shared network.
   ii. **Frame format:** A frame consists of two parts, namely a frame header which contains mainly the addresses of the source and destination and the frame type as the first part followed by the second part known as the payload which is the data part being sent and much larger than the first part. A format of the frame as defined by ethernet is shown in Figure 12.17.

The 64-bit preamble contains alternating 1s and 0s and is used to synchronize the receiver hardware with the incoming frame. Ethernet uses static addressing with 48 bits. The 16-bit frame type contains a unique value for each possible use of the network. The receiver examines the frame type field to determine the mode of handling the frame.

12.7 LAN Extension

LAN technology as such is best suited in case of computers located in a single building or office at a distance limited to few hundred metres. However, there are mechanisms for LAN extension using fibre modems, repeaters, bridges or switches. Fibre modems in a pair with optical fibres are used to connect a computer to a distant network hub. Since the fibre has low transmission time and high bandwidth, it allows longer distance (several kilometres) transmission than the typical cable LAN.

A repeater is an analog electronic device which joins together two LAN segments by monitoring the electrical signals in either of the two and transmits the signal with amplification to the other. A pair of computers on the extended LAN can communicate with each other without knowing that there is a repeater separating them. The ethernet standard, however, specifies that because of the limitation on transmission delay, the extension network will not function properly if more than four repeaters are used

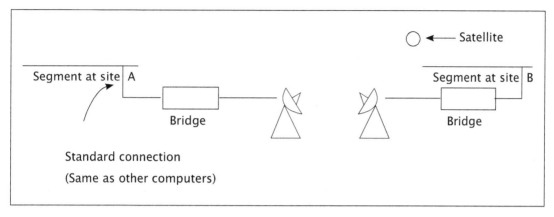

FIGURE 12.18 A Bridge Using a Leased Satellite Channel Connects Two LAN Segments at Two Sites

to separate any pair of stations. Repeaters, however, have several disadvantages. The most important disadvantage is that repeaters cannot understand complete frames. Therefore, in addition to propagating copies of valid signals from one ethernet segment to another, a repeater also transmits other electrical signals such as collisions, or electrical interference from one segment to another. Bridges are also electronic devices that connect two LAN segments. However, unlike repeaters, bridges are digital devices having the same network interface as a computer and thus can handle frames. Bridges are more advantageous than repeaters because unlike repeaters, bridges will not propagate any electrical interference caused by lighting and other reasons from one segment of ethernet to another segment. Bridges will simply discard an incorrectly formed frame in much the same way as a network computer discards a frame with error. Similarly, a bridge will not forward a collision from one segment to another. A bridge using a leased satellite channel can connect two LAN segments at two sites across a long distance as shown in Figure 12.18.

Switching is another mechanism of connecting one or more computers with an electronic device known as switch. A switched LAN consists of a single switch that transmits frames among many computers.

A switch consists of processors and interconnect such as an electronic crossbar. The processor being an intelligent device is capable of finding the destination address of an incoming frame from a computer connected to one of its ports and then uses the interconnect to transfer the frame to the correct output port. Figure 12.19 shows the concept of a switched LAN.

A switch differs from a network hub in that the hub connects computers with no understanding of the frames it transfers. It simply receives a frame of data and transfers (broadcasts) the same to all other connected devices irrespective of which one device responds as the final destination. The network bandwidth is split being used by all the connected devices or computers, which naturally implies slower transmission speed. On the other hand, a switch receives a frame of data from a computer and determines which computer or device the frame is intended for and sends it to that computer or device only. Obviously, the network bandwidth is not shared by all connected devices as in the case of hub and makes the speed of transmission much faster and the network efficient. Hence, switches are preferred over hubs.

Router is another hardware which connects two heterogeneous networks. A computer network can be connected to the Internet through router. A router contains a processor and memory and a separate

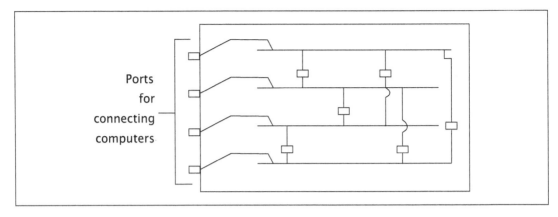

FIGURE 12.19 Concept of a Switched LAN

network I/O interface for each network it connects. The basic difference between a switch or hub and a router is that unlike a switch or hub, which transmits data packets among local computers, router routes frames of data to other networks. Routers have more logic built in it and can determine the best path or route for transmitting the data packets.

12.8 Long-distance and Local-loop Digital Technologies

The two main limitations of the LAN are its inability to connect any arbitrary number of computers and to connect computers located at sites large distances apart. In order to overcome the above two limitations, the following two developments were made.

12.8.1 Digital Telephony Circuits

Digital telephony circuits developed by telephone companies were adopted for the purpose of long-distance connections in a large network. Digital telephony circuits designed to carry voice traffic in a digital form through analog to digital form and vice-versa through appropriate converters (analog to digital and digital to analog) have been used for data traffic also. The digital circuits leased from telephone companies form the fundamental components for long-distance computer networks. However, a special hardware device is needed to interface a computer in a network to a digital circuit developed by a telephone company. This hardware device contains two functional parts known as data service unit (DSU) and channel service unit (CSU). The need for the hardware device DSU/CSU arose because of the different standards developed by telephone companies for their digital circuits and the same developed by the computer industry. A DSU/CSU is required at end of a leased digital circuit as shown in Figure 12.20.

The DSU of the device handles the data, whereas the CSU handles line termination, diagnostics and a loop-back test facility to send a copy of all data that arrive at the circuit back to the sender without further processing. Network interface unit (NIU) shown in Figure 12.20, is an equipment provided by

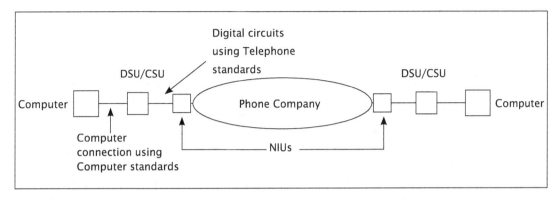

FIGURE 12.20 Illustration of a Digital Circuit with a DSU/CSU at Each End

Source: Comer (2004, 180).

the telephone company and is an interface between the facilities of the phone company and those of the subscriber.

Digital signal (DS) level multiplexing facilitates multiple phone calls onto a single carrier system connection. For example, DS1 denotes multiplexing of 24 phone calls onto a single circuit. The other important standards which classify the digital circuits of the carrier system are the T-standards, which define the underlying carrier systems based on their data rates in mbps and the number of voice circuits such as 24 and 96. Some of the popular T-standards are as follows:

Name of T-Standard Line	Bit Rate	Voice Circuit Channels
T1	1.5444 mbps	24
T1C	3.152 mbps	48
T2	6.312 mbps	96 (4 × 24)
T3	44.736 mbps	672 (28 × 24)
T4	274.176 mbps	4,032
T5	400.352 mbps	5,760

It may be noted that T3 circuit can multiplex 28 numbers of T1 Circuits.

TDM technology is used to further subdivide T1 circuit, and one such popular fractional T1 capacity is 64 kbps leased by the telephone companies, who do not need T1 capacity.

A DS1 telephone circuit is made up of 24 8-bit channels and is full-duplex circuit. The bandwidth is achieved by a pulse code modulation (PCM) of 8 khz (8,000 frames per second) for each of the 24 channels. The calculation is as follows:

> (8 bits per channel × 24 channels × 8,000 frames/sec)
> = 1,544,000 bits per second
> = 1.544 mbps

In the late 20th century, parts of the network created primarily to transmit voices were upgraded with large-scale digital services to subscribers under the name of integrated services digital network (ISDN) and DSL to handle traffic of digital data. In telecommunication arena, DSL is now widely understood as the asymmetric digital subscriber line (ADSL).

ISDN handles data and voice in a digitized form for subscribers over conventional local loop wiring with twisted copper wires. It provides three separate digital channels to subscribers. The three are B, B and D usually denoted as 2B + D. The 'B' channels are for carrying digitized voice or compressed video and operate at a speed of 64 kbps. The 'D' channel which operates at 16 kbps is basically a control channel. Subscribers use the 'D' channel to request for services (data, fax or voice), which are then supplied through the 'B' channels. The subscriber also uses the 'D' channel to manage a session in progress or to terminate the same. However, with the development of dial-up modems and other technologies such as the Internet providing higher data transfer rates across the local loop wiring at lower cost, ISDN has now got limited application.

ADSL is one of the most important DSL and is a local loop technology that accommodates users who receive much more information (a higher bit rate downstream) than they send (a lower bit rate upstream). Hence, the name of the DSL is prefixed with the word 'asymmetric'. In case of a typical ADSL, the maximum downstream rate can be as high of 6.144 mbps; whereas the upstream rate is a mere 640 kbps. Because the mandatory network control channel requires 64 kbps, the effective upstream rate is (640 − 64) = 576 kbps only. In order to achieve high bit rates downstream over conventional twisted-pair wiring, ADSL uses an adaptive technology in which a pair of modems (one providing digital connection to local loop network and the other to provider of service) probe many frequencies on the line connecting them and select frequencies and modulation techniques best suited to the line condition.

12.8.2 Wireless Networks

Technologies such as DSL and ADSL have limitations particularly in remote areas. Further, copper wiring for ADSL networks needs sufficient gauge as otherwise, the digital signals will be attenuated. In order to overcome such limitations of wired networks, wireless networks have been developed. WiMAX developed by IEEE is a high-speed wireless network used in metropolitan area with a throughput of up to 155 mbps. WiMAX is capable of spanning larger distances than a LAN but obviously less than wide area network (WAN). WiMAX can either replace a local loop technology or can link an Internet service provider with a neighbourhood in a city providing high-speed access. Another wireless alternative for digital communication is through broadcast satellite systems. However, in order to devise a low-cost local loop system through satellites, two developments were made. First, instead of treating satellites as a point-to-point communication system, a broadcasting system was devised. Second, for low-cost solution instead of a large ground station, an alternative uplink transmission path was made. The first development enabled the satellite to broadcast each packet, a copy of which can be received by all stations tuned to the satellite. Each station is assigned a unique address, the station filters incoming packets and a packet is accepted by a station only when the address of the packet is the same as the address of the station; other packets are discarded by the station.

The uplink transmission path was taken care of by adopting the concept of asymmetric delivery by the broadcast satellite technology. In such situations, the broadcast satellite is used for downstream traffic only and upstream traffic travels over a low-capacity network such as a conventional dial-up telephone connection.

Synchronous optical networking (SONET) and synchronous digital hierarchy (SDH) are standardized protocols that transfer multiple digital bit streams synchronously over optical fibre using lasers or light from LED. SONET specifications include framing of data, multiplexing circuit capacity enhancement and synchronizing clock information along with data.

12.9 WAN Technologies

Unlike LAN and MAN (metropolitan area network such as WiMAX), WAN can connect sites located in multiple cities, countries and continents. The other distinguishing feature of WAN is its scalability to connect many sites with many computers in each site. Because of its scalability, a WAN can connect computers located in offices or business units of a multinational company with large geographical dispersions. In spite of large scalability, WAN is capable of connecting large number of computers without any trade-off in its performance of speed and efficient communication.

WAN is made up of many switches to which individual computers are connected. The switches are known as packet switches because they move complete packets of data from one connection to another. The digital connection may be from one switch to another or may be from a computer to the switch as shown in Figure 12.21.

A packet switch is conceptually a small computer having its processor, memory and I/O devices for sending and receiving packets. The I/O connectors which connect a packet switch to a digital circuit leading to another packet switch operate at high speed, whereas the I/O connectors which connect individual computers to the switch operate at lower speed. The digital connections in a WAN can include leased data circuits, optical fibres, microwaves and satellite channels depending upon the particular WAN design. The interconnections among switches and their capacities are chosen according to the traffic expected and additional redundancy to take care of contingencies such as failures. In that sense, a WAN need not be symmetric.

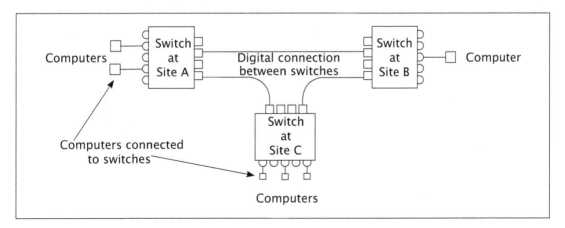

FIGURE 12.21 WAN Formed with Packet Switches and Computers

12.9.1 Store and Forward

WAN permits many computers to send packets simultaneously by the Store and Forward technique. The technique allows a packet switch to store in buffer a short burst of packets that arrive at a time to the switch. The store operation, which occurs first, stores a copy of the packets received by the I/O hardware of the packet switch into its memory. Next, the forward operation takes place. If the device is not already busy, the processor of the packet switch checks each packet for its destination, determines the interface over which it should be sent and starts the output hardware device over which it should be sent, or else the processor places the outgoing packets in a queue associated with the output device. As soon as the device finishes sending a packet, it extracts and begins sending the next packet in the queue on a first-come-first-serve basis.

12.9.2 Physical Addressing Method in a WAN

Each address in a WAN consists of two parts: the first part identifies the particular packet switch and the second part identifies the computer connected to the switch. Figure 12.22 illustrates the addressing method in a WAN.

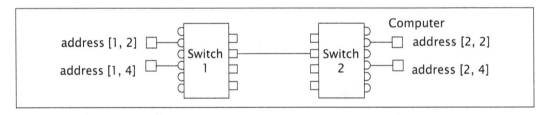

FIGURE 12.22   Addressing Method in a WAN

The two-part addressing in a WAN as shown in Figure 12.22 is also known as the hierarchical address of a WAN. In actual practice, the address is represented as a single binary value, with some bits of the value to represent the first part of the address and the remaining bits to represent the second part. Because each address in WAN is represented as a single binary value, users and application programmers treat the address as an integer and need not know that addresses are hierarchically assigned.

A packet switch in a WAN works on the principles of 'source independence' and 'next-hop forwarding', which means that a packet switch has to keep the information about the next place (technically known as 'next hop') where to forward the packet so as to eventually reach its destination, without any dependence on either the original source of the packet or the path already traversed by the packet before arriving at the particular switch. This mechanism of 'next-hop' forwarding with 'source independence' in a WAN makes the computer network compact and improves its performance.

12.9.3 Routing Table in a WAN

Routing table is a table used by a WAN to store next-hop information of its packet switches. Figure 12.23 illustrates a routing table. (Routing table for each switch is stored in the same switch.)

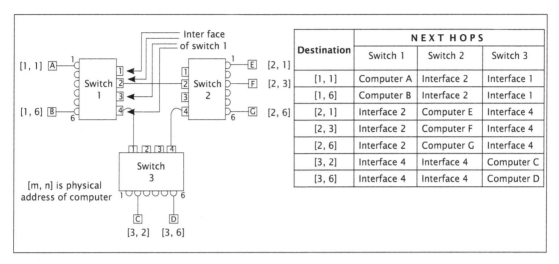

FIGURE 12.23 Illustration of Routing Table

Note: Routing table for each switch is stored in the same switch.

12.9.4 Interior and Exterior Switches in a WAN

Interior packet switches in a WAN are those which do not have any computers attached. Such switches are only to handle traffic (load). Exterior switches have computers attached to them.

For any WAN to function correctly and optimally, both interior and exterior packet switches must have a routing table for each, and both types must forward packets through the 'next-hop forwarding' mechanism. Moreover, the routing table for each packet switch must have values to fulfil the following criteria:

1. **Universal routing:** It means the routing table in each switch must have a next-hop route for each possible destination.
2. **Optimal routes:** In a packet switch, the next hop value in the routing table for a given destination must point to the shortest path to the destination.

Based on the above criteria, computer-based algorithms are used to compute routing table entries for each packet switch in a large WAN. The computation follows two basic approaches as explained below:

1. **Static routing:** A computer program computes the routes when a packet switch boots. The routes once computed do not change with the changes in the network conditions such as traffic.
2. **Dynamic routing:** In this case, the program develops an initial routing table when a packet switch boots, but the table is subsequently altered as and when condition of the network changes.

Although static routing is simple and having less network overhead, it is inflexible. Therefore, many networks follow dynamic routing because of its obvious advantages such as handling of dynamic network traffic and in case of failure of network hardware its capability to modify the routes to take care of the failure.

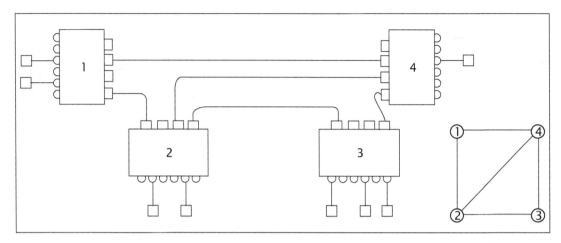

FIGURE 12.24 WAN and the Corresponding Graph

The software for computation of entries for a routing table is based on shortest path from a particular source to each of the destinations adopting the famous Dijkstra's algorithm. In order to facilitate the application of the same algorithm, a WAN is treated as a graph with the nodes of the graph corresponding to the packet switches and with each edge of the graph connecting two nodes to represent a digital connection between the corresponding packet switches as shown in Figure 12.24. The routing table corresponding to each node of the graph is shown in Table 12.2.

The Dijkstra's algorithm finds the distance along the shortest path from a single source node to each of the other nodes (destination) in the graph, and accordingly, the next-hop routing table is constructed during the shortest path determination. The distance of each edge is the weight assigned to the edge during the computation of the shortest path. Thus, a path with least number of edges may not be the path with least weight. For example, in the graph shown in Figure 12.24, the path from node 1 to node 3 could have been either (1, 2) → (2–3) or (1–4) → (4, 3). However, the next hop has been shown as (1, 2) as the former path (1, 2) → (2–3) might have been less in weight compared to (1–4) → (4, 3).

TABLE 12.2 Routing Table for Each Node of the Graph Shown in Figure 12.24

Node1		Node 2		Node 3		Node 4	
Destination	Next Hop	Destination	Next Hop	Destination	Next Hop	Destination	Next Hop
1	—	1	(2, 1)	1	(3, 2)	1	(4, 1)
2	(1, 2)	2	—	2	(3, 2)	2	(4, 2)
3	(1, 2)	3	(2, 3)	3	—	3	(4, 3)
4	(1, 4)	4	(2, 4)	4	(3, 4)	4	—

12.9.5 Popular WAN Technologies

Few of the popular WAN are the Advanced Research Projects Agency Network (ARPANET), X.25, Frame relay, switched multi-megabit data service (SMDS) and ATM.

ARPANET was developed by the US Defence Department in the late 1960s and is a legacy WAN technology with leased data lines connecting packet switches at a slow speed of 56 kbps.

X.25 was a standard for WAN technology developed by the Consultative Committee for International Telephone and Telegraph (CCITT) using two or more X.25 packet switches connected by leased line. X.25 operates at a speed of maximum 100 kbps.

Frame relay is a high-speed WAN used by many phone companies to provide high speed WAN service up to 1.5 mbps. Frame relay service is designed to accept and deliver blocks of data, each block containing up to 8K octets of data. Frame relay can bridge two LAN segments located in two different distant geographic locations, such as two cities. In order to connect two LAN segments, a frame relay can be designed to operate at a high speed of 4 mbps or more. However, in practice, frame relay subscribers choose to operate at either 1.5 mbps or a lower 56 kbps. SMDS is also a high-speed (1.544–44.736 mbps) WAN data service offered by long-distance carriers. SMDS is designed to carry data instead of voice traffic to achieve the highest speed of 44.736 mbps over DS Level 3 (DS–3) transmission. ATM also provides WAN technology developed by the telecommunication industry to handle both conventional telephone voice traffic and data traffic. ATM was also designed to serve both LAN and WAN technologies.

12.10 Network Characteristics

Apart from the underlying technologies, which classify networks into various categories such as LAN, MAN and WAN, there are additional characteristics such as ownership, service paradigm and performance of the network in terms of its transmission delay, and throughput.

Ownership of a network can be either private or public, and accordingly there can be private networks or public networks. A network is called a private network if its use is limited to a single individual or a company.

A public network, on the other hand, is owned and operated by a service provider such as a common carrier such as a telephone company. Any subscriber can avail of the service of a public network to communicate with any other subscriber to the service. A virtual private network (VPN) is one having the advantages of both private and public networks because it allows an individual company with multiple sites to have the feel of a completely private network although using a public network to carry the traffic between the sites, because the VPN system restricts incoming and outgoing packets at each site so that no packet can enter the site of a company unless it arrived from one of the other sites of the same company. Likewise, no outgoing packet can leave the site of a company unless its destination is another one of the same company sites. Moreover, VPN systems use encryption to assure absolute privacy of the packets sent by a company. Even if anyone who is not connected with the company obtains a copy of a packet, the same person will be unable to decipher the contents of the packet.

12.10.1 Service Paradigm

For the sake of explaining the variety of services by a network to the computers attached to it, networks can be broadly categorized as connection-oriented (CO) service or connectionless (CL) service.

A connection-oriented service requires a connection to be established between two computers before any data can be transferred from one to the other and when transfer of data is complete, the connection is terminated. This is similar in concept to telephonic communication.

A connectionless service requires a computer to arrange the data to be transmitted in the appropriate frame and to attach the address of the computer to which the data have to be delivered and then pass the frame to the network for delivery. The connectionless network system then transports the frame to the destination computer and delivers the same. Connectionless network system is analogous to the postal mail system where the sender writes his message (data) and places the same in an envelope on which the address of the receiver is written and then the envelope is mailed for delivery. Both connection-oriented and connectionless networks have their own service paradigms. For example, connection-oriented network technologies have design features to provide variations in service such as continuous traffic at a uniform rate to handle voice or video or burst traffic which is typical of computer communication. The other variations are simplex (one-way traffic flow) or full duplex (two-way traffic flow in one connection), permanent or switched connection that can be established or terminated fast automatically, service guarantee in terms of throughput rate and maximum packet-loss rate, stream data or message data interface depending upon whether the data interface accepts continuous data even though the sender generated the data in blocks or accepts the same data in the same block size as the sender transmitted. Likewise, connectionless network technologies differ in terms of addressing scheme (length of address and method of assigning the same), maximum frame size and minimum packet size.

It may be worthwhile to mention that a network may have different mixed-service paradigms—one for interior and another for exterior. For example, ARPANET provides connectionless service to attached local computers while its internal services are all connection oriented. Table 12.3 shows the service paradigms offered by a few popular network technologies.

In a connectionless network, each packet contains the address of remote destinations, whereas in case of connection-oriented networks, the destination address is required only when establishing a new connection, thereafter the packet flowing through the connection contains only a connection identifier which is much smaller than a full address.

TABLE 12.3 Service Paradigms Offered by Few Popular Network Technologies. The Technologies Suitable for WAN Are Used in Public Networks

Technology	Connection Oriented	Connection Less	Used for LAN	Used for WAN
Ethernet		√	√	
Token ring		√	√	
FDDI		√	√	
Frame relay	√			√
SMDS		√		√
ATM	√			√
Local talk		√	√	

Source: Comer (2004, 243).

12.10.2 Performance Characteristics of a Network

Performance characteristics of a network mainly include delay, throughput and jitter. Delay and throughput together provide a quantitative measure relating to the network capacity. Delay specifies the time taken by a data bit to travel through the network from one computer to another, measured in seconds or fractions of a second (milliseconds). The total delay comprises propagation delay, switching delay, access delay and queuing delay. Propagation delay is the time taken by a signal to travel across a wire or optical fibre and depends upon the distance of travel. It is a significant part of total delay being of the order of milliseconds. Switching delay is much smaller than propagation delay and is the small amount of time taken by bridges or packet switches to choose and send a received packet to the next hop. Access delay is also significant and is the time a LAN has to wait before a shared medium is available to a particular computer in the shared LAN. Queuing delay occurs in case of packet switched WANs only when an incoming packet to a switch may have to wait in a queue when the CPU forwards the packets which arrived earlier. This delay is associated with the store-and-forward process of a packet switch. Propagation delay is the major delay associated with network performance.

Throughput is the second performance parameter of a network, and it is the rate at which data can be transmitted through the network. It is usually expressed in bits per second (bps) or million bits per second (mbps). Another way of specifying throughput is the bandwidth which is the upper limit of throughput of a network. This is because a frame contains a header which is an overhead and reduces the effective throughput obtained with a particular bandwidth. However, throughput is a measure of the network capacity.

It may be emphasized that throughput and delay are not independent of each other. As the utilization of network capacity increases (the throughput increases), network delay also increases because of increased traffic congestion. The relationship can be expressed as

$$D = \frac{D_0}{(1-U)}$$

where D is the delay associated with utilization U, and D_0 is the delay when the network is idle ($U = 0$). U can have values between 0 and 1. When $U = 1$, that is, 100% utilization, delay (D) becomes very large. Therefore, network designers prefer to keep the utilization of network capacity below 90%.

Transit volume of data in a network is the total number of data bits in transit in the network at any point of time and is obtained by multiplying delay (D) with throughput (T).

The third performance characteristic of a network is jitter. Jitter is the measure of variance in delay in a network. It is a very important parameter for networks that handle voice and video traffic as any variation in the network delay may cause flawed output. If the jitter is zero, the audio/video output will exactly synchronize with the input and the output will be flawless. Networks with zero or very less jitter are known as isochronous networks in which case the separate paths transmitting digitized voice/video data have all the same delay. However, asynchronous networks for which the delay in the separate paths transmitting packets varies require additional protocol support (protocol has been explained in subsequent paragraphs of this chapter) to offset the jitter when audio and video are transmitted across such network.

12.11 Protocols and Layering in Network Communication

Similar to a diplomatic protocol, a term used by diplomats as an agreed set of rules followed while communicating with each other for exchanging messages, a set of rules that specify the format of messages and the actions associated with each such message is known as a network protocol or communication protocol in computer or internetwork parlance. The software which implements such protocol is called a protocol software. A protocol software similar to a high-level language provides an interface between the application programs that make use of a network and the network hardware. An application program interacts with the protocol software which follows the rules of any given protocol to communicate with the network hardware.

12.11.1 Protocol Suites and Layering

Instead of having a single large protocol to specify all rules of the protocol for all possible variations in the forms of communication, protocol designers preferred to divide the communication protocols into pieces according to the various problems associated with the communication. This facilitates ease of design, analysis, testing and implementation of each protocol.

The pieces which together describe the complete protocol suite are known as layers and the tool that describes the layers is known as protocol layering model. The layering of a protocol suite, however, must ensure the following aspects:

1. The entire suite is designed to make the communication system efficient and effective.
2. Each layer of the protocol suite handles part of the communication problem not handled by the other protocols.
3. Layers of protocol should be so designed that they can share structures of data and information.
4. The combination of all protocol layers should handle all possible communication problems including failures and other exceptional conditions.

A historic seven-layer OSI reference model and the five-layer internetwork TCP/IP reference model (described in subsequent paragraphs) have been shown in Figure 12.25.

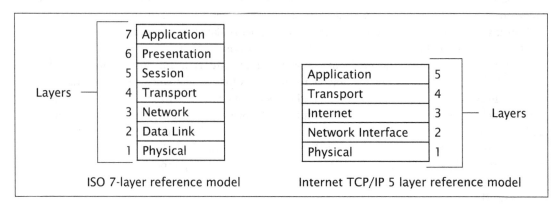

FIGURE 12.25   ISO Seven-layer and Internet TCP/IP Five-layer Model

In the ISO model as well as the Internet model, the first layer (physical layer) relates to the network hardware and the other higher layers (2–7) relate to the software that uses the hardware, the highest seventh layer being the application layer.

Data link protocols (second layer) contain rules for organizing data into frames and mechanism of transmission of frames through a network. Frame format, byte stuffing, checksum and CRC computation as explained in Section 12.4 are included in layer 2.

Layer 3 (network) relates to the addressing system for the packet switches and computers and the method of routing the packets from source at one end to the destination at another end of the network.

Layer 4 (transport) protocols specify the details of reliable transfer of packets in a network. Transport protocols make use of a number of tools to tackle complicated communication problems such as out-of-order delivery of packets and their proper sequencing, duplicate packets and their elimination, lost packets and their retransmission, replay caused by excessive delay and flow control through suitable rate control mechanism which monitors the rate of production of packets and reduce the same when congestion occurs till the congestion is overcome.

The out-of-order deliveries of packets are taken care of by transport protocols through sequencing of the packets. The sending side attaches a sequence number to each packet it transmits and receiving side stores the sequence number of the last packet received and separately the list of packets arrived out-of-order. If the next packet received has a sequence number higher than the sequence number of the last packet, the protocol software delivers the packet to the next higher layer protocol and then checks the list of out-of-order packets to see whether additional packets can be delivered out of the same. Sequencing also helps in eliminating the problem of duplicate packets. Packet loss is a basic problem in computer networks and arises mainly due to two reasons: first, because of transmission errors making bits corrupted resulting in an invalid frame and second, due to congestion in the network traffic. Transport protocols use two different methods to take care of the above two causes for ensuring reliable transmission without any packet loss. The first method is to send an acknowledgement (ACK) which is a small message sent by receiving transport protocol when it receives a frame intact. The sender starts a timer for a small-time duration when it sends a packet successfully and waits for the acknowledgement. If the same is received before the timer expires, the sender protocol software cancels the timer. However, if the timer expires before the acknowledgement arrives, the sender protocol software sends another copy of the packet and sets the timer to start again. The second copy is called a retransmission. However, retransmission will fail in case there is crashing of the receiving computer or the network gets disconnected due to hardware failure. Therefore, transport protocols usually have a bound on the maximum number of retransmissions and beyond that, it stops retransmitting.

Replay caused by excessive delay happens when there is heavy delay in a route, and consequently the protocol software changes the route and retransmits the delayed packet and the subsequent packets. However, this replay may affect the later communication because the delayed packet from the earlier (old) conversation might be accepted by the receiving computer and the correct packet discarded as a duplicate. In order to avoid replay, protocol software marks each session of communication with a unique session ID such as the time of commencement of the session and the session ID is incorporated in each packet transmitted during the session. In order to avoid replay, the protocol software discards any packet at the receiving end that contains inconsistent session ID.

Flow-control mechanism handles data overrun and consequent network congestion. Data overrun occurs when the sending computer transmits data through the network at a faster rate than the capacity of the receiving computer to receive data. Obviously, such a situation gives rise to network congestion which may eventually result in data loss. One of the flow-control techniques used by protocols is known as 'sliding window' which efficiently prevents data overrun while maintaining high throughput rates consistent with network capacity. In case of a sliding window, the sender and receiver agree as per protocol to use a fixed amount of data in terms of number of packets (window size) that can be sent by the sending side before receiving an acknowledgement from the receiving side for the window-size packets. Figure 12.26 illustrates the 'sliding window' mechanism with a window size of three packets, and total nine packets are transmitted.

The advantage so far as throughput is concerned is obvious from Figure 12.26. It can be seen that through a window size of 3 packets, 9 packets have been transmitted in $3 \times (2\sigma)$ time, where σ is the transmission delay for a packet to reach from sending computer to receiving computer. If, otherwise without a sliding window, the packets would have been sent one at a time at an interval of 2σ, the time

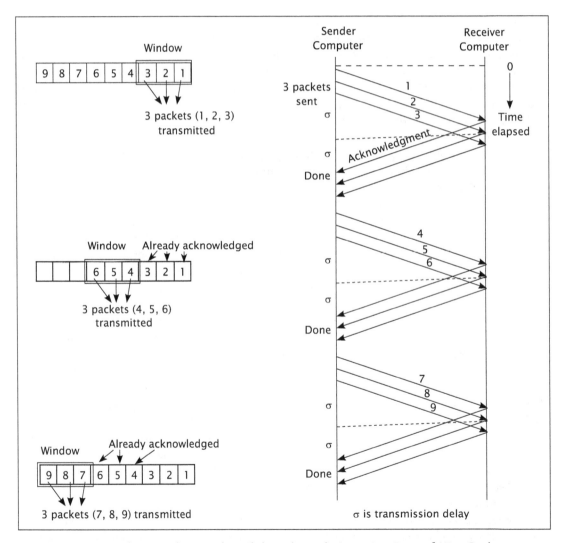

FIGURE 12.26 A Three-packet Window Sliding through Outgoing Data of Nine Packets

delay between sending one packet and waiting till the acknowledgement is received by the sending computer; total time would have been $9 \times (2\sigma)$ which is 18σ, three times more. Hence, the throughput with a window size (W), T_w can be written as:

$$T_w = W \times T_0$$

Here, T_0 is the throughput without a sliding window.

By increasing the window size, the throughput can be increased, but a large window size may give rise to data overrun; hence, an optimum size of the sliding window is decided to be commensurate with the underlying hardware capacity (bandwidth).

Congestion in network results in packet loss. Retransmission can recover lost packets, but retransmission reduces effective throughput. Hence, protocols try to avoid congestion by arranging packet switches to send a special message to the source of packets to control the rate of transmission of packets, when congestion occurs. Further, protocols adopt the quantum of packet loss as an estimate of congestion in the network for remedial measures.

Layer 5 protocols specify the method of starting a communication session with a remote system. Layer 6 protocols specify how data are represented in various computers, and Layer 7 protocols specify how any particular application uses a network.

Finally, designing protocols is very important for eliminating the problems associated with network transmission as mentioned earlier. A systematic and detailed study is essential for the sake of protocol design as protocols can interact adversely in unexpected ways.

12.12 Internet Working Technology

We have seen in earlier sections of this chapter that the network technology varies depending upon the user needs. For example, LAN is a technology suited to high-speed communication across short distances, whereas WAN is designed to communicate across large distances. Therefore, no single network design is best for all-purpose use or universal service. However, need was greatly felt to have a communication system which would provide such universal service by connecting the heterogeneous networks so that any pair of computers connected to arbitrary network technologies can communicate with each other. Network designers and researchers finally devised a scheme known as internetwork or the Internet which provides such universal service among heterogeneous networks. Internet uses both additional hardware and software on attached computers which provide universal service.

Additional hardware includes a basic component known as 'router' to interconnect a set of physical and heterogeneous networks. A router such as a bridge has got a processor, memory and a separate I/O interface for each network to which it connects. A network treats a router as a computer. Figure 12.27 shows a router connecting two physical networks depicted as clouds since the network may be using different technologies, media, frame formats and addressing schemes.

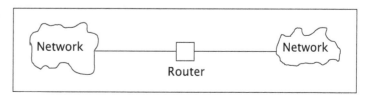

FIGURE 12.27 Two Physical Networks Connected through a Router

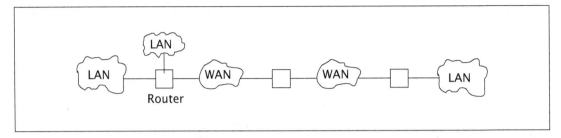

FIGURE 12.28 Three Routers Connecting Five Networks (Three LANs and Two WANs)

An Internet can be formed by using more than one routers to connect a set of physical networks. The number and type of networks and the interconnection topology decide the number of routers. Figure 12.28 shows an Internet to connect five physical networks having different technologies.

12.12.1 Internet: A Virtual Network

Internet is not restricted in size. It can contain hundreds of networks and each network can connect hundreds of computers. However, the Internet protocol software (known as transmission control protocol/Internet protocol, abbreviated as TCP/IP) provides the illusion to the computers attached to a single seamless communication network known as a virtual network system. The name virtual network for an Internet arises because the system is an abstraction. Figure 12.29 illustrates the abstraction concept of a virtual network and the corresponding physical networks.

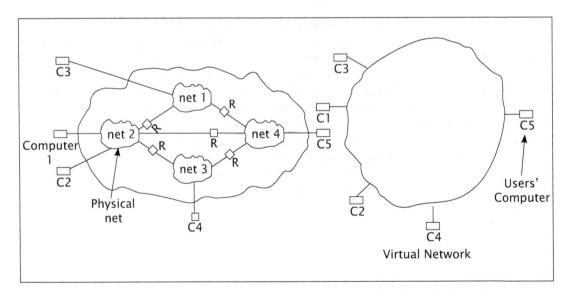

FIGURE 12.29 The Illusion of a Single Network (Virtual Network) That TCP/IP Software Provides to Users/Applications

TABLE 12.4 Layers of TCP/IP Reference Model and Corresponding ISO Model Layers

Layers of TCP/IP Model	*Corresponding Layers of the ISO Model*
Layer 1: Physical layer relates to basic network hardware.	Layer 1: Physical
Layer 2: Network interface specifies organization of data into frames and transmission of frames across the network.	Layer 2: Data link
Layer 3: Internet specifies format of packets sent across Internet and method of forwarding packets from source to destination through routers.	No corresponding layer
Layer 4: Transport specifies how to ensure reliable transmission of data in the form of packets.	Layer 4: Transport
Layer 5: Application specifies how an application makes use of Internet.	Layer 6: Presentation and Layer 7: Application

12.12.1.1 Layers of TCP/IP Protocols

TCP/IP protocols are organized into five layers: physical, network interface, the Internet, transport and application. These layers of TCP/IP layering model, also known as the Internet layering model, have been shown in Figure 12.26 along with the ISO seven-layers model.

Four of the layers (physical, network interface, transport and application) of the TCP/IP model correspond to one or more layers of the ISO model. However, ISO model has no Internet. Likewise, TCP/IP model has no session layer.

Table 12.4 shows the purpose of each of the five layers of TCP/IP reference model and the corresponding layers of the ISO seven-layer model.

Layering principle stipulates that a particular layer, say, Nth layer at the destination applies the inverse of the transformations applied in the same Nth layer at the source. The collection of the modules is known as a protocol stack. Therefore, layering principle implies that outgoing data pass down through the layers of the stack on the sending side and pass up the stack on the receiving side as shown in Figure 12.30.

12.12.1.2 Protocols for Routers

Unlike host computers, TCP/IP protocol software for routers usually does not contain Layer 5 (Application) as because routers generally do not run applications as do host computers.

12.13 IP Addressing

In TCP/IP, the Internet protocol specifies the addressing scheme. IP divides Internet address for each computer attached to a two-level hierarchy.

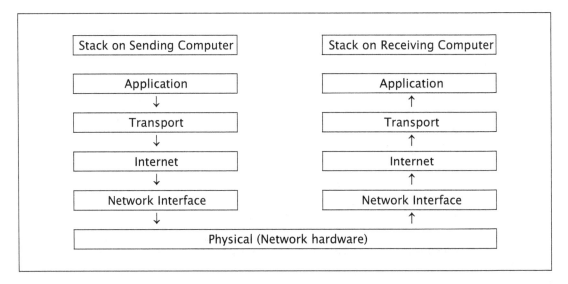

FIGURE 12.30 The Conceptual Path of Data from an Application on Computer Sending Data to an Application on Computer Receiving Data

The two levels are the prefix of an address, which identifies the network to which the computer is attached, and the suffix which identifies the particular computer on the network. In order to ensure unique addresses throughout the Internet, a central authority assigns network prefixes in the address hierarchy. Once a prefix has been assigned, a local network administrator (such as the Internet service provider) can assign a unique suffix to each host on the network. For example, if an Internet contains four networks, the four can be assigned prefixes as 1, 2, 3 and 4. If four computers are assigned to network 1, those can be assigned suffixes 1, 2, 3 and 4, while four computers attached to network 2 can also be assigned suffixes 1, 2, 3 and 4. However, the four computers attached to network 1 will have different prefixes (being 1) from those of network 2 (being 2), and thus all computers attached will have unique addresses. User application programs and other higher layers of protocol software use the abstract IP addresses as explained in order to communicate. The IP address is a unique 32-bit binary number assigned to a host for communicating with the host. The address bits are numbered from left to right, and the first (left most) bit is numbered 0 and the right most bit 31.

The 32-bit address is divided into three parts. The first four bits determine the class of the address, the next part represents the prefix and the last part the suffix of the IP address. There are five classes of IP address, of which three (classes A, B and C) are primary classes used to denote host addresses. The fourth class (class D) is used for multicast address, where a set of host computers share the multicast address and a copy of any packet sent to the same address will be received by each host belonging to the set. Class E, the fifth class, has been reserved for future use only. Class A addresses have '0' as the first bit, and the boundary between prefix and suffix is at the end of first octet. Class B has '1' and '0' as the first-two bits and places the boundary between prefix and suffix after the second octet. Class C has '1', '1' and '0' as the first three bits and places the same boundary after the third octet. The five classes of IP addresses have been shown in Figure 12.31.

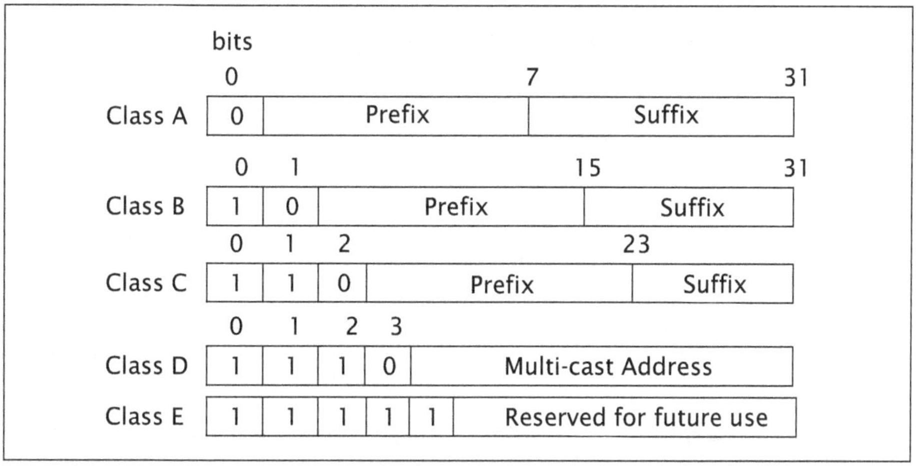

FIGURE 12.31 The Five Classes of IP Address

12.13.1 Dotted Decimal Notation for IP Addresses

Although IP addresses are 32-bit binary numbers, the software uses a notation known as 'dotted decimal notation' for the IP addresses for interacting with users for their convenience.

The 'dotted decimal notation' consists of four decimal values separated by periods (.), and the values correspond to the four octets of binary digits in the 32-bit IP address of the three primary classes A, B and C. Table 12.5 shows examples of 32-bit binary addresses and the equivalent dotted decimal addresses.

Dotted decimal addresses can range from 0.0.0.0 to 255.255.255.255 equivalent to binary octet of 00000000 and 11111111 respectively. All the addresses mentioned above are examples of class full addresses. It may be mentioned that increasing the number bits in the prefix will enable a greater number of networks to be accommodated and a smaller number of bits in suffix, which results in a smaller number of hosts per network. Accordingly, the maximum number of networks and hosts per network have been calculated for the three primary address classes A, B and C as shown in Table 12.6. It can be noted that the size of a network determines the address class.

TABLE 12.5 Examples of 32-Bit Binary Addresses and Their Equivalent Dotted Decimal Addresses

32-Bit Binary Address				Equivalent Dotted Decimal Address			
00001111	00000100	00000000	00100101	15.	4.	0.	37
10111111	00011100	00000111	00000011	191.	28.	7.	3
11011111	01110000	11111111	01010101	223.	112.	225.	85
10101111	10000111	11001011	00000000	175.	135.	203.	0

TABLE 12.6 The Maximum Number of Networks and Hosts per Network for Each of the Three Primary Address Classes

Class of Address	Bits in Prefix	Maximum Number of Networks	Bits in Suffix	Maximum Number of Hosts per Network
A	7 (8 − 1)	128	24	16777216
B	14 (8 − 2 + 8)	16384	16	65536
C	21 (8 − 3 + 8 + 8)	2097152	8	256

12.14 Classless Addressing, Address Masks and Classless Inter-Domain Routing (CIDR) Notation

One serious limitation of class full addressing scheme is the non-utilized address spaces. Suppose a network has got only 10 hosts, obviously class C address which has the minimum number of hosts possible (256) will be chosen. However, for 10 hosts only, four bits of suffix will be needed and therefore the remaining four bits will be non-utilized. In order to overcome the above limitation, a classless addressing scheme was invented in which the division between prefix and suffix in the 32-bit address can occur at any arbitrary bit boundary. In the above example of a network with 10 hosts, the protocol for classless addressing will assign a prefix 28 bits long so that the suffix with four bits can accommodate up to 15 hosts.

The classless addressing scheme divides an IP address range using a combination of the IP address and the associated 'address mask' or 'subnet mask' which specifies the boundary between the network prefix and suffix. Address mask is also stored along with the 32-bit IP address as a 32-bit binary value wherein '1' bits mark the network prefix and '0' bits mark the suffix or the host portion. For example, in the previous example of a network with 10 hosts only and a prefix of 28 bits, the address mask will be: 11111111 11111111 11111111 11110000 which is 255.255.255.240 in dotted decimal notation.

CIDR notation, which stands for classless inter-domain, routing specifies the address mask associated with an IP address by appending with the IP address in dotted decimal a slash (/) followed by the size of the mask (for '1' bits).

Examples of CIDR address block:

1. 128.211.0.16/28 represents
   10000000 11010011 00000000 00001 0000
                       Prefix   Suffix
2. 128.211.0.32/28 represents
   10000000 11010011 00000000 0010 0000
                                   Suffix

   Prefix is different from the same in Example 1.
3. 192.168.12.0/23 = 192.168.12.0/24 + 192.168.13.0/24
   It means 192.168.12.0/23 is a combination of two class C subnets 192.168.12.0/24 and 192.168.13.0/24

12.14.1 Special IP Address

IP reserves host address (suffix) as all zeroes to denote a network with the assigned prefix. Thus, the address 128.211.0.16/28 denotes a network with prefix as:

10000000 11010011 00000000 0001 and suffix 0000. Similarly, a network suffix with all ones identifies a directed broadcast address as follows:

128.211.0.15/28 which in binary form is:

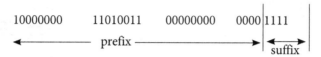

In case of directed broadcast, transmission of a packet will reach all host computers on the network.

12.14.2 IP Addressing for Routers

Routers which connect more than one physical network have more than one IP address. Each such IP address for a router has got a prefix, which specifies one physical network. Figure 12.32 illustrates the concept of multiple IP addresses assigned to two routers. IP does not require that same suffix is to be attached to all interfaces of a router.

12.14.2.1 Address Resolution

The protocol addresses described in the earlier paragraphs are only IP addresses maintained by the protocol software and those addresses are not understood by the networks or host computer hardware. Therefore, a packet transmitted across a physical network pre-requires that the IP address of the receiver computer must be translated into its equivalent hardware address. The process or technique of translating a computer's protocol address into the equivalent hardware address is called 'address resolution'. There are three basic techniques of address resolution. They are (a) table lookup meant primarily for WAN hardware, (b) closed-form computation where the algorithm for address resolution can translate the protocol address of a computer into the hardware address of the hardware using Boolean and arithmetic

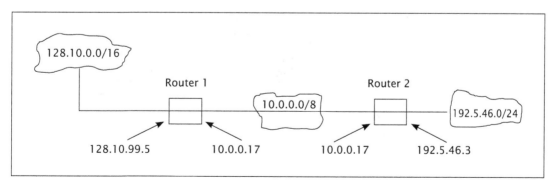

FIGURE 12.32 Illustration of Addresses Assigned to Two Routers—Each Interface of the Routers Is Assigned an Address Containing the Prefix of the Network to Which the Interface Connects

TABLE 12.7	Example of Address Binding Table
IP Address	*Hardware Address*
128.211.5.1	0A—07—4B—12—82—36
128.211.5.2	9C—AD—97—84—6A—8D
128.211.5.3	A0—14—52—44—F2—91
128.211.5.4	0A—04—BC—00—03—28

operations and (c) message exchange used with LANs having static addressing. In this case, one computer sends a message requesting for an address translation and another computer sends the requested information. The three basic techniques have been illustrated below as examples. Table lookup contains a table having two columns, the IP address and the corresponding hardware address as shown in Table 12.7. Each entry (row) of the table corresponds to one computer of the network.

This table contains the IP address and the corresponding hardware address of the four host computers attached to the physical network prefix 128.211.0.0/16 which is a B-class network. A separate address binding table is needed for each physical network of the Internet. The hardware address is also known as its physical or media access control (MAC) address, which can be found for a host computer with window operating system invoking the command prompt and then typing the command:

```
C: > ipconfig/all
```

The physical address of the hardware of the computer is a 48-bit unique address consisting of 6 bytes (6 × 8) having hexadecimal values. The structure of the address is as shown in Figure 12.33.

Address Resolution with Closed-form Computation

Unlike a static physical address as described in case of table lookup, closed-form computation for address resolution adopts configurable addressing of the network interface hardware by a suitable mathematical function that maps an IP address to a hardware address. For example, the IP address suffix representing a host can be matched to be the hardware address of the host.

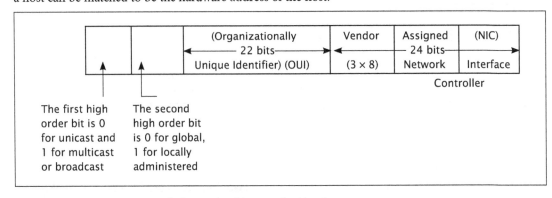

FIGURE 12.33 Structure of Physical Address of a Hardware

Thus, a network 128.211.0.0/16 can have the first host computer IP address as 128.211.5.1 with a matching hardware address as 1 and so on.

Address Resolution with Message Exchange

Message exchange is used with LANs having static addressing. In this case, a computer attached to a network that requires an address resolution sends a message as request with an IP address and receives a reply with the corresponding hardware address. The protocol for address resolution with message exchange can be of two types or designs. In the first case, dedicated servers are earmarked in the network to answer all address resolution requests. In the second case, no special address resolution servers are used, instead each computer in a network participates in address resolution by agreeing to reply any request for its address. Any computer in the network, in order to resolve an address, broadcasts the request to all other computers in the network. All computers receive the request and examine the requested address, and if it matches with a computer's address, the same will respond. The TCP/IP suite contains a standard address resolution protocol (ARP). The ARP standard defines two basic message types—a request and a response. A request message contains the IP address, whereas a reply (response) contains both the IP address and the hardware address requested for. Finally, although ARP message format for both the request and the response is sufficiently general to allow arbitrary protocol and hardware addresses, ARP almost always resolves a 32-bit IP address into a 48-bit (6 bytes of 8 bits each) ethernet address.

12.15 IP Datagrams and Forwarding Datagrams

The Internet protocol defines an Internet packet format that is independent of the heterogeneous networks and their hardware.

This packet, which is universal and virtual, is known as IP datagram and is the basic unit of transfer of data across a TCP/IP Internet. The format of an IP datagram is similar to a hardware frame like it begins with a header followed by a data area which contains the data to be transferred across the Internet. Figure 12.34 is a general format of an IP datagram.

Header	Data Area

FIGURE 12.34   General Form of an IP Datagram

The header contains IP addresses of source and destination of the datagram and other information as fields. The fields of the header of a datagram along with size in bits have been shown in Table 12.8. The amount of data carried in the data area of a datagram is variable and depends upon the type of application. IPV4 (Internet Protocol Version 4), which is the current IP version, permits a datagram size from one octet of data up to a maximum of 64K octets inclusive of the header. However, the header is usually much smaller in size as compared to data area as because the header is an overhead associated with cost of transmitting data.

TABLE 12.8 Fields in the IP Datagram Header

Header Fields	Size in Bits
First 32 bits	
Version number of protocol (4 for current version)	4 (0 to 3)
Header length (in number of 32 bits)	4 (4 to 7)
Service type (a value to specify minimum delay or maximum throughput for a data datagram)	16 (8 to 15)
Total length in 16-bit integer to denote the total no. of octets in the datagram (both the header and data)	16 (16 to 31)
Second 32 bits	
Identification: Unique identification number for each outgoing datagram	16 (0 to 15)
Flags (to specify a fragmented datagram)	3 (16 to 18)
Fragment offset (to indicate the position of a fragment in the original datagram)	13 (19 to 31)
Third 32 bits	
Time to live (a positive integer value between 1 and 255 specifying a time to prevent a datagram traveling indefinitely around a path containing a loop due to error in configuring the root)	8 (0 to 7)
Type (datagram data: audio, video or key stroke and so on)	8 (8 to 15)
Header checksum (to ensure that bits of datagram header are not changed in transit)	16 (16 to 31)
Source IP address	32 (fourth 32 bits)
Destination IP address	32 (fifth 32 bits)

12.15.1 Mechanism of Forwarding an IP Datagram

Datagrams travel across an Internet from initial source to the final destination. In this travel path, datagrams pass through one or more heterogeneous networks connected by routers. Each router plays a vital role in receiving a datagram, extracting its destination address and forwarding the datagram according to its destination address either to a next-hop router or to the final destination network. In order to facilitate the same, each IP router keeps a routing table which contains a set of entries for each destination and the corresponding next hop used to reach the same. Figure 12.35 illustrates a routing table for a router in an Internet with five networks. The destination addresses shown in the routing table are the network prefix of the network, and hence the second field in the table contains the address mask to specify the bits of the destination corresponding to the network prefix. Each router has got two or more interface IP addresses depending upon the networks it connects. It may be noted that each destination in a routing table is a network and not an individual host. The purpose is to keep the size of the routing table small. The destination network receiving a datagram can deliver the same locally to the particular host (suffix of IP address).

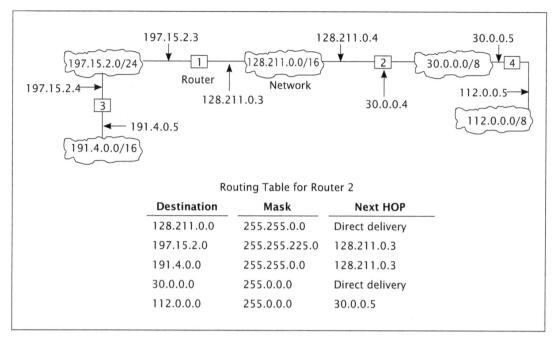

FIGURE 12.35 An Internet of Five Networks and Four Routers with Routing Table for Router 2

It may be stated that once a router forwards a datagram to another router or network, the destination address contained in the header of the datagram remains as it is and always refers to the ultimate destination and the next hop address never appears in the datagram header. It may further be stated that IP does not guarantee handling the problems of datagram duplication, delayed/out-of-order delivery of datagrams, datagram corruption and loss in order to ensure best-effort delivery of datagram. Higher layers of protocol software that uses IP take care of such errors for best effort delivery to take place.

12.16 IP Encapsulation, Fragmentation and Reassembly

12.16.1 Encapsulation

In the previous paragraph, we have seen that an IP datagram, in the course of its traverse from a source (host or router) to the destination through one or more next hops, passes through one or more heterogeneous networks, whose hardware do not understand datagram format. This is because each heterogeneous network hardware understands its own frame format which may differ among the networks, through which the IP datagram has to pass in its traverse across the Internet from source to destination. The technique adopted to transmit a datagram across a network that does not understand its format is known as 'encapsulation'. Encapsulation is the method of placing the entire datagram in the data area of the frame of the network through which the datagram has to pass. The network hardware treats a frame containing a datagram exactly similar to any other frame except that the frame-type field of the frame contains a special and agreed value for all networks to identify a frame with a datagram.

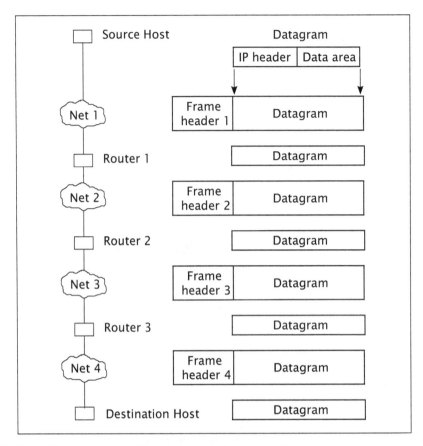

FIGURE 12.36 A Datagram as it Travels across the Internet

The destination address in the frame containing a datagram is the address of the next hop to which the datagram should be sent, and the same address is obtained by translating the IP address of the next hop to an equivalent hardware address using address binding as described in earlier paragraphs. Figure 12.36 illustrates how a datagram is encapsulated and unencapsulated as it travels from a source host to a destination host through four networks and three routers.

It may be seen that hosts and routers store a datagram in memory with no additional header. Further, when a datagram is encapsulated during its traverse through a physical network as a frame, the header of the frame such as Header 1, Header 2, ... as shown in Figure 12.37 depends on the particular network. For example, the header can be ethernet header. Every time the datagram reaches a network or the final destination, it is extracted and the frame that carried the datagram is discarded.

12.16.2 Fragmentation

Every network hardware technology has a limit on the maximum amount of data that a frame can carry through the network. This limit is known as 'maximum transmission unit' or MTU of the network. In case of an Internet consisting of heterogeneous networks, the MTU may be different for the networks

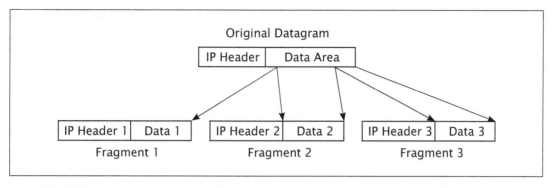

FIGURE 12.37 An IP Datagram Divided into Three Fragments, IP Headers of the Three Are Similar to the Original Datagram IP Header

through which the datagram has to traverse. This implies that the datagram travelling across the Internet has to be smaller or equal to MTU of each physical network as otherwise it cannot be encapsulated. Obviously, this creates a problem as the router, which connects two networks with different MTU values may receive a datagram from the network with higher MTU but cannot send the same through the network with lower MTU if the datagram size is equal to the higher MTU. An IP router uses a 'fragmentation' technique to take care of such problem of heterogeneous MTUs. If a router has to send a datagram through a network whose MTU is less than the size of the datagram, the router fragments the datagram into pieces and sends each piece or fragment separately through the network. Each fragment has the IP datagram format but carries only part of the data of the original datagram. A bit in the flag field of IP header (please refer Figure 12.37) indicates whether a datagram is a fragment or a complete one, and the fragment offset field of the header of a fragment indicates the position of the fragment in the original datagram. Figure 12.37 illustrates the 'fragmentation' process.

12.16.3 Reassembly

Reassembly of the fragments to create a copy of the original datagram is done at the destination which is the same for all the fragments as also the original datagram. The destination receiver host performing the reassembly ensures arrival of all fragments through the offset field of the fragments and also an additional bit to indicate the final fragment.

12.17 IPV6 (Future IP)

IPV4, the current version of IP, has been successful for the Internet to handle data transmission through heterogeneous networks while also taking care of large scalability. However, with exponential growth of the Internet worldwide, a need was felt, first, to increase the address space to accommodate the growth. Second, need was also felt for changes in IP to take care of newer Internet applications, such as audio and video conferencing in a real-time delivery environment. Therefore, researchers started developing a new version of IP for the future—IPV6.

2.17.1 Features of IPV6

The distinctive features of IPV6 include the following:

1. **128-bit address**: A 128 bits address (unlike 32 bits for IPV4) to accommodate the future growth of the Internet worldwide. Further, unlike the dotted decimal notation as in case of IPV4, IPV6 uses a more compact form of address in colon hexadecimal notation in which each group of 16 bits is written in hexadecimal with colon (:) as the separator between two successive groups and there are eight groups (8 × 16 = 128 bits) as shown below:

   FFFF: 8 COA: B1: 1280: 0: 0: 0: C1

   Moreover, in order to further reduce the address size, the zeroes are replaced with successive colons (::) as follows:

   0: 0: 0: 0: 0: 0: B1: F F F F

   Replaced with: B1 : F F F F

2. **Header format**: Unlike IPV4 which has a single header format for all datagrams, IPV6 has a compulsory header followed by one or more optional extension headers. A datagram in case of IPV6 consists of the base header followed by zero or more number of extension headers and then followed by data area. The length of a datagram (payload length), unlike IPV4, specifies only the size of the data area and the size of header is excluded. The general form of an IPV6 datagram has been shown in Figure 12.38. The reasons for having extension headers are economy and extensibility. It is economical because it saves space by having a small subset out of many features of the IPV6 protocol. Extensibility allows IPV6 to add any new feature to a protocol which is not possible in case of IPV4 without a complete change in the design of its fixed header.

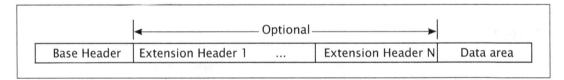

FIGURE 12.38 Format of an IPV6 Datagram

   The base-header format is as shown in Table 12.9.

3. **Support for audio and video traffic**: IPV6 allows a sender and receiver to establish a high-quality or a low-cost path through the internetwork in order to associate use of audio and video applications in one hand and other datagrams on the other hand through the low-cost path. Further, IPV6 addresses are of three types basically—unicast, multicast and anycast. Unicast address corresponds to a single host computer and a datagram meant for any unicast address is routed to that host computer address through the shortest path. When a datagram is sent to a multicast address, IPV6 delivers a copy of the same to each member of a set of computers belonging to the same multicast address. Anycast address corresponds to a set of computers that share a common address prefix such as a single local network. A datagram destined for 'anycast' address is routed and delivered to any one of the computers nearest to the sender through the shortest path.

TABLE 12.9 Base Header Format (IPV6)

Header Fields	Size in Bits
First 32 bits	
Version (IPV6)	4 bits (0–3)
Traffic class (such as keystrokes, real-time audio, video and so on)	8 bits (4–11)
Flow label (specifies the path through the network depending upon traffic class)	20 bits (12–31)
Second 32 bits	
Pay-load length	16 bits (0–15)
Next header (to specify the extension header or the type of data in data area if there is no extension header)	8 bits (16–23)
HOP limit: Time-to-live for a datagram before it reaches the destination	8 bits (24–31)
Source address	128 bits (next four 32 bits; 4 × 32 = 128 bits)
Destination address	128 bits (next four 32 bits; 4 × 32 = 128 bits)

4. **Fragmentation, reassembly and path MTU:** Unlike IPV4, in case of IPV6, the base header does not include fragmentation information fields and instead places such information in a separate fragment extension header for each fragment as illustrated in Figure 12.39.

   Further, unlike IPV4 wherein fragmentation is done by the routers, the fragmentation in case of IPV6 is done by the host computer sending a datagram. In order to facilitate the same, the sending host in case of IPV6 contains the MTU data for each network, which the datagram has to traverse along its path to destination, and chooses a fragment size to fit the smallest MTU. The minimum MTU in a path from source to destination is known as the 'path MTU' which is determined by the sending host following an iterative procedure in case of IPV6.

5. **Error reporting mechanism:** In spite of best-effort delivery by IP, it attempts to avoid errors and therefore has got an error detection and reporting mechanism included in the TCP/IP suite. The

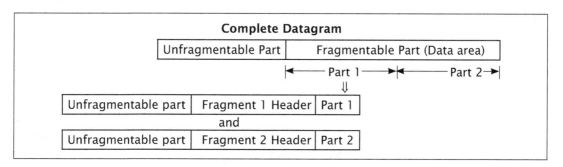

FIGURE 12.39 Illustration of Fragmentation in Case of IPV6

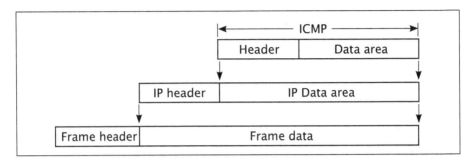

FIGURE 12.40 Two Levels of Encapsulation for Sending ICMP Message

mechanism is known as the 'Internet control message protocol' abbreviated as ICMP. IP and ICMP are codependent. IP uses ICMP to send an error message, and ICMP uses IP to transport message identified by an 8-bit type of message field. Figure 12.40 illustrates how a router sends an ICMP message through an IP datagram using two levels of encapsulation: the first level encapsulates the ICMP header and data area together inside an IP data area and the second level encapsulates the complete IP inside a frame data area. It may be mentioned that ICMP messages can be both error and informational messages. For example, source quench is a type of ICMP error message which a router sends to the source host to reduce its rate of transmission because the router has to discard an incoming datagram as its buffer space is full. The echo request and reply messages of ICMP are used by a host computer to determine whether a destination is reachable. ICMP messages can also be used by a host to determine path MTU for a given destination. Routers send ICMP error messages to the original source of a datagram that causes any error.

12.18 User Datagram Protocol (UDP)

UDP takes care of the need for end-to-end transport protocols. We have seen from the previous paragraphs that IP provides a service through which a datagram can pass from a sending computer to a receiving computer traversing across one or more physical networks. However, IP lacks its ability to support multiple applications running simultaneously on the same computer. This is because the datagram headers that IP supports contain information about the source and destination address for the host computers only but not about the application programs on those hosts. A protocol which allows an individual application program to serve as the end point of communication is known as the 'end-to-end transport protocol' or simply a 'transport protocol'. The transport protocol has been designed as layer 4 of TCP/IP protocols. Further, this layer 4 of the TCP/IP suite contains two protocols for transport, namely the UDP and the TCP.

12.18.1 Protocol Port Numbers for Endpoint Identification

UDP defines an abstract set of identifiers known as protocol port numbers for different application programs run on each computer independent of its operating system (OS). This is because heterogeneous computers can run applications on different operating systems such as windows, MAC and Linux

(Ubuntu or Red Hat). Some OS uses daemon or process identifiers, others may use job names or task numbers to identify individual application programs.

Port numbers in the range from 0 to 1023 are the well-known system ports. For example, port number 50 is for 'remote mail checking protocol', 118 for 'SQL services' and so on. All computers with UDP can recognize the standard protocol port numbers independent of the underlying OS. Thus, when an UDP message arrives to a computer for port 118, the software protocol for UDP must identify which program on the computer implements the SQL services and then forwards the message to that program.

12.18.2 UDP Datagram

Each UDP message makes a user datagram which consists of a header of 64 bits (8 octets) followed by the payload that carries the UDP data. The total size of UDP message is measured in octets. The format of the UDP user datagram header is as follows:

Header Fields	Size in Bits
First 32 bits	
UDP source port (contains port number of sending application)	16 (0–15)
UDP destination port (port number of the application to which message is sent)	16 (0–31)
Second 32 bits	
UDP message length (message length in number of octets)	16 (0–15)
UDP checksum (optional if it is not there all bits will be zero)	16 bits (16–31)

It may be noted that user datagram header has no field for either source IP address or destination IP address. Those addresses are contained in the IP datagram that carries UDP message consisting of UDP header and the UDP data. Similar to ICMP, UDP is also encapsulated with two levels of encapsulation as shown in Figure 12.41.

UDP offers the same best-effort delivery to the applications as in case of an IP, which means a UDP message can be lost, duplicated or delivered out of order. However, applications such as audio or video can sustain packet delivery errors, but for other applications, such errors can be of serious consequences.

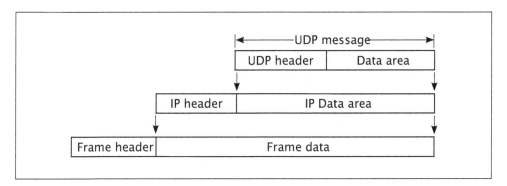

FIGURE 12.41   Two-level Encapsulation of UDP Message

Finally, UDP allows arbitrary interaction involving one-to-one (one application exchanges messages with only one other application), one-to-many (one application sends a message to multiple recipient applications), many-to-one (one application receives messages from multiple sender applications) and many-to-many (applications exchange messages with one another).

12.19 TCP for Reliable Transport

TCP is the main transport protocol in TCP/IP suite and ensures reliable delivery of packets. It ensures connection-oriented, full duplex, stream transport service (an application can send a continuous sequence of octets without the concept of records and similarly data can be delivered in a stream of octets), end-to-end service with complete reliability. TCP guarantees data transmission with zero missing or out-of-order delivery. Further, TCP connection is started reliably in which case two applications create a new connection with no duplicate packet from any previous connection allowed. Similarly, the connection is shut down with all data delivered before the connection is terminated.

TCP uses IP to carry messages known as 'segment'. Each TCP segment is encapsulated in an IP datagram and sent across the Internet. When the datagram reaches the destination host, IP passes the segment to TCP. IP never reads or interprets the TCP segments. It only acts as a communication system between two hosts at two end points of a connection.

Some of the distinctive features or techniques adopted by TCP for achieving reliability are (a) adaptive retransmission, (b) flow control through window advertisement, (c) three-way handshake to ensure start up and termination of connections reliably and (d) mechanism to control congestion in the Internet by measuring packet loss and responding to congestion by reducing temporarily window size to reduce data transmission rate.

Through the adaptive retransmission for packet loss, TCP measures the current round trip delay (the time delay between the sending of a TCP segment by a sending host and the receipt of the acknowledgement from the receiving host) for each connection and then estimates statistically time out for each connection to set the retransmission timer for the same.

In order to control the flow of data, TCP uses a window advertisement technique. Whenever TCP establishes a connection, each end of the connection earmarks a buffer to hold incoming data and sends information about the size of the buffer to the other end. As data arrives, the receiver sends acknowledgement, which also specifies the remaining buffer size, known as 'window' through a notification known as 'window advertisement' in TCP parlance. A receiver sends a window advertisement with each acknowledgement. If the sender transmits faster than the receiver can consume in its application, the window size will gradually reduce and at one time becomes zero, thereby causing receiver to advertise a 'zero window'. The sender, on receiving a 'zero window' advertisement, has to stop transmission till the receiver again advertises a positive window along with an acknowledgement of the last data octet received.

The three-way handshake guarantees reliable start-up or termination of a connection by exchange of three messages between the two hosts located at the two ends of the connection. TCP uses the term 'SYN' segment (synchronization segment) to establish a connection and the term 'FIN' segment (Finish segment) to describe messages in a three-way handshake to terminate a connection. Figure 12.42 illustrates the three-way handshake used to terminate a connection.

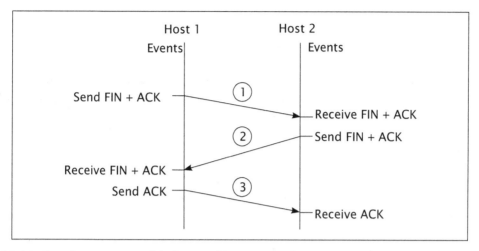

FIGURE 12.42 Three-way Handshake Used by TCP to Close a Connection

12.20 Private IP Addressing and Network Address Translation (NAT) Private IP Addressing

In an attempt to conserve address spaces, in addition to subnet and classless addressing schemes described in earlier paragraphs, the private addressing scheme was invented and introduced. A private network is a network with computers attached to it, however the network administrator assigns a locally unique address to each computer connected to the private network known as its private address or non-routable address which are not valid on global Internet. The private network will have a single globally valid IP address. Routers at the site with private addresses are configured to forward datagrams containing source with private addresses. However, before allowing a datagram with a private address of source to the Internet, a device known as NAT translates the private IP source address into a global IP address recognized by the Internet. Similarly, in case of an incoming datagram from a computer in the global internetwork to a private address, NAT translates the global IP address of the private network to a private address used at the site. The conservation of address spaces arises because in case of a site with private addresses, all the individual nodes or computers will not have separate globally valid IP addresses but the whole set of computers with the private network will have one globally valid IP address assigned to the private network site.

The private IPV4 address space specified in request for comment 1918 (RFC 1918) is defined by the following address blocks:

1. 10.0.0.0/8, which is a single class A network with an IP address range from 10.0.0.0 to 10.255.255.255. The host ID size is 24 bits and can accommodate 16,777,216 number of addresses.
2. 172.16.0.0/12, which is a 16 contiguous class B networks with an IP address range from 172.16.0.0 to 172.31.255.255. The host ID size is 20 bits and can accommodate 1,048,576 number of addresses.
3. 192.168.0.0/16, which is a 256 contiguous class C networks with an IP address range from 192.168.0.0 to 192.168.255.255. The host ID size is 16 bits and can accommodate 65,536 number of addresses.

12.20.1 NAT Technology

NAT basically provides two views:

1. From the Internet perspective, the private site appears to have a single host computer with a single global IP address assigned to it. Datagrams appear to have originated from the same IP address and responses are sent to the same IP address.
2. From the perspective of any one computer in the site, the Internet appears to accept and route private addresses.

In order to provide the above views or illusion, the NAT device processes each incoming datagram to a private site and each outgoing datagram from a private site. The process is rewriting of IP addresses in the datagram as illustrated in Figure 12.43.

12.20.1.1 Network Address and Port Translation (NAPT) and Translation Table

NAPT is the abbreviated from of 'network address and port translation' and is a more popular form of NAT. NAPT takes care of two limitations of NAT. First, if more than one computer at a site with private addresses communicate with the same destination D, basic NAT will fail because there will be more than one private address corresponding to a same destination address D. Therefore, it will not be possible for NAT to identify the particular source of the private site from which an incoming datagram arrives for D.

Second, if more than one application running on a particular computer at the private site communicate with different destinations on the Internet, NAT cannot manage the situation since its translation does not involve the port number for any particular application running on a computer.

NAPT allows a private site to have more than one application running on one or more number of computers to communicate with one or more destinations on the global internet. In order to facilitate the above feature, NAPT translates both IP addresses and protocol port numbers, unlike NAT which only translates IP addresses. NAPT uses a translation table, which contains both old value and new value of IP addresses and protocol port numbers. However, in case two computers in a private site send datagrams using the same local port number (similar application) and both form a TCP connection to a web server at a particular port number through a NAPT device, to avoid such conflicting situations,

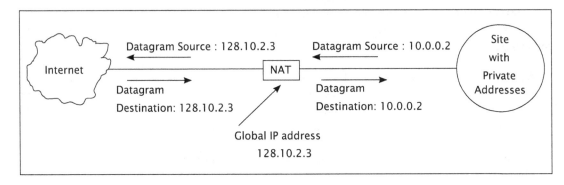

FIGURE 12.43 Illustration of the Process of NAT Translation

TABLE 12.10	An Illustration of NAPT Translation Table for TCP Connections		

Direction	Fields	Old Value	New Value
Outgoing	IP source: TCP source	10.0.0.207 : 7000	128.10.2.3 : 7101
Outgoing	IP source: TCP source	10.0.0.208 : 7000	128.10.2.3 : 7102
Incoming	IP destination: TCP destination	128.10.2.3 : 7101	10.0.0.207 : 7000
Incoming	IP destination: TCP destination	128.10.2.3 : 7102	10.0.0.208 : 7000

NAPT assigns different TCP source port numbers to the two computers running similar applications. This is illustrated schematically with a NAPT translation table in Table 12.10.

Private addresses with NAT find common use in residential networks, since most 'Internet service providers' (ISPs) only allocate a single routable public IP address to a residential customer, but many homes have more than one computer or other Internet-connected devices, such as smartphones. In such cases, a NAT gateway is used to provide Internet connectivity to multiple hosts. Private addresses are also often used by corporate networks because of security reasons. Such networks are not connected directly to the Internet. Private addresses thus enhance network security for the internal network, since it is difficult for an Internet host (external host) to connect directly to an internal network. Finally, NAT can be implemented in software on a conventional PC (software defined NAT) or as a dedicated hardware device.

12.21 Internet Routing Protocols

We have seen from the previous paragraphs that IP uses routing tables contained in both hosts and routers to facilitate forwarding of datagrams. IP routing deals with the propagation of routing information for creating and updating routing tables. There are several routing protocols for global Internet. Certain concepts such as static routing and dynamic routing related to IP routing need elaboration. Static routing relates to routes, which do not change unless any error in the network is detected. Dynamic routing, on the contrary, changes routes and updates the routing tables of the routers to learn about optimal routes for each location to ensure datagrams to follow the same routes. Static routing is simple, easy to specify but inflexible. It is mostly used by hosts particularly in cases where the host has one network connection as in case of ethernet and the network is connected to the rest of the Internet by a single router. The routing table in case of static routing for a host has only two entries, one for the network to which it is attached and the other for a default route meant for all other destinations as shown in Figures 12.44a and 12.44b.

Static routing is limited to simple configuration as shown in Figure 12.44. However, when there are more than one router, each connected to separate ISPs, and the ISPs also connect with each other through a network, the routers have to exchange routing information and update the individual routing table dynamically. The architecture for a dynamic routing situation has been illustrated in Figure 12.45.

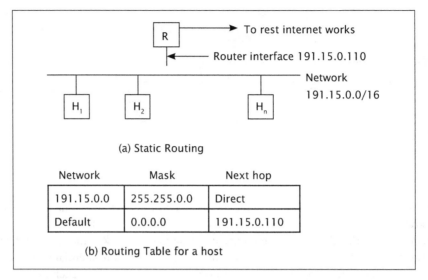

(a) Static Routing

Network	Mask	Next hop
191.15.0.0	255.255.0.0	Direct
Default	0.0.0.0	191.15.0.110

(b) Routing Table for a host

FIGURE 12.44   (a) Static Routing (b) Routing Table Used by a Host

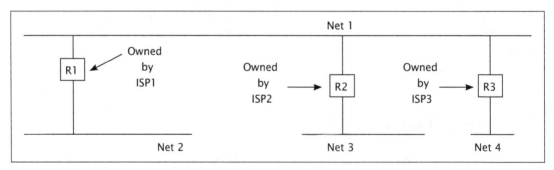

FIGURE 12.45   Four Networks Connected by Three Routers Belonging to Three ISPs Leading to Dynamic Routing to Propagate Routing Information

12.22 Autonomous System (AS) Concept

Basically, a route propagation protocol allows each router to exchange routing information with another router. However, in case of the global Internet if each router exchanges routing information with another router the total routing information traffic will become enormous and will not be scalable by the Internet works. In order to limit the routing traffic, routers and networks are divided and grouped into 'autonomous systems' numbered as AS_1, AS_2, ... AS_n such that routers within a particular AS exchange routing information among themselves. Then, at least one or more router in each AS summarizes the routing information within the autonomous group before passing it to the other AS. AS is a contiguous set of networks and routers under the control of one administrative authority such as an ISP, one small corporation or a large corporation with number of sites in a metro city.

Internet routing protocols within an autonomous system are collectively known as Interior gateway protocol (IGP) which governs exchange of routing information among the routers within the system.

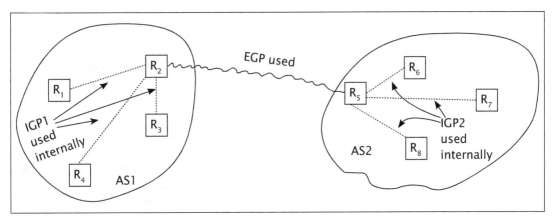

FIGURE 12.46 The Internet Routing Architecture with IGP and EGP

TABLE 12.11	The Internet Routing Protocols for IGP and EGP	
IGPs *(Interior Gateway Protocols)*	**EGPs** *(Exterior Gateway Protocol)*
RIP (routing information protocol)	EGP
OSPF (open shortest path first)	BGP (Border Gateway Protocol) version 4
IGRP (interior gateway routing protocol)	EBGP
EIGRP (enhanced interior or gateway routing protocol)	
IS—IS (intermediate system to intermediate system)	

A router in one AS uses an exterior gateway protocol (EGP) to exchange routing information with a router in another AS. In order to save traffic, an EGP passes only summarized routing information from one AS to another AS. Figure 12.46 illustrates the IGP and EGP routing architecture of the Internet.

In the figure, AS1 uses IGP1 to use internally the exchange of routing information among the routers R_1, R_2, R_3 and R_4. Similarly, AS2 uses IGP2 internally. R_2 summarizes routing information for AS1 and R5 does the same for AS2. R_2 and R_5 use EGP to communicate the summarized routing information between AS1 and AS2. Additionally, R_2 and R_5 accept the summary from each other and propagate the same to their routers in AS1 and AS2 respectively.

Some of the important Internet routing protocols belonging to IGP and EGP have been shown in Table 12.11.

12.22.1 Optimal Routes, Routing Metrics and Administrative Distance

In principle, Internet routing protocols find all possible paths from a router to each destination and then choose a path that is optimal for each destination and update the routing table accordingly. However, there is no universally agreed criterion of optimality of a path. The optimal path selection is based on a number of parameters such as type of application, associated delay, throughput and jitter. Routing protocol designers refer to a term known as 'routing metric' as a measure for selecting an optimal path. Although it is possible to use parameters as mentioned above such as throughput, delay or jitter as a routing metric, in practice, Internet routing is often based on two metrics, namely hop count (the number of intermediate routers or networks on the path to destination) and administrative cost assigned manually as per corporate policy to control the traffic flow along different paths. Moreover, decision as regards choosing a particular Internet routing protocol is based on its reliability for selecting the optimal routing. A number of arbitrary units known as 'administrative distance' are assigned to dynamic routes, static routes and directly connected routes. The value of administrative distance is used to rank routes from most preferred (with low administrative distance value) to least preferred (with high administrative distance value).

Administrative distance assigned to Internet routing protocol bears an inverse relationship with its reliability for optimal routing. The lower the administrative distance value, the higher is the reliability. The default administrative distance for various routing protocols used on Cisco routers have been shown in Table 12.12.

TABLE 12.12 Administrative Distance for Various Routing Protocols Used on CISCO Routers

Routing Protocol	Administrative Distance (Arbitrary units based on reliability)
Directly connected interface	0
Static route out at interface	1
Static route to next-hop address	1
Dynamic mobile network routing	3
EIGRP summary route	5
External BGP	20
Internal EIGRP	90
IGRP	100
OSPF	110
IS-IS	115
RIP	120
Exterior gateway protocol (EGP)	140
On-demand routing (ODR)	160
External EIGRP	170
Internal BGP	200
Next-hop resolution protocol (NHRP)	250
Floating static route (Ex. DHCP)	254
Unknown others	255

An administrative distance of 255 will cause the router to remove the route from the routing table and not use it because of very poor reliability for optimal routing. It may be noted that within an AS, IGP software uses a routing metric to determine the optimal path to each destination. However, EGP finds only the path to each destination but cannot determine an optimal path as it cannot compare the routing metrics from more than one AS, which may vary for the various AS. In case of IGP, the routers mainly exchange routing information and update the individual routing tables and the hosts listen passively to the routing information to update their individual routing tables.

The Internet routing protocols for IGP can be broadly categorized into two groups. One group consists of distance-vector-based protocols and the other link-state-based protocols. Typical examples of the distance-vector-based IGP protocols are: routing information protocol (RIP), interior gateway routing protocol (IGRP) and enhanced interior gateway routing protocol (EIGRP), whereas open shortest path first (OSPF) and intermediate system to intermediate system (IS–IS) are examples of link-state-based protocols.

Distance-vector protocols are based on calculating the direction and distance to any link in a network within an administrative system. 'Direction' here means the next-hop address together with the exit interface. 'Distance' here is a measure of the cost to reach a certain node. The minimum cost route between any two nodes is the route with minimum distance. Each node (router or host) maintains a vector (array or table) of minimum distance to every node. The cost of reaching a destination is calculated using various route metrics. RIP uses the hop count as a measure of distance to destination, where each network between the source and destination counts as a single hop. It also uses origin as one counting, meaning that a directly connected network is one hop away and not zero. IGRP, however, takes into account other information such as node delay and available bandwidth for considering distance.

A router informs its neighbours of topology changes periodically so that updates are performed by the neighbours, and these are configured to use the same distance-vector routing protocol. Distance-vector routing protocols use various algorithms to calculate paths such as Bellman-Ford, Ford-Fulkerson or dual finite state machine (FSM).

The basic concept of link-state routing is that every switching node (router) constructs a graph of the connectivity to the network; the edges of the graph show which nodes are connected to which other nodes. This is illustrated in Figure 12.47. Each node then determines the next best path from it to every possible destination in the network.

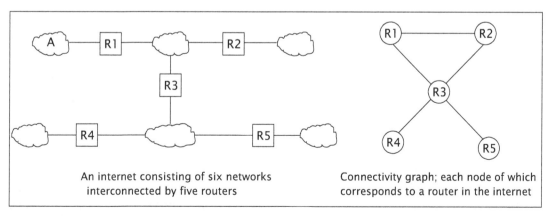

An internet consisting of six networks interconnected by five routers

Connectivity graph; each node of which corresponds to a router in the internet

FIGURE 12.47 Illustration of Link State Graph Corresponding to an Internet Consisting of Six Networks Interconnected by Five Routers

The consolidation of the best path for a particular node will be its routing table. The difference between distance vector routing protocols and link state routing protocols lies in that in case of the former, each node shares its routing table with neighbours, whereas in case of the latter, the information exchanged among the nodes is connectivity oriented.

RIP was among the first routing protocols based on the distance–vector approach. It is simple and requires little configuration. It has important features such as hop count metric, use of UDP for all message transmission, broadcast or multicast delivery, support for default route propagation and passive version for hosts as explained earlier. OSPF is an interior gateway protocol that uses a link-status algorithm to propagate routing information. It supports multi-access networks also. Each router participating in OSPF periodically broadcasts link status to adjacent routers which use Dijkstra's shortest path first algorithm to compute the shortest path. The following table shows important differences between RIP and OSPF as discussed earlier also.

RIP	OSPF
It is a distance-vector protocol.	It is a link-state protocol.
The metric used in RIP is hop count.	The metrics used in OSPF are bandwidth and delay.
RIP uses distance vector algorithms such as Bellman Ford, Ford-Fulkerson or Dual FSM to determine best path.	OSPF uses Dijkstra's SPF algorithm to determine the best path.
In RIP, networks are not divided in areas or tables.	OSPF allows partitioning of the routers and networks in an autonomous system into multiple areas, subareas and backbone areas. OSPF can handle a large number of routers than RIP.
Maximum hop Count is 15.	No hop count
Periodic routing updates every 30 seconds convergence time is high.	Much less convergence time[a]
RIP routes have an administrative distance value of 120.	OSPG routes have an administrative distance value of 110.
Routing is both class full and classless for different versions of RIP.	Classless
RIP uses UDP.	OSPF uses IP.

Note: [a] Convergence time is a measure of how fast a group of routers attains the state of convergence (a state of a set of routers that have the same topological information about the internet in which they operate).

12.22.1.1 Border Gateway Protocol (BGP)

BGP version 4, the current version is the most important EGP and is used to exchange routing information among AS in the global Internet. BGP version 4, abbreviated as BGP-4, ensures correct transmission of a datagram from an arbitrary source host to any arbitrary destination through consistent global routing information propagation. BGP-4 has important features such as provision for policies enforced by the sender and receiver (regarding routes, security restrictions and advertisements), transit routing and reliable transport using TCP. The TCP ensures that data arrive in correct order without any loss.

12.22.1.2 Multicast Routing Protocol

Since Internet multicast allows dynamic grouping and further because an arbitrary source can send information to a multicast group without being a member of the group, multicast route propagation is a very complex and difficult situation. Even though there are several multicast routing protocols, global Internet-wide multicast protocol technology exists.

12.23 Client–Server Paradigm of Interaction

Network application software provides high-level services available on an Internet. Further, application programs that communicate with each other on a network or on the Internet use the client–server paradigm of interaction. In this paradigm, two applications are involved in the communication process: client and server applications. A server program or application waits passively for contact or being invoked, while a client application initiates communication actively. A client application software is an arbitrary program invoked directly by a user and runs locally on the computer of the user to actively initiate contact with a server program. The client application software can access multiple server programs running on a single-server computer or on more than one server computer. It can actively contact one remote server at a time. Generally, client application does not require any sophisticated hardware or operating system.

Server software, on the contrary, is a single dedicated service-oriented privilege program which can serve multiple remote clients at a time. In other words, it waits passively for contact from one or more arbitrary remote clients to whom it offers a single service. The server software gets invoked when the server system boots and continues to execute through many sessions. The server software runs on a shared computer with powerful hardware and sophisticated multi-user operating system such as UNIX.

Information flow between a client and a server can be in either one or both directions. In general, a client sends a request for a service to a server and the server returns a response to the client. In some cases, however, a client sends multiple requests such as queries and the server sends more than one responses. For example, a database client may seek from overseas employment database server all openings for civil engineering graduates and the server sends responses for more than one opening at a time. Bi-directional information flows also involve a case of a file server receiving copy of files from a client for storage and sending a particular file to the client on request. A client or server application interacts with the transport layer of the TCP/IP suite to establish communication. The transport layer, in turn, uses lower-layer protocols to send and receive individual packets. Thus, both the computers for a client and a server need the complete stack of protocols.

A server-class computer can offer more than one service at the same time. The computer in that case must have large memory, fast processor and an operating system such as UNIX or windows which can run multiple application programs concurrently. The computer offers more than one service and waits passively for client active communication for the offered services. Likewise, more than one remote client may like to avail of the same service from a server-class computer at the same time. This is facilitated due to a feature known as 'support concurrency' which allows multiple copies of a server offering a single service. The application program having more than one thread of control or execution is known as a concurrent program. Concurrent execution is essential to the client–server model of interaction as a concurrent server offers the same service to multiple clients simultaneously without any client to wait for any other previous client to finish availing of the service. In a concurrent server, the main server thread

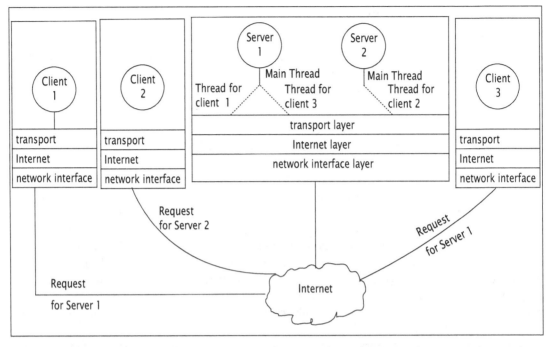

FIGURE 12.48 Two Servers on a Single Computer Accessed by Three Clients on Three Other Computers with Concurrent Support by the Server 1

creates a new service thread to handle each client. The service thread entertains one particular client request and then terminates, but the main thread keeps the server alive for another one or more requests to arrive. Thus, if N number of clients are using a service on a single computer, there will be (N + 1) threads providing the service. N threads will be providing service to N clients, and the main thread waits passively for additional requests. Figure 12.48 illustrates the arrangement of multiple services with multiple copies of a single service on a computer accessed by remote clients through the Internet.

A question arises as to how to identify a particular service being offered by a server (such as web server or file server) and how a client will specify unambiguously the service it requests for. For this, client–server interaction paradigm assigns a unique identifier for each service, and the same identifier will be used by both the server, which offers the same service and the client, which actively communicates for the service. Protocol software uses the identifier to direct each incoming request to the correct application server. As for example of service identifier, the TCP uses 16-bit integer values known as TCP port numbers to identify services and assigns a unique port number to each service. TCP software on the server-side computer uses the protocol port number in an incoming request from a client to determine the server which should handle the request. In case of multiple copies of a server to handle multiple clients requesting for the same service, the transport protocols, in practice, assign each client a unique identifier and require the particular client to include its identifier while making a request. Transport protocol software on the server computer uses both the client and server identifiers to seek the copy of the server created for the client. In case of TCP, each client selects a local protocol port number, which is not assigned to any service and specifies the same in the source port field and the protocol port number of the server in the destination port field of the TCP segment, which the remote client sends.

TCP on the server's machine uses the combination of client and server port numbers to choose the correct copy of a concurrent server.

Finally, clients and servers can use either connection-oriented interface (as in case of TCP) or a connectionless interface (as is case of UDP).

In case of connection-oriented transport, a client first forms a connection to a specific server and then sends requests and receives responses till it finishes using the service and closes the connection. In contrast, connectionless protocols allow clients and servers to exchange individual messages.

For example, a client can send each request and the server can return each response as a single message.

12.24 Application Programming Interface (API)

The interface between an application program and the transport protocols for communication is known as API. Most APIs define a set of procedures (one for each logical function) such as one procedure to establish communication and another procedure to transmit data. In addition, API specifies the arguments associated with each procedure and the data type.

The standard API available with various operating systems such as Microsoft's windows and also UNIX systems is the socket API often abbreviated as 'sockets'. Vendors of various operating systems created a 'socket library', which provides applications with a socket API on a computer system which has no native sockets. When an application calls for one of the socket procedures, control passes to a routine in the socket library to implement the socket procedure. Sockets were originally developed as a part of the Berkeley software distribution (BSD) UNIX operating system.

Before an application can use protocols to communicate, the application must request the operating system to create a socket that will be used for communication. The operating system returns a small integer descriptor, which will be used by the application to reference the socket. The socket procedure which creates a socket for an application and returns a descriptor is as follows:

Descriptor = Socket (proto-family, type, protocol)

These three arguments are:

1. **Proto-family:** Proto-family specifies the protocol family to be associated with the socket. For example, proto-family PF_INET indicates TCP/IP protocol suite.
2. **Type:** Type specifies the type of communication the socket will use; the typical values are SOCK_STREAM for connection-oriented type and SOCK_DGRAM for a connectionless message-oriented transfer.
3. **Protocol:** Protocol permits a single protocol suit to include two or more protocols to provide the same service.

The other common procedures with their formats are as follows:

1. **Close (socket):** Here, socket is the integer descriptor for the socket being closed. It immediately terminates use of the socket, and the descriptor is released preventing the application from sending or receiving any further data.

2. **Bind (socket, localaddr, addrlen):** It allows a server to supply the protocol address at which the server will wait passively for contact. The argument 'socket' is the descriptor of the socket created but not bound, 'localaddr' specifies the local address assigned to the socket, and 'addrlen' is an integer specifying the length of the local address.

3. **Listen (socket, queuesize):** This is for a socket for a server computer to be in passive mode awaiting contact from clients. It has two arguments, namely 'socket', which is the descriptor of a socket that has been created and bound to a local address by the 'bind' procedure and the 'queuesize', which specifies the length of queue for the socket's requests. If the queue is full, no further request will be accepted by the socket.

4. **Newsock = Accept (socket, caddress, caddresslen):** It is associated with the call for the procedure 'accept' in case of connection-oriented transport to accept a new connection request from a client. The argument 'socket' is the descriptor of a socket that the server has created and bound to a specific protocol port. The 'accept' procedure fills in the argument 'caddress' with the address of the client that formed the connection and sets 'caddresslen' as the length of the same address.

   The 'accept' procedure creates a new socket for the new connection request from a client and returns the descriptor of 'newsock' to the caller (client). The server uses the new socket to communicate with the client and closes the socket 'newsock' when finished. However, the original socket remains as it is and is used by the server to accept the next connection from any client.

The procedure connect (`socket, saddress, saddresslen`) is used to establish connection by a client with a specific server where 'socket' is the descriptor of a socket on the client computer for the connection, 'saddress' specifies the end point address of the server (a combination of server address and the protocol port number), 'saddresslen' specifies the length of server address in octets:

```
            send (socket, data, length, flags)
  send to (socket, data, length, flags, destaddress, addresslen)
            sendmsg (socket, msgstruct, flags)
```

The 'send', 'send to' and 'sendmsg' procedures are used to send data/information by both clients and servers.

The 'send' procedure is used to send data when the socket has been created and connected whereas both 'send to' and 'sendmsg' are procedures used by either a client or a server to send a message using unconnected sockets. It has four arguments, namely 'socket', 'data', which is the address in the memory of the client or server computer where the data to be sent exist, 'length', an integer which specifies the number of octets of data and 'flags', which contains bits for special option request such as debugging of the system.

The 'send to' procedure contains two additional arguments, namely 'dest address' and 'addresslen' to specify the address of the destination and the length of the destination address.

The 'send msg' procedure performs the same procedure as 'send to' but has only three arguments.

The arguments 'socket' and 'flags' are similar to 'send to' procedure. However, 'msgstruct' is a structure, which contains information about the destination address, the length of the same, the message to be sent and the length of the message:

```
            recv (socket, buffer, length, flags)
  recv from (socket, buffer, length, flags, sndaddress, saddrlen)
            recvmsg (socket, msgstruct, flags)
```

The procedures 'recv', 'recvfrom' and 'recvmsg' are used by a client or a server to receive data/information sent by the other. They are very similar in form to the three send procedures as explained earlier except that the argument 'buffer' specifies the address in memory where the incoming message (data or information) should be placed and argument 'length' specifies the buffer size. The 'recv' procedure is for connected socket, whereas 'recvfrom' and 'recvmsg' are for socket not connected.

The arguments 'sndaddress' and 'saddrlen' are the pointers to a socket address structure to denote the sender's address and the length of the same. The argument 'msgstruct' gives the address of a structure that holds address for an incoming message and the location for the sender's IP address.

Sequence of 'socket' procedure calls: Figure 12.49 illustrates the sequence of socket procedures for a client and server calls. It may be noted from the figure that the server must call 'listen' before a client calls 'connect'.

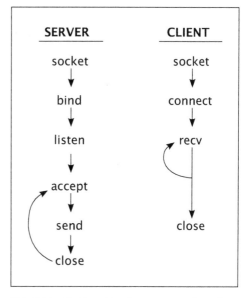

FIGURE 12.49 The Sequence of Socket Procedures for a Client and Server Calls

12.25 Domain Name System (DNS)

Internet users do not always require to remember IP addresses of the destination computers. Instead, they can remember with much more ease symbolic names assigned to such computers. For example, in case of a client-server interaction, the client can send a message to a recipient server and use a string specifying the name of the server computer. Likewise, a computer name can be specified as a string by a user to reach a particular site on the World Wide Web.

A question arises as to how the computers will understand symbolic names. In other words, although application software permits users to enter symbolic names, the Internet protocol requires equivalent IP addresses, and therefore an application program must convert every symbolic name into its equivalent IP address before transmitting the message. In order to facilitate the conversion of symbolic names into equivalent IP addresses, a structure of symbolic computer names, known as 'domain name system' (DNS), has been designed. Further, the database of computer names resides on a number of computers located at different sites across the Internet. The servers which handle the naming information are known as the DNS servers. An application program converts the computer symbolic names into the equivalent IP addresses with the help of DNS servers through client–server interaction, which has been explained in subsequent paragraphs of this chapter.

12.25.1 Structure of DNS

Domain names are hierarchical and consist of alpha-numeric parts separated by periods. The hierarchy order follows that the most significant part of the name is on the extreme right and the other parts on

Top-Level Domain Name (TLDs)		Assigned to
com	...	Commercial organization
edu	...	Educational institution
org	...	Non-commercial organizations
gov	...	US Government
aero	...	Air transport industry
arpa	...	Infrastructure domain
museum	...	Museums
net	...	Major network support centre
biz	...	Businesses
country code (such as uk, in, etc.)	...	A country

FIGURE 12.50 Some Typical Values for Top-level Domain Names

the left, one before the other in order of significance. The left-most part indicates the name of a computer. For example, the domain name 'apple.econ.jadavpur.edu' symbolically indicates a computer named 'apple' in the economics department of 'Jadavpur University', an educational institution. Similarly, a domain name 'macintosh.cognizant.com' symbolically indicates a computer named 'macintosh' at 'cognizant' a company.

The domain name system neither puts any stipulation on the number of parts or segments in each name, nor does it specify what those segments represent. However, DNS specifies the values for the most significant part (right most part) of a domain name, which is known as TLD (top-level domain). TLDs are assigned and controlled by the 'Internet Corporation for Assigned Names and Numbers' (ICANN), and some typical values of TLDs have been shown in Figure 12.50. It may be stated that DNS does not differentiate between names in upper or lowercase characters.

In order to obtain a domain, an organization has to register with an approved registrar and a unique domain suffix is assigned to each organization from among the list of TLDs. DNS allows an organization to use a suffix to denote geographic location (country, state and city). For example, 'incometax.gov.in' is the domain registered by the income tax department of Government of India.

Likewise, UK universities register under the domain 'ac.uk', where 'ac' stands for academic and 'uk' for United Kingdom.

DNS also permits hierarchical order of names within an organization. Even individual groups or departments within an organization can have appropriate hierarchical structure of the names. Each name in the hierarchy has a corresponding segment in a domain name, and there is no universal standard for the names in the hierarchy. Similarly, there is no restriction regarding the levels of the naming hierarchy in DNS. The naming hierarchy facilitates achieving autonomy by allowing an organization to control all names with a particular suffix.

For example, Figure 12.51 shows graphically the DNS hierarchy of a company named Zenith which has two broad divisions—pump and motor—and pump has two subdivisions, namely centrifugal and submersible. Motor division has three subdivisions, namely synchronous, induction and series.

Individual computer names within the sub-divisions can be the domain names as follows:

computer.centrifugal.pump.zenith.com
computer.submersible.pump.zenith.com
computer.synchronous.motor.zenith.com
computer.induction.motor.zenith.com
computer.series.motor.zenith.com

Although in the names shown above, the first name is the name of a computer, the same first label can be used for denoting a service that a computer provides. For example, the first label www indicates the name of a computer which runs the web server. However, this is merely a naming convention for helping users to remember the service that a first name provides.

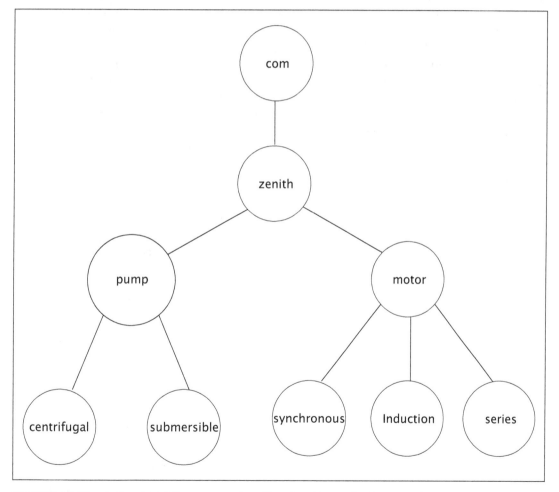

FIGURE 12.51 A Graphical Representation Showing How a DNS Hierarchy Can Be Structured in an Organization

DNS uses a client–server interaction model, wherein the entire naming system (the domain names along with the equivalent IP addresses) operates as a large and distributed database. Each organization with Internet connection runs a domain name server which is linked with other domain name servers and the integrated set of DNS servers functions as the database of domain names. A user application becomes a client of the DNS server when it needs to translate a name into an IP address. The client sends a DNS request message with a particular domain name to be translated to a DNS server. The server extracts the name from the message, translates the name to an equivalent IP address and returns the same to the client as a reply message. The translation of a domain name into an equivalent IP address is called 'name resolution', and the software which performs the 'name resolution' is called 'name resolver' or simply 'resolver' software. Operating systems in general have the name 'resolver' software as an in-built library routine, which an application program can invoke. For example, in case of UNIX operating system, the library routine to resolve a name is called as 'gethostbyname'. The argument of 'gethostbyname' is the domain name as a character string. If the domain name can be successfully resolved 'gethostbyname' returns a list of one or more IP addresses corresponding to the argument. However, if the name in the argument cannot be resolved a 'NULL' is returned instead of any IP address. In order to understand how the resolver works to resolve a name with the help of the DNS servers, let us look into the hierarchy and architecture of the DNS servers.

DNS servers are arranged in a hierarchy, which matches with the naming hierarchy with each one server corresponding to a part of the naming hierarchy. The root server sitting on the top of the hierarchy is meant for the top-level domains (such as .edu) as mentioned in Figure 12.50. The root server contains information about other servers to fetch all possible domain names. It may be mentioned that although the hierarchy of DNS servers matches the naming hierarchy, the structure or the architecture is not identical and the same is designed or chosen by every organization depending upon how it divides names among one or more servers. For example, Figure 12.52 illustrates two different architectures (a) and (b) for the DNS servers for the same name hierarchy shown in Figure 12.51.

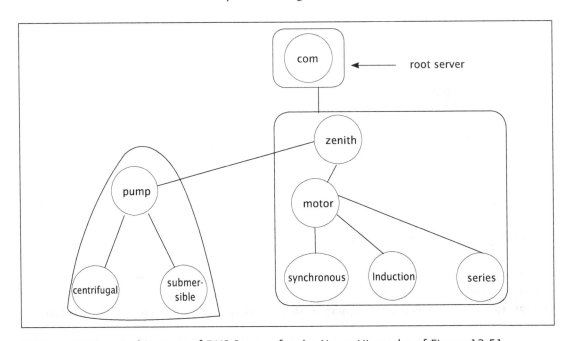

FIGURE 12.52a Architecture of DNS Servers for the Name Hierarchy of Figure 12.51

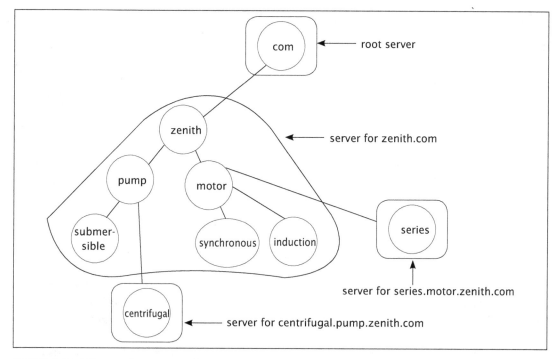

FIGURE 12.52b Architecture of DNS Servers for the Name Hierarchy of Figure 12.51

The resolver software in a host goes by a recursive resolution to find the equivalent IP address for a name. Each resolver is configured with the address of a local DNS server. The resolver becomes the client of the same DNS server and sends a DNS request message to the local server and waits for a reply. If the local server is an authority for the name specified in the request message from the resolver, the server directly replies after searching for the name in its local database. However, if the name with the request is beyond the authority of the local server (that is the name with the request is not available with the local database), the local server for the time being becomes a client for another name server and further client–server interaction takes place. When the other server returns and answers, the original server sends a copy of the answer back to the resolver who sent the request. This type of iterative search begins with the root server whose address is known to each other DNS server. Further, the iterative search for resolution proceeds through the server hierarchy beginning with the root server one level at a time.

12.25.2 DNS Entry Types

The DNS database records have got three elements, namely domain name, record type and a value for the equivalent IP address. The record type indicates how the value is to be interpreted. For example, type A addresses are for computer name for applications such as file transfer protocol, Internet browser and many other programs, whereas type MX is for mail exchanger, which maps computer name found in an email address into the equivalent IP address.

Whenever a resolver looks up a name, the resolver has to specify the type that is desired in order to enable a DNS server to return only entries that match the specified type.

12.25.3 Optimization Techniques for Performance of DNS Servers

Two optimization techniques, namely replication and caching, are adopted by DNS servers to improve performance in terms of response. Replication is carried out by creating multiple copies of the root server around the world in order to reduce the load on any particular server.

The local DNS servers pertaining to any site are configured with the list of all the root servers. The local server for a site uses a root server that is most responsive at a given time.

DNS caching is more important because of the principle of locality, that is a tendency for a user to look up the same name repeatedly. Each server maintains a cache of names with already resolved bindings. When an application looks up for a name for the first time, the local DNS server places a copy of resolved binding into its cache. The server can then entertain subsequent requests by checking first its cache instead of contacting the authoritative server again.

12.26 Electronic Mail (Email) Transfer

Email is a type of client–server interaction involving the basic mail transport, mail forwarding and access to mailbox. An email is a message that consists of a header followed by the body which is the text of the message. The header specifies the sender of the message, one or more recipients, a subject and date the message was sent.

The address of either the sender or the recipients of an email is a string divided into two parts by the '@' (at sign) character. The first part (left part) is a mailbox identifier, and the second part denotes the name of the computer on which the mailbox resides. The mailbox is a storage area assigned to a participant of email (a sender and each recipient) into which messages (emails) can be stored. The email box is a private mailbox with permission to allow the email software to place or store incoming mails into it but denies permission to anyone except the owner of the mailbox to read the messages or remove them. A few examples of email addresses are as follows:

jaytilak.biswas@yahoo.com
12345.6789@zenith.com
ibmnce@cal3.vsnl.net.in

The first example indicates the mailbox of user with firstname 'jaytilak' and last name 'biswas' residing on the computer of yahoo commercial organization. The second example indicates the user's login id '12345.6789' as his/her mailbox identifier which is resident on a computer of Zenith Corporation.

Figure 12.53 illustrates an email message. The header lines begin with a keyword and colon. The typical keywords are From, To, Date, Subject, CC (carbon copy) and BCC (blind carbon copy). The email uses the keyword 'CC' to denote a carbon copy similar to the conventional office memos. The message (email) will be received by all recipients whose email addresses are specified against the keyword 'CC'. The keyword 'BCC' stands for blind carbon copy and the recipients whose email addresses are specified against the 'BCC' keyword will all also receive a copy of the message each similar to CC but the difference is that neither the BCC field itself nor the email addresses in it will appear in any of the copies and even to the original recipient whose address appears after the keyword 'To'. The 'BCC' line will appear blank to all recipients. A blank line separates the header from the body.

From : ray_debansu@yahoo.co.in
To: jaytilak@yahoo.com
Date: Fri, 11 Nov at 9.30 PM
Subject: Examination schedule
CC: rita_nce@yahoo.com

Sir,
Please confirm through return e-mail whether you have received
the Examination Schedule for 1st semester 2016.

Debansu Ray

FIGURE 12.53 An Example of Email Message

After composing an email message and specifying the recipients, when a user submits the same by pressing the 'send' button, the email software transfers a copy of the message to each recipient. The email software basically performs two functions: first, it allows a user to interact with email interface program to compose messages or read messages. Second, the software handles an email transfer program for sending a copy of a message to a remote computer. The mail transfer program on the sender's computer becomes a client of the remote mail server, and the same uses the second part of the email address of the recipient to select the destination.

The mail transfer program receives composed messages, places the messages in a queue and then transfers a copy of each message to each recipient. The message is appended in the mailbox of each recipient. Figure 12.54 illustrates the path of an email message from user (sender) to the mailbox of a recipient.

The simple mail transfer protocol (SMTP) is used to transfer email between the sender computer and the recipient computer. The connection is first formed as a TCP connection and through the same connection, both the client and server identify themselves. It may be mentioned that SMTP uses ASCII

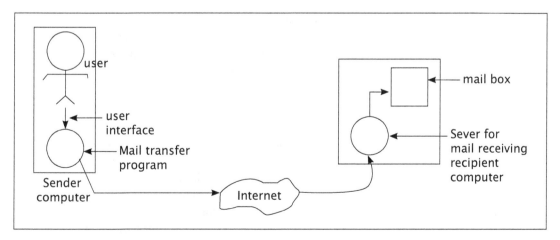

FIGURE 12.54 The Path of an Email Message

TABLE 12.13	An Example of Mail Exploder Database
List	*Email Addresses of Members*
Students	anita@zenith.com, smita@jadavpur.edu, benoy@stxaviers.edu, rita@wbu.edu
Teachers	asit@cu.edu, bimal-mitra@tcs.com, palash@nexus.com

text for all communication. After a message is transferred, the sender (client) sends a QUIT command to terminate the connection and the server of the recipient computer replies to end the connection. Each side then closes the TCP connection.

Mail transfer programs are capable of handling multiple recipients on a given remote computer. For example, if a user on computer zenith.com sends an email to three separate recipients at computer nexus. com, the mail transfer program on zenith.com does not establish three separate connections at nexus. com, but it establishes a single connection to the server on nexus.com and multiple RCPT TO commands to specify all three recipients before sending the body of the message. The server accepts the message and delivers to each of the three recipients.

A mail exploder program uses a database of a group mail participants with a common group mail name. When a message is sent to the group mail name, the mail exploder program forwards a copy of the message to each member of the group. Table 12.13 is an example of mail exploder database. Each entry in the database has a group name and contains a list of email addresses. The database shown in Table 12.13 has got two mailing lists.

12.26.1 Mail Gateways

In case the mail lists of mail exploder database become large enough, it occupies considerable storage space and also processing time on conventional computers. In such a situation, organizations select a dedicated set of computers to store the mail exploder database and run exploders to forward emails. Such dedicated computers for processing emails are called mail gateways or email gateways. However, the mailing lists maintained on mail gateways are public, which means that any user can join the list or any user can send a message to the list. Figure 12.55 illustrates how the mail transfer program interacts with the exploder when any user sends a message to a mailing list on a mail gateway computer.

12.26.2 Mailbox Access

Usually a mailbox is a storage location, and it is accessed by a mail server program which receives incoming email and stores the same in the appropriate mailbox. In case of a powerful computer system, the mail server program operating in the background allows more than one client to send emails simultaneously. However, a mailbox cannot be placed in a computer without running a mail server continuously. Such a computer system needs to have enough memory, high-processor capacity, an operating system, which permits mail server programs to run in the background with other application programs and most importantly cannot be disconnected from the Internet at any point of time. Therefore, a personal computer or any computer, which has to be switched off or disconnected

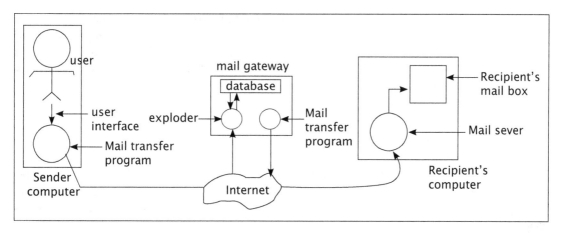

FIGURE 12.55 The Path of a Message as It Passes from Sender to Recipient through Mail Gateway

from the Internet beyond working hours, will not suffice as an email receiver and hence cannot accommodate a mailbox.

TCP/IP, therefore, includes a protocol known as the 'Post Office Protocol' (POP) and a user runs a 'POP' client to access mailbox kept on another computer, which runs the mail server round the clock and an additional POP server. The separate computer, which contains the mailbox, runs two servers: mail server which receives emails and stores it in the correct mailbox and POP server which allows a user on a remote machine to access the mailbox. However, the former uses SMTP, while the latter uses the POP. Unlike SMTP, POP allows a user to access the mailbox after proper authentication such as a password. Further, a POP server also provides the user with information about the mails contained in the mailbox.

12.27 File Transfer Protocol (FTP)

FTP is a standard Internet protocol for providing file transfer service between computers using TCP/IP connections. FTP is a general-purpose client-server protocol, which can be used by a client to upload, download, delete, rename, move and copy files from a server. FTP permits transfer of files with arbitrary data. It also transfers a copy of files between any arbitrary pair of computers. A very important feature of FTP is that it has a feature which allows ownership of files and access restrictions to files.

12.27.1 FTP Prompt and Commands

A user invokes FTP either through a program or interactively. When a user invokes FTP interactively, the interactions are command-driven one. In order to enable a user to enter a command, FTP issues a prompt (ftp>) and the user enters one of the FTP commands which is executed and then another prompt is issued by FTP for the next command.

For example, FTP commands to connect to the FTP server it.ju.edu is:

```
ftp> open ftp.it.ju.edu
```

It may be stated that by default, the 'open' command uses the TCP port 21 to make the control connection.

Similarly, in order to get file or files from the server to the user computer, the 'get or mget' commands are used. Of course, before the same, the username and password prompt will appear, and the user has to enter those to complete the authentication. However, some FTP servers allow 'anonymous' login using 'guest' or an email address as password.

```
ftp> get coursefile.htm (to get coursefile.htm)
ftp> mget*.htm (to get all files that end with.htm)
```

FTP allows file transfer in either direction. After a user establishes a control connection to a remote computer, he/she can either obtain a copy of a remote file or transfer a copy of a local file to the remote computer subject to access permissions. The transfer of file either way is completed through a data connection separately from the control connection, which has been explained in a subsequent paragraph of this chapter.

FTP is not an encrypted transmission, which means data sent through it, including the authentication username and password, can be accessed by others. In order to ensure secured file transfer, another version of FTP known as SFTP (Secure File Transfer Protocol) is used to encrypt the contents. FTP is often also secured with secured shell (SSH) FTP, which has a technology different from the same for the usual FTP.

12.27.2 File Types and Transfer Modes

Even though files can be represented differently by two different computers, FTP does not handle all different possible file representations and instead defines two basic transfer modes for files: textual used for text files and binary for non-text files. However, in case of binary mode, the transmitted copy may be meaningless as FTP does not convert values to the local representation.

12.27.3 Control and Data Connections

FTP is built on a client–server interaction model which uses separate control and data connections between the client and the server. The control connection is meant for sending commands and receiving responses, whereas the data connection is for file transfer. After sending one file either way (client to server or server to client), the data connection is closed. If the user requests another file transfer, a new data connection is established. However, the control connection remains open. In order to avoid conflict between the control and data connections, separate protocol port numbers are used for each of the above connections.

FTP sessions may run in either active or passive mode depending upon how the data connection is established. In both cases, the client creates the TCP control connection from an arbitrary port to the FTP server command port 21. In the active mode of FTP session, after the client initiates a session through the command channel request, the server initiates a data connection back to the client and begins data transfer. However, in the passive mode, the server instead uses the command channel to send to the client the information needed by the client to open a data channel. As the passive mode has the client initiating all connections, it works well across firewalls and NAT gateways. The main difference between the two modes is that in case of active mode, the client initiates the control

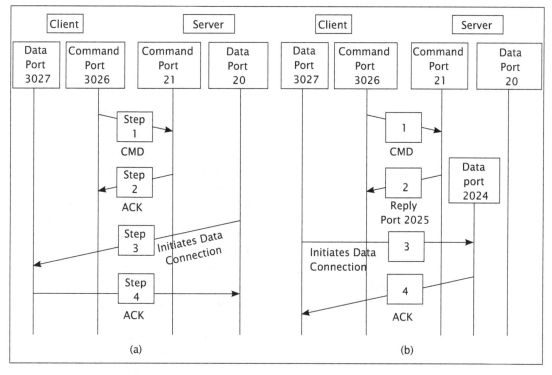

FIGURE 12.56 Illustration of (a) Active Mode and (b) Passive Mode of FTP

connection and the server initiates the data connection, whereas in case of passive mode (PASV is the command for passive mode) the client initiates both the connections. Both the modes of FTP have been illustrated in Figure 12.56 (a) and (b) respectively.

12.27.4 Trivial File Transfer Protocol (TFTP)

TFTP is a second Internet protocol for file transfer service using UDP instead of TCP. It only supports file transfer and does not support interaction that allows user to list contents of a directory, file name translation and setting file transfer mode for textual and binary files. As such, TFTP is simpler with a small set of commands and it does not have provision for authorization with login name and password. Also, the code for TFTP requires lesser memory compared to the same for FTP, thereby making TFTP useful for bootstrapping a hardware device with a small read-only memory (ROM) in which TFTP, UDP and IP can be put.

12.27.5 Network File System (NFS)

NFS provides a file access service used with TCP/IP which allows an application to read or modify parts of a remote file without copying an entire file. It also allows file sharing in which more than one client can access a file over a server. Unlike FTP, NFS is integrated into a computer's file system. Whenever an application performs a file operation on a file kept on a remote computer, NFS client software communicates with the remote computer to perform the desired operation. NFS provides for the conventional file operations such as 'open', 'read' and 'write'.

12.28 Configuration

Configuration refers to the initialization of the variables and the steps needed to be taken before a protocol software gets ready for use. Configuration or initialization is in fact one of the application programs that use client–server. A protocol software contains parameters. The parameters correspond to internal values such as the address that corresponds to the host computer or externally to the default router. Values of parameters are required to be supplied before protocol software can be used, and the process of supplying values to parameters of the protocol software is known as 'protocol configuration'. There are two methods of reading configuration information: some operating systems read configuration information from a file on permanent storage, whereas in the other case the operating systems use a network through which the information is obtained. In the second method, layers of protocol software are configured in order from lowest to highest, making it possible for each layer to use layers beneath it in order to communicate with the network to obtain configuration information.

The items of information that TCP/IP protocol software needs to configure consist of IP addresses, default IP router address, address mask(s), DNS server address and printer server address.

The protocol software converts values supplied during configuration to a form used internally (such as value in ASCII text to binary) and stores the same as an appropriate variable in memory. Because computers require protocol configuration information to change frequently, automatic update becomes necessary using automated protocol configuration. Thus, with a portable laptop which needs to be connected to different networks at different locations, the configuration information relating to each new environment must be changed before using it in the new environment.

The use of separate protocols to obtain each item of configuration information results in a sequence of configuration steps. For example, a computer can use the Reverse Address Resolution Protocol (RARP) to find out its IP address and use a separate protocol ICMP to find the subnet mask of the default router. Although using a separate protocol to obtain each individual piece of configuration information has flexibility, it suffers from a serious disadvantage of network traffic and results in delay. In order to overcome the above-mentioned disadvantage, two more protocols, namely the 'Bootstrap Protocol' (BOOTP) and 'Dynamic Host Configuration Protocol' (DHCP), were invented by TCP/IP designers.

The BOOTP is a computer networking protocol used in 'Internet protocol' networks to automatically assign IP addresses to network devices from a configuration server. BOOTP software broadcasts a BOOTP 'request message' to obtain configuration information. When the BOOTP configuration server receives the request message, it finds out multiple pieces of configuration information for the computer, which sent the request and places all those information in a single BOOTP 'response message' and sends the message to the requesting computer. Thus, in a single step, a computer can obtain multiple configuration information such as the IP address of the computer, the IP address of the server and IP address of a default router. The BOOTP configuration server assigns IP addresses based on the request from a pool of addresses configured by an administrator. The BOOTP message (request) from a computer gets invoked when the computer connected to the network is powered up and the same boots in the operating system. BOOTP uses the UDP as the transport protocol, BOOTP server uses port 67 to receive requests, and port 68 is used by the client to receive server responses. BOOTP operates only on IPV4 networks.

The DHCP is also a standard network protocol used by IP networks. It extends beyond BOOTP in the sense that unlike the BOOTP server wherein a network administrator manually enters the configuration information for computers that enter the network into the server's database, the DHCP server dynamically assigns network configuration parameters such as IP addresses into its database.

DHCP permits completely automated address assignment. This implies that DHCP permits a computer to join a new network and obtain a valid IP address for using the address for configuration without any administrator to enter the information about the computer in the server's database.

Another important feature of DHCP is that its server never assigns an address permanently. It specifies a lease during which the address can be used, and a computer has to either extend the lease or stop using the address when the lease period is over.

12.29 Network Security Aspects

Network security is not absolute in the sense that each organization defines the level of access to its network that is permitted or denied such as read only, read and amend data, and read and execute operations on data.

There are important aspects based on which organizations define their computer network security policy. Those are generally data integrity, data availability without disruption, data confidentiality and data privacy.

Data integrity refers to protection of data from change or accidental damage. It is ensured through various mechanisms such as parity bits, checksums and CRCs, which have already been described. However, such mechanisms fail to support data integrity in case of compensating alteration of the data and the value of the checksum in which case, the alteration of the data remains unnoticed. Therefore, there are other methods to ensure data integrity such as encoding of transmitted data with a Message Authentication Code, which makes it impossible for unauthorized persons to break or forge the data. Data availability refers to protection against disruption of data transmission. Data confidentiality refers to safeguard against unauthorized data access and is facilitated through access control or a password assigned to each user. Whenever a user needs to access protected resource, the user is asked to enter the assigned password. Data confidentiality is also ensured through encryption and decryption using two keys (public key and private key). Encryption basically scrambles the message bits in a form that only the receiver and no one else can unscramble (decryption). In many encryption schemes, the key for encryption must remain secret to anyone else other than the sender and the receiver of the encrypted message to avoid compromising data security. However, in case of encryption using the two keys, the encryption function has the mathematical property that a message encrypted with the public key cannot be easily decrypted except with the private key. Similarly, a message encrypted with the private key cannot be decrypted except with the public key. The keys are basically long random numbers generated by key generator algorithm using randomizing routines (an example is 'PuTTY' key generator). An example of a public key is as follows:

3 4 0 1 0 1 4 3 0 0 C 9 1 8 F A C F 8 D E B 2 D E F D 5
B A F A 3 6 2 F 9 2 2 B F 0 1 B 2 F 4 0 C 7 4 4 2 6 5 4 C O D

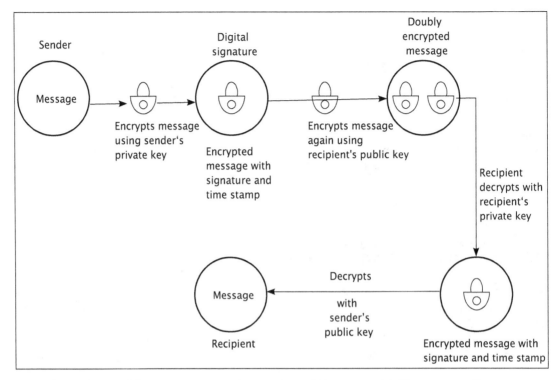

FIGURE 12.57 Double Encryption and Decryption of Message with Signature to Guarantee Authentication

The public key, as its name suggests, is made available to everyone through a public repository or directory, whereas the private key remains confidential except with its respective owner.

Privacy refers to the ability of the sender of a message to remain anonymous. An encryption mechanism can be used to authenticate the sender. The mechanism is known as 'digital signature'. In order to digitally sign a message, the sender encrypts the message using a key known to the sender only. The recipient uses the inverse function to decrypt the message. The recipient knows who sent the message because only the sender can perform the same encryption using the key which the sender only has got. Moreover, the encryption of message with digital signature has the time stamp of the signature which uniquely identifies the time of the signature. In order to ensure authentication and confidentiality, a message can be encrypted doubly, first the message is signed using the sender's private key to encrypt it and then the encrypted message is again encrypted using the recipient's public key. At the recipient end the decryption processes are just the reverse of the two encryption processes. The encryption and decryption processes have been illustrated in Figure 12.57.

12.29.1 Internet Firewall

Internet firewall is another technology to protect an organization's computers and networks from undesirable Internet traffic. A firewall as shown in Figure 12.58 is placed between an organization's network and the rest of the Internet. Obviously, if an organization has more than one Internet connection, a firewall has to be placed at each such connection.

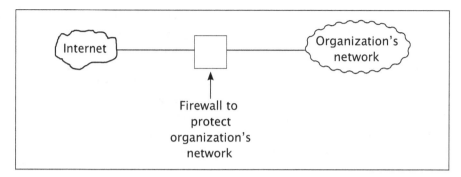

FIGURE 12.58 Illustration of a Firewall

The basic mechanism adopted to build a firewall consists of packet filters in routers as well as in the secure host that runs application gateways. A packet filter consists of a software configured by the network administrator or manager to check the header of each packet to determine the packets which are to be allowed to pass through the router and the packets which are to be discarded. For example, in order to allow a computer with IP address 192.5.48.37 on a network to communicate with any computer on another network, a manager specifies that the filter in the router connecting the two networks should allow all IP packets with source address 192.5.48.37 to pass on to the other network. Similarly, to allow a computer in a network with IP address 128.10.0.20 to receive any packet from another network, the filter in the router connecting the two networks should allow all IP packets with destination address 128.10.0.20. A packet filter software permits complex boolean combinations of source, destination address and service type.

12.29.2 Security Technologies

In order to detect unwanted attacks, an organization uses various security technologies with the Internet. Some of them are listed as follows:

1. Intrusion Detection System (IDS);
2. Pretty Good Privacy (PGP);
3. SSH based on encrypting data before transmission;
4. Secure Socket Layer (SSL) based on encryption;
5. IP security (IPSec) using cryptographic techniques;
6. Remote Authentication Dial-in User Service (RADIUS);
7. Wired Equivalent Privacy (WEP).

12.30 Software-defined Networking (SDN)

SDN is a networking architecture that separates the network control from the forwarding functions. This facilitates the network control directly programmable and the underlying infrastructure to be abstracted for application and network services. The SDN is based on open flow protocol, which makes it extremely dynamic, manageable, cost-effective and adaptable to an architecture that provides network administrators whit high degree of programmability, automation and control. The open flow standard protocol advocated by the Open Networking Foundation (ONF) enables remote programming of the forwarding plane. The architecture of software-defined networking has been shown in Figure 12.59. It has been modelled as a set of client–server interactions with SDN controller at the core of the controller plane. The service client manages and controls network services through the SDN controller. Thus clients/applications interact directly with network control. Clients also send/receive data using network resources.

Network service provider maps client service intent onto resources which include forward processing and storage domains. The service provider recursively maps services and resources to scale to multiple administrative domains to take care of large-scale parallel processing algorithms associated with mega data sets known as 'Big data' across an entire computing pool. 'Orchestration' shown in the architecture is to orchestrate resources to meet client service needs.

The SDN architecture facilitates network control as directly programmable by decoupling it from forwarding functions. The other features are its agility to adjust network-wide traffic flow to changing needs, centralized control of network intelligence, automatic configuration and most important open-standard based, which make it independent of vendor specific devices and protocols.

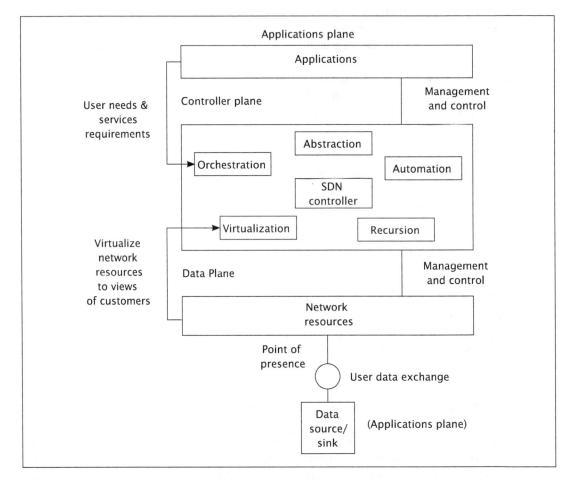

FIGURE 12.59 Architecture of Software-defined Networking

The purpose of SDN is to reduce cost and improve user experience by automating the full range of network services from end user to network elements.

CASE STUDY: SHI INTERNATIONAL IMPLEMENTS SOFTWARE-DEFINED NETWORKING FOR A GLOBAL PACKAGING COMPANY FOR IMPROVED PERFORMANCE, MANAGEABILITY AND SAVING IN NETWORKING COST

Customer Profile and the Background

A global leader in consumer packaging and dispensing systems employing more than 13,000 employees spread across 40 locations all over the world was experiencing frequent network delays in their main data centre, adversely affecting their manufacturing operations in various geographical locations. An inspection of its existing network equipment revealed that the data centre switches and network-interface hardware were very old and lacked flexibility and also not dynamic with respect to network traffic.

The packaging company decided to go for a replacement of its age-old Cisco Nexus 5,600 series infrastructure. The company needed a robust solution that could be managed easily and is financially feasible at the same time. They got an offer from a vendor, but the same was overpriced. The company thereafter approached Software House International (SHI) for feasible alternative solution for their primary data centre networking.

It is worth mentioning that SHI is a US$10 billion global provider of IT products and services. SHI offers custom IT solutions for its customers such as software and hardware procurement, deployment planning, configuration, data centre optimization, IT asset management and cloud computing.

Solution

During an initial 'whiteboard' session, SHI solution architects familiarized themselves with the offer on table and predicted the performance of the same in the customer's desired environment. Subsequently, SHI recommended several alternate Cisco solutions designed to improve the networking performance within the budgetary constraint of the company.

After evaluating the alternative solutions as recommended by SHI, both from technical and program angles, the packaging company decided to replace the existing Nexus 5600 series infrastructure with four 93180 and two 93108 Nexus switches. The company also purchased and installed Cisco's application centric infrastructure (ACI) which is a SDN and controls all other network devices from a single location. The company also purchased two Nexus 9K ACI spines and ACI mentored implementation services from SHI. The whole project took only 5 months.

Benefits and Results

The above-mentioned replacements and the new solution made it possible for the company's IT team to manage and monitor all the devices from one place. Further, with easy access, the server team could make changes and create configurations without engaging the networking team, thus reducing the number of touch points. The new solution also offered scalable growth options and the choice to utilize copper cable or fibre optic connections.

Finally, the network performance improved significantly and the packaging company saved 30% expenditure compared to the originally offered solution.

Review Questions

1. Draw the waveform diagram that results when the word 'CAB' is sent in ASCII across an RS–232 connection (use: 7-bit ASCII character code table from the Internet).

2. Suppose you want to send 5,000, 7-bit characters across an RS–232 connection. How much time does the transmission require?

3. What happens if an RS–232 transmitter and receiver are programmed to send and receive at different band rates?

4. If amplitude modulation with a sine wave operates at a frequency of 500 HZ, how many bits per second can be encoded and why?

5. FDM can improve throughput if it replaces a multiplexor with TDM. Do you agree? If so, why?

6. What is half- and full-duplex asynchronous communication?

7. What is the difference between a packet and a frame? What do you understand by the term 'packet switching'?

8. Suppose malfunctioning hardware in a character-oriented transmission system sets all bits transferred to zero. Does a parity bit catch the problem? Why or why not?

9. What is CRC? What are the hardware components required for CRC computation?

10. Classify the topology of computer networks in a particular site. What is CSMA/CD?

11. What data values in an Ethernet packet result in the maximum number of voltage transmissions when the packet is transmitted using Manchester encoding?

12. Illustrate the general frame format used with Ethernet.

13. What are the functions of repeaters, bridges, switches and routers?

14. Consider a packet sent across a bridged LAN to a non-existent address. How far will bridges forward the packet?

15. Can a bridge connect a Wi-Fi network to an Ethernet? Why or why not?

16. Explain the terms 'store and forward', 'next-hop forwarding and 'universal routing'.

17. What are 'ARPANET' and 'frame relay'?

18. What is a 'VPN'?

19. Explain the terms 'delay', 'throughput', 'bandwidth' and 'jitter' with respect to network performance.

20. State the names with brief explanation of the TCP/IP layers based on the following:

    i.   I am responsible for the routing of information and managing the logical addressing. What layer am I?
    ii. I am responsible for the initial request for network communication. What layer am I?
    iii. I am responsible for ensuring packets are assembled in the correct order and ensuring that the information has been delivered. What layer am I?

    iv. I am responsible for the physical addressing and conversion of packets to electrical signals. What layer am I?

    v. I am responsible for placing the electrical signals on wire. What layer am I?

    vi. I am responsible for establishing and managing the session. What layer am I?

21. Draw a TCP/IP Internet that consists of two networks connected by a router. Show a computer attached to each network. Show the protocol stack used on the computers and the stack used on the router.

22. What are the five classes of IP addresses in class-full scheme? Explain with examples 'dotted decimal notation'.

23. What are 'address masks'? What is the chief advantage of CIDR over the original class-full addressing scheme?

24. Explain why a router is assigned two or more IP addresses.

25. How does a computer know whether an arriving frame contains an IP datagram or an ARP message?

26. What is an IP datagram? What it its general form?

27. If a datagram contains one 8-bit option and one 8-bit data value, what values will be found in header fields HLEN and total length?

28. Why is fragmentation needed on an Internet but not on a typical WAN?

29. Why is encapsulation needed for transmitting a datagram?

30. What are 'MTU' and 'path MTU'?

31. Suppose a datagram passes through N routers on a trip across an Internet. How many times is the datagram encapsulated?

32. What are the features of IPV6 which are not there with IPV4?

33. How many octets does the smallest possible IPV6 datagram contain? The largest?

34. What do you understand by UDP? What is the size of the largest possible UDP message?

35. What is NAT? What is the difference between NAT and NAPT?

36. What is dynamic routing? Explain the terms 'EGP', 'IGP', 'BGP' 'RIP' and 'OSPF'.

37. What is 'concurrency' with reference to client-server paradigm?

38. What do you understand by 'socket API'?

39. Many companies prefer to use the organization structure for domain names instead of the geographical structure. What is the main advantage for the same?

40. What is DNS server hierarchy? Does limiting the number of levels in a DNS hierarchy result in faster name resolution? Explain you answer.

41. What is an email gateway? What is 'Post Office Protocol' (POP)?

42. Explain with suitable illustration the difference between active and passive mode of FTP.

43. What is DHCP? Explain.

44. What is the difference between a 'private key' and a 'public key'?

45. Explain the advantages of SDN. What is open flow protocol? Show the SDN architecture.

Bibliography

Comer, D. E. *Computer Network and Internet: With Internet Applications*, 4th ed. London: Pearson Education, 2004.

Gorranson, P., C. Black, and T. Culver. *Software Defined Networks: A Comprehensive Approach*, 2nd ed. Waltham, MA: Morgan Kaufmann, 2016.

Patil, S., and M. S. Subhedar. 'Analyzing MPLS Performance by SDN.' *Proc. of IEMIS* 3 (2018): 589–598.

Sybex. *Networking Complete*, 3rd ed. New Delhi: BPB Publications, 2002.

CHAPTER

Big Data Analytics and Cloud Computing

13.1 Introduction

D ata in an organization that cannot be processed using traditional data management techniques and technologies can be broadly categorized as 'Big data'. Big data are characterized by important dimensions known as the V's of 'Big data'. IBM data scientists defined four such dimensions as the four V's, namely volume, variety, velocity and veracity. **Volume** implies large scale of data generated worldwide every day expressed in zettabytes (1 zettabyte = 1 million petabytes and 1 petabyte = 10^{15} bytes). It is estimated that 2.3 trillion gigabytes ($2.3 \times 10^{12} \times 10^9 = 2.3 \times 10^{21}$ bytes) of data were created every day in 2016, and at this rate, by 2025 about 175 zettabytes of data will be created. **Variety** implies the different forms of data such as numbers, text, string, images and networked graph data generated through different sources such as social networks, stock exchange, logistics, health care, hospitality sector, security devices and sensors such as CCTV and surveillance cameras, weather and aviation data generated by radars, defence, infrastructure sectors, baking and insurance and many others. For example, during 2011, about 30 billion pieces of content were shared on Facebook every month. During 2014, about 400 million tweets were sent per day by about 200 million monthly active users, 4 billion hours of video were watched on YouTube every month and about 421 million wearable and wireless health monitors were in use. The traditional data or small data that were created in the past were structured data which could be stored in columns and rows as relational databases. However, big data generated by the organizations today are not only structured or semi-structured but also unstructured in nature because of the wide variety of the data. Big data, therefore, requires a different approach and techniques of storage and analysis. **Velocity** refers to huge rates of influx and analysis of data. For example, about 1 terabyte of trade information is generated by the New York Stock Exchange during each trading session. About 18.9 billion network connections globally in 2016 transmitted data at high speed. **Veracity** implies the uncertainty of the data because of inaccuracy and poor quality, which make them less credible. Therefore, organizations need to ensure that both the data and analysis are correct and trustworthy.

13.1.1 Three Additional V's

Apart from the four V's as described above, three additional V's, namely variability, visualization and value are worth mentioning as those are also important for organizations to consider while developing their big data strategy. Variability is not the same as variety. Variability can be explained with a simple example of a bread shop which sells breads of different brands. Variety, in this case, implies the different brands. However, if the taste of the bread of a particular brand differs every day, the same is due to variability of the same brand. The same concept is true for data; if the same data carry different meaning under different situations or contexts, it will have great impact on data homogenization. Variability of data is an important factor to be considered in sentiment analysis. In order to perform such analysis properly, algorithms need to be developed to understand the context and accordingly decipher the exact meaning of data (words) in that context, which is a complex task. Data visualization is very important to facilitate proper decision-making. For example, using graphical representation of large amount of complex data is much more effective in conveying the meaning of the data than spreadsheets and allied reports full of numeric figures and formulae. Huge amount of raw data remains useless without proper comprehension.

13.1.2 Value

Big data, if analysed properly and utilized, facilitate creation of value for organizations, the society at large and the consumers. Of course, data in itself are not valuable at all. Proper analysis of the data and transformation of the data into information and knowledge to turn organizations into information-centric companies create value for those companies. According to McKinsey, the potential value of big data to US healthcare industry is about US$300 billion annually, which is a lot of value.

Besides the volume, variety, velocity, veracity, variability, visualization and value, there are a number of practical issues that can make things more complex with big data than with small data. Let us elaborate on those issues. The first is the goal. Unlike small data, which are gathered for a specific goal, big data may serve multiple goals such as providing valuable information for use of consumers, predictive marketing strategy and fraud detection. Second, the location of the data is usually a single one, usually a single computer file for small data. However, for big data, it may be distributed in multiple files on different computers located in various geographic locations. Third, data preparation and analysis for small data are done by the end users for their own purposes, but with big data, the same is often prepared by one group, analysed by a second group for ultimate use by a third group. Fourth difference is in the retention period or longevity of the data. Small data is preserved for a small- and specific-time duration, whereas big data, as it is associated with high cost of storage and analysis and often get converted into other form of data, have to be retained for a very long time. Fifth difference is in the measurement protocols. Small data are usually measured with a single set of units under a single protocol, whereas big data being located in different locations involving different computers, organizations and people are measured often using different protocols. Sixth difference is in reproducibility. Small data can be reproduced in their entirety, if something gets wrong with it. Big data being stored in different computers located at different places may not be reproduced totally if some problem crops up with the data. Seventh difference is in the stakes. In case of small data, the cost of corruption or loss is limited, but in case of big data such loss of data can cost enormous amount of time and money. Finally, the analysis of small data is usually done in a single procedure from a single computer file. However, with big data, because data are so enormous and spread across different files and servers, analysis is carried out using multiple procedures such as extraction, reduction, normalization, transformation and other steps. Moreover, big data analysis deals with part of the data at a time to make it more manageable and then summarizes the results.

We can summarize the major differentiators of big data as follows:

- No *finite* structure.
- High *volume.*
- *Ambiguous* in metadata. Metadata is data about the nature, location, time stamp of actual data.
- *Loosely* connected in structure.
- If data are linguistic oriented, processing will be heavily *contextual.*
- If data are numeric oriented, processing needs more granular data.
- *Number crunching.*
- If semi-structured data, it needs more expansion and can have a *mixed workload.*

13.1.3 Various Sources of Big Data

The sources of big data can broadly be divided into two categories: one is generated by human beings and the other generated by machines including mobile apps and sensors.

Big data generated by human source can be again classified into the following groups:

1. **Social media:** Twitter, LinkedIn, Facebook, Blog, SlideShare, YouTube, Google+, Instagram, Pinterest, Vimeo, WordPress, Chatter and many such sources of data.
2. **Public web services:** Government, weather, traffic, regulatory compliance, health care, economic, census, public finance, stock market, World Bank, Reserve Bank of India, other nationalized banks, Wikipedia and similar web services.
3. **Business operations and functions:** Project management, marketing functions, logistics and supply chains, production and productivity, CRM, ERP systems, human resources, human skill management, financial management, Google documents, intranets, web portals and so on.
4. **Documents and files:** Excel spreadsheet (XLS), portable document format (PDF), comma-separated values (CSV), email, Word, PPT, hypertext markup language (HTML), plain text, XML and JSON (XML and JSON stand for extensible markup language and JavaScript object notation respectively). XML and JSON represent mainly semi-structured data as explained in a subsequent paragraph.
5. **Media:** Images, videos, audio, flash, live streams and so on.
6. **Database and data storages:** SQL, NoSQL, Hadoop Distributed File System (HDFS), document repository, various other file systems.
7. **Archives:** Archives of scanned documents, newspapers, rare collection of literary works, trade and industry journals, bulletins, medical records, contracts, customer correspondences, feedback forms and such other archives.

Machine- and sensor-generated big data are as follows:

1. **Machine log data:** Event logs, server logs, application logs, business process logs, audit trails, call records, mobile location and app usage data, click stream data, data generated by IOT and

machine to machine data generated by a machine for communicating with another machine. The concept of IOT has been explained in a subsequent paragraph of this chapter.

2. **Sensor data:** Medical devices such as electrocardiogram data, smart utility metre readings, car sensor data, surveillance camera images, satellite data, traffic recording device data, weather radar data, video device images, household appliances data, radio frequency identification device (RFID) data, assembly lines, smart buildings, cell towers, jet engines, thermostats and cut-off relays for refrigerators and air conditioners, and proximity devices for entry and exit control.

The above lists are only illustrative and not exhaustive. However, those only show the broad categories of big data sources.

13.2 Structure of Big Data

Big data can be structured, unstructured or semi-structured. Data are said to be structured when those are placed in a file with fixed fields of variables. A simple example of structured data is the spreadsheet, where every column is a variable and every row is a particular case or observation. Large amount of structured data are stored in rows and columns as relational databases. For example, Table 13.1 is a structured data table having two columns indicating different games in the first column and the team names associated with the games in the second column. Each team will have one row.

However, if we write the above data in a different way as a natural language (text), the same become: two football teams are 'East Bengal' and 'Mohun Bagan' and two Indian Premier League (IPL) teams are 'Mumbai Indians' and 'Kolkata Knight Riders'.

While the above data are very easy to be understood by a person knowing English, it is much more difficult for a machine to understand the same. This is because the above data cannot be easily sorted, rearranged or appended to other data and also to count the number of teams is not easy and hence is unstructured in nature. We have to adopt techniques of text mining or semantic analysis (as explained later) to analyse such type of unstructured data. Incidentally, it may be stated that majority of big data relating to business environment are unstructured data in the form of text, images, presentations and so on. A third type of data is semi-structured data, which are not in fixed fields such as the rows and columns of a spreadsheet, but the fields and the data thereof are identifiable. Two very common formats

TABLE 13.1 Illustration of Structured Data Table

Games	Teams
Football	East Bengal
Football	Mohun Bagan
Cricket	Mumbai Indians
Cricket	Kolkata Knight Riders

for semi-structured data are XML and the JSON. The same game data as above can be represented in the XML format as follows:

```
<games>
<football>
<team>East Bengal</team>
<team>Mohun Bagan</team>
</football>
<cricket>
<team>Mumbai Indians</team>
<team>Kolkata Knight Riders</team>
</cricket>
</games>
```

The above XML format is good for nested data or hierarchical structures, though it is a little wordy. A more recent format is JSON which is similar to XML but there is not much text and the brackets will be there as curly brackets. The above game data expressed in JSON will be as follows:

```
{
  "games": {
    "football": {
      "team": {
        "East Bengal",
        "Mohun Bagan",
      }
    },
    "cricket": {
      "team": {
        "Mumbai Indians",
         "Kolkata Knight Riders"
      }
    }
  }
}
```

13.3 Big Data Applications

The major applications of big data can be broadly grouped as consumer applications, business applications, research applications and IOT applications. Consumers use big data for a variety of applications. The first one is that through an Apple iPhone or iPad and using Siri (a computer program which acts as an intelligent personal assistant and knowledge navigator) for big data analysis, consumers can find out the available sources of goods or services they want to avail. For example, one can search for restaurants of a particular type such as Thai, Mexican or Chinese in one's convenient location and also get a recommendation for the same based on a lot many reviews from those who had been to those restaurants earlier. Also, recommendation engines are capable of making specific suggestions based on big data analysis techniques such as data mining or text analytics. For example, when we search for a book a particular subject or title, Amazon.com makes recommendations for the books of our requirement. Another important consumer application for big data is through the use of photos taken by powerful cameras, Google maps, satellites and so on and analysis of the generated big data. Valuable information can be provided thereby regarding traffic condition or weather forecast to the interested persons.

Big data have revolutionized the business world by changing the way people do commerce. There are a number of applications of big data in business. The first application is pertaining to the search for anything of interest through search engines such as Google. Besides getting the search result, people also get through big data analysis a number of advertisements based on what a person searches but also suiting his/her likes or dislikes as known to the search engines during all previous searches. Google or any other search engine analyses all the things that the user searched for on all earlier occasions along with any other pertinent information about the users available with Google and attempts to place advertisements that the users will most likely select. The next important area of business application is what is known as predictive marketing. Predictive marketing means making decisions by predicting which marketing actions are more likely to succeed and which are more likely to fail. It has profound implication throughout the marketing process.

Big data are used to identify the target consumers while launching new products or services. This is based on a study of major life events. Major life events such as getting a good job, marriage or childbirth are associated with a whole series of commercial transactions. Similarly, companies going for predictive marketing look at consumer behaviour. Consumer behaviour study is linked with customer sentiment analysis which is a popular technique of big data analytics. Just to illustrate sentiment analysis, the following statements representing customer sentiments for particular types of health drinks, such as 'Horlicks' and 'Frooti' are reproduced below:

'I personally like the **taste** of Horlicks and while the **price** is much higher than I would like to pay, I would pick up Horlicks at Frank Ross in the **evening**.'

'I occasionally pick up a **Frooti Juice** in the **morning** but this is a little **cheaper** and packs more **calories** and gives **nutrition**.'

'Of course at ₹10 a pack, I will stick to my Sumit Power Juicer and make my own.'

The sentiment analysis based on the above statements yields the following:
A number of technologies for semantic analysis of textual contents include:

- Clustering algorithms for obtaining semantic word cluster.
- Algorithms for extracting salient phrases and ranking them using context.

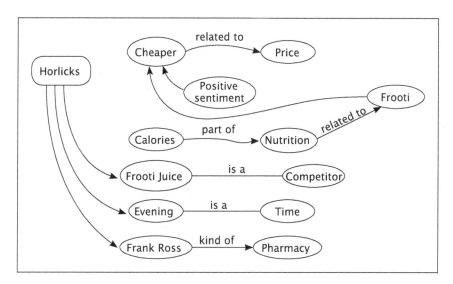

- Random tree algorithms.
- Bayesian models and associated algorithms.

A study of consumer behaviour also calls for consumer habits such as how often one logs into different websites and looks for particular items. A lot many data regarding consumer habits can be made available through websites browsing history.

Similarly, demographic information such as age, marital status, family size, salary, home address and the credit cards one holds are of importance for predictive marketing. Another important use of big data relating to business and commerce is in the area of trend prediction. For example, big data analysis has its use to predict fashion trends. It means telling retailers in advance what the most popular colours, styles and brands are going to be and when those are going to be popular. Obviously, such kind of information relating to future trend of different products will be of paramount importance to the companies who will be selling those products in future. A very important use of big data in commerce is for fraud detection. Fraud detection has become a major issue in case of online business transactions. The gravity of this issue can be visualized by the fact that in the USA alone online retailers lose about US$3.5 billion every year due to online fraud. Fraud detection is based on analysis of data concerning point of sale (POS), the website being used for online transactions, physical location of the persons making online transactions, the IP addresses of the computers, log in time of usual transactions for a particular computer and a lot of many other data. Biometric data also help detection of fraud. For example, the way people move their mouse, the response time to online queries or the time between two successive pressing of keys on the computer keyboard are distinctive measures of individuals. All these data comprise big data sets which enable analysts to determine whether the genuine persons are making online transactions and which in turn facilitate detection of anomalies leading to potential frauds.

Finally, big data facilitate risk management. Technologies relating to big data can help risk managers gain more accurate risk intelligence, drawn from a variety of data sources for structured as well as unstructured data in almost real time. It can improve the predictive capability of various risk models involving credit risk, money laundering risk, market risk, operational risk, compliance risk and churn analysis.

Credit risk models derive better predictive power by the real-time big data drawn from data lakes of new data sources such as social media and marketing databases. Financial institutions have thorough knowledge of their clients and can harness big data to develop more robust predictive indicators (such as credit score) in the credit risk domain. Besides traditional data such as income, profession, property details of the customers, big data sources can reveal vital information such as a costly divorce, an expensive purchase or a gambling habit for any customer, which will go a long way towards credit risk prediction. Credit firms can take full advantage of big data technologies to detect early warning signals by observing customer behaviour on real time and act in time.

So far money laundering risk is concerned, big data can provide real-time actionable insights to risk managers. The recent money laundering scandals of some non-banking financial institutions and terrorist financing have prompted banks, financial and credit guarantee institutions to look for innovative ways to address the limitations of the traditional approaches to anti-money laundering. Traditional approaches are again based on structured data, and the analysis thereof is rule based. Obviously, such approaches suffer limitations of laborious manual searches of keywords through the reports. For example, a financial institution in its payment advice specifies State Bank of India (SBI) only. SBI branch can be at New Delhi, Kolkata or Chennai. So operational staff responsible for anti-money laundering to whom the transactions were routed have to manually review the transactions for the particular branch of SBI which is a time-consuming and error-prone task. Big data analytics, however, allow both advanced statistical analysis of structured data and statistical analysis such as 'text mining' ('text mining' has been explained in a subsequent paragraph) of unstructured data to facilitate proper visualization of hidden links between transactions and accounts leading to detection of suspicious transaction patterns. Advanced analytics can generate real-time actionable insights preventing potential money laundering and at the same time allowing fund transfers for genuine cases.

In case of market risks involving market price/volatility, new client trades and counter-party credit risk management, volume and velocity of data are the prime factors. Counter-party credit risk assessment has now become more complex and involves: (a) debt valuation adjustments (DVA), (b) credit valuation adjustments (CVA) and (c) funding valuation adjustments (FVA), all in sets with different pricing data for getting 'risk neutral' CVA. The above exercise needs to be repeated at different frequencies for reporting monthly, weekly or daily. The calculation involved for finding the above risk components is highly data-intensive, and processing has to be done speedily. For example, to fully simulate all the potential scenarios of all path-dependent derivatives as structured portfolios, banks need to run about 1 lakh Monte Carlo scenarios. Traditional data analysis techniques are not capable of processing such high volume of data at high speed. Big data analytics technologies such as Hadoop and its ecosystems (described in subsequent paragraphs of this chapter) can provide enormous help in this type of increasingly data-heavy market risk assessment by bringing out accurate and incremental 'what-if' statistics. In other words, banks with increased Monte Carlo abilities will be able to price 'path dependent' derivatives at better levels than their competitors.

According to Andy Smith–Managing Director, operational risk management–Bank of New York Mellon,

In operational risk the power of big data lies in the ability to integrate vast information from legacy platforms into a single highly flexible solution. For example, we can leverage big data solutions to gain superior insights for access control management across the various platforms in which our clients interact with us, helping us to ensure the safety, security and confidentiality of client transactions at all times.

13.3.1 Compliance Risk

Compliance risk is the threat posed to an organization's financial, organizational or reputational standing resulting from violations of laws, regulations, codes of conduct or organizational standards of practice. Big data analysis enables continuous compliance risk assessment and automated operational risk management that can be used by various stakeholders including senior management, audit and risk committees and even external regulatory and audit organizations.

13.3.2 Churn Analysis

Churn analysis is another analytic application, also called churn prediction. Churn means a customer who discontinues getting service from any service provider or products from any company or who switches from one company to another company for any service or product. Churn analysis aims at retaining existing customers and keeps them satisfied instead of inducting new customers into the customer base of a company or service provider such as the telecom companies. The reason behind the same is that inducting new customers costs high specially in saturated markets, whereas retaining existing customers results in lower cost and also augments loyalty benefits. Therefore, companies should make dedicated efforts to retain their existing customers. Churn analysis helps identifying the determinants of churn so that improvement can be made in those areas to retain customers. The analysis is based on big data mining to arrive at a good churn prediction model. The objectives of the model are to correlate churn and customer attributes, predict future churn based on past churn and target a retention campaign towards high risk customers who are most likely to churn or leave. Churn prediction models are based on logistic regression, decision trees, support vector machines, neural networks, survival (time-to-churn) analysis and relational classifiers (customer social network analysis). Social network analysis also often leads to additional customer attributes, which are relevant for the analysis. Churn analysis input data source may be more than one. For example, to understand the churn behaviour of customers of a mobile telephone operator, the input data are collected from the following data tables.

1. Customer table, which contains basic customer information such as customer identification (say, mobile number, customer account number), address, age, gender, education and monthly income.
2. CDR table contains details of all call data records in transactional form. Each record provides the duration of specific type of calls such as local, STD and international calls on a daily basis aggregated over a month.
3. Billing data table which contains monthly usage, monthly billing, average billing, payment, number of delayed payments, mode of payment of bills and so on. Customer service data table, which contains basic information concerning service subscribed by the customer such as handset model/class, length of service in months, tariff plan and type, number of complaints in the past made to customer care executives and the churn state (active or deactive). Apart from the above sources of data, social networks also form a vital input data source for churn analysis. The churn prediction process can be described by a flow diagram depicting the steps as shown in Figure 13.1.

IOT is a very recent development for connecting various objects through the Internet. It makes great use of big data analysis of the data generated by sensors or machines. It has been described in subsequent paragraphs of this chapter.

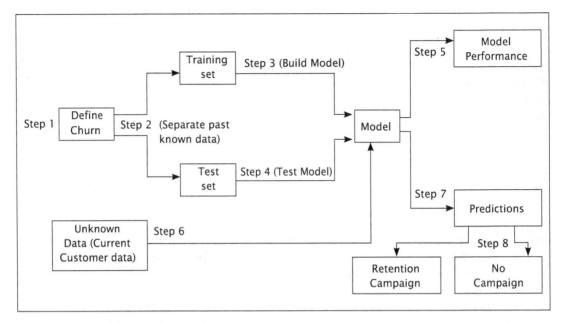

FIGURE 13.1 Churn-prediction Process

13.4 Data Mining

Big data analysis involves a popular technique known as 'data mining'. The technique facilitates the process of extraction of knowledge from huge amount of data stored in databases. Knowledge extraction or discovery process is also known as 'KDD' (Knowledge Discovery in Databases) process. Data mining is one of the steps in the same (KDD) process and can be compared with gold mining from rock or sand. The knowledge discovery process involves data cleaning, data integration, data selection, data transformation, data mining, pattern generation, pattern evaluation/presentation and finally knowledge discovery as 'knowledge nuggets' such as the gold nuggets produced out of rock and sand. The KDD process along with the sequence of the above-mentioned steps has been shown in Figure 13.2.

Data cleaning refers to removal of noise, inconsistent or irrelevant data to achieve data quality. Next step is integration of data from multiple sources both formal and informal. Careful integration of data avoids redundancies and thus enhances the speed of data mining. Data selection picks data which are relevant for analysis.

Data transformation converts the selected data in a format to suit the analysis and to speed up data mining process. For example, daily sales figures may be aggregated to generate month-wise sales figures or item-wise total monthly sales figures. Data mining refers to application of various algorithms to generate data patterns. It adopts various techniques such as association rule, clustering and classification of data. It generates interesting data patterns which are evaluated to obtain the useful patterns and present the same to users to get some inference on the data.

The last step is the knowledge discovery, which presents the knowledge to the users. The three important techniques of data mining have been described as follows with suitable examples.

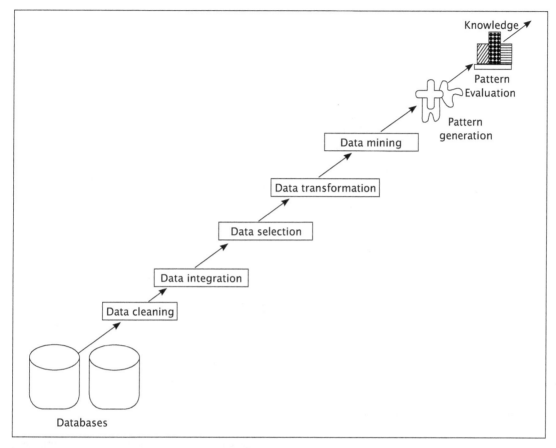

FIGURE 13.2 Knowledge Discovery in Databases

13.4.1 Association Rule of Data Mining

Association rule of data mining is a method of finding useful relations or associations among the variables in a large database. Association rules help prediction of customer behaviour while marketing various products.

Example 1: Bread $\Rightarrow$ jelly,
which means that when a customer buys bread from a shop, he/she is quite likely to buy jelly also. Hence, the sale of bread is associated with sale of jelly also.

Example 2: Buys (salt, chilli powder) $\Rightarrow$ buys (pepper), which means a customer buying salt and chilli powder is also very likely to purchase pepper also.

Association rules are expressed in the form of if-then statements and are useful in case of market-based analysis for product marketing and pricing. Two parameters are associated with association rules known as 'support' and 'confidence'. Support is a measure of the probability of buying both bread and jelly by a customer in case of Example 1 above, whereas confidence is a measure of the probability that a transaction involving bread also contains jelly. Here, bread is an antecedent and jelly is consequence. Suppose in the case of Example 1, the support is 60% and confidence is 80%, the association rule can be expressed as bread $\Rightarrow$ jelly (60%, 80%) and which is a knowledge discovered by data mining. Let me illustrate how to calculate support and confidence with an example involving 5 items in 10 transactions as shown below:

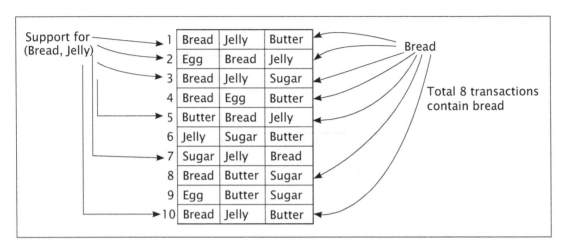

In the case of above 10 transactions involving 10 customers:

Support for (Bread, Jelly) = 6/10 = 0.6, that is, 60%

Confidence for Bread $\Rightarrow$ Jelly = 6/8 = 0.75, that is, 75%

Out of eight transactions with bread as one of the items; six times, bread was purchased with jelly. Therefore, we can say with 75% confidence that if a customer buys bread, he/she will also buy jelly. Association rule mining makes use of a very important algorithm known as the 'Apriori' algorithm to find frequent item sets. The 'Apriori' algorithm can be stated as follows:

'For a given minimum support S as the interesting criterion, all item sets of interest having i elements are a subset of all item sets of interest having $(i + 1)$ elements', which means that to find the interesting association of i items having required minimum support, we have not to search all the associations of all items, but only to search the interesting association of $(i - 1)$ items having support of the required minimum and to join $(i - 1)$ item sets within itself and then prune the subsets of i item sets, which are not of interest (do not have the minimum support). Let me explain the Apriori algorithm with the previous example of 5 items (bread, jelly, butter, egg and sugar) with 10 customer transactions of buying.

Let the minimum support be 0.3, that is, 3 out of 10.

1. **Interesting (1-element) item sets:** That is, one item set with three or more transactions are (bread), (butter), (jelly), (egg), (sugar)
2. **Interesting (2-element) item sets:** That is two item sets with three or more transactions.
   (bread, butter), (bread, jelly), (bread, egg)
   (bread, sugar), (butter, jelly), (butter, egg)
   (butter, sugar), (jelly, egg), (jelly, sugar)

3. **Interesting (3-element) item sets:** We have to search from 3-element possible combinations out of 2-element sets. There is only one set of three items having the required minimum support. (Bread, butter, jelly). Furthermore, the subsets of (bread, butter, jelly), that is, (bread, butter), (bread, jelly) and (butter, jelly) are all having the minimum support of 0.3.

The above shows that in order to find the interesting set with a particular number of items, we do not have to search the entire data sets but only to search the previous iteration of interesting sets with one less number of items.

13.4.2 Data Classification

Data classification is another important technique of data mining. Classification consists of predicting outcome based on certain input parameters. It follows a systematic approach and uses a number of algorithms such as decision tree, random forest, rule-based induction, neural networks and Bayesian network.

The application of classification technique in data mining finds use in fraud detection, credit risk assessment, weather prediction and many other big data applications. The classification process consists of a learning phase based on training data followed by the classification model development phase with the help of classification algorithms such as decision tree to predict unknown values. Let me illustrate data classification process with a simple example as shown in Figure 13.3.

13.4.2.1 Clustering

Clustering in data mining is the grouping of objects based on similarity of their characteristics. Cluster analysis is one of the main and most important tasks of data mining process. Clustering can be performed using various methods based on algorithms. Clustering methods basically partition the data based on similarity into clusters such that there exists similarity among the data points within a cluster, but no similarity exists between the data points of two different clusters. For example, if we collect the data relating to monthly income and expenditure of people of a locality and cluster the data into three different clusters, the clusters may be represented as shown in Figure 13.4.

Clustering of data has important applications in various fields such as:

- Market research, market segmentation and target market
- Pattern recognition
- Image processing
- Social network analysis
- The World Wide Web and search engines
- Genetics

For example, if we search the web through Google search engine to find books on 'Environmental ecology', it will retrieve the cluster of all relevant books belonging to the Environmental ecology subject. Similarly, in case of social network analysis, clustering helps finding communities among a large number of people. In case of marketing, clustering helps marketing managers of companies in fast-moving consumer goods to cluster the customers according to their income and apply different pricing policy for customers belonging to different income groups and who buy the company products.

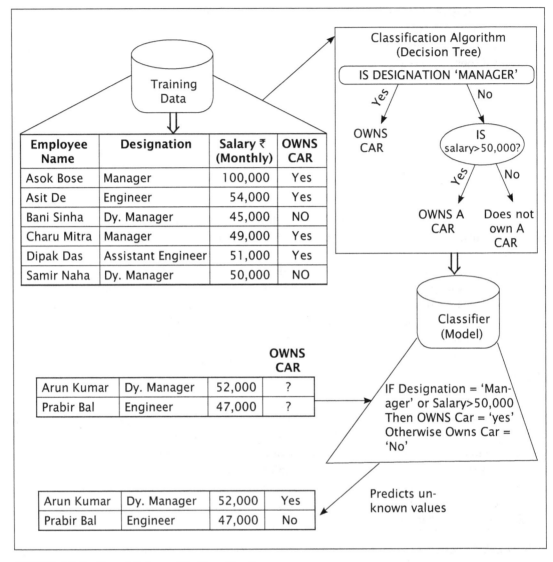

FIGURE 13.3 Data Mining with Classification

Clustering in data mining of big data has its distinctive advantages such as:

1. **High scalability:** Clustering algorithms are capable of handling large amount of data.
2. **High dimensionality:** Clustering algorithms can handle multidimensional data. For example, it can cluster consumers based on income, expenditure, credit ranking and many similar dimensions.
3. **Comprehensibility:** The results of clustering can be easily interpreted, understood and used in practice.
4. **Interoperability:** Clustering algorithms are simple and can be operated on databases stored in different platforms.

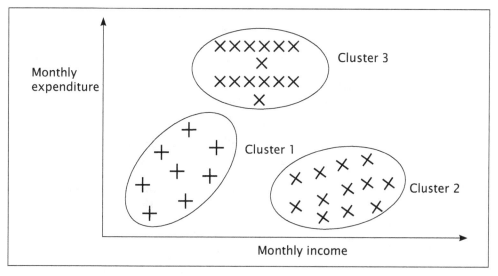

FIGURE 13.4 Representation of Clusters

Clustering adopts various approaches such as partitioning, model, hierarchy, density and constraint-based approaches.

There are a number of clustering algorithms such as:

1. K-means
2. Fuzzy C-means
3. Hierarchical clustering
4. Mixture of Gaussian

The most popular and widely applied clustering algorithm is the K-means clustering. K stands for the number of clusters, and the K clusters are based on least aggregate distance of the data points of clusters from the mean or centroid of the same cluster.

Let us illustrate the K-means clustering algorithm with an example of one-dimensional data say the annual income of few people in lakhs of ₹ as follows:

$$3 \quad 5 \quad 7 \quad 8 \quad 11 \quad 12 \quad 15 \quad 18 \quad 29 \quad 32$$

Let us take K = 3 (3 clusters), that is, let us group the above data into 3 clusters.

Step 1: Select cluster centres (three) from the above data points such that the centres are farthest apart from each other.

③	5	7	8	11	⑫	15	18	29	㉜
C1					C2				C3

Step 2: Now check all other data points as regards to their nearness to the cluster centres C1, C2 and C3 and assign the label of any centre which is nearest. The result will be as follows:

③	5	7	8	11	⑫	15	18	29	㉜
C1	C1	C1	C2	C2	C2	C2	C2	C3	C3

Step 3: Recalculate the cluster centres by finding the mean of the data points belonging to the same cluster formed with data points labelled as in Step 2.

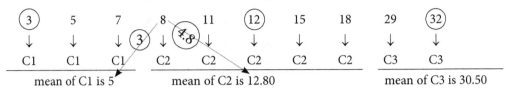

| mean of C1 is 5 | | | mean of C2 is 12.80 | | | | | mean of C3 is 30.50 | |

Step 4: Now repeat Steps 2 and 3 till convergence is reached when data points do not move between clusters and cluster centres stabilize and do not shift. The iteration is as follows:

3	5	7	8		11	12	15	18		29	32
↓	↓	↓	↓		↓	↓	↓	↓		↓	↓
C1	C1	C1	C2		C2	C2	C2	C2		C3	C3

| mean = 5.75 | | | | mean = 14 | | | | mean = 30.5 | |

The result finally has been obtained as above and all the data points within a cluster are near to the cluster centre than the cluster centres of the other clusters. Hence, the algorithm K mean clustering has formed the three clusters of follows:

3 5 7 8	11 12 15 18	29 32
Cluster 1	Cluster 2	Cluster 3

It may be noted that the K-means clustering as illustrated above is suitable for data mining of numeric data and not suitable for text data mining. Text mining also known as 'text analytics' is typically achieved through the devising of patterns and trends of association and frequency of occurrences through techniques of statistical pattern learning. However, in almost all text mining applications, we need to assess the quality of text retrieval which is denoted by the relevance of such retrieval of text data or generation of patterns on the basis of usefulness of the patterns to the users. Usually, there are three primary metrics for assessing quality of text data mining. They are (a) precision (b) recall and (c) F-score.

Precision is denoted by the fraction of retrieved text data that is relevant to the user. Recall is the fraction of text data that are relevant to the user and is actually retrieved. The above measures can be expressed as follows:

```
Precision = [{Relevant} n {Retrieved}]/[{Retrieved}]
Recall = [{Relevant}n{Retrieved}]/[{Relevant}]
```

F-score is a measure of trade-off between precision or otherwise and is defined as the harmonic mean of recall or precision and expressed as follows:

```
F-score = (recall × precision)/(recall + precision)/2
```

The above measures can be visualized by a diagram as shown in Figure 13.5.

Text mining can help an organization derive potentially valuable business insights from text documents such as word documents, emails and postings on social media streams such as Facebook,

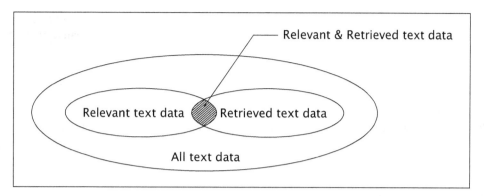

FIGURE 13.5 Measures of Quality of Text Data Mining

Twitter and LinkedIn. Text data mining is often challenging as because natural language text is often ambiguous due to inconsistent syntax or semantics. Text analytics software, however, can help by transposing words or phrases in unstructured data into numerical values, which can then be linked with structured data in a database so that traditional data mining techniques can be applied.

Example of R-codes for clustering of cricket players of IPL:

R-codes for cluster analysis of cricket players of the Indian Premier League (IPL):

The following is the R-script for cluster analysis which was done for 22 players based on 13 parameters of past performance in various matches. The parameters are like number of wickets taken, maiden overs bowled, number of matches played, number of boundaries, over boundaries, ducks and many more. The purpose of the script is to form a dendrogram which is a diagrammatic representation of the clusters. Four clusters were formed and the cluster having the maximum values of the descriptive statistics was considered as the best cluster consisting of efficient players.

```
ipl <-read.csv("D:\\BISWAS 19.03.17\\E Drive Backup\\R\\R CSV\\
Cluster_ipl.csv",header = T)
view(ipl)
iplstandard<-scale(ipl[,2:14])
```

Remarks: The first code imports the IPL file. Next, we are viewing the file with 22 players and their 13 performance parameters from column 2 to 14. The first column contains the names of the players:

```
distmat<-dist(x=iplstandard,method = 'euclidean')
```

Remarks: The above code finds the Euclidean distance:

```
summary(distmat)
```

Remarks: The descriptive statistics of the calculated Euclidean distance are found out:

```
Cluster_result<-hclust(d=distmat^2,method ="ward.D")
```

Remarks: The above code finds the Euclidean distance and squaring the same to avoid negative values and storing the same in cluster_result. Here, we are using the Ward's minimum variance method:

```
plot.new()
plot(cluster_result)
```

Remarks: First, we are creating the new plotting window and in the next line of code plotting cluster_ result. This is the diagrammatic representation of clusters known as dendrogram and the same shows the cluster information.

```
View(iplstandard)
clus1<-ipl[clusterNum==1,]
clus2<-ipl[clusterNum==2,]
clus3<-ipl[clusterNum==3,]
clus4<-ipl[clusterNum==4,]
```

The above codes are forming subsets. When clusterNum=1, the data will be stored in clus1 and so on for the other 3 clusters:

```
summary(clus1)
summary(clus2)
summary(clus3)
summary(clus4)
```

Remarks: The above codes calculate the descriptive statistics of each cluster. The values of the descriptive statistics were found to be maximum for Cluster 4 in the above case:

```
View(clus4)
```

Remarks: We are viewing the best or most efficient cluster 4 consisting of efficient players of IPL.

13.5 Machine learning

In Chapter 5, we have seen the various methods through which machines learn such as supervised, unsupervised, reinforced learning, analytic learning and also deep learning. Let us elaborate a little more on machine learning in the following paragraphs in the context of data mining.

Human beings learn by experience; machines also learn through data. According to Ron Bekkerman, 'Machine learning develops algorithms for making predictions from data.' In that sense machine learning is quite similar to data mining because data mining also uses techniques to generate patterns and make predictions of values of unknown data. However, data mining generates data sets as patterns which give rise to knowledge, whereas machine learning also uses training data and test data for a particular purpose or task and accordingly makes a classifier model to derive a data set B similar in properties to the original data set A. In fact, machine learning applies statistical methods to real-world tasks and thereby predicts outcomes related to the tasks.

Data for the sake of machine learning consist of data instances (similar to the rows of a relational database), and the data instances are represented as feature vectors (similar to the data attributes or columns of a relational database). Features are chosen in machine learning based on the specific tasks. For example, if the task is to select basketball players, the features such as height and weight are relevant, whereas if the task is to select candidates who can teach machine learning such features are of no use. Hence, feature vectors of data instances for machine learning are task-specific.

Machine learning is all about making sense of existing data and then making predictions about new data instances. For example, if we group people according to their annual income into high-, medium- and low-income groups, then if a person with a particular income becomes a new data instance then we can say 'this person belongs to high income group', if his income is matching with income of our existing classification for the high-income group.

Machine-learning process can be either supervised or unsupervised. Supervised learning takes place when there is pre-defined knowledge about the data items as to their structure or the target associated with each input data, whereas unsupervised learning takes place when the structure of the data is not known and the learning process tries to find the similarities of the data items based on certain distinctive features. For example, clustering is a process of unsupervised learning since the grouping of items or objects is done based on certain features or attributes such as colour, shape or size. Classification is, however, a supervised-learning process since the classification of data items or objects is made based on predefined knowledge and training about the rules of classification. Both the above types of learning have been illustrated with some practical examples.

Example 1: A basket of fruits and vegetables can be left with a child. The child can segregate the items in the baskets in the following ways depending on whether the child has been taught (supervised learning) what are vegetables and fruits or not taught (unsupervised learning)

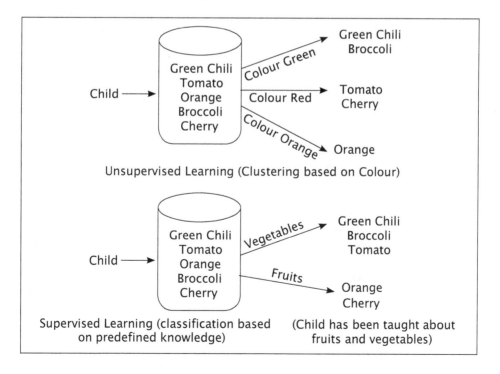

Example 2: Arrival time of flights in a particular airport depending upon weather conditions.

The historical data regarding arrival of flights on time, ahead of time or late and the corresponding weather conditions can be our training data sets for supervised learning based on which we can predict arrival time of flights given a particular weather condition. However, in case of unsupervised learning, we can only group the flights depending upon arrival pattern and cannot make any prediction. This is explained as follows:

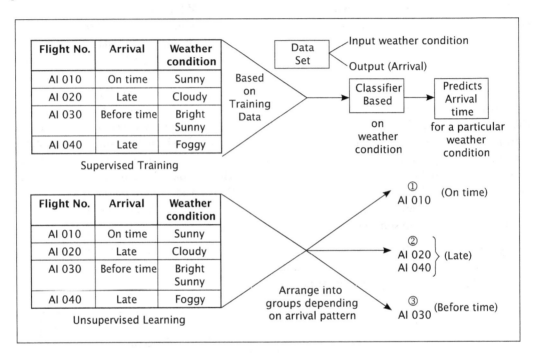

Machine-learning tasks use techniques of data mining, namely classification and clustering heavily and also association. However, machine learning also uses both linear and logistic data regression. Some interesting machine learning examples are the classification of incoming emails into spam and non-spam groups based on some classifier algorithm and handwritten numbers recognition based on classifier features. Figure 13.6 illustrates the machine learning process for handwriting recognition using classifier features and a decision tree.

Out of the techniques adopted by machine-learning tasks, classification, clustering and association of data have been explained in earlier paragraphs on data mining. The remaining technique of data regression which is also widely used by machine-learning tasks can be either linear or logistic regression.

Regression is basically a relation of the value of one variable (output) which is called the dependent variable with the corresponding values of one or more independent variables. For example, there may be a relation between the university grade point average (GPA) of a person with his/her school GPA. Here, university GPA is the dependent variable and depends on the school GPA which is the independent variable. In case of linear regression, the relationship can be expressed as a linear equation of the form:

$$Y = \beta_0 + \beta_1 \times X$$

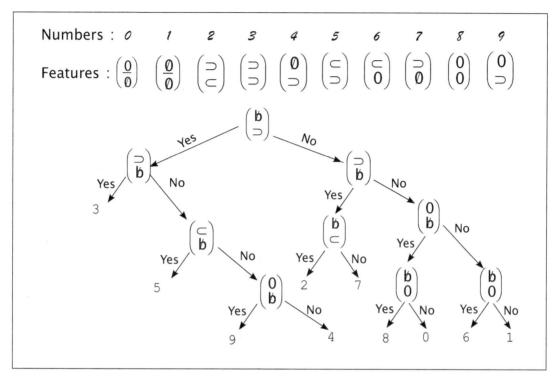

FIGURE 13.6 Illustration of Handwritten Number Recognition

where Y is the dependent variable and X is the independent variable. In this case, the output or dependent variable (say Y) can be a continuous variable, that is, it can have many numbers of possible values such as age, income, height expressed as numerical values. Linear regression consists of finding the best fitting straight line through the actual data points.

In case of logistic regression, however, the output or dependent variable is a categorical variable such as gender (male or female), city or 'Yes or No', which has a finite number of values (usually binary) or outcomes. Just to illustrate binary outcomes, the following are the examples:

- Is a bank transaction fraudulent?
- Is a customer likely to buy a new product?
- Is a tumour benign or malignant?

The outcome can be either 0 or 1, 0 if 'No' and 1 if 'Yes'. Here, the outcome is represented by a dummy (zero-one) variable. Figure 13.7 shows a linear regression model and a logistic regression model with Y, the dependent variable and X, the independent variable.

Now, if we convert the binary outcome of a logistic regression model into a probability, we can get a continuous value of p (Y), where p (Y) is the probability of the outcome of the binary variable Y and the value of p (Y) can be represented as 0 < p (Y) < 1. Hence, the logistic regression model of Figure 13.7 can be represented as shown in Figure 13.8.

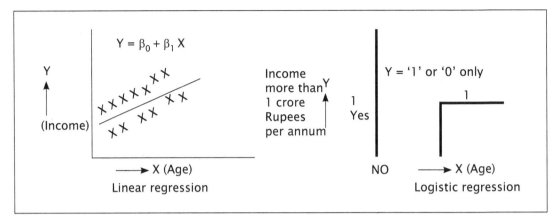

FIGURE 13.7 Linear Regression versus Logistic Regression

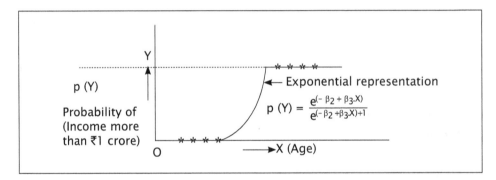

FIGURE 13.8 Logistic Regression Model

13.6 Metadata

Metadata is another example of big data. For example, email metadata, cell phone metadata consisting of time and location of calls, photograph exchangeable image file (EXIF) metadata and metadata related to social networks, such as twitter form a considerable chunk of big data which can be analysed to furnish information for predictive marketing, market research and e-commerce. The following is a simple example of the volume of data generated by the log file of a particular Gmail account. Each email (incoming or outgoing) will have one usual entry as follows:

<u>date time From/To Subject/Body Attachments</u>

Assuming about 100 kB of storage space will be required for each mail and on an average 10 such mails are received per day, in a month the total data volume generated for the log file will be $10 \times 100 \times 30 \simeq 30$ MB, which is a high volume indeed. The log file has no finite or fixed structure as some of the fields can have different types of contents.

13.7 Attributes of Highly Effective Big Data Environment

Big data environment has got certain distinct attributes as we have seen in the preceding paragraphs of this chapter. Those can be listed as follows:

1. **Seamless integration:** Seamless integration of data through mixing, combining and contrasting of data sets. Forrester Research has mentioned that 80% of the value of big data comes through integration.
2. **Flexibility with low cost:** Low cost and low complexity with sufficient flexibility to scale the feed needs is the target.
3. **Stability:** Users need to easily access and interact with data and in this sense, infrastructure performance with stability is a key to boosting business performance through big data.

Big data thus pose some challenges as shown in Figure 13.9.

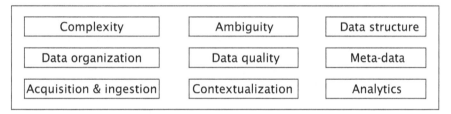

FIGURE 13.9 Big Data Challenges

13.8 Big Data—Infrastructure Requirements

Infrastructure for storage, processing and retrieval of big data has the following requirements:

- Scalable platform.
- Database independent.
- Fault tolerant.
- Low cost of acquisition.
- Capable of processing dynamic and unstructured data.
- Capable to perform complex operations within reasonable response time.
- Scalable and reliable storage.
- Supported by standard toolset.
- Data centre ready.

13.9 Hadoop Story Line

Google was the first to conceive the idea of developing a distributed file system to process big data and published a paper in 2004 that described the architecture of Google's distributed file system known as GFS. In the same year, Google also published a paper on the MapReduce (MapR) framework explaining a system that they used to scale their own search system. Doug Cutting immediately saw the suitability of the Global Forecast System (GFS) and MapR technologies for Nutch, which is an open source web search engine and a part of Lucene project widely used in text search library. Later on, in late 2005, Nutch was rewritten by Doug Cutting and his team to use MapR to boost Nutch's scalability. In 2006, Hadoop was born out of Nutch and Yahoo hired Doug Cutting in 2006 itself to work with a dedicated team on improving Hadoop as an open source project. In 2007, 'Times Machine' came as a backup software application, which creates incremental backups of files that can be restored at a later date. 'Times Machine' was based on the concept of distributed file system. In 2008, Hadoop became a top-level Apache project. Later on, at the end of 2008, Hadoop achieved the TerraSort benchmark (209 seconds!) and Yahoo announced that Hadoop running on a 10,000+ core Linux clusters was in a production system for indexing the web (http://developer.yahoo.net/blogs/hadoop/2008/02/yahoo-worlds-largest-production-hadoop.html).

The name Hadoop was adopted by Doug Cutting as the name used by his son as a toddler for a yellow-stuffed elephant toy.

13.10 Apache Hadoop

Apache Hadoop is a platform for data storage and processing which is scalable, fault tolerant and an open source. It has two core components, namely HDFS and MapR/Yet Another Resource Negotiator (YARN). The two core components have been described in the subsequent paragraphs. However, some of the features of Hadoop are listed as follows:

- Consolidates mixed type of data.
- Complex and relational data into a single repository.
- Inexpensive storage because of use of commodity hardware (daily usable hardware).
- Keeps raw data available at all times.
- Processes data at the source.
- Eliminates ETL bottlenecks.
- Mines data first, governs later.

13.11 Hadoop Distributed File System

HDFS is a specially designed file system to store huge data files in a cluster of commodity hardware. Here, by commodity hardware, we mean daily usable hardware built on inexpensive servers.

A data file may be stored in more than one storage device, hence the name Distributed File System. Hadoop is based on the concept of distributed storage coupled with distributed processing of the data in a file. This means storage and processing need to be tightly coupled in a high-volume data-based distributed environment.

13.11.1 HDFS Building Blocks

On a fully configured cluster of Hadoop, daemons or services run. These daemons which are basically resident processes have specific roles and some exist only on one server, while some of them may exist across multiple servers. Further, the daemons follow a master–slave architecture. Master daemons activate the slaves and at the same time, master services can talk to each other and similarly the slave daemons can also communicate among themselves. The daemons are grouped accordingly and shown in Figure 13.10.

Each daemon and its role in Hadoop have been described as follows:

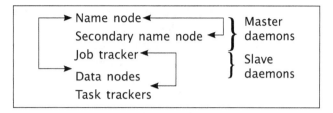

FIGURE 13.10 Master and Slave Daemons in Hadoop

NameNode: It is the most important daemon of the Hadoop daemons and is the master of HDFS that directs the slave data nodes daemons to perform the low-level tasks. NameNode is the metadata of HDFS and keeps track of how the files are split into various blocks and stored in data nodes. NameNode also monitors the health of the DataNodes and the entire distributed file system. The NameNode server is a single one and does not store any user data or perform any computation process. However, NameNode can be a single-point failure of the entire Hadoop cluster if it does not function.

DataNode: Each slave storage device hosts a DataNode daemon to perform the read and write operations of the actual file on HDFS. A file is broken into blocks of data of typical size 64 MB and stored in one or more DataNodes. NameNode keeps the account of the individual blocks and the DataNodes on which they reside.

HDFS sits on the top of local and traditional file systems and supports write-once-read-many times with read at streaming speed. The typical block size of 64 MB on the data nodes can be increased to blocks of 128 MB also. Further, a DataNode may communicate with other DataNodes to replicate its data blocks for redundancy. The default replication factor is 3. Figure 13.11 illustrates

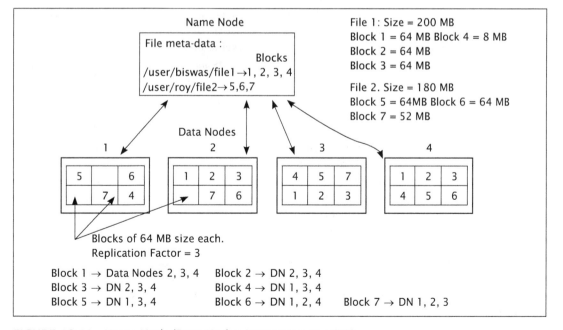

FIGURE 13.11 Name Node/Data Nodes Interaction in HDFS

the way files are stored among DataNodes with three replicas and the role of NameNode as a metadata for the data files in the DataNodes.

Each DataNode constantly informs the NameNode about the blocks in which it is storing data and also receives instructions to create, move or delete blocks from the local disk. NameNode monitors continuously the health of DataNodes by sending heartbeat signal for 10 seconds. In case it does not receive response within 10 seconds, it sends the second heartbeat for another 10 seconds and finally a third heartbeat signal for 10 seconds. If the DataNode does not send a response within 30 seconds, the NameNode declares the DataNode as problematic and informs the other DataNodes having the replica of the affected DataNode blocks accordingly.

Secondary NameNode (SNN): The SNN is an assistant daemon which acts as a backup node for the NameNode. Like the NameNode, each HDFS cluster has one SNN which typically resides on its own machine (server) and no other DataNode or task tracker daemon runs on the same server. SNN does not record HDFS metadata on a real-time basis but it only communicates with the NameNode to take snapshots of the HDFS metadata as available on the NameNode at intervals as defined by the HDFS cluster configuration. In case of Hadoop 1.0 the interval is 1 hour.

JobTracker: The JobTracker daemon acts as a liaison between individual client application and Hadoop. JobTracker determines the schedule of execution of tasks involved with the client application and assigns the tasks to TaskTrackers of different nodes. JobTracker performs the following services:

1. It communicates with the NameNodes to determine the location of data (file splits).
2. JobTracker communicates with TaskTrackers to locate available slots.
3. JobTracker submits the tasks to the chosen TaskTrackers.
4. After submission of tasks, JobTracker monitors all the TaskTrackers by the use of heartbeat signals. If no response is received up to a predefined limit of attempts, the JobTracker will automatically reschedule the task to a different TaskTracker.
5. JobTracker decides whether to declare a TaskTracker as unreliable.
6. When the client job is finished, JobTracker updates its status to signal back to NameNode.

Any client application can pool the JobTracker for output or for information logs.

There is only one JobTracker per Hadoop cluster. It typically runs on a server as a masternode of the cluster.

TaskTrackers: TaskTrackers are computing daemons and slaves to the master JobTracker, which oversees the overall execution of MapR job. TaskTrackers manage the execution of individual tasks allotted to each slave DataNode. It is interesting to note that although there is a single TaskTracker per DataNode, each TaskTracker can create multiple Java Virtual Machines (JVMs) to handle many parallel MapR tasks. Map and Reduce are basically Java programs. Figure 13.12 shows the interaction among client application, JobTracker and the TaskTrackers.

The architecture of a typical Hadoop cluster has been shown in Figure 13.13.

As already stated in earlier paragraphs, Hadoop consists of HDFS, the distributed file system and the MapR the distributed processing associated with each distributed DataNode. MapR is the data processing or analysis function which again comprises ETL and analytics using various statistical and simple analytic techniques.

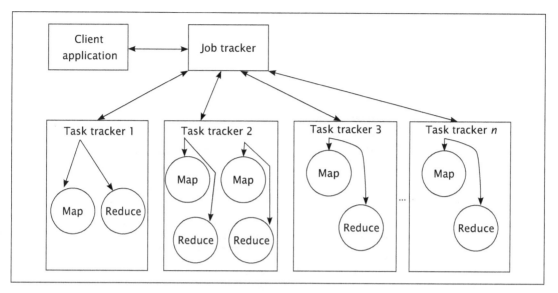

FIGURE 13.12 Interaction among Client Application, Job Tracker and Task Trackers

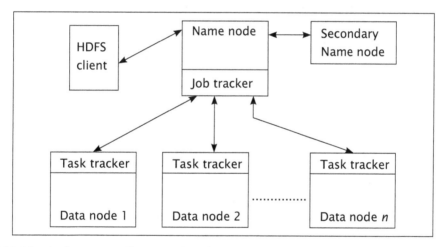

FIGURE 13.13 Architecture of a Typical Hadoop Cluster

13.12 MapReduce

Before we discuss about the MapR framework consisting of InputSplit, RecordReader, mapper, intermediate grouping, shuffling and reducer, MapR function has been explained with a simple word count example. Let us consider a text file as follows:

> hi how are you
> how is your job

how is your bro
how is your sis
how is your spouse
how is your family
what is your hobby

Suppose we want to count the number of each word in the above file. Let us assume that the size of the file is 200 MB. For the purpose of the word count, we split the input into four blocks of 64 MB each as follows and then proceed to find the word count for each InputSplit separately. Map function has been explained below:

Input split 1 (64 MB)	Input split 2 (64 MB)	Input split 3 (64 MB)	Input split 4 (8 MB)
hi how are you how is your job	how is your bro how is your sis	how is your spouse how is your family	what is your hobby
(hi, 1) (how, 1) (are, 1) (you, 1) (how, 1) (is, 1) (your, 1) (job, 1)	(how, 1) (is, 1) (your, 1) (bro, 1) (how, 1) (is, 1) (your, 1) (sis, 1)	(how, 1) (is, 1) (your, 1) (spouse, 1) (how, 1) (is, 1) (your, 1) (family, 1)	(what, 1) (is, 1) (your, 1) (hobby, 1)

Next, the intermediate output of the Map function as explained is shuffled and each grouped word-wise which is the key as shown below. Each time a word appears, we put a count 1.

```
hi, (1) how, (1, 1, 1, 1, 1, 1) are, (1) you, (1)
is, (1, 1, 1, 1, 1, 1) your, (1, 1, 1, 1, 1, 1) job, (1) bro, (1)
sis, (1) spouse, (1) family, (1) what, (1)
hobby (1)
```

After shuffling as above, the Reduce function reduces the individual counts of each word into a total count and the output of the Reduce function will be as follows:

```
hi, (1) how, (6) are (1) you, (1) is, (6)
your, (6) job (1) bro, (1) sis, (1)
spouse, (1) family, (1) what, (1) hobby (1)
```

The output is the word count and in the key-value format.

MapR framework has been shown in Figure 13.14.

Both Mapper and Reducer are small programs. Mapper does computation on InputSplit line by line, each line being read by the reader as byte offset entire line as shown below:

```
                                 1 2 3
        Input          Line # 1   0,  hi ↓ how are you
        Split 1 ——→    Line # 2   15, how is your job
```

The byte offset is the number of characters that exist from the beginning of a line. In the above case, byte offset for line 1 is 0 and the same for line 2 is 15. The byte offset is used as a key by Hadoop while mapping (key-value).

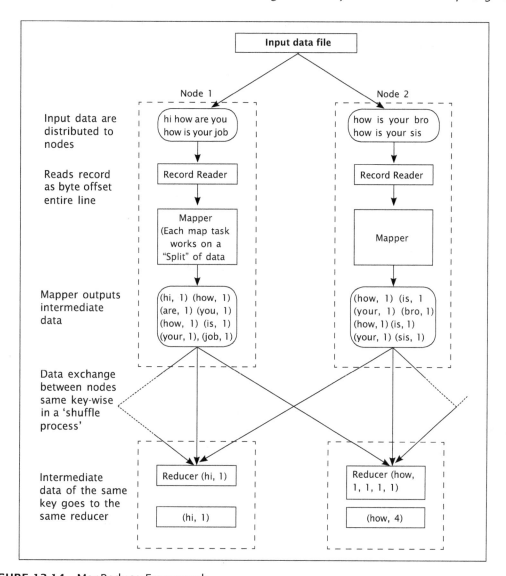

FIGURE 13.14 MapReduce Framework

The anatomy of a MapR program as obtained by manipulating (key-value) pairs in the general form is as follows:

$$\text{Map} : (K_1, V_1) \rightarrow \text{list } (K_2, V_2)$$
$$\text{Reduce: } (K_2, \text{list } (V_2)) \rightarrow \text{list } (K_3, V_3)$$

Here Map (K_1, V_1) is input to Mapper and refers to key K_1 as byte offset and V_1 as the value. For example, for Line 1 of InputSplit 1, the entire line read by the reader relates to $(K_1 = 0)$ and the same line is 'hi how are you'. Similarly, for the Line 2 $(K_1 = 15)$, the line is 'how is your job'.

The Map program converts the same to a list (K_2, V_2), where K_2 is the keyword such as 'hi' and 'how' and V_2 is its value as integer 1:

$$\text{list } (K_2, V_2) = \text{(hi, 1) (how, 1) (are, 1) (you, 1)}$$
$$\text{(how, 1) (is, 1) (your, 1) (job, 1)}$$

which is the intermediate output of Mapper.

After shuffling, list (K_2, V_2) results in $(K_2 \text{ list } (V_2))$ which is as follows:

```
(K₂ list (V₂)) = (hi, 1) (how, (1, 1))...
```

$(K_2, \text{ list } (V_2))$ is fed to Reducer and the output is list (K_3, V_3) where K_3 is the keyword and V_3 is the total count for the same. For our example:

```
list (K₃, V₃) = (hi, 1) (how, 2)...
```

A listing of a partial view of word count program in Java is as follows:

Public class word count extends configured implements Tool {public static Class Mapclass extends MapR Base implements Mapper < Long Writable, Text, Text, Intwritable> {private Text word = new Text ();

```
public void map (Long Writable key. Text value, output
collector < Text, Intwritable > output, Reporter reporter) throws
IOException {
String line = value. tostring ();
String Tokenizer itr = new string Tokenizer (line); while (itr.
hasMore Tokens ()) {
word.set (itr.next Token ()); output. collect (word, one);
}
}
}
public static class Reduce extends MapReduce Base implements
Reducer < Text, Intwritable, Text, Intwritable > {public void reduce
(Text key, Iterator
< Intwritable > values, output collector < Text,
Intwritable > output, Reporter reporter) throws IO Exception {
int sum = 0;
while (values.has Next ()) {sum + = values.next () .get ();
}
output.collect (key, new Intwritable (sum));
}
}...
```

For the word count example with multiple reducers shown in Figure 13.14, shuffling is done with a default behaviour to hash the key (word such as hi, how...) and depending on the same, the reducer is determined. For example, all 'hi' in one reducer, all 'how' in another reducer and so on. However, in case of sorting of the output of the mapper or any other type of analysis, we have to customize the partitioner for directing the mapper output for the particular application to different reducers through shuffling. Such type of hash partitioning with multiple reducers facilitates parallel computation. Combiners are optional, and they perform local reduce for the intermediate output of the mappers before we distribute the mapper results through shuffling. Each mapper has its own combiner. Combiners increase the speed and efficiency of intermediate storage as well as shuffling of mapper output.

For example, in the case of word count, if a document for the job contains the word 'how', say 200 times, it is much more efficient to store and shuffle the pair ('how', 200) once instead of the pair ('how', 1) 200 times. This processing step of local reduce is known as 'combining'.

13.12.1 Data Flow in a MapR Program in Hadoop

Figure 13.15 illustrates the data flow in a MapR program in Hadoop.

Before we go into details of components of Hadoop 2.0, let us get into the architecture of both Hadoop 1.0 vis-a-vis Hadoop 2.0 as shown in Figure 13.16.

APP Master stands for application master. There is one APP Master for every application instance. Basically, it manages the application life cycle and task scheduling. APP Master gets MapReduce status from each container and also sends request for resource allocation to resource manager.

A container is a pool of resource in terms of memory and processor. The entire resource of a DataNode is divided into a number of containers. For example, if the total memory of a node is 100 GB, it may be sliced into 25 containers of 4 GB each and say one core of processor. The resource manager allocates resources to each APP Master in terms of containers. For a MapR application, the total number of containers is equal to the sum total of number of Mappers and number of Reducers. Containers hold a predefined quantity of memory and processor. For instance, in the above example, if an application requires a memory of 5 GB, it will be allotted 2 containers of 4 GB each.

Node manager administers resources of a node, and there is one node manager for each DataNode. It also furnishes the node status to the resource manager. Resource manager is a central agent (similar to JobTracker), and it manages and allocates cluster resources. Hadoop 2.0 obviously has got several advantages over Hadoop 1.0 such as its horizontal scalability, higher availability of resource manager as

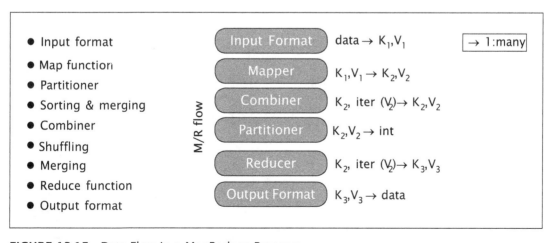

FIGURE 13.15 Data Flow in a MapReduce Program

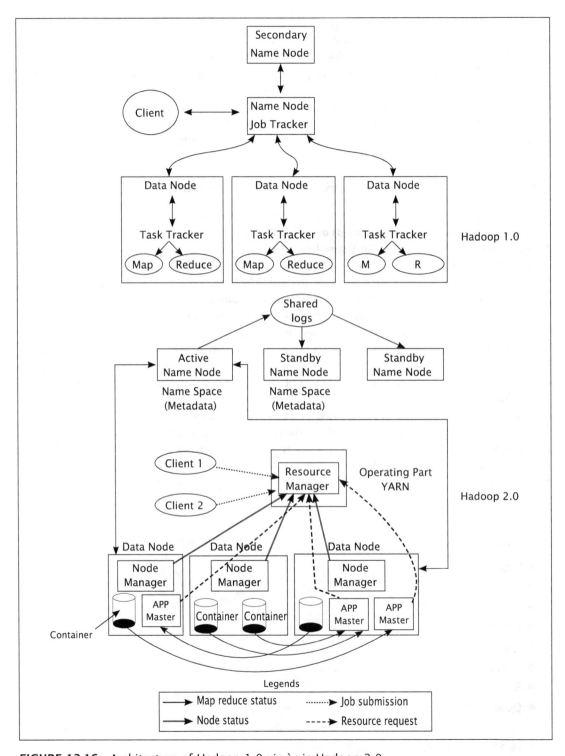

FIGURE 13.16 Architecture of Hadoop 1.0 vis-à-vis Hadoop 2.0

compared to the same for JobTracker in case of Hadoop 1.0. It may be stated that JobTracker is overburdened in case of Hadoop 1.0 because of its multiple functions such as assignment of jobs to TaskTrackers, submission of the outputs of the jobs by TaskTrackers to JobTracker, monitoring of the TaskTrackers and communication with the clients (users) of Hadoop 1.0.

Hadoop 1.0, the first-generation Hadoop, is made up of HDFS, MapR, NameNode, SNN, JobTracker, DataNode and TaskTracker. However, in case of the second-generation Hadoop 2.X, YARN, is a new component known as 'MRV2' which is now characterized as a large scale, distributed operating system for big data applications. YARN is a software which separates resource allocation and scheduling of task from data processing function enabling Hadoop 2.0 to handle more varied applications and their processing. Besides in case of Hadoop 2.0 and above, there are multiple NameNodes, one being the active NameNode and the others the SNN. Each SNN shares the logs of active NameNode continuously and the Namespace (metadata) of active NameNode is maintained on real-time basis by all the standby NameNodes as a federation. This has a distinct advantage of immediate recovery of Namespace of active NameNode in case of its failure unlike in case of Hadoop 1.0 in which case the SNN maintains the Namespace at hourly intervals only.

13.13 Hadoop Installation

Hadoop software can be installed in three modes of operation, namely (a) stand-alone mode, (b) pseudo-distributed mode and (c) fully-distributed mode. In the stand-alone mode, Hadoop is installed on a single node and there is no need to communicate with other nodes and as such no use of HDFS is made in stand-alone mode. Further, Hadoop daemons are not launched in this mode. All the Hadoop configuration files (XML extension) remain empty in this mode which is the default mode of Hadoop. This software in the stand-alone mode runs as a single monolithic Java process. This mode of operation of Hadoop is primarily used for developing and debugging the logic of MapR program on small data sets before actually executing the same with big data and with additional complexity of interactions of the Hadoop daemons.

The pseudo-distributed mode runs Hadoop on a single-node cluster with various daemons of Hadoop running as separate Java processes on the same node or machine. In this mode NameNode, DataNode, SNN, JobTracker and TaskTracker run on the same machine. This mode of operation of Hadoop also facilitates debugging of MapR code with memory usage, HDFS issues and with interaction among the daemons. Before beginning the installation steps of Apache Hadoop (Apache Hadoop is an open source software) which is a Java framework and can be installed with ease on Linux operating systems such as Ubuntu (various versions). It is therefore recommended to install Apache Hadoop on Ubuntu, and some knowledge of basic Linux commands will be helpful in normal operation connected with the installation task.

The prerequisites for the installation are Java Development Kit (JDK) 1.6 and onward versions and a SSH. The listing for installation of Hadoop 2.6 on Ubuntu is as follows:

```
# Installation of Java #
: ~ $ Sudo apt-get install openjdk-7-jdk
: ~ $ java-version # # To check whether, Java downloaded # #
java version "1.7.0.79"
# Creating a Hadoop user for accessing #
```

```
# HDFS and Map Reduce #
# We will create hadoop as system group #
# hduser as system user #
: ~ $ Sudo addgroup hadoop
: ~ $ Sudo adduser hduser
# installing SSH #
# SSH is a protocol for securely accessing one machine from another #
: Sudo apt-get install open SSH-server
# configuring SSH #
# To do this we need to copy generated RSA Key #
# (id-rsa.pub) pairs to authorized_keys folder of SSH #
: ~$ Sudo Su hduser
# Generate SSh key for hduser account
hduser@ubuntu: ~ $ ssh-keygen-t rsa-p" "
# Copy id_rsa.pub to authorized keys from hduser
# Disabling IPV6 since Hadoop does not work on IPV6
# Need to update/etc/sysctl.conf by adding following lines
hduser@ubuntu: ~$sudo vi/etc/sysctl.conf
# Add following lines after the end of the file
    net.ipv6.conf.all.disable_ipv6 = 1
    net.ipv6.conf.default.disable_ipv6 = 1
    net.ipv6.conf.IO.disable_ipv6 = 1
# Hadoop installation from Apache Hadoop 2.6.0
# Source from Apache download Mirrors
# Location for installation is/usr/local/hadoop
hduser@ubuntu: ~ $ cd/usr/local/
## Extract Hadoop Source from hadoop-2.6.0.tar.gz
hduser@ubuntu: ~$sudo tar-XZvf hadoop-2.6.0.tar.gz
## Move hadoop-2.6.0 to hadoop folder
: ~$ Sudo mv hadoop-2.6.0/usr/local/hadoop
## Assign ownership of this folder to Hadoop user
: ~$ Sudo chown hduser: hadoop-R/usr/local/hadoop
: ~$ ssh local host
## Create Hadoop temp directories for Name Node and Data Node
: ~$ sudo mkdir-p/usr/local/hadoop_tmp/hdfs/name node
: ~$ sudo mkdir-p/usr/local/hadoop_tmp/hdfs/data node
## Again assign ownership of this hadoop temp folders to Hadoop user.
: ~$ sudo chown hduser: hadoop —R/usr/local/hadoop_temp
## update hduser configuration files by appending the
## following environment variable at the end of
##. bashrc file.
: ~$ sudo gedit. bashrc
# - - HADOOP ENVIRONMENT VARIABLES START--#
export JAVA_HOME = /usr/lib/jvm/jdk 1.7.0_79
export HADOOP_HOME = /usr/local/Hadoop
export PATH = $PATH: $ HADOOP_HOME/bin
```

```
export PATH = $ PATH: HADOOP_HOME/sbin
export HADOOP_MAPRED_HOME = $ HADOOP_HOME
export HADOOP_COMMON_HOME = $ HADOOP_HOME
export HADOOP_HDFS_HOME = $ HADOOP_HOME
export YARN_HOME = $ HADOOP_HOME
export HADOOP_COMMON_LIB_NATIVE_DIR = $ HADOOP_HOME/lib/native
export HADOOP_OPTS = "—Djava.library.path = $HADOOP_HOME/lib"
# — — HADOOP ENVIRONMENT VARIABLES END — — #
# Configuration file : hadoop.env.sh
# To edit the file, the following command to be executed
hduser@ubuntu : /usr/local/hadoop/etc/hadoop $ sudo gedit hadoop-env.sh
# update JAVA_HOME variable
export JAVA_HOME=/usr/lib/jvm/jdk 1.7.0_79
## configure file: core—site.Xml
hduser@ubuntu:/usr/local/hadoop/etc/hodoop $ sudo gedit core-site-Xml
# Paste these lies into<configuration>tag
<property>
<name>fs.default.name</name>
<value>hdfs://local host: 9000</value>
</property>
## configure file : hdfs—site.Xml
hduser@ubuntu : /usr/local/hadoop/etc/hadoop $sudo gedit hdfs-site.Xml
# Paste these lines into<configuration>tag
<property>
   <name>dfs. replication</name>
   <value>1</value>
</property>
<property>
   <name>dfs.name node.name.dir</name>
   <value>file: /usr/local/hadoop_tmp/hdfs/name node</value>
</property>
<property>
   <name>dfs. data node. data. dir</name>
   <value>file : /usr/local/hadoop_tmp/hdfs/data node</value>
</property>
# configure file :yarn—site.Xml
hduser@ubuntu :/usr/local/hadoop/etc/hadoop $sudo gedit yarn-site.Xml
# Paste these lines into<configuration>tag
<property>
   <name>yarn.nodemanager.aux-services</name>
   <value>mapreduce_shuffle</value>
</property>
<property>
   <name>yarn.node manager.aux-services.mapreduce.shuffle-class</name>
   <value. org.apache.hadoop.mapred.shuffle Handler</value>
</property>
```

```
# configure file : mapred-site.Xml
# copy template of mapred-site.Xml.template file
cp/usr/local/hadoop/etc/hadoop/mapred-site.Xml.template/usr/local/
hadoop/etc/hadoop/mapred—site.Xml
# To edit the file
hduser@ubuntu: /usr/local/hadoop/etc/hadoop $ Sudo gedit mapred-Sie.Xml
# Paste these lines into<configuration>tag
<property>
   <name>mapreduce. framework.name</name>
   <value>yarn</value>
</property>
cd..
cd..
hduser@ubuntu: /~$ Sudo chmod—R 777/usr/local/hadoop
# Format name node
hduser@ubuntu: /~$ hdfs name node—format
# Start hdfs daemons
hduser@ubuntu: /usr/local/hadoop $ start-dfs.sh
# start Map Reduce daemons
hduser @ ubuntu: /usr/local/hadoop $ start-yarn.sh
```

Instead of the two above commands, we can also use start_all.sh but that is now deprecated and so not recommended to be used for better Hadoop operations.

```
# verify Hadoop daemons
hduser@ubuntu :jps
```

13.13.1 Hadoop 2.6.0 Installation in Fully Distributed Mode

Let us now install Hadoop 2.6.0 on Ubuntu in a cluster of three nodes: one master (NameNode) and two slave nodes (DataNodes).

The steps and listing are as follows:

1.0: Installing Java oracle version 1.7.0_45 in all three machines (nodes):

```
: ~ $ Sudo apt-get update
$ Sudo add-apt-repository ppa: webupd8team/java
$ Sudo apt-get update
$ Sudo apt-get install oracle-jdk 7-installer # To check Java
version #
$ java-version
java version "1.7.0_45"
```

2.0: Add all host names to/etc/hosts directory in all three machines (master and two slaves):

```
: ~ $ Sudo getdit/etc/hosts
# Add following host names and their IP addresses
```

```
# host table
192.168.2.10 Hadoop Master
192.168.2.11 Hadoop Slave 1
192.168.2.12 Hadoop Slave 2
```

3.0: Creating a Hadoop user for accessing HDFS and MapR:

```
# we shall Create hadoop as system group and
# hduser as system user in all the three nodes
: ~ $ Sudo addgroup hadoop
: ~ $ Sudo add user ─ingroup hadoop hduser
: ~ $ Sudo usermod─a─G
: ~ $ Sudo hduser
```

4.0: Download Hadoop. Let us download Hadoop 2.6.0 from apache mirror.gtcomm.net/hadoop/ common/hadoop─2.6.0/hadoop─2.6.0 tar.gz

```
# issue wget command from shell hduser@Hadoop Master: ~$ Wget
http: //apache.mirror.gt comm.net/hadoop/common/hadoop─2.6.0/
hadoop─2.6.0. tar.gz
# unzip the file
: ~ $ Sudo tar ─XZVf hadoop─2.6.0 tar.gz
# For ease of operation and maintenance let
# us rename the 'hadoop─2.6.0' directory to 'hadoop'
: ~ $ mv hadoop─2.6.0 hadoop
```

Repeat Step 4.0 for slave 1 and slave 2 also.

5.0: Verify SSH installation. If not, open SSH in the same way as we did for the single node Hadoop installation for master and the two slave nodes.

6.0: Configuring password-less key-based logins on servers. After setting up SSH in every node, we have to use ssh-keygen on the master of Hadoop Masternode to generate the Rivest, Shamir, Adleman (RSA) key pair in order to enable the Hadoop Master node to communicate with the other nodes without any prompt password.

```
hd user @ Hadoop Master: ~$ Sudo hduser
hd user @ Hadoop Master: ~$ ssh-keygen-t rsa
# Generating public/private rsa key pair
```

Enter the file in which to save the key: (/home/hduser/.ssh/id_rsa) Enter passphrase (empty for no passphrase):
Enter same passphrase again:

```
#/home/hduser/.ssh/id_rsa
#/home/hduser/.ssh/id_rsa.pub (public key)
# Distribute public key and validate logins
```

Copy the public key to every slave node as well as the master node by secure copy (SCP)

```
hduser@Hadoop Master: $ scp ~/hduser/.ssh/id_rsa.pub
hduser@Hadoop Master: ~/hduser/master-key
hduser@Hadoop Master: ~ $ mkdir ~/hduser/.ssh
hduser@Hadoop Master: ~ $ chmod 700 ~/hduser/.ssh
hduser@Hadoop Master: ~ $ mv ~/hduser/master-key ~/hduser/-ssh/
authorized keys hduser@Hadoop Master: ~ $ chmod 600 ~/hduser/.ssh/
authorized-keys
# Secure copy public key to master key in slaves
hduser@Hadoop Master: ~ $ scp ~/hduser/.ssh/id_rsa.pub
hduser@Hadoop Slave 1
: ~/hduser/master-key
hduser@Hadoop Master: ~ $ scp ~/hduser/.ssh/id_rsa.pub
hduser@Hadoop slave 2: ~/hduser/master-key
```

Next, manually log in to slave nodes and set the master key as an authorized key and change the mode to 600 for the authorized key as done above in case of Hadoop Master.

7.0: Setting up environment variable for hduser. Update the .bashrc file to add important Hadoop paths and directories.

```
Navigate to home directory hduser @ Hadoop Master: $ cd
# open.bashrc file in Vi editor
: ~ $ Vi. bashrc
# Add following at the end of file
export HADOOP_CONF=/home/hduser/hadoop/conf
export HADOOP_PREFIX=/home/hduser/hadoop
# set JAVA_HOME
export JAVA_HOME=/usr/lib/jvm/java-7-oracle
export PATH=$PATH: $ JAVA_HOME/bin
# Add Hadoop bin/directory to path
export PATH=$ PATH: $ HADOOP_PREFIX/bin export
PATH=$ PATH: $ HADOOP_PREFIX/S bin
```

Save and exit. Repeat 7.0 for the two slave machines (nodes).

8.0: Hadoop cluster configuration:

We have to configure the following:

- hadoop-env.sh (for JAVA_HOME)
- core-site.Xml (key property fs.default.name for NameNode configuration)
- hdfs-site.Xml (key property-dfs.replication-by default it is 3)
- mapred-site.Xml (for MapR framework which is YARN)
- yarn-site.Xml (for node manager and resource manager)

We will first start with master (NameNode) and then copy the above XML changes to the two slave nodes.

```
# hadoop-env.sh
: $ vi $ HADOOP_CONF/hadoop-env.sh
```

```
export JAVA_HOME=/usr/lib/jvm/java-7-oracle
# Core-site. Xml
: $ Vi $ HADOOP_CONF/core-site Xml
```

We are going to add two properties:

1. fs. default.name will point to the NameNode URL and port (9000 usually)
2. hadoop.temp.dir—A base for other temporary directories. It is important to note that every node needs hadoop.tmp directory. We shall create a new directory 'hdfstmp' as below in all the three nodes.

```
: ~ cd
: ~ $ mkdir hdfs.tmp
<configuration>
<property>
<name>fs.default.name</name>
<value>hdfs://Hadoop Master: 9000</value>
</property>
<property>
<name>hadoop.temp.dir</name>
<value>/home/hduser/hdfstmp</value>
</property>
</configuration>
# hdfs-site.Xml on master
```

We are going to add the following properties:

1. dfs.permissions.enabled with value 'false'. If 'true' means permission checking is enabled.
2. dfs.replication. Default value is 3 since we have two slave nodes, we will set the same value to 2.
3. name node.name directory and data node.data directory.

```
<configuration>
<property>
<name>dfs. replication</name>
<value>2</value>
</property>
<property>
<name>dfs.permissions</name>
<value>false</value>
</property>
<property>
<name>dfs.name node.name.dir</name>
<value>/home/hduser/hdfs_tmp/hdfs/name node</value>
</property>
<property>
<name>dfs.datanode.data.dir</name>
<value>/home/hduser/hdfs_tmp/hdfs/data node</value>
```

```
</property>
</configuration>
```

Open mapred-site.Xml and replace configuration as follows:

```
<configuration>
<property>
<name>mapreduce.framework.name</name>
<value>yarn</value>
</property>
</configuration>
```

Next open and configure yarn-site.Xml on Hadoop Master:

```
<configuration>
<property>
<name>yarn.node manager.aux-services</name>
<value>mapreduce_shuffle</value>
</property>
<property>
<name>yarn.node manager.aux-services.mapreduce_shuffle.class</name>
<value>org.apache.hadoop.mapred.shuffle Handler</value>
</property>
<property>
<name>yarn.resource manager.resource-tracker.address (/name)
<value>Hadoop Master: 8025</value>
</property>
<property>
<name>yarn.resourcemanager.scheduler.address</name>
<value>Hadoop Master :8030</value>
</property>
<property>
<name>yarn. resource manager.address</name>
<value>Hadoop Master :8033</value>
</property>
</configuration>
```

8.0: Move configuration files to slaves using scp. Start with Slave 1 from Hadoop Master shell:

```
hduser@Hadoop Master :~/hd user/hadoop/conf$scp
hadoop-env.sh core-site.Xml hdfs-site.Xml mapred-site.Xml
yarn-site.Xml hduser@Hadoop Slave1 :/~hduser/hadoop/conf
```

Repeat the above SCP for slave 2 also.

9.0: Configure master and slaves. Every Hadoop distribution comes with master and slave files. By default, it contains one entry for the same files, and we have to edit these two files on both 'masters' (Hadoop Master) and 'slaves' (Hadoop slave 1 and Hadoop slave 2) machines as follows:

Edit/modify masters file on master machine.

```
$ Vi$HA DOOP_CONF/masters
```

📄 masters ×	
Hadoop Master |	

Next, edit/modify slaves file in master machine.

```
$ vi $ HADOOP_CONF/Slaves
```

📄 Slaves ×	
Hadoop Master | Hadoop Slave 1 | Hadoop Slave 2 |	

Next, configure master and slaves on 'slaves' node since we are configuring slaves (Hadoop Slave 1 and Hadoop Slave 2), masters file on Slave machine is going to be empty. We edit the 'slaves' file on the slave server (Hadoop Slave 1).

```
$ Vi $ HADOOP_CONF/masters
$ Vi $ HADOOP_CONF/Slaves
```

📄 slavess ×	
Hadoop Slave 1 |	

Similarly, update masters and slaves for Hadoop Slave 2.

10.0: Hadoop daemon setup. The first step for starting up the Hadoop installation is formatting the Hadoop file system which runs on top of the local file system of our cluster. We need to do it the first time we set up a Hadoop installation. However, we must format a running Hadoop file system, which will cause all our data to be erased.

We have to format the NameNode (only on master machine). To format the NameNode, the command is as follows:

```
$ hadoop name node-format
```

Let us now start all hadoop daemons from the Hadoop NameNode:

```
$ cd $ HADOOP_CONF
$ start-all.sh
```

Next, we can check all the daemons running on both master and slave machines with the command: jps.

```
hduser@Hadoop Master: ~/hadoop/conf $ jps
16883 Node Manager
16116 Name Node
16582 Resource Manager
20784 jps
16431 Secondary Name Node
16255 Data Node
hduser@Hadoop Master : ~/hadoop/conf $.
```
On master

```
hduser@Hadoop Slave 1 :~ $ jps
11816 jps
12211 Data Node
11977 Node Manager
hduser@Hadoop Slave 1 :~ $ jps
```
On Slave 1

```
hd user@ Hadoop Slave 2 :~ $ jps
10815 Data Node
11210 jps
10976 Node Manager
```
On Slave 2

13.14 Ecosystems of Hadoop

Hadoop ecosystems run on HDFS and YARN. Each member of the ecosystems is in particular application-oriented. For example, 'Mahout' is one of the ecosystems of Hadoop and pertains to machine-learning applications based on HDFS and the Hadoop daemons. Figure 13.17 shows the major ecosystems of Hadoop.

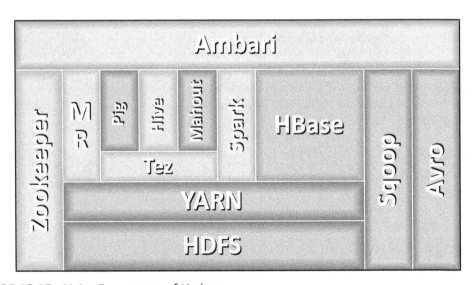

FIGURE 13.17 Major Ecosystems of Hadoop

We are already familiar with HDFS, YARN and MapR. Pig, often referred to as Pig Latin, has no revision or version. It is a scripting language having two major components. One is a high-level data processing language and the other is a compiler that compiles and runs Pig Latin scripts in a choice of evaluation mechanism. Pig uses ETL tools and facilitates rapid development because of the ease of programming. It is considered as a data-flow language. It should be used for structured or semi-structured data such as web logs, click streams, search platforms involving large data sets, time-sensitive data analysis such as weather data. However, Pig is generally not used for audio/video and human readable text data. It can be run in two modes: (a) local mode and (b) Hadoop (MapR) mode. In order to run Pig in local mode, we need access to a single machine, and in order to run it on the Hadoop (MapR) mode, we need access to a Hadoop cluster and HDFS installation. The corresponding commands are:

1. Local mode:

   ```
   $>Pig-X local
   grunt>
   ```

2. Hadoop (MapR) mode on HDFS:

   ```
   $>Pig
   grunt>
   ```

Pig shell is the 'grunt' interactive shell. Pig-script files are saved with '.pig' extension. Pig scripts can be embedded into other scripts also. Pig Latin scripts usually consist of loading a file, identifying the fields in the tuple and the data types of the fields, then filtering or grouping the tuples based on given criteria and finally generating counts for the groups. In addition, it has two more functions namely 'DUMP' and 'DESCRIBE'; the former prints the entire file or the computational output, while the latter describes the data types of the fields or computed fields. It may be mentioned that Pig assumes default data type as byte array. 'STORE' function is similar to 'DUMP' except that it dumps the file tuples as a separate file storage.

Example 1: Let 'word count' be a file containing—hi how are you.
Then,

```
grunt>abc=Load 'word count' USING Pig Storage (' ')
As (word chararray);
```

This will Load the file as character array as follows:

abc ⇒　　　　　hi,　　how,　　are,　　you
　　　　　　　↓　　　↓　　　↓　　　↓
　　　　　　　$0　　　$1　　　$2　　　$3

grunt > describe abc;

abc : {word : chararray}

grunt > DUMP abc;

hi, how, are, you

```
grunt>STORE ABC INTO 'output',
grunt>DUMP 'output';
output, hi, how, are, you
```

In Pig, we have data models as follows:

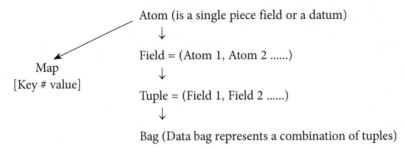

Atom (is a single piece field or a datum)

Field = (Atom 1, Atom 2 ......)

Tuple = (Field 1, Field 2 ......)

Bag (Data bag represents a combination of tuples)

Atom is the basic datum for Map function.

Example 2: Let us consider the following car data set as an example:

```
Id, car_name
01, Santro
02, Swift
03, Alto
```

A field is a piece of data such as car_name consisting of atoms which are Santro, Swift and Alto. A tuple is a set of fields such as (01, Santro). In the above example, there are three tuples. A bag is a collection of tuples. In the above example Bag is {(01, Santro), (02, Swift), (03, Alto)}. A map is a set of key/value pairs. A key must be unique and be a string (chararray). The value can be of any type.

13.14.1 Pig Architecture

Pig Latin consists of the basic Pig script for which no Java codes are required. However, the core architecture of Pig is Java in the form of pig.jar class files. Finally, the execution plan consists of map, filter, reduce and count. Figure 13.18 shows the Pig architecture.

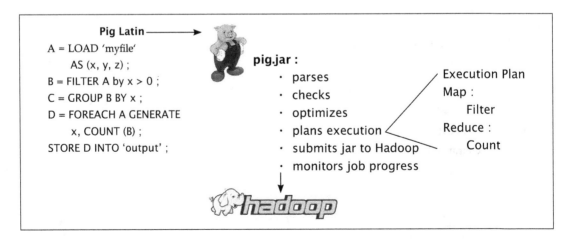

FIGURE 13.18 Pig Architecture

13.14.1.1 Sample Pig Scripts

It may be stated that Pig supports schemas in processing structured data, yet it is flexible enough to work with unstructured text or semi-structured XML data. Two sample Pig scripts with and without schema are illustrated as follows:

Without Schema	With Schema
grunt > A = load 'passwd' using Pig Storage (' : ');	grunt > A = LOAD 'student_data' AS (name:chararray,age:int,gpa:float);
> B = foreach A generate $ 0 as id;	> B = FOR EACH A GENERATE myudfs. UPPER (name);
> store B into 'id.out';	

Word count using Pig Latin script:

```
grunt > a = Load '/user/file path';
    > b = foreach a generate flatten (TOKENIZE (chararry)
          ($0)) as word;
    > c = group b by $0;
    > d = foreach c generate cout (b), group;
    > dump d
```

The function flatten (TOKENIZE ((char array) $0)) as word, arranges hi how are you

```
as (hi)
   (how)    hi, {hi.}
        ⟹ how, {how…} as data bags
   (are)    are, {are.}
   (you)    you, {you.}
     ↓
   $0
d: (hi, 1)
   (how, 1)
   (are, 1)
   (you, 1)
```

Pig atomic data can be of various types as shown in Table 13.2 below:

Pig allows use of expressions and functions to data fields to compute various values. It has two types of functions—built-in and UDF. Built-in functions are 'AVG' for calculating average, 'MAX', 'MIN ', 'SUM' for finding the maximum, minimum value in a single column bag of numeric or array type and sum of numeric values in a single column bag and many similar built-in functions.

TABLE 13.2 Atomic Data Types in Pig Latin

int	signed 32-bit integer
long	signed 64-bit integer
float	32-bit floating point
double	64-bit floating point
chararray	character array (string)
bytearray	Byte array (binary object)

The UDF are always written in Java and packaged in jar files. In order to use a particular UDF's class files, Pig supports two main categories of UDFs: eval and load/store. We use load/store functions only in LOAD and STORE statements to help Pig read and write special formats. Most UDFs are eval functions that take one field value and return another field value. In order to create an eval UDF, we make a Java class that extends the abstract Eval Func <T> class. It has only one abstract method that we need to implement, for example, abstract public T exec (tuple input) throws IO exception. This method is called on each tuple in a relation, where each tuple is represented by a tuple object. The exce() method processes the tuple and returns a type T corresponding to a valid Pig Latin type. T can be any one of the Java classes listed in Table 13.3, some of which are native Java classes, and some are Pig extensions.

TABLE 13.3 Pig Latin Types and Their Equivalent Java Class

Pig Latin Type	Java Class
bytearray	Data byte array
chararray	string
int	Integer
long	Long
float	Float
double	Double
tuple	Tuple
bag	Data bag
map	Map <object, object>

13.14.1.2 Relational Operators

The most salient characteristic of Pig Latin is its relational operators which make Pig Latin a data processing language. Some of the common relational operators are 'UNION ', 'SPLIT', 'FILTER ', 'FOREACH ', 'JOIN ', 'GROUP ', 'ORDER' and so on. A few illustrative examples of use of relational operators in Pig are as follows:

```
grunt>x=load 'A' using Pig Storage (', ') as (x1 : int,
x2 :int, x3 :int); grunt>y=load 'B' using Pig storage
(', ') as (y1 : int, y2 int, y3 :int), grunt>DUMP x;
(1, 2, 3)
(4, 5, 6)
grunt > DUMP y;
(7, 8, 9)
(1, 3, 5)
grunt>C=UNION x, y;
grunt>DUMP C;
(1, 2, 3)
(4, 5, 6)
(7, 8, 9)
(1, 3, 5)
```

```
grunt>SPLIT C INTO d IF $0==4, e IF $0==1;
grunt>DUMP d;
(4, 5, 6)
grunt>DUMP e;
(1, 2, 3)
(1, 3, 5)
```

One important application of Pig Latin is in analysis of stock data relating to stock exchange trading of listed shares of various companies. The data volume is huge and streaming in nature. Figure 13.19 shows a (.CSV) file containing data related to daily opening, maximum, minimum, closing price and the total number of shares traded for various groups of companies in the National Stock Exchange. The file was analysed to find the annual average opening price of the companies, namely ABB, HCL, NTTM, ABCSE, GARTNER and HOST.GTR using Pig Latin script as shown in Figure 13.20. The result has been dumped on the terminal shown in the same figure such as (ABB, 7917.2099) and (H CL, 8426.27999…).

13.14.2 Hive

Hive is a SQL-like data warehouse infrastructure tool which is built on Hadoop to process structured data. It was developed by Facebook to suit non-Java programmers and its query language known as Hive QL or HQL facilitates query and analysis with big data. The target users of Hive are data analysts who

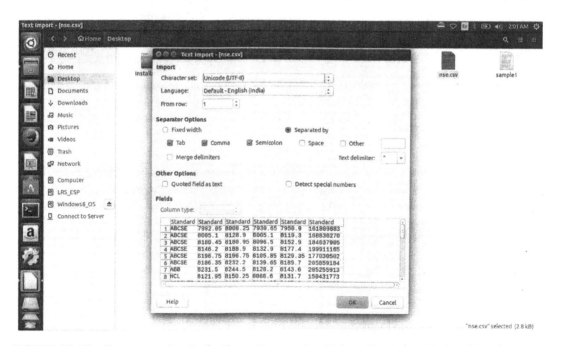

FIGURE 13.19 Company-wise Daily Share Transaction Values Traded in National Stock Exchange

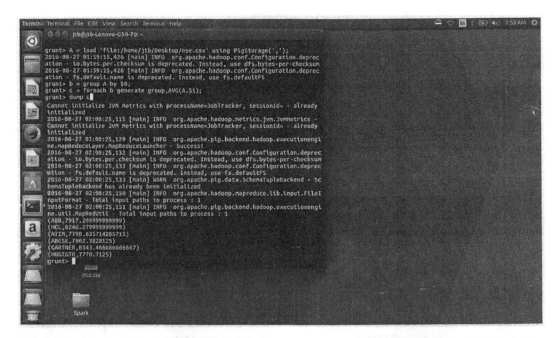

FIGURE 13.20 Pig Latin Script for Generating Average Value of Opening Stock Price and the Result Dumped on Terminal

are comfortable with SQL. We interact with Hive by issuing queries in a SQL-like language, the HQL. For example, a query to get all active users from a user table looks as follows:

```
INSERT OVERWRITE TABLE user_active
SELECT user.*
FROM user
WHERE user.active=1;
```

Hive also uses familiar concepts from RDBMS such as rows, columns, tables and schema to facilitate learning Hive. Further, in order to improve upon query performance, Hive can use directory structures. Another important feature of Hive is its 'meta-store' which stores schema information. The meta-store resides in a relational database. The architecture of Hive on Hadoop has been shown in Figure 13.21.

We can interact with Hive using several methods as shown in Figure 13.21 such as Web, GUI, Java database connectivity (JDBC) and command line interface (CLI). However, major interactions take place over a CLI. Hive stores metadata in a standard relational database, which in case of a multi-user environment uses a shared SQL database such as MySQL, Postgre SQL and Oracle, although any JDBC compliant database will also do.

13.14.2.1 Hive Data Types

Hive supports the following simple data types:

```
TINYINT: 1-byte signed integer, for example, 100
SMALLINT: 2-byte signed integer, for example, 100, 100
```

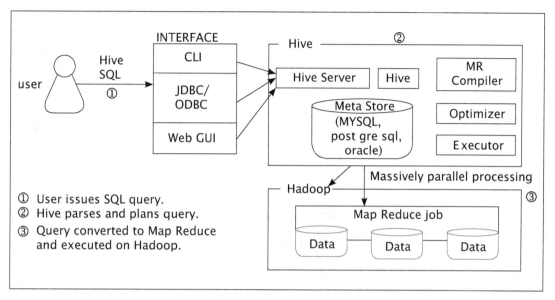

FIGURE 13.21 Hive Architecture

```
INT: 4-byte signed integer, for example, 100, 1000, 5000
BIGINT: 8-byte signed integer, for example 100, 1000, 10¹⁰
FLOAT: 4-byte single-precision floating point, for example, 1500.00
DOUBLE: 8-byte double-precision floating point, for example, 750000.00
DECIMAL: 17-bytes precision up to 38 digits, for example, DECIMAL (5, 2)
STRING: Sequence of characters, for example, 'Welcome to Hive'
VARCHAR: Maximum length allowed is 65355 bytes. Similar to SQL's
         VARCHAR, for example, 'Welcome to Hive'
CHAR: Similar to SQL's CHAR with fixed length. Values shorter than
      fixed length (of 255 bytes) are padded with spaces,
      for example, 'Welcome to Hive'
DATE: Values are represented in YYYY-MM-DD format,
      for Example, '2017-04-08'
TIMESTAMP: yyyy-mm-dd hh:mm:ss
```

In addition to the above data types, Hive also supports complex or collection data types, which unlike the simple data types, are not available in many relation DBMS. Complex types are built up from simple types and other composite types. Hive currently supports four complex data types, namely array, map, struct and union.

Array is an ordered sequence of similar type elements which are indexable using zero-based integers. For example, array ('Ram', 'Lakshman', 'Sita'). Second element can be accessed with array {1}.

MAP is a collection of key-value pairs. Fields are accessed using array notation of keys.

Example: 'first'→'Ram', 'last'→'Sita' is represented as map ('first', 'Ram', 'last', 'sita'). Now 'Sita' can be accessed with map {'last'}.

Struct is similar to STRUCT in C language. It is a record type which encapsulates a set of named fields of simple data type. Elements in STRUCT type are accessed using the dot (.) notation.

Example: For a column C of type STRUCT {a INT; b INT}, the 'a' field is accessed by the expression 'c.a'

Union Type is similar to unions in C. At any point of time, a union type can hold any one data type from its specified data types.

Example:

```
CREATE TABLE test (Col 1 UNIONTYPE<INT, DOUBLE, ARRAY<VARCHAR>,
STRUCT<a: INT, b. CHAR>>);
```

Then retrieving results from Column 1 of test table can be any one of the following:

```
SELECT col 1 FROM test;
{0: 1}//Matching INT types
{1: 10.0}//Matching DOUBLE types
{2: {"MY" "SQL"}}//Matching ARRAY with VARCHAR type
```

The difference between traditional relational database and Hive lies in the feature that in the case of the former, insert, delete and update of data in a table take place one at a time, whereas in the case of the latter (Hive), bulk insert, delete and update are possible. For example, we can drop a whole table at a time using Hive.

13.14.2.2 Hive Tables

Hive deals with two types of data tables, namely the managed or internal tables and the external tables.

In case of internal table, the schema (table metadata) as well as the data of the table both reside inside the warehouse directory of Hive. If the table is dropped, then the table metadata as well as the data will be deleted. In case of an external table, the data of the table reside on HDFS or local file system and the metadata is only stored in the Hive meta-store. If the external table is dropped, then only the metadata is deleted in Hive, whereas the table data remain intact on HDFS or local File system. Figure 13.22 shows the difference between an Internal and External employee table in case of Hive.

13.14.2.3 Partitioning and Bucketing in Hive

A Hive table can be partitioned to slice the data in the table horizontally using one or more columns either for the entire range or a smaller range of values.

It may be mentioned that Hive physically stores tables as directories under the path/user/Hive/warehouse. For example, if we create a student table for a 3-year degree college for year (1st, 2nd and 3rd), stream (Science, Arts and Commerce) and name of the students as the three columns, the data will be stored under the/user/Hive/warehouse/students directory.

If we partition the same student table on two columns year and stream, the table will have each partition as a directory and a structure of the table will be as follows:

```
/user/Hive/warehouse/students/year=1ST/stream=Science
/user/Hive/warehouse/students/year=1ST/stream=Arts
/user/Hive/warehouse/students/year=1ST/stream=Commerce
```

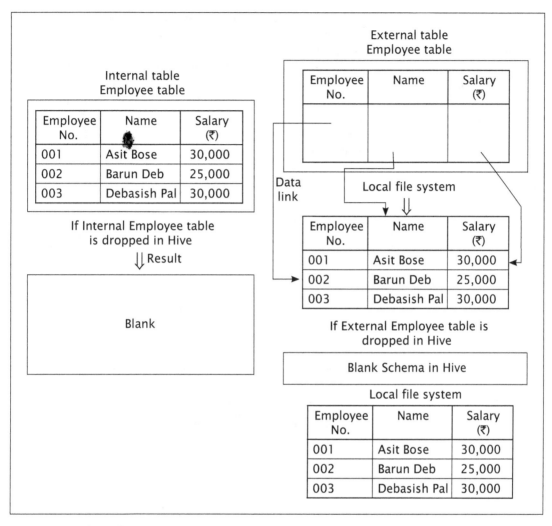

FIGURE 13.22 Difference between Hive Internal and Hive External Tables

```
/user/Hive/warehouse/students/year=2ND/stream=Science
/user/Hive/warehouse/students/year=2ND/stream=Arts
/user/Hive/warehouse/students/year=2ND/stream=Commerce
—
/user/Hive/warehouse/students/year=3RD/stream=Science
/user/Hive/warehouse/students/year=3RD/stream=Arts
/user/Hive/warehouse/students/year=3RD/stream=Commerce
```

All student names for Science stream of 1st year will reside in one directory and similarly, data for other partitions will reside in other directories. There will be 3 × 3 = 9 directories corresponding to 9 partitions. It may be stated that partitioning reduces query time since depending upon a query, Hive has to search a particular partition and not the entire data table of students. In addition to partitioning, Hive data tables adopt a concept of buckets, which provide efficient query handling in random sample of data. Bucketing divides data into a specified number of files based on a hash algorithm of the bucket column. For example, in the above students table, if we specify four buckets based on student names, the student names appearing in each partition under a directory will be stored in four buckets (each bucket being a file) depending on hash algorithm like all student names beginning with say, letters A–F in one bucket, G–M in the second bucket and so on. In order to search a particular student name beginning with say letter C in 1st year Science stream, Hive has to search the first bucket in the partition directory of 1st year Science stream and not to search the other buckets improving query handling efficiency greatly. The full directory and file structure of the student table will look as follows:

```
Partition Directory→/user/Hive/warehouse/students/year = 1ST/
stream = Science
```

	Name	Type	Size	Replication	Block Size	Permission	Owner	Group
	000000–0	file	0.02 KB	1	64 MB	rw-r--r-	root	Super Group
4 Buckets (files) in a Partition	000001–0	file	0.03 KB	1	64 MB	rw-r--r-	root	Super Group
	000002–0	file	0.04 KB	1	64 MB	rw-r--r-	root	Super Group
	000003–0	file	0.03 KB	1	64 MB	rw-r--r-	root	Super Group

```
Partition Directory→/user/Hive/warehouse/students/year=1ST/stream = Arts
```

Name	Type	Size	Replication	Block Size	Permission	Owner	Group
000000–0	file	0.03 KB	1	64 MB	rw-r·--rm	root	Super Group
000001–0	file	0.04 KB	1	64 MB	rw-r-·-rm	root	Super Group
000002–0	file	0.02 KB	1	64 MB	rw.-r.--r̄m	root	Super Group
000003–0	file	0.02 KB	1	64 MB	rw-.r--rm	root	Super Group

Each file representing a bucket contains the names of students as per hash.

As we know the number of reduce task determines the number of output files, so in the above example, we have defined the table as four buckets and accordingly, the number of reduce task is four as highlighted above.

Examples of Hive queries:
Let us see a few Hive queries from CLI. We assume we have the employee data Emp.txt on our local machine and it is a comma-separated data set of employees. In Hive, we first define a table that will store the data:

```
Hive > Create Table Emp (id INT, name STRING, sal FLOAT)
     > Row format delimited
     > fields terminated by ','
```

```
> stored as text file;
  OK
Time taken: 0.246 second
```

It may be noted that HQL statements are terminated by semicolons. If we want to see the tables available with Hive, the command is:

```
Hive > show tables;
       OK
       Emp
    Time taken: 0.053 second
Hive > describe Emp;
       OK
       id int
       name string
       sal float
    Time taken: 0.13 second
```

Let us now load the employee data from Emp.txt into the Emp table on Hive.

```
Hive > Load data local inpath 'Emp.txt'
     > overwrite into table Emp;
       copying data from file: /root/Emp.txt
       Loading data to table Emp
       OK
    Time taken: 9.52 seconds
```

The above command tells Hive to load data from a file called Emp.txt in the local file system into Emp table. Underneath the hood, the local machine uploads this data into HDFS under some directory managed by Hive under/user/Hive/warehouse.

The command, if we transfer data from HDFS to Hive table will be, however, as follows:

```
Hive > Load data inpath 'Emp.txt'
     > Overwrite into table Emp;
```

It may be stated that while loading data, Hive will not load any data into a table that violates its schema. In place of such data, Hive will substitute a null. For example, if we have the column names in the Emp.txt as the first line and then we use SELECT command to list data from the Emp table, the result will be as follows:

```
Hive > SELECT * from Emp limit 5;
       OK
```

NULL	NAME	NULL
001	A.K.Bose	50000
002	C. Prasad	25000
003	J. K. Lahiri	30000
004	S. K. Singh	40000

The lines after the CREATE TABLE command instructs Hive how the data are stored as a text file and how the data should be parsed, that is, each line of data is stored in a row and the fields are separated by commas.

A table can be deleted or dropped by DROP TABLE command:

```
Hive > DROP TABLE Emp;
   OK
Time taken: 0.34 second
```

To terminate the Hive session, we use the exit command.
Some more Hive commands:

```
Hive > create database if not exists emp_table;
       OK
Hive > create Schema emp_table;
Hive > Drop database if exists emp_table;
Hive > drop schema emp_table;
Hive > create table if not exists Emp_table (id int, name string,
       Sal float)
    > row format delimited
    > lines terminated by ' n'
    > fields terminated by ' t'
    > Stored as text file;
```

13.14.2.5 Commands in Hive for Managing Tables

Complicated tables can be created part by part using commands such as page_view followed by partitioning and bucketing as described earlier.

```
Hive > Create Table page_view (Empid int,
       Name string, Sex string, Sal float)
       Comment 'This is the page-view Table' partitioned by (joinyr
       string, Dept string
       Clustered by (Empid) into 32 Buckets Row Format Delimited
       Fields terminated by ' t'
       Lines terminated by ' n'
       Stored as Sequence File;
```

The first part of the above commands specifies the name of the table (page_view) and its schema which includes the name of the columns as well as their types.

The next part of the CREATE TABLE statement specifies the partition columns: joinyr and Dept which are both string type. The partition columns are distinct from the data columns of Empid, Name, Sex and Sal. The Value of a partition column for a particular row is not explicitly stored with the row; it is implied from the directory path. The last part: clustered by (Empid) into 32 buckets specifies the number of buckets based on the column (Empid) that random samples will be taken from and the number of buckets depend upon (i) the size of data under each partition and (ii) the size of the sample we intend to use.

13.14.2.6 Word Count Using Hive Command

Figure 13.23 shows the Hive command for word count.

```
Hive > SELECT word, COUNT (*) FROM doc LATERAL VIEW explode (split
       (text, ' ')) ltable as word GROUP By word;
```

which was run to count words from table doc which was created and loaded from a local file system abc shown in Figure 13.24 using following Hive commands:

```
Hive > CREATE TABLE doc (text string) row format delimited fields
       terminated by ' n' stored as text file;
       OK
Hive > Load data local inpath '/home/jtb/Desktop/word count/abc'
       overwrite into Table doc;
       Ok
```

13.4.3 Sqoop

Sqoop is a tool designed for seamless import or export of bulk data between Hadoop or HDFS or related Hadoop ecosystem (Hive, HBase and so on) and external data stores such as relational databases or enterprise data warehouses. Sqoop (SQL + Hadoop) works with relational databases such as MySQL, PostgreSQL, Oracle and Teradata.

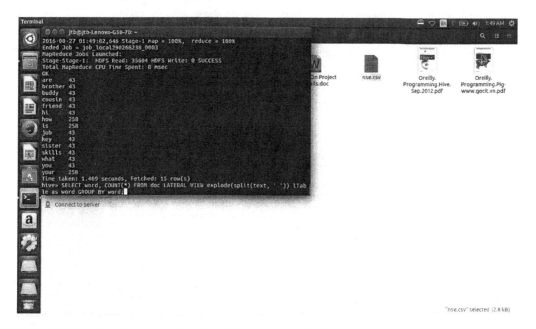

FIGURE 13.23 Hive Command for Word Count from Table Doc

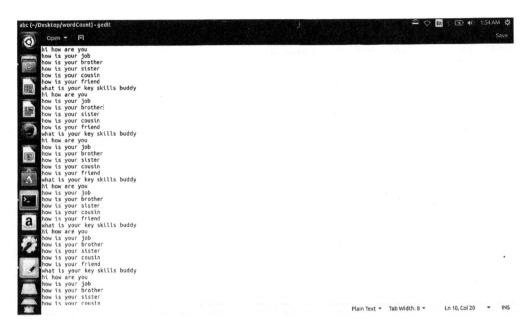

FIGURE 13.24 Local File 'abc' Created for Word Count with Hive Command

We can import/export all the tables in a database or part of a table or part of a database using Sqoop. It may be stated that Sqoop uses MapR framework to import or export the data, which provides parallel mechanism as well as fault tolerance. Sqoop allows CLI for developers who just have to provide information regarding source, destination and database authentication details in the Sqoop commands and Sqoop takes care of other details. Sqoop commands of the end users are parsed by Sqoop, which launches Hadoop map task to import or export data. Figure 13.25 shows the architecture of Sqoop on Hadoop.

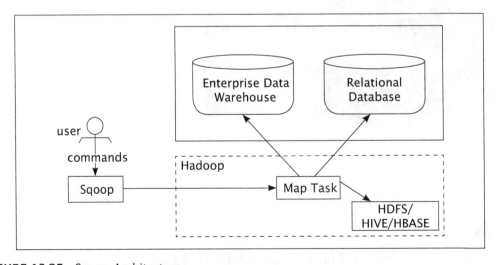

FIGURE 13.25 Sqoop Architecture

13.14.3.1 Basic Sqoop Commands and Syntax

1. Importing a table into HDFS. Syntax:

```
$ Sqoop import—connect jdbc: mysql: //<host name>: port No./
— table<table name>—username<username>
— password<password>— fields terminated by ‘ t’—target-dir<target
directory>⤶
```

The above sqoop command takes JDBC URL and connects to the database.

Database host should not be used as 'local host' as sqoop launches mappers on multiple data nodes and the mapper will not be able to connect to the DB host. '—target-dir' is the specified directory to which data are imported. The default port number is usually 80.

2. Importing part of a table. Syntax:

```
$ Sqoop import—connect jdbc: my sql//<host name>.port No./
— table<table name>—username—password
— fields-terminated by ‘ t’—columns “id,
name, salary”—where “salary>15000” ⤶
```

Here, '— columns' selects subset columns and '— where' retrieves the data, which satisfy the condition (in the above case salary > 15000). '—password' parameter is insecure as anyone can read it from the command line. '-p' option can be used in lieu, which prompts for password in console.

3. Importing all tables in a RDBMS database to HDFS:

In this case, data from each table is stored in a separate directory in HDFS syntax:

```
$ Sqoop-import-all-tables—connect jdbc: my sql: //<host name>port
No./<database
name>— username<username>
— password<password>
— fields terminated by ‘ t’ ⤶
```

In order to use 'Sqoop-import-all-tables' command, the following conditions need to be fulfilled:
a. Each table should have a single column primary key.
b. All columns of each table have to be imported.
c. No splitting of any column or any check condition using 'where' clause is allowed.

4. Exporting data from HDFS directory back to RDBMS table: The target table should already exist in the database.

Syntax:

```
$ Sqoop-export
$>—connect jdbc: mySql://<host name>: port No./<database name>—username
<username>
— password<password>
$>—table<table name>—input-fields-terminated-by ‘/t’
$>—export-dir<HDFS directory path>⤶
```

The Sqoop-export command prepares INSERT statements with sets of input data, then hits the database. If the table has unique value constant with primary key, export fails as the insert statement fails. Thus, it is for exporting new records only.

5. Listing all Database available on RDBMS server: Syntax:

```
$>Sqoop list-databases—connect jdbc: my sql: //<host name>port no/
— username<username>
—password<password>
```

6. Listing all tables in a specified database: Syntax:

```
$ Sqoop list-tables
— connect jdbc: my sql: //<host name>: port no./database name/$
— username<username>—password<password>
```

If the above command is executed successfully, then it will display the list of tables in the specified database.

13.14.4 HBase and Zookeeper

In Chapter 10, we have seen HBase as a column-oriented NOSQL database capable of handling and processing a large volume of tables having millions of rows and columns speedily. We also know about the HBase data model consisting of rows, columns, column families and row keys as the primary keys. In the subsequent paragraphs of this chapter, let us see how the HBase architecture falls in line with its data model and makes it capable of large storage of data together with high-processing speed. HBase has got a master slave architecture consisting of HMaster, HBase region servers (slaves), Zookeeper and the combination runs on Hadoop. Before we go through the details of the above components of HBase including their functions, the total HBase architecture is shown in Figure 13.26.

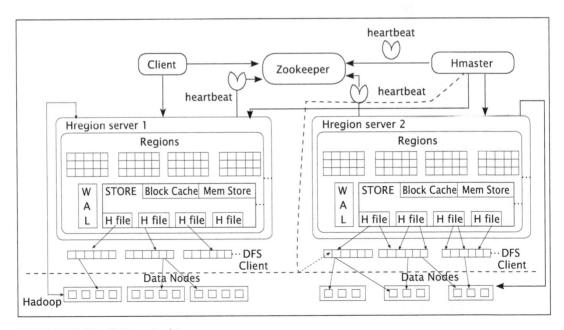

FIGURE 13.26 H Base Architecture

H Master is responsible for the following actions:

1. Coordinating with the region servers for assigning regions (portion of the whole HBase table) at the start and thereafter reassigning regions for recovery or load balancing.
2. Interfacing with regions for creating, deleting and updating of tables.

In short, Region assignment and DDL (create, delete tables) operations are the main functions handled by HMaster.

Region servers serve data mainly for reads and writes. Clients communicate with HBase region servers directly for accessing data. Region servers consist of regions which are obtained by partitioning the HBase tables horizontally according to row key range. For example, a HBase table having 10,000 rows can be divided into five regions having rows from 1–2000 | 2001–4000 | 4001–6000 | 6001–8000 | 8001–10000 |

Each region is identified by the starting row key and the end key as shown below.

A region server can serve up to about 1,000 regions and runs on a HDFS DataNode which stores the data managed by the region server. Partitioning the HBase table into regions and putting the data of the regions into region servers enable handling huge data at a fast speed. Region servers perform write, read and other HBase operations with the help of its components as follows:

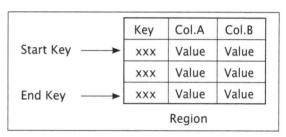

1. **Write Ahead Log (WAL):** It is a file on the HDFS and is used to store new data before putting the same into permanent storage. It is basically used for data recovery in case of failure of a region server.
2. **Block cache:** Block cache is the read cache. It stores frequently read data into memory. Least Recently Used (LRU) data are evicted when block cache gets full.
3. **MemStore:** This is the write cache which stores new data which have not been written to disk. It is sorted row key-wise, and there is one MemStore per column family per region. The MemStore stores updates in memory as sorted key value per column family with the version (time stamp) of each particular update. When the MemStore accumulates enough data, the entire sorted set is written to a new HFile in HDFS and the MemStore is flushed. HBase uses multiple HFiles per column family which contain the actual cells or key value instances. When the MemStore is flushed into HFile, the last written sequence number is also saved in HFile metadata so that the system knows what persisted till the time the flushing took place. The MemStore writes the sorted set of key-values into a new block of HFiles on HDFS sequentially and very fast.
4. **HFiles:** HFiles store the rows as sorted key values on disk.

Zookeeper provides the coordination service in HBase. HBase uses Zookeeper, which maintains server state in the cluster. Zookeeper maintains the state of servers (HMaster as well as region servers) as alive and available and provides server failure notification. The Zookeeper maintains ephemeral nodes for active sessions through heartbeats as shown in Figure 13.26. Zookeeper also has another important function of holding the location of a metatable, which in turn, contains the location of regions in the cluster of region servers.

13.14.4.1 Functioning of the HBase Components Together

Region servers and the active HMaster connect themselves in a session to Zookeeper. Each Region server creates an ephemeral node and the HMaster monitors these nodes to find out the available region servers. HMaster also monitors the failed server nodes. HMasters also create ephemeral nodes and Zookeeper finds the first one and uses the same to make sure that only one master is active at a time. If at any time, either the active HMaster or any region server fails to send a heartbeat, the session is terminated and the corresponding ephemeral node is deleted.

13.14.4.2 HBase Search Mechanism

In order to facilitate search of a particular row key and the corresponding region, HBase has a special catalogue table, the metatable. It maintains the list of start keys of the regions with its ID and the corresponding region server value which is the path of the same region server. Metatable has been shown in Figure 13.27.

For a first-time read or write operation, the client gets the region server that hosts the metatable from the zookeeper. Next, the client finds from the metatable server the particular region server corresponding to the row key the client wishes to access. The client caches this information along with the metatable location. Then the client gets the desired row from the corresponding region server and the region.

13.14.4.3 HBase Write Mechanism

The client willing to write data on HBase, first writes it to the WAL. Once the data have been written on WAL, the same is copied from WAL to MemStore. After the data have been fully copied to MemStore, WAL sends an ACK to the client. The MemStore always updates the data stored in it sequentially as

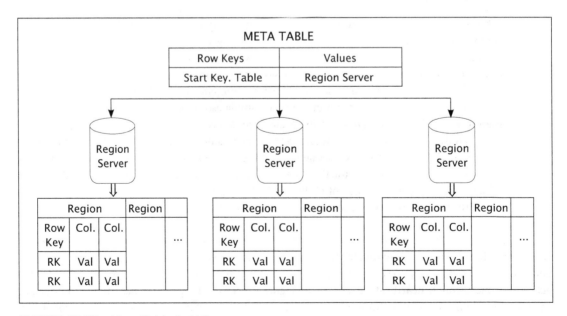

FIGURE 13.27 Meta Table in H Base

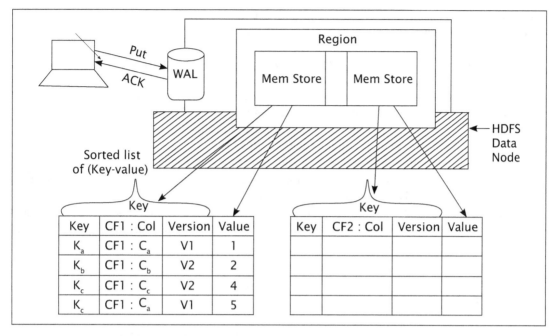

FIGURE 13.28 Write Mechanism in H Base

sorted key values for each column family. When the MemStore becomes full or reaches its threshold, it dumps all the data in a new HFile in a sorted manner and saves the data on HDFS. Figure 13.28 shows the write Mechanism as explained above.

13.14.4.4 HBase Read Mechanism

A HFile has got a multi-layered index which allows HBase to seek and read the desired data without reading the whole file. The index is loaded when the HFile is opened and kept in memory in order to facilitate look ups to be performed with a single seek.

We can see that the key value cells corresponding to a row can be in multiple locations such as HFiles for saved row cells, MemStore for recently written (updated) cells and block cache. Therefore, HBase reads data and merges the same in the following steps:

1. First, it looks for the row key-value cells in the block cache.
2. Next, it looks for the row cells in the MemStore.
3. If all row cells are not found in MemStore or block cache, HBase read-merge operation will look for row cells in HFiles. However, as discussed earlier, there may be many HFiles per MemStore which implies for a read, multiple HFiles may be required to be looked into which is known as read amplification in HBase.

Besides the above, HBase performs other operations such as major and minor compaction, region split, read-load balancing, data replication and crash recovery. We have already become familiar with several ecosystems of Hadoop such as MapR, Zookeeper, Pig, Hive, HBase, Sqoop, Yarn and HDFS. However, there are some more ecosystems of Hadoop such as Mahout, Tez, Avro and Ambari as shown in Figure 13.18. A brief introduction for each of these ecosystems of Hadoop has been given below.

> **Mahout:** It is an open source project mainly used for developing scalable machine-learning algorithms. Mahout runs on top of Hadoop.
>
> **Tez:** It acts as an interface between applications such as Pig (scripting) and Hive (SQL) and Yarn to reduce operations and complexity of backend processing. Tez reduces or saves on MapR or hard-disk operations. It provides a 'service' which always attempts to decrease start times of jobs. Tez also allows caching of data in memory.
>
> **Avro:** It is a serialization framework developed within Apache's Hadoop. Its primary use is in providing a serialization format for persistent data. Avro facilitates conversion of unstructured and semi-structured data into structured way using schemas.
>
> **Spark:** It is a separate and fast MapR such as engine for very fast iterative queries. Spark is up to 40 times faster than Hadoop. Spark can also read from/write to any Hadoop supported system such as HDFS, HBase and sequential files.

13.15 Cloud Computing

The practice of using a network of remote servers hosted on the Internet to store, manage, process and retrieve data, rather than a single local server or a personal computer, is known as cloud computing. It is a model for enabling ubiquitous and on-demand access to a shared pool of configurable computing resources such as computer networks, servers, storage devices, applications and services, which can be provisioned and released with least management effort. The term cloud computing is a metaphor because to a user of cloud computing, the elements providing the computing services remain invisible or obscured like a cloud as shown in Figure 13.29.

Cloud computing has got an inherent advantage of resource sharing to achieve coherence and economy of scale. It enables companies to lay emphasis on their core business instead of developing in-house elaborate IT infrastructure. Moreover, cloud marketers allow users to pay according to their requirements of computational facilities.

13.15.1 History of Development of Cloud Computing

Cloud computing came into existence in 2000. In August 2006, Amazon introduced the Elastic Computing Cloud (ECC). In early 2008, NASA introduced 'open Nebula', the first open source software deploying private and hybrid clouds. Simultaneously, efforts were there for providing quality service to cloud-based infrastructures to facilitate real-time interactive applications. In July 2010, Rackspace Hosting and NASA jointly launched an open-source cloud software known as 'OpenStack'. The project was intended for organizations offering cloud computing services running on standard hardware. Thereafter in March 2011, IBM announced its 'SmartCloud' framework to support cloud computing. On 7 June 2012, Oracle announced the 'Oracle Cloud' which is supposed to be the first to provide users access to an integrated set of IT solutions under the cloud layers of applications–software, platform and infrastructure. In May 2012, Google released 'Google Compute Engine' in preview before being rolled out into full-fledged general availability in December 2013.

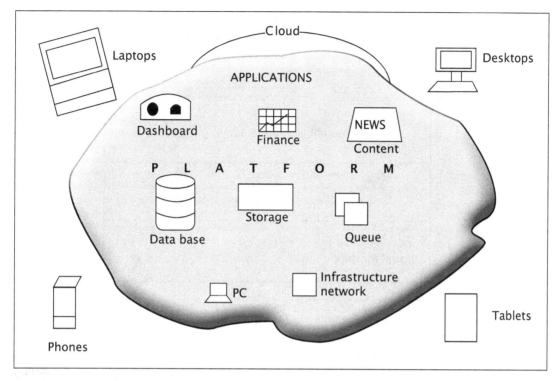

FIGURE 13.29 Cloud Computing

13.15.2 Service Models of Cloud Computing

Cloud-computing service providers offer their services according to different models. Three such standard models as per National Institute of Standards and Technology (NIST) of the USA are (a) software as a service (SaaS) (b) platform as a service (PaaS) and (c) infrastructure as a service (IaaS).

NIST defined the above service models as follows:

Software as a Service (SaaS): The service provider's applications are accessible to the users through a client interface such as a web browser or a program interface. The user does not manage or control the underlying cloud infrastructure such as network, servers, storage devices and even the individual application capabilities. SaaS is sometimes referred to as 'on-demand software' and usually priced on a pay-per-use basis or a subscription fee per user per month or year.

Platform as a Service (PaaS): The service provided to the user is to deploy on to the cloud infrastructure user-created or acquired applications developed adopting programming languages, libraries, services and tools supported by the cloud-service provider.

The user has control over the deployed applications including possibly configuration settings for the application-hosting environment only. However, the user does not have any control on the cloud infrastructure, including network servers, operating system or storage. PaaS vendors offer to application developers a development environment.

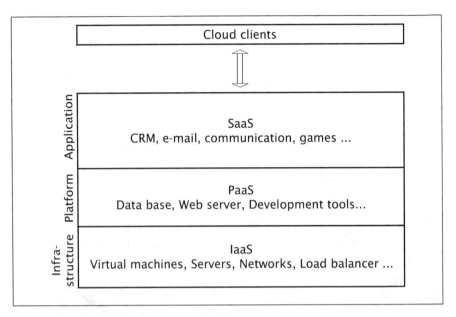

FIGURE 13.30 Cloud Computing Service Models

Infrastructure as a Service (IaaS): The capability provided to the user is to provide processing, storage, networks and other fundamental computing resources using which the user can deploy or run arbitrary software such as OS and applications.

In the IaaS model, the user does not control the underlying cloud infrastructure except limited control on some networking components such as host firewalls. IaaS is the most basic cloud-service model providing computing infrastructure such as the virtual machines and other resources. Pools of hypervisor run the virtual machines with an ability to scale services up and down according to users' varying requirements.

The cloud-computing service models have been shown in Figure 13.30 as layers in a stack but they are not related.

Besides the above three types of service models, there is a mobile 'backend' as a service (MBaaS) also known as Backend as a service (BasS). In this service model, web application and mobile-application developers link their applications to cloud storage and cloud computing services with APIs pertaining to their applications and software development kits. BaaS includes many services such as client management and integration with social networking services. BaaS start-ups date back from 2011 and onwards and these services are gaining significant mainstream traction with enterprise consumers.

13.15.2.1 Server-less Computing

Server-less computing is a cloud computing code execution model in which the cloud provider fully manages starting and stopping virtual machines to serve user requests and the billing is done based on the resources actually utilized to satisfy the request, instead of per virtual machine (VMs) per hour rate. However, server-less computing is really not executing codes without servers. It only signifies the fact that the service provider does not have to purchase, rent or provision servers or VMs for the backend code to run on.

13.15.2.2 Cloud Deployment Models

Cloud deployment models include mainly private, public and hybrid clouds. Private cloud is cloud infrastructure operated solely for a single entity or organization, managed either internally or by a third party and hosted either internally or externally. Private cloud for an organization is generally resource intensive because of space, hardware, software and the necessary environmental controls. Moreover, security issues need to be addressed properly to rule out severe vulnerability. However, private cloud if properly managed can improve business decisions and performance.

Public cloud provides services over a network which is open to public for use. Public cloud-service providers, such as Amazon Web Services (AWS), Microsoft and Google, own and operate the infrastructure at their data centres and access to the public is through the Internet. Community cloud is a particular type of cloud similar to public cloud, wherein the cloud infrastructure is shared by a few organizations belonging to a specific community with common concerns for security, areas of operation, compliance and so on. The cost of operation is shared by the few users unlike a public cloud.

Hybrid cloud obviously, as the name signifies, is a cloud composed of two or more clouds (public, private or community) that remain distinct entities but tied together and offer benefits of more than one deployment models. Gartner Inc. defined a hybrid-cloud service as a cloud-computing service that is composed of some combination of private, public and community cloud services provided by different service providers. Besides the above deployment models, there are other types of cloud deployment such as distributed cloud, intercloud and multicloud also.

13.15.3 Cloud Architecture

Architecture of the cloud software system for the delivery of cloud-computing service typically involves multiple cloud components such as cloud platform, cloud infrastructure and cloud storage communicating with each other over a loose coupling mechanism such as a messaging queue.

13.15.4 Limitations and Disadvantages

Cloud computing has got some limitations and disadvantages also. First of all, cloud computing has limited scope of customization for users. Moreover, the control of the backend infrastructure is limited to the cloud vendors only and cloud users have little control over their applications, data and services. Privacy and confidentiality are big concerns for cloud users because the service provider can access the data that is in the cloud at any time. Many cloud providers can share information with third parties if necessary for purpose of law and order even without prior permission or notice. This is permitted in their privacy policies which cloud users have to agree as a precondition for using cloud services. According to the Global Cloud Security Market Professional Survey Report 2016, the top three threats in the cloud are insecure interfaces and APIs, data loss and leakage and hardware failure which accounted for 29%, 25% and 10% of all cloud-security outages respectively. Together the above security concerns form shared technology vulnerabilities.

13.15.5 Popular Cloud Services

Three popular cloud-computing services are Microsoft Azure, IBM Bluemix and the AWS. Microsoft Azure cloud-computing service was created by Microsoft for developing, deploying and managing applications and services through Microsoft managed-data centres all over the world connected through a global network. Azure provides SaaS, PaaS and IaaS besides supporting many programming languages, tools and frameworks developed by Microsoft and a third party also. Microsoft Azure came into existence in March 2014 when Microsoft renamed Windows Azure as Microsoft Azure. There are about 600 Azure services available today such as VMs, compute services, mobile services and storage services.

IBM Bluemix is a cloud platform as a service developed by IBM. It supports several programming languages such as Java, Node.js, Python, PHP, Ruby and Swift. IBM Bluemix also provides integrated software development and IT operation services to build, run and deploy applications on the cloud. The initial release of Bluemix was made by IBM in June 2014.

AWS are, by far, the most popular and widely deployed cloud services. One can hire computing and storage services on demand from AWS as per the scale of requirement for the same. Because of its flexibility and cost effectiveness, running Hadoop on AWS cloud has become a popular setup. AWS offers its Elastic Compute Cloud (EC2) and Simple Storage Service (S3) as the two core services. EC2 service provides compute capacity for running Hadoop nodes. We can think of EC2 as a large collection of VMs. An EC2 instance is in AWS terminology a virtual compute unit and each Hadoop node will take up an EC2 instance. One can rent as many EC2 instances matching the requirement as long as one needs and pays on hourly basis. Whenever the requirement scales down, one can terminate the instances not required and need not pay rental. It is because of the above feature that the name is Elastic Compute Cloud.

The Amazon S3 service is a cloud storage service provided for storing all data pertaining to an EC2 instance, which is deleted when the instance is terminated by a user and the user may use the data in future.

Each EC2 instance functions like a commodity Intel hardware which one can access and control over the Internet. We can boot up an instance using an Amazon Machine Image (AMI). Some images are only basic OSs. EC2 supports more than six variants of Linux, Windows server and OpenSolaris. It is worth mentioning that AWS offers preconfigured images of Hadoop running on Linux and Hadoop in turn has inbuilt support for working with both EC2 and S3.

13.16 Internet of Things (IOT)

The term IOT was first used in 1999 by British technology pioneer Kevin Ashton to describe a system in which objects in the physical world could be connected to the Internet by sensors. There is, however, no single universal definition for IOT. The term 'Internet of things' refers to a scenario where network connectivity and computing extend to objects, sensors (also referred to as 'smart devices') and everyday items not normally considered as computers such as vehicles, garage doors and buildings. IOT allows these devices to generate, exchange and consume data without human intervention.

13.16.1 IOT Connectivity Models

There are four common connectivity models used by IOT. They are (a) device-to-device (b) device-to-cloud (c) device-to-gateway and (d) backend data sharing.

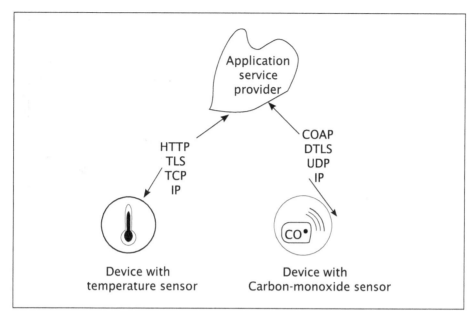

FIGURE 13.31 Example of Device-to-Cloud IOT Model

Source: TSchofenig, Arkko and Thaler (2015).

Device-to-device communication involves two or more devices that directly connect and communicate among themselves through various types of networks such as IP networks of the Internet and Bluetooth. This model is very common for home automation systems to transfer small data packets of information between devices such as thermostats, light bulbs, light switches, door locks and timers. Device-to-device communication is also popular among wearable IOT devices used for healthcare such as a heart monitor connected to a valve controlling flow of saline (electrolyte) into the patient's body.

Device-to-cloud communication enables an IOT device to connect directly to an Internet cloud-service provider, to exchange data and control message traffic. Figure 13.31 shows an example of device-to-cloud communication model where two devices with temperature and carbon monoxide sensors communicate with cloud application service provider.

Device-to-gateway is similar to a device-to-cloud model except that in this case, IOT devices basically connect to an intermediary device usually a local gateway device such as a smartphone or a hub to access a cloud-service provider. The intermediate gateway provides security and other functionalities such as data or protocol translation.

Backend data sharing essentially is a single device-to-cloud communication model extended to more than one application service provider as shown in Figure 13.32.

13.16.2 IOT Applications

According to Gartner Inc., there will be 30 plus billion permanent devices on the IOT by 2020. The former British Chancellor of the Exchequer, George Osborne posited that the IOT is the next stage of the information revolution and mentioned about the interconnectivity of everything from urban transport

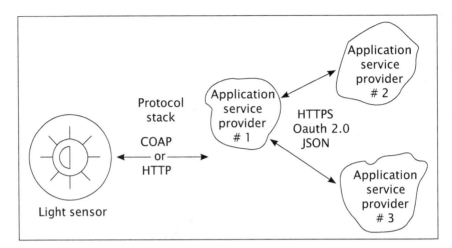

FIGURE 13.32 Backend Data Sharing IOT Model

Source: Tschofenig, Arkko and Thaler (2015).

to medical devices and to household appliances. It is obvious that the growth of IOT to connect very large number of devices through the Internet over the years is tremendous. IOT finds applications in nearly every field starting with media to environmental monitoring, infrastructure management, manufacturing, energy management, healthcare management, building and home automation, transportation, management of urban facilities, consumer applications and many other similar fields.

Not all connected devices contribute to big data, but connected devices are large and visible portion of what makes up the IOT and are the source of a variety of new data inputs and data considerations. IOT goes hand in hand with big data and advanced analytic due to the variety of data it produces. There are numerous connected home appliances in the field from security systems and thermostats to keyless entry, refrigerators and garage doors. Today, about 56% of big data and advanced analytics developers work on projects for which connected devices are client devices, which besides personal computers include home devices or appliances, wearable devices, industrial sensors, automotive devices and so on.

An overview of some of the major application areas of IOT are provided as follows:

1. **Smart home:** There are many smart home products which are connected as IOT to facilitate home automation. Some activities such as setting up a light to turn on or off at the whims of the occupants are simple and relatively inexpensive, whereas sophisticated access control and modern surveillance cameras require more investment of money. However, a smart home has got the following major features:
    i. IOT-driven efficient building energy management system.
    ii. Real-time monitoring of energy consumption and occupant behaviour for controlling energy consumption.
    iii. Integration of home devices for control of operations relating to garage door, door lock security and access control, surveillance, watering of plants in the garden, fire and obnoxious gas detector and alarms and so on.
    iv. Temperature and humidity control for comfort.
2. **Wearables:** Wearables are smart electronic devices which can be worn on the human body as implant or accessories. Examples include smart watches, fitness trackers and sport trackers. Such

devices belong to IOT that enable objects to exchange data through the Internet with a manufacturer, operator or other connected devices without human intervention.

3. **Manufacturing:** Process control, production scheduling and control, dynamic response to product demands and real-time optimization of manufacturing and supply-chain networks bring IOT within the realm of smart manufacturing applications. It also extends itself to asset management through predictive maintenance and statistical evaluation to maximize reliability.

4. **Retail smart store:** A smart store is a retail store which uses smart technologies such as smart shelves, smart cards and smart carts. Smart stores generally deliver retail services to customers through the Internet, smartphone apps and augmented reality applications in real stores. Such technologies enhance the productivity of store space and inventory. For example, RFID technology allows for the use of kiosks and self-checkout terminals for keeping track of all incoming and outgoing goods.

5. **Transportation and automotive:** The IOT can facilitate dynamic communication and control among the components of various transportation systems such as the vehicle, infrastructure, driver or user. Some of the features of such dynamic communication are intra-vehicular communication, smart traffic control, smart parking bay, toll collection, fleet management, vehicle movement control including speed limit, safety and road assistance.

6. **Environmental monitoring:** Environmental monitoring applications of the IOT typically monitor quality of biophysical environment such as air, water, soil as well as environmental stress of various types involving even movements of wildlife and habitats. The purpose is to protect the environment. Further, early warning systems for disaster management involving earthquake and tsunami with devices connected to the Internet form another important application area. IOT devices for environmental monitoring typically span a large geographical area and can also be mobile.

7. **Health care:** Connected devices are essential for healthcare IOT. They collect data, communicate with each other and integrate with larger systems through high-speed data networks, cloud computing and mobile technology. Such devices create new possibilities in healthcare and patient care also. A few examples are location monitors, defibrillators, tele-health, and temperature and humidity sensors.

   Another healthcare application area is the stationary medical device. These devices are used for prevention, diagnosis and treatment of diseases. For example, hospital telemetry monitors, imaging machines, intravenous infusion equipment, ventilators and similar other life-sustaining equipment work over WiFi or cellular 'Medical Body Area Networks' (MBANs). The devices can be linked together through different enterprise platforms for data transfer among healthcare systems.

   A very recent development is the internally embedded medical devices such as insulin pumps, pacemakers, drug dispensers, nerve simulators and artificial body implants. Those often use proprietary and secured wireless protocols or Bluetooth to connect themselves with larger systems. A good example is a pacemaker which continually transmits data to cardiologists over WiFi and artificial pancreas having a continuous glucose monitor connected through WiFi to an insulin pump. Another example is chip-based orthopaedic implants which can communicate information about wear and tear, alerting a patient when an artificial joint needs replacement. Ingestible and adhesives are pill-like devices (also known as e-pills) that monitor internal physiological data such as temperature, activity level, flow rate and reaction to a particular medication. For example, health care equipment companies have developed ingestible pill-like sensors, which can reach a patient's stomach and through a miniature Bluetooth antenna send vital data of stomach to smartphones accessible to healthcare providers including physicians.

Many health-related things such as drug inventory, pill bottles, medical insurance cards, hospital wrist bands and sleep monitors can be made 'smart' by equipping them with radio frequency identification tags or other sensors that can work with near-field communication (NFC), WiFi, cellular data or Bluetooth. A sleep monitor attached as a wristband can work on mobile phone technology to furnish data relating to hours of sound sleep, number of tossing on bed, hours of no sleep and so on pertaining to a continuous night the patient spent. Similarly, Adhere Tech's pill bottles track and improve medication adherence. The bottles, which again work on mobile-phone technology, light up and sound an alert when patients forget to take their medicine in the prescribed time.

8. **Sports/fitness:** Devices and apps used by consumers to track health, fitness and wellness are gaining lot of importance of late. Examples are Jawbone, Fitbit, Smartphone apps for tracking calories and menstrual cycles. Other advanced examples include smart toothbrushes, wireless elementary monitors for blood pressure, blood sugar and smart clothing. Apple Inc. is working with large healthcare systems to integrate its health app data into electronic medical records (EMRs).

   The IOT is revolutionizing the sports world. The richness and the speed at which data are captured during a sporting event with IOT devices are certainly innovative. Smart sportswear allows us to transcribe body data into training advice and all kinds of sports equipment are increasingly capable of measuring our performance and reporting the same to our smartphones.

9. **Infrastructure management:** Monitoring and controlling operations of urban and rural infrastructures such as tunnels, bridges, highways, railway tracks and on-and-offshore wind farms are key applications of IOT relating to infrastructure management. Scheduling and control of repair and maintenance activities in an efficient manner for infrastructures can be undertaken by communication and coordination of tasks among different service providers and users of the facilities.

10. **Smart cities:** IOT has brought about the smart city concept. A 'smart city' is an urban region that is highly advanced in terms of overall infrastructure, sustainable real estate, communication and market. It is a city where IT is the principal infrastructure and forms the basis for providing essential hi-tech services to residents. There are identified indicative areas which make a smart city. Some of those areas are listed as follows:
    i.   Water supply
    ii. Air quality
    iii. Healthcare
    iv. Education
    v.   Intelligent transport system
    vi. Waste management
    vii. Safety and security
    viii. IT/WiFi connectivity
    ix. Intelligent government service
    x.   Online shopping mall
    xi. Walk-ability, which is an important concept in sustainable urban design

CASE STUDY: *THE NEW YORK TIMES* CONVERTED 11 MILLION ARTICLES AS IMAGES INTO PDF VERSION

In the year 2007, *The New York Times* decided to make all the public domain articles from 1851 to 1922 available on their website free of charge. These articles were in the form of images scanned from the original papers. Each article actually composed of numerous smaller tag image file format (TIFF) images that needed to be scaled and combined together coherently. Doing this required a scalable image conversion system.

Previously, the Times had generated all PDFs dynamically. Although the same approach worked reasonably well, the same might not scale up to handle significant traffic increase possibility due to free availability of the articles. Pregenerating all these articles as PDF files and statically serving them would be a challenging option because of the massive archive of 11 million articles consisting of 4 TB of data.

Derek Gottfrid, a software programmer at *The New York Times* got the idea of using Amazon's S3 service for storage and retrieval of the 4 TB of TIFF images and also the converted PDF version of the articles. He also thought of writing some code that would run on multiple instances of EC2 under Hadoop framework to generate the PDF.

Derek copied the 4 TB TIFF images into S3. Next, he 'started writing code to pull all the parts that make up an article out of S3, generate a PDF back in S3. This was easy enough using the JetS3t–open-source Java toolkit for S3, iText PDF library and installing the Java advanced image extension'. After tweaking and bug fixing, Derek deployed Hadoop and his code running on 100 EC2 instances (nodes). The job took only 24 hours to churn through 11 million articles and generated another 1.5 TB of data to store in S3.

Assuming an EC2 reserved instance's price about $0.05 per hour in all, the above conversion was completed with a cost of only $120 (100 instances × 24 hours × 0.05)! This is amazing.

Review Questions

1. What are the characteristics and sources of big data? Illustrate with suitable examples.

2. Mention some major applications of big data.

3. What is 'churn analysis'? What is its scope and applicability?

4. What is KDD process? What are the major techniques of data mining?

5. What are the measures of quality of text mining?

6. What is machine learning? What is the basic difference between supervised and unsupervised learning?

7. What are the master and slave daemons of Hadoop? What is the default replication factor of Hadoop?

8. What is the function of combiner in Hadoop? What is shuffling in MapR?

9. What are the differences between Hadoop 1.0 and Hadoop 2.0? What does 'rsa' stand for?

10. What are the major ecosystems of Hadoop? What are their basic functions?

11. Which ecosystem of Hadoop has 'grunt' shell?

12. What are the functions of 'WAL' and 'Zookeeper'?

13. What is 'time stamp'? How it facilitates analysis of streaming data?

14. What is cloud computing? Explain the three service models of cloud.

15. What is elastic cloud? What are its advantages? Mention the name of any popular elastic cloud-computing service provider.

16. What is IOT? Illustrate with examples.

17. What is the importance of wearable technologies in overall healthcare?

18. How do you think IOT can provide a business with competitive advantage?

19. What is collaborative technology? Explain.

Bibliography

Bughin, J. 'Big Data: Getting a Better Read on Performance.' *McKinsey Quarterly* (2016, February). Available at: https://www.mckinsey.com/industries/technology-media-and-telecommunications/our-insights/big-data-getting-a-better-read-on-performance (accessed on 29 March 2020).

Dasgupta, N. *Practical Big Data Analytics*. Birmingham: Packt Publishing, 2018.

Dean, J. *Big Data, Data Mining and Machine Learning: Value Creation for Business Leaders and Practitioners*. Hoboken, NJ: Wiley, 2014.

Evans, J. *Business Analytics, Methods, Models and Decisions*, 2nd ed. London: Pearson, 2017.

Harrison, G. *Next Generation Databases: NoSQL and Big Data*, 1st ed. New York, NY: Apress, 2015.

Inmon, W. H., and K. Krishnan. *Building the Unstructured Data Warehouse*. Bradley Beach, NJ: Technics Publications, 2011.

Karen, R., D. E. Scott, and C. Lyman. 'The Internet of Things (IOT): An Overview—Understanding the Issues and Challenges of a More Connected World.' Internet Society, USA, October, 2015.

Krishnan, K. *Data Warehousing in the Age of Big Data*. Waltham, MA: Morgan Kaufmann, Elsevier, 2013.

Krishnan, K., and S. Rogers. *Social Data Analytics: Collaboration for the Enterprise*. Waltham, MA: Morgan Kaufmann, Elsevier, 2015.

Shmueli, G., P. C. Bruce, I. Yahav, N. R. Patel, and Kenneth C. Lichtendahl Jr. *Data Mining for Business Analytics*. Hoboken: NJ: John Wiley & Sons, 2018.

TSchofenig, H., J. Arkko, and D. Thaler. 'Architectural Considerations in Smart Object Networking.' *Internet Architecture Board* RFC 7452, March 2015.

Business Process Re-engineering

14.1 Introduction

BPR is the *fundamental rethinking* and *radical redesign* of *core business processes* to achieve *dramatic improvements* in critical, contemporary measures of performance such as *quality, cost and cycle time.*

The words *in italics* are very important. Fundamental rethinking implies that re-engineering of business processes has to start from scratch considering the ground reality and without any bias towards the existing processes or systems. Michael Hammer, the founder of the BPR concept, published the article 'Re-engineering work: Do not Automate, Obliterate' in 1990. In this article, what Hammer wanted to mean is that re-engineering is neither simply automating the existing systems including the legacy systems, nor is it for obliterating those systems. Radical redesign involves transformation of business processes and every aspect of the organization to avail of the full benefits of the BPR exercise. Dramatic improvements imply a quantum jump and not continuous incremental business improvements. Quality, cost and cycle time are key-performance indicators, which lead to customer satisfaction.

Re-engineering focuses on rethinking for more efficient ways of working and eliminating unproductive work or processes which do not add value to the customers. Companies reduce organizational layers and eliminate unproductive work in two significant areas. First, they change functional departmentalization into cross-functional teams and second, they employ information, communication and other state-of-the-art technologies to facilitate data and information dissemination for effective and efficient decision-making and resource management.

A business process is a collection of activities which together produce something of value to the customers. According to Thomas Davenport, 'A process is simply a structured, measured set of activities designed to produce a specific output for a particular customer or market.' A business process is characterized by its (a) specific sequence of work activities across time and space; (b) a beginning and an end; (c) clearly defined inputs and outputs; (d) customer focus; (e) work procedure; (f) process ownership and (g) measurable performance indicators of quality, cost, cycle time and overall customer value addition.

Let us illustrate business process with some real-life examples:

- Customer-order processing is a business process consisting of the activities of customer-order acceptance, resource utilization, local purchase of input materials, input material receipt and delivery of goods and services to the customer.

- Student admission in a business school is a business process consisting of receiving application forms for admission, scrutiny of the forms, written test, group discussion, personal interview, selection, publication of admission list, collection of fees from the students selected for admission and registration of the students.
- Accounts receivable process in a manufacturing organization consists of customer order, preparation of invoice, dispatch of invoice and dispatch of finished products, receipt of cash/cheque/bank draft/real-time gross settlement (RTGS)/National Electronic Funds Transfer (NEFT) from the customers and preparation of accounts receivable statement.

BPR also includes innovation of new products and services. It may be stated that BPR changes business processes and not functions, activities, tasks or departments. Some proponents of BPR consider the same as a business management strategy because it focuses on the analysis, design and workflow of business processes within an organization in order to improve customer service, cut operational costs and to become a world-class competitor.

BPR is exercised through the six R's of re-engineering, namely *realization* for change, *requirement, rethinking, redesign, retooling* and the last but not the least important *re-evaluation*. It is an all-pervasive organizational development exercise to improve existing business processes by way of changing organizational structure, improving systems and procedures, introducing better work culture, replacing old business practices with new ones and diversifying the products and services to suit the customer needs. Success of BPR largely depends upon correct assessment of the shortcomings in the existing organizational systems and the measures to eliminate the same. However, proper risk analysis of the changes with technical and operational feasibility studies is an essential pre-requirement.

BPR needs an effective planning for the changes to be introduced in the business processes with priorities for each individual change and the modalities for effecting the changes. Obviously, it involves a lot of trial-and-error exercises. Also, the right kind of analysis of causes of failures, if any, is needed during the re-engineering exercise to avoid mistakes and achieve ultimate success. Transformation of employees particularly their behaviour and attitude towards change is of paramount importance as the success of BPR largely depends upon the extent of cooperation and involvement of the employees of an organization.

14.2 BPR Methodology

BPR involves the following methodology broadly:

1. **Process identification through business process mapping (BPM):** The steps of BPM have been listed in a subsequent paragraph.
2. **Process rationalization through value-chain analysis:** In this phase, the value addition of each process is critically examined in order to eliminate non-value adding or non-essential processes.
3. **Process simplification through redesign:** The processes retained after 2 above are redesigned to make them work more efficiently.
4. **Process integration:** The reengineered processes after 3 above are integrated in proper sequence and implemented resulting in effective and efficient performance of the whole organization.

14.3 Steps of Business Process Mapping (BPM)

BPM consists of the following steps:

1. Identification of each distinct process and the start and the end activities of each process.
2. Collection of relevant information about tasks from different people associated with the process. The different categories of the processes such as reactive processes that create bottlenecks in daily activities, strategic processes and customer-oriented processes must be prioritized.
3. Correct sequencing of all activities in between the start and end of the process.
4. Matching of all activities with proper symbols.
5. Preparation of the process flow chart depicting workflow mapping.

The purpose of workflow mapping process is to analyse the existing processes in an organization and to understand if the process workflow is in keeping with the business objectives and strategic plan formulated by the top management of the organization.

14.4 Steps Involved in BPR

BPR is carried out in an organization in the following sequential steps. Each step consists of one or more tasks as mentioned under each step:

1. Initiate organizational changes. The tasks involved with this step are:
   i. Assessment of the current state of the organization.
   ii. Understand the existing processes through process overview, mission, scope and boundaries of each process.
   iii. Understand customers' expectations from the process.
2. Develop and communicate vision for improved processes:
   i. Communicate with all employees to make them aware of the vision of the future.
   ii. Demonstrate to employees the necessity of BPR.
   iii. Clearly identify opportunities for improvement such as quality improvement, cost and time reduction and value addition.
   iv. Resolve inconsistencies among processes if any, and make prediction for the consequences of the changes.
   v. Remove any fear among employees regarding job security.
3. Identify action plans for BPR:
   i. Evaluate the existing business policies and customer requirements.
   ii. Identify new business opportunities and develop an improvement plan which should include diversification plan for products and services.
   iii. Select the core processes which need to be re-engineered.
   iv. Identify the process owners.
   v. Identify potential barriers against implementation.
   vi. Simplify processes to reduce process time and cost.

    vii. Remove no value-added activities.

    viii. Formulate new process-performance strategies.

4. Changes in work culture:

    i. Brainstorm the BPR principles through questionnaires, meetings and focus groups.

    ii. Make customer delight the focal point.

    iii. Explain the new value system and culture to the employees.

    iv. Set up re-engineering team, executive improvement team and cross-functional groups. Re-engineering team has to include BPR leader.

    v. Allow the workers to participate in decision-making.

    vi. Consultants may be engaged for quick implementation of BPR. However, adequate consultation with all employees is needed to ensure initiative on the part of all employees.

5. Establish new business system:

    i. Draw new workflow diagram.

    ii. Document the new organization structure.

    iii. Standardize processes and automation if feasible has to be adopted.

    iv. Upgrade equipment and describe new technologies if adopted.

    v. Redesign the information requirement.

6. Execute the transformation process:

    i. Develop correct change strategy.

    ii. Plan and schedule the changes.

    iii. Map the new skill requirements.

    iv. Train the employees to take care of the new processes.

    v. Reallocate work among the workforce.

    vi. Design performance metrics for the new processes.

    vii. Design and establish a feedback system.

    viii. Benchmark the processes and transform the organization.

14.5 Process Re-engineering Life Cycle

Aphrodite Tsalgatidou introduced the concept of 'process life cycle' based on her comparative study of four popular BPR methodologies, namely Hammer and Champy (2009), Davenport and Short (1990), process analysis and design methodology (PADM) developed by Informatics Process Group of Manchester University, UK in 1994 and the object-oriented BPR by Jacobson and others (1994).

Hammer and Champy definition of BPR has already been mentioned in an earlier paragraph of this chapter. They mentioned 'fundamental rethinking and radical change'. According to them, any BPR effort changes every organizational aspect such as the business processes, employees, jobs and structures, management and measurement systems, values and beliefs as all these aspects are related with the business processes. The 'business system diamond' a term coined by them represents the above-mentioned aspects as the four corner points of the diamond as shown in Figure 14.1. According to Hammer and Champy, IT plays a crucial role in BPR.

Davenport and Short (1990) placed IT at the heart of BPR. Their strategy for BPR is more modest and tempered with the approach of continuous process improvement. They also recommended selecting the critical processes, analysing and redesigning them iteratively.

PADM emanated out-of-process modelling techniques, which describe two phases of the technique, namely representation and refinement phase. Both the phases incorporate continuous and iterative process improvement as key to BPR. PADM, however recognizes the relationship between IT and processes as reciprocal, which implies that changes in IT may require process changes and similarly the changes in process may require changes in IT.

The object-oriented BPR as advocated by Jackobson and others defines an object as an occurrence containing information and behaviour that is meaningful to the business

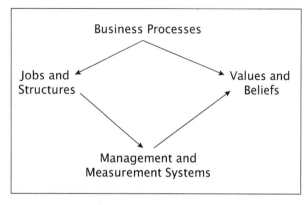

FIGURE 14.1 The Business System Diamond

Source: Hammer and Champy.

organization and hence needs to be described in the organizational environment. For example, supplier, customer, supply order and invoice are objects. The behaviour of the object and related information can be used by other objects also. Work tasks in an organization can be modelled as objects. The processes are modelled with the objects for clarifying the inner working of an organization.

Re-engineering work is performed within the framework of BPR in two steps, namely *reverse engineering* the existing organization, where an abstract model of the business and the processes under study are constructed as it is and *forward engineering* where the reverse-engineered business is redesigned with new processes.

Aphrodite Tsalgatidou recommended, as an outcome of her study, five phases for a BPR project cycle. The phases are as follows:

1. Learning the processes.
2. Creating the business vision.
3. Model and analyse the current (as-is) processes.
4. Model and analyse the future (to-be) processes.
5. Transition to a continuous improvement effort.

The phases form the BPR cycle of continuous process improvement.

14.6 BPR and Its Linkage with IT and ISs

ISs encompass IT and the systems relating to the management and the organization. BPR and IT/IS are closely related to each other. A successful BPR project owes its success to IT/IS. In BPR, an effective IT facilitates sharing of databases, development of expert systems, development of communication networks, use of decision-making tools, effective interaction with customers, retrieval of appropriate information and computation at a high level of aggregation.

On the other hand, BPR projects can be directed towards IT/IS revamping by way of upgrading the client–server technology, mobile computing, data storage and retrieval, BPM, workflow management,

ERP, CRM, SCM, DSS, data mining, BI, and also web-enabled services. ERP is an integrated suite of business management software which helps in managing business needs. Experts believe that BPR makes ERP implementation in an organization faster, less expensive and easier due to acceptability on the part of the employees.

14.7 Some Important Concepts about BPR

1. BPR changes processes and not functions, activities, departments, geographies or tasks.
2. Re-engineering is not reorganizing only. Reorganizing is redesigning an organization structure to support re-engineered business processes.
3. Re-engineering is not downsizing or reduction of workforce to achieve short-term cost saving. Re-engineering, on the contrary, emphasizes rethinking from the point of view of ground reality for more efficient ways of working including elimination of unnecessary work.
4. Re-engineering is not automation of ineffective and obsolete processes.

14.8 Factors Leading to the Success of BPR

The important factors, which lead to the success of BPR in an organization, are listed as follows:

1. Proven and tested methods should be adopted.
2. Employees should be convinced about the need for BPR.
3. Drive for innovation should come from the employees.
4. Prior analysis of business needs should consider strategy and long-term objectives of the organization.
5. BPR team should effectively manage the changes within the prescribed time frame and with least impact on the business.
6. Adequate IT infrastructure is one of the factors which facilitates implementation of the re-engineered processes.
7. Customer needs and customer-centric processes should direct business practices.
8. Ultimate results should be the main focus. The processes should go beyond the traditional tasks and functional boundaries to achieve attainment of the objectives of the organization.
9. Work simplification is to be carried out to eliminate unnecessary complexities.

In the above context, it may be stated that the objectives of BPR are mainly customer delight, effectiveness and efficiency of business processes in terms of cost, quality, time and effort.

14.9 BPR Success Stories in the Real World

Example 1: Ford motor company–Accounts payable process.

Ford's accounts payable process was slow and cumbersome, and 500 clerks were engaged mainly for reconciling mismatches among purchase orders, goods receipt documents and invoices before releasing payment to vendors. The process (as-is) shown in Figure 14.2 was slow, awkward and having frequent mismatches due to mistakes. After re-engineering the process, there was a reduction in head count in the accounts payable process by 75%. Invoices were eliminated and matching was computerized resulting in improved accuracy, faster and a more efficient process. Ford's accounts payable process (to-be) after re-engineering has been shown in Figure 14.3.

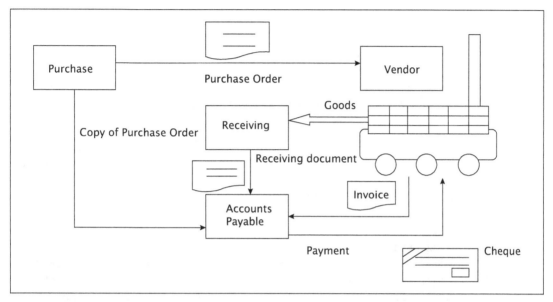

FIGURE 14.2 Ford's Account Payable Process (AS-IS) before Re-engineering

Source: Hammer and Champy (1993).

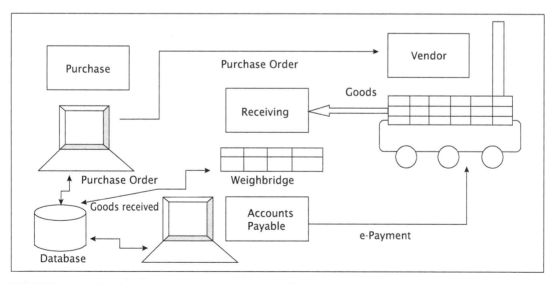

FIGURE 14.3 Ford's Accounts Payable Process after Re-engineering

Source: Hammer and Champy (1993).

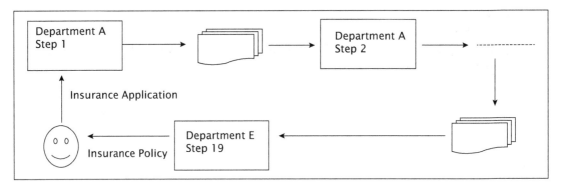

FIGURE 14.4   Mutual Benefits Life (AS-IS) before Re-engineering

Source: Eccles (1991).

Example 2: New life insurance policy application process at Mutual Benefits Life before re-engineering had 30 steps, 5 departments and 19 persons. The insurance application processing cycle time used to vary from a minimum of 24 hours to an average of 22 days even though the actual processing time of an application was only 17 minutes. The workflow process of Mutual Benefits Life before re-engineering has been shown in Figure 14.4.

After re-engineering one mainframe computer, one PC workstation and a LAN server were used to take care of the whole processing. The case manager could handle the same volume of policy applications with a processing cycle time of minimum 4 hours and average 2–5 days. Moreover, the application handling capacity increased two times the same before re-engineering. The life insurance company could also cut 100 number of various positions in the field office. The new life insurance policy application processing method after re-engineering has been shown in Figure 14.5.

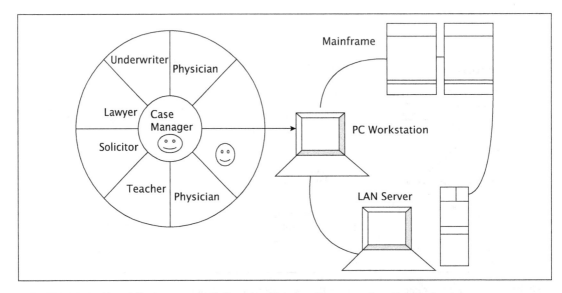

FIGURE 14.5   New Life Insurance Policy Application Process after Re-engineering

14.10 BPR Case Studies in Indian Corporate Sector

CASE 1: BPR IN ICICI BANK

ICICI bank (earlier known as Industrial Credit and Investment Corporation of India) is a large Indian MNC banking entity with a market capitalization of about ₹2,562,055.3 million as on 2 April 2019. The bank has got 4,867 branches and 14,367 ATMs in India and has also got overseas branches in 16 countries including USA, China, Singapore and many more countries. ICICI bank offers a wide range of banking and financial services to corporate as well as retail customers such as investment banking, life and non-life insurance, venture capital and asset management. BPR was carried out in ICICI bank in the year 2000 and onwards when anytime and anywhere banking facilities were introduced in India.

Background and Justification of BPR

The traditional legacy systems at ICICI bank were very much branch-centric. ICICI bank authorities decided to change the branch-centric model in order to make its services available all over India. In order to facilitate the above, it was necessary for ICICI bank to centralize its banking applications and also to have a centralized data repository.

Teams Involved with the BPR for Appropriate Technology Transfer

Infosys was the main technology partner who provided the required assistance to ICICI bank to implement Finacle for handling all the banking activities such as:

- BillDesk for online payment;
- Sybase, an SAP company for systems, applications and procedures;
- SAS for business analytics software and services;

ICICI Infotech which is a company promoted by ICICI, designed the initial network for ICICI group in 1999. The initial design was a hub and spoke architecture.

ICICI had to modify the initial design because the same was not able to cater to the need for centralization of data available with the stand-alone legacy systems of the branches. The data from one branch were not available with the other branches. The above-mentioned problem led the ICICI bank to design a new hub and spoke architecture.

Supporting tools and techniques: The following tools and techniques were used by ICICI bank:

1. Finacle: The core banking and the universal banking solution developed by Infosys. Finacle was needed to seamlessly integrate multiple applications such as credit cards, mutual funds, brokerage, data warehouses and call centres.
2. The network follows a hub-and-spoke architecture consisting of a mix of very-small-aperture terminals (VSATs), leased lines, ISDN and radio links. The network has around 800 number of leased lines, about 600 number of VSATs, approximately 800 number of ISDN lines and multiple 34 mbps lines.

There is a primary site from where the spokes emanate and reach the regional branches and other offices. The secondary site has got the disaster recovery facility.

Hardware at each site varies from low-end new technology (NT) servers to the high-end Sun Enterprises 10k (Sun E10k) along with 12 terabytes of data storage at each end connected through storage area network. Unix is the operating system for the major part of the hardware, while the databases use mainly Oracle and a few use Sybase and MS SQL. High-end Cisco routers and switches have been deployed to establish connectivity. The network is monitored using HP OpenView and CiscoWorks.

More than 30 portals are being operated using highly secured state-of-the-art security features such as firewalls, IDS, antivirus and other security tools. The network architecture was designed to establish a good relation among the technology consultants (network integrators), the vendors and the clients.

Results Achieved

ICICI bank adopting the scalable and open systems-based architecture with Finacle has been able to manage successfully an increased transaction level from 0.4 million in the year 2000 to roughly 2.1 million in 2005, nearly five and a half times. There has been a quantum jump in all other areas of performance of ICICI bank also. On the whole, ICICI bank after BPR has grown significantly resulting in a present net worth of about ₹1,083,680 million as on 31 March 2019.

CASE 2: BPR IN MAHINDRA AND MAHINDRA (M&M) COMPANY

The company was started in the year 1945 by two brothers, namely J. C. Mahindra and K. C. Mahindra to manufacture general-purpose utility vehicles. In October 1947, the first batch of 75 jeeps was produced by the company. In course of time, the company diversified its business into other segments such as hotels, financial services, auto components and IT. In 1994, a major restructuring exercise was initiated as part of a BPR program and the company was regrouped into six distinct autonomous strategic business units (SBUs) with empowered presidents for the SBUs.

Background and Justification for BPR in M&M

Before implementation of BPR in M&M, there were certain factors present which led to manufacturing inefficiencies resulting in low productivity. Moreover, the production cycle time was long due to poor scheduling, frequent imbalance in the assembly lines and idle time of workers due to unorganized processes. The work culture was unhealthy and corruption among employees was widespread.

The top management, therefore, decided to focus on productivity increase and delivery of world-class quality products at competitive cost with the strategic intent of becoming the largest tractor manufacturer in the world. In short, the three C's (customers, competition and change) led M&M to implement BPR.

Business Process Reengineering 493

Major Changes Pursuant to BPR Exercise by M&M

Business of the company was restructured into core and non-core business units as shown in detail in Table 14.1.

Project 'Vishwajeet': A major program conceptualized by McKinsey, was undertaken by M&M to make it the largest global manufacturer of tractors by the year 2005. The project envisaged division of farm equipment business into five distinct departments, namely marketing and customer relations, manufacturing and supply chain, product development and R&D, performance management and internal operations.

TABLE 14.1 Restructuring M&M into Core and Non-core Business Units

	Details
Core Business Units:	
Automotive	MUVs and SUVs
Farm equipment	Tractors and other farm equipment
Non-core Business Units:	
Trade and financial service	Imports, exports, lease financing, hire purchase, domestic trading and marketing
Infrastructure development	Real estate

Project 'blue chip': Due to depressed revenue, high cost and reduced profit margin in 2002 resulting in share price fall from ₹322 in 2000 to ₹114 in 2002 and return on capital employed (ROCE) sliding down from 17.09% to 8.92% during the same period, M&M set up a corporate turnaround program office and articulated the need for a sharper focus on financial returns. Consequently, a restructuring exercise called 'blue chip' was undertaken by M&M to raise the level of performance. The major actions on the part of 'blue chip' for financial revival were as follows:

1. ROCE replaced the benchmarks such as market share, sales and profit.
2. A policy was formulated that business units would have to compete among themselves for capital based on the returns made by them.
3. M&M overhauled operations for cost cutting and streamlining the manufacturing facility.

HR management also underwent crucial changes.

Results Achieved by M&M

Due to BPR, tractor division brought down break-even point from 54,000 to 35,000 units due to cost cutting.

Net sales and operating profit increased by 28% and 34% respectively for the first half of the financial year 2004–2005.

M&M stock touched ₹390 as against ₹112 only a year before the BPR exercise.

CASE 3: BPR IN INDIAN RAILWAYS CATERING AND TOURISM CORPORATION (IRCTC)

IRCTC is a subsidiary of Indian Railways set up by the Ministry of Railways, Government of India. IRCTC started its operations on 27 September 1999. Its corporate office is located at New Delhi. IRCTC is headed by its managing director who is assisted by director (catering services), director (tourism and marketing), director (finance), chief vigilance officer, company secretary and 17 group general managers reporting to him directly. Approximately, 2 million tickets are sold per day through the website of IRCTC.

Background and Justification of BPR in IRCTC

The ticket booking system prior to introduction of BPR was an offline manual system wherein there were many counters, each of which was meant for booking and reservation of a particular train or a few numbers of trains. As a result, passenger rush and waiting time were heavy. In order to avoid this rush in the railway booking-cum-reservation offices, the ticket booking and seat reservation process were re-engineered and with the assistance of M/s Computer Maintenance Corporation (CMC), Indian Railways developed the online booking and seat reservation system using the Customer Information Control System (CICS). It was mainly for the customer (passenger) satisfaction and comfortable journey that BPR was implemented in Indian Railways and IRCTC became operational. Also, prompt delivery of passenger services and eliminating inefficient operations for increased revenue were the other prime considerations leading to the BPR exercise.

Present Scenario of Ticket Booking and Passenger Services in Indian Railways

Today IRCTC is offering various re-engineered services to the railway passengers through online systems some of which are as follows:

1. Passenger information and enquiry;
2. Railway reservation and ticket-booking services which include Internet and mobile ticketing, booking history, ticket printing and cancellation;
3. Catering and vending services;
4. Railway claims and refunds;
5. Booking of retiring rooms at railway stations.

The above services are provided by intelligent use of IT through:

- Freight Operations Information System (FOIS);
- Passenger Reservation System (PRS);
- Unreserved Ticketing System (UTS);
- Interactive voice response system which is a passenger feedback system;
- E-ticketing system;
- Railnet also known as Corporate Wide Information System (CWIS). It connects Railway Board with all zonal, divisional, sub-divisional headquarters, production units, research development and standardization organization (RDSO) and all other units;
- Radio-frequency identification device (RFID) for wagon and consignment tracking system.

Results Achieved by IRCTC

IRCTC made phenomenal improvement in performance in Indian Railways after BPR. Some of those worth mentioning achievements are as follows:

1. Total earning increased by about 17.3% in one year after BPR due to quantum jump in ticket sales through Internet ticketing.
2. Tourism activities through Indian Railways considerably increased.
3. Indian Railways became unit-cost focused rather than tariff focused.
4. The earlier thinking of restructuring and right sizing changed towards competitiveness.

•Review Questions•

1. What is BPR? How is it different from TQM?

2. What are the steps in BPR?

3. What are the roles of ISs and IT in BPR?

4. Why is BPR at all needed in an organization?

5. Why is BPR required for successful implementation of ERP? Which of the two needs to be carried out first?

6. What are the factors leading to the success of a BPR exercise?

7. What is the relationship between BPM and BPR?

8. Which of the following actions on the part of a company are within the scope of BPR?
   i. Outsourcing of components needed for the end products.
   ii. Opening a new retail outlet in a remote location.
   iii. Cutting the strength of office by offering voluntary retirement scheme as a cost-reduction measure.

Bibliography

Davenport, T. H. *Process Innovation: Reengineering Work through Information Technology.* Boston, MA: Harvard Business School Press, 1992.

Davenport, T. H., and J. E. Short. 'The New Industrial Engineering: Information Technology and Business Process Redesign.' *Sloan Management Review* 31 (1990): 11–27.

Eccles, Robert G. 'Rethinking the Corporate Workplace: Case Manager at Mutual Benefits Life.' Harvard Business School, Case 9 492–015, 1991.

Grover, V., S. R. Jeong, W. J. Kettinger, and J. T. Teng. 'The Implementation of Business Process Reengineering.' *Journal of Management Information Systems* 12, no. 1 (1995): 109–144.

Hammer, Michael. 'Reengineering Work: Don't Automate, Obliterate.' *Harvard Business Review* 68, no. 4 (1990): 104–112.

Hammer, Michael, and James Champy. *Reengineering the Corporation: A Manifesto for Business Revolution*. New York, NY: HarperCollins Publishers, 1993.

Jacobson, I., Ericsson, M., and Jacobson, A. *The Object Advantage: Business Process Reengineering with Object Technology*, 1st ed. Boston, MA: Addisson-Wesley, September 1994.

Tsalgatidou, Aphrodite. 'Methodologies for Business Process Modeling and Reengineering.' Department of Information and Telecommunication, University of Athens, Greece, 2014.

CHAPTER

Information Systems for Managerial Decisions: The Future

15.1 The Future: An Overview

Many managers, particularly those in the IT industry, expect that big data analytics and cloud marketing will be the largest employer of IT professionals in the near future. Besides being large in volume or physical output, new data types such as big data, social media data, corporate data and image data all emanating out of smarter consumers, global competition and digitally connected devices will have a larger influence on the world.

Today the world is rapidly changing both socially and technologically. According to Professor Warren G. Bennis (1968), the managerial skills needed for effectiveness in such a changing environment include a knowledge of complex systems and 'an ability to develop and use all types of information systems, including high-speed electronic computers. The job of the leader will be to collect, organize and transmit information'.

Many visionaries and leaders deem digital intelligence derived out of new types of data, analytics and computer-based ISs, a prerequisite for survival and growth in the forthcoming decades. Existence of information-oriented management system is one of the conditions of success of business organizations.

Notwithstanding its importance in managing the business enterprises, it is in other areas that information and communications technology may have its greatest impact in the years to come. More important perhaps is the area of social applications such as healthcare, education, transportation, welfare and urban development. Information and communication coupled with computer technology have made tremendous change in educational methodology. Today, we have smart classrooms where entire lecture sessions can be recorded and also students with the help of the Internet can attend the class sitting at their home. The next decade will see the impact of computer and IT on common people. Computer terminals and mobile phones (Android, IOS or Blackberry) are finding their places in homes, business offices or classrooms in schools.

Current data management and processing platforms mostly do not cater to incessant data growth, elastic scalability, sustained 'Google like' performance, new types of requirements for new data types, new analytics, heavy workload and new metadata.

Next-generation data warehouse will evolve to be a dynamic decision support and analytics platform that needs to be scalable, real time, flexible and also will support hundreds of users whether on site or on cloud.

Hadoop and distributed data processing in general are fast becoming an important skill set for many IT managers. Today, an effective IT manager must have knowledge of relational database, networking and data/information security all of which were considered optional skills about 15–20 years back. Similarly, basic understanding of distributed data processing will become an essential part of every programmer's skill set in near future.

None of these developments will look unusual by the managers of the future. It will be natural for them to face the exponential growth of big data and the analytics thereof in dealing with customers, vendors, government agencies and other stakeholders of the company. The managers will realize that distributed file systems, digitization of data, NOSQL databases, mobile and cloud computing will become important parts of their social and business life as time passes. Rather than being confused by the above-mentioned developments, they will welcome the changes. The future managers will understand the IT and will become involved in the design of ISs affecting their jobs.

15.2 Future Trends in ISs for Managerial Decisions

It is very difficult to forecast the future of ISs for managerial decisions in totality. However, by reviewing the literature, observing the developments and by listening to the experts in the field, we find several trends are emerging that may reflect on the design and development of ISs for managers in the future years to come. We shall discuss those trends under the following headings:

1. The changing nature of managerial decision-making process
2. Real-time systems
3. Big data and analytics
4. The Internet and web technology
5. IOT
6. Cloud computing
7. Social media
8. Mobile technology and wearables
9. Data security and privacy aspects
10. Impact of ISs on management echelon

15.3 The Changing Nature of Managerial Decision-making Process

Managerial decision-making process has undergone significant changes over the last two decades. Today, decisions are taken not only based on intuition and judgement but also on evidence generated by data and business analytics. Decision-making in future, particularly at the strategic and tactical levels, will

TABLE 15.1 Global Internet Growth, 2008–2012

Country	New Internet Users in Millions 2008–2012	Yearly Growth (in Percent)
China	264	10
India	88	26
Indonesia	39	58
Iran	35	205
Russia	33	6
Nigeria	31	15
Philippines	28	32
Brazil	27	6
Mexico	19	9
USA	18	3

Source: Internet World Stats.

become more streamlined due to a consistent structure for addressing ill-structured or unstructured problems based on facts and not on intuition. Rapid evolution in information and communication technology helped the managers in making decisions more on the 'prescriptive model' rather than on the 'descriptive model' in the terminology of Herbert A. Simon (1955). Decisions are taken with more rationality unlike in the past.

Development of the Internet and other communication devices has given rise to continuous globalization. Table 15.1 shows the growth of Internet users during the period from 2008 to 2012.

Globalization of business operations led to managerial decisions more as an outcome of computational thinking—a perfect blend of critical thinking and IT. Beginning with the traditional electronic data processing of clerical applications, there had been evolution of ISs and ITs. Today, business managers in the globalization perspective are applying technology to understand and predict human behaviour.

Big data and predictive analytics will guide managerial decision-making by predicting, forecasting and optimizing through statistical analysis using 'SPSS or R'.

Globalization further enables sharing of data by managers which leads to collaborative decision-making and development of GDSSs.

Many of the operational controls and some of the management controls, which earlier used to be taken by managers have now been automated through sensor driven decision analysis.

The IOT also can support long range and more complex human planning systems that generate a variety of graphical displays for analysing data. Further, automated variance analysis to reveal root causes, 'what-if' analysis and sensitivity analysis led to improved strategic and tactical decisions. Big data analytics and the associated technologies will enable managers to move more towards the upper levels of knowledge and wisdom of the Haeckel's (1993) information hierarchy as shown in Figure 15.1.

The above-mentioned movement in turn facilitates conversion of tacit knowledge (subjective) gained from experience and practice into explicit knowledge based on more of theory and rationality as a continuous process. In future, when decision-makers address problems particularly unstructured and ill-structured ones, they will more often convert knowledge from one form to the other. The future decision-makers will enhance their base of explicit knowledge in extent and function through the above-mentioned conversion process. However, the Internet will play a key role in sharing of tacit knowledge. The outcome will obviously be streamlined strategic and tactical planning, increased business insight, improved and faster strategic decision-making.

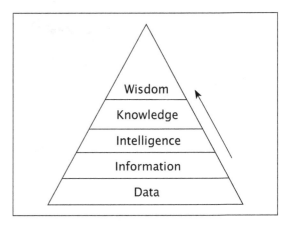

FIGURE 15.1   Haeckel's Information Hierarchy

15.4 Growth of Real-time ISs

Real-time information processing which had its beginning with passenger seat reservation at airline ticket counters or railway berth reservation in trains and even with the inter-state bus seat booking counters has grown over the years in various operational control and even management control areas to facilitate monitoring and control because of its speed of response. Today real-time systems are operational in job progress control in manufacturing, inventory ordering, cash flow analysis and forecasting. Because of its speed of response, real-time systems find great use in the aviation sector for flight control, traffic control in highways and even in automation of process control in manufacturing such as chemical plants. Compared with batch processing, the real-time applications, though fewer in number, are highly advocated because of their exciting nature and great potential for the future.

Real-time systems have three distinctive features: (a) data are maintained online, (b) data are updated as and when events occur unlike batch processing in which case all master data are updated at periodic intervals and (c) the computer database can be interrogated from remote terminals or other devices by multiple users. Some managers often raise a doubt as to whether they really need the above-mentioned capabilities of real-time systems in more than a small fraction of their daily information needs. However, the fact remains that many current real-time applications are little more than online versions of previous systems and are primarily single application-oriented with little integration between the various functional subsystems. The development in real-time processing coupled with the design of common database systems will provide real-time IS where all information required to run a company will be within the reach of the management of the company. Such an IS will be of immense help for intense monitoring and control on a real-time basis as in the case of a project command and control centre known as a 'dashboard'.

Model building will become easier as system designers and managers familiarize themselves with real-time systems for problem solving. The remote terminals, the integrated data bank, the real-time processing and the library of retrievable programs and mathematical models will provide a business experimentation laboratory in which managers can test the results of their decisions before implementing them.

15.5 Big Data and Analytics

Since the dawn of time up to 2003, mankind has created 2 exabyte of data, but today at least that much data are created each and every day! New technologies are changing the way we design and build data warehouses.

The new technologies are evolving to effectively link unstructured and semi-structured data with traditional relational data to support our information requirement to meet the business needs and organizational goals. We have already become aware of Big data—its sources, characteristics, storage, processing, and analysis of the same. We became also familiar with Hadoop and its ecosystems. Storage of big data emanating from business environment, corporate world, social media and sensors in the form of structured as well as unstructured or ill-structured data, scientific data, streaming data and analysis of such huge data are subjects of continuous research. Furthermore, many new ecosystems of information storage and retrieval for managerial decision-making will emerge in the future. Because of advancement in big data analytics using statistical techniques, decision-making at the strategic level will become more rational and streamlined and uncertainties in the decision-making process will be considerably reduced, if not totally eliminated.

Future ISs for managerial decision will be addressing more and more ill-structured or unstructured data and will have more flexibility, scalability, speed and predictability to evolve a dynamic decision support and analytics platform. Big data and predictive analytics will make prediction models based on patterns of behaviour of performance variables and the patterns will become institutional knowledge for managers. The future trend of ISs will be integrated DSSs providing BI. Figure 15.2 shows the paradigm shift with big data from the traditional-structured data.

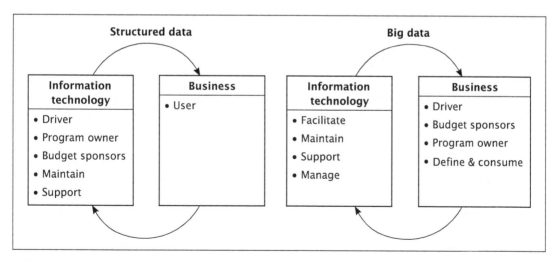

FIGURE 15.2 Paradigm Shift with Big Data from the Traditional Structured Data

Source: Krishnan (2015).

15.6 Internet and Web Technology

As stated earlier in this chapter, the Internet accelerated globalization through sharing of knowledge and information across the world. Rapid development of the Internet made information and knowledge available online to grow exponentially. This had a profound effect on organization structure and its functioning. As information is available to the managers who need it and when they need it, line of control and influence becomes distinct and departments often self-organize in new and more effective ways. The result is not only flattening of organization structure but also changing of skill mix of employees.

The Internet has made it possible to establish direct contact between buyers and sellers, thus eliminating the middle layer in distribution channels besides significantly reducing inventory costs. Since the advent of the Internet, retail marketing has been transformed largely. CRM by companies using the Internet has become dynamic with the changing nature of customer needs.

The Internet's capabilities to empower consumers, to facilitate dynamic information exchange among organizations and to flatten organization echelons, promise to result in new operational strategies, business models, service delivery models and above all improved organizational decision-making.

Business applications are now web-based to increase flexibility with accessing systems and upgrades. Today organizations have adopted web 2.0 applications such as Facebook, Google Plus, email, blogs, Wiki and many others to interact online with clients and customers. Web technology switches from a keyword-based search to semantic technologies in which search is conducted by context analysis and word meanings. The semantic web is not only more accurate in search but also extracts information from multiple sources and their comparison permits a variety of services such as e-commerce and e-health services. It is important to mention that e-commerce encompasses business processes to include the entire value chain comprising of purchasing, marketing, sales, customer service and business relationships.

15.7 Internet of Things

The 'IOT' as we have seen in Chapter 13, refers to the idea of physical objects being connected to the Internet. Developments in the field of wireless technologies and sensors allow physical objects to transmit and also receive data about themselves. Many applications involving IOT are already available today.

Mckinsey & Company in a report in 2010 broadly identified six such application areas of IOT. Those are as follows:

1. **Tracking behaviour:** When products are embedded with sensors, companies can track the movements of the products and also monitor their interactions. Business models can be developed to make use of such behavioural data. For example, some insurance companies install location sensors in their customers' cars to enable the companies to formulate the base price of policies on how a car is driven as well as the running pattern of the car.

2. **Enhanced sensor-driven decision analysis:** As already stated in an earlier paragraph of this chapter, sensor-driven DSS can support long range and more complex human planning systems that generate a variety of graphical displays for data analysis.

3. **Enhanced security and surveillance:** Data from large number of sensors deployed at sensitive locations including entrance and exits of buildings and roads and analysis of the same data serve detection of security lapses including unauthorized persons entering restricted areas. Similarly, report on environmental conditions including soil moistures, ocean currents and weather can make decision takers aware of early warning for disaster management.

4. **Process optimization:** Process industries, such as chemical plants are controlling the process parameters with the aid of legions of sensors installed along the process flow line. These sensors feed data to computers, which in turn analyse the data and then send signals to actuators that adjust processes by modifying ingredient mixtures, temperature or pressure.

5. **Optimum resource consumption:** Sensors connected to automated feedback mechanisms can change usage patterns for scarce resources such as water, energy and fuel. This can also be accomplished by controlling the price of these scarce resources to regulate demand.

6. **Complex autonomous systems:** A very important application of the IOT involves the sensing of unpredictable conditions and instantaneous responses on a real-time basis guided by autonomous systems. This type of real time decision-making resembles human reactions, but at a very high-performance level. For example, the automobile industry is adopting systems that can detect imminent adverse conditions and take remedial measures.

15.8 Cloud Computing

Cloud computing has become a new model for fulfilling corporate IT needs. Flexible and elastic cloud services deliver resources as required, such as infrastructure, platform and software to corporates similar to other utilities such as water, fuel or electricity. This has resulted in cost saving by organizations as they do not need to create permanent or fixed IT resources. IT departments often face serious problems due to outdated infrastructures, underutilized capacity and rigid architecture particularly with changing technological, economic and other environmental conditions. As businesses nowadays have to survive harsh economic fluctuations, ISs of future have to be agile to save on budget and to face unexpected sudden changes such as enhanced competition and changing customer preferences. Cloud computing and similar latest technologies promise to turn the IT department that had always been viewed as a cost centre into a source of saving money and instilling flexibility and agility to the IS. Flexibility is the adaptability to changing market. Agile methods were used in software development for complex systems that require frequent changes, quick responses and short release times. Research had witnessed that IS agility is one of the most vital factors in sustaining strategic alignment of a company. An agile enterprise builds an agile IS.

However, in order to leverage the full benefit—both present and potential—as promised by cloud services (software as a service [SaaS], platform as a service [PaaS] and infrastructure as a service [IaaS]), numerous challenges such as specific requirements of existing and legacy applications are to be addressed. The agility, which can be driven into IS of any particular organization, has to be judged within the context of the same organization. Imache, Izza and Nacer in 2012 proposed a five-element framework known as process, organization, information, resource and environment (POIRE) to assess an enterprise IS agility. Sawas and Watfa in 2015 conducted an extensive study and research on the impact of cloud-computing services on IS agility and their finding is that there is an association between using IaaS as a cloud service model and improving the technical infrastructure agility or the IT process agility of the IS.

However, there is no evident association between IaaS and other agility categories. They further found that there is an association between using PaaS as a cloud service model and improving the human characteristics or the business aspects of the IS. No other association was found by them between PaaS and other agility categories.

There exist no association between SaaS and any agility category. This finding was quite interesting as it appears that SaaS would normally imply less IT staff and running cost of IT, which in turn normally would mean more business agility.

15.9 Social Media

Social media, an evolving phenomenon, have got the highest impact on continuous communication of an organization with the customers and the public at large. They consist of social networks such as Facebook, Twitter, Instagram, YouTube, Flickr, corporate blogs, multimedia sites, company-sponsored websites and collaborative websites. Facebook helps us to share ideas with people in our life. WhatsApp is a simple, secure and reliable messaging and calling media. Twitter shows happenings. Instagram allows users to sign up and see photos and videos from friends. Social media today play the role of an ever-increasing marketing platform for a company's products and services. They are also recognized as a powerful medium in business environment and have grown from a local niche phenomenon to mass adoption.

Social media form a vital source of information for managerial decisions. Du and Jiang (2015) observed that performance of firms improves due to use of Facebook and Twitter. The present trend of growth of social media indicates that the future opportunities which may be forthcoming will be for creation of new technologies for integration of existing social media into accounting ISs as well as analytical systems for BI.

Perdana, Robb and Rohde (2015) considered social media from the perspective of a vehicle for community learning, information dissemination and for the institutionalization of knowledge. There are many areas in which accounting plays an important role and where social media are particularly influential such as behavioural finance. Moreover, exploration of social media trends would appear to provide powerful insights into organizations that auditors could leverage for engagement planning and risk management.

15.10 Mobile Technology and Wearables

Mobile technology is perhaps the most significant digital innovation in the last decade starting with the simple cell phones in the 1990s, the development of smartphones and finally the tablets of today. The fantastic growth of mobile technology can be witnessed from the following facts:

- In 2011, smartphone sales exceeded the sales of personal computers.
- The number of smartphone subscribers grew by 31% in 2013.
- In May 2013, mobile technology accounted for 15% of all Internet traffic.
- Facebook reported that 68% of its active users used their mobile platforms to access the social network.
- Tablet sales now outpace sale of notebook PCs and desktop PCs. It is predicted that 93% of all connected devices will either be smartphones or tablets by the end of 2020.

15.11 Wearables

On an average, a smartphone user looks at his/her smartphone 150 times a day for functions such as messaging, phone calls, social media and listening to music. In order to facilitate the above functions, the technology can be worn on or physically integrated into human bodies and the same is known as 'wearables'. Wearables such as hearing aids and Bluetooth earpieces are some of the examples of wearable technology. Now we have seen many new innovative wearable technologies such as the 'Google Glass', which one wears over eyes such as a pair of eyeglasses. 'Google Glass' can project images into one's field of vision based on context and voice commands. Wearables are also very common in case of healthcare such as Jawbone which monitors sleep.

As technology continues to evolve in future, there will be many more mobile computational devices and wearables which will generate a variety of graphical displays for analysing data. Moreover with more and more use of smart phones and wearables, storage and analysis of data will be within the reach of many persons and they will be sharing the data and analysis thereof with each other for mutual benefit and group decision support. Some of this data sharing can be done passively, such as disclosing one's location in order to update traffic statistics on a real-time basis.

However, data can also be reported actively such as uploading customer rating of a restaurant to review site. Mobile and wearable technologies will have significant effect on healthcare and traffic ISs. Further, traditional marketing ISs based on market research will be significantly changed by way of compilation of customer ratings for products and services such as restaurants and shopping malls and then allowing consumers back to search through the ratings via their website or mobile phone app which is giving rise to the digital marketing concept of today.

15.12 Data Security and Privacy

In case of all computer systems that maintain and process valuable information or provide services to multiple users concurrently, it is necessary to provide security against unauthorized access, use or modification of any data file. Computer systems must also be protected against disruption of operations and physical damage. The exponential growth of big data and increasing number of computer applications involving valuable information resulted in huge amount of data transmission through networks and shared computing including cloud services. This increased data transmission and shared computing underscore the need for finding effective solutions to computer security problems. In future, data privacy and data security will have to become an integral part in planning and design of computer systems, applications and business models adopting new technologies and services.

Data privacy is an issue that concerns the computer community maintaining personal information of individuals in computerized record-keeping system. Privacy deals with the right of individuals regarding the collection of information in a record-keeping system about their personal data and the processing, dissemination, storage and use of such data in making determination about them.

Turn and Ware (1976) mentioned about five basic principles relating to personal information record-keeping system in the both private sector and government, which are as follows:

1. There must be no personal data record-keeping system whose very existence is secret.
2. There must be a way for an individual to find out what information about him/her is on record and how it is used.

3. There must be a way for an individual to correct or amend a record of identifiable information about him/her.
4. There must be a way for an individual to prevent his/her personal information that was obtained for one purpose from being used for other purposes without his/her consent.
5. Any organization creating, maintaining, using or disseminating record of identifiable personal data must guarantee the reliability of the data for their intended use and must take precautions to prevent misuse of the data.

Maintaining privacy is challenging today with the World Wide Web. Even diligently removing cookies, super cookies and browsing history cannot guarantee that they are entirely invisible. Further, long-term durability of data is a growing concern since the current memory technologies have a data lifetime expectancy of a few decades only. The nano technology being researched to solve this problem is simply amazing and promising durability of billion years and density of one trillion bits per square inch.

Data security includes the procedural and technical measures required:

1. To prevent unauthorized access, modification, use and dissemination of data stored or processed in a computer system;
2. To prevent any deliberate refusal of data service;
3. To protect the data and computer system from physical harm.

Security safeguards include physical safeguards such as lock, fire and water protection, computer hardware safeguards such as memory protect, software safeguards such as file access control schemes, security permissions such as read, write, execute, communication safeguards to ensure secrecy of information in transit over communication channels and personnel safeguards such as background checks and biometric checks. Security safeguards also include all aspects of administrative and management controls such as inspection, test and security audit. A variety of equipment and techniques exist for providing physical security such as fire controllers and digital locks for controlling physical access. Currently, techniques for protection of programs and data within the computer system include positive identification of all users and authentication, isolation of users and their processes from each other and system supervisory programs, concealment of information on removable storage media and in communication channels by encryption techniques. Commonly used identification techniques include a username, personal number or account number. Authentication techniques commonly used include passwords, combinations of locks or some facts about a person's background.

Cryptographic techniques can be used in communication links between computers and terminals to protect information against interception by wiretapping or capture and modification at illicit terminals or computers secretly inserted in the system. Popular algorithms such as RSA and Putty generate unique keys (public and private) to encrypt and decrypt data and information. Integrity and auditing of security safeguards must be a continuous process of monitoring for being effective.

Pitkanen, Sarvas et al. (2011) mentioned about future information security trends. Some of their observations in this regard can be stated as follows:

1. Information security issues become more international.
2. The interdependency between societal processes and ISs increases rapidly.
3. Increasing data gathering and data combination from different sources do occur.
4. The correctness of information becomes increasingly important.

5. Automation/autonomous systems are increasingly employed to effect security.
6. Traceability of persons and goods increases.
7. Malicious action against ISs increases.
8. Commercial interests drive actors to restrict access to proprietary information resources.
9. Governance of access to information resources in organizations becomes more difficult.

Some of the future trends in security techniques are worth mentioning. For example, cloud context will provide a wealth of challenges, such as autonomous checking of cloud security configurations, setting up of security systems known as 'honey pots' to lure intruders and to collect incriminating evidence about them for seeing or overseeing insecure end devices with more sophistication.

The development of new software will also lead to new tools and techniques to cope with information security requirements in a better way.

Future demand for traceability for counterfeit prevention and surveillance of life-saving drugs manufacture will open up possibilities of economic security solutions. Hardware-assisted security of end user platforms as well as the software run on such platforms will improve because of increasing industry investment in these areas. For example, Trusted Platform Modules, processor memory area protection and many other such security functions are likely to come up in future.

Lately, attacks targeting service disruptions, technically known as distributed denial-of-service (DDOS) have gained attention after cyberattacks on Estonia and other places. In future, networks will evolve to provide some automatic response to such cyberattacks but this needs an overhaul of the underlying networks.

Internet and cloud computing technologies will share common ground with the evolution of information networks in future. Both are more likely to prefer true names over IP addresses while discussing with each other. The result will be more complicated networks and more simplified client side and thereby the security issues will be more shifting towards the network. From the end user point of view, there will be no border or gateway within clouds to oversee traffic or to see it at all. This implies that user visibility will be limited to application level and with more emphasis on application level security tools for data loss prevention, identity management, IDS and intrusion prevention system (IPS).

From the cloud service providers' viewpoint, they will need to deploy tools to deter attacks, to detect suspicious user activity and to collect forensic data. Public law enforcing agencies are in the process of engaging 'net traffic police' to ensure fast network traffic response.

15.13 Impact of ISs on Management Echelon

Traditional approaches to decision support and analysis require several management layers, usually the three tiers, namely strategic planning at the top of the hierarchy, management control in the middle and operational control at the bottom. However, with the advances in IT and innovative DSS, many of the decisions taken by managers at the operational control and the management control levels have been automated. Further, the role of management control level which was earlier translating the strategy formulated by the strategic planning level of managers into operating plans for the operational control level of managers had diminished with the advent of communication technology such as the Internet and knowledge-based systems giving rise to computational thinking. It is likely that in future the management

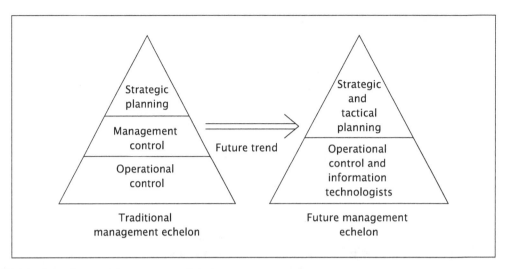

FIGURE 15.3 Future Management Echelon

control level will split up into two parts, one part consisting of managers who are experts in systems approach, big data analytics and the like will merge with the strategic planning level to create knowledge and wisdom for strategic and tactical decision-making. The other part will join with the operational control level to monitor and control the operations and implement the decisions of the higher echelon of managers.

The future management echelon will consist of two levels only, the top and the bottom levels. The top level will consist of managers who will be concerned with organizational goals and will be understanding the need to bring the diverse elements of the organization together in a system. The bottom level will be having managers who will be in the implementing role for the decisions of the top level, and they will also look after the operations and maintenance of the advanced technology of hardware, software and communication devices. Figure 15.3 shows the future trend of management echelon with the advancement of IT.

Bibliography

Krishnan, Krish. 'Big Data: Architecting for Business Intelligence and Data Warehousing in Your Organization'. Data Management Forum Seminar on the Big Data, Hotel Pennsylvania, New York City, September 2015.

Bennis, Warren G. 'New Patterns of Leadership for Tomorrow's Organizations'. *Technology Review*, April 1968, p. 37.

Simon, H. A. 'A Behavioral Model of Rational Choice'. *The Quarterly Journal of Oxford University Press*, February 1955, 69(1), pp. 99–118.

Haeckel, S. H., and Nolan, R.L. 'The Role of Technology in an Information Age: Transforming Symbols into Action'. *The Knowledge Economy: The Nature of Information in the 21st Century.* Queenstown, MD: The Aspen Institute, 1993, pp. 1–24.

Chui, Michael, Loffler, Markus, and Roberts, Roger. 'The Internet of Things'. *McKinsey Quarterly*, March 2010.

Imache, Rabba, Izza, Said, and Nacer, Mohammad Ahmed. 'An Enterprise Information System Agility Assessment Model'. *Computer Science and Information Systems*, January 2012, 9(1), pp. 107–133.

Sawas, M. S., and Watfa, M. K. 'The Impact of Cloud Computing on Information Systems Agility'. *Australasian Journal of Information Systems,* 2015, 19, pp. 97–112.

Du, H., and Jiang, W. 'Do Social Media Matter? Initial Empirical Evidence'. *Journal of Information Systems,* Summer 2015, 29(2), pp. 1–4.

Perdana, A., Robb, A., and Rhode, F., 'XBRL Diffusion in Social Media: Discourses and Community learning'. *Journal of Information Systems,* 2015, 29(2), pp. 71–106.

Turn, R., and Ware, W. H. 'Privacy and Security issues in Information Systems'. *IEEE Transactions on computers,* C-25, 1976, pp. 1353–1361.

Pitkanen, Olli, Sarvas, Risto, Lehmuskallio, A., et al. 'Future Information Security Trends'. *Research Publication.* Helsinki: Aalto University, 2011.

Index

CPSIA information can be obtained
at www.ICGtesting.com
Printed in the USA
BVHW010239300822
645835BV00010B/291

9 789353 883416